CENTRE FOR EDUCATIONAL RESEARCH AND INNOVATION

Co-ordinating Services for Children and Youth at Risk

A *World View*

ORGANISATION FOR ECONOMIC CO-OPERATION AND DEVELOPMENT

ORGANISATION FOR ECONOMIC CO-OPERATION AND DEVELOPMENT

Pursuant to Article 1 of the Convention signed in Paris on 14th December 1960, and which came into force on 30th September 1961, the Organisation for Economic Co-operation and Development (OECD) shall promote policies designed:

- to achieve the highest sustainable economic growth and employment and a rising standard of living in Member countries, while maintaining financial stability, and thus to contribute to the development of the world economy;
- to contribute to sound economic expansion in Member as well as non-member countries in the process of economic development; and
- to contribute to the expansion of world trade on a multilateral, non-discriminatory basis in accordance with international obligations.

The original Member countries of the OECD are Austria, Belgium, Canada, Denmark, France, Germany, Greece, Iceland, Ireland, Italy, Luxembourg, the Netherlands, Norway, Portugal, Spain, Sweden, Switzerland, Turkey, the United Kingdom and the United States. The following countries became Members subsequently through accession at the dates indicated hereafter: Japan (28th April 1964), Finland (28th January 1969), Australia (7th June 1971), New Zealand (29th May 1973), Mexico (18th May 1994), the Czech Republic (21st December 1995), Hungary (7th May 1996), Poland (22nd November 1996) and Korea (12th December 1996). The Commission of the European Communities takes part in the work of the OECD (Article 13 of the OECD Convention).

The Centre for Educational Research and Innovation was created in June 1968 by the Council of the Organisation for Economic Co-operation and Development and all Member countries of the OECD are participants.

The main objectives of the Centre are as follows:

- *analyse and develop research, innovation and key indicators in current and emerging education and learning issues, and their links to other sectors of policy;*
- *explore forward-looking coherent approaches to education and learning in the context of national and international cultural, social and economic change; and*
- *facilitate practical co-operation among Member countries and, where relevant, with non-member countries, in order to seek solutions and exchange views of educational problems of common interest.*

The Centre functions within the Organisation for Economic Co-operation and Development in accordance with the decisions of the Council of the Organisation, under the authority of the Secretary-General. It is supervised by a Governing Board composed of one national expert in its field of competence from each of the countries participating in its programme of work.

Publié en français sous le titre :

COORDONNER LES SERVICES POUR LES ENFANTS ET JEUNES A RISQUE
Une perspective mondiale

FOREWORD

The research reported in this book develops a theme identified from previous work described in *Our Children at Risk* (OECD, 1995) which noted the integration of services as a way to provide more effective, holistic, client-oriented and preventive support to families and to children who are at risk of failing in school and the transition to work.

The book complements the publication *Successful Services for our Children and Families at Risk* (OECD, 1996), by providing detailed accounts of how countries have developed co-ordinated service systems which establish their effectiveness through being sensitive to the needs of clients. Often the approach goes beyond statutory services and involves business and charities as well as other parts of the community.

The complexities of systems such as these are addressed by considering their operation at four levels: mandating is concerned with laws and policies; strategic with the ways those policies are interpreted by senior management, in the context of guiding system management; operational with the ways in which the delivery of services are managed on the ground; and the field level with the ways in which services are working for professionals and clients.

At each of these four levels, information is presented following Stufflebeam's CIPP approach (Stufflebeam, 1988). This model stresses the importance of considering the *Context* leading to the need for change, the *Input* that helped to bring the change about, the *Process* of the change itself and finally the *Product* or the outcomes of the changes.

The book provides an introduction to the issues of services co-ordination based on available international literature commissioned by CERI from researchers who are nationals of the countries involved. Detailed case studies then follow, based on work carried out in Australia (New South Wales, South Australia and Victoria), Canada (Alberta, New Brunswick, Ontario and Saskatchewan), Finland, Germany, the Netherlands, Portugal and the United States (California, Missouri and New York City).

The work took place between 1993 and 1995 and would not have been possible without generous support by the countries involved and in particular by grants from the United States Department of Education, the United States Department of Health and Human Services, the Dutch SVO and the Charles Stewart Mott Foundation of the United States of America.

This book is published on the responsibility of the Secretary-General of the OECD.

TABLE OF CONTENTS

Part I
CASE STUDIES CARRIED OUT BY THE OECD SECRETARIAT

ACKNOWLEDGEMENTS

The work described in this book was made possible by the full co-operation of a very large number of individuals and institutions.

The following experts, Mrs. Josette Combes of ACEPP (*Association Collectifs Enfants, Parents, Professionnels*), Paris, France; Mrs. Jennifer Evans of the Institute of Education, University of London, United Kingdom; Professor Mary Lewis of the University of Houston, Texas, United States; Mrs. Lucienne Roussel, Inspector General of the Ministry of National Education, Paris, France; and Professor Richard Volpe of the University of Toronto, Canada, helped to conceive and execute the work with great enthusiasm and commitment.

The following institutions gave their total support during the completion of the case studies.

AUSTRALIA

Canberra: The Department of the Prime Minister and Cabinet; The Department of Employment, Education, Training and Youth Affairs; The Department of Human Services and Health; The Department of Social Security; The Attorney General's Office.

New South Wales: In *Sydney*: Arthur Phillip High School; Burnside (Uniting Church in Australia); South Sydney Youth Services; City Central Youth Access Centre; Inner West Youth Access Centre; Cleveland Street High School; Cranebrook High School; Jamison High School; Nepean High School; Barnado's Penrith Centre; Penrith Police Citizens' Youth Club; The Wirraway Community Centre. In *Newcastle*: Newcastle Youth Access Centre; Jasper-Gateshead High School; Lake Macquarie Police Citizens' Youth Club; The Eastlakes Community Network Committee; Jesmond High School – Hunter Adolescent Support Unit; The Annexe – Worimi School.

South Australia: In A*delaide*: The Commonwealth Employment Service; Department for Education and Children's Services, Family and Children's Services, Child and Adolescent Mental Health Services; The Beafield Education Centre; Paralowie R-12 School; Fremont High School: Seaton High School; Port Adelaide Youth Access Centre; Salisbury Youth Access Centre; Possibility 14. Ceduna Murat Bay District Council; The Aboriginal Pre-Kindergarten, Murat Bay Children's Centre; Crossways Lutheran School; Ceduna Area School; Spencer Institute of Technology and Further Education; South Australia Independent Schools Board Inc., Malvern.

State of Victoria: In *Melbourne*: The Directorate of School Education; The Catholic Education Office; Melbourne Deaneries STAR Project; Preston Koori Youth Access Centre; Brunswick Youth Access Centre; Footscray Youth Access Centre; Melbourne Youth Access Centre; Crossroads Housing and Support Network Collingwood College; Kensington Community High School. In *Bendigo*: Bendigo Senior Secondary College.

CANADA

Toronto: The Council of Ministers of Education.

Alberta: In *Edmonton*: The Ministry of Education; Ministry of Health; Ministry of Family and Social Services; Ministry of Justice; Commissioner of Services for Children; Community Services Consultancy Ltd; Wellington Junior High School; St Nicolas Catholic Junior High Programme: Partners for

Youth. In *Lethbridge*: Lethbridge City Council; Lethbridge Co-ordination of Services for Children Initiative; Preschool Assessment Treatment Centre; Lethbridge Regional Hospital; Parents Place; Family and Community Development Program; School Districts 9 and 51; Canada Employment; Youth Employment Centre; Paediatric Neuromuscular Unit; Programme Outreach. In *Calgary*: The City of Calgary; Calgary Board of Education; Calgary Catholic School Board; Alcohol and Drug Abuse Commission (AADAC); Calgary Health Services; Alberta Mental Health; Alberta Children's Hospital; Federation of Calgary Communities; Opening Doors Steering Committee; Adolescent Treatment Centre; Thornhill Community services; McDougall Centre; Huntington Hills University of Calgary.

New Brunswick: Department of Education; Department of Health and Community Services. In *Woodstock*: The Office of the Mayor; School District 12; Atlantic Provinces Special Education Authority; Family and Community Social Services; Centennial Elementary School; Woodstock Junior High School; Woodstock High School; Carelton Victoria Child Development Services Inc.; The Woodstock Access Centre; The Probation service.

Ontario: The Ministry of Education and Training; Ministry of Health; Ministry of Community and Social Services; Ministry of Inter-Governmental Affairs; Ontario Association of Children's Aid Societies. In *Timmins*: The Office of the Mayor; Ministry of Education and Training; Ministry of Health; Ministry of Community and Social Services; Ministry of Northern Development and Mines; MPP; The Area Inter-Ministerial Management Committee; Laurentian University; Integrated Services for Northern Children; South Cochrane Child and Youth Service (Children's Mental Health Centre); Jeanne Sauve Youth Services; Children's Treatment Centre. In *Kitchener*: The City of Kitchener; Eastwood Collegiate Institute; The Waterloo County Board of Education; The Mutual Insurance Group; The Rotary Club; The Volunteer Action Centre of Kitchener. In *Sudbury*: The Ministry of Education and Training; Ministry of Health; Ministry of Community and Social Services; Federal Department of Indian and Northern Affairs; Better Beginnings, Better Futures Association.

Saskatchewan: Saskatchewan Education; Saskatchewan Social Services; Saskatchewan Health Services; The League of Educational Administrators; Saskatchewan School Trustees Association; Saskatchewan Federation of Home-school Associations; Princess Alexandra Community School; Princess Alexandra Community Association; Riversdale Community and School Association; Riversdale Business Improvement District; Saskatoon Police Service; Planning and Development, Saskatoon; Saskatoon Prince Albert Regional Education Services; Prince Albert Regional Social Services; Prince Albert Police Department; St. Mary's School; Prince Albert Regional Health Services; West Flat Citizens' Group.

FINLAND

Hameenlinna: Hämeen lääninhallitus; Hämeen lääninhallitus kouluosasto; Hämeen lääninhallitus sosiaali-ja terveysosasto; Hämeenlinnan kaupungin erityispalvelut; A-Klinikka; Ammatillinen opettajakorkeakoulu (Hämeenlinna); Hämeenlinnan kaupungin nuorisotoimisto; Hämeenlinnan seudun kansanterveystyön kuntayhtymä; Hämeenlinnan perusturvavirasto; Vanajan koulukoti; Harvialan koulukoti; Hämeenlinnan perhetukikeskus; Hämeenlinnan ammattioppilaitos; Hämeenlinnan poliisilaitos; Kiipulasäätiö.

Helsinki: Opetushallitus; Sosiaali-ja terveysalan tutkimus-ja kehittämiskeskus, STAKES; Äitiys-ja lastenneuvola, Myllypuron terveyskeskus; Oulunkylän erityisensikoti; Käpylän pikkulastenkoti; Koulupsykologipalvelut (Helsingin kaupunki); Kotipalvelu (Helsingin kaupunki); Päiväkoti (Helsingin kaupunki); Helsingin yliopistollinen keskussairaala; Auroran lastensairaala; Helsingin kaupungin sosiaalivirasto; Ensikotien liitto.

Jyväskylä: Keski-Suomen lääninhallituksen kouluosasto; Keski-Suomen lääninhallituksen sosiaali-ja terveysosasto; Keski-Suomen perheneuvola; Mannerheimin Lastensuojeluliiton Keski-Suomen piiri; Suomen mustalaislähetys; Jyväskylän kaupungin hallinto; Jyväskylän yliopisto; Nenäinniemen ala-asteen koulu ja päiväkoti; Huhtaharjun koulu; Huhtasuon sosiaali-ja terveyskeskus; Hovilan nuorisokoti ja työpaja.

GERMANY

Deutsches Jugendinstitut (DJI).

Bremen: Senator für Gesundheit, Jugend und Soziales; Stadtteilkonferenz, Huchting; Stadtteilfarm Huchting; Kindertagesheim (KTH) Dietrich Bonhoeffer; Kindertagesheim (KTH) Höpost; Mütterzentrum; Haus der Familie.

Duisburg: Industrie- und Handelskammer Duisburg; Dezernat für Schule und Jugend der Stadt Duisburg; Jugendamt Duisburg; Arbeitsamt Duisburg; Stadtrat; Regionale Arbeitsstelle für Ausländerfragen (RAA) Duisburg; auerbetriebliche Berufsbildungseinrichtung; Berthold Brecht Berufsschule.

Leipzig: Sächsisches Staatsministerium für Kultus; Sächsisches Staatsministerium für Soziales, Gesundheit und Familie; Regionale Arbeitsstellen für Ausländerfragen (RAA); Dezernat für Schule, Jugend und Sport der Stadt Leipzig; Jugendamt Leipzig; Christlicher Verein junger Männer (CVJM), Leipzig; 21. und 51. Mittelschule; Schülerclub Grunau.

NETHERLANDS

Zoetermeer: The Ministry of Education, Culture and Science.

Emmen: Bureau of the Drenthe Educational Priority Area; New Dordrecht preschool playgroup.

Rotterdam: City Fund for Reduction of Educational Disadvantages Rotterdam (FAO); Foundation De Meeuw; Protestant Educational Services Foundation Rotterdam (DCO); De Beukelburg school; Foundation for Welfare in Afrikaanderwijk; Erasmus University.

Rijswijk: Ministry of Health, Welfare and Sports.

PORTUGAL

Lisbon: Ministério da Educação; Ministério do Emprego e da Segurança Social; Ministério da Justiça; Casa Pia de Lisboa; Colégio Pina Manique; Colégio de N. St. da Conceição; Direcção de Serviços de Saúde Mental; Instituto de Apoio à Criança; SOS Criança (linha telefónica); Santa Casa de Misericórdia de Lisboa; Jardim Zoológico de Lisboa; Aldeia de Santa Isabel; Câmara Municipal de Lisboa; Junta de Greguesia; Escola do 1° Ciclo No 5 da Amora-Quinta da Princesa; CEBI – Centro Comunitário de Alverca; Núcleo de Intervenção Comunitária para a Prevenção da Toxicodependência; Chapitô; Centro de Observação e Acção Social; Centro de Estudos para a Intervenção Social; Escola Preparatória de Vila Franca de Xira; Escola Secundaria de Linda-a-Velha; Secretariado Eutre Culturas; Centro Social do Bairro 6 de Maio.

Porto: Centro Regional de Segurança Social do Norte; A Casa do Caminho; Projecto de Luta contra a Pobreza de Ringe; Fundação para o Desenvolvimento da Zona Histórica do Porto.

UNITED STATES

Washington: The Department of Education; The Department of Health and Human Services; The Department of Housing and Urban Development; The White House Domestic Policy Council; Council of Chief State School Officers; National Governors Association; The Institute of Educational Leadership.

California: In Sacramento: The Department of Social Services; The Department of Health Services; The Department of Education; California Child Development Programmes Advisory Committee; California Assembly Office of Research; California Legislature Assembly, Committee on Human Services; California Research Bureau; The Foundation Consortium for School Linked Services; California Legislative Budget Committee. In San Diego: The Office of the Superintendent, San Diego City School District; Department of Health Services; Department of Social Services; Department of Health Services; The Private Industry Council; The Children's Hospital and Health Centre; Alexander Hamilton Elementary School; Hoover Health and Social Services Centre; New Beginnings Council; The Healthy Start Program.

Missouri: Missouri Department of Social Services; Department of Elementary and Secondary Education; Department of Health; Department of Mental Health; The Family Investment Trust.

Kansas City: LINC (Local Investment Commission); Futures Advisory Committee; 21st Century Communities; Heart of America Family Services United Way; Women's Employment Network; KCMC Child Development Corporation; Goppert Child Development Centre; Southeast High School; Swope Parkway Neighbourhood Clinic; Family Focus Centre; Partnership for Kids; Full Employment Council; Adult Basic Education; Employment Security; Penn Valley College.

St Louis: Grace Hill Neighbourhood Services; Family Preservation Services; LINC, Parents as Teachers (PAT); 21st Century Communities; Crisis Nursery; Penrose Family Support Centre; St Charles Employment Training Office; Caring Communities.

New York: The National Centre for Social Work and Education Collaboration; The Edwin Gould Foundation; The Fund for New York City Public Education; The Aaron Diamond Foundation; The Youth Development Institute; The Children's Aid Society; The Door; Community School, IS 218/PS5; Project Highroad, IS 183; The Clearpool School and Camp Clearpool.

AN INTRODUCTION AND REVIEW OF THE LITERATURE

by

Philippa Hurrell and Peter Evans

> Anita, 24, is a single African American mother with three children aged
> 16 months, 4 and 5. She dropped out of school at the age of 15 and is
> unemployed. Her 4 year old son, Thomas, has a speech impediment. She is
> ashamed of being on welfare. A programme called New Start in Kansas City
> (United States) has enabled Anita to study for a high school diploma equivalent
> while Thomas is cared for in a child care centre on the same site. Through New
> Start, Thomas benefits from dental and medical services, and is receiving special-
> ist help for his speech. With the support of New Start, Anita feels optimistic about
> her future and is beginning to regain her self-esteem. Thomas is very happy at
> the child centre. He thoroughly enjoys visits to museums, theatres and zoos
> which, in other circumstances, he might never have experienced.

INTRODUCTION

OECD Member countries have become increasingly concerned about the growing number of children and families who are living in disadvantaged situations and, as a result of school failure and unemployment, find themselves excluded from mainstream society. Many of these people have multiple economic, educational, social and health difficulties which prevent them from enjoying full and rewarding social and working lives.

The integrated provision of education, health and social services is regarded by many Member countries as the most promising solution to this problem. It is widely believed that, by working together, human services can provide more effective and appropriate services – and at a reduced cost to governments.

As a result of the strong interest among Member countries in the integration of services for children at risk, the Centre for Educational Research and Innovation (CERI) at the OECD initiated a three-year study (between 1993 and 1995) to explore policy and practice in this area. "Services integration" was defined in the study as "co-ordination, co-operation or collaboration" between two or more services (OECD, 1996). "Children at risk", on the other hand, were defined as "children who are failing in school and unsuccessful in making the transition to work and, as a consequence, are unlikely to be able to make a full contribution to active society" (OECD, 1996). A total of fourteen Member countries took part in the study including Australia, Belgium, Canada, Finland, France, Germany, Italy, the Netherlands, Portugal, Slovenia, Sweden, Turkey, the United Kingdom, and the United States. The main results of the research, including case study abstracts from seven countries, are outlined in the publication *Successful Services for our Children and Families at Risk* (OECD, 1996), which provides an important synopsis.

The Secretariat as well as participating Member countries agreed, however, that the case study reports that are summarised in this main publication contained important and useful detail, and deserved to be published in their own right. It was felt that great benefits could be derived from planting these case studies firmly in the context of other national research in the field. The purpose of this book, then, is to draw out the main themes of other key national studies in the field, to reproduce the country case studies in full, and to allow useful comparisons to be drawn between the findings of national research and the conclusions of the international OECD study.

Internationally, there is a very wide body of literature on integrated services. In some countries, such as the United States, it is relatively sophisticated; in other countries, such as Portugal, it is just developing. The OECD study has a number of key features which distinguish it from other studies published around the world. First and foremost, it is international and comparative – few other research projects involving several countries have been carried out. Second, it looks at the integration of services at different levels in the services hierarchy – namely, mandating strategic, operational and field – considering changes in the legal and policy frameworks along with the perspectives of administrators, professionals and clients. Third, it considers the provision of services for three different groups of children – preschool children, school children and youth in the transition to work – as well as their families. Fourth, it considers several different dimensions of human services including the context in which they operate, financial and other inputs, the process of service delivery, and outcomes for clients. Finally, it looks at many different programmes in particular locations thus making it possible to describe the functioning of complex community networks.

In the early part of this report, the focus is on the existing literature on the subject of services integration in Germany, Finland, Portugal, the United States, Canada and Australia (a review of the Dutch literature has been published by the Dutch government separately in Geelen *et al.*, 1994). The discussion is based on commissioned literature reviews written by national experts in the field. This is followed by a summary of the common and country-specific themes which emerge from the literature. Finally, case studies of examples of "best practice" in integrated services in Europe (Germany, Finland, Portugal and the Netherlands), the United States (Missouri, New York City and California), Canada (Saskatchewan, Alberta, Ontario and New Brunswick) and Australia (Victoria, South Australia and New South Wales) will be reproduced. These cases studies provide rich and detailed descriptions and analyses of integrated services in different locations which, it is intended, will be useful for administrators and professionals who are designing integrated systems or who are wrestling with their implementation.

This report aims to make available international "know-how" in the field of integrated services – to describe different approaches to achieving integration, to outline the obstacles to co-ordinated working methods, and to offer potential solutions to these problems based on international experience.

NATIONAL REVIEWS OF EXISTING RESEARCH ON INTEGRATED SERVICES

The OECD commissioned a total of six national literature reviews, on integrated services in Germany, Finland, Portugal, the United States, Canada and Australia. The aim was to identify key pieces of academic research and government reports in the field, although in some countries, where research on integrated services is prolific, this proved to be a complex task. The following discussion of national research, plots out the main preoccupations and concerns of leading national "thinkers" and decision-makers in relation to services integration.

Providing a literary back-drop to the case studies, which are the main focus of this publication, this summary of national research and analysis is necessarily quite brief.

Germany

According to Haubrich and Zeller (1994), there is very little reference to "services integration" in the German literature. Instead, the terms "co-operation" and "co-ordination" are used. However, these terms are similar in meaning to "integration" as defined by other countries.

A large segment of the German literature on integrated services outlines the historical development of this approach. Haubrich and Zeller (1994) report that the co-ordination of social services first came to the fore as a national issue during the anti-authoritarian movement of the late 1960s. Critics of the social services system pointed to the need for a new approach in which the needs of customers were analysed in the context of their social environments and in which customers were able to participate in the process of services provision (Barth, 1993). During the 1970s and 1980s, efforts were made to re-organise communal social welfare offices to make them more citizen-oriented and effective. Central goals were to encourage social welfare offices to become more neighbourhood-focused and to reduce fragmentation and duplication in services provision (Bronke and Wenzel, 1980; Reichhwein and Kirchhoff, 1980; Jordan and Sengling, 1992). Many model projects were developed to re-organise communal social services during the 1970s and 1980s; however, according to Olk (1991), they often failed to achieve real changes in services delivery.

In recent years, the dominant concept in political and professional discussion on education and social welfare has been the "world-of-life", or social environment, of individuals (Habermas, 1981). It has led to an increased interest in analysing customers problems in the context of their socio-economic environment, and support for the "decentralisation and regionalisation" of social services so that they can meet customer needs at the local level (Haubrich and Zeller, 1994).

A number of German studies outline legislative measures which have promoted services integration, and their impact in both the old *Länder* (the former Federal Republic of Germany) and the new *Länder* (the former German Democratic Republic). Haubrich and Zeller (1994) report that since 1990 in the new *Länder* and 1991 in the old *Länder*, the Children and Youth Services Act has been in force to promote prevention, customer empowerment, and the integration of services. However, Haubrich and Zeller claim that a lack of funding has impeded the implementation of the recommendations inscribed in the Act. They observe that the Children and Youth Services Act has affected the old and new *Länder* quite differently – largely because they have sharply contrasting traditions of social welfare provision. In the old *Länder*, the principle of "subsidiarity" (according to which the voluntary sector has priority over the public sector) has led to widespread private sector provision of social services whereas, in the new *Länder*, public sector agencies predominate. Furthermore, in the old *Länder*, the social work profession is strongly established, whereas in the new *Länder* social work is almost non-existent as a profession (Backhaus-Maul and Olk, 1992). The outcome is that, in a resource limited environment, the new *Länder* are struggling even more than the old *Länder* to implement change. Local governments simply perform obligatory tasks, and leave innovative work to publicly or privately funded "model projects" (Thole, 1993).

Many detailed accounts of integrated programmes for preschool children, school children and youth in the transition to work have been written by German authors. According to the principle of integrative social work, services for preschool children, including crèches, kindergartens and day nurseries, are expected to co-operate with each other (Jordan and Sengling, 1992). Being part of the educational system, kindergartens traditionally have been oriented towards schools. However, in the last few years they have made efforts to become more integrated into the community. Provision for young children at risk has moved away from residential care towards family support and care in the community, involving a network of local services. Counselling and support services, which traditionally have operated independently, have become increasingly community-oriented and willing to co-operate with other agencies. A number of pilot projects, involving co-operation between kindergartens or day care centres and child guidance services have been developed. Evaluations of these projects have pointed to the need for increased funding, more training and supervision, and the eradication of hierarchical relationships (Haberkorn *et al.*, 1988).

As part of the new "world-of-life" oriented perspective, social services for school children increasingly are looking towards co-operation with educational institutions, in which students spend a large part of each day. Indeed, under the Children and Youth Services Act and other education laws, statutory youth services and schools are obliged to co-operate with each other. Youth services have been made responsible for making programmes available to schools which promote the educational success of disadvantaged students. With the rise in serious problems in schools, such as violence and political extremism, many teachers have embraced school social work as a necessary part of school life (Raab, 1994). However, there are still large differences between the German *Länder* as to the extent to which the integration of youth services and schools has been achieved. A barrier to co-operation has been the different philosophic outlooks of teachers, who see their role as imparters of knowledge, and social workers, who aim to address all of children's needs (Glanzer, 1993). Although, some teachers have been unwilling to accept social workers in schools, many researchers see them as a vital resource to identify individual and organisational problems and to find appropriate solutions (*e.g.* Kunkel, 1990).

The spectre of unemployment has stimulated the development of a system of vocational assistance for disadvantaged young people, including career preparation and vocational training programmes (Raab, 1992). Most of these programmes are funded jointly by the Federal Institute of Labour, free (private) agencies providing social and youth services, and communities. Up until recently, statutory agencies provided little input, although the Children and Youth Services Act has now obliged them to address the needs of untrained and unemployed youth (Braun *et al.*, 1993). Since school failure constitutes the biggest threat to disadvantaged children, many vocational programmes are provided in schools. These have a social pedagogical quality and usually involve collaboration between several different agencies.

The German case studies carried out by the OECD provide up-to-date information which reflects the extent to which the Children and Youth Services Act has achieved its goals.

Finland

Academic or policy research which has the integration of services as its main focus is relatively uncommon in Finland; however, a number of studies touch on this area. These have been summarised by Syväniemi (1994) who claims that national interest in services integration is far greater than is reflected in the literature.

Syväniemi (1994) observes that most day care services for preschool children are provided by the social welfare authorities, although the education authorities also offer day care and preschool education for six-year-olds. Ojala (1989) suggests that although welfare and education services have different priorities – the sufficiency and appropriateness of child care arrangements on one hand, and the quality of preschool education on the other – it is in the interest of children that collaboration between these services is developed further. This conclusion is echoed by research on preschool education carried out by the Ministry of Social Affairs and Health (Aalto, 1991).

Other studies have emphasized the importance of an even broader pattern of collaboration, including child guidance clinics and other child agencies. Research on children who start primary school late has indicated that co-operation is necessary between service providers to prevent this delay, although in practice it is uncommon (Linno 1990a, 1990b). Niemi (1992) points to the need for more co-operation between child guidance clinics and welfare services, but identifies an ignorance of each other's roles as an important obstacle. Tarpila's work (1992) also emphasizes the need for multi-service co-operation – including mental health centres, family guidance clinics, day care centres, child guidance clinics and schools – but, like Niemi, recognises certain barriers. In particular, he points to problems arising from the contrasting fields of work and educational backgrounds of different professional groups. Kauppinen and Sarjanoja (1991) also point to the need for wider professional co-operation, emphasizing the avoidance of duplication in services as a valuable outcome. In addition, they recommend greater co-operation between day care personnel and parents so that they can exchange information and experiences relevant to children's upbringing.

According to Syväniemi (1994), welfare and health services for school children concentrate their activities in schools. In his doctoral thesis, Jauhiainen (1993) describes in detail the evolution of school-based integrated services in Finland, dividing it into three historical periods. The hunger and disease period, from 1866-1920, witnessed the birth of support institutions and services to provide the physical and material prerequisites for school attendance, including school dormitories, school kitchens and summer camps. Early health care was provided by school doctors. During the building period, from 1920-1960, school health care continued to develop, and psycho-social provision began to grow from rudimentary beginnings. In the 1920s, the Mannerheim League for Child Welfare, in providing training for school nurses, played a significant role in the development of school health services. The League was also responsible for the initial development of the Finnish system of Child Guidance Clinics which worked in close co-operation with schools. Vocational counselling services based on psychological premises also developed at this time, and became statutory towards the end of the period. The psycho-social period saw the further development of school health care, and following comprehensive school and public health reforms in the early 1970s, it became statutory in both comprehensive and post-compulsory educational institutions. In the 1970s and 1980s, increasing attention was paid to mental health care and, today, special psychological examinations in school are necessitated by law. Child Guidance Clinics were made statutory in the early 1970s, after which the network of nation-wide clinics grew quickly. However, co-operation with schools has decreased over the years as they have became more family-centred in their approach and as the number of school-based psycho-social staff has grown. The role of psychologists and student counsellors was written into the Child Protection Act in the 1990s, although the Act does not oblige municipalities to establish these positions.

Jauhiainen concludes that the modern day Finnish school is in many respects like a "miniature welfare state" which, in addition to its job of teaching, functions as a centre for social welfare, health care and employment advice. As such, it acts to identify and protect those students who are in danger of failing or dropping out of school. Special educators in educational institutions also contribute to this role. However Jauhiainen's predictions for the future of school welfare provision are bleak: he warns that the economic recession may lead to the "dismantling" of the social welfare system, and is particularly pessimistic regarding the future of psycho-social and preventive care.

While many researchers and practitioners fear cutbacks in spending on psycho-social services, Terho and Vakkilainen (1993) argue that more rather than less attention needs to be given to pupils' mental health problems, particularly in respect of prevention. For the provision of effective mental and general health care, co-operation between health and social welfare professionals, teachers, parents and children is regarded by them as vital. Co-operation between the different professionals in schools is also identified as an important ingredient for the provision of effective health education (Liimatainen-Lamberg, 1993). However, on the basis of a study of anti-smoking health education in Finland, Liimatainen-Lamberg concludes that, without the supplementary involvement of parents and the community, within-school collaboration is impotent as a means to change pupils' behaviour.

Syväniemi (1994) claims that schools also are important focal points for the provision of services for youth in the transition to work. In a study of young people with "school allergy" (unemployed school drop-outs), Takala (1992) concludes that this can only be prevented if schools are willing to cross traditional boundaries and co-operate with other human services such as social welfare, health and leisure. Also regarded as important is the increased integration of education and work, a conclusion shared by Valde (1993).

The Finnish case studies which follow, confirm Jauhiainen's conception of schools as "miniature welfare states", and add to the rather sparse literature addressing the issue of services integration.

Portugal

In Portugal, Cardoso (1994) reports that few examples of integrated services exist and that, as a consequence, research studies in this area are rare. She links limited development in the field of services integration to the relatively recent creation of an effective national social security system (in the late 1960s), and the decentralisation of administrative and political powers (making the implementation of national strategies harder). She reports, however, that there is a strong political interest in services integration, and that it is much discussed at senior levels.

Many co-ordinated initiatives, according to Cardoso, are experimental, at the local level, and address the problem of poverty. Within these programmes, social workers have been particularly quick to embrace the concepts of "partnership" and "multidimensionality" and have emerged as key players in integration efforts. In addition to inter-professional collaboration, increasing attention has been given to community participation, and to public input into strategic planning and decision making. Traditionally, community people have been excluded from these processes. Many experimental programmes receive mixed public and private sector funding and several receive financial support from the European Union.

The concept of integration is attracting growing interest in schools. This has been stimulated by recent studies in Portugal demonstrating the multiple causes of educational failure. These studies have reported the need for: more co-ordination between school support services; improved relationships between schools and families; and better links between schools and employers. Equally they have emphasized the need to address all of students' needs (not just their educational ones), and to involve families more fully in the educational process, as well as in decisions made by service providers. Services integration is reported to be particularly vital when children make important transitions, such as those from family to school and school to work.

Portuguese writers on services integration have identified several key benefits to this approach including: improved economy in services provision; enhanced effectiveness; and change and innovation. However, they also point out important obstacles to integration. Most notably, they emphasize the compartmentalisation of services, differences in the nature and responsibilities of various professions, the "absence or distortion of information", and bureaucratic inertia.

Some of the most significant work in the field of services integration in Portugal has been carried out by Gracio (1988). According to him, one of the main goals of the integration of children's services should be to "provide a coherent system of activities to solve the problems that arise, be it at the level of health, education or social security". He argues that integration makes services more accessible, and can achieve "rationalisation and economy on the one hand and, on the other (...) social justice [through attempting] to solve the serious problems that place children at a disadvantage". He regards administrative, technical and financial support as vital if services integration is to be successfully achieved, and is a supporter of an ecological approach to its implementation. According to this approach, a broad range of bio-medical, behavioural, educational and social services should be provided in a co-ordinated fashion to meet clearly defined community needs.

The Portuguese case study which follows reflects many of the themes apparent in the national literature on services integration. It provides further evidence of the lack of far-reaching developments at the strategic level to achieve integration, and the existence of only a small number of locally initiated co-ordinated services on the ground. At the same time, it adds to the existing literature in exploring the effects of government policy, including decentralisation and privatisation, on services integration, and in providing in-depth analyses of government-nominated examples of best practice.

United States

The American literature on services integration is immense, documenting numerous and varied federal, state and local level initiatives to integrate services over the last three decades. The literature emanating from the political sciences is based on formal organisation theory, while that arising from the social and administrative sciences is concerned with the formulation and implementation of social policy. This literature includes many practical guides which provide step-by-step advice on how to develop integrated service systems.

Lewis (1993) observes that in the vast literature on services integration the "language, concepts and theories are murky and imprecise" (p. 2). The term "services integration" is used in many different ways although many authors cite the definition furnished by Elliot Richardson who was the Secretary of the Department of Health, Education and Welfare in the early 1970s: "services integration refers primarily to ways of organising the delivery of services to people at the local level" (Kusserow, 1991, p. 10). Other common terms, according to Lewis (1993), are the "three C's", co-operation, co-ordination and collaboration. Authors such as Bruner (1991), Kagan (1991), Melaville and Blank (1993), and Mulford and Rogers (1982), describe and contrast the different modes of services provision implied by these terms. The literatures on networks (Alter and Hage, 1993) and case management are also relevant to the concept of integration. Case management approaches have been advocated in the United States for decades and are rooted in the work of Richmond (1901). Current theory and practice in this area have been well documented by Weil and Karls (1985).

The historical development of services integration in the United States has received much attention. During the 1960s, many of the integrated services which developed – including neighbourhood service centres, family planning agencies and Head Start programmes – were community-based. A significant number were community initiated, and received much of their funding support from the federal government, which tended to bypass state government agencies (Resnick *et al.*, 1992). During the 1970s, a major services integration initiative was launched by Secretary Richardson. In contrast to the previous decade, a top-down approach was used in which efforts were made to simplify and integrate over 500 federal programmes and to re-organise state level departments and agencies. In the 1980s, changes in rules allowed for the more flexible use of categorical funding, but deep budget cuts under the Reagan Administration limited integration efforts (US *Budget in Brief*, 1989). Subsequent governments have supported the devolution of responsibility for human services to the state level.

Reviewing federal initiatives to integrate services, the United States Inspector General observed that while services integration efforts "have been instrumental in making human services more accessible to clients and more responsive to their needs", they have had "little institutional impact on a highly fragmented human services system" (Kusserow, 1991, p. i-ii). He suggests that future efforts to integrate services should be targeted at well-defined groups within categorical programme areas. The United States General Accounting Office (1992), on the other hand, points to the need to develop programmes which are "service-oriented" (implying the development of links between customers and services) rather than "system-oriented" (implying the transformation of human services systems).

Many authoritative sources in the United States have indicated their pessimism about the future of services integration, and some have argued that categorical programmes which generate more interest and publicity are better than non-categorical programmes (*e.g.* Ooms and Owen, 1991). However, public outrage and alarm about the failure of the human services system to meet society's needs, combined with disapproval of federal initiatives to create new, narrow and limited categorical programmes, have led to an upsurge of support. Many authors claim that new knowledge and technologies and changing values are creating a more favourable climate for services integration (Kagan, 1991; Kahn and Kamerman, 1992; Schorr *et al.*, 1991).

A new feature which distinguishes services integration efforts from those in the past is the involvement of the education system. Recent laws, including the Hawkins-Stafford Elementary and Secondary School Improvement Amendments (1988), have encouraged collaboration between schools and community-based organisations to provide special programmes for children at risk (Allen-Meares, 1990). Numerous reports have been written which describe efforts in various states to integrate services for preschool and school children (*e.g.* Hendrickson, 1993; Levy and Shepardson 1992; Mitchell, 1992; State Co-ordinating Council, 1993). While many state initiatives involve school-based services on the grounds that they are accessible to all children, some authors have questioned whether any one agency should be allowed to predominate (Chaskin and Richman, 1992).

The American literature on services integration is probably the most sophisticated and expansive in the world. However, in spite of its good advice, federal and state governments and private sector organisations have failed to provide a comprehensive and effective system of services for children at risk. The American case studies which follow consider examples of integrated services provision from an "international" perspective, in which programmes are analysed with the experience of other countries as an available reference point.

Canada

In Canada, the main responsibility for education, social welfare and health services rests with its provinces and territories. Government departments in nearly all of Canada's ten provinces and two territories are interested in promoting the integration of services, and this is reflected in the large body of literature on the subject emanating from government administrations.

According to Volpe (1996), a weak national economy, deep cuts in public spending, and a rise in the number of children and families in disadvantaged situations, are important contextual factors in understanding both the need for, and interest in, services integration.

The available government literature on services integration reveals that nearly all of Canada's provinces and territories are moving in the same direction, namely towards increased integration, and that this is happening at a very rapid pace.

In Alberta, an influential report published in 1994 highlighted the need to eliminate gaps in services provision, reduce the fragmentation of services, and to move beyond co-ordination towards full integration (Commissioner of Services for Children, 1994a). It also recommended that integrated services should be community-managed, should focus on early intervention and prevention, and should recognise cultural diversity. In response, the Alberta government published a provincial Action Plan which proposed changes, in the direction recommended in the report, over a three-year period (Commissioner of Services for Children, 1994b). At around the same time, an interim evaluation of an inter-ministerial initiative, called "Co-ordination of Services for Children", was produced, assessing the success of efforts to promote services co-ordination in five separate communities (Community Services Consulting Limited, 1994). It concluded that the co-ordination of services was essential to provide accessible and effective support to individuals. Other government documents on the provision of integrated and other services have emphasized the importance of children's and parents' rights, including the right to be heard and the right to decide (e.g. Premier's Council in Support of Alberta Families, 1994).

In Ontario, impetus was given to services integration by a report, published in 1988, called "Investing in Children" (Ontario Ministry of Community and Social Services, 1988). This document asserted the need for inter-ministerial collaboration in providing services for children. Two years later, "Children First" set out a comprehensive plan involving several ministries to deliver integrated services with a focus on schools (Maloney, 1990). This was followed by "For the Love of Learning" which proposed that schools should become more community-oriented and that they should be at the hub of integrated services provision (Royal Commission on Learning, 1994). In the same year, "Yours, Mine and Ours: Ontario's Children and Youth" reviewed research about major life transitions and concluded that cross Ministry collaboration was vital (Offord, 1994). The culmination of these reports and recommendations is the government's "Children's Services Policy Framework" which provides a strategic plan for change in the direction of integration, co-ordinated access, enhanced local planning, equity in resource distribution, the establishment of priority groups and enhanced accountability (Ontario Ministry of Community and Social Services, 1994). More recently (in 1995), the Royal Commission on Learning called for additional reforms, including greater participation in services provision by parents and community agencies, and more substantial integration in Ontario's schools.

In Saskatchewan, a government report called "Children First: An Invitation to Work Together" has had an important impact of the development of children's services (Government of Saskatchewan, 1993). This document maps out an Action Plan to promote the well-being of Saskatchewan's children. It recommends that efforts need to be made to further integrate services in the province, and states that existing services are fragmented and therefore ineffective. It proposes that the departments of Social Services, Health, Education, Training and Employment and Justice should work together in the best interest of children by sharing resources, information, skills and knowledge. The report also places a strong emphasis on public participation in strategic planning and on children's rights as laid out in the UN Convention on the Rights of the Child. The Action Plan has spawned an initiative, described in the report "Working Together to Address Barriers to Learning", to provide integrated services in community schools (Department of Education, Training and Employment, 1994). This document points to the various benefits of an integrated approach and outlines the types of programme which could be offered in schools. It also provides examples of existing school-linked services in Saskatchewan.

In New Brunswick, efforts to co-ordinate services for preschool children are documented in a report called "Early Childhood Initiatives" (Department of Health and Community Services, 1993). This describes a programme, developed jointly by the Public Health and Medical Services Division and the Family and Social Services Division, which seeks to promote healthiness and "readiness to learn" among very young children. In the following year, a report by the Department of Education on children of school age stated that it was essential for educators to collaborate with other government and non-government agencies to meet pupils' wide-ranging needs (Department of Education, 1994). It announced that various departments, covering education, employment, health, community services, mental health, human resources and justice, had agreed to work collaboratively in order to develop programmes and services for students with severe behavioural problems. In the same year, three reports by the Department of Health and Community Services described and evaluated a five-year programme, organised in conjunction with the Department of Education, to provide multiple services in schools to support students with language, learning, psychological, social, physical and health needs. It was found that this programme (entitled "Support Services to Education") was highly effective in promoting students' well-being (Dilworth, 1994; Dilworth and Sanford, 1994; Lapointe, 1994).

Similar government reports, either recommending services integration or providing a strategic plan to achieve it have been published by a number of other provinces including British Columbia (Gove, 1995), Manitoba (Postl, 1995), Prince Edward Island (Youth Services Review Committee, 1993) and Quebec (Government of Quebec, 1990). And this list is by no means complete. Common themes across these reports are an emphasis on children's rights as defined in the UN Convention and a concern about the rights of aboriginal groups.

The Canadian case studies which follow show how four provincial governments' strategic plans to integrate children's services have been put into practice and with what level of success.

Australia

According to Batten (1995), services integration in Australia has been stimulated by numerous studies which have highlighted the multiple causes of school drop-out. Drug and alcohol abuse, family conflict, fragmentation and dislocation, homelessness, pregnancy and motherhood, and social and emotional problems, have all been linked with early school leaving or poor educational achievement (South Australia, 1993; Holden and Dwyer, 1992; Maas and Hartley, 1988; Cornwell et al., 1989; Candy and Baker, 1992).

A large number of studies in Australia have examined interventions to meet the needs of students at risk. They indicate that the majority of programmes have been school-based or school focused (i.e. off-site but with strong school links). Often, services integration is viewed by writers as one of a broad set of strategies that should be used in such initiatives. Bradley (1992), for example, lists nine areas of school life which need to be addressed to help keep students in school. These are the curriculum, teaching/learning processes, assessment and credentials, relationships and climate, discipline and control, school organisation, environment and resources, external links and staffing. Similarly, Corbitt (1993) and Holden (1993) refer to a range of features which need to be in-built into programmes for the homeless. Several of these, including financial and physical assistance, emotional support, adult support work, health and guidance counselling, and the provision of advocacy, indicate the need for services co-ordination.

According to two government reports, school counsellors are key to addressing the needs of students who are homeless or who have behavioural problems (Burdekin, 1989; House of Representatives, 1994). The Burdekin Report recommends an expanded role for school counsellors, suggesting that they undergo intensive training to perform a welfare (as well as an educational) role. The House of Representatives report deplores the decreasing numbers of counsellors and psychologists in schools (due to reduced education budgets), and recommends a ratio of one counsellor per 500 students in all Australian states.

Services integration in Australian secondary schools recently has been promoted through a Students at Risk (STAR) Programme which began in 1990. This programme aims to identify those students most at risk of dropping out, and to encourage their continued participation through a range of school-based or school-focused projects. A national evaluation of the programme by Coopers et al. (1992) concludes that "an outstanding feature of the STAR Programme is that so much has been done with very little". Their evaluation includes a series of case studies which describe the different locally designed programmes implemented at each site, and the main outcomes of these initiatives. Most outcomes are reported to be positive, although the evidence is largely anecdotal.

A number of other reports provide descriptions, analyses and/or evaluations of integrated programmes for disruptive or disinclined secondary students and unemployed youth (Turner, 1988; Withers and Batten, 1988; Russell, 1994), pregnant teenagers and adolescent mothers (Education

Department of South Australia, 1991; Milligan and Thomson, 1992), homeless students (Holden, 1993; Coopers *et al.*, 1992), and students who use drugs (Kelly, 1987; Garrard and Northfield, 1987).

Australian authors also have addressed difficult or unresolved issues connected with the implementation of co-ordinated services. Several have questioned whether or not it is appropriate for schools to extend their responsibilities beyond education. A study by Coopers *et al.* (1992) found that school staff viewed housing, financial, health and social welfare services as essential for homeless students to be able to learn efficiently. However, other research warns of the legal and resource implications of school involvement in this field. The issue of parental involvement in integrated programmes has also been raised. Some authors, including Laurie and Collings (1993), point to the fact that behavioural problems amongst students can be caused by their parents. Parenting programmes in schools are viewed by them as an important means to address children's problems. Important concerns have also been raised regarding services for young adults (Burdekin, 1989). Indeed, recently the Committee on Youth Affairs (Western Australia Legislative Assembly, 1992) reported that the youth affairs field was "in a state of considerable disrepair because of poorly resourced central policy mechanisms and fragmented local co-ordinating structures" (p. 13). At an even more fundamental level, some authors are worried that services integration can have little impact without "far-reaching changes in societal equity and access" (Abbott-Chapman and Patterson, 1990, p. ix).

In spite of these concerns, the concept of services integration is widely supported as an effective means to address the problems of children at risk in Australia, and Batten (1995) predicts that services integration "is likely to grow and strengthen in the years ahead".

The Australian case studies which follow provide new descriptions, analyses and evaluations of integrated programmes. In doing so they confirm many of the findings reported in the existing (and very rich) literature in the field. However, in considering integration at state and local levels, and in examining programmes for different age and at risk groups, they provide a uniquely broad perspective on the topic.

INTERNATIONAL THEMES AND ISSUES

It is apparent from the international literature that "integration" is only one of many different terms, including co-operation, co-ordination and collaboration, which are used to describe the process of creating a network of services which work together. In some countries, such as Germany, the use of the term is in fact rare; in others, notably the United States, it is common. In all of the countries reviewed, however, services integration (in the broadest sense) is seen as having enormous potential as a strategic option. Integration is seen as a means to improve the effectiveness of services while at the same time reducing public costs; in other words, it is regarded as cost-effective. Seemingly paradoxically, in addition to relieving public financial pressures it is viewed as demanding additional funding provision. But this paradox is resolved by the argument that "short-term costs achieve long-term gains".

For preschool children, governments and academics alike have concluded that social welfare and health services, including day care centres and mental health centres, should form integrated networks, and that day care services and schools should work closely together. For school children, school-based or school-focused integrated services are regarded as particularly appropriate. And for youth in the transition to work, many authors recommend closer links between schools and employers.

In the international literature, services integration is spoken of in the same sentence as a number of other related issues. These include the decentralisation of services, preventive and holistic care, community involvement and client participation, and an outcomes-driven approach to services provision. Interestingly, the same constellation of concerns is apparent from country to country.

By definition, OECD Member countries are liberal market economies which emphasize cost-efficient public spending. The priority given to social exclusion on the agendas of both the OECD and the European Union shows that Member countries also are deeply disturbed by the growing proportion of individuals who are living in "marginal" situations. It is, then, not surprising that services integration is a strategy which enjoys world-wide support. And it is, perhaps, also to be expected that countries who adopt integration as a policy face the same set of issues and concerns – which, by and large, they do. As a result, there is great potential for international collaboration and information sharing in the field. The case studies which follow aim to facilitate this process.

RESEARCH METHODOLOGY

A central aim of the OECD research was to collect information on examples of best practice in integrated services for children in three distinct phases, namely, preschool children, school children and youth in the transition to work. The decision to study them separately was based on the different spectrum of services they require. Families with preschool children are important consumers of health care; school children are important users of educational services; and youth in the transition to work are more likely to take advantage of vocational and employment services. Hence the character of "integrated services" for each of these age groups will differ in a significant way.

While the term "integrated services" often seems to imply collaboration between professionals at the front-line, the ability to work together is frequently dependent on initiatives to support integration at the administrative and management levels. Therefore, for the case studies, OECD experts interviewed actors from the strategic and operational levels as well as field level workers. They also interviewed service users to elicit the degree of success of integrated services in meeting individual needs.

In order to collect a comprehensive body of information which would allow us to analyse how and why integrated services "work" (or fail to work), we addressed four conceptual areas: context, input, process and product. These have been widely used in North America and elsewhere to study human services (Stufflebeam, 1988; Volpe, 1996). Context refers to the history and background to integrated services, providing a setting in which to contextualise them. Input refers to the different resources which have been invested in integrated services by both public and private bodies. Process alludes to ways in which services are planned, organised and delivered by administrators, managers and professionals. Finally product refers to the outcomes of service delivery, such as the level of client satisfaction and the success of treatment programmes.

To assure consistent and systematic data collection between the case study sites, the experts used four semi-structured interview schedules. These posed questions – grouped according to CIPP (Context, Input, Process, Product) structure – relevant to each of the four interest groups described earlier (strategic, operational and field level personnel, and clients; for details see OECD, 1996). While some issues were only relevant to one particular group, others were asked at more than one level in the services hierarchy. This provided an interesting window on the similarities and differences in perspective amongst administrators, managers and professionals.

At each case study site the main body of the research centred around one-to-one or, where appropriate, group interviews. However, interviewees were also asked to complete a self-completion questionnaire containing a more general set of questions on services integration, and other elements of the research included tours of institutions, observation of the service delivery process, informal discussion, and the collection of relevant literature.

A team including two members of the OECD Secretariat and five OECD experts, carried out the research over a period of between three and five days in each country. The European case studies (Germany, Finland and Portugal) were carried out in 1993; the American and Canadian case studies (Missouri, New York City, California, Saskatchewan, Alberta, Ontario and New Brunswick) in 1994; and the Australian case studies (Victoria, South Australia and New South Wales) in 1995. Additional case studies were completed by the Finnish government in 1995 and the Dutch government in 1996.

In practice, the data collection was less systematic than was planned. The nature of the visits to the case study sites, arranged by Member countries, differed markedly and this, of course, influenced the kind of data that could be collected. Differences between the visits reflected the different emphases and concerns of the organisers and professionals on the ground, and variation in the nature of service networks. In hindsight, these differences are regarded as valuable and interesting, providing important insight into the unique features of each location. Each case study, then, has its own particular character, although all of them share the same basic research themes (described above).

REFERENCES

General

GEELEN, H., VAN UNEN, A. and WALRAVEN, G. with BUIS, C. (1994), *Services Integration for Children and Youth at Risk in the Netherlands*, SARDES, The Hague.

OECD (1996), *Successful Services for our Children and Families at Risk*, Paris.

STUFFLEBEAM, D. (1988), "The CIPP model for programme evaluation", in G. Madaus, M. Scriven and D. Stufflebeam (eds.), *Evaluation Models*, Kluwer-Nijhoff, Boston.

VOLPE, R. (1996), "The CIPP model and the case study approach", *Successful Services for our Children and Families at Risk*, Annex 2, p. 325, OECD, Paris.

Germany

BACKHAUS-MAUL, H. and OLK, T. (1992), "Die Konstitution kommunaler Sozialpolitik; Probleme des Aufbaus sozialer Versorgungsstrukturen in den neuen Bundesländern", in C. Rühl (ed.), *Probleme der Einheit, Band 5: Institutionelle Reorganisation in den neuen Bundesländern*, Marburg.

BARTH, K. (1993), "Aspekte der Organisationsberatung in der Sozialarbeit/Sozialpädagogik", in E.J. Brunner and W. Schöning (eds.), *Organisationen beraten: Impulse für Theorie und Praxis*, Freiburg im Breisgau.

BRAUN, F., LEX, T., SCHAFER, H. and ZINK, G. (1993), "Öffentliche Jugendhilfe und Jugendberufshilfe – Ergebnisse aus der wissenschaftlichen Begleitung des Bundesjugendplan Modellprogramms 'Arbeitsweltbezogene Jugendsozialarbeit'", *Jugend Beruf Gesellschaft*, 44, pp. 182-187.

BRONKE, K. and WENZEL, G. (1980), "Neuorganisation – staatliches Handeln in der Krise?", in *Sozialarbeit als Sozialbürokratie? Zur Neuorganisation sozialer Dienste, Neue Praxis*, Sonderheft, 10, pp. 121-132.

GLANZER, W. (1993), "Schulsozialarbeit in den neuen Ländern – Schlagwort oder zukunftsweisende strukturelle Manahme", *Jugendhilfe*, 31, pp. 19-22.

HABERKORN, R., HAGEMANN, U. and SEEHAUSEN, H. (1988), *Kindergarten und soziale Dienste*, Freiburg im Breisgau.

HABERMAS, J. (1981), *Theorie des kommunikativen Handelns*, 2 Bände, Frankfurt.

HAUBRICH, K. and ZELLER, M.C. (1994), "Services integration for children and youth at risk: A review of the German literature", unpublished, OECD, Paris.

JORDAN, E. and SENGLING, D. (1992), *Jugendhilfe. Einführung in Geschichte und Handlungsfelder, Organisationsformen und gesellschaftliche Problemlagen*, Weinheim und München.

KUNKEL, P.-C. (1990), *Jugendhilfe und Schule. Zum Verhältnis beider Institutionen nach dem neuen Jugendhilferecht*, Kehl.

OLK, T. (1991), "Die professionelle Zukunft sozialer Arbeit", in H. Oppl and A. Tomaschek (eds.), *Soziale Arbeit 2000, Modernisierungskrise und soziale Dienste*, Freiburg im Breisgau.

RAAB, E. (1992), "Berufsausbildung und Arbeitsmarktchancen Jugendlicher in den alten Bundesländern", *Aus Politik und Zeitgeschichte*, 38, pp. 36-46.

RAAB, E. (1994), "Schulsozialarbeit – Perspektiven für die 90er Jahre", *Jugend Beruf Gesellschaft*, 44, p. 5.

REICHWEIN, A. and KIRCHHOFF, G. (1980), "Integration sozialer Dienste als Problem, Sozialarbeit als Sozialbürokratie?", *Zur Neuorganisation sozialer Dienste, Neue Praxis*, Sonderheft, 10, pp. 132-139.

THOLE, W. (1993), "Strae oder Jugendclub. Zur Reaktivierung der auerschulischen Kinder und Jugendarbeit in den neuen Bundesländern", *Neue Praxis*, 23, 3, pp. 185-206.

Finland

AALTO, V.-L. (1991), "Esiopetuksen järjestämisestä", *Sosiaalinen Aikakauskirja* (on organising preschool education), Vol 6, p. 32.

JAUHIAINEN, A. (1993), "School, student welfare and the welfare state: The formation of the student welfare system in the Finnish compulsory education system and its network of experts from the late 1800s to 1990s", *Publications of the University of Turku C 98*, University of Turku, Turku.

KAUPPINEN, M. and SARJANOJA, M. (ed.) (1991), *Erilainen lapsi päivähoidossa* (a different child in day care), WSOY, Porvoo.

LIIMATAINEN-LAMBERG, A.-E. (1993), "Changes in student smoking habits at the vocational institutions and senior secondary schools and health education", *Studies in Sport, Physical Education and Health 30*, University of Jyväskylä, Jyväskylä.

LINNO, T. (1990a), "Ketkä kompastuvat koulun kynnykseen? Koulun, päiväkodin ja neuvolan mahdollisuudet ennaltaehkäistä lieviä oppimisvaikeuksia Vantaalla", *Koulutuksen Palvelukeskuksen julkaisuja 1990* (who stumble on the school threshold?), 1, Vantaan kaupunki.

LINNO, T. (1990b), "Jotta koulun kynnykseen ei kompastuttaisi", *Koulutuksen Palvelukeskuksen julkaisuja 1990* (so as not to stumble on the school threshold), 2, Vantaan kaupunki.

NIEMI, A. (1992), "Neuvolatyö muuttuvassa terveydenhuollossa" (child guidance within changing public health work), *Lapsen maailma 3*.

OJALA, M. (1989), "Early childhood training, care and education in Finland", in P.P. Olmsted and D.P. Weikart (eds.), *How Nations Serve Young Children: Profiles of Child Care and Education in 14 Countries*, The High Scope Press, Ypsilanti, Michigan.

SYVÄNIEMI, U. (1994), "Services integration for children and youth at risk: A review of the Finnish literature", unpublished, OECD, Paris.

TAKALA, M. (1992), "'Kouluallergia – yksilön ja yhteiskunnan ongelma", *Acta Universitatis Tamperensis*, ser. A, Vol. 335, Tampereen, Tampere.

TARPILA, J. (1992), "Neuvola ja sosiaalityö – yhdessä lapsen hyväksi" (child guidance clinic and social work – together for the good of the child), *Lapsen maailma 3*.

TERHO, P. and VAKKILAINEN, E.-L. (1993), *Kouluterveydenhuollon tukiaineisto* (support material for school health care), STAKES, Helsinki.

VALDE, E. (1993), "The role of student counselling in senior secondary school in orientation towards working life and in vocational choice", *Publications of the University of Turku C 94*, University of Turku, Turku.

Portugal

CARDOSO, A. (1994), "Services integration for children and youth at risk: A review of the Portuguese literature", unpublished, OECD, Paris.

GRACIO, R. (1988), *Integração de Serviços para a Infância/Metodologia de Projectos*, Fundação Aga Khan/Fundação Calouste Gulbenkian, Lisbon.

United States

ALLEN-MEARES, P. (1990), "Elementary and secondary school improvement amendments of 1988 and the future of social services in schools", *Social Work in Education*, 12, pp. 249-260.

ALTER, C. and HAGE, J. (1993), *Organisations Working Together*, SAGE, London.

BRUNER, C. (1991), *Thinking Collaboratively*, Education and Human Services Consortium, Washington.

CHASKIN, R.J. and RICHMAN, H.A (1992), "Concerns about school-linked services: Institution-based versus community-based models", *The Future of Children*, 2, pp. 107-117.

HENDRICKSON, J.M. (1993), *School-based Comprehensive Services*, unpublished paper presented at the Obermann Faculty Research Seminar, Centre for Advanced Studies, University of Iowa, July 13.

KAGAN, S.L. (1991), *United We Stand: Collaboration for Child Care and Early Education Services*, Teachers College, Columbia University.

KAHN, A.J. and KAMERMAN, S.B. (1992), *Integrating Services Integration: An Overview of Initiatives, Issues and Possibilities*, Columbia University School of Social Work, New York.

KUSSEROW, R.P. (1991), *Services Integration: A Twenty-one Year Retrospective*, Department of Health and Human Services, Office of the Inspector General, Washington.

LEVY, J.E. and SHEPARDSON, W. (1992), "A look at current school-linked service efforts", *The Future of Children*, 2:1, pp. 44-55.

LEWIS, M. (1993), "Services integration for children and youth at risk: A review of the American literature", unpublished, OECD, Paris.

MELAVILLE, A.I. and BLANK, M.J. (1993), *Together We Can*, US Government Printing Office, Washington.

MITCHELL, A. and THE EARLY EDUCATION/CHILD CARE WORK GROUP (1992), *Moving Toward a Unified System of Child Development and Family Support Services in Vermont*, Department of SRS, Child Care Services Division, Waterbury, VT.

MULFORD, C.L. and ROGERS, D.L. (1982), "Definitions and models", in D.L. Rogers and D.A. Whetten (eds.), *Interorganisational Co-ordination: Theory, Research and Implementation*, Iowa State University Press, Ames, Iowa.

OOMS, T. and OWEN, T. (1991), *Co-ordination, Collaboration, Integration: Strategies for Serving Families More Effectively, Part 1: The Federal Role*, AAMFT Research and Education Foundation, Washington.

RESNICK, G., BURT, M.R., NEWMARK, L. and REILLY, L. (1992), *Youth at Risk: Definitions, Prevalence and Approaches to Service Delivery*, Urban Institute, Washington.

RICHMOND, M.E. (1901), "Charitable co-operation", in I.C. Barrows (ed.), *Proceedings of the National Conference of Charities and Correction*, George H. Ellis, Boston.

SCHORR, L.B., BOTH, D. and COPPLE, C. (eds.) (1991), *Effective Services for Young Children*, National Academy Press, Washington.

STATE CO-ORDINATING COUNCIL (1993), Third Annual Report of the State Co-ordinating Council for Early Childhood Services, Tallahassee, FL.

US Budget in Brief: Fiscal Year 1990 (1989), Government Printing Office, Washington.

US GENERAL ACCOUNTING OFFICE (1992), *Integrating Human Services*, Washington.

WEIL, M. and KARLS, J.M. (1985), *Case Management in Human Service Practice*, Jossey-Bass Publishers, Washington.

Canada

COMMISSIONER OF SERVICES FOR CHILDREN (1994a), *Finding a Better Way: The Consultations and Research Leading to the Redesign of Children's Services in Alberta*, Government of Alberta, Alberta.

COMMISSIONER OF SERVICES FOR CHILDREN (1994b), *Focus on Children: A Plan for Effective, Integrated Community Services for Children and their Families*, Government of Alberta, Alberta.

COMMUNITY SERVICES CONSULTING LIMITED (1994), *The Co-ordination of Services for Children*, Edmonton, Alberta.

DEPARTMENT OF EDUCATION (1994), *Children and Youth with Severe Behavior Disorders*, Government of New Brunswick, New Brunswick.

DEPARTMENT OF EDUCATION, TRAINING AND EMPLOYMENT (1994), *Working Together to Address Barriers to Learning*, Government of Saskatchewan, Saskatchewan.

DEPARTMENT OF HEALTH AND COMMUNITY SERVICES (1993), *Early Childhood Initiatives*, Government of New Brunswick, New Brunswick.

DILWORTH, C. (1994), *Support Services to Education (SSE) Evaluation Project, Phase I, Section I: Service Delivery*, Department of Health and Community Services, Government of New Brunswick, New Brunswick.

DILWORTH, C. and SANFORD, S. (1994), *Support Services to Education (SSE) Evaluation Project, Phase I, Section II: Case Count*, Department of Health and Community Services, Government of New Brunswick, New Brunswick.

GOVE, T.J. (1995), *Executive Summary: Report of the Gove Inquiry into Child Protection*, Ministry of Social Services, British Columbia.

GOVERNMENT OF QUEBEC (1990), *Health and Social Services in Schools*, Quebec.

GOVERNMENT OF SASKATCHEWAN (1993), *Children First – An Invitation to Work Together: Creating Saskatchewan's Action Plan for Children*, Saskatchewan.

LAPOINTE, R. (1994), *Support Services to Education (SSE) Evaluation Project, Phase II: Perception of Effectiveness*, Department of Health and Community Services, Government of New Brunswick, New Brunswick.

MALONEY, C. (1990), *Children First*, Ontario Ministry of Community and Social Services, Toronto.

OFFORD, D. (1994), *Yours, Mine and Ours*, Premier's Council on Health, Well-being and Social Justice, Toronto, Ontario.

ONTARIO MINISTRY OF COMMUNITY AND SOCIAL SERVICES (1988), *Investing in Children*, Toronto, Ontario.

ONTARIO MINISTRY OF COMMUNITY AND SOCIAL SERVICES (1994), *Children's Services Policy Framework*, Queen's Printer, Toronto.

POSTL, B. (1995), *The Health of Manitoba's Children*, Government of Manitoba, Manitoba.

PREMIER'S COUNCIL IN SUPPORT OF ALBERTA FAMILIES (1994), *Coming of Age in Alberta: An Overview of Parents' and Children's Rights and Responsibilities*, Edmonton.

ROYAL COMMISSION ON LEARNING (1994), *For the Love of Learning*, Government of Ontario, Ontario.

VOLPE, R. (1996), "Services integration for children and youth at risk: A review of the Canadian literature", unpublished, OECD, Paris.

YOUTH SERVICES REVIEW COMMITTEE (1993), *Youth, Families and Communities: The New Paradigm for Action*, Government of Prince Edward Island, PEI.

Australia

ABBOTT-CHAPMAN, J. and PATTERSON, C. (1990), *Evaluation of the Students at Risk Programme in Tasmanian Schools*, Report 1, Youth Studies Centre, Hobart.

BATTEN, M. (1995), "Services integration for children and youth at risk: A review of the Australian literature", unpublished, OECD, Paris.

BRADLEY, G. (1992), "Increasing student retention", *Youth Studies Australia*, 11 (2), pp. 37-42.

BURDEKIN, B. (Chair, Human Rights and Equal Opportunity Commission) (1989), *Our Homeless Children: Report of the National Inquiry into Homeless Children*, AGPS, Canberra.

CANDY, L. and BAKER, M. (1992), "What Berengarra School has learned about working with families", in J. Elkins and J. Izard (eds.), *Student Behaviour Problems: Contexts, Initiatives and Programmes*, ACER, Hawthorn, pp. 276-282.

COOPERS AND LYBRAND CONSULTANTS and ASHENDEN MILLIGAN (1992), *Students at Risk Programme: Case Studies*, AGPS, Canberra.

CORBITT, B. (1993), "Helping homeless kids break the transition gap", in D. Evans, M. Myhill and J. Izard (eds.), *Student Behaviour Problems: Contexts, Initiatives and Programmes*, ACER, Hawthorn, pp. 50-64.

CORNWELL, E., HARKIN, P., PRICE, R., ROWE, J. and THOMPSON, L. (1989), "The Rosemount Day Programme", *The Bulletin of the National Clearinghouse for Youth Studies*, 8 (3), pp. 44-48.

EDUCATION DEPARTMENT OF SOUTH AUSTRALIA, EDUCATION OF GIRLS UNIT (1991), *Supportive Learning Environment: Pregnant Girls and Teenage Mothers*, Education Department of South Australia, Adelaide.

GARRARD, J. and NORTHFIELD, J. (1987), *Drug Education in Victorian Post-Primary Schools*, Faculty of Education, Monash University and Health Department of Victoria, Melbourne.

HOLDEN, E. (1993), *Services and Early School Leavers: Policies, Programmes and Practices*, Working Paper No. 10, University of Melbourne, Institute of Education, Youth Research Centre, Melbourne.

HOLDEN, E. and DWYER, P. (1992), *Making the Break: Leaving School Early*, Working Paper No. 8, University of Melbourne, Institute of Education, Youth Research Centre, Melbourne.

HOUSE OF REPRESENTATIVES COMMITTEE ON EMPLOYMENT, EDUCATION AND TRAINING (1994), *Sticks and Stones: Report on Violence in Australian Schools*, AGPS, Canberra.

KELLY, A. (1987), "Preparing school-based staff to manage drug-related incidents", *Drug Education Journal of Australia*, 1 (3), pp. 245-254.

LAURIE, R. and COLLINGS, Y. (1993), "Helping kids by helping the parents", in D. Evans, M. Myhill and J. Izard (eds.), *Student Behaviour Problems: Positive Initiatives and New Frontiers*, ACER, Hawthorn, pp. 143-147.

MAAS, F. and HARTLEY, R. (1988), *On the Outside: The Needs of Unsupported, Homeless Youth*, Australian Institute of Family Studies, Melbourne.

MILLIGAN, S. and THOMSON, K. (1992), *Listening to Girls: A Report of the Consultancy Undertaken for the Australian Education Council Committee to Review the National Policy for the Education of Girls in Australian Schools*, Australian Education Council, Carlton.

RUSSELL, V.J. (1994), *Post-Compulsory Education and Training Arrangements in the Australian States and Territories*, AGPS, Canberra.

SOUTH AUSTRALIA, EDUCATION DEPARTMENT (1993), *Students at Risk Programme in South Australia*, Education Department of South Australia, Richmond, South Australia.

TURNER, D. (1988), "It means a lot more than business: Young people and enterprise skills", *The Bulletin of the National Clearinghouse for Youth Studies*, 7 (2), pp. 2-7.

WESTERN AUSTRALIA LEGISLATIVE ASSEMBLY (1992), *Select Committee on Youth Affairs*, Discussion Paper No. 2, Government Printer, Perth.

WITHERS, G. and BATTEN, M. (1988), *For National Consideration: Improving Post-Compulsory Curriculum Provision*, Curriculum Development Centre, Canberra.

Part I

CASE STUDIES CARRIED OUT
BY THE OECD SECRETARIAT

AUSTRALIA

In this section, the case studies focus on integrated services in three Australian states: Victoria, South Australia and New South Wales.

One of the main federal bodies responsible for the planning of services for disadvantaged young people is the Department of Education, Employment, Training and Youth Affairs. As part of the National Equity Programme for Schools (NEPS), implemented in 1994, the Department funds special programmes for students with physical, emotional or behavioural difficulties, at risk of dropping out of school, from low socio-economic backgrounds, from non-English speaking backgrounds or who are geographically isolated, as well as Aboriginals and Torres Strait Islanders. One such programme is called Students at Risk or STAR. Initiated in 1990, this programme is designed for pupils in danger of dropping out of school, and particularly focuses on the plight of girls, who tend to have more problems in developing a career orientation. All STAR funded projects have to be school-based but the involvement of outside agencies – and therefore co-ordination of some kind – is encouraged.

The Department also is responsible for improving the employment opportunities of young adults at risk. From 1985 onwards, a national network of Youth Access Centres (YAC) was developed. Attached to Commonwealth Employment Services, these are places where young people can obtain information and advice on education, training and employment, income support, health, accommodation and legal issues. YACs are also responsible for facilitating co-ordination among local youth services. Amongst other things, they have been charged to develop youth profiles, circulate this information through inter-agency networks, identify gaps and duplication in services provision, develop linkages with other service providers, assist in the development of inter-agency strategies, and participate in co-ordinated planning.

Since NEPS, the STAR Programme and Youth Access Centres are central to local level efforts to integrate services in the Australian states, these will be discussed in more detail within the three case studies which follow.

VICTORIA

COHESION AND CONFLICT IN FEDERAL, STATE AND LOCAL LEVEL EFFORTS TO INTEGRATE SERVICES

by

Jennifer Evans and Josette Combes

THE RESEARCH

The research sites in the State of Victoria were located in Melbourne and Bendigo. They consisted of four secondary schools, four Youth Access Centres, and a scheme run by the Salvation Army (Crossroads) which linked housing aid with employment and training. This report is based on our site visits, talks with senior managers from the Victorian Education Department, the Commonwealth Employment Service (CES), and Youth Access Centres (YACs), and documentation provided by the federal government, the Victorian government and the sites themselves.

MAIN AT RISK GROUPS

For the purposes of our visit, at risk young people appeared to be defined as those who were at risk of dropping out of school, and those who were at risk of long-term unemployment. Thus it focused on older children and young people in their last years of schooling or who had just left education.

The first section of this report focuses on programmes delivered in schools for pupils whose education is at risk for various reasons, such as homelessness, an unstable home background, lack of resources or problems with drugs. The second section of the report focuses on the operation of the Youth Access Centres (YACs) which were set up specifically to target young people in the transition from secondary school to work or further/higher education. They are part of the Commonwealth Employment Service (CES). The third section reports on the work of Crossroads, a project managed by the Salvation Army (a non-government organisation or NGO).

CONTEXT

Australia has a total area of 8 million square kilometres (about the same size as mainland United States). The population is 17 million, most of whom live in the coastal cities. Some 2 per cent of the population are of aboriginal descent, and 20 per cent were born outside Australia. Up until 1945, the majority of immigration was from Britain and Ireland. After the Second World War, immigration from Europe increased, and in the past ten years, a sizeable proportion of immigrants have come from the Asia Pacific region.

Australia has a federal system of government, with six states and two territories. The federal capital is Canberra. Each state and territory has its own government. The provision of education is a state responsibility, but the Department of Employment, Education, Training and Youth Affairs (DEETYA) is the Commonwealth Department responsible for national education policy.

The economy has been heavily dependent on agriculture and the extraction of natural resources. More recently, the greatest expansion in employment has been in the service sector, in areas such as finance, tourism and government.

Around 4.9 per cent of GDP are spent on education. The major portion of the funding for education (90 per cent of the cost of government schools and 35 per cent of the cost of non-government schools) comes from the state and territory governments. About 25 per cent of children attend private schools, the majority of these being Catholic.

Although the state and territory governments have the major responsibility for schools and non-advanced technical and further education (TAFE), the Commonwealth Government takes special responsibility for the delivery of education to Aborigines, migrants and disadvantaged students. These programmes are the responsibility of DEETYA. The Department is responsible for higher education, research, overseas students, Aboriginal and multi-cultural education, assistance to schools and TAFE, and the provision of financial assistance to students, notably ABSTUDY (for Aboriginal students at all levels) and AUSTUDY (means-tested assistance for secondary and post-secondary students aged 16 and over).

Altogether the two school sectors, government and non-government, cater for over 3.1 million children. There are approximately 10 000 schools in Australia, of which around 70 per cent are primary schools, 16 per cent secondary schools, 8 per cent combined primary and secondary schools, and 4 per cent special schools. School is compulsory from age 6 to 15 (16 in Tasmania). Most children enrol at five in a preparatory year. Primary education lasts six or seven years, followed by five or six years of secondary education. The student/teaching staff ratio is around 18:1 in primary and 12:1 in secondary schools.

The Commonwealth provides funds in four broad areas:

- general recurrent grants to assist with on-going costs;

- capital grants to assist in the provision of school facilities;

- targeted programmes designed to assist schools and students with special needs; and

- grants to promote activities in areas of national education importance.

The Commonwealth administers policies and programmes related to these broad areas of funding. Total expenditure on schools in Australia is estimated to be over A$13.5 billion per year.

In 1989, Commonwealth and State Ministers of Education signed a document known as the Hobart Declaration which was a commitment to collaborate towards a significant improvement in Australian schooling.

BRIEF REVIEW OF SOME OF THE MAIN PROGRAMMES

National Equity Programme for Schools (NEPS)

The NEPS brings together in a single framework a range of formerly separate programme components. It came into full effect in 1994. Total funding under the NEPS is about A$280 million. The objectives of the NEPS are to provide target groups (e.g. students disadvantaged by poverty, by being Aboriginal or Torres Strait Islander, by poor literacy, family breakdown violence or abuse, homeless or substance abuse) with equal opportunities to take advantage of their schooling.

The NEPS is made up of eleven programme components grouped into four elements. These are listed below:

- The *access element*:

  • English as a second language component for students with non-English speaking backgrounds (NESB); and

  • special education component for children with special needs.

- The *equity element*:

  • disadvantaged schools component for schools located in communities with low socio-economic status; and

  • country areas general component for isolated students in remote areas.

- *The national priorities element*:
  - literacy and learning national component;
  - early literacy component;
  - students at Risk (STAR) component for those students most at risk of not finishing secondary school;
  - gifted and talented component to enrich the learning experience of gifted and talented students particularly when they have disabilities or social handicaps; and
  - transition support component to help disabled students in the transition from school to further education or employment.
- *The incentives element*:
  - gender equity component, which provides grants per capita to encourage girls to study maths or physics in years 11 and 12; and
  - students with disabilities component per capita incentive to help schools meet operational costs associated with disabilities.

There is no NEPS component dedicated to the needs of Aboriginal children and Torres Strait Islanders, but they are considered as the main target group of almost all of the other components. In addition, there is a major educational programme operated under the Aboriginal and Torres Strait Islander Commission (ATSIC).

There are now agreements between the Commonwealth and education authorities covering declared objectives, targets, mechanisms for community involvement, evaluation and the provision of nationally consistent data on equity outcomes.

Students at Risk (STAR) component of NEPS

STAR is a Commonwealth initiative introduced in 1990 as part of the Youth Social Justice Strategy. In 1995, A\$7 077 million were allocated under STAR, A\$5 055 million for the government sector and A\$2 022 million for the non-government sector.

STAR is aimed at those students most a risk of not completing secondary school and who need extra help to finish their schooling. At risk students have been identified as those up to 19 years of age who are ready to leave school or have already left and whose level of achievement is affected by circumstances such as family dislocation, itinerancy, violence or abuse, homelessness, truancy and substance abuse.

Special attention is given to the needs of Aboriginal, Torres Strait Islander and NESB students, students from low socio-economic backgrounds, young offenders and students not aiming at tertiary education but who may go on to further education or training. Projects must be school-based, but those involving non-school organisations are encouraged.

The schools visited during the OECD survey had been allocated STAR Programmes. Before reporting on the visits to schools, some of the main issues arising from a preliminary meeting with senior managers from the state education system will be presented.

MEETINGS WITH SENIOR MANAGERS IN EDUCATION, MELBOURNE

The STAR project focuses on curriculum and welfare support and targets those students at risk of not completing their secondary education due to living or family circumstance such as homelessness or other unstable situations. Even though STAR projects themselves are new, they reflect what has been happening for some time and are currently running in about 10 per cent of secondary colleges.

Following a failed attempt to enforce co-operation at the local level the approach has now been modified to support co-operation by helping to facilitate on-going collaboration which has been emerging for a considerable period of time in response to the need to meet a range of student needs, cost effectively. There are good communication networks between local providers about students at risk.

The STAR managers will look at what works well at the local level and then create frameworks and protocols. However, there is still a need to provide opportunities for other agencies to link into schools. For instance, health services would like to run parent education programmes in schools.

According to the report given at the meeting, it is important that change and co-operation at the field level are reflected in policy. The initial thrust was to harness all services for children at risk at the municipal level with schools being the focal point inviting other services to be part of the provision – in other words, at a political level, the establishment of a "one stop shop". This initiative resulted in the Extra Edge Programme.

Extra Edge is a student-youth services co-ordination project. It involves Education, the Office of Youth Affairs, Municipal Association of Victoria, Health and Community Services, plus NGOs (such as the Salvation Army and private foundations). It involves providing someone at the local level who takes responsibility for co-ordination (an additional teacher). A staff post and a grant over three years were made available to schools which were asked to justify how they would use the position. The new posts were filled through a decision making process at the local level. There are currently 18 projects in Victoria, two of which are very new. The funding comes from the Commonwealth, the State and other Government departments. By putting education, social and health workers together, they find that they have common ground and this process helps to break down the barriers between services.

THE BENDIGO SENIOR SECONDARY COLLEGE

Context

Bendigo is located about 156 kilometres north of Melbourne and is the largest city in the area, with remaining signs of the wealth deriving from gold mining. Nowadays, Bendigo is a regional city in central Victoria servicing a population of 85 000, mainly employed in agriculture and manufacturing industries. Although the heritage is predominantly white Anglo-Saxon, it has well established Chinese connections and culture (the Chinese arrived in Bendigo in 1854).

Established as one of the first state funded secondary schools in 1907, Bendigo Senior Secondary College (BSSC) is the first Senior College established in Victoria (1976). It now caters for over 1 500 students in years 11 and 12 (16-18 year-olds). It is the largest college in the area, providing students with a full range of VCE (Victorian Certificate of Education) subjects and has established links with TAFE/Dual Recognition to offer more vocational options. It also offers accelerated learning and bridging programmes with work placements.

The following is an abstract of the BSSC Annual Report 1994. Most of the information for this report is taken from it, and completed by interview material and a contribution from the Extra Edge co-ordinator.

College goals are:
- to provide a quality learning environment;
- to promote excellence in all aspects of student learning;
- to deliver quality teaching;
- to have management practices which support the delivery of the college curriculum, and encourage effective decision making and communication; and
- to involve the wider educational community and the general community in the college.

Input – strategic level

Financial input

After nearly five years of controversy, community discussion and numerous reports and enquiries, the Ministry for Education decided to allocate A$3 million for the completion of the master plan designed to provide a better and larger learning site at the college.

An injection of A$8 million during the previous three years had allowed dramatic improvements such as: a new three-storey arts, science, technology and physical education complex; refurbishment of the music, drama and information technology areas; and, landscaping of the recreation areas in the college. The new budget will be devoted to BSSC consolidation on one site to accommodate more students without having to split the school population on two smaller campuses.

Annual budget

The budget of the college is approximately A$6 million including salaries, allowances and on-going costs. It is funded, according to normal state-wide formulae on a cost per head basis. In 1994, parents' levies were A$122 000 for a total budget of A$4 800 000, having decreased by about 10 per cent over the last four years. The total budget of the college is slightly less than A$4 000 per student and the College Council is greatly concerned by cost-efficiency strategies to meet both a high level of quality and a prospective new technology provision in order to meet future educational trends.

Input – field level

Policies and strategies

Special emphasis is put on attendance to lift the retention rates. A new attendance policy, introduced in 1994, resulted in a decrease of unexplained absences by 66 per cent. Students who miss lessons are required to go in for a four-hour mandatory Sunday class to catch up with work. Each student belongs to a form group and the group teacher is initially responsible for student welfare. A year level co-ordinator is responsible for five or six form groups. Two student welfare co-ordinators, two careers advisers, and nine-year level co-ordinators make up the student management and welfare team. Pastoral care is implemented through group teachers and VCE management. A literacy co-ordinator assists students at risk through literacy tutoring.

A youth development worker and a youth activities services worker have been appointed and located at the college as part of the Resource Centre. Two psychology and guidance workers are re-deployed from the Regional School Support Centre which, as part of its regional role, links with and assists in providing services within the college. The Extra Edge state funded project aims at the co-ordination of education and youth services to eliminate gaps in services and to avoid duplication. The college has an Extra Edge co-ordinator, who is a key worker in the STAR initiative.

Process – operational and field levels

According to the College Principal and College Council President, BSSC is a "pilot school of the future". In order to provide the best quality learning environment the Council has fought to obtain financial support to provide appropriate space and equipment.

The introduction of Schools of the Future (or self-management) in Victorian schools has led the college to undertake a thorough review of its organisational structure. The objective was to reduce ambiguity and uncertainty, to devolve to the college management a considerable degree of responsibility, authority and accountability, and to improve internal and external communications for allocation of resources, decision making, evaluation and outcomes.

Staff training

Professional development is seen as paramount to ensuring high quality teaching, collaborative activities and the achievement of self-management. Teachers are trained through a variety of staff development sessions such as computer workshops, international and local conferences, a mandatory reporting programme (all staff), global budgeting, administrative computer systems, personnel management and staff selection.

Collaborative process

Each student belongs to a form group. The nine group teachers are initially responsible for student welfare. They report concerns about any student to the student welfare co-ordinator (SWC). The Welfare Support Team adopts a holistic approach to meeting and dealing with student needs and is responsible for helping students to solve any problem arising from their family situation, such as family disruption resulting in homelessness or lack of money to survive. A nearby hostel (St Lukes) offers accommodation for young homeless people. It is supervised. There are good links between St Lukes and the school. Some students will self refer to St Lukes, others will be referred by the school. According to the student welfare co-ordinator, about 80 students a year see her with some kind of problem to solve.

The Extra Edge Programme supports student with extra needs. The college has established a data collection process to identify students at risk. The Extra Edge co-ordinator's responsibilities include:

- definition and identification of students at risk;
- identification of the factors that make students at risk;
- establishing priorities and time lines;
- development and implementation of programmes and alternative curriculum options for students, for example the bridging programme and work placements; and
- co-location and co-ordination of resources and personnel to assist and support students at risk within BSSC and within the wider community.

They liaise with the year 7-10 colleges to collect students' records and find out who is at risk and what the risk factors are. Level co-ordinators, careers advisers and SWC visit the year 7-10 colleges to inform students about enrolment and VCE subjects in BSSC. The year 7-10 college staff pass on information to the Extra Edge staff. They make recommendations and supply information to assist in developing programmes and selecting courses for incoming students. Information supplied by the SWC is also vital in identifying students at risk. Careers Advisers visit schools to provide students with advice and assistance. Any change to courses requires parent/guardian approval unless the student is classified as independent.

Home Group teachers provide pastoral care to students throughout the year.

VCE Management is a unit which assists students in organising their schedule and their work so that they achieve their VCE. Those identified as at risk are mandatorily referred to the VCE management unit.

As part of the school's Literacy Policy, a literacy co-ordinator links with the year 7-10 colleges to identify students who need support and a literacy programme is implemented according to an assessment of their needs.

A Youth Development Worker has been appointed to build a bridge between the school and the community. The role is apparently not too well defined, which has led to a turn-over of staff in the position. The person in the post at the time of our visit had been appointed very recently. The Youth Development Worker and the Youth Activities Services Worker operate from the Resource Centre located close to the SWC and the careers room. The base provides facilities such as a coffee corner, a meeting room, and an information shop. The present plans are to co-locate all school support staff in a single access room.

Involving the wider educational and general community

- The Principals of BSCC and its feeder year 7-10 colleges meet fortnightly and regular meetings occur attended by the Student Support staff.
- Parents and students attend a two-hour information session before enrolment at BSSC.
- An electronic link between libraries allows access to information.
- Dual Recognition Courses emphasize vocational education and allow students to achieve both a VCE qualification and a TAFE certificate over a two- or three-year period.

- A traineeship programme in hospitality has involved extensive developmental work with the Central Victorian Training Company and DEETYA. The programmes are funded by Extra Edge.
- Strong links exist with La Trobe University, Bendigo, with some VCE students undertaking accelerated learning courses and the majority of post-VCE students enrolling in the Bendigo campus of La Trobe University.
- The business community is involved in curricula development and provides work site visits and presentation sessions.
- The Parents' and Citizens' Association gives beneficial input into college operations and policies.
- Other partners, such as DSS, CASA, Health Clinics, Family Planning, Community Police, accommodation agencies, and psychiatric centres, meet regularly.

Several agencies provide services, but there is a lack of co-ordination to best maximise the use of resources.

Products

In recent years, 98 per cent of students who enrol and complete their VCE courses at BSSC have successfully obtained their VCE. These results are significantly better than the state-wide average.

There has been a dramatic decrease in the absenteeism rate (66 per cent less) since the 1994 new attendance policy.

A satisfaction survey shows global satisfaction with BSSC education amongst students (97 per cent) and parents (97 per cent).

Teachers felt that work strain and work demands were significantly greater at BSSC than in other places (staffing levels decreased by 16 per cent over the last two years in spite of more work due to the new self-management structure).

The students we met reported that the support staff had helped them to settle in and find their way when they were having a hard time. The parents were very satisfied with the way staff and teachers respect both the students and their families instead of being negative and discouraging as they had previously experienced in other schools.

Self-management has substantially modified the structure of the school and improved cost-effectiveness. Both parents and students are very satisfied with the management and the opportunity to participate effectively.

Improvements still need to be made in co-ordinating the relationships of the different agencies to maximise their efficiency. Liaison with TAFE is still not sufficient to provide full potential for students to obtain dual recognition for courses.

MELBOURNE DEANERIES STUDENTS AT RISK PROJECT

Background and context

A deanery is a grouping of ten parishes. Four deaneries are funded under this project – one on the Mornington Peninsular, one in Dandenong and two in the western suburbs of Melbourne. One of these deaneries was visited, the Sunshine Deanery, which is located in a traditional manufacturing area in the west of Melbourne.

In this area, average home incomes are lower than in other regions of the metropolitan area. There is a relatively high unemployment rate, especially among youth and people from a non-English speaking background. The area has a diverse ethnic mix resulting from successive migrant waves from southern Europe and recent waves from Indochina and Africa. This area has been popular to these groups due to the availability of unskilled factory work and relatively low cost housing.

The Sunshine Deanery consists of a group of Catholic secondary schools, parish primary schools and community services. The deanery model aids cluster of schools in identifying and assisting target groups of students. This model emphasizes the links between the secondary school, the home, parish communities and church, municipal and other agencies. The deanery model enables resources beyond those generally available to schools to be assembled and used from the variety of sources within the parish groups to assist children and youth at risk.

The Sunshine Deanery STAR Project has enabled a range of programmes and strategies to be explored, attempting to build upon the ways in which schools work with young people at risk. The integration of services at the school level is aimed at holistically meeting the needs of young people. This involves staff from community agencies and services working with school staff, young people and their families using the school as a base. This approach also positions the school as a central focus in the life of the young person.

Input – strategic level

The Catholic System has a budget of A$392 000 for the STAR Programme. Maria Minto Cahill is in charge of co-ordination and evaluation, professional development, and management of support structures. The Sunshine STAR Programme involves four secondary schools and eight parishes.

A meeting was held in June, 1993 with the purpose of clarifying the STAR project and developing a framework for STAR in the Sunshine Deaneries.

Input – field level

The colleges provide accommodation and facilities for the STAR co-ordinator, and staff are encouraged to contribute to the development of the programme. Every secondary school has a welfare co-ordinator who is also a teacher.

Process – strategic and field level

The Sunshine Deaneries STAR project has two main objectives: to keep children in school and reduce the drop out rate; and to give children a positive experience in school that goes beyond academic achievements – to help them to build self-esteem and hope.

Initially, those involved spent six to nine months trying to answer questions such as:

- How to find a way to change schools? It is important that the STAR Programme should not operate on the fringes as a "Band aid".
- How to become clearer about identifying students at risk?
- How to give young people the opportunity to demonstrate competencies?

The key outcomes of this reflection and collaborative work were the following:

- The realisation of the need to better assess needs and keep records with great emphasis on what should be confidential and what should be shared.
- The realisation that schools are a central place where children at risk can be reached. Once children fail they are often "lost" to the mainstream and most attempts at remediation are not successful.
- The realisation that community involvement is vital to project achievement.

Time has to be dedicated to build trust between schools and external staff. The school culture has to be explored so that approaches can be refined (*i.e.* its hierarchy, approach to discipline and curriculum needs to be modified).

Integration of services at the school level is an emerging response and structural changes are needed to match with the design of the programme.

STAR reference group

A STAR reference group has been established and is responsible for the on-going management and co-ordination of the STAR Programme within the Sunshine Deaneries. It involves representation from the Catholic Education Office, School Principals, Priest's Deanery Representatives, staff representatives from each of the schools, and the STAR Project Officer. They meet regularly to contribute to evaluation and programme guidelines.

Objectives of the programme

Eight main objectives have been defined and programmes aimed to fulfil each of them have been implemented or are under way.

Objective 1: The development of basic skills, with programmes designed to improve literacy, numeracy, social and other skills necessary for students to function effectively in society.

Programmes include:

– Vietnamese Girls Group: With the aid of a Vietnamese Support Worker the Group aims to help Vietnamese girls solve family conflicts. They mainly occur because of the difference between traditional family expectations and the amount of freedom the girls would see as "normal" in a western society. Many of the girls have been separated from their families in camps for some years, before being re-united in Australia.

– Stress management or anger management.

– Negotiating positive family relationships.

– Support groups: To improve self-esteem and skills.

– Exploring Together Programme: Eight staff were trained to help parents in developing parenting skills.

– Alternative School Programme: This provides part-time placements for students. The City Sunshine youth worker ran a two-week alternative schooling programme, including outdoor activities and "risky physical experiences", every Thursday with thirteen students. This is aimed at motivating students towards other goals when they have experienced that they can "make it".

– Mentor Programme: A student from Western Metropolitan College of TAFE helps students develop organisational and coping skills for VCE.

– Community Linkage Programme: Students are offered work experience in the local area in primary schools, nursing homes, kindergartens, etc. We met three girls whose experience had been positive and rewarding. One of the challenges is to set up programmes which can be part of the normal curriculum of schools, so that students are not marginalized and receive credit for work done in the community.

– Case Management: If a student is identified as severely at risk the STAR co-ordinator would initiate a case conference. Together they would plan and co-ordinate a response to the student's needs. This would involve members of staff within the school and representatives from the community.

Objective 2: Development of a range of in-service strategies which support the continued involvement of young people at risk in mainstream education.

This has been tackled through staff presentations and teachers' meetings to discuss strategies. These include issues related to STAR as part of the normal school schedule to bring about improvements in flexibility and co-operative teaching methods. Non-teaching staff have been informed and trained. Priests from the Parish have been involved in different meetings and seminars to develop a "shared vision of the Deaneries" and a better knowledge of STAR objectives and strategies. Seminars and workshops have allowed the participants to share information and views about students at risk, and to collect data and better assess needs.

Objective 3: Strengthening home-school relations through greater involvement of and feed-back to parents of students at risk.

This has occurred through school-based programmes, referrals and home visits and has involved agencies such as the City of Sunshine Youth Workers, Vietnamese Laos Cambodian Support Centre staff, and the City of Sunshine Family Counsellor. It is felt that the quality of the relationship between parents and schools has a direct influence on students' positive or negative feelings about school.

Objective 4: Development of screening strategies so that counsellors, year level co-ordinators and teachers are better able to identify students at risk prior to their becoming alienated from schooling.

This is essential to setting up pro-active programmes, preventative work and crisis management.

Objective 5: The development of innovative organisational arrangements in school.

These can be mixed ability programmes, community placements, flexible time-tables, as well as modifications of work requirements and report systems to adjust to individual needs. Some schools have developed more flexible exit and re-entry policies which allow, for example, students to go back to school on a part-time basis. It takes time to convince teachers that the structural changes are essential and that all students are worthwhile.

Objective 6: The development of enterprise skills through school-based and community-based activities.

This involves part-time job placements (*e.g.* in nursing or floristry), tutorship by college students in the primary school, and community initiatives, such as establishing a Gardening Club at the Sunshine Adult Activity Unit. Students get opportunities to show their skills in a non-academic framework. The community gets a chance to better know those at risk and develop a more positive image of them. The schools can reflect on curriculum and strategies to facilitate "success for all".

Objective 7: The development of projects which involve cross-agency collaboration and co-ordination.

Apart from programmes already described above which have been jointly managed with staff from other agencies, STAR has launched a Directory of Resources/Contact People to Support Young People in the West, with information contributed by many local agencies. Its purpose is to provide access to services and information for youth. A grant of A$30 000 from the Department of Justice has been dedicated to providing a youth project and programmes at Highpoint Shopping Centre. This is a Youth Crime Prevention Programme, based on the idea that when young people find ways to be useful to their community, they are less inclined to become offenders. It gives agencies opportunities, through their collaboration with schools, to deliver sustainable and long-term supervision while youth are reachable, in a safe and caring place.

Objective 8: Documentation, evaluation and dissemination of information on successful strategies.

Reports and databases are shared within the Deaneries and circulated among the agencies involved. Forums and seminars are held on the subject of students at risk. A Student at Risk Kit aimed at classroom teachers and year level co-ordinators is being developed. It is seen as essential for the adults in charge of students to get information and guidelines to improve their own approach. Dissemination of outcomes is the best way to encourage their motivation to move towards good practice.

Outcomes

STAR is a Commonwealth funded project. As usual when different levels of intervention are to be matched there is always a need for adjustments. Field workers and local agencies have to be informed and consulted in order to allow flexibility between general guidelines and local realities and practices. This is time-consuming, since trust and links between all partners and new structural options take a while to accomplish.

According to the clients (youth) that we interviewed, the programmes were effective in creating a positive feeling towards school, improving self-esteem and encouraging personal development. The girls who went to the primary school to teach children reported that they felt more confident and understood better what education as a whole involved. The boys were more motivated to stay in school and found that teachers and non-teaching staff were more ready to listen to their questions and give positive responses. The alternative programmes gave them the chance to confront the "real world" and show off skills that had been overshadowed by academic expectations. All of them felt that it helped them to see the benefits they could expect from attendance at school. The traditional punitive approach has changed towards a more trusting attitude towards children's abilities to cope with challenging tasks.

The programme is carefully evaluated. It has contributed to the Federal Government STAR evaluation. It now involves nine agencies including the TAFE college, Community Department of the University, Footscray YAC, Laos, Cambodian Young People's Support Group and Highpoint Shopping Centre, amongst others.

Most of the programmes could be replicated and the schools are willing to work on curriculum development and in-service training to promote equity and support for all the children.

COLLINGWOOD COLLEGE

Context and background

Collingwood school is a primary and secondary state school with 450 pupils in the secondary sector and 350 in the primary. They predominantly have clientele with a non-English speaking background (NESB), including Vietnamese, Turkish, Greek and African children.

They have two special English as a Second Language (ESL) programmes: STEP UP for refugee students and LINK, an intensive course for those who are literate in their own language. The school is directly adjacent to a large Ministry of Housing Estate and its clientele fall into a low socio-economic bracket. The school provides a mainstream education with support staff in the specialised areas of careers, integration and student welfare. The Extra Edge project has the role of co-ordinating the school and community services available to students, aiming to more effectively support students at risk.

Input – strategic and field level

The Extra Edge project is an inter-departmental initiative involving the Directorate of School Education which has allocated a project teacher, the Office of Youth Affairs which has provided an establishment grant of A$10 000, and Health and Community Services, which has provided a A$5 000 grant for accommodation-oriented projects. About 28 agencies are involved, public and private, whose representatives form the reference group in charge of the co-ordination and evaluation of the project. They meet fortnightly.

Process – field level

Quite a lot of cross-working and cross-referencing procedures are shared by agencies. For example, housing, health and welfare staff work together. The project teacher's task is to collaborate with all of the services available in and outside of school to organise a sensible response to children's needs.

Tensions between the welfare staff and the school occur over the amount of time young people take out of class when trying to solve their housing problems. A discussion paper on this subject has been written to be discussed by staff, teachers and others at the school. Cuts in AUSTUDY grants, to support children's schooling costs and directly given to recipients, are having dramatic effects and may defeat the attempts to help children.

A co-located Student and Youth Services Centre is still at the planning stage, discussion being under way regarding the location of the Centre – on or off the school site. As there is competition between schools for students, there is tension between policies like Schools of Tomorrow, which are about excellence and achievement of high educational standards, and programme such as Extra Edge. One obstacle is the school management's fear that the image of the school could be spoiled by the presence in the area of young men taking advantage of the openness of the school and smuggling in drugs.

Examples of the Extra Edge components include:

– *Parent education programme for Vietnamese parents*: There are a number of homeless and at risk Vietnamese young people. There is a particular refugee issue: families have been separated for quite a long time, three or four years sometimes, which results in family dislocation, communication difficulties, etc. A number of the workers on the project decided that they needed a different approach to parent education to prevent family break-down. The approach had to be culturally sensitive, so they decided to use the medium of Vietnamese opera to get the message across. They worked with parents, students and community leaders to produce an opera which tackled the themes of parent-child relationships. This has been very successful. When setting up something like this, there needs to be an awareness of the impact of other services on family life (such as health and education, etc.).

– A *"peer education" project*: This project organised with the local council caters for students who have dropped out of school. The project uses a "peer education" approach which involves inviting young people who have dropped out to take a course which will train them to work with other young people who are at risk of dropping out. The participants are paid A$20 per week. This project is aimed at the 15-19 age group.

– A *project which involves asking the school to identify young women at risk*: The youth worker will run a programme using drama to look at how to resolve conflict. This is for year 7-8 students. A psychologist works with the youth worker.

– *The Island*: The Island is an alternative school for those who have rejected – or have been rejected by – mainstream education. It started in the mid-1980s. It was the product of a shared vision between building workers and a "visionary" who felt there was a need for students to have a place outside school where they could be released from pressure and could build their own strengths and interests. In 1991, it changed from being a part-time to a full-time programme. The site is a warehouse with a tin roof and concrete floor, and is up a cobbled lane. The project is supported by the Building Workers Redundancy Fund. They have a number of teachers (they call themselves instructors) including a builder, a wood-worker, a nutritionist, a computer operator, and an automotive engineer. All of them were actually engaged in the crafts they teach. The Island also has the support of a part-time physical education teacher, jeweller, music teacher, and community care worker. There is also a co-ordinator. The Island takes 15-20 year-olds for an open ended length of time – on average one year. It caters for the needs of outer suburban students. It takes 25 students at any one time, mostly males. Four girls were present at the time we were carrying out our research. The culture of the Island is based around the workplace; technical education is declining and this fills a gap. The Island caters for students who have floundered academically and have expressed an interest in learning by doing. They will move on to part-time and full-time employment or apprenticeships. According to their follow-up records, a small number of the Island's clients go back to school, but very few continue to be significantly at risk. Schools, peers and parents refer young people to the Island which has established strong community links.

The reference group also has links with the school because the curriculum co-ordinator and the welfare co-ordinator are part of the group, and some of the discussion is linked to the curriculum.

Outcomes

Very little material has been provided to document this issue. The achievements of the Extra Edge Project are to be found in the progress registered in the collaboration process, curriculum cross-working, and the success of the programmes among youth. The large number of agencies involved (28) is a good indication of commitment to and interest in an approach which is sensitive to the concerns of the school. This is vital to avoid the danger of marginalizing the school. Advocacy among the community also has to be fully supported.

There is some joint training of staff. For example, Extra Edge professional development programmes are attended by members of the reference group.

Many of the agreements are not yet formalised and sharing of data should be easier once the Student and Youth Services Centre starts to operate. It should play the role of a single access point to a number of co-ordinated services.

KENSINGTON COMMUNITY HIGH SCHOOL (KCHS)

Background

KCHS is situated in the Inner Western region of Melbourne. It is a relatively high density area, with three Ministry of Housing "High Rise" estates in the local area. Traditionally this has been a working class area of Melbourne, but over the past ten years the neighbourhood has become increasingly gentrified.

The school is a state funded secondary school which started in 1975 at a time when alternative models were popular in Victoria. It enrols 7 to 12th grade students, but mainly from grade 9 onwards.

KCHS was established to meet the perceived needs of local Kensington students who were failing to continue in education past the minimum age. Initially the school had a direct neighbourhood focus, but over time it changed to become a wider community focus. In the early to mid-1980s, the school's intake area grew rapidly to include students from virtually all areas of Melbourne. By the early 1990s the school population was mostly made up of Anglo-Australian students from second or third generation welfare families, as well as a fair percentage of Aboriginal students who later moved on to enrol elsewhere. There was a high student turn over and many students displayed severe psychological disturbances. Physical attacks on staff were not uncommon and the place became quite unbearable for girls. Many students were returning to study after long absences, and currently 35 per cent are homeless or under government care. The number of NESB students is increasing. Many come from single-parent families or families on welfare.

In 1992 the school undertook a year-long self-imposed evaluation to identify its focus, client groups, intake procedures and curriculum delivery.

Since 1984, the staff have operated the school on a collective basis, jointly sharing all administration duties and all carrying an extensive teaching load. Other professionals are made to feel supported when participating in school programmes.

KCHS caters for some 100 students. It is committed to equal opportunity principles, especially gender equity, and to respectful attitudes between teachers and pupils. They introduced an Extra Edge Programme called KEEP (Kensington Extra Edge Programme) aiming to co-ordinate and co-locate services to eliminate service gaps and avoid duplication.

The DOXA Youth Welfare Foundation supports ROCKS (Real Opportunities for Careers at Kensington). DOXA is sponsored by enterprises and private donors, who also provide work places to give students vocational training. DOXA currently operates the Hollingworth Cadetship Programme in Victoria. This state-wide programme was launched in 1992 and supports students who complete their VCE and obtain tertiary entrance, but lack the financial support to adequately undertake such studies. The programme covers all books, fees, transport costs and provides clothing, personal development courses and tuition. Each student is assigned a corporate sponsor (mentor) pertinent to their field of study, who provides paid work experience to the value A$5 000 per year for the duration of their studies. On completion of their studies each graduate is guaranteed three years full employment. This programme is currently assisting 80 students at a total cost of A$350 000.

The ROCKS Programme is modelled on this, but supports a younger non-academic group of students. The key aim of the ROCKS Programme is to provide students at risk with necessary life skills to make the transition from school to full-time employment. It is managed at the school level through a co-ordinated approach in conjunction with KEEP, whilst still maintaining its autonomy.

Input – strategic level

The approximate current school budget is A$640 000 inclusive of all wages. The school also receives funding under the Extra Edge Programme totalling A$135 000 over two years. The DOXA Youth Welfare Foundation will fund a pilot project for three years for A$150 000. The annual budget altogether is A$757 000.

Process – field level

Following the year-long evaluation, it was decided to introduce changes in enrolment procedures to emphasize gender equality and a case-by-case basis to prioritise "at risk" enrolment. The curriculum focus is based on a practical self-esteem building "Learning by Doing" approach, yet it provides a whole range of VCE academic programmes. Emphasis is put on art subjects such as drama, dance and music which are seen as good elective choices to help students find their own voice.

Atmosphere and philosophy

Mainstream schools are generally very petty about things like uniform or discipline whereas KCHS tries to create more of an adult learning environment. They respect students as individuals. For example, a teacher will apologise to a student if he has made a mistake. Instead of punitive and controlling attitudes, they prefer to discuss and find out whether the blame should be placed on an inadequate policy rather than on students when they fail to adjust.

Children come to the school for the following reasons:

– as they have failed elsewhere, it is their last chance;

– it is their local school;

– it is the only place where they can fulfil their particular interest (*e.g.* drama).

It is felt that smaller schools are better for students. They have networks of friends within the school, which is especially important for children who have moved around and lost their social contacts.

The school has a flexible way of allocating staff, so classes can be smaller. Recruitment is not imposed on the school by the local education department, as usually happens. Rather, staff are recruited because of their motivation to work in KCHS. There have been a lot of people on the staff who were politically active. Staff have undertaken re-training, which involved a process of discussion in detail about programmes and philosophy. They operate as a collective and share responsibilities. Administrative tasks are done after school hours. The school co-ordinator (principal) is elected by the staff for a three-year term. Until recently, it used to be a yearly selection and was rotated by gender. They do a lot of team teaching and try to have a consistency of approach to the students. They do a lot of one to one support. Each student has a key worker for pastoral care. The school is staffed on the same basis as all others in the state, but the way in which staff are deployed and administrative tasks are shared means that the ratio of students to staff is 10:1.

Non-teaching staff

The community health nurse is based at the community health centre and comes into the school once a week for a couple of hours. She does direct work with students, providing information, health education, etc. Youth welfare workers work with young people at risk. They refer people to the school, including school refusers. They offer an alternative service. One worker supports a group of young males in the school, doing social skills training. The youth worker for the girls offers workshops on body image, stress management, self-esteem building and runs recreational programmes such as horse riding, netball and pool.

Collaboration

KEEP is in the beginning stages, although the co-ordinating process is under way. For example, they are making joint submissions for funding for cross-agency projects. They occasionally have access to Health and Community Services planning meetings or are asked to provide written submissions. The school is concerned that a change in the residence of a student can and does often mean that he or she will move school, losing the only stable thing in his or her life. The school can call for case planning meetings when trying to gain support for a child whom they believe is in need of specific help for issues other than schooling. They try to avoid duplication and refer students to appropriate agencies if they need housing or special support.

The school and the projects based on site have community links. For example, parents are involved in the school council and help with the everyday routine when necessary. The school is trying to set up a parenting programme to help parents get positively involved in their children's education. They organise community get together at least once a term and other opportunities to meet are frequent.

Support services are available through a referral system the same as that for any school in the state system.

They also have developed informal relationships with agencies due to the number of clients they share and, as a result, an informal network of workers has grown.

Membership of the school council is open to a range of people. There is nothing to preclude the involvement of local agency workers. In the past they have had various local workers on their council and the school staff have held and currently do hold management positions on a range of local agency committees, as well as being involved in one-off events and joint funding applications.

Although not formalised, the network seems to work and fulfil its role of avoiding duplication on the one hand and serving those most at risk on the other.

Outcomes

We met two students in years 10 and 11 and three parents. The students expressed the feeling that mainstream schools are very traditional and restrictive and that a lot of young people are very creative and have no outlet for their creativity. Respectful attitudes, time, space and caring staff dedicated to students' need to talk about their problems are vital to their own growing process.

Retention rates are higher since they changed the policies of the school. They have managed to achieve a gender balance. Half the students are girls and they resist pressure to fill a place or a teaching position by males if it threatens this balance.

Parents' comments were positive. They experienced good communication with the school. The school had a bad image before restructuring, and parents would hesitate to send their children there. But more recently, it has been reported as successful at the local level "through word of mouth".

The fact that teachers work with a core of students like a primary school system for basic literacy and numeracy is seen as very effective. The size of the classes is small enough to ensure individual support.

The staff find the job very demanding but rewarding as well. Now staff are willing to work in the school, whereas it was harder to get staff before. At the moment, the school spends a lot of time linking with outside agencies according to the needs of the students at the time. Despite the lack of a formal protocol, co-operation happens at field worker level, mainly on an interpersonal level. They are looking to formalise things, perhaps by co-locating workers on-site.

They would like to be able to bring people in to offer individual counselling to students. Services are invited into the school and can become involved in their clients' education. It helps the students to see that they are considered in a holistic way.

Conclusions

Concerns expressed both at national, state and local levels have led to the setting up of some innovative programmes for students at risk of not completing their education. The emphasis is placed on supporting students before they drop out, as well as providing opportunities for re-entry.

At the local (field) level, the commitment of staff and their willingness to work collaboratively was most impressive. Teachers and other workers were willing to look at and change structures and programmes to meet the needs of students more flexibly. It was notable that this was one of the key aspects which students valued highly.

Aspects of the projects which supported collaboration appeared to be:

– good communication between staff;

– joint training of staff;

– cultural sensitivity;

– the presence of a co-ordinator;

– clear goals;

– thorough evaluation leading to adaptation of programmes;

– keeping the needs of the child as a central focus; and

– the availability of funding.

YOUTH ACCESS CENTRES (YACs)

This section of the report will focus on the work of the Youth Access Centres in Melbourne. The research in Australia focused on the needs of young people at risk of dropping out of school or those in the transition from school to work, or to further study. This section of the report focuses on the second of these groups, and the operation of the Youth Access Centres (YACs) which were set up specifically to target young people in the transition from secondary school to work or further/higher education. They are part of the Commonwealth Employment Services (CES).

Context

The YAC network was set up in 1985 and was designed as a local information, advice, counselling and referral service. They provide a central point in the local community for young people to obtain advice on a range of matters including:

– education, training and employment opportunities;

– income support;

– health;

– accommodation; and

– legal issues.

In 1991, YACs were given specific responsibility for facilitating co-ordination among youth services at the local level. This role was called for in a report entitled: "Towards a Fairer Australia: Social Justice Strategy 1991-92". In a section on the evaluation of the Youth Social Justice Strategy (set up in 1989), it was noted that a particular concern was that the services available to young people at the local level had not been integrated and co-ordinated as well as possible. This role, which was to support rather than to direct local service providers, was to be given to the YACs and was to be reviewed in 1992. The co-ordination process was aimed, in particular, at meeting the needs of four groups identified as particularly disadvantaged and as receiving inadequate support from the system as it was then operating. These were:

– urban homeless young people;

– young offenders;

- Aboriginal and Torres Strait Islander youth; and

- young people from non-English speaking backgrounds.

The co-ordinating functions of the YACs were described as follows:

- developing local youth profiles, including information on young people and service givers;

- circulating and using the profile information;

- identifying gaps and duplicated servicing;

- developing linkages with other youth service providers;

- participating in co-ordinated planning; and

- assisting in the development of inter-agency strategies, including some joint projects, to overcome these problems.

Guidelines were issued to the YACs on how to go about this Local Level Co-ordination. These covered the following topics:

- co-ordination and the Youth Social Justice Strategy;

- co-ordination responsibilities;

- the YAC co-ordination role;

- promoting co-ordination through co-location; and

- co-ordination of DEETYA programmes and services.

The co-ordination responsibilities of DEETYA, in partnership with state and community agencies, are described as to:

- monitor local level access points to ensure a sufficient number of appropriate services within the community;

- monitor the range of available services to ensure the complex needs of young people can be addressed;

- foster and/or support links between services to improve outcomes for young people;

- actively support common planning arrangements with other youth services to minimise gaps in services and to identify and examine priorities collectively; and

- encourage youth services to develop a shared appreciation of issues and subject knowledge by disseminating appropriate research material and data.

Thus the role of the national Commonwealth agency is one of support and monitoring of co-ordination efforts.

At the state level, youth co-ordination committees are responsible for co-ordination and planning between Commonwealth and state departments. Special emphasis is placed upon drawing together the delivery of programmes and services for disadvantaged young people and policy development at the state level. Representatives on the committees include Commonwealth department, state government and local government staff.

At the local level, YACs are involved in a variety of activities to support their co-ordination role. These include:

- developing local youth profiles. This includes the collection of information on young people and service providers, particularly Commonwealth government programmes and services;

- circulating and using this information through local inter-agency networks;

- identifying gaps and duplication in services and assisting in the development of inter-agency strategies to overcome these deficiencies;

- developing linkages with other youth service providers;

- participating in co-ordinated planning, including the development of measurable outcomes for inter-agency activity, where possible; and

– assisting in the development of inter-agency strategies, including some one-off joint projects with other youth services.

Although they are expected to facilitate inter-agency co-operation, YACs are not expected to take a lead role in co-ordination at the local level. They have a remit to support local co-ordination arrangements by providing facilities such as a venue for meetings, secretarial support, youth profile information and information about YAC services, and the YAC co-ordination role.

Thus the role of the YACs at the local level is an advisory and facilitating one rather than a managing or leading one.

An evaluation of the co-ordination role of the YACs was carried out in 1992, and a report published (Waller, 1992). It stated that there was "confusion and uncertainty at the local level surrounding the YACs role in co-ordination" (p. 13). This had affected the YACs' and Youth Services' reaction to the YACs' role and their opinions of its appropriateness. There were three main areas of uncertainty:

– the extent of the YACs' responsibilities;

– the YACs' role in co-ordination; and

– what was to be co-ordinated.

More fundamentally, there was confusion about what the term "co-ordination" meant. There appear to be a number of processes and activities which are involved in co-ordination, according to the Youth Services surveyed for the evaluation. These are:

– information sharing;

– identification of gaps in services;

– occasional joint projects;

– integration of services (a one stop shop); and

– lobbying for change.

As outlined above, however, the remit of the YACs given by the National Government extends across the first three of these, but not to the last two. This confusion led to some suspicion at the local level about the intentions of the government in promoting the YACs' role as a local co-ordinator. There was a feeling, at the local level, that the government had a hidden agenda to cut back on funding, and that this was at the heart of the drive for better co-ordination of services.

Despite the initial negative reaction from some services, however, others were reported to have found the information sharing and inter-agency meetings very useful. They wanted to extend these to cover, not just information sharing, but also planning and joint projects. Thus, the remit given to YACs was confirmed by reactions at the local level. This is despite initial problems, where local agencies were already working together and saw the YACs' interventions as cutting across co-ordinating mechanisms which they already had in place.

Thus, although the need for co-ordination was identified, the fact that a local co-ordinating role was given to a national organisation caused some initial problems.

One aspect of co-ordination is that of the co-ordination of the delivery of services to clients. This is focused on the individual's experience and is designed to ensure that vulnerable young people do not "fall through the net" or do not get referred inappropriately. However, the remit given by the government to the YACs refers to structural processes of co-ordination which are defined as information-sharing, identification of gaps in services, and one-off projects.

An evaluation published in 1994 reported a high level of satisfaction among young people with the service they had received (Budd and Cameron, 1994). This related mainly to information about jobs and job interviews or financial support for study. However the survey reported that there was a relatively low awareness and understanding among clients of the role of the YACs. Nevertheless, considering the wider remit of the YACs to provide a co-ordinated service which meets the multiple needs of clients, over 40 per cent of clients were given advice on other government benefits or allowances, or health, accommodation or personal matters, and of these, over 85 per cent were satisfied with the service they received.

The YACs' liaison with schools and youth service providers was also covered by the survey. Schools appeared to be satisfied with the service provided by the YACs, which consisted mainly of giving information on job or study-related topics. The survey reported that YACs targeted students at risk of leaving before grade 10 in only 48 per cent of the schools visited.

The types of youth services responding to the survey included: youth refuges; drop-in centres; youth housing agencies; welfare agencies; state/territory government agencies; local government agencies; legal centres; employment centres; health services; counselling services; drug rehabilitation centres; training providers; and, a number of other miscellaneous services, mainly educational or church-based organisations.

These organisations had less contact with YACs than schools. Overall 64 per cent had had contact with a YAC in the previous six months. Of the 36 per cent who had had no contact, 40 per cent said that they had not been approached and 35 per cent said they did not know enough about YACs to judge whether contact would be useful.

When asked about the co-ordination process, those services which had had contact gave the highest rating for effectiveness to participation in inter-agency meetings and the lowest to planning with other providers and promoting government youth policy. Nationally, 57 per cent of youth organisations were satisfied or very satisfied with the co-ordination activities of YACs.

The report concludes that "co-ordination activities were identified by youth service providers and schools as the main areas for improvement" (ibid., p. 52).

The data presented in this part of the report are taken from discussions with managers and field workers in the CES and YACs and from self-completion questionnaires returned by YAC managers.

Before reporting on the four YACs, some details will be presented of a preliminary meeting with senior managers, in which some of the crucial issues affecting the co-ordination of services were discussed.

Meeting with senior managers from CES and YACs

We had a preliminary meeting with a group of senior managers. The following issues emerged:

– There is a problem with the three levels of government: federal, state and local district. YACs are trying to link education and training to employment, but DEETYA (which manages the CES and YACs) is a federal responsibility and education is a state responsibility. So policy about employment and the role of YACs in the transition from school to work is made at the federal government level, and policy about education and schooling is made at the state level. This makes joint action more problematic. "The three levels of government are doing the same thing at the same time, but not communicating with one another." Getting people into work is a local issue, depending on local knowledge of the job market and the needs of the local population for training, etc. It is therefore difficult to achieve a co-ordinated approach.

– At the senior (strategic) level, the CES manager runs employment services. The YACs are a small part of his work. The YAC managers are relatively junior managers (this is reflected in their age – they all appeared to be in their late 20s or early 30s). It appears, therefore, that work around transition is not high status or high priority.

– YACs are moving to a "case management" role, rather than an "outreach" role. That is to say, they will be concentrating their efforts on a smaller number of young people who are long-term unemployed, or who are in danger of becoming long-term unemployed.

– Some YAC staff are resistant to this change in approach. They value the work they were doing with a wide range of young people and the liaison work they were doing with schools and other agencies. They are now being required to monitor closely the progress of a smaller number of more problematic clients.

- The case management work is also being offered to local agencies, so that YACs will be in competition with private providers. If YACs lose business to private providers, then the number of YAC staff will be cut. This is part of a government drive to bring down costs.
- This change was brought about after the publication of a report which was highly critical of DEETYA and the way the department was serving clients. The report concluded that the department was trying to do too much and expectations of staff were too great. The report called for a more focused approach.
- As the more general service offered to young people contracts, so co-ordination with a wide range of youth services will also contract. The focus will be on those most at risk of long-term unemployment.
- The funding of education and other state level welfare services has been cut by the present state administration. Thus many of the provisions made to support youth at risk have been cut back, making co-ordination more difficult.
- Service provision is more integrated at the field worker level.

Visits to YACs

We visited four YACs in Melbourne: Footscray, Brunswick, Preston Koori and Melbourne (City Centre).

All of these YACs were located in areas of relative socio-economic deprivation. The profiles of the areas show a high proportion of people from non-English speaking backgrounds; a shifting, migrant population; a high proportion of families with below average incomes; a declining industrial base leading to above average levels of unemployment; and, a high proportion of clients who left school before the age of 17.

Preston Koori YAC was aimed at Aboriginal youth and staffed by Aboriginal women. These women were in an older age group than the staff members we met at the other three YACs.

Melbourne YAC was in the city centre, near the railway station. It shared its premises with the Young People's Health Service and the Youth Information Service. This co-location of services provided the opportunity to offer integrated services to a very needy clientele. It also provided a location for outreach workers from other agencies to work with the client group. At the time of the study these included workers from the Department of Social Security, the Centre for Adolescent Health, and the North Melbourne Legal Service.

All the YACs we visited were dealing with young people with multiple problems: homelessness, mental health problems, health problems, family problems. This necessitated linking in with other agencies. The linkages were mainly in the form of net-working across local agencies, rather than any form of integrated approach (apart from the Melbourne YAC described above).

Process

The role given to YACs in 1991 by government policy is to facilitate co-ordination at the local level among services for youth. The YAC co-ordination functions are to:
- develop youth action plans;
- identify service gaps;
- develop links with other service providers; and
- assist in the development of inter-agency strategies, including joint projects to overcome problems.

Their job is not to initiate social reform (*i.e.* systemic reform), but to carry out social policy, as defined from the "top down". There is often weak linkage between the central policy-making level and the local offices. For example, Jobs, Employment, Training (JET) funding was allocated for "family mediation" as part of a joint initiative between the Department of Social Security and DEETYA but this was not identified as a priority in local areas by YAC staff. Similarly, there appeared to be deep resentment among the YAC staff about the change in their role towards case management. The YAC review was not endorsed at the local level.

At the local level, it was perceived that there was a lack of co-ordinated planning efforts at the strategic and mandating levels, and that links at the operational and field levels were better. There were also difficulties with links and co-ordination between the State and the Commonwealth at the strategic level, including problems with duplication. The government will not fund structures, but it will fund programmes. In north-west Melbourne, there was a project set up to co-ordinate youth services, but this has now closed down. The current change in policy towards much more "office-based" case management threatens to cut across the co-ordinating role given to YACs under the previous policy. "Co-ordination is no longer a priority. At the moment, the major pre-occupation is case management. The focus is now totally on outcomes."

However, the YACs we visited are moving only slowly in the direction of case management and are continuing to participate in networking activities such as attendance at joint committees of various local agencies concerned with youth, and to use their networks to resolve the multiple problems of their clientele. For example, the YACs were involved in projects to help young homeless people. They linked with both statutory and voluntary agencies to provide welfare advice and material aid.

The Preston Koori YAC had a slightly different mission from the other YACs we visited, in that it was set up to cater for Aboriginal young people, and its networks were focused on the Aboriginal community. It is funded jointly by three DEETYA offices. Its staff were involved in extensive outreach work and see their role as welfare work and counselling, rather than primarily focusing on getting young people into employment. However, they link into schools and provide links to other services for Aboriginal people. For example, they have sent their clients on a LEAP (environmental work) programme which had a specific Aboriginal focus. They encourage young people to take advantage of grants such as ABSTUDY, which will enable them to continue their education. They work within the community and will undertake activities such as accompanying young Aboriginal people to visit the university, to encourage them to think about higher education.

The aim of the staff at the Koori YAC is to provide a more casual and friendly environment than other YACs. The two staff are Aboriginal, as is one of the staff from the mainstream CES, with which the YAC is co-located.

The Melbourne YAC was, as already mentioned, the only one of the four we visited co-located with other services. It was set up in 1990 by DEETYA central office in Canberra. It was an experiment to see what would happen if a YAC was co-located with a community agency. It was set up with seed money from Canberra to concentrate on homelessness among young people. The Youth Information Service was co-located with Health and Community Services. This would give clients access to a range of services under one roof.

The target group was young people 15-20 years old who were homeless or in insecure accommodation. The long-term aim was to get them into employment. Most clients do not realise there are three different services. They try as much as possible to have an open referral system. There are two broad categories of clients: the chronic homeless and the emergency/acute homeless.

The chronic homeless are aged 12-21 years. They have been in prison, in care, etc. They are early school leavers or have poor literacy skills. They are on welfare, victims of violence, drugs or alcohol. They have a gang mentality.

The emergency/acute homeless might make the first contact by phone, or may be referred by their school or by friends. They have usually just left home and have no experience of welfare. They are usually still in school. The aim is to get them into long-term accommodation and on a benefit programme. They try to prevent them getting into a long-term situation.

The office is staffed by the three services. Staffing consists of social workers, doctors, nurses, psychologists, DEETYA staff and social security staff.

The YAC has three staff and a manager, all full-time. The staff are all experienced CES workers. They needed to recruit specialist workers and came up against bureaucracy, because they were assigned staff who could not adapt to the new way of working.

The Young People's Health Service has sessional and part-time staff. There is a co-ordinator and two nurse practitioners. Doctors come in for sessions. There are a psychiatrist and a psychiatric nurse.

The Youth Information Service has a co-ordinator and two full-time youth workers.

As well as carrying out individual work with clients, they also do joint work with schools and youth groups.

The view of the YAC manager was that to set up such a system, each service's line management had to be aware of what they were committing themselves to. For this project, they have produced joint protocols across the three services involved. The advantage for clients is that there is a full range of services available quickly and efficiently. But for the workers and managers, it is more complicated. They needed to evolve new ways of working together. There is an informal agreement for resource sharing (photocopier, fax, etc.). There are no structural problems with the set up of the project, but there are sometimes personality clashes. However, having no structure at all is problematic. There are some confidentiality issues (*e.g.* with health workers).

There was no overall line management to say, "How is it working overall?". Currently, there is an informal arrangement between the three levels of government, but this needs to be put into a memorandum of understanding. Without this it is difficult to establish a model and to evaluate the strengths and weaknesses of this way of working.

Conclusion

The role of the YACs in the co-ordination of services for young people

Overall, the impression gained was that the role of YACs was primarily to engage in networking to provide access to a range of services for their clients. There was no integration of services, and apart from the Melbourne YAC, no co-location. We had no opportunity to talk to workers in other agencies about their links with the YACs, and so our analysis is based mainly on the accounts given by YAC managers. It may be that, given the complexity of the organisation of services, with responsibilities shared between local, state and national agencies, the networking and co-ordinating role given to YACs is the optimum approach to providing holistic support for unemployed youth. However, there was no opportunity to test out the perspective on "at risk" status accorded to the YAC clients. This focused almost exclusively on the problem of unemployment. Other problems, such as homelessness or drug addiction, were seen as aspects which needed to be addressed in order to render the young person able to seek work and to stay in employment once a job had been found. Other agencies may have felt that the focus on employability was not always appropriate. However, we had no opportunity to find out whether this was the case.

Moreover, the recent changes in the mode of services delivery were perceived by the staff and management as likely to limit the scope for networking and outreach work, as staff concentrated on case-management of the clients most at risk. However, it may be that these clients are the ones most in need of an integrated approach to their problems.

THE SALVATION ARMY CROSSROADS HOUSING AND SUPPORT NETWORK

Introduction

The Crossroads network consists of a number of projects designed to support homeless people. In addition to dealing with housing issues, it also deals with a range of problems which homeless people face.

Data for this section of the report are taken from a report on the Crossroads Project and discussions with senior staff at Crossroads (McDonald, 1993).

The services offered by the Crossroads project include:

- *Crisis services*:
  - information referral;
  - syringe exchange;
  - material aid; and
  - emergency accommodation.

- *Housing services*:
  - rooming house programme;
  - family housing;
  - young adults housing;
  - youth statutory support;
  - youth housing specialist service housing; and
  - youth refuges.

- *Employment*:
  - three labour market business programmes.

- *Training*:
  - three Skillshare training programmes;
  - job placement service.

Input

They describe themselves as "a medium- to large-scale non-government multi-disciplined organisation". The annual budget is A$5.8 million. Although they work with a number of other professionals, including social security department personnel and lawyers, most of the staff are employed by the Agency.

Process

In their leaflet, "Homelessness – An Integrated Response", the scope of the work of the organisation is described. They operate a Crisis Centre in St Kilda, an inner-city area of Melbourne. It provides crisis counselling, intervention, emergency relief and financial assistance. It also operates the largest needle exchange programme in Victoria. The centre is open seven days a week.

The St. Kilda crisis accommodation centre provides emergency accommodation, advocacy and support for people aged 15-30 years and families who are homeless. In addition, the centre helps them into secure, stable, long-term accommodation by placing them in Crossroads longer term housing programmes. These cater for different housing needs, such as those of families, single people, young people and those who have been chronically homeless for a long time. It also provides a refuge for young people aged 16-20 years, which is designed to help them into independent living, and a youth support service for 13-16-year-olds who are under judicial or statutory orders. This service attempts to reconcile them with their families or to establish them in a supported environment.

The emphasis of this work with the homeless, or those in danger of becoming homeless, is on supporting them to secure long-term accommodation.

Another aspect of the work of Crossroads is the provision of training and employment. They have three projects which offer work: a furniture manufacturing company called "This Way Up"; a cleaning company; and a retail shop. These provide employment and training for 65 homeless or at risk young people each week. The programmes are part-funded by DEETYA.

They also operate a Skillshare training programme, which offers training to the long-term unemployed. Training is provided in woodwork, furniture restoration, office, computer, catering and hospitality skills. The programme facilities are funded by DEETYA.

Another aspect of the work of Crossroads is an education project, to enable young people who have dropped out of school to complete their education.

A Job Placement Project provides work experience opportunities and support for those who have found work and their employers. A Job Club provides a three-week intensive programme to support those looking for work.

Crossroads also provides pastoral care and counselling through their Salvation Army Chaplains.

They are members of a number of local forums such as: the West Region Child Protection Group; the West Region Adolescent Psychiatric Services; the Council to Homeless Persons; the Regional Disability Services; the state-wide Homeless Families Forum; and the Victorian Dual Disability Group.

There are a number of staff working for Crossroads who have been seconded from other agencies. For example, a psychiatric worker seconded from the Royal Children's Hospital and a teacher from Broadmeadows TAFE College.

Crossroads sees itself as the lead agency in providing support and training to other agencies engaged in similar work. It provides staff training for professionals from other agencies. It also provides training places for clients of other agencies and preferential access for clients of other agencies which work with the homeless.

Thus, in the course of their work with homeless people and those in crisis situations, Crossroads staff work with a range of other agencies. There is no doubt that they are providing a highly valuable service to very disadvantaged clients. However, their view of integrated services is focused mainly on the integrated network of support provided within the Crossroads projects which has enabled them to deal so effectively with clients with multiple problems. Such close co-ordination of services is, unfortunately, much harder to achieve when separate agencies are involved.

FINAL CONCLUSION

Federal and state government support for co-ordinated programmes for children at risk in Victoria is strong. However, while they may provide the funding, decisions about the kind of services to be delivered are often made at the local level. This is consistent with a state education policy to devolve management responsibility to schools. Programmes which allow flexibility at the local level, such as the Students at Risk initiative, have proved to be well supported as well as effective in meeting the needs of disadvantaged children.

Victoria schools not only emphasize educational achievement but also play a very active role in student welfare (which is itself a determinant of educational success). A broad range of welfare staff can be found in local schools. In addition, teachers play an important role in welfare provision, and a growing number have formal training in this field. They are not only willing to work directly with children at risk but also to collaborate with other professionals who have special responsibility for welfare needs.

Youth Access Centres in Victoria play an important role in assisting disadvantaged young people who are looking for work. They are responsible for supporting existing networks of co-ordinated services or creating new networks where they do not exist. However, at times they have been seen as competitors by other services. While they have a mixed record, it seems that greater co-operation between federal, state and local employees responsible for YACs could make them powerful instruments in combating youth unemployment.

REFERENCES

BUDD, N. and CAMERON, M. (1994), *National Survey of Client Satisfaction with Youth Access Centres (YACs), December 1993 – March 1994,* Department of Employment, Education and Training, Canberra.

McDONALD, P. (1993), *Confronting the Chaos. A Report of the SANS Project,* Salvation Army, Melbourne.

WALLER, V. (1992), *Review of the Interim Co-ordination Role of Youth Access Centres* (YACs), Department of Employment, Education and Training, Canberra.

SOUTH AUSTRALIA

A LEADER IN BUILDING EFFECTIVE STRUCTURES
FOR SERVICES INTEGRATION

by

Mary Lewis and Lucienne Roussel

INTRODUCTION

The study visit to South Australia (SA) portrayed five main aspects of services integration: 1) specific programmes undertaken by the Commonwealth government and SA, working together, to target educationally disadvantaged youth; 2) Youth Access Centres; 3) an Interagency Referral System developed in South Australia to co-ordinate services to the 5 per cent of youth who require multi-disciplinary services; 4) specific school-based strategies to combat educational disadvantage that included services integration components; and 5) the steps taken by the Murat Bay District Council to co-ordinate its work with the Aboriginal community.

The hosts for the visit were the Commonwealth Department of Employment, Education, Training and Youth Affairs (DEETYA) and the SA Department of Education and Children's Services (DECS). The partnership between DEETYA and State Departments of Education provides a rich example of co-ordination and services integration on behalf of disadvantaged youth who are at risk of leaving school early without a qualification for work and of facing prolonged unemployment and poverty. Explicit youth policies within a social justice framework draw many agencies together to address issues of educational disadvantage from many perspectives.

PROGRAMMES OF THE COMMONWEALTH DEPARTMENT OF EMPLOYMENT, EDUCATION, TRAINING AND YOUTH AFFAIRS

Since 1987, the Commonwealth through DEETYA has co-ordinated education, training and employment policies concerned with restructuring and rationalising national manpower programmes in order to address the changing needs of industries, to assist disadvantaged groups to gain employment, and to improve labour market efficiency. A Youth Social Justice Strategy embodies many approaches to compensate for educational disadvantage. One is the National Strategy for Equity in Schooling that was developed to combat educational inequities for the following six groups whose educational participation and outcomes are significantly lower than the total population's:

– students with disabilities, difficulties in learning and/or emotional or behavioural disorders;

– students at risk of dropping out of school;

– students from low socio-economic backgrounds or living in poverty;

– aboriginal and Torres Strait Islander students;

– students from non-English speaking backgrounds (NESB) who need assistance with English as a Second Language; and

– geographically isolated students (Ministerial Council on Education, Employment, Training and Youth Affairs, 1994).

The Students at Risk (STAR) Programme is another example of a Commonwealth strategy started in 1990. Its objective is to provide specially designed programmes to encourage continued schooling for identified students, in government schools, who are most at risk of not completing secondary schooling. Generally, the STAR Programme has targeted girls because they are predominant among those who leave school early without having a particular pathway to employment. STAR grants were made to thirteen secondary schools/school clusters in SA. Research on these programmes often found that STAR participants had experienced one or more of the following factors that influenced school attendance and participation: poverty, abuse, homelessness/independent living, family dysfunction, sexual or racial harassment, pregnancy or parenting responsibilities, grief from personal loss, family responsibilities, and significant interruptions in schooling (Paterson, 1993).

DEETYA also operates a network of about 128 Youth Access Centres (YACs) throughout the nation to offer specialised services for youth, aged 15-20 or older, who require information and referral services concerning benefits to which they are entitled and assistance with employment, education and training. YACs have been the subject of considerable evaluation which, on the whole, has been positive. Areas for improvement were noted and are being addressed (Budd and Cameron, 1994). Many YACs are located in the offices of the Commonwealth Employment Services, but others are located at sites tailored to induce the most disadvantaged, isolated and alienated youth to come in. Through case management services, youth who have left school with no qualification, are unemployed or have other unmet needs can be guided through the maze of bureaucratic red-tape to get benefits. Any youth is eligible for case management services after being registered with the CES for three months. The reason for the waiting period is that many youth will find their own job or solve other problems within this time. However, the identified at risk groups, such as Aboriginals, the homeless, the disabled, non-English speaking minorities, truants, and children who did not complete year 10 of school, have immediate access. In addition to assistance with gaining employment or job training, concrete problems are addressed, such as housing, health and other welfare issues like financial assistance. AUSTUDY, which is a means-tested benefit, provides monetary grants to poor students 16 years of age and over and homeless youth, who undertake approved full-time secondary and tertiary studies. ABSTUDY is a similar programme for Aboriginal and Torres Strait Islander students. YACs are constructed as nurturing environments as much as technical reference centres. At the local level, YACs have been assigned the responsibility of co-ordinating youth services, defined as "supporting rather than dominating the co-ordination process between government and community agencies, accepting the legitimate role that local government and the community sector can play" (Waller, 1992, p. 5). However this role varies widely among YACs.

Two YACs were visited in SA. One, located in a modern shopping mall and integrated with the CES, served Salisbury and Woodville which have large numbers of non-English speaking people. At this site, one section of the CES called Employment Assistance Australia provided case management for youth aged 18 and older. The YAC unit concentrated upon youth under the age of 18 who qualified for the new Youth Training Initiative (YTI) that provides access to case management earlier than in previous years and a Youth Training Allowance (YTA) that is paid at three rates, depending upon the living arrangements of recipients. The manager of the CES emphasized the pressing need for assistance to youth because there has been a severe recession since 1991. She stated that around 30 per cent of teenagers have been unemployed for the last two years in South Australia.

This CES manager and the YAC case manager discussed their efforts to establish co-ordination with industries and other service providing agencies in the area. They liaise with seven high schools and an alternative school, providing video-tapes about a range of career opportunities, informing school personnel about new programmes, and engaging in other outreach efforts to seek referrals for the new YTI. Links with the Technical and Further Education (TAFE) College are essential for developing appropriate local training programmes. There is an occupational psychologist on site who provides a variety of services, for example, testing for assembly positions. Testing can be provided for some industries upon request. One strategy is to offer industries a free recruiting service if they will agree to employ a certain number of disadvantaged youth. Advertising job vacancies on self-service bulletin boards is a free service across the nation. Advice is provided to industries about Commonwealth subsidy schemes and training programmes. For example, some labour market programmes will provide consultation with a clinical psychologist or a person specialising in suicide for locations experiencing high rates of youth suicide. DEETYA has a Special Interventions Programme (SIP) with a flexible budget from which individually or locally tailored projects can be funded. For example, one youth was assisted with the expenses of repairing his automobile which was essential for him to be able to continue in a job. Funds have been used to make adaptations facilitating the employment of disabled youth. SIP funds are being used to develop the Salisbury Youth Annexe, an alternative educational programme described below.

The CES manager emphasized the point that the CES and YAC are strategically located to participate in negotiations among federal, state, local and industrial organisations in the region. She is working closely with the Commonwealth Department of Housing and Regional Development, businesses, unions, local governments and education agencies to promote industrial and commercial development and to develop a Northern Adelaide Regional Education, Employment and Training Committee (NAREET). Other regional co-operative ventures to provide specific solutions to problems of youth unemployment are: 1) the first Youth Enterprise curriculum for unemployed disadvantaged people that teaches small business development skills, supports the creative ideas of the participants, and tries to turn them into real jobs (*e.g.* food outlets at baseball stands); 2) training programmes in automotive and computer skills for youth in detention centres where some may be confined for three years; and 3) an Offenders and Rehabilitation Service (OARS) for individual offenders of all ages to develop short range career plans.

The YAC case manager supervises three counsellors and has recently been elected Chairman of an informal youth network whose membership includes workers from various agencies. Its goal is to provide education and information about resources for youth workers and it meets every three months. An executive committee meets monthly in order to administer a budget received from the states crime prevention programme. The CES manager emphasized the point that much networking is essential to keep abreast of changes in available services and to help forge the best organisational solutions to recent decentralisation trends and retrenchments in several big government agencies.

The other YAC site visited was in Port Adelaide, a section of the city that has the highest percentage of people receiving public assistance. Port Adelaide has its own local government council and functions more like a country area. This YAC is not located in the CES and is designed to meet the needs of its multi-cultural and Aboriginal population through co-operation with local schools and TAFE colleges.

CHARACTERISTICS OF SOUTH AUSTRALIA AND ITS POPULATION

SA is one of six states and two territories that constitute the federal Commonwealth of Australia. It is situated on the South-central edge of the country and has been described as "the harshest, driest state in the most arid of the Earth's populated continents" (Fodor's, 1995, p. 353). The country and each state have Parliamentary governments. Almost 99 per cent of South Australia's population live in a fertile area around Adelaide, the state's capital. The northern half of the state remains virtually unchanged since the first settlers arrived in Australia. Briefing papers for the study visit estimated the total population to be about 1.5 million of whom 29 per cent are under the age of 29. Also, however, South Australia has a more rapidly growing population and larger percentage of ageing people than other states. Ten per cent of people in the state were born overseas and about 15 per cent speak a language other than English at home. About one per cent of the total SA population are Aboriginals or Torres Strait Islanders, including 1.5 per cent of the northern sector population and 0.6 per cent of those in the southern sector. This is a larger percentage than in any other state. In March 1995, the unemployment rate for SA was 10.3 per cent compared to 8.7 per cent for the nation. Sole parents in SA have an unemployment rate of about 18 per cent. It was noted that 21.1 per cent of job seekers in the northern area and 14.4 per cent in the southern area are single parents with dependants. Higher than average unemployment rates are experienced by people born overseas, and Aboriginal people experience rates that are about three times the level of the total population. The children at greatest educational risk are often in families with these characteristics.

Throughout South Australia, agriculture is a dominant sector of the economy with 18 600 firms, but 25 per cent employ less than five people. Most people are employed in community services (20.9 per cent), the wholesale and retail trade (18 per cent), manufacturing (12.4 per cent), and in finance, property and business services (10.9 per cent). Percentages in different job categories vary between the two areas. For example, in the southern part of the state where bigger cities are located, there are similar percentages among managers (12.8 per cent), professionals (14 per cent), clerks (14 per cent), and salespersons (14.5 per cent). In the northern part there are fewer managers and administrators (10.8 per cent) and more labourers (14.5 per cent compared to 11.7 per cent in the southern part). Also, the percentage of professionals is smaller (9 per cent instead of 14 per cent).

EDUCATION SYSTEM

In Australia, state governments have the constitutional, administrative and major financial responsibility for education and there are diverse systems among the states. However, in 1989, the ministers of Education from federal, state and territory governments agreed to national collaboration and signed the Hobart Declaration endorsing ten national goals for schools in Australia. Since then, a national curriculum framework has been developed in eight broad learning areas. In addition to the government schools, there are two organisations of independent schools in SA, the Catholic association and an association of all other independent schools. In the whole country, 25 per cent of the schools are non-governmental and they serve 28 per cent of the school population (DEETYA, 1993). In SA, about 10 per cent of children attend independent schools. The SA government provides about 90 per cent of funding for schools, including funds for independent schools. Independent schools must meet minimum educational standards set by the State and they may charge fees.

In all states, education consists of four stages: preschool, primary, secondary and tertiary. Attending school is compulsory up to the age of 15 or after completing year 10 at school. Those who want to access tertiary education must have two more years of schooling. In SA, the system includes one preparatory year for children aged 5, called reception or kindergarten, which is not compulsory but is widely utilised. Local voluntary bodies played a major role in establishing preschools. Government preschools were first established in socio-economically disadvantaged areas, then in well populated areas with inadequate or no preschools, and finally in isolated rural areas. There are seven years of primary school and five years of secondary school. Government preschools and primary and secondary schools are free for Australian citizens and permanent residents but some fees may be charged for textbooks or the use of school equipment.

An important feature of tertiary education for youth at risk is the system of Technical and Further Education (TAFE) colleges. They offer a wide variety of courses to year 10 leavers, such as trade training and paraprofessional courses, which may be part-time or full-time, and may lead to certificates or advanced certificates. Courses may be combined with practical experience, such as apprenticeships. The State Government provides about 85 per cent and the Commonwealth 15 per cent of funding for TAFE colleges. Although TAFE colleges are organised on a State basis, certifications are co-ordinated through a national nomenclature that was established in 1989.

SA's Department of Education and Children's Services (DECS) set performance targets in its three-year social justice strategy that was released in 1992. It specifically mentioned that the following groups should be targeted, in addition to those named above in the Commonwealth strategy: victims of abuse, pregnant girls and teenage mothers, and students in itinerant families. One performance target was a 15 per cent increase in attendance of Aboriginals and school card holders (children with below average means who receive a small amount of financial assistance). In some schools, especially in urban areas, as many as 66 per cent of pupils have a school card. Statistics indicate that in August, 1991 all but three schools in South Australia recorded a school card holder enrolment. There are about 67 500 in the State. Another target was a 20 per cent increase in retention to year 12 of such students. Briefing papers reported that the school retention rate to year 12 in South Australia has increased steadily and was 86.3 per cent in 1993. Female retention rates were 89.7 per cent compared to 83.0 per cent for males that year. The highest overall retention rate recorded was 92.7 per cent in 1992.

Social justice concepts permeate the language and strategies of DECS to deal with educationally disadvantaged children and youth. For example, the official use of the term "behaviour support" refers to what are often called discipline policies in many other places. This term implies that there is an understandable reason for unacceptable behaviour and that both pupil and teacher may need additional support to comprehend and address the underlying difficulties. DECS provides a programme of behaviour management support to school personnel in dealing with difficult students in the most disadvantaged environments. It includes 80 primary counsellors whose services are often engaged before utilising a referral outside the school. Fueloep (1995) noted that, now, attention is turning to a small group of pupils with unpredictable violent behaviour who are not psychotic but very disturbed, for whom existing facilities are not appropriate or the professional repertoire of skills not good enough. They are seeking ways to identify and provide help earlier to these youth whose struggles make them likely to become behaviour problems, but who have not yet required removal from the school setting or absented themselves completely. Sweetman (1995) described them as active or passive truants, youth who have major problems outside the school environment, such as being penniless, victims of abuse, drug abusers, involved in petty crimes that verge on major crimes, teenage mothers, or living in families experiencing crises. As many as 50 000 young people are at serious risk of becoming homeless. When such a youth is identified, Sweetman's programme is able to utilise an extra person, designated as a student at risk teacher, to provide a quick response and seek the needed resources, to keep the youth in school and to prevent the situation from deteriorating. Usually, a contract will be negotiated with the youth that includes attending class and undertaking individually designed learning tasks. In order to make this type of approach successful, training about social justice issues is being utilised with principals and teachers to help them envision more facilitative roles with such students. Sweetman, Principal Curriculum Officer for Equity, oversees the preparation of teaching materials that reflect the experiences and interests of the most disadvantaged targeted pupils. For example, some teaching units deal with the construction of disadvantage, such as how sexual harassment and domestic violence are linked to the concept of gender. Officers in the Equity Section also work with others in the Curriculum Division to ensure that all teaching materials provided by DECS are inclusive of all students. The Principal Curriculum Officer for Equity also manages the STAR projects, the country areas programme, and the disadvantaged schools programme throughout the state. DECS makes its training available to independent schools through purchase, but they are rarely used. Sweetman (1995) said that the Catholic schools "endorsed DECS behaviour management policy and Catholicized it".

Dillon (1995) said that, in principle, the behaviour management programme embodies school reform and a success orientation for every student. The new documents about it being prepared for distribution will emphasize the curriculum aspect. In this spirit, home-based or alternative schooling can be made available for children and youth who can not be managed in regular school, while needed multidisciplinary and interagency services are marshalled to restore equilibrium and facilitate a return to regular school if possible.

One example of an alternative programme is Possibility 14, a voluntary one-term programme which accommodates nine 14-year-olds who are causing disruptions to schools and the wider community and who have required considerable resources from DECS, Family and Children's Services, and the juvenile justice system. Although the programme is officially connected to one high school, the participants do not interact with pupils at that school. They are chosen through the Interagency Referral Process described later in this report. The curriculum is activity-oriented and conceptualised to develop self-confidence and career pathways. For example, there are units in self-defence, health and personal development, kayaking, swimming/diving, rock climbing, decision making/problem solving, first aid, literacy, numeracy, resume writing, computer technology and word processing. An effort is made to identify any possible career interest of participants and one whole day per week is devoted to work experience at a relevant site. This training helps to prepare the youth for what to expect at work, how to interview, how to develop a personal portfolio, and how to recognise and deal with sexual harassment. The programme is viewed as a manifestation of services integration because it was a grassroots development and funded from a variety of community sources, including DECS, YACs, businesses and churches. Also, some agencies provide instructional or activity modules. For example, Child and

Adolescent Mental Health Services offered the health and personal development course. The police division has offered challenge activities as a way to give youth a better view of police, to see different aspects of police work, and to assist with some of the daily work, such as cleaning stables and caring for horses. There are three paid staff who work as a team. One is a teacher/director, one is a mentor, and one provides behaviour support. Additional volunteer mentors were recruited from the community. Because of some incidents where volunteers wanted to be too protective of participants, a decision was made not to use volunteers in the future. Some of the best will be retained with additional training and paid A$12 per hour plus expenses. The project has been evaluated as highly successful. Only two participants have dropped out. Eighty per cent of the participants have returned to mainstream school at the end of the programme. Some get jobs or go into further training through TAFE or on-the-job training opportunities. Boys and girls both participate in the programme. Most in the next group are expected to be girls and a social worker will be added to the team. Another available component of the programme is a wilderness trek with the army and the police, moving to seven different sites. This offers opportunities to learn how to live in the bush, group and team skills, and survival problem-solving skills, such as how to get everything across a river or over a bridge or an electric fence. Although future funding is uncertain, the leaders were optimistic and are making plans to offer a similar programme for 15-year-olds.

OTHER SCHOOL-BASED PROGRAMMES TO KEEP AT RISK YOUTH IN SCHOOL

Paralowie R-12 School's Student Services Team – a prevention approach

Paralowie School is designated a Disadvantaged School, which makes it eligible to receive about A$70 000 annually in extra funds that can be used to obtain additional teachers and staff, as well as literacy, technological and other resources. There are 1 100 pupils, aged 5 to 15, attending this school and approximately 65 teachers. The average class size is 27. There are many pupils from multicultural and non-English speaking backgrounds or with other indicators of disadvantage.

The Principal expressed the view that, during the last 20 years, the education system in SA has had to absorb health, mental health and family services because the resources available to the other sectors have become more restricted. There has been a focus upon bringing together services within schools as one way of avoiding duplication of effort. The school can provide a single point of access for community agencies whose personnel can also provide advice to school administrators.

He has mobilised an impressive Student Services Team that has developed a variety of programmes and approaches to prevent school failure and dropping out. The team consists of the following people employed by the education system: the Principal, two secondary counsellors, a primary counsellor, a teacher whose programme is named Middle School Enterprise, a co-ordinator of accelerated learning (special education), a community liaison officer, and the Manager of the Salisbury Youth Annexe which is an alternative, residential educational programme for older youth who cannot live at home. A nurse employed by the Child, Adolescent and Family Health Services (CAFHS), the STAR Project Co-ordinator and her apprentice employed by DEETYA are based at the school and are members of the team also. The roles of these key players will be described.

DECS's job description for a primary school counsellor involves utilising preventative and developmental models of school counselling. This view recognises the developmental needs of all members of the school community in contrast to crisis-counselling approaches that exclude most members of the school community. Crisis intervention and case management are only part of the work. The counsellor negotiates with the whole school community to achieve needed changes, to provide leadership in developing school behaviour management policies, and to access resources and services for the entire school community. Also, one is expected to model methods to enhance teachers' skills in managing student behaviour. A counsellor must have teacher and counsellor qualifications. Also, one must be able to organise and conduct training programmes about student behaviour management both within the classroom and throughout the buildings and grounds. The primary counsellor at Paralowie School gave examples of his work, such as conducting groups for angry boys and withdrawn girls. He engages in team teaching with regular classroom teachers about conflict management, peer mediation, and protective behaviours. He works with parents to identify needed agency services. He utilises his special training in work with Aboriginals and other minorities.

He introduced a creative planning mechanism used by the Student Services Team called Kid Map. This involved the team in identifying about 14 areas of concern relevant to pupils in all grades in the school, such as attendance problems, abuse, withdrawn behaviour, self-esteem difficulties, friendlessness, violence, harassment, bullying, grief issues, eating disorders, homelessness, sexuality issues and interagency relations. Then they identified the pupils who were facing these difficulties through discussions with teachers and staff. This process brought fuller awareness that family problems were the basis for many symptoms, and of what service gaps were. Having identified groups of pupils dealing with the same problems, the team was able to devise many group, rather than individual, programmes to address them. This engendered the development of friendships and support networks among pupils. The Kid Map also influenced decisions about other school issues, such as the health and personal development curriculum, distribution of school support resources, training and development for teachers, and the overall objectives and strategies for the school development plan. The Kid Map is treated confidentially by the team. As situations change for children, families and teachers the map is modified. It has become a dynamic and continually evolving document that assists the team to address issues of pupil welfare and to reduce the frequency of crisis situations.

The secondary counsellors who work with older pupils said that the majority of their work is to help individuals deal with conflict situations and to obtain needed services. They also work with small groups of victimised youth to develop survival skills. They counsel pupils about subject enrolment and career development.

The Middle School Enterprise offers an alternative within school for disruptive boys who still attend some regular classes. For example, they might learn how to repair or restore bicycles, to play the guitar, or to use computers to improve numeracy and literacy. The programme offers a reward rather than a deficit model. It aims to keep pupils in school and to prevent their alienation. Goals include assisting teachers and training them to be more inclusive about curriculum development. It was stated that absenteeism in this school is now lower than ever. Research funded through the Workmen's Compensation Programme is being conducted on this programme.

The special education teacher said that 10 per cent of this school's population have been assessed by the school psychologist as having cognitive learning difficulties. Many of them are boys who live in poverty and have behaviour and learning problems with maths and literacy. Three teachers are involved in special education, but the school does not utilise any withdrawal classes for pupils. They focus upon developing teaching skills throughout the faculty and provide some tutorial services and special sports programmes for pupils.

The Community Liaison Officer and the nurse involve parents in parent support groups, home-based programmes and other school activities. One example is a programme called Partners in Education that involved nine to twelve parents for two hours weekly for nine weeks in literacy work and learning how to use the library.

The STAR counsellor focuses on girls in grades 8 to 12 who were identified by school personnel as being at such high risk that they might not be in school at all without individualised assistance. More girls are referred for the STAR Programme than can be accommodated. Therefore she interviews them and determines priorities for offering her services. She uses both individual and group methods that are relationship-oriented. She develops individual goals with each girl that focus upon a future career orientation and makes agency referrals for needed services. Group methods focus upon developing peer support, problem-solving and assertiveness skills. Some of her efforts address whole school problems, such as promoting the concept that women have successful careers. For example, she initiated the idea of having a forum in which successful career women were featured in order to provide role models.

Two teachers are employed by DECS to develop and administer the Salisbury Youth Annexe, a unique residential programme for older youth from Paralowie and another high school who are in jeopardy of being excluded from school or not continuing beyond the compulsory attendance age.

Twenty youth can be accommodated, ten from each school, in a large home acquired for the programme because the community has a high rate of youth homelessness. The programme includes both education and other services. It gets support from DEETYA, the Salisbury District Council, the Salisbury Youth Network, and the Together Against Crime Committee. The Metropolitan Youth Association takes responsibility for liability. The programme is activity-oriented and focuses upon developing skills for small enterprise development, such as dealing with second-hand furniture, restoring guitars, catering and dealing with bicycles. The project has been operating for three years. Plans are underway for expanding the property to include a farming component.

Fremont/Elizabeth City High School – linking with community agencies

Fremont and Elizabeth High Schools also qualify as disadvantaged schools and make heavy use of the Interagency Referral Process described below. The disadvantaged nature of the school is indicated by the fact that 54 per cent of the youth at Fremont H.S. are school card holders, 2.7 per cent have NESB, and 3.1 per cent are Aboriginals. At Elizabeth H.S. 66 per cent are school card holders, 13 per cent have NESB, and 4.2 per cent are Aboriginals, the highest percentage in the metropolitan area. High proportions of students are involved in behaviour management issues. The numbers of suspensions and interagency meetings related to pupils are amongst the highest in the state. The area, an industrial suburb where the main manufacturer has departed, suffers from structural long-term unemployment with many youth being the third generation to face unemployment. There is a 75 per cent unemployment rate among youth in the area aged 15-18 years.

The STAR Project Co-ordinator at this school developed the strategy of creating a team of representatives from the major youth-serving agencies in the neighbourhoods served by these two schools, which are amalgamating and together serve 1 057 secondary pupils. He emphasized that the pupils need help while they are still in school and it is impossible for school personnel, alone, to help the students access all of the benefits and services which they need and are entitled to. Youth under the age of 16 are particularly likely not to know how to access services for which they may be eligible. Therefore, this STAR Co-ordinator decided to work with other organisational representatives rather than to create a new STAR service within the school. At the visit to this school, representatives from a wide variety of types of public and private agencies explained how they work with the STAR Co-ordinator to facilitate service provision and problem-solving for individual pupils. The STAR Programme allows flexibility in methods of identifying target pupils. At these schools, the main criterion is low participation and most STAR pupils are girls. Before this STAR Programme began, there was no organised way within the school to link pupils with services in the community. By creating a community-based team for this work, school personnel are left free to continue with their main educational work. This STAR Co-ordinator also believes that some alternative educational programmes marginalize students further and he tries to use psycho-social approaches to working with families and community agencies to address the underlying problems that interfere with pupils' participation in the school's programmes. He brings pupils, their parents, and potential sources of help together around the table to engage in problem-solving.

SOUTH AUSTRALIAN GOVERNMENT INITIATIVES TO PROMOTE SERVICES INTEGRATION

A major SA government initiative was started in 1987 to promote more effective co-ordination of health, education and welfare services for the school-aged population with serious social and behavioural difficulties. A high level team of senior directors and planners was established jointly by the ministers of Education, Health and Community Welfare (now named Family and Children's Services: FACS) to investigate the extent of the problems posed by such children, to review existing provisions to assist them, to address the feasibility of a multidisciplinary interagency approach, and to recommend future action. Based upon their extensive study of processes across the three government sectors of health, education and welfare, the final report of this team (Stratmann, 1988) made 32 recommendations for improving interagency co-ordination. The State Cabinet approved the implementation of these recommendations over the three-year period, 1989-91. Funding to implement the recommendations was allocated from the government's social justice budget and the responsibility for implementation was placed with the Human Services Committee, a group composed of senior government ministers with portfolios in health, education, welfare, housing, local government and related services. About 50 per cent of the recommendations involved actions that could be taken on by one organisation or two working together. These were implemented within twelve months.

The study process as well as the recommendations of the Stratmann Report were influenced by a literature review concerning the co-ordination of human services. Some of the key points that influenced the study process and the outcomes are summarised.

"(...) it is uneconomical to bring a multi-disciplinary, multi-agency structure into play in situations where the required response is simple or straightforward (...). It is estimated that a multi-disciplinary, multi-agency response is required for approximately 5 per cent of the student population with 4 per cent of these being supported in schools and 1 per cent being supported in alternative settings (...). In its simplest form, co-ordination involves responding to the multiple needs of clients by creating networks which bring the relevant services together into a coherent whole characterised by a unified approach to policy development, planning, and service delivery. The components which both create and characterise co-ordinated services are as follows: common service areas; co-location of a number of services in a local setting; common eligibility; joint intake, assessment, case planning, management and review; decentralisation of administrative authority; the development of a functional role for a generalist manager; the operation of a co-ordinated service network structure; and a common client/management information system.

Service co-ordination involves the three aspects of comprehensiveness, compatibility, and co-operation being applied to the four key elements: programmes and services, resources, clients, and information. The first aspect, comprehensiveness, means that all necessary services needed for the client group exist or are argued for, otherwise co-ordination simply reinforces the status quo. Compatibility, the second aspect, requires all existing services to be properly linked and sequenced in terms of clients' needs. Co-operation acknowledges that the quality of relationships between providers and between providers and recipients is important.

The four elements require co-ordination at a specific level for optimal effect. Resources are best co-ordinated by mandate at a state or county level, programmes and services by each organisation involved in the co-ordination initiative, clients by the local network through an individual case co-ordinator, and information across all levels (...).

The main criterion for an effective, co-ordinated, service delivery structure involves a state or county level formal coalition of service-providing organisations, represented by their programme and executive directors. Set within a state or county level mandate for interagency service delivery, this coalition enables organisational benefits to be maximised and costs to be minimised. Regular interactions on the coalition committee create the structural imperative for information flow and enable programme directors to become aware of the need for certain programmes and services to be co-ordinated to meet the diverse needs of mutual clients. The coalition provides the arena and the expertise for working out the co-ordination, whilst the executive directors provide the necessary organisational support and commitment. This arena dramatically increases the visibility and hence the accountability of programmes because they are subjected to the scrutiny of professionals from other agencies.

On its own, a coalition does not provide a structure for effective, integrated service delivery. The second criterion is a working arm or unit that provides a fixed point of referral and case co-ordination. The third requirement is a regional group which has broad responsibilities for monitoring local outcomes and clients' well-being, for co-ordinating local services and resources, and for obtaining local political support" (Stratmann, 1988, pp. 8-10).

Attention focused upon how to implement recommendations that involved all three major service sectors to serve the small percentage of youth who required co-ordination involving them all. An interagency planning and development process was initiated at the highest administrative levels. Specific management responsibility was lodged in a committee of senior directors from the Health and

Education departments and FACS, named the State Interagency Committee (SIC), and chaired by a representative of the Director-General of Education. This committee reported to the Human Services Committee every six months about progress. Also, an evaluation by an independent researcher was completed, as mandated, within the three years following the implementation of the recommendations. The SIC provides the overall structure for interagency co-ordination through its state and regional committees. The Interagency Referral Process (IRP), which began functioning throughout the state in 1991, provides the local fixed point of referral, assessment, case co-ordination and review. It is a voluntary, not a statutory process.

The model for interagency co-ordination that was implemented state-wide was derived from bottom-up discussions beginning with direct service personnel. It was then endorsed by the SIC, the chief executive officers of the three sectors, and the Australian Governments Human Services Committee. The SIC now consists of:

- the Director of programmes for the Department for Education and Children's Services (DECS) who serves as Chairperson;
- the Deputy Chief Executive of Family and Children's Services (FACS);
- the Director of Primary Health Care, South Australian Health Commission (SAHC);
- the Executive Director of Child and Adolescent Mental Health Service (CAMHS) Northern;
- the Executive Director of CAMHS Southern; and
- the Manager of schools programmes, Child, Adolescent and Family Health Services (CAFHS).

This SIC now meets every three months to consider issues relating to interagency service delivery to school children with social and behavioural problems. Its role is to:

- monitor the progress of organisations at state and local level in relation to the implementation of shared responsibilities and commitment to interagency work;
- co-ordinate all interagency initiatives to support school children with social and behavioural problems;
- support and evaluate the implemented recommendations from the Stratmann Report;
- recommend changes to existing policies where necessary and assist in assuring the consistency of newly developed policies in interagency work; and
- investigate effective, proactive and early intervention strategies for this target population and to promote their implementation;
- report regularly to chief executive officers, ministers, and relevant cabinet committees.

There are regional interagency groups comprised of regional managers from DECS, FACS and SAHC that meet regularly to:

- monitor existing interagency initiatives targeting school aged students with social and behavioural problems;
- develop co-ordinated service delivery plans and joint performance outcomes;
- investigate and put into practice co-location and co-working opportunities; and
- report their findings and policy/planning needs to the SIC.

Service planning and provision is managed at a local level, since the nature of service delivery is dependent on the needs of the community and other local factors (Fueloep *et al.*, 1995).

THE INTERAGENCY REFERRAL PROCESS

An unanticipated and highly valued product of this initiative was the SA Interagency Referral Process. It was designed to facilitate services to the 5 per cent of school-aged people who have significant social and behaviour problems and need multidisciplinary and multiagency services. In order to begin identification of these youth, the working definition of the target group became, school-aged children and adolescents whose chances of successfully completing school were being reduced and whose successful transition to employment and adult life was being endangered by one or more of the following:

- severe withdrawal or emotional disturbance (e.g. depression, suicidal tendencies, chronic substance abuse, psychotic incidents);
- serious disruptive, violent or illegal acts; and
- absence from school because of truancy, family mobility, etc.

The structure and process of the IRP require one contact point in each geographic area through which all health, education and welfare services external to a school can be accessed to assist a student with complex social and behavioural difficulties. The IRP concept includes the following requirements:

- an integrated holistic approach to case assessment, management and review;
- contact points to give health and welfare sectors improved education services for their clients;
- link people appointed in the health and welfare sectors to facilitate access to services in these sectors;
- a number of different pathways to cater for individual needs;
- quality control to prevent duplication and over-servicing, as well as to ensure that students were not unnecessarily accelerated out of their usual school settings;
- sensitivity to the ethnicity, the aboriginality or the disability of the individual; and
- an interagency protocol for information exchange about clients.

The IRP process can be conceptualised in four stages: 1) referral, 2) assessment, 3) case planning and management, and 4) case review. There are six key points of referral based in the six regional offices of DECS, including four metropolitan and two country sites. Referrals can be made from a variety of sources, including school principals, middle management personnel from the health and welfare sectors, non-government agencies and private practitioners. Each site has an Interagency Referral Manager (IRM) who receives the referrals and co-ordinates inter-agency involvement through a group of field managers from the health, welfare, and education offices in the area and through other types of networks developed in more sparsely populated country areas. The IRMs are paid by DECS. They have different ways of working, depending upon their areas and personal working styles. They are people with teaching and counselling backgrounds. Sue Jager and Janine Harvey, two IRMs in the Adelaide metropolitan area, were interviewed. Jager is Manager of the Beafield Education Centre, an alternative education programme which offers a variety of programmes and sites for youth with severe social/ behavioural difficulties, who cannot function in a mainstream school. Harvey is Co-ordinator of School Support Services for CAMHS. In addition to their graduate diplomas in primary and secondary counselling, they completed a three-year course in family therapy. In DECS they are classified as deputy principals. They noted that their additional training does not affect their salary levels. Others present at this meeting included Gerri Walker, Principal of the Beafield Education Centre, Chris Seeboth, Co-ordinator of School Support Services for CAMHS, and Alana Cox, Supervisor of the Adolescent and Family Team at FACS. A group composition such as this would be typical of membership in interagency consultancy groups of senior managers who convene periodically with a IRM to review the status of referrals, and to focus on management decisions, resource commitments, referral trends and future requirements.

When an agency has developed concerns about a student and a belief that interagency planning is needed, the worker can communicate this to the IRM, without parent or student knowledge before making a formal referral for interagency services. This initial phase assists workers in determining whether further interagency collaboration is appropriate. These consultations could involve:

- exchanging sufficient information to identify the student and the reasons for the consultation;
- the nature of the agency(s) involvement;
- the current worker(s);
- the proposed steps to be initiated with the student/family;

- the need for interagency collaboration and, if so, who will talk with the parent/guardian and student to fully inform them and to seek their co-operation;
- any information critical to ensuring the safety or protection of the student(s); and
- what steps could be taken in the short-term (South Australia DECS, 1992).

When the IRM receives a formal referral from an agency, she ascertains which agencies and who has been involved in the case in the past. She convenes an appropriate group of people and agency representatives to develop a clear picture of:

- what assessments have been conducted already;
- the opinions of the professionals who have been involved;
- insight into what has worked with the student;
- directions on what areas may still require evaluation/intervention; and
- how to prevent duplication and over-assessment of the student (South Australia DECS, 1992).

A management strategy is evolved. A decision is made about who should be involved in an initial meeting with a pupil and his/her family and who should negotiate the agreement with them to participate. Voluntary co-operation of the student and parent/guardians must be obtained to initiate an interagency case management process. The nominated worker should discuss in a careful and sensitive manner the concerns of the referring source, including:

- specific details regarding the student's needs and difficulties;
- where violent or seriously destructive actions are occurring, the school's obligation to care for the student and all other members of the school community;
- the need for further support for the student; and
- the alternatives if the student and/or parents decide against interagency case management, such as suspension, truancy charges, or other legal actions that might be invoked by an appropriate authority.

Clients who become involved in the IRP sign a voluntary agreement to participate and often there will be a meeting that includes the student and family members as part of the assessment process. The IRM must ensure that parents/guardians and students, if age appropriate, sign Involvement and Information Release Forms. The knowledge and permission of the student and parents/guardians must be gained for non-Education Department information to be obtained. Student participation in the process is encouraged commensurate with their age and cognitive ability. Students 13 years of age and older must be fully involved and informed about all aspects of the process and are allowed to nominate a responsible support person to assist them when participating in case meetings.

A decision is made about who will provide the case management. Usually this is determined by the most fundamental service need that has been assessed. If the basic problem seems to be one of mental health, CAMHS will provide the case management. If it is a welfare or child protection issue, FACS will provide the case management. Once agency responsibility for case management has been determined, that agency decides which staff member will provide the direct services. Sometimes the decision about case management must be influenced by statutory authority, such as in child abuse or other juvenile justice cases. After these steps have been taken, there will be another meeting, involving the IRM, the case manager, and other direct service personnel to devise the service plan. The roles and responsibilities of all participants, in particular the client and care givers, are mutually agreed upon when developing the case management plan.

One source reported that case planning and management usually follow one of the following four pathways that are designed to provide a flexible approach for each individual:

- an in-school programme, supervised by school personnel;
- a programme involving student support personnel from outside the school but within the Education Department;
- a programme involving student support personnel from health or welfare; and

- an interagency programme involving joint services, or additional problem solving due to the complexity of the individual situation.

This same source reported that case review meetings are convened by the designated case manager to:

- review the progress of the student and resolve problems;
- assess the student's current needs and develop additional case plans;
- involve new supports as needed;
- cease agency involvement if no longer needed;
- continue the programme with the student and school, making any adjustments to the case plan as needed; and
- set the next review date or close case involvement.

If a student's problem behaviour escalates, or remains of concern, re-referral occurs. In collaboration with the referral source, the IRM will facilitate a re-assessment of the students situation and develop a new programme. This programme is then re-negotiated with school personnel and the student and family. If the student's behaviour continues to be of serious concern, the manager will negotiate an alternative placement with the school and the family. It would involve one of the following placements:

- an alternative school (either mainstream or specialist);
- an appropriate area withdrawal facility or programme;
- supervised open access schooling where a worker supervises the student's educational output and progress in behavioural change, and provides support and counselling;
- an option such as on-the-job training, job skills training, etc.; and
- an option related to creative behaviour change (*e.g.* wilderness trekking).

Where an alternative placement cannot be negotiated, or where serious disruptive behaviour continues, the IRM will initiate an Alternative Placement Review. The outcome of the review will be to direct that an appropriate alternative placement as recommended by the manager be implemented.

In the period from term 4, 1990 to term 3, 1991, 1 436 school-aged pupils (0.79 per cent) were referred to the IRP. Jager and Harvey (1995) reported that now the service is accessed by approximately 2 per cent of the government school population, including about 3 700 pupils.

The success of the SA government in establishing and sustaining the IRP can be attributed to the leadership of top and middle management and their commitment to continued interaction, learning and enhancing the IRP. Also, the thorough process that produced the Stratmann Report, and the commitment of additional resources that made possible initial implementation of all of its recommendations, created a climate that was receptive to co-ordination in all of the three major child-serving agencies. The IRP has been operational for over four years and commitment to it has been renewed formally by ministers of the newly elected government. However, current economic problems and fiscal restraints are putting new pressures upon maintaining the system.

Members of the IRP interviewed at Beafield Education Centre expressed some concerns about its future as well as enthusiasm for its benefits. They recalled several aspects of the start up phase and the first three years of operation that had been helpful. In addition to the SIC, there were regional policy and planning groups of directors. During the first three months there was wide consultation to learn about existing informal co-ordinating networks and to identify best practices in the existing system. There were also numerous local interagency committees that looked continuously at what would interfere with making the new IRP function. Their input was considered by other over-arching planning committees so that barriers to implementation were addressed. Two project officers were employed, one from welfare and one from education. Training materials were designed to be appropriate for all three sectors. Now there is no project officer from FACS or CAMHS. There are two in DECS, one who oversees behaviour management policy and planning and another whose current major function is to establish links with law enforcement and crime prevention initiatives. Seeboth (1995) believes that it would be helpful to maintain project officers in FACS and CAMHS. Concern was voiced about whether important links had been lost between the SIC and the field level of the IRP, although the agency managers in their region have continued to meet regularly. There are still some complicating issues that need resolution. For example, the geographic organisational boundaries of agencies are not contiguous. The agencies involved in the IRP activities are run by the state government. Other relevant service providing agencies who should become involved belong to local and federal government sectors. Information about the IRP does not get through to direct service people in a planned manner so that it is difficult to keep up with important new developments. Due to turnover in personnel, there are now many employees who did not receive staff development about IRP and there is no systematic periodic training about it. FACS employs many individual staff on a contract basis for short periods of time and many of them do not know how to utilise IRP. IRP responsibilities are not written into the job descriptions of all of the positions that are routinely involved. This means that the work may not receive the attention or recognition that it warrants. The type of strategic planning that characterised the first three years of operation would still be helpful. Although there was unanimous agreement that the IRP results in improved support for youth and their families and improved educational outcomes, several sources suggested that a more systematic way of documenting the benefits and outcomes is needed.

Senior programme managers in DECS reported that, through IRP, the personnel in the ministries, at all levels, have learned much about each other's clients, programmes, services and use of language. They have been able to identify and address duplicated efforts, barriers to co-ordination and factors that tend to include or exclude clients. Other government sectors are becoming interested in applying the IRP model to their arenas, such as the Children's Court and law enforcement. The model permits flexibility of structure which is important because the supportive structures in rural or isolated communities often differ from those in urban areas. For example, there may be a IRM but no specific facility operated by DECS. In the country the same people conducting the IRP may also be the behaviour support team (Dillon, 1995). Fueloep (1995) believes that the networking required at all levels to make the IRP viable is more possible in a small than a large state.

Cox, a supervisor of a FACS adolescent and family team, described a case handled by the IRP process which portrays the complexity of the interagency work often required. The severity of the case also illustrates the reality that many youth referred to the IRP will remain in the case-load indefinitely as every effort is made to sustain a connection with home and school. The youth, aged 13, presented serious behavioural problems at school. He was violent to other pupils and could stay on task for no longer than one minute. For two years, the school attempted to deal with him using a behaviour support team provided by DECS to advise the teacher and a school support officer to work with him. Behaviour support team members all have teacher and perhaps other qualifications, but school support officers are non-professionals. These measures did not solve the violent behaviours and other problems. The case was referred to the IRP. A decision was made that CAMHS should provide the primary case management and child and family therapeutic interventions. During this process domestic violence and neglect issues were identified. The youth had to be excluded from school for four to six weeks with an alternative school programme because his behaviour was dangerous and unacceptable. If space had permitted, he would have been placed at a Learning Centre that offers both individualised academic programmes and therapeutic services. Because no space was available, he was placed in "open access college", which meant that he stayed at home with contact by telephone to his teacher regarding his academic assignments. His mother was supposed to supervise him, but she could not cope. At this time of crisis, the parents agreed to sign a voluntary custody order through FACS. Then through the IRP it was agreed that case management leadership would shift to FACS. He was placed in foster care, with the goal of staying for at least six months. Gradually he started attending the Learning Centre. In the opinion of the FACS and education personnel, he was making progress until he told his father that a worker involved in foster care had engaged in an inappropriate act with him. The FACS and education authorities believe that he lied. At this point, the parents revoked the voluntary custody agreement and took the youth home. The child's behaviour regressed and several mandatory notifications were made to FACS about bruises on his body. He became violent again. He was re-referred to the IRP. FACS and CAMHS became involved once again, but the parents made a complaint to a federally funded multidisciplinary management assessment panel whose role is to assess service delivery to people with intellectual disabilities, convene agencies involved, and to recommend how to improve services. The composition of these panels includes psychiatrists, educators, psychologists and other related disciplines in an attempt to replicate the professions that have provided the direct service under review. This panel recommended a care and protection order. FACS believed this was appropriate, but did not have sufficient hard evidence to go to court. The family dynamics are still counter-productive as long as they allow the youth to play off one agency against another or to divide his parents from the professional personnel. He is still violent and recently assaulted his mother and two education workers. He is able to stay in school only three days a week for two hours per day, with one-to-one support. When educators attempt to apply more structure to his programme, his behaviour deteriorates. He has had some contact with police youth officers and has made appearances in court. FACS is now considering whether to attempt to utilise family preservation services. This case illustrates the necessity of involving several agencies to provide direct services and for statutory reasons. It illustrates how important it is to agree through interagency co-ordination which agency and person will assume case management leadership at different phases of work with a young person and their family. This example involves a destructive hostile youth and family who could not break out of a cycle of self-defeating manipulative actions. The IRP made the manipulation transparent. Although many resources have been required, even more might have been expended in frustration if agencies acted independently.

OTHER LINKS WITH THE MENTAL HEALTH SECTOR

The SA Child and Adolescent Mental Health Services started a School Support Service in 1990 to follow recommendations made in the Stratmann Report (1988). A variety of services are provided in the most disadvantaged clusters of schools in the Northern and Western parts of Adelaide. They include health promotion and prevention strategies and also therapeutic services to individual students and their families. The individual and family services were restricted to four clusters of schools including 16 primary and four secondary schools. A review of the School Support Service found that in 1994, 22 training and development services for students and school personnel were offered, reaching 589 participants. Additionally, twelve group programmes reaching 229 pupils and twelve teachers were offered that focused upon educative and therapeutic issues (Lock *et al.*, 1995).

ISSUES RELATED TO ABORIGINALS AND TORRES STRAIT ISLANDERS

Several Commonwealth publications provided documentation of the disadvantaged position that indigenous people have throughout Australia and also of policies initiated to address the inequities.

- Income: The mean income figure for indigenous people is less than two-thirds of the national figure (ATSIC, 1994a).
- Education: Between 1985 and 1992, the retention rate to year 12 of indigenous students rose from 14 per cent to 25 per cent. Rates for other students rose from 58 per cent to 78 per cent (ATSIC, 1994a).
- Unemployment: Between 1986 and 1991 unemployment in the total Australian labour force increased from 9.2 per cent to 11.7 per cent, but the unemployment rate for indigenous Australians in 1991 was 2.6 times the level for other Australians. This was an improvement over the 1986 rate which was 3.8 times higher. High levels of long-term unemployment among indigenous people are particularly worrying, ranging from 60 per cent to 70 per cent of all indigenous people unemployed compared with 46 per cent of all unemployed Australians. An Aboriginal Employment Development Policy (AEDP) was launched in 1987 with the goal of achieving indigenous employment and income equity with the wider Australian community by the year 2000. The basic elements of the policy include: 1) training and labour market assistance to facilitate access to mainstream employment in the public and private sectors; 2) assistance with employment through Community Development Employment Projects (CDEP); 3) assistance in developing enterprises that are owned and controlled by indigenous people; and 4) enhancing the

involvement of indigenous people in and control over development and delivery of programmes (ATSIC, 1994a).

- *Health*: Life expectancy at birth for indigenous males is up to 18 years less than the national figure. For females, the gap is 20 years. Infant mortality rates in some locations can be more than three times the rate for the total Australian population. In 1990, the Commonwealth Government committed A$232 million over five years to implement a National Aboriginal Health Strategy (NAHS) on condition that, from 1991-92, the states and territories would match the commitment. Thus spending has increased on health, housing and infrastructure for indigenous people (ATSIC, 1994a).

- *Criminal justice*: Indigenous people are over-represented in the criminal justice system. In 1992 they were in police custody at 26 times the rate for non-Aboriginals. In 1993, one in seven prisoners were indigenous people. They are over-represented by a factor of 15 in Australian prisons. In 1992, the government addressed these issues with two funding packages to be spent over five years. The first focused upon measures to reduce indigenous contact with the law and the second on measures to improve the employment prospects and general socio-economic status of indigenous people. Some existing programmes were supplemented, such as legal representation, land acquisition and CDEP. Some new programmes were established, such as the Community Economic Initiatives Scheme. Most of the funding that became available is being channelled through ATSIC (ATSIC, 1994a).

- *The Aboriginal and Torres Strait Islander Commission* (ATSIC): This was established in March, 1990, giving indigenous Australians the right to make decisions affecting their communities for the first time. ATSIC replaced the former Department of Aboriginal Affairs and Aboriginal Development Commission. This marked a radical departure from the previous policy approach and is designed to effect the principle of self-determination for indigenous people and to achieve more social justice and equity for them. It has a decentralised organisation, combining representative, policy-making and administrative elements. There are 35 regional councils elected by indigenous people. There are 17 commissioners elected from the 35 council chairpersons. The main task of the commissioners is to develop national policies for all indigenous people. The 1993-94 expenditures of A$928.1 million by ATSIC included A$251.9 million for Community Development Employment Projects (CDEPs). They offer an alternative to regular unemployment benefits. Participants, otherwise eligible, work two days per week in return for receiving a financial benefit comparable to and in lieu of unemployment benefit. Examples of projects are beautification, building and/or maintenance, workshop/mechanical, yard maintenance, gardening, women's groups, administration/office, shop assistants, oyster or emu farm, store persons, drivers, health workers, cleaners, welding, wood collection, fishing, poultry farm, child care, home duties, security services, music and television production. Other expenditures were A$199.4 million for community housing and infrastructure, A$115.9 million for the administrative arm, A$75.7 million for health, substance abuse prevention, sports and recreation, A$40.4 million for community training and planning, A$40 million for the aboriginal hostels commercial development corporation, A$32.4 million for indigenous legal services, international issues and human rights, A$29.4 million for Community Economic Initiatives and Enterprise Employment Assistance, A$28.9 million for housing loans, A$22.9 million for family reunification, child care, youth affairs and family support, A$22.8 million for payments to the Regional Land Fund, land acquisition and maintenance, A$16.8 million for local government, art and culture, and language maintenance, A$15.3 million for native title, heritage protection and the environment, A$15.1 million for the elected arm, A$11.1 million for the business funding scheme, A$5.1 million for public awareness and women's issues, and A$5 million for other activities (ATSIC, 1994a and 1994b).

- *MABO Judgement and the Native Title Act* 1993: In the MABO decision on 3 June 1992, the Australian High Court overturned the *terra nullius* concept that Australia had belonged to no one when the British arrived. On the contrary, the court ruled that in 1788, the land of Australia was owned by indigenous peoples under their own laws and customs, and that they continued to have title to their land so long as they still observed their traditional laws and so long as their land had not been validly alienated by governments. It found also that the Racial Discrimination Act 1975 protected native title from extinguishment without compensation, throwing doubt on the validity of some leases that had been granted since 1875. Therefore, the Native Title Act 1993 was enacted to: 1) provide for validation of past grants of land or water rights which might have been invalid because of native title rights; 2) set up a Native Title Tribunal to decide where native title still exists; 3) provide for compensation where native title has been lost validly; 4) give negotiation rights to native title where other interests want to mine or buy the land; and 5) create a Land Fund to help indigenous people who are no longer native title holders (ATSIC, 1994*a*).

– *Reconciliation*: Reconciliation, the bringing together of indigenous and non-indigenous citizens into a united Australia, became a formal government policy with Commonwealth legislation creating a Council of Reconciliation in 1991 consisting of twelve Aboriginals, two Torres Strait Islanders and eleven non-indigenous Australians. The results of its initiatives include creating a Joint Committee on Aboriginal Land and Mining that brings together leaders of Aboriginal Land Councils and senior executives of prominent mining companies, establishing a network of Australians for Reconciliation, Study Circles of self-guiding groups who learn about Reconciliation with the aid of material on the history of indigenous people, and an annual Week of Prayer for Reconciliation (ATSIC, 1994*a*). Many of the policies described above express the principle of self-determination for indigenous Australians, but the concept of reconciliation moves the country toward fuller social integration.

The specific measures taken by governments to create more social justice and equity for and reconciliation with indigenous Australians create new pressures upon governments at all levels and upon public and private institutions to develop co-ordinate services integration efforts on their behalf.

SERVICES INTEGRATION IN A SMALL COMMUNITY ON THE FAR WEST COAST OF SOUTH AUSTRALIA

Focus of study visit to Ceduna

Ceduna was selected for a site visit for several reasons. One was because the Murat Bay District Council has received national recognition for its creativity and initiative in working with the Aboriginal community. Their local economic plan, being jointly developed with the Aboriginal community, is a project of national significance. It is being documented as a model that other local governments might adopt. This is the only local government in Australia that has such an agreement with the Aboriginal community (Irvine, 1995). ATSIC reported the following view of this accomplishment:

"Successful negotiations have commenced with the Local District Council of Murat Bay to develop an integrated Community Plan to address efficient and effective service delivery networks within the entire Local Council boundaries."

"The Community Plan will seek to address both the Regional Council Plan as well as the needs of all community residents. It is hoped that the compilation of a Community Plan for Ceduna and its process will be used as a blueprint for other Local Government authorities in the region" (ATSIC, 1994*a*, p. 260).

Also, the Crossways Lutheran School demonstrates the role that an independent school is playing in reconciliation with the Aboriginal community. Additionally, Ceduna has the first district council in the state to develop a youth network, as an arm of the council, to co-ordinate the work of all organisations serving youth in the community. The findings relative to each goal will be discussed after a description of the characteristics of the area.

Social, economic, political and demographic characteristics

Ceduna, a small, isolated town set on the shores of Murat Bay, is 780 kilometres west of Adelaide on the Murat Bay, and 480 kilometres east of the Western Australian border. In the 1991 census, the population served by the District Council of Murat Bay was 3 654 of whom 551 (15 per cent) were Aboriginal. In comparison with other District Council areas based upon 1986 census data, the Murat Bay

District has a relatively young population. It was among the top quarter of districts in the state in terms of percentages of people aged 10-17 years, young adults aged 18-24 years, unemployed 15-19 year-olds, single parent families, and families with incomes below A$9 000 per year. By contrast, it was also in the second quarter of districts for the percentage of individuals with incomes of more than A$26 000 (Collins and Miller, 1992).

Ceduna is the focal point and business centre of the far west coast and the centre of a large cereal growing and grazing area. Bulk handling of grain, gypsum and salt is the main business of the port which is two kilometres away at Thevenard. The education sector provides the most employment. The area of Ceduna offers a wide range of sporting and recreational facilities such as swimming, surfing, sailing and fishing. Ceduna houses the regional headquarters of ATSIC and is also the regional headquarters for several other government departments. The area has no major industries. Irvine (1995) commented that 80 per cent of small industry efforts fail because of lack of needed skills.

The Director of the local TAFE campus described Ceduna as a marginal agricultural community and not a wealthy town. Many farmers have experienced very difficult times in recent years because drought and rural economic depression have forced them off their land or encouraged them to seek alternatives to wheat and sheep. Many people who live in Ceduna receive government welfare benefits. Ceduna has high crime and unemployment rates. A significant proportion of students do not complete year 12 and do not gain an educational qualification for beginning level jobs which limits their future opportunities.

The Murat Bay District Council has the largest percentage of Aboriginal citizens of all local government areas in SA. Aboriginal and Torres Strait Islander people comprise over 4 per cent of the ATSIC Region served by the Wangka Wilurrara Regional Council which is directly elected by Aboriginals living in an area of 355 000 square kilometres. This must be compared to the 1.2 per cent figure for SA as a whole (ATSIC, 1994a, p. 259). Irvine, Chief Executive Officer of the Murat Bay District Council, said that Ceduna had been the most affected by Aboriginal mobility caused by the atomic bomb tests at Maralinga during the 1950s because the displaced Aboriginals were moved to nearby areas. At the government school, 190 of the 500 students (38 per cent) in kindergarten through grade 12 are Aboriginals. About 60 per cent of the students in reception through to year 7 at the Lutheran School are Aboriginals. The concept of the family in Aboriginal communities is much broader than in most European societies. For example, the concept of cousin includes far more distant relatives. School and social adaptation problems in mainstream society can emerge for a child who is moved during the school year from one part of a family to another part of the extended family in a different location. The Aboriginal people of this region have a variety of traditional and non-traditional life styles. ATSIC (1994a) reported that:

> "Many Aboriginal and Torres Strait Islander families are unhappy living in townships such as Ceduna and Port Lincoln and are now opting to move to homeland areas to escape many of the social problems which exist in the towns.
>
> In the region, 11 per cent owned their own homes or are in the process of buying homes with 50 per cent living in State Housing Commission homes.
>
> The provision of housing to communities/organisations and newly established homelands throughout the Ceduna region remains one of the Regional Council's highest priorities" (p. 259).

Co-ordination between the District Council in Ceduna and the Aboriginal community

Money flows into the Ceduna area through the ATSIC regional office to provide services to Aboriginals. The Far West Aboriginal Progress Association (FWAPA) is the local funding body for projects in the town of Ceduna that are funded through ATSIC. Also, money flows into the town through the federal and state governments for any eligible citizen or programme. A significant proportion of the revenue of the District Council comes from formula grants that are influenced by the number of persons resident in the area, including Aboriginals. Financial assistance grants in Australia are based on needs. There is the possibility of duplication of effort on behalf of the Aboriginal community without effective co-ordination between the District Council, federal and state agencies, the FWAPA, and other voluntary and Aboriginal organisations.

For a long time, there have been many Aboriginal transients going through or stopping over in Ceduna, and Irvine (1995) believes that their needs have been a neglected issue. Responsibility for the provision of temporary accommodation for campers and visitors lies with the local government, and this became a high priority of the current District Council when they obtained outside consultants to appraise the issues (Nicholas Clark and Associates, 1994). The recommendation about how to fund, design, build, and manage a Town Camp that would be a joint venture between the District Council and the Aboriginal communities is now being implemented.

The Murat Bay District Council is the only one in Australia that has a specific agreement with the Aboriginal community to develop a joint economic development plan for the area. When developing programmes that target the same problem, population or issue, the District Council and the ATSIC Regional Council, or its local affiliate, FWAPA, look at each other's budgets and have agreed to make joint plans that avoid duplication of effort and expenditures and that make joint management possible.

Lewis and Roussel had two opportunities to meet with the entire District Council and the Co-ordinator of the Crime Prevention Programme. The commitment to reconciliation and co-ordination with the Aboriginal community was manifest. They openly discussed the legacy of the history of racism during which Aboriginals had experienced discrimination from mainstream institutions. They expressed their desire to establish different, more inclusive and socially just relationships. They noted how the social policy developments concerning indigenous Australians, described above, precipitated changes that directly affect the economic, social, educational, justice and service dimensions of life in Ceduna. These changes in social policies also open new opportunities for mutual and co-operative develop-ments. However, they are not easy to achieve. The District Council took the initiative to reach out to leaders in the Aboriginal community to begin the process. They have experienced some rejection and difficulties in the process, but persist. When asked how they explained their success in generating joint planning with the Aboriginal community, they attributed some of it to developing personal relation-ships with local resident leaders of the Aboriginal community. They also felt that the local press had been unfair in its reporting of some issues relating to District Council initiatives and Aboriginal issues. They "took the press to task" (Irvine, 1995) and it changed its tone. They also generated interest and support by involving the entire Ceduna community in developing a television advertisement and a series of video-tapes about the economic and recreational opportunities of the 1 500 kilometre area around Ceduna. Local people instead of professional actors were used in these products which portray the multi-cultural lifestyles, people and resources of Ceduna. They have been shown all over Australia and have helped to develop and reinforce a positive self-image in the community.

The District Council's Crime Prevention and Youth Network Initiatives

The District Council also took advantage of another dynamic force, the SA Attorney General's crime prevention initiative. Local authorities may apply for available funds to study the forces contributing to crime and to utilise strategies to combat them. The philosophy behind it is preventive and permits a wide range of strategies, such as community development initiatives that will impact a total population, enhance collective self-esteem, and contribute to economic development, as well as safety and social justice. Community policing, a law enforcement approach that promotes preventive interventions, is practised in SA. The initiative in Ceduna began in 1990-91 with the organisation of a Steering Committee under the auspices of the District Council. Letters were sent to the CEOs of local government and non-government organisations, inviting them to join the efforts to develop a proposal that could be funded. Two qualified researchers were employed to conduct a survey of community perceptions of the crime problem and to compile relevant official statistics. A total of 296 groups and individuals participated in the study process and in public meetings (Collins and Miller, 1992).

Community respondents perceived five major areas that needed to be addressed to combat crime: youth, domestic violence, alcohol and drug abuse, education and skills development to combat unem-ployment, and community development. Available statistics revealed the third highest incidence of child abuse among city areas in the Northern Country Division of FACS. Official statistics on the incidence of domestic violence in SA were not available. The nearest Women's Shelter is about

440 kilometres or four hours driving time from Ceduna. The Sobering Up Centre reported 591 admissions during 1990-91, but only five beds are available there, revealing an urgent need for a Rehabilitation/Detoxification Centre in Ceduna. Official SA police statistics for 1990 revealed that Murat Bay had a higher rate of violent offences (3 426.3 per 100 000 population) than SA as a whole (1 076.1 per 100 000). It also had a higher rate of property offences (19 043.8 compared to 11 035.2). Juveniles comprised 20 per cent of alleged violent crime offenders and 47.6 per cent of alleged property offenders (Collins and Miller, 1992, p. 28).

The following specific programme needs were identified through the community consultation process: 1) a homework centre away from the school environment for youth who lack the necessary supports or environment at home (this had been tried, but failed, at school due to inadequate facilities and students' feelings about having been at school all day); 2) a school breakfast programme; 3) a local women's shelter/hostel/accommodation centre and crisis intervention services for domestic violence and child abuse; 4) a detoxification/rehabilitation centre; 5) literacy programmes for youth and adults; 6) a mediation service; 7) more police aides to assist with communication with specific groups; 8) support services for victims of crime; 9) more cross-cultural information, interaction and integration; 10) more involvement of the elderly with youth to alleviate fears about each other; 11) family support systems related to child rearing; 12) more adequate parental supervision of children; 13) easily accessible information on parental rights and responsibilities; 14) housing facilities for homeless youth; 15) more employment opportunities for the entire population; 16) availability of and access to leisure facilities for those under the age of 18; 17) transportation to cater to the needs of youth; and 18) more adequate street lighting and public telephones in the Housing Trust area (Collins and Miller, 1992).

The Ceduna Together Against Crime Committee was formed in May, 1991. Also, committees were established for each of the five main areas of need that had emerged in the community consultation process. Their function is to determine priority areas for funding, to give advice about implementation, to evaluate the results, and to submit progress reports to the District Council. A proposal to address each of these five areas was funded in October, 1991, by the Attorney General's Office (A$250 000 over a two year period). A crime prevention officer was employed by the District Council to administer programme activities. An Aboriginal Project Officer was employed in June, 1992, to undertake the Aboriginal community consultation process. A review of the international literature about crime prevention revealed that a community development approach is essential to success (Collins and Miller, 1992).

The District Council believes that there should be more planning and co-ordination among agencies concerning the use of available money from a variety of sources that comes into the area to serve youth. In this way, duplication of effort can be avoided and resources can be used more efficiently to provide additional needed services. The creation of the Ceduna Youth Network is one of the major outcomes of the District Council's initiatives and the Together Against Crime Committee. All of the youth serving agencies in the area were invited to a Youth Workers and Agency Workshop held on November 2, 1994. It was well attended and revealed widespread commitment to improving the delivery of services to youth in Ceduna. Following the workshop, a Ceduna Youth Network was formed that had its first meeting on November 30, 1994. It is recognised by the District Council as an Advisory Committee. A Memorandum of Agreement between the District Council and the Youth Network Committee enumerated the terms of agreement that are operating for a period of two years ending 31 January, 1997. The roles and responsibilities of the network are to: 1) implement youth projects and be accountable for the funding that is provided for them; 2) provide opportunities for people and organisations to register interest and participate in developing and implementing local strategies and programmes; 3) negotiate with agencies on funding agreements with programme sponsors; 4) provide direction and support to staff employed for the implementation of supported projects; 5) amalgamate resources and finances for youth in the District area; 6) improve resources and communications for youth; 7) be a vehicle to seek, gain and control funding for youth training and community projects; and 8) provide six monthly written performance and financial reports to the Council.

The District Council is using the Youth Network as the forum through which agencies share information about their available resources, mandates, goals, gaps in services, and through which they agree to plan jointly to combine efforts, resources, avoid duplication, and develop additional services for youth.

Agencies participating in the network have agreed to this process. Initially, the Ceduna Area School authorities were reluctant to participate in this degree of openness and sharing, but now they are participating more fully. Members of the council expressed the view that many of the community's problems begin at the Ceduna Area School and that school facilities are under-utilised. The network decided to establish a Youth Information Room at the Ceduna Area School to be supervised by network members and volunteers during lunch times, beginning in the first school term of 1995. The council has nothing to say about the selection of the Principal and they believe that decisions about such key public community leadership positions should be more decentralised and influenced by local government authorities.

District Council members believe that youth do not have enough opportunity to participate in the definition of their own problems and the design of strategies to address them. A long-term goal of theirs is to create a mini-council of youth who will be an advisory body to the council. At the time of the study visit, a survey of youth aged 13-19 years was just beginning. A comprehensive survey instrument had been developed to be used in conjunction with an interview strategy.

The Crime Prevention Officers role is to provide liaison with organisations. She chairs a variety of types of meetings, and prepares minutes and a newsletter. She plans and executes some projects and co-operates actively in the ones being directed by others. One exemplary project was the first Australian Surf Culture Camp on the far west coast. It was funded primarily by the Together Against Crime Committee. Surfing lessons and equipment were purchased from Surf Culture Australia, a leading commercial source of surfing teachers, coaches and necessary equipment. The FACS supplied food, camping equipment, and some of the participants. A total of 19 youth attended the camp, including at least eight Aboriginals. As a result of that and a subsequent camp three months later, three Aboriginal participants competed for and were included in the South Australian open men's surfing team that competed against other states' teams at an annual Koori national competition at Wreck Bay, New South Wales. Some camp participants expressed their intent to enrol in more advanced surfing courses. Increased skill and interest in surfing could lead to vocational opportunities as Murat Bay has excellent surfing beaches. Youth learned about both safety and health aspects of surfing. More surfing camps and inter-club competitions are being planned. Similar camps have been held, focused on fishing, football and swimming. They have been well attended by Aboriginal and other youth, aged 8-15 years. A three-day residential Adventure Camp was held for girls that focused on self-awareness, relationships, conflict resolution, self-esteem, drugs, alcohol, AIDS and legal issues. Numerous other recreation projects that also have the potential to develop a career path have been sponsored, involving many organisations. A domestic violence awareness agenda and a workshop about the need for a women's shelter are planned.

The education sector in Ceduna

The Ceduna agenda included visits to a preschool for Aboriginal children aged 3-4 operated by FWAPA, the government sponsored kindergarten for children aged 4-6, the Ceduna Area School (CAS) with classes from kindergarten to year 12, and the Crossways Lutheran School, with classes from reception (age 5) to year 7. The Principal of the Crossways Lutheran School was one of our hosts in Ceduna. His school was on the agenda as a good example of an independent school that has taken seriously the mission of integration and reconciliation with Aboriginals and has provided leadership in the community. Aboriginal children may attend primary school in their own communities, but must attend the secondary schools in Ceduna. Bus transportation from nearby Aboriginal communities is provided. We also visited the Spencer Institute of TAFE Ceduna Campus.

Aboriginal pre-kindergarten: We interviewed the Director of the Aboriginal pre-kindergarten and saw the facility when no children were there. The programme was created 20 years ago at the initiative of Aboriginal parents and under the auspices of FWAPA. Most of the funds that support it come through FWAPA, except for the Director's salary. Ms. Armstrong would prefer to have a management committee of parents instead of the present governance arrangement. She is an Aboriginal from a community in a different part of Australia and is a qualified primary-trained teacher. She has one aide. DEETYA provides books and supplies. Children aged 3-4 are eligible to attend. At the time of the visit, 21 were enrolled with an average of 15 attending for one-half day on four days each week. A primary goal is to socialise the Aboriginal children in an environment that is sensitive and responsive to Aboriginal culture to prepare them to enter a regular kindergarten. Another goal is Aboriginal language retrieval.

Kindergarten: The Murat Bay Children's Centre is a government operated kindergarten where attendance is voluntary. We interviewed the co-directors, one of whom is Aboriginal. During the interview they conveyed a comfortable way of sharing leadership. The annual budget varies, determined by how many children attended in the prior term. The co-directors have academic qualifications for director's positions, and two other staff members have early childhood education diplomas which prepared them to work with children aged from 0-8. The government classifies this kindergarten as a high needs centre, therefore funds it at a higher rate than average. However, it is necessary for its voluntary Local Management Committee to raise additional funds for the operational budget. The budget depends also upon parent fees. FWAPA provides the bus that is shared with the pre-kindergarten to provide transportation for some children. Some children from outlying areas are brought by the government's school buses. Aboriginal health services are provided within the centre. School dental services are also available. Now that the new SA Department of Education and Children's Services has responsibility for kindergartens, there may be more sharing of resources with the area's public schools. The co-directors said that some of their greatest challenges lie in dealing effectively with cultural diversity and with the bureaucratic red-tape of government agencies that have difficulty being flexible. Because Ceduna is so far away from the rest of inhabited South Australia, it becomes necessary to share resources. In-service training of staff is regarded as important. They participate in an interagency in-service training group that shares resources. Outside experts have been brought in to deal with topics such as racism, social development, social services, mandatory reporting of child abuse, protective behaviours, and health services.

The 62 enrolled children are divided into three groups. One group comes four mornings per week, and the other two come two days each. The programme is child-centred, recognising their cultural diversity and different learning styles and socio-economic backgrounds. Some of the children come from farms on a bus and some are members of Ceduna's Greek community. About half of the children are Aboriginals. Many of the children are transients whose basic needs have not been addressed adequately. Centre staff co-ordinate with the local Child Care Centre and Family Day Care about approaches to behaviour management because some children attend both kindergarten and the child care facilities.

The staff-child ratio is 1:10. Both centre and mobile services, and a toy lending service, are provided to families within a 300 kilometre radius. The mobile service focuses upon isolated families and early intervention with disabled children or others with special needs. There is also a parent-run play group for children aged 0-6. Occasionally, the kindergarten provides emergency care of a child. Co-ordination with FACS is crucial when there is concern about child abuse or neglect.

Transition programmes assist children and their families with entering the Ceduna Area School or the Lutheran School. These involve kindergarten staff meeting with staff from a primary school and with parents, assisting with enrolment procedures, sharing other information, and arranging for kindergarten children to visit the schools. The Lutheran School has a transition worker who provides a transition package and a specific strategy for involving parents in taking responsibility for their child's transition to school. Transition planning with parents and schools for a child with special needs begins earlier. The successful transition of these children may require the involvement of a team of specialists and a guidance counsellor.

Crossways Lutheran School: The Principal of the Crossways Lutheran School is committed to reconciliation with the Aboriginal community. Since his arrival, the proportion of Aboriginal pupils at Crossways Lutheran School has increased to 60 per cent. The curriculum has been adapted to accommodate differing learning styles, such as using more hands-on learning, and including more observational and imitation techniques. The curriculum must be culturally inclusive and now includes Aboriginal studies for all pupils. The Principal believes that having many Aboriginal pupils has promoted goodwill throughout the community. It is school policy that every teacher must visit every child's home. When going, a teacher may choose to be accompanied by an Aboriginal aide. Aboriginal parents now come more frequently to the school, including visits to classrooms, than in the past. Establishing close links with the Aboriginal Health Service resulted in a plan for every child in the school to receive health examinations from an Aboriginal physician, with parents' permission. This is viewed as one step toward social integration. The Principal established a link with the local CDEP programme, through which he has obtained six people to work two days per week at his school. Under this programme, the school does not pay anything. The CDEP programme, which provides an alternative to unemployment bene-fits, provides the compensation. These additional staff have brought additional skills in working with children and other attributes such as artistic abilities. Several of them have volunteered to work at the school for more than two days per week.

The annual budget of Crossways School is A$430 000. Independent schools in Australia receive financial support from Australian federal and state governments. In addition, Crossways Lutheran School charges parents annual fees of A$400 with a downward sliding scale for second and third children. If a child is deemed to be a government assisted child, the school gets a government allowance to help pay for fees and books. Consequently, the parents' fees are reduced to A$100. Over 50 per cent of the children at Crossways School fall into this category. The organisation known as Parents and Friends of the School raises additional money for specific projects. Also, there is an Aboriginal Students Support and Parent Awareness Programme which has given A$200 per child for activities. These voluntary contributions are not part of the formal school budget, but made possible, for example, the purchase of computers and some of the excursions for pupils.

The principals in the far west area meet together twice per term, discuss their programmes, exchange ideas, share in-service programmes and some equipment. Also, all schools in the far west area share a bus that is used primarily for taking children on excursions and to camps. The Principal also established links with the District Council and its Together Against Crime initiative. He sees their preventive efforts as relevant to his school because children as young as the age of 9 have been involved in petty crime. As many of the children in Crossways School have unmet basic needs and family problems, he would like to find more ways to co-ordinate with agencies and programmes that provide family and social services.

Ceduna Area School: The Ceduna Area School serves children from kindergarten age through to year 12. Of the 500 pupils enrolled, 190 (38 per cent) are Aboriginal. The school has an Aboriginal teaching team consisting of two teachers and three Aboriginal education workers. A sixth person conducts home liaison. These people provide role models for Aboriginal children. One function of the team is to keep track of what happens to pupils who quit coming to school. Some of the absenteeism is related to the cultural patterns of Aboriginals who move often or who may send their children to live with a relative in another community during the school year without notifying the school. Consequently, school authorities must make every effort to find them and provide assistance with the transition into another educational programme in order to fulfil their statutory responsibilities. The Assistant Principal who was interviewed stated that this school is one of twelve in Australia that have been funded to make individual plans for youth at risk based upon their individual aspirations. In addition, efforts are being made to obtain funding to create a mobile pupils' project that would develop a curriculum that could follow Aboriginal youth wherever they go. Many of the individual plans are arranged through the local TAFE campus as the situations of some pupils indicate that they will not continue in a regular school programme. A few pupils will be assisted to make another plan because they are too disruptive. Others will not perform well enough in the traditional curriculum to pass into the next grade and would drop out altogether if an alternative plan was not offered. In these situations, the school personnel must negotiate with both the pupil and parents to convince them that a competency-based course at the TAFE campus would be worthwhile. Some individual planning requires negotiating with other agencies or businesses to design a work-study programme.

TAFE (*Technical and Further Education*): The Spencer Institute of TAFE Ceduna Campus is one of 287 sites in the nation. The study programmes offered here are mainly in the following areas: business studies, Aboriginal education, community services, mechanical engineering, adult literacy and numer-acy. In developing the Aboriginal education component, extensive consultations occur with Aboriginal community organisations and government agencies. However, flexible delivery methods are used to design individual programmes to suit the interests and capabilities of students. This campus serves about 350 people in one year, many of whom attend part-time. There are six to seven full-time teachers. In addition, the TAFE Campus employs specialists to teach specific courses. Also, there is a part-time student counsellor, a part-time librarian, a caretaker and a receptionist.

Through planning with the Ceduna Area School personnel, a Special Initiative Vocational Training Programme (SIVTP) was designed for youth who refuse to continue in the school. It is funded in cash or in kind by a national youth grant from DEETYA, the local Crime Prevention Committee, TAFE, the Ceduna Area School, the Rural Access Programme, Kickstart (a SA government initiative for young unemployed people), and others in the local community. Funding was arranged for twelve months. New funding is needed in order to continue the programme which is considered successful. SIVTP has a Management Committee of five people representing TAFE, the Crime Prevention Programme, the Ceduna Area School, the Family and Children's Service, DEETYA, and the lecturer/co-ordinator. She promotes peer group processes, monitors each individual closely, provides inspiration, counselling and support to the students, and academic leadership. Since its inception in May, 1994, 27 youths have been served. Six of these secured either full- or part-time employment. Six continued their education for obtaining the South Australia Certificate of Education (SACE). Twelve are still in the programme. Three others have an uncertain outcome. The majority of students were unemployed and disaffected from school at the time of enrolling in the programme. Although the programme was designed with the intent that both Aboriginal and other students would participate, staff were disappointed that no Aboriginal students enrolled. Also, more boys than girls have been served through this programme because of the difficulties of arranging child care. In working with the students, near-term rather than long-term goals are set initially according to the ability of the youth. They are approached as adults more than as young people and are expected to take responsibility for their decisions and themselves. Being in an institution attended by other adults, such as the TAFE college, seems to appeal to some who did not like being in the Area School. The curriculum utilises practical activities that involve students in work, special projects, job searches, interviewing skills, and resume writing. There are also traditional classroom, reading and writing components. In the first six weeks of the programme, students studied computing, minor car servicing, communication and career awareness, and study skills. Also, they were able to obtain a Senior First Aid Certificate. Afterwards, they were encouraged to pursue studies relevant to chosen career pathways. Some studied modules from the Business Studies and Community Services curricula. Others enrolled in Occupational Health, Safety and Welfare or Grooming, Sewing, Woodwork, Maths, or Plant Propagation. Instruction in computing continued throughout, focusing upon word processing, database management and spreadsheets. In the final term, studies were offered in two blocks. Hospitality was the content of the first and was taught in the context of a bistro by a professional. For the second block, learning packages were purchased from the Retail Industry Training Council, and students studied Customer Relations and Service. The campus manager attributed the success of the first year's plan to the direction, commitment and problem-solving efforts of the Managing Committee and to the leadership and personal qualities of the co-ordinator. He said that the biggest hindrance to co-ordination of efforts on behalf of at risk youth is social policy or the administration of it. He believes that flexibility is essential to design individual programmes for youth at risk, who have left or are likely to drop out of school. Although the government intends to have a seamless system of benefits and services to meet individuals' needs, there is often so much red tape that individuals cannot be served holistically and it is difficult to merge funding streams that have similar policy objectives. For example, AUSTUDY, the Commonwealth programme for subsidising individual students, is designed primarily for full-time students. This works to the disadvantage of youth at risk who might respond to a part-time or other individualised study programme. It requires much negotiation with relevant authorities to get permission to use such funds for the individualised programmes of the TAFE campus. He noted that sometimes the local government authority is able to obtain money for TAFE programmes when it cannot receive money directly. The co-ordinating role being played by the current District Council has been effective in bringing the TAFE campus together with other youth serving agencies.

SUMMARY AND CONCLUSIONS

One pervasive theme in the SA study visit was social justice for disadvantaged older youth who do not complete or are at risk of not completing secondary education. The equity, financial assistance, housing and targeted programmes of the Commonwealth Government provide a cushion to meet the basic needs of youth whose disadvantage stems from deprivation, discrimination, insensitivity of systems to cultural differences, and other factors beyond the control of youth themselves. The Commonwealth Government has the political sanction of the Australian people to co-ordinate education, training and employment policies concerned with national manpower and labour supply issues. Unemployment rates among youth are very high in some areas. The fact that the Commonwealth addresses so many policies and programmes specifically to educationally disadvantaged youth makes a powerful statement about the nation's commitment to them. An arm of the Commonwealth Employment Service (CES), the Youth Access Centre, has been designated responsibility to co-ordinate youth services at the local level. Yet success in this role depends upon the co-operation of state and local governments and other public and private organisations. Another key ingredient is the leadership and co-ordinating capabilities of managers of local CES offices and the designated YAC personnel. There are no specific qualifications required for YAC case manager positions. The YACs visited portrayed wide variation in focus. At some, the core is case management which is services integration at the individual level. A focus upon planning and co-ordinating with industries and other education or service organisations to address underlying problems was demonstrated at the Salisbury YAC. The latter role requires investment of time in analysing and understanding the local labour market, offering specific services and programmes in a systematic way to industries and schools in order to encourage youth employment.

The leadership of state government agencies must be committed to the same goals in order for Commonwealth targeted programmes to have maximum impact in fighting educational disadvantage. Additionally, the State Government must supplement Commonwealth programmes. The SA government, at the highest levels, offered this type of leadership and commitment in its 1987 initiative to promote services integration for the school-aged population with serious social and behavioural difficulties. The Stratmann Report (1988) produced recommendations for each of the large bureaucracies that provide crucial services for these youth. The SA government also provided the means for implementing most of the recommendations through its social justice budget.

An Interagency Referral Process (IRP) was carefully designed and implemented to facilitate multidisciplinary and interagency work with youth and their families who require the services of two or more of the largest public agencies. Interviews with middle management and direct service personnel involved in the IRP reflected keen clinical understanding of clients and mutual respect for professional competencies. They also demonstrated skills in exchanging management responsibility for difficult youth and families in order to enhance the therapeutic possibilities of statutory mandates and professional relationships while respecting the rights of youth and parents. They communicated enthusiasm for the IRP process but also expressed concern about maintaining and improving system capabilities to sustain the IRP and also to make it more inclusive.

A notable feature of the SA case study is that the education sector has demonstrated leadership and commitment of major resources to sustaining services integration efforts. Within schools, there is a preference for education professionals to fill non-teaching positions focused upon service provision to at risk youth. But SA is one place where the education sector clearly recognises its need for the services of other agencies and professions in order to keep some youth in school. DECS also sees curriculum innovation as essential to breaking down discriminatory racist and sexist attitudes, facilitating multicultural understanding, and attaining social justice goals.

Services integration and reconciliation with Aboriginal Australians was another pervasive theme of the SA case study. Related issues came up at every site, but they were a major component of the work of the Murat Bay District Council in Ceduna, a small isolated town on the far west coast of SA. Here the local government has initiated services integration efforts using a community development approach. The geographic area for which this council has responsibility includes the largest percentage of indigenous Australians of all local government jurisdictions in South Australia. A local economic plan, being jointly developed with the Aboriginal community, is a project of national significance. The work of this Council is being discussed at conferences of local government officials and is a model that other areas may adopt. Co-operation and efforts at services integration with Aboriginal organisations were evident in several areas that are crucial to the well-being of local people, for example, housing, services relating to alcohol and drug abuse, education at all levels, recreation, law enforcement and crime prevention. Co-ordination in financial planning has been initiated to maximise the possibilities of utilising the funds that flow to the District Council, other local organisations, and to the Aboriginal organisations for the same programmatic goals and objectives. These are promising strategies that are basic to attaining effective services integration.

Australia's extensive youth policy has penetrated the Far West Coast. This District Council is the first one to organise a youth network consisting of representatives of all of the youth serving organisations in the District to serve as an official advisory arm to the Council. It has been empowered for a two-year period to co-ordinate the youth services in the area. A sound community development approach was used in the process leading to establishing the network. First the opinion of the community was sought through a survey of their perceptions of need. The results were used by the Council to establish five separate working committees to develop plans to address the major areas of concern that were identified. The Committee on Youth has evolved into the youth network. The other four areas are also in a dynamic process of development. Success in those areas can also affect the well-being of youth. During the interviews and experiences in Ceduna, one could sense the cohesion and pride that has developed.

REFERENCES

ATSIC (Aboriginal and Torres Strait Islander Commission) (1994a), *Annual Report, 1993-94,* Canberra.

ATSIC (1994b), *What is ATSIC?,* Canberra.

Australian Conference of Directors-General of Education and the Commonwealth Youth Bureau, Department of Employment, Education and Training, "Children and youth at risk: Effective programmes and practices", mimeo.

BUDD, N. and CAMERON, M. (1994), *Client Surveys Report: National Survey of Client Satisfaction with Youth Access Centres, December 1993-March 1994,* DEETYA Economic and Policy Analysis Division, Evaluation and Monitoring Branch, Canberra.

COLLINS, R. and MILLER, V. (1992), *Draft Two Year Crime Prevention Plan for Ceduna, Together Against Crime,* District Council of Murat Bay, Ceduna, SA.

DEPARTMENT OF EMPLOYMENT, EDUCATION AND TRAINING (1993), *Education at a Glance,* Commonwealth of Australia, Canberra.

DILLON, G. (1995), Project Manager, Interagency Student Behaviour Management, DECS, Personal interview, 5 April, Adelaide, South Australia.

FODOR'S 95 AUSTRALIA AND NEW ZEALAND (1994), Fodor's Travel Publications, Inc., New York.

FUELOEP, S. (1995), Director, DECS Programmes Personal interview, 5 April, Adelaide, SA.

FUELOEP, S., JOHNSON, W. and DILLON, G. (1995), Self-completion questionnaire for OECD-CERI study visit to South Australia, April.

IRVINE, T. (1995), Chief Executive Officer of the District Council of Murat Bay, personal interview, 5 April, Ceduna, SA.

JAGER, S. and HARVEY, J. (1995), Self-completion questionnaire for OECD-CERI study visit to South Australia, April.

LOCK, C., BROWN, C. and SEIBOTH, C. (1995), "Review of school support service: Strategic directions for promoting mental health in schools", Child and Adolescent Mental Service (Northern), Adelaide, mimeo.

MINISTERIAL COUNCIL ON EDUCATION, EMPLOYMENT, TRAINING AND YOUTH AFFAIRS (1994), *National Strategy for Equity in Schooling,* Curriculum Corporation, Carlton, Victoria.

NICHOLAS CLARK AND ASSOCIATES (1994), *Accommodation of Aboriginal Visitors, Appraisal of Issues and Options,* Sydney.

PATERSON, J. (1993), *Students at Risk Programme in South Australia,* Education Department of South Australia, Adelaide.

SEEBOTH, C. (1995), Co-ordinator of School Support Service, CAMH Services, Personal interview, 6 April, Adelaide, SA.

SOUTH AUSTRALIA, DECS (1992), *The Interagency Referral Process, A Service for Students with Social and Behavioural Difficulties.*

SOUTH AUSTRALIA, STATE INTERAGENCY COMMITTEE (1992), *Final Report on the Implementation of the Recommendations from the Interagency Responses Report.*

STRATMANN, P. (1988), *Interagency Responses to School Children with Social and Behavioural Problems,* Department of Premier and Cabinet, Adelaide, SA.

SWEETMAN, S. (1995), Principal Curriculum Officer for Equity, DECS, Personal interview, 5 April, Adelaide, SA.

WALLER, V. (1992), *Review of the Interim Co-ordination Role of Youth Access Centres (YACs),* DEETYA, Evaluation and Monitoring Branch, Canberra.

NEW SOUTH WALES

HOW INTEGRATED SERVICES CAN BE USED TO ADDRESS BROAD RANGING PROBLEMS, FROM BAD BEHAVIOUR TO VIOLENT CRIME

by

Richard Volpe and Philippa Hurrell

INTRODUCTION

Australia's current economic and political situation supports the reduction and privatisation of government services. Like other OECD Member countries, Australia has targeted services for children and youth as some of the first to be reduced when programme cuts are made. Health, education and welfare have been most vulnerable at a time when budget balancing is a preoccupation. In keeping with a world trend, human services integration is seen by Australian policy makers both as a way of improving services and of economising. What follows is a descriptive evaluation of eight government selected integrated youth service programmes in New South Wales that were visited by the OECD team.

BACKGROUND

Policies governing the provision of services for children and families are divided among six states and two self-governing territories which are represented in the bicameral Australian Parliament in Canberra. Each state has areas of guarded sovereignty, a Governor, Constitution, Parliament, executive branch and judiciary. The Australian Constitution provides for a parallel system of federal courts, a parliament and an executive branch. Although the federal government has jurisdiction over divorce, marriage and social security, it does not have the authority to make laws in respect of children. In this area state legislation takes precedence over federal legislation. Most policies affecting children (health, education and welfare) are created by the states. As a result, there are many inconsistencies in practice, regulations and service organisation throughout the country. Where a child lives matters because services are administered through state laws, agencies and programmes. Consequently, no national children's policies exist. Where national programmes are clearly needed, however, Australians have been creative in using federal laws to supply comprehensive services to youth. This is especially true in the area of youth employment services. Unlike many parts of the world that provide traditional youth services through health, education and welfare, Australia links mental health, suicide prevention, sex education, drug abuse prevention, educational remediation and criminal rehabilitation initiatives to employment services.

According to the last official census in 1993 the population of Australia was 17.6 million. New South Wales is the richest and most populous state (close to 5 million people). As in the rest of Australia, most of the population of this state is concentrated in coastal areas. Sydney (the largest city) and Newcastle (a major coal producing city and port) are the study sites for this report. Both of these cities have been hit hard by a recession that has kept unemployment at unprecedented levels since 1990.

A report on the distribution of wealth in Australia by the Roman Catholic Bishops in 1992 drew national attention to the impact of the recession and consequent poverty on families and children. They concluded that Australia had become the least egalitarian of the western nations (Australian Catholic Bishops, 1992).

The nature of risk factors for youth throughout Australia is well documented. The Australian Youth Foundation concludes in the report "A Lost Generation" (1994) that more than half a million young people, aged between 15 and 24 years, are living on the margins of Australian society, participating in neither work or full-time education. Australian youth suicide rates are the highest in the world. In actual numbers there are around 2 000 teen suicides each year. This figure refers to actual deaths, not attempts, and has been dramatically broken down as follows: 40 teen suicides a week, six a day, or one death every four hours. Suicides among 14-19 year-olds have risen 600 per cent in the last 25 years. More young people die at their own hands in Australia than in road accidents each year. Drug abuse is also a major problem with half of illegal drug users being under 20 years of age. Australian youth have been characterised as discouraged and in deep despair. With its highly dense urban areas, New South Wales is over-represented in these figures. Youth alienation is also more pronounced in the large population of Aboriginal people living in this region.

Youth unemployment is considered a major risk factor. Forty per cent of those unemployed are under 25 years of age. The Australian Youth Foundation (1995) claims unemployment to be the number one problem faced by youth. It estimates that it takes on average 20 months for a 15-24 year-old to find a job. When jobs are found they are usually low paid, without training and insecure. The Centre for Labour Studies, University of Adelaide predicts that there will be no full-time jobs for those under 19 years of age by the year 2000.

Although a slight surge in economic growth occurred in early 1994 (unemployment fell from a high of 11.4 per cent to 9.4 per cent), the country has remained in the grip of a severe recession. Three million people are out of work. Youth unemployment is running at about 25 per cent. In response to official recognition of the depth of this recession, the Australian government produced a major policy paper on employment and growth. The paper called "Working Nation" (1994) outlined a plan to spend 6.5 billion Australian dollars over four years to reduce the unemployment rate to 5 per cent by the year 2000. Programmes were set up to deal with long-term joblessness and job training for youth.

The milestone policy articulation and implementation efforts surrounding a National Strategy for Equity in Schooling (Ministerial Council of Education, Employment, Training and Youth Affairs, 1994) have given prominence to a set of goals and priorities that reflect Australia's long-term commitment to dealing with the economic and social basis of school failure. The programmes that have resulted from this and other recent policy initiatives are comprehensive. Moreover, they have culminated in the government's 1994 Youth Social Justice Strategy (YSJS) that specifically attempts to ensure co-ordination of local and Commonwealth programmes and services in order to improve outcomes for children and youth at risk. This programme provides a full range of youth services that includes accommodation for the homeless, income support, labour market assistance, education, health, information and counselling. The overall consequence of these policies has been the creation of good examples of integration based on local communication networks and efforts by providers to co-ordinate youth services.

STATE AND FEDERAL EDUCATION POLICIES AND STRUCTURES

Constitutional responsibility for education and training is held by the states and territories. The Federal Government is, however, significantly involved in this area because of its responsibility for national economic development. There are three education sectors: elementary and secondary schools (public and private), vocational education and training (VET) mostly provided through the Technical and Further Education (TAFE) system, and universities.

Many of the policies impacting directly on children and youth are implemented through the education system. One third of all primary and secondary students in Australia attend schools in New South Wales. The New South Wales Department of School Education implements many of the policies developed at both state and federal levels. The objectives set by the state for public (government) and private (non-government) schools reflect world-wide interest in outcomes, accountability, quality assurance, equity, curriculum reform, and integration of special needs students (Ministerial Council on Education, Employment, Training, and Youth Affairs, 1993). Community consultation and involvement are implicitly seen as a means to enhance school effectiveness and vehicles that facilitate collaboration between schools and children's services. Both of the two schools visited were coincidentally undergoing quality assurance reviews when attended by the OECD research team. It was interesting to find that one of the criterion used in evaluating the schools concerned the effectiveness of personnel in collaborating with other community agencies. In spite of this observation, no explicit local level policies on services integration were presented or referenced. Moreover, no mention was made of the potential of services integration in discussions of special needs and socio-economically disadvantaged students.

Integrating youth services

The Department of Employment, Education, Training and Youth Affairs (DEETYA) is attempting to provide comprehensive co-ordinated integrated services through an initiative called Youth Networking. This undertaking is designed to bring together the services of three Commonwealth Government Departments: the Department of Health, Housing, Local Government, and Community Services (funder of AIDS, drug and alcohol, refuge, housing and Medicare programmes); the Department of Social Security (funder of Job Search Allowance, Newstart Allowance, Young Homeless Allowance, Sole Parent Pension, and JET-Jobs, Education and Training Programmes); and the Department of Employment, Education, Training and Youth Affairs (funder of AUSTUDY to help financially eligible youth aged 16 or older to stay in school and ABSTUDY a similar programme for Aboriginal and Torres Strait Islander youth). The Department also runs Career Reference Centres, the Assistance for Isolated Children Scheme, and the Higher Education Contribution Scheme. The youth serving efforts of DEETYA are embodied in Youth Access Centres (YACs) that run alongside, and are often co-housed in, centres providing Commonwealth Employment Services (CES). Since a review of services by Chesterman and Schwager (cited in Waller, 1992) identified problems in existing co-ordination efforts, YACs have been given the responsibility of co-ordinating youth services. Co-ordination is defined in this context as more effective planning of services provision, networking between services and management of individual cases. The ultimate aim of this undertaking is to provide youth with financial support, career information, job training, jobs, housing, and help with personal and health problems.

Youth Access Centres (YACs)

The YACs embody the most explicit attempt to integrate youth services in Australia. They were created to provide information, advice, counselling, and referrals to other service providers. These special information and help centres are designed to provide one stop shopping in a friendly, non-threatening and relaxed setting. A summary of three National Surveys of client satisfaction reports that over 85 per cent of youth, youth serving organisations and participating secondary schools were satisfied with information provided by the YACs (Department of Employment, Education and Training, 1994). Although they are specifically assigned the responsibility of co-ordinating youth services, their role is limited to services co-ordination through information sharing and the identification of gaps. This role has evolved in response to resistance by state and local youth providers to any Commonwealth agency taking responsibility for integrating programmes and agencies. The shared fear amongst providers was that integration efforts would eventually lead to programme amalgamation as a means of reducing costs. Consequently, YACs have a clearly restricted mandate to only "support the co-ordination process between government and community agencies. Providers appear to have a philosophical preference for co-ordination of youth services being the responsibility of local government or community organisations" (Waller, 1992).

Students at Risk Programme (STAR)

DEETYA funds a special initiative called the Students at Risk Programme to identify students who are not likely to complete school, and to provide them with services that will increase their chances of finishing an educational programme. Aspects of the programme include teacher support to maintain at risk students in mainstream programmes, special efforts to strengthen home-school relations and communication, the development of more effective screening methods, targeting the need for more flexible organisational structures that facilitate school re-entry, and establishing means to improve school-business community exchange. An in-depth portrait of these efforts has been provided by a summary of ten case studies commissioned by DEET (Coopers and Lybrand, 1992). The report concludes that an outstanding feature of the STAR Programme is "that so much has been done with so little (...) to improve the education of students at risk for leaving school early". In addition, the study highlights the importance of allowing schools to operate autonomously in playing a welfare role for students and the effectiveness of focusing on youth as individuals as opposed to being members of a particular group.

Three YACs were visited: City Central (Sydney) YAC, Marrickville YAC, and Newcastle YAC. STAR supported programmes existed in most of the schools and service settings observed.

INTEGRATED SERVICES IN SYDNEY

South Sydney Youth Services

Context

South Sydney is a large inner city community which is mainly working class (population 78 000). The largest number of urban Aboriginals in Australia lives in this area along with a diverse group of immigrants. The community suffers from common big city problems such as air pollution, overcrowding, insufficient recreational areas, and problems that threaten personal security. Unemployment runs at three times the national average. Although there is a large number of low income earners and a high number of public housing residents, the cultural mix of the population provides an energy that, when coupled with deliberate community development, makes it an interesting place to live and work in.

The service is a response by twenty provider groups to the complex problems facing young people in this community. The interagency group responded to a grassroots call for collaborative comprehensive services for youth in this part of the inner city.

Input

The service model is based on individual respect, the recognition of rights, social justice, self-determination, and the importance of self-efficacy based on necessary skill and knowledge acquisition. The operation of services is comprehensive and collaborative. Services include: 1) Streetwork; 2) Community development; 3) Assistance with employment and employment training; 4) Access to income support; 5) Education programmes; 6) Health education and services; 7) A juvenile justice programme and paralegal support; 8) Counselling; 9) Music and video programmes, community arts; 10) Sport and recreational programmes; 11) Small business development; 12) Publishing; 13) Casework and counselling; 14) Literacy and numeracy training; and 15) Advocacy.

Funding has been obtained from a variety of sources at both the state and federal levels. Large one-off payments have been obtained for special programmes. Five on-site staff operate out of the service centre. Sessional workers and graphic professionals are employed in a graphics printer company that recently has been made operational. All staff receive two weeks in-service training per year. Counselling staff are expected to be under on-going supervision.

Process

The aim of the service is to involve youth in community life in such a way that they develop a sense of self-efficacy and optimism in their potential to solve the problems of adolescence, and the structural (socio-economic) barriers they face, through co-operative and constructive initiatives. Most (80 per cent) of the 450 or so clients served each year are self-referrals. The other 20 per cent are referred by outside agencies or the courts. Unlike many specialised providers, the service developed as an inter-agency response in 1978 and has maintained and developed close working relationships with a number of services and government departments (Health; Employment, Education, and Training; Employment Services; Social Security; and Community Services). The service facilitates bi-monthly youth agency meetings and has drawn its financial support from a wide range of sponsors.

Product

High participation rates for targeted groups (Aboriginal youth; non-English speaking youngsters; youth involved in the criminal justice system; early school leavers; and young women) suggest that current outreach and involvement strategies are effective.

Cleveland Street High School

Context

This secondary school serves one of the most economically disadvantaged areas in Sydney. The area has the linked social problems of poverty, unemployment, domestic instability, divorce, single parenting, child abuse, and high levels of crime and violence.

Input

In addition to programme and salary support for the operation of the school along with the usual associated services, significant special programme grants have been obtained for a school re-entry programme for Aboriginal youth and an English language study centre. The Back-to-School Programme targets Aboriginal street youth (12-15 years of age) who have been long-term school non-attenders. The Intensive English Centre provides initial language training for non-English speaking immigrant youth. This off-site programme is offered in blocks of 30 to 50 weeks.

Process

Although the school has no formal protocols for co-operation between itself and other youth serving agencies it works closely with them on the basis of well established long-standing personal ties. The school has participated in the inter-agency meeting sponsored by South Sydney Youth Services. Relations with police, medical, Aboriginal, and technical school services are particularly good. Outside agencies often provide in-service programmes for teachers and special programmes for students.

Product

This facility has been successful in retaining Aboriginal students and offering them opportunities for school re-entry. Through a concerted effort to develop mutual respect and an appreciation of Aboriginal culture this school provides a supportive and effective educational environment.

Arthur Phillip High School

Context

This comprehensive school is located in the central business district of Paramatta. The school blends both progressive and traditional aspects of schooling. Illustrative is the use of a local area computer network along with the maintenance of a classroom as it was furnished in 1875. Over the 120 year history of the school it has produced an unusually high number of internationally known artists, actors and writers. The school serves a diverse multicultural non-English speaking population of 870 students with over 90 per cent of them coming from 60 or more countries. Most student families receive social and financial assistance of some kind.

Input

The school is staffed by 75 professionals involved in regular education, and has six special education classes with six support staff. The school also participates in specially funded programmes for disadvantaged and at risk students. The teaching function is supported by advanced computer and information technology. A number of formal structures exist that encourage and enable student, parent and community involvement in school-related policy making and decision making.

A School Study Centre has been established through special funding provided by the Department of Education STAR Programme and Burnside, a child and family service agency of the United Church of Australia. The Centre operates two days a week from the library as an after school study aid to students referred by staff. The Centre provides tutorials, opportunities to interact with staff and complete homework, and afternoon tea for 20 students each term. Tutors are selected from the student population to assist programme participants with their academic studies. The Centre aims to improve academic performance, increase self-esteem, improve attitudes towards education, increase social skills, and extend use of school resources.

Process

Most interaction with other agencies is done on a co-operative basis. Although the Centre adheres to the Burnside agency model for after school programmes, it is not a co-located service as much as an extension of the school's education mandate. A Management Committee involving school, agency and government participation is involved in the governance of the Centre.

Product

Student retention beyond the age of compulsory attendance is exceptionally high. The Study Centre is undergoing formal evaluation. Initial indicators suggest the Centre is effectively meeting its objectives. Site visit interviews and documentation provided by students reveal that students are satisfied with the service and see it as a means to achieve their educational objectives.

Cranebrook High School and Jamison High School

Context

Cranebrook High School serves the new and growing housing area of Penrith in Western Sydney. Families in this area are middle to low income. Unemployment, family violence and youth crime plague the community. The major social problems it must deal with are unemployment and family breakdown. In contrast, Jamison High School is in a nearby largely middle class area.

Input

Committed staff from the schools work with a variety of social service agencies through collaborative programmes that are primarily supported from funds made available through Commonwealth sources such as the previously described STAR Programme.

Barnado's Penrith Centre

Barnado's is a major charity-based child and family service working in New South Wales and Canberra. The aim of the service is to support families in the least intrusive way. The concept of permanency planning has evolved in this agency to mean the prevention of foster care. The Barnado's Penrith Centre operates from premises opposite Cranebrook High School and provides a variety of welfare programmes to 1 500 clients a month. As part of its Street Work and Youth Services Programme (ADAPT), the Centre operates in conjunction with Cranebrook and Jamison the STAR funded Radical Adolescent Programme (RAP) and Project Links. The Penrith Police Citizens' Youth Club and the Department of School Education along with Barnado's Penrith Centre are the major partners in Project Links. These programmes try to help children complete their schooling in spite of risk factors such as homelessness, family dysfunction and peer problems.

Penrith Police Citizens' Youth Club

The Penrith Police Citizens' Youth Club is the service organisation of the local police department. It is part of a federated effort of police throughout New South Wales and most of Australia to help youth between 8 and 21 years of age. This organisation, established in 1937, is an autonomous branch of the police service and a registered charity. It provides a wide range of crime prevention programmes through 22 metropolitan and 31 county clubs. Each branch develops specific programmes in response to particular community needs. Services range from providing meeting space to camping and sports activities.

Worklink and vocational education

These programmes have been developed as a response to the need for increased vocational education. The programmes facilitate the transition from school to work and school-community connections. A number of community agencies are involved such as Wirraway (a private community centre). The overall aim is to help students remain in school and thereby increase their life chances.

Process

The Radical Adolescent Programme provides skills groups to students at risk of dropping out of school. The weekly one-hour groups focus on basic skills, information, communications, self-esteem, and social and after care support. Project Links aims to facilitate the return of students to school after suspension through the development of academic and social skills. This programme is housed in the Penrith Police Citizens' Youth Club.

Product

Evaluation of the programmes has been encouraging. School attendance and classroom participation of clients have improved. They also exhibit less aggressive behaviour and a more positive attitude towards school and family life.

Nepean High School

Context

The City of Penrith is a medium density somewhat isolated and conservative suburban community. A recent move to deregulate school boundaries has dramatically increased the diversity of students attending Nepean. Currently this comprehensive high school receives its 900 students from three nearby primary schools. Although most of the students in the school are Anglo-Australian, Nepean has an academically and socio-economically varied population. Alcohol and drug abuse, truancy and teen pregnancy are considered primary risk factors in the school.

Input

The school describes itself as "a caring school community committed to achievement, responsibility, identity and concern". A close alliance exists between the school and the community. The federally supported STAR Programme provides special support to youth having academic and adjustment problems. Through this programme the services of the Vocational Guidance Bureau, the Penrith Youth Drop – in Centre, and the Insearch Camp Organisation, are co-ordinated. The criteria for entry into this programme are that a student must be 14-15 years of age, at risk in one or more ways, academically able to achieve a High School Certificate, and success oriented. Students also must have supportive parents who share the aims of the school and STAR Programme.

Process

Students are expected to set their own academic goals. These goals become part of the school culture and are reflected in adherence to a common Conduct Code. STAR workers provide outreach and co-ordinate community programmes. They also facilitate school team co-ordination to integrate services around the needs of programme students.

Product

Students participating in the STAR Programme have displayed "marked [positive] changes in behaviour". Student drug and alcohol use during school time has declined. Moreover, truancy has decreased and staying on in school beyond the permitted school leaving age of 15 has increased.

INTEGRATED SERVICES IN NEWCASTLE

Jasper-Gateshead High School

Context

The City of Newcastle is in the 35 000 square kilometre Hunter Region of New South Wales. In addition to traditional coal and steel industries, the area is the centre of diverse manufacturing, agricultural, wine and electrical generation commercial activities. Newcastle, the largest city in the region, suffers from high levels of unemployment and poverty. A total of 37 per cent of families are headed by a single parent, and 25 per cent are considered below the poverty line.

The Jasper-Gateshead Programme, serving 15 students from high schools in the region, is located in the Windale suburb of Newcastle. The suburb has a high concentration of poor single parent families. Students in this programme are largely streetwise youth who have been expelled or suspended from area schools. The programme is led by the Head Teacher (Welfare) from Gateshead High School and is operated by a non-permanent teacher five days a week as an alternative to regular school. As an alternative to correspondence and distance education, this voluntary programme provides a high level of motivational support and individual attention. Close scrutiny is paid to conduct and attendance. The programme seeks to enhance academic skills and achievement, provide positive role models, increase self-esteem, and overcome alienation.

Input

Lake Macquarie Police Citizens' Youth Club provides the space for this programme. Officers participate in outings and act as positive role models. The local bus service has made passes available for students enrolled in the programme.

Process

In addition to the direct involvement of the Home School Liaison (Truant) Officer (the main referral source) and a Police Constable, there is extensive formal and informal co-ordination of other agencies and services. Jasper staff are members of the Eastlakes Community Network Committee. Almost all welfare agencies in the community are members of the Committee.

Product

Although student attendance in the programme is uneven, there is widespread satisfaction with the programme amongst participants, families and other community members. The majority of students have shown improved attendance, attitudes toward school and goal orientation, and increased self-esteem. Jasper received a special award from the Australian Institute of Criminology in 1994.

Hunter Adolescent Support Unit (HASU) – Jesmond High School

Context

Twenty six of the 36 schools in the region are served by this service. Although most referred students are from lower socio-economic backgrounds, they represent a cross-section of the community. The most defining characteristic of the students is that they have been charged with a criminal activity of some kind. The programme is often tied to school re-entry after suspension, bail and probationary decisions. The programme is designed for 24 students, mainly with conduct disorders.

Input

The programme is staffed by 5.8 teachers, two aides, a part-time psychologist, a careers teacher and clerical staff. The programme is housed in an attractive and well equipped section of Jesmond High School.

Process

Case planning occurs monthly in association with the Community Adolescent Team of the Department of Health. Extensive interaction occurs with services involved in individual cases. There has also been some involvement in a new series of inter-agency youth service meetings.

Product

Two external programme evaluations indicate that acts of violence by programme participants have been reduced. This decrement appears to be stable. One indicator, school reintegration, showed that HASU students reintegrated at a rate of 37 per cent while the figure for students in other programmes across the state was 24 per cent. The programme was assessed to be an exemplary programme, provide good value, and to show promise for even greater future success.

Worimi School (The Annexe)

Context

This school and its half way type programme (The Annexe) are part of a detention centre that houses 38 children and youth between the ages of 10 and 20 years. The reasons why youth are held in detention range from their committal for murder to providing them with protection from violent parents. Philosophical differences between school and detention staff are marked. Detention staff find the school too easy-going and relaxed about security issues. School staff are more focused on the present social and educational needs of students than their crimes or reasons for detention.

Input

The school has four teachers and a nurse. This staff draws on the Centre's psychological and social services.

Process

The school offers a wide ranging and flexible programme. An Education Plan is developed for each pupil that can be continued after they have left the Centre. Co-ordination of services through the local YAC allows former students to attend HASU or a Technical and Further Education College.

Product

Although co-ordination of school services with outside agencies is good, internal co-operation between teaching staff and detention centre youth workers is problematic. The youth workers as a group feel undervalued because of low pay and professional expectations. In contrast, the teaching staff would like to operate a case management model and expect a higher level of commitment and skill from youth workers. In spite of their differences the value and effectiveness of the school's work with youth are widely recognised by other agencies.

CONCLUSION

The Youth Social Justice Strategy reviewed in a previous section is a full-scale initiative designed to achieve integration of services for youth through co-ordination of planning and service delivery between all levels of government. Such a national attempt to provide services integration through the Youth Access Centres is a rarity among OECD countries. The explicit mandate of the YACs is to network and provide information, referral, advice and counselling services to Australian youth. The clue to the nature of limited services integration in New South Wales is, however, the necessarily delicate efforts of YACs to provide services co-ordination. The role of the YACs from their inception has been restricted to information sharing and identifying gaps and duplication in efforts.

There has been a concerted effort to restrain the YACs from controlling the process of integration. Waller (1992) notes that "(...) youth services react negatively to the idea of a Commonwealth agency being responsible for ensuring the co-ordination when it involved integration of service or lobbying for change. This was largely due to a perception that Commonwealth agencies often have a hidden agenda of rationalisation, with an end result of less dollars and cuts to function". Consequently, as Waller (1992) concluded that "co-ordination of services at a structural level needs to be recognised as separate from co-ordination of the delivery of services to a young person (...) the former facilitates the development of a cohesive network of services while the latter ensures that individual clients are helped through this network of services". Within these boundaries the work of the YACs as co-ordinators has been appreciated and well received by service providers. In New South Wales YACs expressed awareness of the discrepancy created by their limited co-ordination role and the needs of youth at risk for services.

At best the New South Wales services reviewed were found to operate at a level of integration that can be described as informal and co-operative. This makes network development and programme co-ordination dependent on the diplomacy and interpersonal skills of current administrators. The fragile and somewhat temporary nature of these alliances creates, especially when higher levels of effectiveness in service delivery are achieved, a yearning for structure and stability. Community building in the form of professional liaisons and networks has resulted from current policies that charge YACs with services co-ordination. The tendency of these arrangements to seek a formal structure should not be surprising. In fact, it is a desirable step as part of efforts to increase the effectiveness of services, and needs to be anticipated and supported in the next round of policy development.

REFERENCES

AUSTRALIAN CATHOLIC BISHOPS (1992), *Catholic Bishops Report,* Sydney, Australia.

AUSTRALIAN YOUTH FOUNDATION (1994), *A Lost Generation*, Sydney, Australia.

COOPERS AND LYBRAND (1992), *Students at Risk Programme: Case Studies,* DEET, Canberra.

DEPARTMENT OF EMPLOYMENT, EDUCATION AND TRAINING (1994), "National survey of client satisfaction with Youth Access Centres (YACs)", DEET Evaluation and Monitoring Branch, DEET, Canberra.

DEPARTMENT OF EMPLOYMENT, EDUCATION AND TRAINING (1995), "Briefing package for OECD Delegates".

MINISTERIAL COUNCIL OF EDUCATION, EMPLOYMENT, TRAINING, AND YOUTH AFFAIRS (1993), *National Report on Schooling in Australia,* Curriculum Corporation, Victoria.

MINISTERIAL COUNCIL OF EDUCATION, EMPLOYMENT, TRAINING, AND YOUTH AFFAIRS (1994), *National Strategy for Equity in Schooling,* Curriculum Corporation, Victoria.

RILEY, M. (1995), "Outlook for jobs begins to dim", *The Sydney Herald,* Sydney, Australia

VOLPE, R. (1995), *Doing More with More: A Report on Ontario Efforts to Integrate Children's Services,* OECD, Paris.

WALLER, V. (1992), *Review of the Interim Co-ordination Role of the Youth Access Centres (YACS),* Evaluation and Monitoring Branch, Australian Government Publishing Service, Canberra, Australia.

Working Nation (1994), Australian Government Publishing Service, Canberra, Australia.

2

CANADA

The following case studies describe integrated services programmes in four Canadian provinces: Saskatchewan, Alberta, Ontario and New Brunswick.

Most of the Canadian programmes discussed in the case studies are the product of state level initiatives; federal government and community initiatives are much rarer in Canada than in the United States. The limited role of the federal government in human services planning and provision has its origins in the British-North America Act of 1867 which laid down the foundations for the relationship between the national government and the provinces. Interestingly, while the provinces are able to act relatively independently in the provision of education, health and social services, almost all of them have embraced the concept of integration.

Even though the federal government has limited power to influence the provision of human services at the state level, it has for a long time recognised the importance of integration. As early as 1970, a national report called "One Million Children" by the Commission on Emotional and Learning Disorders in Children (Toronto) concluded that, in providing help for children, a lack of co-ordinated services was the "number one problem". Today, the Canadian Action Plan Programmes, which have been implemented nation-wide, show a continuing national commitment to providing effective (and integrated) services for children at risk.

The following case studies reflect the relatively autonomous efforts of provincial governments to integrate services.

SASKATCHEWAN

UNITED EFFORTS TO INTEGRATE SERVICES FROM THE TOP-DOWN AND BOTTOM-UP

by

Josette Combes and Jennifer Evans

INTRODUCTION

Saskatchewan is one of the ten provinces in Canada. Its name comes from the Plains Cree Indian word *kisiskatchewan* meaning "the river that flows swiftly". It is located in the middle west of Canada and is well known for its large plains from which its farmers produce half of Canada's six major export crops (wheat, oats, barley, rye, flaxseed and canola), and raise cattle, poultry, pigs and sheep. About 60 000 farms with an average size of 440 hectares, mostly in the southern part of the province, use about one third of the total land area which is 651 900 square kilometres. Another third is commercial forest and the last third is Precambrian rock, located in the north of the province. The other sources of income are potash (two thirds of the world's recoverable reserves), uranium (10 per cent of the world's recoverable reserves), and gas.

DEMOGRAPHY

The population (census 1991) is 988 930, one third being rural, two thirds urban. Although containing only 3.6 per cent of the total Canadian population, Saskatchewan comprises 6.5 per cent of the total land mass. There are thirteen cities, 146 towns and 376 villages. It has a high rate of participation in the labour force (67.1 per cent compared to the national rate of 66.6 per cent) and an unemployment rate of 7.4 per cent (the national rate is 8.2 per cent). As in all of Canada, the ancestors of the people living in Saskatchewan are from very diverse origins (British, German, Ukrainian, Scandinavian, French, Native Indian, Dutch, Polish, Métis, Hungarian, Chinese, Russian). The population is characterised by a higher proportion of children and youth than in the rest of the country.

Saskatchewan became a province in 1905. Its provincial legislature has 66 members and is located in Regina, the capital. Its leadership has recently changed and is now in the hands of the New Democratic Party. According to the new representatives, the previous government implemented severe cuts in the social and education budgets which resulted in disaster in terms of the number of people in need.

Saskatchewan has been hit by recession in the same way as most of the developed countries. As in other countries, one of the consequences has been that the level of poverty has increased in the lowest classes of society.

GROUPS AT RISK

In Saskatchewan, the common definition of children at risk is used (for the definition, see the Introduction of this volume). A very well documented paper issued by the Saskatchewan Education, Training and Employment Department defines the high risk population as being divided into "three main groups: children, youth and families living in poverty; Indian and Métis people; and, single and teen parents" (Government of Saskatchewan, 1994*b*). The extracts below are taken from this report.

Children, youth and families living in poverty

"Based on after-tax income, 10.9 per cent of Saskatchewan families (1991) and 16.1 per cent of children under 16, live in poverty (...)."

"In December 1993, there were 38 973 Social Assistance cases involving 78 406 people (...)."

"The unemployment rate increased and unemployment insurance benefits were reduced. In addition, the federal government transferred responsibility for off reserve Indian people to the provinces (...)."

"One Ontario study has shown that poor children have more than twice the rate of emotional and behavioural disorders, poor school performance, regular tobacco use, and social impairment" (p. 3).

Once again it is more the cumulative effect of factors that is significant, but they are often related.

Indian and Métis people

80 000 Indian and 40 000 Métis people live in Saskatchewan, 12 per cent of the total population. The proportion is projected to be around 18 per cent in 2006. About one third of the recipients of social assistance have an Indian or Métis ancestry (p. 3).

Single and teen parents

Single-parent families represent 12 per cent of Saskatchewan families, 82 per cent being headed by a woman and 56 per cent relying to some extent on social assistance. The great majority (85 per cent) receive this support for a relatively long time – the average being 15 months.

In 1992, out of 14 951 births, 34 were to girls aged 10 to 14 years and 1 590 to young women aged 15 to 19 years. The babies born show a high risk of prematurity, low birth weight, developmental delays and abuse (p. 4).

The report lists the following risk factors (p. 11):

- *Poor housing.* This concerns 13.4 per cent of families, urban families slightly more than rural ones. The situation is worse since the federal decision to stop funding social housing (except for those on reserves).

- *Poor prenatal care.* Low birth weight is associated with increased infant mortality and disability. Low birth weight is due mainly to poverty and substance abuse (including smoking).

- *Hunger.* Ten food banks deliver free food, both in Regina and Saskatoon, the main towns. These were used on around 79 000 occasions by families in the area. Around one million meals were served to hungry children in 1992-93 by the Child Nutrition and Development Programme.

- *Poor health.* The link between poverty and poor health is well established. Saskatchewan's relatively high poverty level means that the health of many children is at risk.

- *Sexually Transmitted Diseases* (STDs). In 1992, the highest number of cases of STD was among the 15-19 age group.

- *Child abuse and neglect.* From 1987 to 1993 the number of cases increased from 2 600 to over 3 476 with 30 child deaths attributable to abuse and neglect (1989-93).

- *Family violence.* 46 per cent of Saskatchewan women report experiencing some type of violence by men during their lifetime and 25 per cent report violence from their partner. Women who suffered from paternal violence are more likely to face a violent relationship with their partner. One third of children living in violent homes are abused.

- *Sexual abuse.* In a survey carried out in 1993, 32 per cent of Saskatchewan women and 37 per cent of Canadian women reported some kind of sexual assault during their lifetime. It has been estimated that one girl in four and one boy in ten is sexually assaulted before they become adults (from touching to injury).

– *Substance abuse*. Thirty-two Alcohol and Drugs Services in Saskatchewan Health Centres provide help to clients. The figures show a dramatic growth of clients under 15 years of age (22 per cent) but a 7 per cent decrease for the 15-19 age group. Altogether about 18 per cent of youth are involved in substance abuse.

– *Youth suicide*. In 1992, the highest level of suicide in ten years was recorded for the age group 15-19, namely 25.1 per 100 000 people.

– *Children and youth in conflict with the law*. 4 791 young offenders (77 per cent male, 23 per cent female) were found guilty in 1992-93, some for more than one case. A total of 86 per cent of the cases heard were non-violent cases. Some 291 youth were in custody (both open and secure) and 2 350 were enrolled in a community programme.

– *School drop-out rates*. A 1991 Statistics Canada survey indicates that 16 per cent of Saskatchewan students drop out of school before completing grade 12. But the rate is very high among Indian and Métis students. Up to 90 per cent of them drop out before completing grade 12. Dropping out of school is strongly related to the need for Social Assistance. A total of 56 per cent of recipients have less than a grade 10 education and 84 per cent less than grade 12.

– *School behaviours and challenges*. Teachers report an increase of violent incidents such as verbal and physical assaults together with a lessening in the age of the perpetrators.

To conclude this description, it may be useful to stress the fact that the higher risk groups are the Indian and Métis populations. One can easily deduce from the figures that the Indian and Métis people are more exposed to most of the risk factors such as hunger, poor care during pregnancy, teenage pregnancy, low level of education, and troubles with the law.

Out of these established facts, the current government has launched an Action Plan for Children (Government of Saskatchewan, 1993), a discussion document to promote "a common approach for individuals, governments, organisations and communities in their work together towards the well-being of children". This plan is considered as the corner-stone of efforts to initiate a new type of inter-ministerial and inter-agency collaboration. It will be detailed further on, before the presentation of the site visits.

EDUCATION, SOCIAL AND HEALTH POLICIES

Education

Education is a provincial responsibility; there is no federal (*i.e.* national) structure. Saskatchewan Education, Training and Employment is a provincial government department with responsibility for education programmes for kindergarten to grade 12 and post secondary levels. The department develops overall plans, policies and directions, and determines courses of study and programming for students with special needs. Within the broad definition of an educational programme, the department develops curricula, provides in-service training, facilitates educational change and provides a range of support and personnel to meet the learning needs of children and youth in the province.

In 1992-93, the annual budget was $888.6 million, the majority of which was allocated to school divisions in the province, half of it to K-12 schools. There are seven regional offices and 114 divisions with seven elected people in charge in each. Most divisions have less than 1 000 students (*i.e.* those in rural areas). About 50 per cent have less than 100 students. Each elected person represents a subdivision. There are four types of school divisions – Public, Catholic, Francophone and Independent – giving a total of 849 publicly funded schools. Of these, 734 are public schools, catering for 161 386 students, and 115 are separate schools catering for 33 849 students. There are a further 3 392 students in independent schools (1992-93 figures). These figures are taken from the Saskatchewan Education Indicators Report (Saskatchewan Education, Training and Employment, 1994).

Funding for schools comes 50 per cent from the province and 50 per cent from local taxes within each school division. It is largely unconditional and given on a per pupil basis.

There are a number of community schools in the system. These have been in existence in urban areas since 1980. A grant is provided on the basis of the characteristics of the school – $125 000 for each school. This pays for staff to work with the community, nutrition programmes, and teacher associates (often of Indian or Métis background), to increase the staff ratio and to bring people of Aboriginal ancestry into school. There is a Community Schools Council made up of representatives of parents and the community. Schools on reserves are a federal responsibility, but they follow the public school curriculum.

There are a number of associations which are influential within education such as: SSTA (Saskatchewan Schools Trustees' Association), a voluntary organisation of all elected school district members; STF (Saskatchewan Teachers' Federation), a professional association and union of all teachers of the province; and LEADS (League of Educational Administrators, Directors and Superintendents), chief executive officers of each school division.

The student/educator ratio in Saskatchewan is slightly higher than the Canadian average, being 17 students for one educator (including both teaching and administrative staff) (Canada = 16:1).

Social services

This is the largest government department employing more than 2 000 staff. It deals with income security, family and youth services (including child welfare and young offenders services), and community living aimed at disabled people. Child care is administered at the provincial level (licences, support, development of new facilities, start up grants, operating costs, and assistance grants to low income families). About 116 child care centres and 458 family child care homes were operating in 1992-93, serving an average of 3 617 children each month. Around 2 700 families per month received assistance with child care expenses.

Despite recent efforts towards improvements in provision of early childhood education in terms of quantity (an increase of 104 places) and quality (introduction of a training subsidy), it was reported that the level of resources remains very low compared to needs. Most of the social services budget of $424.1 million in 1992-93 was spent on income security (62.7 per cent), family/youth services (14.10 per cent), and child care (3.13 per cent).

The services were recently restructured into eleven regions which are not co-terminous with education's seven regions. Every programme reports centrally but now services are procured in the regions. Some programmes are not yet devolved (*e.g.* child welfare and community living still reported centrally in 1994). There are no boards in social services regions (as there are in education regions). There are small local agencies but these are not brought together under a board.

Health services

The Department of Health has been going through a period of change. Saskatchewan has a universally accessible health care programme. The key concept is "wellness" which describes a complete state of physical, mental and social health, and not just the absence of disease or infirmity. Viewed from this perspective, the current Canadian health system has several short-comings:
- an emphasis on insured services has led to a health *care* system, not a *health* system;
- the system is not client-centred;
- there needs to be a more holistic approach.

The reforms in Saskatchewan were part of a general move to redefine the goal of the Health Service as "wellness" or general personal well-being. This concept was defined in the Canada Health Act. The need to reform the system has led to restructuring of the health units into 30 district boards composed of appointed members nominated by residents. A total of 52 hospitals have been closed and replaced by Health Centres. The inappropriate use of hospital beds had distorted the funding and delivery of services. The provincial health budget was $1.6 billion. The Federal ministry participated in the cost change of the programme.

$4 million was allocated to health districts to put towards preventive health care. But there were many changes to manage at one time. Professionals had to change their way of working which came from the institutional background of the health system. They had to overcome "the culture shock" of the closure of the hospitals for example. The recurrent key words used to describe the goals of the changes are "client-centred health system" and "integrated community based services".

The health district boundaries are the result of the communities' answer to the Minister's invitation to form themselves into Health Districts. The consequence of this is that these health districts are not co-terminous with social services or education districts. This may pose some problems for the integrated delivery of services.

The first step towards structural realignment has been the development of District Health Boards to take on the management and delivery of services for acute care, long-term care, and home-based and emergency medical services. The second step will be taken depending on the readiness of the district and will involve the devolution of community-based services (mental health, public health and addiction services).

SASKATCHEWAN ACTION PLAN FOR CHILDREN: A FRAMEWORK FOR INTEGRATION OF SERVICES

In 1992 an Ombudsman's report on the deaths of a number of children from neglect or abuse led the government to concentrate means and resources on child protection. In June of 1993, the Saskatchewan Department of Education, Training and Employment launched a discussion paper, "Children First: An Invitation to Work Together", which proposed a common approach to children's issues and provincial goals for achieving the well-being of children (Government of Saskatchewan, 1993).

The goals listed in the Plan stated that children must be:

– *valued* (children's needs must be given priority in legislation, policies, programmes and services' agendas);

– *safe* (from injury, trauma, death, physical and sexual abuse, neglect and exploitation);

– *secure* (with adequate nurturing , financial, social, emotional, recreational and spiritual support);

– *healthy* (including good self-esteem and self-acceptance);

– *culturally connected* (respected for their cultural values and with respect for those of others);

– *socially responsible* (given the opportunity to be self-reliant and to make a meaningful contribution to others);

– *knowledgeable and skilled* (given the means to achieve their full potential) (p. 19).

The guidelines stress seven major expectations:

– Action to enhance the welfare of children should be preventive, primary, culturally appropriate, supportive, collaborative, holistic, empowering and community-based.

– To ensure the achievement of the Action Plan, different levels of follow-up should be implemented.

– *Provincial Health Council*: This community-based group will provide strategic direction to the government on public health policy and advocate for those actions which should be taken.

– *Council on Children*: This body comes under the Action Plan. It is an elected committee from the community. The Provincial Health Council and the Council on Children will be connected and will report to ministers on the Action Plan.

– *The Educational Council*: This will work with the above committees to ensure that the process of change remains on course. It will act as a "watch dog" inside the government itself.

– *The Interdepartmental Steering Committee*: Staff appointed to the committee from different departments will work together with regional and provincial staff of the various provincial government departments to review proposals issued from different bodies and provide recommendations.

– The government branches involved should be the Saskatchewan Alcohol and Drug Abuse Commission, Education, Training and Employment, Social Services, Health, Justice, the Women's Secretariat, the Indian and Métis Affairs Secretariat and the Municipal Government.

Besides realignment of their own districts and procedures, the Action Plan for Children gives grants to community-based initiatives providing they comply with the objectives of the Plan.

The government published in 1994 an impressive list of provincial and local actions taken to implement the Action Plan goals, thus keeping up the momentum for change (Government of Saskatchewan, 1994*a*).

WORKING TOGETHER TO ADDRESS BARRIERS TO LEARNING: INTEGRATED SCHOOL-LINKED SERVICES FOR CHILDREN AND YOUTH AT RISK

"The aim is to develop a new culture among human service providers characterised by co-operation and collaboration and new configurations of service delivery that provide comprehensive and integrated responses to the needs of Saskatchewan children and families" (Government of Saskatchewan, 1994*c*).

This is the message from the ministers of Education and Social Services at the beginning of the policy document. It provides a clear statement of commitment to the policy of services integration at the government level.

The Integrated School-linked Services Initiative is a major activity under the umbrella of the Saskatchewan Action Plan for Children and is considered as a first step towards meeting children's needs through a collaborative process and a holistic approach. A total of 20 pilot projects have been evaluated and the outcomes have been taken into account to build new guidelines and definitions.

The programme involves members of several government bodies including: Education, Training and Employment; Health; Social Services; Municipal Government; Justice; and the Indian and Métis Affairs Secretariat. Also included are the Federation of Home and School Associations; Teachers' Federation; School Trustees' Association; League of Educational Administrators, Directors and Superintendent; and the Métis Nation. At the local level, integrated services initiatives involve business partners, churches, community associations, non-government human service agencies, and Aboriginal organisations.

Integrated School-linked Services emphasises the importance of preventive measures. A School Trustees' Association Research Centre Report issued following a forum on integrated school-based services (November 9 and 10, 1992) quotes the United States Committee for Economic Development's statement that "every dollar spent on preschool programmes eventually saves six dollars in remedial education, welfare and losses to crime" (Loraine Thompson Information Services Limited, 1992).

From a literature review, the report identifies nine principles as being key to ensuring the success of integrated programming:

– respond to what people want for their children;
– see the child in the context of the family and the family in the context of its social network and community;
– identify and capitalise on the strengths of children, families and communities;
– give programme staff the time, training and skills to build sustained, trusting relationships with children, families and communities;
– provide prevention as well as intervention for high risk children and youth;
– ensure that the needs of the child are given priority over institutional and other concerns;
– involve all stakeholders in decision-making;
– offer a comprehensive range of services;
– be flexible in the planning and delivery of services (p. 11).

The 1994 draft report of Department of Education, Training and Employment, "Working Together to Address Barriers to Learning", cited above, proposes eight guiding principles and strategies to create a collaborative culture:

- child-centredness;
- prevention;
- co-operation;
- empowerment;
- equity;
- holistic, comprehensive approaches;
- cultural sensitivity;
- affordability (p. 15).

"In addition, the movement toward integrated school-linked services is a shared responsibility between the provincial government and schools and communities in the province. Community-based participation and shared ownership with government in initiating, guiding and managing all aspects of the change process are critical to its success. The province can provide the overall vision, policy, co-ordination supports, and work to remove structural and other barriers. Schools and communities need to provide leadership in developing collaborative relationships and processes. The aim of these collaborative relationships is to identify local needs and solutions which are relevant and effective in addressing the unique situations in the community with resources available."

The report gives examples of existing collaborative projects and provides an outline of possible contributions, roles, responsibilities and areas of expertise of the various organisations and individuals who might be involved in integrated services.

Interviews with senior personnel in education, social services and health, as well as discussions with the Ministers' Working Committee on Integrated School-linked Services produced the following observations.

Resources and training

The Department of Education, Training and Employment provides a wide range of programmes and services from kindergarten to grade 12 as well as post-secondary education in the province.

Such things as curriculum development, in-service training for teachers, grants to school boards and scholarships are provided. Regional Directors of Education work with stakeholders to implement the new collaborative and integrated approach to meet the multi-faceted needs of children and families at risk. Regional Directors and Regional Co-ordinators of Special Education participate in regional Inter-agency Committees which bring together representatives of the regional branches of each of the departments involved in Saskatchewan's Action Plan for Children.

Professional development for teachers is planned and conducted with input from other agencies. The Department of Education, Training and Employment generates data on students, schools and programmes and makes it available to the public. An electronic Bulletin Board system has been developed which enables school divisions and schools to access information and to communicate and exchange information with colleagues.

Collaboration

A single access point for funding is the goal for government and local agency personnel. A good example of this is the new funding arrangements instituted to approve Prevention and Support Grants for new initiatives for children. Community agencies may apply through the Inter-agency Prevention and Support Grants Review Committee which works with regional and provincial staff to review proposals.

Exchanges of resources (*i.e.* staff, equipment and transportation) are more likely to happen at the local level within project boundaries.

Work spaces can be available for partners to meet clients for a specialised purpose (*i.e.* health professionals in schools, social workers in health premises, etc.). Shared Service Agreements between school divisions allow them to share psychologists, counsellors and speech pathologists who provide services on a rotating basis. The integrated school-linked service approach is based on the assumption that because school is a mandatory universal provision, clients are most likely to be reached through their attendance as pupils or parents. The schools, therefore, play a central role in planning and organising integrated services.

Inhibiting factors

There is not yet a critical mass of people working in a collaborative way. Even within departments there is fragmentation in structures and processes. The "collaborative culture" has not yet totally overcome the old sectoral approach to operating. Among the main reasons for enhancing collaboration were: overlapping of different agencies; inadequate use of resources; and the confusion for clients trying to access services. Though there is real commitment from government at senior levels to collaborate, there is uneven implementation of integrated services at the field level. Collaboration needs financial input and different structures at the local level to support the process. The collaborative process goes along with realignment of services at all levels. "There are so many things to manage at one time". There are different professional cultures and values among agencies and individuals. Protocols, guidelines and recommendations are sometimes established, but there is work to be done in establishing common values and goals towards collaboration.

A lot of activity has gone on in Saskatchewan, at all levels, from government through to the community, to discuss and promote the change towards integrated service provision. Some examples of existing collaborative projects are given below. These accounts are based on site visits, interviews with key people involved in the projects (including clients), and responses to a written questionnaire, as well as other written documentation supplied by the sites.

SITE VISITS

These were thoroughly organised and planned and the expert team was welcomed with constant care for their needs (be they professional or personal). The high degree of dedication to meeting the expectations of the OECD research team reflected the commitment of all those involved to the success of the challenges emanating from the Action Plan for Children. At every level people showed deep involvement and great enthusiasm for community-based services and inter-disciplinary action. Despite all kind of difficulties linked with the nature of the complex situations they have to cope with, people were wide open to our questions, prepared to talk frankly about their work, including the difficulties.

The two site visits were organised according to a similar protocol: a short meeting with key people; a tour visit of the school and area; and, sets of interviews with a variety of local people. Every level of involvement was represented from senior managers to field workers, teacher associates, parents and pupils. Information and material such as leaflets, drafts, evaluation reports and data sets were generously provided. Saskatchewan is very interested in the findings of the OECD research and is looking forward to accessing information about other Member countries.

Princess Alexandra Community School, Saskatoon

Background

Saskatoon, founded in 1883 and incorporated as a city in 1906, is the largest city in Saskatchewan with a population of 194 000 inhabitants. It is built on the banks of the South Saskatchewan River and is the result of the amalgamation of three settlements, Saskatoon (west side), Nutana (east side) and Riversdale (west of the railway tracks). The name "Saskatoon" is derived from the Cree Indian name

Mis-sask-quah-toomina. These words are in the plural. The singular is secured by dropping the final "a". The name was given by Indians to the berry which is found in such profusion in this vicinity.

The city consistently ranks among the top ten major cities in Canada with the cost of living 25 per cent below the national average. The combined municipal and regional burden for property and other business taxes is 47 per cent below the national average.

The University of Saskatchewan attracts over $46 million annually in research funding, placing it among the most prestigious research universities in North America. The major industries are agriculture, mining, manufacturing, food processing, tourism, transportation, technology, construction and finance. Known as the advanced technology centre for the province, Saskatoon specialises in areas such as bio-technology, micro-electronics, computer software, aerospace, food processing, agriculture, pharmaceuti-cals and animal health products. Saskatoon is the leader in agricultural bio-technology in North America, with 600 scientists in the industry. Saskatoon and the province are world leaders in radio-telemetry, satellite communications, digital communications, mining robotics and energy-efficient con-struction. Innovation Place, Saskatoon's research park, provides the largest and most diversified techni-cal resource centre in Western Canada.

Saskatoon is characterised by a fairly small Central Business District surrounded by eight Core Neighbourhoods which have many housing and population characteristics in common and yet signifi-cant differences. Saskatoon witnessed an apartment boom following a federal tax incentive programme aimed at alleviating the shortage of rental units around the country. This created, as a side effect, uncontrolled and unbalanced situations. In 1977, the Council declared an "apartment freeze" to permit time to complete a comprehensive study. That provided the City Council with policies to guide decisions about density, zoning and future development.

Demographic data based on the 1991 census show the major population trends. The major age group is composed of adults aged 20-40. A total of 84.2 per cent are English speakers. Other languages are shared by less than 3 per cent of each community. Total school enrolment was 22 315 in public schools and 13 826 in Catholic (no data available for others). There are 42 elementary schools, eight high schools and a University.

The average family income was $49 032 and the average family size was three persons. The rate of single-parent families was 10 per cent.

From one neighbourhood to another, some variations do exist which are significant. The level of family income varies, with some neighbourhoods having an average income four times that of others ($24 006 being the lowest and $98 479 the highest). The proportion of single parent families varies from 27.8 per cent to less than 1 per cent. Not surprisingly, the data are correlated: the lowest income with the highest rate of single parent families and the lowest education level.

Princess Alexandra School is located in the Riversdale neighbourhood which shows most of the risk indicators: low family income, a high rate of single-parent families (15.3 per cent), a high percentage of non-English speakers (40 per cent), and a low level of school achievement (66.2 per cent grade 9-13 or without a diploma). The majority of the students (approximately 80 per cent) are of Aboriginal ancestry. The other 20 per cent is made up primarily of Asian and Caucasian students. Each year approximately 66 per cent of the student body is new and there is a 66 per cent turnover again during the course of the school year. One of the consequences of the high transience rate of students is that the majority tend to be two to four grades below their peers in suburban schools. On average, approximately 80 per cent of families have direct involvement with social services and/or the justice system, and 60 per cent are on welfare.

Input – strategic level

The Community School concept: "A community school is concerned with involvement of all residents of its Community. It seeks to improve the total environment and quality of living for children, families, older people, all who live in the neighbourhood. It brings the services of health, welfare, recreational and educational agencies so close to the people that they are readily available" (Jack Stevens, a Community School Co-ordinator of Vancouver, quoted in Community Schools Programme, March 1990).

The Community School approach first began in Canada in 1966 at Flegmington Road Community School in North York, Toronto. Community Schools were supposed to serve three major roles:

- to offer a community-centred curriculum;
- to be a centre of community living;
- to provide community services.

Therefore the Saskatchewan programme goals are:

- to encourage community involvement in and understanding of school affairs;
- to provide for the development of activities which: a) enhance the learning of both children and adults; b) foster racial and cultural understanding, particularly of groups within the neighbourhood; c) assist in creating a safe neighbourhood environment for the physical well-being of the children;
- to involve parents and other community residents in discussions of school policy, procedures, curriculum, finance and facilities;
- to contribute to a sense of community in the local school neighbourhood;
- to communicate educational information and special events to the parents and area residents;
- to involve community residents in the identification and initiation of adult activities in the school and the community;
- to involve community residents in discussions on the use of community resources and agencies to support the educational programme and meet the community's needs.

A key element of the Community School model is the addition to the regular school staff of Native teaching associates, a Community School co-ordinator, administrative support to the Central Office, and a nutrition co-ordinator hired to implement the nutrition programme.

In 1990, the Saskatoon Board of Education held a symposium to develop a concept plan for its inner city elementary schools. The plan identified the four following major goals:

- to increase academic achievement;
- to encourage appropriate student behaviour;
- to enhance each child's self-esteem;
- to empower inner-city communities and parents.

In its Concept Plan for Inner City Elementary Schools, the definition of at risk students is as follows: "those students whose unmet social, emotional, physical and/or intellectual needs lead to chronic and urgent situations which impede individual academic success and personal and social development".

Context

The government of Saskatchewan developed criteria to be used in the determination of schools that would be eligible for Community School designation. Princess Alexandra School, located in the Riversdale community, met all of the criteria with the following statistics:

- 47 per cent of the population 15 or over are not in the work-force;
- 22 per cent of families are headed by a single parent;
- 28.3 per cent of homes do not have English as a first language;
- 36.6 per cent of homes have highest education level less than grade 9;
- 42.6 per cent of families live on an income of less than $20 000 per annum;
- 63.6 per cent of the school population are of Indian or Métis origin;
- 56 per cent of households are rental (Saskatoon Board of Education, April 5, 1994).

Princess Alexandra is one of the four Inner City Community Schools which operate under the Concept Plan for Inner City School. The development of the Concept Plan began during the 1988-89 school year. It currently has about 150 students. The main problems recorded are transiency of the students, cultural gaps between home and school, delay in achievement, low level of self-esteem, street wandering and precocious prostitution, delinquency, high numbers on social assistance, and high numbers of children in need of protection.

Process – field level

Atmosphere: The principal and staff decided to respond to students' needs by making their school more "intentionally inviting" and endeavouring to make the school gradually reflect the surrounding community by incorporating the Native American culture of many of its students. At one level, this culture was celebrated in the art work around the school and in the establishment of a school Hoop Dance Troop. In a deeper way, the educational needs of Native American students were met through adopting classroom structures which used family grouping, and by using a thematic approach through-out the school. Family grouping was seen as being more in tune with the "holistic philosophy of the Native American community". It enhances self-esteem and cultural affiliation. One of the first aims identified by staff at the school was that of encouraging co-operation among students. Placing students in clusters or family groups, where ages and abilities are mixed, stimulates more positive interaction.

One of the recommendations of the Saskatoon Concept Plan is to enhance the physical appearance and comfort of the inner city schools. During the tour of the school, Principal John Barton emphasized this part as being paramount to the success of other attempts towards enhancing school achievement. The walls were repainted, giving space to the exhibition of children's drawings and paintings which are renewed throughout the year. Basic things, such as the way the principal's office was organised or the placing all over the school of green plants, posters, positive incentive sentences, pictures and photo-graphs of successful or well respected First Nations people, were part of this approach.

Eight programmes are currently offered by the school to meet the needs of the community: a re-entry programme; reading intervention; family groupings for instruction; school-wide themes; quality daily physical education; a preschool programme; a Learning Resource Centre extension (open from 07.00 to 21.00); and an Alternative School Day.

Other programmes involve community agencies. These include: the Hoop Dance Troop; Saint Paul's Hospital Volunteers; partnership with the Star Phoenix and Nutana Collegiate; delivering stu-dents' progress reports to their homes; the Inner City Police Liaison Programme; and the home and school liaison programme.

During the interviews, we met some of the staff of the school and some partners of the different programmes.

The preschool: The four public community schools, community associations and interested citizens formed the Inner City Preschool Committee (ICPC). The ICPC has two major functions: one is to ensure uniformity in the preschool programmes based in the four community schools, and the second is to co-ordinate fund raising for the programmes.

The preschool operates on the school premises but is run by a community elected person and the board (made up of the Principal, community workers and parents). It is funded 75 per cent by the government and 25 per cent through fund raising. The churches and service clubs have been involved. There are 20 places. It runs three days per week from 09.30 to 12.30 and enrols 3 and 4 year old children. There are different community oriented activities along with preschool activities such as a "come and read with me programme" to give parents examples and ideas to read with their children; tea parties; and, healing circles (a Native cultural formula to help people talk about their problems). It is difficult to convince Natives to bring children in, even though it is free, and the adult groups are focused on helping parents to understand the benefits of preschool for their children.

The Re-entry Programme: It is handled by Radius Tutoring, a Community Centre for Education and Employment Training. Students are sent, generally after dropping out of school, to acquire new ways of coping with school. The strategy is based on individual relationships, individual responsibility and a personal skills assessment process. It is not an alternative school but rather a behaviour change programme. After re-entry into school, a liaison worker will follow up. About 20 places are booked to provide for Princess Alexandra students. A total of 31 students were helped between September and December 1993. The ratio is six to eight students for one adult. It is funded year to year through federal grants (as part of the Stay-in School Initiative). The other funds derive from the Saskatoon Board of Education, which purchases seats, as well as from the Saskatoon Social Services Branch (10 per cent) and private donors.

Family groupings: There are now six regular classes in Princess Alexandra Community School, as well as special education groupings. The two classes in each "cluster" or "family" incorporate the same grade span. So there are two K-1-2 classes in the primary cluster, two 3-4-5 classes in the middle cluster, and two 6-7-8 classes in the senior cluster. Weekly cluster meetings usually involve the two classroom teachers, teacher associates, special education staff (including the resource room teacher), and the librarian. Within each class there is a wide age range, with sometimes as much as five years separating the youngest from the oldest class member. Teachers and students alike think that this enables students to forget about age and grade labels. Having a wide age range within one class allows more developmentally appropriate activities for students. For example, some grade 2 students need toys and activities; in the primary cluster it is acceptable for older children to engage in play.

The school system: The school is open from 07.30 to 23.00 and provides breakfast and lunch. It is open after school hours to provide leisure activities such as Hoop Dance, art, craft and cooking, literacy classes for adults, and to allow use of the Learning Resource Centre as a quiet place to work. It has an alternative school day, which creates a safer place for students, an internal mail system to encourage literacy, and the staff deliver Progress Reports to students' homes.

The Hoop Dance Troop: It was created to develop community pride in Aboriginal culture. The group has performed in four Canadian provinces and has been featured in a television commercial. Dedicated staff have served as resources to many local and provincial groups. They have made presentations at provincial and national conferences and hosted over 20 tours of the school. The troop kindly performed during the visit of the OECD experts and demonstrated their skill. The hoop dance involves many rings which the dancers display around their bodies creating metaphorical images of the world. They do it while dancing at a relatively high speed. The performance as a whole was very impressive.

School partnerships: A partnership with the Star Phoenix and Nutana Collegiate has been established to encourage art performance, through exchanges between the two schools with the help of the newspaper's great public relations value. A total of ten people from the company have links with pupils as role models and for tutorship. The Star Phoenix is a major Saskatoon newspaper. A partnership was established to link the business world and the schools. Through the partnership, student art exhibitions were arranged where student pieces were sold and proceeds went to the artists.

The Inner City Police Liaison Programme: The police department has an education unit. A decision was made to send a police officer into elementary schools to deal with communities which were suspicious of the police. The police officer would wear his uniform and would establish relationships with the students.

The Community and Police Help Centre is housed in a building leased by the BID (Business Improvement District) which also provided computers and office equipment. The centre provides literacy programmes with computers. It is a centre for crime prevention where anyone who has a complaint can drop in. It is open from 09.00 to 21.00. Community Partners work as volunteers. The Zero Tolerance Group, a citizen's group tied up with the community association helped to rid the place of prostitution by taking pictures of prostitutes' clients. The police department funds the officers' salaries and supplies. But the core of funding is from the community as a whole. It is a partnership between the school, the community association and the police.

Students from the Human Justice Programme at Regina and from Saskatoon University participate. A doctoral student currently is completing a survey of the scheme.

The Riversdale Business Improvement District (BID): The BID Board consists of nine people (eight men and one woman) and a councillor appointed by the City of Saskatoon. They have a meeting once a month. It was set up in March 1990. Its purpose was:

- to upgrade the commercial area which has suffered in the recession;
- to combat the strength of the big shopping areas;
- to enhance the multicultural aspect of the area.

The area was very depressed. There were two public houses which were very badly managed. BID had them closed and they were re-opened under new management. This stabilised the situation. The street walkers disappeared too. The BID Board is concerned about the number of children wandering, vandalising property and grouping into gangs. It launched initiatives such as a front- and side-walk clean sweep programme and supported wall paintings and other attempts to improve the shopping environment. It is a funding partner for some special events and contributes resources to the police centre.

Collaboration input – strategic, operational and field levels

The Saskatoon Education Branch gives additional resources to pay the Community School Co-ordinator, teacher associates and for extra activities for children. The Community School Co-ordinator described her role as "to plan extra programmes for the kids, to try to provide opportunities for the families, and to work with the community association to plan special events".

The role of Native teacher associates is to help the teacher and to facilitate the class routine and the non-traditional grouping of students. "The teaching associates should be Native people from the community in which the school is located. As a cultural interpreter, the teaching associate will become a voice for the community in the classroom. He/she can help teachers be more aware of and sensitive to the cultural dissonance between the environment of the home and the school. The associate and the regular classroom teacher will form a co-operative team relationship, where the professional teacher is generally responsible for planning teaching activities and diagnosing learning difficulties, and the teaching associate acts as a support, assisting with the teaching and helping to make the professional teacher aware of the social environment of the students" (Community Schools Programme, March, 1990).

The City of Saskatoon directly assists neighbourhoods in delivering programmes to the residents of the city through their Leisure Services Department. It supports 43 Community Associations, ensuring that they have an organisational structure and training, and providing grants and funding for programming. The Community Associations deliver the programmes. The Community Associations are combined into six area groupings throughout Saskatoon. There is also joint programming across areas. For example, there was a joint programme involving the Planning, Fire and Health departments looking at the quality of the housing stock.

They have run programmes with the Aboriginal community. For example, they wanted to increase the use of swimming pools by Aboriginal children. By involving the community, they found out that these children were not going because they did not know how to use the swimming pool. For example, they did not know whether they should keep their underwear on under their swimming costume. So the Community Association employed more Aboriginal life-guards.

They have set up a down-town youth centre as an inter-agency effort. A high proportion of Aboriginal young people use this facility (EGADZ). It involves a number of agencies. It runs "back to school" programmes, health programmes and food programmes. It was a first attempt at inter-agency involvement in this type of work. To be on the Board, an agency must be part of the programme.

The process of collaboration – strategic and operational levels

The Saskatoon Board of Education has seven elected board members on a three-year term. The board sets policies, and then, as administrators, implements the policies. School principals and central office administrators meet bi-monthly to deal with administrative issues, planning and professional development. Elected board members visit schools in teams of two in order to maintain communication links with parents and communities. Superintendents from the central office visit schools on a regular basis to maintain communication with staff, students and parents.

The Regional Directors of Education: They liaise between the government and the local level, and regulate school spending. They give advice on the interpretation of government regulations. For this purpose, there is a curriculum specialist and a special education specialist. They are supposed to work with their equivalents in Social Services and Health Services, despite the fact that regions of responsibility are not co-terminous between the three departments.

The Saskatchewan Council on Children: The Saskatchewan Council on Children was created under Saskatchewan Action Plan for Children. The Council is made up of members who are at the strategic and operational levels of human services and who are involved in the integrated services process. The principal of Princess Alexandra School is a member of the Saskatchewan Council on Children. The Council reports to the Inter-departmental Steering Committee, which is made of representatives from each government department. The Steering Committee oversees the implementation of Saskatchewan Action Plan for Children.

The process of collaboration – field level

Planning and decision making are carried out by the whole staff and the community in monthly meetings. The entire staff meets weekly outside of school hours, and monthly during school time to discuss issues, plan and engage in professional development. The role of the Community Association is a major one. The Aboriginal Recreation Committee helps to provide programmes for Aboriginal young people (*e.g.* Hoop Dancing, Native Arts and Crafts). It works with the Multicultural Council to meet the needs of other cultures.

Initially set up by the Leisure Services for organising programmes of leisure activities, it has recently become more focused on problems and neighbourhood issues. One of its goals is to stabilise the population by providing better accommodation, increasing home ownership from 47 per cent to 54 per cent. One programme, in collaboration with the Housing and Fire Department, was to control the quality of housing. It discouraged slum landlords and forced some out.

Training: There is limited training in the regular teacher education programme to prepare teachers to work with Native students. The ITEP (Indian Teacher Education Programme) trains Natives with extra support for a specifically designed training curriculum (two years separated, two years mixed). Most of the Indian teachers choose to go back and teach in the reserves. There is a lack of Native teachers in local schools. An annual two-day retreat has been organised between 1990 and 1993, focused on bringing together all inner city administrators, teachers, paraprofessionals, support staff and parents to refocus attention on the Concept Plan, develop new ideas and stimulate initiatives.

Products

An evaluation of the Implementation of the Concept Plan for Inner City School (1990-93) was published on April 5, 1994 (Saskatoon Board of Education, 1994). The evaluation was conducted by an Evaluation Management Committee comprised of staff from the Saskatoon Board of Education. Mr. Don Hoium wrote the final report. Dr. Angela Ward of the University of Saskatchewan co-authored a report on the Cluster Approach to Instruction at Princess Alexandra Community School. It provides figures such as enrolment statistics and student mobility rates. It makes a number of recommendations, among them:

- emphasizing preschool provisions. In fact, the four Inner City Community Schools do provide preschool facilities;
- establishing Extended Readiness Programmes to accommodate students not ready to begin to read after one year of kindergarten;
- providing access to computers;

- working towards an "ideal" student-teacher ratio of 15:1;
- enhancing the Co-operative Learning Model to personalise and individualise instruction;
- providing nutrition and hygiene facilities;
- increasing the allocation of time that Pupil Services Staff offer to schools;
- supporting re-entry programmes aimed at students who frequently truant or are transient;
- reinforcing curriculum relevance by emphasizing appropriate content, language enrichment, heritage languages, life skills, work experience and inter-cultural harmony;
- developing appropriate criterion tests;
- improving the physical appearance and comfort of schools;
- providing annual orientation meetings and follow-up in-service sessions;
- continuing the Education Equity Programme to provide successful teacher role models for students, particularly those of Aboriginal ancestry;
- emphasizing contact with parents, home visits, parent education and parenting skills;
- establishing an inter-agency planning council of all agencies involved;
- pursuing support for community agencies;
- pursuing and ameliorating joint funding, enrolling all levels from federal to provincial and municipal;
- exploring the construction of an integrated community centre.

All these recommendations are currently being followed with some noticeable differences from one school to another.

When asked about their perceptions of change, staff reported general progress, and the usefulness of Aboriginal oriented themes and activities, language and social skills programmes, and sport and leisure opportunities. However, the effort to adapt curricula is seen as impeded by lack of additional funding. Staff development programmes were seen as paramount to the creation of collegiality and collaboration among teachers. Staff members' reports referred to improved classroom behaviour and increased student pride in schools. The general atmosphere and physical appearance of the schools have improved. Yet there is a continual need for repair and renovation.

OECD experts' interviews add to this general overview the assessments of a number of people directly involved in Princess Alexandra School, who reported a number of beneficial outcomes. There has been an improvement in children's social skills, pride and commitment in school. Students appear to be better linked to the community. There has been an improvement in inter-cultural relationships, despite surrounding racism. There has been a decline in crime rates, truancy and transience, although these are still regarded as the key problems. Parents' willingness to visit the school is slowly improving, but still not enough. Natives are involved in community boards and decision making. The usefulness of cluster classrooms, resource teachers, and teacher associates was recorded. There was a general feeling that good work was being accomplished under the strategy. More collaboration at every level was reported. Now teachers stay or apply to work in Princess Alexandra School. The school is becoming a resource centre for the community where families can drop in at any time during after school hours. Additionally, there has been a general improvement of the whole neighbourhood.

Problems and challenges in collaboration

The main problem is the unbalanced representation of Natives in the whole process. Only three teachers are from a Native background, the board members of the Community Association are mostly white, and only two nations out of the twelve in the area are represented. Attendance of Native parents at the meetings is poor because "they don't understand how they function (...) they feel powerless to change things" (David Fineday, parent, board member of the Community Association). Princess Alexandra Community School attempts to serve the needs of all of the students and families in the community. Therefore, it is by design that the Hoop Dance Troop is open to all students. This enhances the school's philosophical base of harmony and education. The dance troop consists of Native, Métis and several non-Native boys and girls. The drummers and singers are usually Native men and boys.

Another inhibiting factor is that there is no community space in the school premises, which could be used as a specific place for parents to use.

There is still a bad perception of the neighbourhood, which is not congruent with the actual facts, according to some of those interviewed.

The judicial system, which is perceived as lacking equity in its treatment of the Natives, does not help rehabilitation efforts.

Factors which help collaboration

The following factors appear to be helpful in bringing about collaboration:
- A clear framework with appropriate funding, a common vision and a core of relevant guidelines.
- A clear monitoring of the process with regular evaluation sessions.
- The dedication of staff and readiness to give up routines and to get involved far beyond normal activities.
- Good management by the Principal who should be confident and optimistic, flexible and able to adjust to situations, able to hand over responsibility to staff and community members, and open to others' points of view. John Barton, the Principal of Princess Alexandra School, was unanimously credited with these qualities.
- Careful and detailed planning of activities.
- Adequate pre- and on-going training for all staff.
- Community and family involvement.
- Equity and liaison between staff and volunteers.

Impediments to collaboration

Bureaucracy is seen as time-consuming by those at the field level. There is conflict related to ownership of the process and the difficulty of giving up control. The severity of situations being tackled sometimes discourages attempts to improve them. Often the clients for the services are passive or resistant. Despite efforts, gaps in liaison exist between services due to different boundaries and lack of time at the strategic level. Another factor is exhaustion of staff linked to extra work, events and activities taking place after normal school hours (including time which has to be spent on fund raising because of a shortage of funding). Finally, there is a lack of training in collaborative processes.

West Flat Citizens' Group, Prince Albert

Background

Prince Albert is located north of Saskatoon, at the borderline of the two main geographical regions of Saskatchewan: to the north is the park land and the beginning of the Canadian shield and to the south is the commencement of the prairies and the flat grasslands. Its population is 33 000 and its main economic resources are agriculture, forestry, mining to a lesser extent, and tourism. Prince Albert has a number of jobs generated through correction facilities: two Provincial institutions and a federal penitentiary. Large spin off services are derived from primary industries such as the pulp mill, processing and tourism. A large proportion of the population of the city is of Aboriginal descent (30-40 per cent) and is estimated to be 50 per cent by the year 2000.

Prince Albert Region has 14 First Nations Tribes with a population of approximately 25 000. The decline of their traditional sources of income has resulted in a large influx of Indians from the reserves.

The district as a whole has suffered from low crop prices and high production costs.

The West Flat area: This area comprises approximately 25 per cent of the total city population. In it are concentrated risk indicators such as:

- high unemployment therefore low income;
- high number of rental properties and substandard housing;
- high transiency rate;
- high number of single parent families and "blended" families;
- highest rate of teenage pregnancy in the province (17 per cent of births);
- high density of school age children (60 per cent compared to 30 per cent in the rest of the province).

Many residents are of Aboriginal ancestry and their first language is not English. Many of them were raised in residential schools (a common feature until about 20 years ago) and had no chance to learn parental roles and experience parental skills. They lack support from family networks. Many parents have minimal education and do not see education as a high priority for their children. Therefore there is high level of functional illiteracy. There are problems with alcohol, crime and the fear of crime particularly among senior citizens.

There is "a high level of frustration and anger, combined with learned hopelessness and learned helplessness. They don't see a way out" (Yvonne Gryoerick, community member, West Flat Survey).

The area as a whole suffers from a negative image, negative public perception, uninformed public opinion and to some extent from the excess of "publicity" through the media.

West Flat Community Programmes: In 1991, three or four women became concerned with the amount of police calls coming from the West Flats. The feeling of insecurity led seniors to be afraid to leave their homes. The main problems were alcohol abuse, violence, bootlegging and property crimes. The rates of adolescent truancy and teenage pregnancy were also a worry. In order to change this complaining attitude into an active involvement in improving the situation, a survey was carried out.

A steering committee was created to do the work over the summer. They got help from a member of the Tribal Council, who used computers to input data and do the basic analysis. The principal of St. Michael Community School wrote the report. In August and September of the following year, the St. Michael School building was due to become vacant. The person who was running a "food bank" and the Senior Citizen Group wanted the building but it was too big for them on their own. So the Community Association offered to join forces with them. The Regional Director of Social Services, obtained $9 000 to be made available to rent the building for a six-month period.

The West Flat Citizens' Group was created then to take ownership of the grant. The basic structure was of a non-profit association with a board of volunteer directors. A proposal was then developed by the Citizens' Group with the help of the departments of Education, Training and Employment, Health and Social Services. The integrated and community-based approach was considered as the best solution to existing problems. The City of Prince Albert then acquired the property and agreed to renovate the facility in order to accommodate the different programmes derived from the survey and the proposal. The project falls under Saskatchewan Action Plan for Children.

The following programmes are operating:

- *Education*: Preschool for children aged 3 and 4; EAGLE Programme for youth aged 15 to 18 who cannot cope with the regular school system; parent education provided by a Teen and Young Parent Worker; health and nutrition education; speech and language services are provided in the centre by nurses from the Health Department.

- *Recreation*: Recreation programmes are offered on a regular basis for children and youth, including skating, swimming, movie nights, teen dances, Family Fun Days and gym nights.

- *Housing*: House repairs are arranged for senior citizens and low income families. Labour is provided at no cost through the New Careers Corporation. Home owners supply materials. Saskatchewan Housing has approved 20 housing units adjacent to the Community Centre to accommodate seniors and families.

- *Policing*: A neighbourhood Police Office is operated by West Flat volunteers. Prince Albert City Police are involved. Neighbourhood patrols take place with volunteers' involvement.

- *Seniors programming*: This is to be developed along with the housing project.

The preschool: It opened on October 4th, 1993. There are 73 children currently enrolled and 90 could be accommodated. Children come twice a week for half a day. We visited two different groups of about 15 each. The staff includes the director, a half-time family support worker who leads the teenage parent programme and makes home visits, and four teachers (two for each class). Five parents come in every day as volunteers. Funding for the project is provided through three government departments: Social Services, Education, Training and Employment, and Health. The Department of Health carries out health screenings. Health and development work is done jointly with the public health nurse. A nutritionist prepares breakfast twice a week. A dental nurse does dental screenings. The preschool committee consists of members from the Department of Social Services, chairpersons of the West Flat Citizens' Group, the principals and school co-ordinators of the two Community Schools based in the area, and representatives of the Department of Public Health (a nurse, nutritionist, dental nurse, speech and language pathologist and day care consultant). They meet monthly and participate in meetings with a Family Support Network group.

The aim of the preschool is to give children a head start, and to develop cognitive, physical, social and communication skills. Most of the children are of Indian or Métis background and English is a second language at home. Although access is preferential for West Flats children, if demand for places came from another part of the city, it would be considered according to the remaining spaces.

EAGLE *Programme* (*Education, A Good Learning Experience*): Funding is provided by the departments of Social Services and Education, Training and Employment. The programme has been set up to address the problem of too many students dropping out of school. The programme provides a mix of education, life skills and employment skills training. The staff is composed of a teacher and a social worker. The programme accommodates 15 students at the most. There were nine of them when we visited the centre including a pregnant teenage girl.

Besides regular courses, the programme provides counselling, follow up of health checks, nutrition courses and recreational opportunities. It uses the High School's facilities, including its computers and swimming pool, and the staff work with the High School to reintegrate students when they feel ready.

Students are picked up at home by the social worker if they need transportation. Meals are prepared on a rotating basis by students. We interviewed a 16-year-old pregnant girl (whose mother gave her birth when she was herself 16). She said that she would have never been able to cope with her situation in a normal High School, and that she had already truanted many times. She felt she needed help to face up to and cope with her approaching motherhood. She said that it was helpful to be among other teenage people with a similar background and problems.

Community policing: In 1991, in response to an outcry from seniors citizens of the West Flat district, and following the survey for needs assessment, it was felt that a higher police presence was needed in the area. Because of a shortfall in the City Police budget and a growth in their work load, it was decided that volunteers would take on duties in a police substation, the site of which was chosen to get "right into the middle of it". As a result, some of those creating a nuisance moved out of the area. The volunteer staff at the substation provide referrals for complaints to the police station, help with missing people and intervene whenever they find police action is needed. They work in four shifts. There is also a mobile crisis centre which provides social intervention.

The Volunteer Citizens operate from their own cars. They patrol in twos and have radio communication with the police station. Around 50 to 60 volunteers are involved, including some parents from the preschool. A community liaison officer supervises the citizens' involvement. He gave two sessions of three hours on the legal position of patrollers who are not "auxiliary officers allowed to be actively involved in catching wrong-doers". Advice was given on when and for what reason it is useful to call in the regular police, what should be reported and what should not. The aim is to reduce the fear of crime, which is regarded as being greater than the actual level of crime, together with providing an awareness among citizens. The substation and the patrols have alleviated fear and given to residents, at least those involved, a sense of ownership of their own security needs.

Input – strategic level

According to interviews and self-completion questionnaires, one could say that almost every service is involved in everything.

The preschool was a grassroots initiative but it has been promoted to become one of the two pilot projects of the Region V Saskatchewan Education Training and Employment Office under the Children First Plan. It will operate for three years and will be evaluated. Based on the evaluation information, further discussions will be undertaken regarding its future.

Social Services have ultimate responsibility for children's services but focus on financial assistance and child protection services. They are currently putting 8.5 workers into the area. There is a supervisor, three preschool workers, two family support workers, one teen parent worker, a clerical worker and a half-time parent worker who provides services to the preschool programme. Four positions are new and the others are filled by existing staff. They are directly funded by social services. Funding goes directly to the preschool (mostly from the Education budget) and EAGLE. Health Services provide on-site nursing and specialists such as a speech therapist, dietician and psychiatric social worker. The City provided the building facilities and has allocated a post from the City Planning Department to work on planning renovations. Inter-agency committees are involved in the two Community Schools in the area. Three departments – Health, Education, Training and Employment and Social Services – are involved.

The City Police Department provides funds to pay the rent and related expenses of the substation and the community liaison officer's salary (he is not only employed for West Flat Citizens' Group activities).

Not counting the cost of manpower, the budget allocated to these programmes is:

Preschool	$98 000
EAGLE	$96 000
Co-ordinator	$30 000
Evaluation	$20 000

Input – field level

A lot of work is done on a voluntary basis. The substation was furnished with items given by citizens, and patrollers use their own money to pay for gasoline. They spend time raising extra money. Repairs to housing are done at cost. Most of the direct commitment is coming from field workers.

Process – strategic and operational level

Most of the OECD questionnaire respondents report meeting attendance as part of their routine. Planning and management are joint concerns and, depending on their part in the whole programme, some representatives of the above Provincial or Municipal services are involved. The City has been a constant partner since one of the West Flats Citizens' became Major of the town. This person was already involved as a member of the City Council. Her new position helped to speed up decision making.

The Director of the Regional Department of Social Services in his statement about inter-agency consultation gives an amazing list of committees and reviews in which agencies get together.

These include:

- The Children First Programme, which involves the separate and public school boards, personnel from Queen Mary, St. Michael and Carleton schools, and Mental Health and Social Services.
- The Family Support Network which consists of 32 departments, agencies and interested people who information share and problem-solve on an on-going basis.

- Regular meetings are currently taking place which involve on a collective or more reduced level the following: the Family Support Network; 18 non-government organisations; Mental Health Services, Catholic Family Services, Mobile Crisis and the Children's Haven (treatment of sexually abused children); Mental Health Services, City Police and Mobile Crisis (crisis services); the Mayor's Committee on Community Development (hunger, family violence, street youth, housing and racism); West Flat School Children's First Programme; Mental Health Services and the separate and public school boards (programme development for a Therapeutic Group Home); and Prince Albert Partnership in Family Violence (involving all stakeholders in the community).

Also, the Prince Albert Partnership on Family Violence has developed a case management model. Any of the stakeholders can call for a case conference and a joint planning conference will be called to develop a shared plan and identify a case manager.

Training: A wide range of training for inter-agency work has been offered. Staff of the "Nobody's Perfect" parent education programme trained agency and inter-departmental personnel who then jointly provided training to all agency and department clients. The Community Service Centre Interval House has provided family violence training to department and other agency staff. Child Protection Service training has been provided to all Mobile Crisis staff and has been offered to Aboriginal tribal staff. Case Management Training has been provided to some Mobile Crisis staff and has been offered to band staff. The Prince Albert Child Abuse Council has provided training opportunities for all agencies and departments in the city on child abuse. Joint training was developed by the Provincial Foster Parent Association and the Department of Social Services. Regional training teams were then developed and training was provided jointly to prospective foster parents.

Sharing of resources and data: A city-wide data base procedure is still in the developmental phase. Non-government organisations and community programmes have access to public facilities such as photocopiers, paper products, and articles or other professional materials. Vehicles from the government may be leased for staff of the Community Association or may be hired for transportation of staff or children.

Government agents are commonly involved as counsellors to help grassroots initiatives find their way through the administrative labyrinth in order to speed up the referral process.

There is no single entry point as such, nor does any service actually provide leadership. One respondent stressed that it is for the better – one entry point could lead to rigidity. "Whatever the access point, there needs to be a natural and easy transfer to the full range of support that is called for in a particular situation".

Process – field level

To begin with, the West Flat Citizens' Group is a non-profit organisation open to anyone who volunteers (potentially the 8 000 to 10 000 people living in the area). The three or four women who initiated the project organised a "bitch tea party" to put an end to the complaining attitude of local people and transform it into a positive, active and comprehensive attempt to bring about change. They liaised from the outset with resourceful persons from the City Council and Department Services. Planning of programmes came about as the result of consultation, and brain-storming among citizens and counsellors from various services. Every programme board is composed of representatives from the community, and the services. Staff participate in planning and evaluation.

Training: Preschool staff attend Child Day Care training through the Saskatchewan Institute of Applied Arts, Sciences and Technics (SIAST). They have also attended other day care training events sponsored by the Local Child Care Association and Saint John Ambulance. EAGLE staff take part in professional development meetings with staff from the Prince Albert Roman Catholic Separate School Division. In-service training in policing was planned with police and delivered by police, lawyers and a local judge. Boards and staff have taken part in community meetings and workshops (*i.e.* on family violence). Preschool and EAGLE workers participate in case conferences.

Resource sharing: The preschool and EAGLE share resources, such as materials or sport and leisure facilities, with the elementary schools and high schools. They share some transportation facilities. They have not yet set up a collaboration protocol with each other but they are reflecting on the idea of asking EAGLE students to lead art workshops for the 3rd and 4th grade classes.

Products

Parents show satisfaction and report progress in the speech abilities and social skills of their children. Nevertheless, some parents see the preschool merely as "glorified day care". However, professionals stress the strength of preventive programmes for developing in parents a sense that they should value their children. Social Services have set up a three-year evaluation follow-up project.

The attendance rate at EAGLE is 98 per cent. It is too new to obtain any success indicators. The young pregnant girl whom we interviewed felt that the programme had helped her to sort out her relationship with her father which had been badly affected by her pregnancy, and she said she was ready to cope with studies in order to better manage her future life.

Fear of crime had reduced following the community policing initiative.

Most of the partners considered that the best achievement of the programme was its high level of community involvement. The wide range of programmes, from those aimed at 3- to 4-year-olds to those for seniors including health, educational, recreational and housing components, reflects the holistic approach attached to integrated services. Community members expressed the feeling that they were "doing the right thing" after so many years of helplessness. Voluntary work gives people self-worth. A large number of Métis and Aboriginal people are involved, although it is sometimes hard to identify them.

Factors supporting collaboration

The West Flat Citizens' Group initiative came at the "right time". It occurred almost at the same time as the provincial launch of the Action Plan for Children. Funds were allocated to pilot community-based projects. This helped to prevent discouragement due to delays and postponement of decisions. A new culture of partnership emerged which led to planning partnerships and resource sharing. The provincial government established a general atmosphere of support for collaboration.

The small scale of the City, allowing everyone to know each other, was a factor which made collaboration easier, as was the power of a community which had defined its own needs and had decided to do something about them.

Barriers to collaboration

Despite the impressive level of collaboration in Prince Albert, there were still factors identified by respondents which impeded it. These included the lack of co-terminous boundaries between the various services such as education, health and social services, and the reluctance of bureaucracies to allow "mixed marriages". In addition, time needs to be allocated during the working day to allow collaboration.

There are still barriers remaining in terms of government legislation and protocols (for example, data protection legislation restricting the transfer of information from health to education services).

At the community level, there are still problems getting people to live harmoniously. The basic fear is that people with negative attitudes might take over and undo what has been achieved.

CONCLUSION

The concept of integrated services was embraced at strategic, operational and field levels. In Prince Albert, it has demonstrated its relevance and efficiency. However, the process is time-consuming and difficult when people are given no extra time for collaboration. Considering the number of meetings and committees, one wonders whether there is any time left for other ordinary work.

Community involvement and empowerment is a key factor in the setting up of appropriate responses to children's and families' needs.

Natives' willingness to get involved is a controversial issue. Cultural gaps between Whites and Natives are far from being resolved, despite structural changes, such as systematic consultation with the Indian and Métis Affairs Secretariat or Tribal Council. A long history of segregation and injustice has left scars on both sides.

Preventative actions are too new to have achieved their goals of equity, self-confidence, cultural pride and social balance. However, Saskatchewan province has obviously moved ahead and prioritised the objective of giving every child access to his or her basic rights whatever his or her family background.

The holistic approach is becoming part of the professional culture of field workers as well as top managers.

Whether it is cost-effective has not yet really been assessed. But should this be an impediment to the whole concept if the major expected human outcomes are met?

REFERENCES

COMMUNITY SCHOOLS PROGRAMME (1990), Discussion Paper, Saskatchewan Education, March.

GOVERNMENT OF SASKATCHEWAN (1993), *Children First: An Invitation to Work Together,* Government of Saskatchewan, Regina.

GOVERNMENT OF SASKATCHEWAN (1994a), *Saskatchewan's Action Plan for Children. Overview of Provincial and Local Actions,* Government of Saskatchewan, Regina, April.

GOVERNMENT OF SASKATCHEWAN (1994b), *Saskatchewan Children and Families at Risk, Demographic Risk Factors,* Government of Saskatchewan, Regina, May.

GOVERNMENT OF SASKATCHEWAN (1994c), *Working Together to Address Barriers to Learning. A Policy Framework for Integrated School-linked Services for Children and Youth at Risk,* Draft, Government of Saskatchewan, Regina.

LORAINE THOMPSON INFORMATION SERVICES LIMITED (eds.) (1992), *Building a Community for Learning: Integrated School-based Services,* SSTA Research Centre Report 92-16, Saskatchewan School Trustees Association, Regina.

SASKATCHEWAN EDUCATION, TRAINING AND EMPLOYMENT (1994), *Saskatchewan Education Indicators Report. K-12 Schooling: How Well are We Doing?,* Saskatchewan Education, Training and Employment, Regina.

SASKATOON BOARD OF EDUCATION (1994), *Inner-city School Concept Plan Evaluation,* Saskatoon Board of Education, Saskatoon.

ALBERTA

RADICAL CHANGE TOWARDS SERVICES INTEGRATION

by

Lucienne Roussel and Mary Lewis

INTRODUCTION

Population

The Province of Alberta, in western Canada, is a region of prairies and high mountain ranges (the Rockies). It has a total population of 2 681 300. The figure is stable, even slightly on the rise (up 34 400 between 1992 and 1993). Most of the population lives in the towns, with country-dwellers accounting for only 20.2 per cent. By far the most densely populated areas are to be found in and around Edmonton, the political and administrative capital (933 911 inhabitants), and Calgary (854 934). Aboriginal people, including First Nations (99 650), Inuit (2 825) and Métis (56 310), account for 5.5 per cent of the population in Alberta, compared with 3.6 per cent in the rest of Canada.

Economic situation

In December 1992, male unemployment was estimated at 9.9 per cent (against 11.9 per cent in Canada as a whole) and female unemployment at 8.9 per cent (10.4 per cent nationally). The overall number of unemployed has in fact declined, from 137 733 in 1993 to 132 100 in 1994. The average annual income has risen slightly from C$20 830 in 1989 to C$22 477 in 1991.

Alberta is an agricultural province, and is an important cereal and livestock producer. But it was oil that gave a strong boost to the local economy in the 1950s, and now accounts for over 80 per cent of national output. Thus Calgary became the centre of the oil industry and a city of international standing. In spite of the economic problems that have emerged over the past few years, Calgary remains one of the richest cities in Canada. Edmonton, the seat of the Provincial Government, is also a major business and trading centre. Of course, the overall picture does tend to mask disparities. Edmonton, for instance, has a high percentage of residents receiving financial assistance through the Supports for Independence Programme, 42 per cent of all those in the Province as a whole. In Wetaskiwin, the average income is lower than the average for the Province. Calgary too has pockets of poverty with families in serious financial difficulty.

Administrative organisation

Alberta became a Province of Canada in 1905. The British North America Acts gave the Parliament of Canada the power to legislate "in relation to all Matters not coming within the Classes of Subjects by this Act assigned exclusively to the Legislatures of the Provinces". The Federal government has authority in areas such as defence, tax collection, currency, banks and unemployment. In the event of a conflict of power between Parliament and the Provincial Governments, the Federal authority has pre-eminence.

Responsibility for managing and funding services such as roads, schools and hospitals lies with the Province, which has decisionary powers over taxes levied directly at the provincial and municipal level for provincial purposes. Education, most labour legislation and most of the social security system are also areas in which the provincial legislature has virtually exclusive powers.

Municipal governments in the province are generally responsible for local hospitals and schools, the latter often administered by their own elected board. Resources are derived from local taxation and provincial subsidies.

Services to aboriginal people are a special case, depending on whether or not individuals live on or off reserves. Anything relating to health and social affairs is dealt with by institutions directly managed and funded by the Federal government and not by provincial services as is the case for people living off reserves. Those who live on the reserves have treaty status, which confers prerogatives such as hunting rights and tax exemption, as set out in the treaties drawn up between their ancestors and the Crown. They have their own education system which is funded by the Department of Indian Affairs and Northern Development and meets provincial standards.

MAIN AT RISK GROUPS

Some 40 per cent of the aboriginal people are under 15 years of age (42 405). Between 42 per cent and 47 per cent of all children seen for one reason or another by child welfare services are aboriginal children. The justice system estimates that aboriginal children comprise 31 per cent of all the cases on their books.

The school drop-out rate among young aboriginal people is also beginning to give cause for concern and has in some cases reached 30 per cent. Cultural and language difficulties can create attendance problems. Before 1970, aboriginal children were removed from their homes to attend residential schools. Schools became established on the reserves during the early 1970s. Until then, families were not accustomed to discussing the educational needs of their children.

Unemployment is particularly high amongst the aboriginal population (almost 20 per cent, which is practically 50 per cent more than in other population groups). This is sometimes due to lack of employment opportunities in remote areas.

However, while aboriginal children are at high risk, they are not the only ones with problems and are not alone in the at risk category – a term for which there is no clear, official definition. Despite many hardships, there are many and increasing numbers of successful, healthy aboriginal families.

As in many cities in the industrialised world, violence and crime are increasing among the youngest members of the population. Concern is mounting everywhere about this trend and the high number of young under-achievers with behaviour problems who are totally alienated from the school culture.

By and large, young people in the at risk category are the victims of poor housing, economic problems and family difficulties that may be serious. Single-parent families, for instance, account for 15 per cent of all the families in Edmonton, and a similar figure is found in every area, city and county. A proportion of these families fall under the poverty line for the country, especially those headed by females.

DEPARTMENTAL ORGANISATION AND FUNDING AT THE PROVINCIAL LEVEL

Social services

The main areas covered by these services are income and employment programmes, child welfare, day care and services to persons with disabilities (SPD). There are also programmes focusing on the prevention of problems raised by domestic violence.

Current support is targeted at low-skilled, unemployed people on welfare. A project is underway to assist individuals to develop skills for job hunting and to provide work-related training. Its aim is to help clients move from welfare to employment and to become self-sufficient.

The Federal government is redefining the whole of Canada's social policy and its national social security system. Until now, the cost of these programmes has been shared by the province and the Federal government. The exact nature of the reform has not yet emerged in any detail, but there appears to be a consensus on the need to reform funding methods. Funding to Alberta from the federal government for social programmes has been in decline since 1992 and new cuts are planned every year until 1996.

Health services

Albertans are very proud of their health system. Statistics reveal that the average life expectancy has increased considerably and is now slightly higher than that of Canada as a whole. An improvement also has occurred in infant mortality, which dropped from 17.5 per thousand in 1972 to 8.1 per thousand in 1990.

The health system is going through major changes. Seventeen Regional Health Authorities are assuming responsibility for health care services in the province. The Alberta health care insurance plan, a comprehensive plan which covers doctor's fees and hospitalisation, provides for at least 95 per cent of the population. The Federal government helps fund this programme.

The 1994-95 budget allocates C$3.77 billion for health expenditure, plus C$133 million for building, facilities and services. Provincial health care includes all aspects of hospital provision (*i.e.* intensive care, long stays, mental health and public health), since the delivery of special services is the responsibility of the Provinces. Public health covers a variety of sectors ranging from home care to environmental and health education. It was allocated a budget of C$264.3 million for 1994. All these features make Alberta the third Canadian Province in terms of health expenditure per capita.

Until 1993, the Health department comprised nine divisions, covering sectors such as public health and mental health. However, health services are being restructured and replaced by 17 regional authorities, each with their own Board. Each authority will be responsible for every aspect of health. A provincial administration has been set up to liaise with local authorities and draw up a project to organise local service delivery for mental health services.

Education services

Education comes exclusively under the authority of each Province. Federal government provides funding for schools on reserves which meet provincial standards.

Alberta has two ministries of Education, one for children of school age, the other for higher education. There are major universities in Edmonton, Calgary and Lethbridge, as well as various technical and vocational colleges. The Province is divided into 170 school districts, with 1 500 schools and 500 000 pupils in basic education. The average number of pupils per district is therefore quite low; while some, like Calgary, have 100 000 pupils, others have only a hundred or so.

School is divided into twelve grades, with the first six forming elementary school and the other six the secondary level. Schooling begins at 5 and a half as a preschool option, but 98 per cent of all children attend from that age.

The education system includes public schools, and a network of Roman Catholic schools, also funded by government. In Alberta, this network forms a separate school district in its own right. There are also a number of private schools, for which the Province provides 75 per cent funding.

The responsibility for running schools is delegated to local school boards with elected or appointed members. They supervise the construction of school buildings, school transport, and the recruitment of staff. Their budget is subject to ministry approval.

Formerly, 60 per cent of funds came from the Province and the rest from local taxation but the system is now being changed. The plan is to transfer all decisions concerning staff recruitment and school curricula to the local level; however, funding will come entirely from the Provincial Government. It will collect all taxes and redistribute them across the Province as a whole to provide more even resources and greater equity for all residents in the Province wherever they may live. This should also enable schools to deliver more services.

Another major change involves the way schools are funded. Instead of receiving an annual payment based on enrolment figures at the start of the school year, they will receive their funds in two instalments: one at the start of the school year and another in the course of the year, based on the number of pupils on the register at each time. Funding will follow pupils if they change schools, and will disappear if they drop out altogether. The hope is that this will encourage schools to do all they can to prevent pupils from changing schools or dropping out of the education system altogether.

Department of Justice

The legislation on young offenders is being reviewed. For the moment, half the costs are shouldered by the Province and half by the Federal government. The budgetary cuts planned will affect adult rather than youth programmes.

Many programmes are run in co-operation with other departments and are therefore funded from two or more sources. The Department of Health, for instance, provides resources for the assessment of young offenders.

Generally, there is an obvious need to co-ordinate with other services, for instance, when young offenders are released from prison or put on probation in the community. Many rehabilitation schemes are in fact run by the community.

ORIGIN AND DEVELOPMENT OF SERVICES INTEGRATION

Government policy

Major shifts are occurring in government policy, which is now undergoing massive changes.

For some years now, the Federal government and the Province have been seeing disturbing increases in their budget deficits. It has become essential to review policy in all areas in order to examine cost-effective ways of providing services. Safeguarding the future for individual families and the economy as a whole has meant radical restructuring and new priorities.

Furthermore, various surveys indicated that in some instances the public had poor access to services and that, in spite of a host of service providers, output and quality were not always up to standard. A joint report by the Ministry of Education and Calgary services found that many services and associations were looking after the same families or children and therefore duplicating effort. On the other hand, there were also gaps and breaks in service delivery.

The drive to enhance efficiency and quality, stemming from the need to manage a smaller budget as cost-effectively as possible, meant taking the whole system back to the drawing-board, and changing the thinking and culture prevailing in each government department.

While the policy review stemmed from determination on the part of the Provincial Government, it also reflected concerns and efforts at the grassroots level. In many cases, initiatives had been launched in the community to achieve a better level of service delivery to improve efficiency and services to children and families.

The Province accordingly drew up a three-year plan, which, it is hoped, will eventually make the system more operational and bring costs into line with the economic situation. Its goals are as follows:

– to eliminate waste and duplication;
– to increase productivity;
– to encourage teamwork and innovation;
– to cut red-tape and abolish pointless regulations;
– to turn the Provincial Government from a direct service-provider into a facilitator for the institutions subsequently appointed to deliver the services;
– to make the Provincial Government responsible for regulating policy, monitoring and funding;
– to state objectives and define stages;

- to create more scope for private sector involvement; and

- to ask clients to participate in the cost of the services they use.

All this is to be achieved without raising taxes; rather than finding more resources, it is more a case of changing the way available funds are spent.

Each ministerial department is undertaking discussions along these lines and reviewing its objectives, structures and working methods accordingly.

The Education Department, for instance, has set itself nine objectives, one being to improve co-ordination between ministries, local services and the various associations dealing with disabled or problem children. The same applies to the three other ministries concerned (Health, Justice and Social Services), which emphasize strongly in their plans the need for co-ordination and efficiency.

A Commissioner for Children's Services was appointed in 1993 to look at ways of reforming services for families and the young as provided by the ministerial departments in charge of health, social services, education and justice. The Commissioner is submitting a set of recommendations in June 1994, and the implementation process for the new system should begin in June 1995. The direction given to the Commissioner specifies that the new services should aim to be effective within the budget available, to be readily available to the public, and to take into account community needs and priorities; services must be managed and provided at community level; and, finally, they must form a network allowing services integration.

Clearly, then, this new policy is aimed at considerable decentralisation, viewed as the most efficient solution in every area since it delegates responsibility and commitment to private individuals and the community as a whole.

Co-ordination of Services for Children

The Co-ordination of Services for Children scheme was launched so that four government departments (Justice, Health, Education and Social Services) could work in partnership with communities to develop better services for children. The idea was to see how officials in central government could work with communities to remove administrative barriers and introduce practices based on multidisciplinary integrated approaches to service delivery.

At the central level (i.e. that of Assistant Deputy Ministers or ADMs), a working committee has been set up with two representatives from each ministry. Each member of the working committee also liaises with specific pilot sites to assist them and find how best to overcome any remaining obstacles that affect services to families. Each local project is monitored by two people from any two ministries. They are both official representatives of departments and human resources. One of the two always attends meetings on site, while the other provides support for evaluation activities.

The two members of the working party delegated to each pilot site are in charge of communication and refer back to the central level any problems that might arise. Of course, working at the grassroots level gives them a good grasp of local issues and problems, and they become better intermediaries and even advocates for local projects.

Research and evaluation

A sub-committee of the central working group has set up a monitoring and evaluation procedure for the Co-ordination of Services for Children initiative. A draft survey has been drawn up for interim evaluation purposes. It will take stock of working methods and actions affecting service planning and delivery, both at provincial and local level. The second part of the evaluation will look at results from the viewpoint of children and families to see what kind of services are received and how this compares with the previous situation.

The draft evaluation will be used by external evaluators, both for basic data collection and for the preparation of summary reports on local evaluation results.

The draft will also be used as a starting-point for discussions with teams working in the field, who will be free to adapt it for their particular use. Although communities are probably more interested in the part of the questionnaire that directly concerns them, they have also been sent the other part concerning the province, to show them how every level involved in the initiative interacts. In fact there is nothing to stop communities adding their own comments. They may, if they wish, request the assistance of ministerial experts in conducting the evaluation. In any event the experts must be kept informed of the evaluation method eventually selected.

The draft was prepared in collaboration with ADMs, the interministerial working group, and local groups. The purpose is to obtain at least thirty responses from each community, if possible at every level of authority.

Internal evaluation is a key factor in the scheme. A consultant has tested the questionnaire in the field and will help to analyse the responses. The evaluation sub-committee will also help to interpret findings and will write the report. The communities of Edmonton and Calgary have signed a contract with the same consultant to evaluate their own programmes. As for the final evaluation, the plan is for communities to be represented on the sub-committee. The evaluation will probably be high on the agenda at the Autumn Forum bringing together all the communities involved in the initiative.

Three ministerial departments – Health, Social Services and Education – are providing C$ 100 000 per annum to fund evaluation, consultation, facilitation and planning at the sites. Expenditures are monitored by the interministerial ADM's committee.

LOCAL INITIATIVES AS PART OF THE CO-ORDINATION OF SERVICES FOR CHILDREN SCHEME

Five sites have been selected for study in the Co-ordination of Services for Children initiative, namely Calgary, Edmonton, Lethbridge, Wabasca-Demarais and Wetaskiwin. The descriptions below will show how local officials have been involved in a process of change.

In Calgary, the Opening Doors project focuses on the community, but school administrators and teachers are very closely involved, both at district level and in individual schools. The project is an attempt to create mechanisms to provide linkages between service providers, their superiors and administrators in the various departments and will try to break down barriers and compartmentalisation between all services targeting families and children. Community people are also involved in planning their own services. In one community in the city, families were faced with 82 different services and associations, all available to address different family problems.

In Edmonton, the Partners for Youth scheme has a multidisciplinary approach but with the focus on schools, where families have access to a whole range of services.

The Lethbridge project is more diversified. The idea is to involve as many members of the community as possible in discussions and work. There are three focuses in Lethbridge. One is a programme known as "5th on 5th", an alternative high school, and the other two are amalgamations, the first merging the Family and Community Development Programme with another programme called Parents' Place, and the second merging the Preschool Assessment Centre with the Paediatric Neuro-muscular Unit.

Action in Wabasca-Demarais and Wetaskiwin focuses on social and health issues from a broad community perspective.

A short description is given below of each pilot site, the institutions concerned and how they are organised. Each one is then analysed in terms of the type of support they receive in their drive to integrate services, the resources and training they have available to them, any positive or negative factors that might have been perceived and the outcome of their progress towards integration.

Pilot sites

Calgary is one of Canada's largest cities with a population of 727 719. After becoming a major business centre thanks to expansion in the oil industry in the 1950s, Calgary is now a prosperous city where most of the population enjoys a good standard of living and education. Unemployment stands at around 10 per cent.

Edmonton is the administrative capital of the province, with a population of 627 000. It is also a major centre for trade and commerce. The unemployment rate stands at about 11 per cent. The school drop-out rate is 8.5 per cent and regrettably youth unemployment is particularly high (10 to 20 per cent). Edmonton is a quiet, friendly city but recently, as in many other cities, there has been an increase in violence among young people.

Lethbridge is a smaller town of 63 000 inhabitants, but it is a major business centre serving the whole of southern Alberta. This is a predominantly agricultural area, where livestock farming is a major activity. Its population covers a wide range of ethnic groups and cultures. In particular, two large Indian reserves are located close to the town. Under-18s make up 28 per cent of the population. Although the area is still expanding, unemployment stands at 12 per cent.

Wabasca-Demarais is part of an aboriginal community. It is the first to be included in the Co-ordination of Services for Children scheme. It covers a vast area 385 km north-east of Edmonton. There are six reservations and some 5 000 inhabitants. The cost of living is quite high and the average income per capita is low. Jobs are scarce and there are major social problems. The area has several local facilities, including a hospital, mental health services, childcare facilities and adult training pro-grammes. There are also schools, each with its own counsellor, and one family counsellor for the three schools in the community. However, a number of residents in the area remain very isolated and have no access to services.

Wetaskiwin is a small community with a population of 10 700. The area is mainly agricultural with some minor industries. Many of the inhabitants travel to Edmonton to work every day. Personal incomes are quite low and below average for the province, with 30.9 per cent earning less than C$20 000 per annum. The standard of education is not very high either, and there are many single-parent families (16.5 per cent). This area is also close to a large Indian reserve. There are numerous services for children and many initiatives are run jointly by the community and school districts.

How the projects began

Calgary's Opening Doors project began in 1991. At the time, the Board of Education and the Ministry held a meeting with all the services and associations dealing with young people at risk and their families. The purpose was to respond more closely to these people's needs. A report had revealed a large number of gaps in the system, as well as room for improvement in communication between service providers and the public. The report also emphasized public frustration and discontent with the way in which services responded to their needs. Parents and pupils regretted not being consulted and found it hard to use the services. The Thomas Report was used as a basis for further discussions and staff were invited to participate. This was how the Opening Doors initiative came into being.

The education authorities were at the cutting edge of the initiative. Calgary is one of the largest public school districts in the province, with 130 000 pupils, including 96 000 in the public school system alone. Emphasis was put on locating co-ordinated services in schools to make them more accessible to parents and children; it was also hoped that the initiative would improve conditions in the classroom.

In 1992, the Board of Education acknowledged the importance of collaboration between services and the need to work together. Then in August 1993, the Provincial Government launched discussions on co-ordinated services (Co-ordination of Services for Children) and asked Calgary to become one of the five pilot sites to participate in this joint initiative with the four government departments.

Edmonton's Partners for Youth project came into being following a congress on prevention, called "Safer Cities", held in Montreal in 1989. In 1990, the Mayor set up a working party that included 15 members of the public, chosen for their expertise rather than as representatives of any institution. The police and the Department of Employment each sent a representative too. Discussions were based on the idea of preventing crime through social action.

Reports drawn up in liaison with the communities involved were published between May 1991 and May 1992. The 149 recommendations they put forward emphasized the importance of setting up closely targeted social initiatives that involved the whole community in order to foster a sense of responsibility.

In Edmonton, as elsewhere in Alberta, the fact that services were fragmented raised a genuine problem. Some were provided directly by the Province and others by local departments or associations. Edmonton's services for children and young people were also organised on a highly specialised basis, with each service addressing a single problem only. The co-ordination of services for children and young people was therefore at the top of the agenda.

Partners for Youth is a pilot project to group several services in one place, thereby facilitating public access.

In April 1992, senior officials from each service met to refine the idea of and make arrangements for a multi-disciplinary, multi-service unit that would be school-based. By September 1993, two pilot sites had begun to operate, one in Wellington Junior High School and the other in Saint Nicholas' Catholic Junior High School.

The Lethbridge project was set up in a community that has a history of collaboration between services. Examples include the Preschool Assessment and Treatment Centre (PATC), the Paediatric Neuromuscular Unit (PNMU) and the Family and Community Development Programme (FCDP) which themselves are the result of a co-ordination drive that began in 1978. The PNMU was set up following co-ordination between parents, the regional hospital and the Alberta paediatric hospital; the PATC was established by the three health districts in 1982; and the FCDP is a joint project bringing together Alberta's social services, the town of Lethbridge and the two school districts. In 1987, discussions and a prevention initiative were also under way to target children at risk between the ages of 5 and 13. It was against this background that the community of Lethbridge was invited to become one of the five pilot sites.

In the Lethbridge initiative, Education and Family and Social Services are the ministries that provide site liaison and support. It was important in Lethbridge to achieve the direct involvement of as many people as possible, rather than concentrating on a single project. Consequently three local projects were selected:

- the amalgamation of the PATC and the PNMU;

- the amalgamation of the FCDP and Parents' Place, an organisation for parental support; and

- the Outreach Programme, which provides young people aged 15 to 24 with a variety of resources to them with training, employment and personal development (the programme is carried out by the district, the youth employment centre, Provincial training services and the Federal employment service).

Wabasca-Demarais was chosen by the interministerial working party on the grounds that the community already had some experience of interdisciplinary or joint services work. In the area, the large number of aboriginal Canadians receiving services from both the federal and provincial governments makes it particularly important to ensure strong interlinkage between all the different institutions and governments. After a crisis in 1982 when a teenager committed suicide, the community became fully aware of the need to join forces, first and foremost by addressing the emotional problems of young people. Hence the creation of the "Let's Talk" committee, a local mental health service set up as a non-profit making association. Its aim is to help local residents become self-sufficient and assist one another. A local pilot group was set up with volunteers from various institutions in the community, and representatives from the four ministries, some at federal and some at provincial level. It has been running since 1993.

The Wetaskiwin project was also chosen because the community had some experience of interdisciplinary work, in particular the Wetoka Health Unit which was set up in 1982 to enhance and promote health initiatives in all fields for all sections of the population. Every year, the project is reviewed to ensure that it caters properly for identified needs. The work focuses mainly on prevention and is intended to be comprehensive.

The main aim of the current interdisciplinary project, as part of Co-ordination of Services for Children, is to enhance services for children by facilitating access to a system that had proved much too complex to be of maximum use to local residents. The idea was therefore to introduce co-operation between the ministerial departments concerned and the community, to optimise resource use and share responsibility when treating cases, and to set up concerted strategies and eliminate obstacles, gaps and unnecessary overlapping.

Financial resources and training

In Calgary, the operation has the support of senior level officials, but receives no special funding. Funds come from the services involved and through the usual channels.

One issue on the agenda is that of further training for staff involved in making the change to holistic service delivery. It would take the form of joint discussions on how to organise a team, thereby making it possible to give a clear idea of individual expectations, envisage possible approaches to case management and help to resolve conflict. The staff involved encounter different problems and work differently from the staff in the same services who are not involved in the initiative. This must therefore be taken into account by their superiors when their work is assessed.

Training sessions on joint services have been introduced, including courses by specialists from the paediatric hospital of Alberta showing school auxiliaries how to deal with disabled children, and courses by the social services for the Federal human resource departments and the Training and Assessment Centre.

This joint training work is essential and the ideal way to build up team spirit.

The initiative redistributes resources, with the mental health service sending three specialists into schools to assist teachers and pupils and two into health services. Similarly, a nurse spends two days per week in schools. Work now focuses on prevention rather than crisis management. Family and social services have assigned two child welfare workers to be part of the interdisciplinary team. The City of Calgary Police have also been assigned staff to work on the project.

For the moment these services are not all housed under one roof, but that is one of the ultimate aims of the initiative.

In Edmonton, the Partners for Youth project has the support and backing of officials at all levels but, once again, has not received any specific funding. Resources are made available on an *ad hoc* basis, depending on the requirements of each service.

The social services, for instance, have allocated a full-time post to the Wellington school which has a particularly high number of children with social problems. A social worker also spends one half-day per week at St. Nicholas school. Under the new system, she has had to change her approach, with the authorisation of her department, from case-by-case crisis management to prevention-based methods. For the rest of the week, however, she carries out her ordinary work as usual. This new approach has the full support of her superiors, but has raised problems with her colleagues.

Staff from the city's social services now devote three days every week to each site. Finally, the police spend at least one half-day per week, and more if necessary, in the field.

The YMCA also participates by providing extra school tuition and literacy training. This involves two people working locally for at least one half-day per week.

All of these resources have in fact been found by redeploying resources from one service to another. Partners have all become involved on an informal basis, and Edmonton's private sector has also played a part. In any event the project is not a financial entity and cannot receive funds directly.

The three Lethbridge projects, namely the amalgamation of FCDP and Parents' Place, that of the PNMU and the PATC, and the Outreach scheme are different approaches to similar problems and concerns.

Although the amalgamation of FCDP and Parents' Place is already well under way, the two are not under the same roof and cases are not dealt with by a single person. There is no pooling of transport or administrative resources either, on a systematic or formal basis. The FCDP allocates one-fifth of a psychologist's post to Parents' Place. In fact, the only additional resource that has been allocated is the time required by staff to develop implementation plans for the project.

In the case of the PNMU-PATC amalgamation, both institutions are used to working on a multidisciplinary basis. The new body will give the public easier access and a wider range of services since they will be housed under one roof. The policy shift will put more focus on prevention than on direct treatment. For instance, the mental health service wanted to be part of the planned new centre in order to work more easily with other services. The Lethbridge regional hospital would like to see the PNMU join this new organisation as it would give it a base in the community and thus bring the service provider closer to its clients, while at the same time freeing some much-needed space in the hospital. And schools are, of course, the closest partners.

The new body will be financed from a community fund similar to the one being used for the PATC. As for the highly specialised equipment that may be required by the PNMU, it will probably continue being funded by voluntary contributions.

For the moment, the PATC is located on the same premises as the speech-therapy department and public health unit, and work is carried out on a joint basis. The PATC has also agreed with the PNMU to provide psychological monitoring services for the children examined by the PATC, in return for payment.

A committee bringing together all the services concerned is studying how best to organise services and enhance interdisciplinary processes.

The Governing Board of the hospital has strongly supported the introduction of the project, insisting in particular that the PNMU retain all its existing resources in the new structure. Clients also back the scheme as they can see the usefulness of improved pooling of resources and staff expertise, not to mention the time families and children will save. Families are in fact the PNMU's closest partners.

The Outreach project, designed to meet the needs of young people who do not fit into the regular school system for a variety of reasons, involves the Federal government, the Ministry of Education and assessment and employment services. All services, including education classes, will be more accessible to the people concerned as they are located on the ground floor of a business centre near a major shopping mall and will have extended hours of operation.

The project has received strong local support, but resources are somewhat limited. For the moment, it does have a building at its disposal but the funds required to develop the premises as required are not yet available. Other services will be joining those already in the scheme and will contribute resources. In any event, uncertainty as to future funding makes it hard to plan for the long term.

The Wabasca-Demarais project has received explicit backing from politicians and administrators at all levels. The "Let's Talk" service has been expanded from one shorthand-typist, a director and a part-time counsellor in 1983, serving 75 clients, to three areas of service delivery with a total of 12 employees serving 480 clients in 1992. Most of the resources are provided under an agreement between the mental health service (one co-ordinator, one counsellor and another full-time post) and the community education service (one director of education, one part-time clerical worker, plus operating resources). Various foundations and training/integration initiatives have enabled requirements to be met each year.

The Wetaskiwin project was set up with the support of the senior government officials present at the initial meetings to launch the scheme, together with elected members of local services. They also sit on the subsequently established steering committee. No further resources were allocated to the initiative.

Collaboration

Different solutions to similar problems in other areas or countries were studied as part of the reflection process when the new projects were being devised, one example being the New Beginnings initiative in San Diego (California).

In the Huntington Hills district of Calgary, chosen as the first demonstration site for Opening Doors, a team of local service providers known as the Community Resource Group (CRG) was set up to supervise the introduction of the initiative. Members were drawn from various local services, including major public agencies such as Education, Social Services, Health and Justice.

Members of the CRG include the school's vice-principal, a member of the police force, a mental health worker, a children's service worker, a representative from Alberta's social service and a parent. They have defined their own role and devised working methods as a team, with the support of their superiors. One reason for selecting them was that they had each sought to innovate in their previous job in order to respond more closely to the needs they had identified in the community. While settling into the system, the group has also worked closely with the pupil resource group, present in schools to deal with pupils' behavioural or academic problems. As well as administrators, the group includes the teacher of the child concerned, and possibly a nurse or educational counsellor.

Until the creation of the CRG, the pupil resource group was unable to address problems involving more than one service. Hence the importance of the CRG, since it facilitates liaison between several services dealing with the same pupil. However, it soon became clear that this kind of body could not be set up in all nine schools in the district. Once the Opening Doors pilot group had looked into existing research on the subject, it decided not to base the scheme in a school but in the community.

Access to the CRG was accordingly given to anyone interested in its services. It meets once a week for half a day. Initially, members of the group had to keep one another informed of their normal working methods, the missions assigned by their own institutions, etc. The purpose was for them to become a real team and build up a foundation of trust.

At first they were all somewhat tied to their usual routine, which was only to be expected given their departmental culture and training, but after a while the barriers began to come down. However, there was no question of losing any of the invaluable and much-needed input they each brought with them from their individual occupations.

Each service has had to accept the changes and allow staff to be flexible and to put the client or the community first, rather than the service itself. In some cases nurses, for instance, have had to act as social workers to reassure the families they visit; one mental health officer had to adopt a new approach because he was meeting his patients in a new environment; and an official from the Social Services now has much more scope for early intervention. Now the case of a specific child is managed by one person only, even if the case is complex enough to involve a variety of different services.

Confidence between the community and the service providers has had to be rebuilt, since budget cuts made in some areas have resulted in specific services being cut back or cancelled.

The steering group for Opening Doors for the whole city meets on a monthly basis and deals with more fundamental, broad-ranging problems such as professional secrecy, priority-setting in each service, and liaising with other associations. The CRG and the steering group meet every six weeks.

No co-ordinator has been appointed, so the task falls to each person in turn, but it will not be possible to continue on this voluntary basis. Also, the importance and role of the teachers themselves has not yet been clearly defined. The working party ought to include one teacher, in some capacity or other. Nevertheless, the unions appear to be backing the initiative.

In the Edmonton Partners for Youth initiative, the partners are the education authorities, Children's Services, Mental Health, Health, Justice, the City of Edmonton (represented by various departments, including Parks and Recreation, and the Police), public and catholic schools, and the YMCA. The Children and Youth Services Association and the Glenrose Hospital are also involved. A team of professionals from the various services and associations is based in each of the schools.

When the survey was carried out, the teams had been working together for only four months and had yet to solve a variety of internal problems, compounded by a general lack of time on everyone's part. Most of the staff had never had the opportunity to work together, so they had to get to know one another, develop a new kind of working relationship and forge a common set of values. At the same time, they still had to deal with their normal workload, which was particularly heavy as one youngster attempted suicide and a parent did commit suicide during that time.

A point worth emphasizing is that relations between members of the various services and the YMCA staff did not raise any problems at all as the latter have a broader, more flexible mandate than provincial or local service staff, and they are recruited partly on the basis of their ability to change and adapt.

Here like everywhere else, confidentiality issues do not really hinder teamwork, since information on a particular child is shared by all those working on the case. Force of habit would seem to be more of a hindrance than the actual rules.

However, it has not proved possible to set up a common database for the all the services involved. Similarly, there is no shared case-book system yet. By and large, few documents have been drawn up; this might raise problems, particularly for evaluation purposes. For instance, the Justice Department is allowed to use information recorded by the police but not by social workers. Locally, the team has agreed on a procedure but it requires clarification, and this highlights how incompatible the information systems used by some of the services actually are.

The Community and Family Services Department does publish an annual report in conjunction with eight other partners, although not specifically on the Partners for Youth scheme.

The project as a whole is supervised by a steering committee set up several months before the scheme was launched. Consisting of top officials from government departments and associations, it met initially on a weekly basis but now meets once a fortnight, each time at a different project site.

One member of the steering committee is more specifically responsible for liaising with a particular site, mirroring the approach adopted by the provincial working committee towards the various pilot sites. This person meets the teams working in the field at least once a month. A weekly meeting for all the service providers is also held in each school.

Here, the integrated service process relies heavily on support from the steering committee. There appears to be a common goal, staff are fully involved, and they have a good grasp of the roles and duties of each partner. The fact that staff are all under one roof is also bound to help bring about a change in attitudes and practice.

In Lethbridge, the two organisations now being amalgamated (Parents' Place and the FCDP) have been working together on an informal basis for seven years. They are on an equal footing and share the view that services should be client-oriented. This is an extremely important point, even more so in their eyes than any strictly technical problems. Changing attitudes is the key issue. This is why it is important for staff who have to work together using a new approach to be able to run discussion groups. Examining the advantages and disadvantages of each organisation is one way of forging new attitudes and breathing life into a new institution.

The PATC and PNMU services organise joint training sessions for a range of professionals (teachers, carers, etc.) called upon to deal with disabled youngsters. They systematically join forces with other institutions for training purposes. However, the services do not have a joint database on the clients they share. During the current transition period, the governing boards of both bodies (the PATC and the hospital governing the PNMU) hold joint meetings where problems arising from the amalgamation can be aired and resolved.

The Outreach project is to have its own watchdog committee, including members of the community, employers and professionals as well as representatives from the services and government. Great care is taken when recording basic information on clients, and this will continue after the reform, but the information is destroyed as soon as the client stops using the service. It may nevertheless be shared with other institutions, with the client's agreement.

The Wabasca-Demarais project is run by a steering committee and various "*ad hoc*" committees that focus on specific problem areas. The inventory of community needs now being drawn up will be used to set top priorities for urgent attention. There will also be an evaluation based on statistics and client responses to a questionnaire. The emphasis is on communication to ensure that members of the community are well informed of the services available. Finally, there are also plans to set up a network and training programme for use by all of the services involved.

In Wetaskiwin, the steering committee organised a discussion workshop to define the goals of the project and the general purpose of the initiative. This led to a major shift in direction, namely to start focusing not only on children at risk but on children in general. Regular reports are sent to all elected representatives, colleagues and joint service groups to keep them better informed. Similarly, all kinds of information sessions were organised for the various population groups to win their collaboration and support.

For the moment, there is no single point of access to the various services. Initial efforts have been directed at regrouping services in a single location. For instance, anything to do with education is located in a school, legal services are grouped in one place, and so on. The Co-ordination of Services for Children initiative is thinking of grouping all services in local schools.

All the services or bodies organise review sessions for individual children's cases.

The justice and health services view it as essential to consult other bodies when introducing their training plans. Nurses, for instance, work with families but also with schools and Social Services staff; schools co-operate with the Wetoka Unit to develop programmes for children with special needs.

For the moment, however, there is no single admission file for use by all the services involved.

The various services are represented in a special body and in the Co-ordination of Services for Children initiative. Regular meetings take place between the assistant director for schools, the head of social services and the regional director in charge of placing children in care.

Joint service training sessions are arranged. For example, the Wetoka Health Unit helps to train school or hospital staff. Internal training sessions for the Justice Department and the Wetoka Unit are open to other professionals.

By and large, databanks are not operated on a joint basis, except in some completely informal cases. As for equipment, only the Wetoka Unit appears to offer free photocopying or typing services, and the school services co-ordinate transport, in particular for disabled children of kindergarten age.

The Wetaskiwin community relies heavily on the Co-ordination of Services for Children initiative to promote co-ordination. For the moment, the project is in its very early stages and there is room for improvement where co-ordination is concerned. Schools and social services, for instance, would do well to pool some of their resources.

By May 1994, several initiatives had been set up on a joint basis, namely a committee for the placement of children in care, a mental health service, as well as various liaison committees and school health services. All these services work on an interdisciplinary basis, in liaison with the community and aboriginal "band" representatives.

Positive and negative factors

In the Calgary Opening Doors initiative, emphasis has been put on the lack of time, since any study work, co-ordination meetings, etc., add to the daily workload.

Officials have also highlighted problems raised by structures, policy and funding methods that are occasionally incompatible from one tier of government to another (Federal, Provincial and Municipal). This seems to be one of the hardest obstacles to overcome. In many cases service rigidity stems from methods of funding and mandates for service delivery. Although considerable resources are available, they are often used to solve a particular type of problem rather than respond to the real needs of families and children. A single service cannot meet all these needs in any satisfactory way.

Furthermore, the various services divide their sectors up differently, and in some cases they overlap. This leads to organisational problems when seeking co-ordination. Red tape can also hamper attempts to make services more flexible. Finally, confidentiality is a problem, but more one of professional culture than a legal barrier.

The general fear – whether voiced or not – is disempowerment or the risk of seeing others "trespass" on one's territory. This is true for every level of responsibility and every post.

Success will not necessarily be visible immediately as the goal is systems change and motivation needs to be kept high all round. The support and commitment of senior officials are vital if sustainable commitment is to be fostered among the staff. In particular, they must be sure that there is no threat to jobs or status.

However, there are already some signs of success. Families appreciate being seen by a single person, especially where education is concerned. The head of services for children also feels that the prevention work now under way gives families greater satisfaction and is appreciated by the community. The police feel that they are already closer to the public and that crime is falling. The community is becoming a little more engaged in the process.

At the grassroots level too, the lack of time and human resources raises similar difficulties, but more emphasis is put on relational and communication problems among professionals, between professionals and the community, and between the various groups, committees and commissions that have been set up. In fact Huntington Hills (Calgary) publishes a regular magazine in an attempt to alleviate the problem. Other staff concerns relate to job stability and the way professions are defined in relation to other specialists and "non-specialists".

The same comments are made regarding the Edmonton project, namely the need for all concerned to develop a common vision and, through joint training or discussion sessions, acquire a better grasp of each other's fields and develop an internal and external communication policy.

The evaluation plan is still in the early stages and no conclusions can be drawn yet. Nevertheless, first impressions are positive. Surveys in schools and amongst the young reveal an improvement in academic achievement and pupils' attitudes. The young appear to have a greater sense of security in the community and in school. Greater efforts to prevent domestic violence are also appreciated.

Professionals find that their new methods are having a beneficial impact on the work they do outside the project itself, so much so that the city has received a large number of applications to set up other similar projects. However, red tape will have to be cut if the system is to become more widespread. Senior officials will also have to accept that their staff are innovating and working outside their normal mandates and will have to find new ways of evaluating and supporting them if internal conflicts arise.

In Lethbridge, there have also been communication problems, stemming partly from the lack of teachers on the pilot committee. Structural rigidity and also corporatism are mentioned as major obstacles to overcome, together with the fear of partial disempowerment. For instance, all service providers must be persuaded not to put children into rigid categories. This will mean a major – and difficult – change in attitudes. There is some doubt as to whether all those involved in the project are really driven by this desire for change, rather than just tempted by the financial benefits to be derived from such reform.

At the grassroots level, changes of direction are already emerging in operating methods and clientele. The FCDP now devotes 74 per cent of its work to service delivery, compared with the 65 per cent originally planned. There has also been a decline in liaison with the community and internal training. In the next few years, there is likely to be a decline in direct service delivery and an increase in prevention but, for the moment, the head of the medical team still devotes a lot of time – and overtime – to treatment. Costs per child have been rising since 1992. Schools remain the main source of referrals but have been referring fewer cases to the FCDP, as the waiting list is so long. The FCDP does however receive case referrals from elsewhere. Strong emphasis is put on the advantages to be expected from amalgamation and a change of location, one being better services to families who will have easier access. In particular, the new approach will give families more say, as many of them had requested. This advantage is particularly appreciated by families who have had dealings with the PNMU or the PATC, where they find themselves more closely involved in their children's treatment. The role played by schools requires clarification, since parents have pointed out liaison problems between schools and services, with schools not appearing to acknowledge or be aware of the expertise that the PATC in particular can bring them.

The difference in management methods between hospital and community services also raises problems. Furthermore, the amalgamation plans have run up against problems relating to the status of staff and the definition of their roles. These problems are delaying the launch of the scheme, in particular making any forward planning difficult, and this is a cause of concern to families.

The new centre will not be able to provide all the services required. Outside staff and other institutions will be called upon for psychological testing, assessment and social work. This will also be a cause of concern to staff.

The Outreach Programme has been drawn up as a positive alternative to the social costs generated by youth unemployment and lack of skills. However, doubts about future funding have not dispelled concern as to whether all the necessary services can be provided.

In Wabasca-Demarais, collaboration between the community and service providers has improved. However, the fact that many services in the community are run from outside the area raises problems when it comes to co-ordination. Finance becomes a problem when someone has to decide which level of government will pay for the services a child requires. The development of community awareness is, it would seem, crucial to improvement in co-ordination. The less attached to jurisdiction the services are, the more efficient they will be. All the resources could then be pooled, but this raises a political issue, as it means giving more power to the community. On the other hand, the community regards decentralisation with some suspicion as it could be a way of disguising budget cuts.

Wetaskiwin is facing possible salary problems in the near future, when all the professionals working together on the same cases and under the same conditions will want to be paid on the same basis. Locally too, there is concern about a change in relations and authority at the central and local levels. Will the Provincial Government manage to give up some control and support local governance for a whole range of initiatives?

Personal commitment from government departments is vital but varies from one individual to another. The problem is compounded by the presence of a large aboriginal community. Much store is being set on the evaluation now under way, which should help to move the initiative forward.

CONCLUSION

In Alberta, services of all kinds are very fragmented. They exist. They are very numerous. But this is the root of the problem, in particular for the most deprived who do not always know where to turn for the best and most effective solution to their problems. At the local level, there appears to be no clear list of all services, agencies and associations available or details of what they do. The need to clarify this and make these services more accessible and integrated is one of the main objectives of the Co-ordination of Services for Children initiative.

At the same time, it emerged that while services in a particular place were being provided by more than one institution, there were also gaps in service delivery. So the idea was to rationalise both the network itself and the costs incurred through poor organisation. Abundant and generous funding in earlier years probably had something to do with this situation, as services were devised to cater for needs as soon as they were perceived, without conducting any systematic prior assessment of the opportunities already available or changes that could be made to existing services. Frequent references have been made to this situation at all levels and there appears to be a consensus on the need to rationalise options and expenditure, given the general economic cutbacks imposed by most funding institutions.

Co-ordination of Services for Children is a highly coherent project, with the determination shown at higher, provincial government level matched by similar determination and drive in individual communities.

One cannot help but be struck by the desire for cohesion and communication shown in the way the initiative is organised – informing from the bottom up, explaining, giving people a say, while at the same time involving the most senior levels of authority. This willingness to let people voice their views and make those views widely available is also reflected in the way co-ordinated local services are organised, namely through the promotion and interlinkage of numerous pilot groups, *ad hoc* groups and committees.

Another substantial form of support was found at the Forum held in Autumn 1993. Each pilot site was able to present its project and discuss any problems with the other communities involved in Co-ordination of Services for Children. They were able to suggest potential solutions to one another or to officials from the Provincial Government. Factors such as a feeling of not being isolated, the opportunity of sharing problems and ideas with others, the perception too that central government really was interested, created an atmosphere of motivation and encouragement for all those involved.

In all of these projects, the initiatives devised at the provincial level clearly coincide with new or long-standing local initiatives. The sites were well chosen and receptive. There may have been very strong pressure from the community on the Federal or Provincial Government for these projects to be launched.

Furthermore, local initiatives were reinforced and boosted in that their objectives and the spirit in which they were undertaken were supported and encouraged by the Provincial Government. The involvement and backing of senior provincial officials is generally seen as key to the scheme's success. The changes were therefore bound to be facilitated since Provincial Government direction was in line with needs and determination at the grassroots level.

"Changing the way we do business", in particular tightening up the network of services and preventing any overlapping, raises a twofold problem of human resource management:

– Redefining positions means redeploying staff and resources, and in some cases this may lead to redundancies. For 1994-95, the plan is to cut central staff costs by 5 per cent. The same also applies at local level.

– Either new jobs descriptions have to be drawn up, or staff will have to learn to change their methods and attitudes to work. This implies a planned effort to re-train staff.

Such work requires openness on everyone's part towards other people, to their methods, language and professional culture. For instance, everyone must be clear about what they understand by "client", as some services give a narrower connotation to the term than others. For the Ministry of Health, it means the whole community, whereas for Social Services the target group, or "clientele" is more specific and restricted.

The various committees already appear to have overcome preconceptions and obstacles, which have in fact proved to be much weaker than first feared. This has forged or strengthened mutual trust and respect. On the sensitive issue of confidentiality in particular, such a change of attitudes does seem to have made useful progress, indicating that – provided certain precautions were taken – there was more scope for sharing information than was initially thought possible. Frequent mention has been made of the work involved and the impact that the new system might have on the jobs of health and social services staff. Teachers have been mentioned much less often, although there have been references to schools. Administrative officials or school principals appear to be much more involved than teaching staff, who do not seem to have participated much at all in the general debate or in questioning teaching methods under the new system.

The new way of doing business may substantially change the working lives of staff and, in spite of efforts to train and inform, concerns persist or are emerging as to whether jobs will be maintained and skills acknowledged. It has been confirmed that skilled specialists will still be needed, but there are frequent references to the need for less skilled staff, or "non-specialists"; and jobs are having to be redefined as they open up to cover a larger field, in some cases giving the impression of encroaching on those of others. Staff involved in the initiative are therefore in an ambiguous situation and require understanding and support from superiors and colleagues alike.

In any event, it is all the more crucial to have the backing of politicians and senior officials since the reform will involve regulatory and organisational change. Even if, as some would have it, this is less important than changing attitudes, the problem must be faced, otherwise it may aggravate existing problems or serve as an excuse for those who are hostile to the change.

Another key factor in the initiative is decentralisation of resources and decision-making. The need to move closer to grassroots can be explained by the wish to focus more on the "client" and the need for individuals and the community alike to become more responsible for determining service delivery. It is quite a sweeping move, since a number of powers are being transferred from federal to provincial level. But the transfer from provincial to the community level tends to provoke two questions, namely "is there some hidden motive for the transfer of authority?" and "will the community actually get the powers and funding it really needs?"

The importance of the community is further reinforced by the fact that it is frequently seen as the right level for introducing co-ordinated services with a single point of access. In the cases in hand, schools were often seen as the ideal place for these "new-style" services. But sometimes there were clearly doubts on this point and it was queried whether schools should in fact be opened up to the public at large. In such cases the community was then given preference over schools.

By and large, there has been no special funding to help organise these pilot schemes. Any additional resources found for some initiatives or institutions are the result of redistributing resources among the various services, depending on the view taken by those in charge, once requirements had been assessed and the local system fully or partially reorganised. All this seems to have been done on a completely informal basis.

A transitional period is inevitable. Service reorganisation and rationalisation should normally lead to savings on some services thus releasing more resources for others. In the meantime, project heads have to get by with the resources at their disposal or apply for outside support. For instance, some foundations have been able to find funds on a provisional basis to cover the cost of the new services during the transition period.

So funding is not always – and never will be – straightforward, and this could give rise to misunderstandings or even tension, to the extent that it impairs the image of the development project presented to "clients".

What is important is the shift to a policy based on prevention, which will affect budget options. Here again, it should be possible to eliminate certain major social costs and so cut the cost of acute crisis care by an equal amount. How long this interim phase will last, of course, remains uncertain.

The projects making up the experimental base for the Co-ordination of Services for Children in Alberta initiative are all very recent and, while it has been possible to discuss the problems encountered and perceived, it is still too early to say what conclusions will be drawn by the evaluation now under way. However, here are some of the benefits to be derived from co-ordinating services:

- better mutual understanding between the services involved and between Provincial and Local Government;
- less compartmentalisation of services;
- satisfaction on the part of parents and professionals;
- better access to services;
- the involvement of most stakeholders, and at every level;
- better care for children; and
- more responsiveness to the actual needs of children and their families.

However, difficulties do remain, including:

- problems of authority involving individuals and institutions;
- differences of approach and departmental culture;
- the time and energy given to the many meetings required at every level to discuss and deal with problems;
- uncertainty about funding and hence about whether all the services needed to treat and follow-up every case will be maintained or introduced; and
- problems involving regulations and professional ethics.

Given such widespread commitment, it is to be hoped that solutions to these problems, already acknowledged at every level, will eventually be found. The partial evaluations expected over the next two years of experimentation should help avoid pitfalls and present recommendations for solutions as the province as a whole moves towards integrated community-based services.

ONTARIO

INTEGRATING SERVICES IN CANADA'S WEALTHIEST PROVINCE

by

Richard Volpe, Peter Evans and Philippa Hurrell

INTRODUCTION

This report is a descriptive evaluation of three prime examples of integrated services for children in Ontario, Canada. The examples are drawn from an ongoing programme and two demonstration projects which provide services to different age groups of at risk children and youth, and their families. These programmes are the Waterloo County Education-Work Connection Demonstration Project which serves youth aged 12-16; the Sudbury Better Beginnings, Better Futures Project which focuses on children aged 4-8; and the Integrated Services for Northern Children (ISNC) Programme which provides services to children aged 0-18. Accompanying the three case studies is a brief discussion of the circumstances and policy history of efforts to provide integrated social, health and educational services to at risk children and families in Ontario. The case studies include information from programme materials, evaluation reports, and interviews with policy makers, programme managers, staff and clients.

GENERAL CONTEXT

One third of Canada's population resides in Ontario. Twenty-seven per cent of those residing in Ontario are under the age of 19 (Statistics Canada, 1993). Although Ontario is Canada's leading manufacturing province, growth in heavy industry has declined considerably over the last ten years. Youth have been one of the most negatively impacted groups by the major recession that has gripped the province since the late 1980s. The current economic circumstances have resulted in reduced public spending and have been an incentive to develop co-ordinated services that reduce duplication and are more cost-effective.

As dollars for services have declined, the needs of children have increased. About 18 per cent of children between the ages of 4 and 16 have been identified as having a conduct disorder and are at risk of social and academic failure (Offord and Boyle, 1987). Some 10-15 per cent of school age children have been identified as having some type of learning difficulty, and approximately 23 per cent of youth (aged 15-24) are considered at risk of dropping out of school.

Youth are the only group in the labour market experiencing both declines in employability and relatively high unemployment rates. The unemployment rate for Ontario youth was 18.7 per cent (59 000) in 1993. This figure is twice the national unemployment total of 9.3 per cent. That is, youth make up 16 per cent of Ontario's labour force and represent 30 per cent of those unemployed. Although they are the largest single source of new entrants into the labour force, they are most at risk of dependency on social assistance.

POLICY INPUTS

Since the late 1970s, the Ontario government has sought to reform children's services through integration, the involvement of local communities in planning, the clarification of accountability, and the use of comprehensive information systems in planning and evaluation. Most important in this undertaking has been an emphasis on human service needs rather than professional services.

The resolution of many issues that arise from co-ordination initiatives involves the development of interagency protocols, bringing together laws that affect children under a consistent statute, and the development of a unified policy and planning framework. Some specific strategies for integration have been the use of multi-service centres (i.e. community schools and one stop shops); multi-agency protocols; omnibus statues; and the actual amalgamation of departments and agencies. Ontario's commitment to these approaches is exemplified in the document, "Investing in Children" (Ontario Ministry of Community and Social Services, 1988), which has provided a basis for current services integration initiatives. The report out-lined a corporate plan enabling relevant sectors of government to focus on child development, health, treatment and intervention. Although the document asserted that *interministerial* co-operation was important, like the current planning framework, it only provided impetus for *intraministerial* integration.

Further support for integrating services has come from two high profile policy reviews. The Report of the Advisory Committee on Children Services, entitled "Children First" (1990), set out an explicit cross ministry integrated service delivery plan. Drawing on Edward Zigler's notion of the school as the hub of services, this proposal set forth a new plan for the comprehensive provision of services, which were claimed to be entitlements. This document was reinforced by the Report of the Premier's Health Council, "Yours, Mine and Ours: Ontario's Children and Youth" (1994). This report reviewed what is known from theory and research about major life transitions and concluded that the facts of human development require cross ministry collaboration. More recently, the Royal Commission on Learning (1994) called for sweeping reforms that include increased participation of parents and community agencies, and greater integration of services, in Ontario schools.

Ontario has passed legislation that supports and complicates integration efforts. The government enacted the Child and Family Services Act (CFSA) in 1984, to bring a wide range of children's services under a flexible funding envelope and one set of legal requirements. This legislation has helped to establish a common set of service principles, definitions, expectations, and funding and accountability requirements. Although the Education Act (1980) does not mention school collaboration with social and health services, many school boards do collaborate with them. The Act allows school boards to construct and operate day care facilities. It also enables schools to provide teachers and cover their costs in social and health services treatment programmes. The Young Offender's Act (1984) changed the minimum age of admission to the adult courts from 16 to 18. This legislation has created difficulties in the division of authority between the Ministry of Community and Social Services and the Ministry of the Solicitor General and Correctional Services. Now the two ministries must work together on cases involving young offenders under the age of 18, and have to co-ordinate social and economic support services and incarceration and supervision services for them.

In April of 1993, the Ministry of Community and Social Services (MCSS) announced a series of new policy directions for children's services funded under the Child and Family Services Act. The new Children's Services Policy Framework (CSPF) consists of six directions for change or development in the current system of MCSS-funded services for children. These are integration, co-ordinated access, enhanced local planning, equity in resource distribution, the establishment of priority groups, and enhanced accountability. Since the initial announcement of the policy, MCSS policy makers, in co-operation with other stakeholders, have been working to provide information on the specific changes it will require in the organisation and delivery of children's services.

WHY IS SERVICES INTEGRATION SO DIFFICULT TO ACHIEVE IN ONTARIO?

The pattern of administration of children's services in Ontario has been one of separate ministries functioning in relative isolation from one another. Although some attempts have been made to rationalise the system (such as the transfer of responsibility for children's mental health services from the Ministry of Health to the Ministry of Community and Social Services), the traditional division of responsibility among ministries has persisted. The Ministry of Community and Social Services is responsible for the provision of all child protection services, most children's mental health services, services for the developmentally handicapped and most services for young offenders; the Ministry of Health is responsible for the provision of institutionally-based health services for children (and adults), community-based physical rehabilitation services and public health services; and, the Ministry of Education and Training is responsible for the provision of all basic education and most special education services for children.

The Ministry of Community and Social Services has a history of creating and funding isolated children's services (*i.e.* Children's Aid Societies, Children's Mental Health Centres, associations and programmes for developmentally disabled persons, and programmes and services for young offenders). The Ministry of Health has created and funded separate institutional and community-based sectors of health care. The Ministry of Education and Training has funded most special education services through autonomous school boards. Services for children and youth are currently located in several ministries, hundreds of local authorities, and over a thousand agencies. Each has its own mandate, catchment area, resources, and accountability mechanisms. No provincial or national policies exist that provide coherence to the myriad of programmes that exist for children and families. The main barriers to services integration are the different areas of authority, funding mechanisms, and management structures of ministries that often serve the same clients. The current organisation of children's services is in both design and operation very far from any form of coherent delivery system.

THE CURRENT STATE OF SERVICES INTEGRATION POLICY IN ONTARIO

The current economic situation and the consequent fiscal crisis have exacerbated the necessity to move from planning to implementation of province wide co-ordinated services that are more effective and less costly. The current policy context for children services reflects this situation. The 1994 Children's Services Policy Framework adopted by the Ministry of Community and Social Services is an integrationist plan for services that was the result of consultations and recommendations from working groups, consumers and communities. At the core of the Children's Services Policy Framework is the mission to create a system of services, funded by the initiative, which ensures that children and their families benefit to the greatest extent possible from available resources. The new Children's Services Policy Framework explicitly recognises that changes will be required in many current service delivery processes and structures, and is intended to influence the deployment of hundreds of millions of dollars of public money on an annual basis.

The Ministry of Education and the Ministry of Health have developed parallel policies in regard to services integration for children and families although they are less explicit. The Report of the Royal Commission on Learning, "For the Love of Learning" (1994), clearly sets out proposals and strategies for opening schools to greater community influence and making them the hub of integrated services. The expectation at this point, however, is that successful within-ministry efforts at integration and several well conceived and supported shared pilot projects will provide the basis for future changes in the direction of increased integration of children's services.

The government of Ontario shows evidence of a strong long-term intention to integrate services. The government appears aware that gaps exist in the way services are currently organised and that many children fall through them. There also is a good understanding amongst policy-makers of current models of human growth and development which stress the importance of considering the needs of the whole child and the vital influence of both the micro- and macro-environments in which children and their families live. Government reports and reviews on integration conclude that it is one way of creating "a more effective and comprehensive service system based on equity" that "is consistent with the goals of healthy child development in which each individual is enabled to develop to his/her potential by providing services as needed".

In an apparent effort to "do more with less", the Ontario government has as its long-term goal the integration of children's services. The implications of such an aim in a period of financial restraint and insecurity has, however, brought massive resistance to change of any sort. There is a suspicion that integration is a euphemism for amalgamation designed not to improve services but to create savings through job cutting. This suspicion has created strong opposition from labour and professional associations. These factors have conspired against the attainment of widespread services integration. The best the Ontario government has been able to achieve is to demonstrate the benefits of integration in a number of special projects. The three projects to be reviewed here constitute exemplary initiatives in this field. Each project represents an effort to support collaboration and co-ordination between education, health and social service ministries. The projects to be described include provision for preschool children, school children and youth in the transition to work, and families of children and youth at risk.

Integration is clearly part of the Ontario policy agenda. The three exemplary programmes reviewed here are organised to represent three different levels of integration (least to most integrated) as described by Swan and Morgan (1993). The Eastwood Project manifests the characteristics of effective co-operation among community agencies. The Sudbury Project exemplifies a community co-ordinating its activities with local services and agencies. The Cochrane/Timiskaming Project illustrates full scale, cross-agency collaboration.

WATERLOO COUNTY EDUCATION-WORK CONNECTION DEMONSTRATION PROJECT

Context

Waterloo county is located in the heart of Southern Ontario and contains the urban areas of Kitchener-Waterloo and Cambridge and the rural townships of Wellesley, Wilmot, North Dumfries and Elmira. It has a population of approximately 387 000. The region's economy is based on a blend of agriculture, business and industry. It can best be described as a middle-class area in terms of income and socio-economic status. The community also has two universities and a community college, and is served by two school boards, one for public school pupils and the other for Roman Catholic students.

There is widespread concern about the student drop out rate which has reached a level of around 11 per cent in the province as a whole. This has stimulated the Ministry of Education to develop policies intended to remove barriers to school efforts to retain students. The reduction of school violence has been seen as a way of maintaining school attendance. Consequently, many school boards have adopted "zero tolerance of aggression" polices. The implementation of these polices has involved the co-ordination of efforts by schools, police and the criminal justice system, to find alternative placements for offending pupils.

The Ontario Ministry of Skills Development (1992) has projected that, by the year 2000, 63 per cent of new jobs in Canada will require more than a grade 12 education. However, the Economic Council of Canada (1992) reported that, in this decade, if present drop out trends continue, Canada's schools will send another one million young people who are functionally illiterate into the work force. Unchecked, current drop-out rates imply an unacceptable loss of human potential, higher social costs, and a serious deficit in the supply of skills needed to expand employment productivity and incomes for all Canadians. The Leaving School Study (1992), commissioned under the federal Stay-in-School initiative, confirmed that "compared with high school graduates, those who do not complete high school have greater chances of unemployment and reduced earnings". The report also suggests that dropping out is linked to crime, delinquency, substance abuse, economic dependency and a lower quality of life.

Each year, hundreds of students in the Waterloo community leave school before completing high school and join the millions of young people who are looking for work but do not possess the skills to guarantee them a job. Some of these students are disillusioned with school because they see no connection between what they learn in school and how this will prepare them for work. Other students are socially disadvantaged and receive no moral support from home.

Thus collectively the challenge is how to deal with a group of students who have tremendous potential, but whose needs go beyond what the school system currently can offer through its regular programmes. These students are not academically driven. In the past students in this situation left school and went to work. Now students have nowhere other than school to go to. Many of them do not fit into the present educational system which is academic, time-based and specialised. As a result they often switch credits, change programmes, and move to different schools, but seldom does this work because they remain in a narrow academic environment. They fall further behind their peer group and their frustration grows.

The Eastwood Collegiate Institute initiative in Waterloo County, as described below, provides a good replicable model that integrates both school and community supports for the purpose of keeping students engaged in the process of acquiring the knowledge, skills and attitudes needed to be successful in the 21st century.

Input

In Waterloo County, a co-ordinated approach to service provision is being developed. The county's two school boards, public and Roman Catholic, meet regularly to investigate areas of common concern and currently share some transportation arrangements and programmes. They also jointly develop procedures to address provincially mandated programmes such as Employment Equity initiatives. The Waterloo Public School Board works co-operatively with a variety of other agencies in the area, including Family Services, the Regional Health Unit, and the Waterloo Regional Police, to provide a continuum of services for students. Public administrators of the universities, hospitals, municipalities and school boards meet on a regular basis to investigate ways of sharing resources.

The Board has worked closely with the Eastwood Collegiate Institute. The Eastwood Collegiate Institute is a composite high school with a population of 1 398 students ranging in age from 13-19. There is a ratio of 718 males to 680 females at this school. The pupil/teacher ratio is 15:1. Eastwood is one of 16 high schools in the Waterloo area. Most of its student population comes from middle and lower-middle socio-economic backgrounds.

In looking for alternative programmes to reduce drop-outs, the Board has recognised the importance of community involvement and has encouraged the use of mentors in the school to help at risk students. In addition, a grants officer works with the Federal Government, foundations and corporations to obtain additional resources. The Excellence in Education initiative has manifested itself in a Stay-in-School Programme for potential drop-outs. This includes an Attendance Works component which encourages employers within the region to offer summer employment to students with perfect attendance. Also, there are incentives to parents to read to their children as well as rewards and recognition for the students. A classroom within the City of Kitchener's Municipal offices has been set up to allow at risk students to combine academic study with on-the-job work experience in City Departments.

The Board of Education provides psychological and social services to the school while the Regional Government provides health services. With school staff, both services are involved in planning an Eating Disorder Programme facilitated by a case manager (school guidance counsellor) who follows agreed procedures and orchestrates the programme.

Both psychological and social services are located in an Education Centre. However, child welfare agencies are located elsewhere. Child welfare staff are allocated to schools and join forces with personnel in the Education Centre to deliver programmes. Even though services for students are school-based, service providers often are located off-site.

There is support from the Ministry of Education and Training for this co-operative approach, although the Ministry also is interested in creating one stop shops in rural areas. In practice, it has been found that integrating two services such as child care and kindergarten at one site (*e.g.* in a community school) is not so difficult, but integrating three or four services is hard. Bringing services together is difficult mainly because agencies have different sources of funding.

Process

At present, the integration of services in Waterloo County is at the level of co-operation. Leadership, as shown by staff at Eastwood, is essential in working through the system (inside and outside the school) to effect change. Any further developments, such as the amalgamation of services, are for the Provincial government to decide. The risk in developing further integration is that it will increase layers of bureaucracy. In Waterloo, an attempt is made to balance co-ordination with innovation from front-line educators. Part of this involves regular meetings with other agencies for case reviews and planning in areas such as special education.

Although schools in Waterloo do not share professional resources with other agencies or jointly hire staff, there are collective agreements making it possible to employ social workers instead of teachers or other staff. This policy has been set up very carefully, and has been achieved through negotiation and attrition of staff. It has led to greater co-operation between services in the region and to the development of case work in schools. As a result, it has become easier to address the problems of street children and truants, to liaise with the courts, and to identify alternative education placements. However, more groups (especially students, parents and business) need to be included in integrated initiatives like this.

The Eastwood Comprehensive Alternative Education Programme Model began in 1990 as a "transition years" project. It comprises a co-operative education programme, a mentorship programme and a needs assessment procedure (see below). It was developed in association with the community to mobilise all services within the school (*i.e.* guidance, special education, library, co-operative education and administration), and to find ways of bringing community partners into the school to support student learning during transition periods. Its primary goal is to induce change and improvement in students' attitudes and understanding of themselves and the world. It is hoped that these changes will lead to a more satisfying life for students and will help them to remain in school until graduation.

The co-operative education programme: Students combine academic study with a graduated co-operative education programme intended to help them to develop the skills, attitudes and knowledge required for work. The co-operative education programme has three components. The first component is a cross-age tutoring placement, as part of which students work as tutors in elementary feeder school classrooms. The second component is a placement in a non-profit or community agency. The third constituent is a placement which the student is allowed to choose, and normally is in the commercial sector (*e.g.* in a retail store, bicycle repair shop or radio station).

The mentorship programme: As part of this programme, students are supported by mentors, who are either senior citizens or representatives of companies that provide workplacement experiences. The senior citizens' role is to relate to students as advisors and to help them develop a sense of community. Senior citizens of both sexes can become mentors. They are difficult to find and, out of 200 applicants, only seven are active. They are volunteers who are retired and have been notably successful in their own lives. This linking of the generations is a very crucial part of the programme. The inter-generational nature of the mentorship adds a dimension that allows the students to relate to experienced, understanding, helpful people who are not teachers and can listen in a different way from teachers. The corporate aspect of the mentorship programme has been developed jointly with the school's business partner, the Mutual Group. Corporate mentors work in local companies. Profiles are developed of twenty to thirty students, and a similar number of mentors, to make a match. They meet for six weeks on the school site. The mentors spend one hour per week with an identified at risk pupil offering "support, guidance and consistency as a role model buddy and friend". The students are exposed to the work that the mentor does, and are involved in a range of activities, including recreation, course planning, and social skills training. The mentor also serves as the corporation's business-education partnership link.

The needs assessment procedure: Following a decision in Ontario to de-stream classrooms, an additional component to the programme was added. This is a needs assessment procedure intended to identify students who need one-to-one academic support in a particular subject area.

To reduce the drop-out rate, a Buddy System for Niners has been implemented, where higher grade students are teamed with grade 9 students to help them with school work (cross-age tutoring). A peer mediation programme is planned which will complement the work of counsellors who are still seen as representing authority. Individual students can either consult with guidance counsellors or employ computerised career counselling.

Eastwood also works with community services such as hospitals, the police, universities, and child and family services. And within the school, there are a variety of activities planned by the student council to create a sense of community (e.g. Special Days such as its car rally, the Spring Fling, the Winterfest, carolling, and intramural sports).

Product

Eastwood was described by students as safe and comfortable. Moreover, they related that it had good teachers who provided opportunities to make meaningful choices. They even felt that many activities such as clubs were fun. Nevertheless the lack of involvement of these students in the school can be illustrated by their lack of knowledge about the structure of student governance. One graduate described why he did not take part in all of the school's activities: "I guess I was really a shy person, and the type that if no one is going to come up to me and ask me to join something, I'm not going to go out of my way for it". This student suggests making the extra activities more accessible to students like himself. One student described the school's guidance counsellors as "understanding, sympathetic and helpful," while another student described them as "formal and impersonal."

The Eastwood Comprehensive Alternative Education Programme Model has been successful, with 90 per cent of participants staying in school and finding work. Clearly the programme attempts to support at risk pupils in many significant aspects of their life inside and outside the school, including fulfilling personal emotional needs and the need for stability.

THE SUDBURY BETTER BEGINNINGS, BETTER FUTURES PROJECT

Context

Sudbury is a medium-sized Ontario city. Known as the gateway to the North, it has in recent years struggled to shake off its dependence on a declining mining industry The population of Sudbury is made up of large native, French speaking, and new Canadian communities.

The Sudbury project involves two adjacent neighbourhoods that locally are known together as the Donovan-Flour Mill. The Flour Mill area is mostly French speaking. The Flour Mill was named after grain silos that provide a distinct area marker. The Donovan area is multicultural, with mainly English speaking European and native families. The project offers programmes in both French and English. In 1986, 4 000 children lived in these largely lower socio-economic status Sudbury neighbourhoods. At that time, 48 per cent of these children spoke English, 38 per cent French, and 14 per cent another language. Approximately 1 in 10 were native children.

The project began in January 1991. The focus of the project is on 4-8 year-old children and their families. Funding for the project comes from the Ministry of Community and Social Services, government agencies, foundations, the federal government, and community sources. It is part of a large-scale province-wide demonstration project called Better Beginnings, Better Futures.

The Better Beginnings, Better Futures Project is a major seven-year interministerial initiative involving the Ministries of Health, Education and Training, and Community and Social Services, and the federal Department of Indian and Northern Affairs. The Project began in 1990. Enough funding was committed to the project to last for five years. Recent allocations have extended the initial commitment. As part of an evaluation, the Ministry of Community and Social Services will provide funds to follow the children into their mid-twenties. Twelve primary prevention demonstration projects in economically disadvantaged communities are involved. Each includes a plan for a comprehensive twenty-year evaluation of the emotional and behavioural development of participating children in two age groups: 0-4 years and 4-8 years. To qualify for funding, communities had to design a community development plan and an integrated model of service planning.

The goals of the project are:

- to prevent serious social, emotional, behavioural, physical and cognitive problems in children;
- to promote the social, emotional, behavioural, physical and cognitive of children;
- to enhance the abilities of socio-economically disadvantaged families and communities to provide for their children.

The legal and administrative sponsor of the Sudbury Project is the N'Swakamok Native Friendship Centre. After April 1, 1995 the newly incorporated Better Beginnings, Better Futures Association will assume all legal and administrative responsibilities for the project. From the programmes beginning, this Association has been responsible for programme development. Membership of the Association is open to anyone who lives in the community and accepts its principles. Associate memberships are available to individuals outside the community.

The project was conceived in 1989 by a committee made up of representatives from the Friendship Centre, the Children's Mental Health Services, the Laurentian University, the Sudbury Board of Education, the John Howard Society, SHARE (the public housing tenants' association), the Sudbury District Housing Authority, the Public Health Unit and the Multicultural Folk Arts Association. The Association has from its beginning operated through participation and consensus. There was a clear commitment to create processes and structures that were not controlled by experts but created by those people who lived or worked closely with children (Reitsman-Street, 1994). The project seeks to represent the native, Francophone, and English cultures of the community. Organisations that provide services for the neighbourhood are represented on a Community Advisory Board. Community involvement has been a major focus of ongoing formative descriptive evaluation.

The articulated vision of the Association is to promote a healthy environment through community decision making that includes and responds to traditional services in organisational forms that are equitable and culturally appropriate.

Input

It is significant that 26 of the 30 staff members associated with the project live in the Donovan-Flour Mill neighbourhood. Therefore project moneys are retained in the community. These community workers and volunteers are at the heart of efforts to build a caring neighbourhood. They work in a variety of ways to support and develop the neighbourhood's capacity to look after its own needs. They go about the business of earning a living, taking care of children, getting an education, and trying to enjoy and make sense out of life as part of the community. Unlike most low income communities, this area is trying to develop, organise and implement services which are controlled and operated by community members. Leadership is developed and resources are garnered by the Sudbury Better Beginnings Project so that programme ownership is retained by the community and a sense of accomplishment and enablement is fostered. The following section describes each of the special programmes designed by the community to serve its collective needs. Each day approximately 150 children and their parents participate in some aspect of the programme.

Process

Community development activities: A Community Advisory Committee has been established to ease communications and facilitate positive working relationships between residents and professionals. Committee members include the Chief of Police, the Mayor, the Executive Directors of the Children's Aid Society and Child and Family Centre, and the Medical Health Officer. Members and agency partners are involved in most special projects. These include work in areas of community interest such as health, education, work and ecology.

Community development involves community direction and control. Leadership development and training are key elements of the Project's activities. Visits with residents and membership recruitment are ongoing. Non-residents who share the Project's vision are encouraged to join. Child care, First Aid and other special forms of training are also provided.

The re-greening of the neighbourhood is a visible part of the community's renewal. Garden planting, yard and park cleanups, and landscaping, have been undertaken to increase the liveability and safety of the community. A foundation grant has made it possible for the Project to hire a project naturalist to facilitate these sorts of activities.

Activities such as special interest workshops, participatory theatre, advocacy, and conflict resolution training, are fostered for recreation and skill building. These sorts of experiences increase group identification and cohesion. Special funds were used to hire a teen facilitator to develop the Learning Centre and obtain stable financial support.

Community economic development: In 1993, the Project created an organisation called GEODE (Grassroots Economic Opportunity Development and Evaluation) to increase the economic viability of the neighbourhood. A barter system and skills exchange programme has increased community participation and served a variety of needs. These activities show the usefulness of micro-economic co-operative activities.

The Better Beginnings Association: With the incorporation of the Better Beginnings Association in April 1995, the Project will be taking a major step toward achieving one of its major goals, the establishment of an independent community-based organisation. The membership has elected a council of thirteen to develop this new organisation.

School development: Members of the community have articulated their concerns about schools and their relationship to the community. To increase cultural sensitivity, a native parent group has been formed. Native, Afro-Canadian, and Latin American cultural programmes that include craft, music and lore, have been developed in four schools. A Playground Peacemakers Programme has been initiated in some schools.

Parent support: Rent free use of a City of Sudbury facility enables special multicultural recreation programmes to take place. Arts, crafts, food preparation, skating, and a variety of co-operative games are provided. Child care programmes based on co-operative activities have been set up in some schools. Afternoon visits to residential developments enable parents and young children to have an opportunity to join other community members in a range of activities. A parent booklet explaining the Project has been developed to encourage their involvement. Community workers do home visits and help parents to participate in the Project. A Teen Mom's Drop In and a Parent Support Centre have been established. Camping experiences and summer programmes mix outdoor activities with field and beach trips, environmental education, art, and summer sports.

Product

Although the longitudinal aspect of the research associated with the Better Beginnings, Better Futures Project is still being planned, the on-site researchers have carefully documented the development of the Project, the process of fostering community participation, and some early positive outcomes (such as a sense of belonging and community identification). Moreover, impressive math and reading score results have been connected to the Project's school programmes.

COCHRANE/TIMISKAMING INTEGRATED SERVICES FOR NORTHERN CHILDREN PROJECT

Context

With almost 90 per cent of Ontario's land mass yet only 10 per cent of its population, Northern Ontario presents a formidable challenge for the delivery of professional services. Consequently, the region has suffered from a lack of services for children. Children in rural or remote regions are particularly underserved. Services that are taken for granted in Southern Ontario are unobtainable for many children. Geographic obstacles to the delivery of traditional children's services were one of the main reasons for the development of the Integrated Services for Northern Children (ISNC) Programme. For example, prior to the implementation of the ISNC Programme, a parent who lived in a rural/remote part of Northern Ontario may have had to drive or fly several hundred kilometres with their child in order to obtain a psychological or speech assessment.

The children most negatively affected by this situation are children with multiple difficulties who must be served by a number of professionals who cross service ministry funding divisions and agency mandates.

Input

Because of a growing recognition of these issues throughout Ontario, the Ministry of Community and Social Services underwent a reorganisation in 1978 in an attempt "to consolidate children's services and to improve the co-ordination across programme streams". To address the situation in the North, a committee was formed (consisting of senior ministry managers in Northern Ontario), and was charged with the responsibility of developing long range strategies. This new committee appointed a number of ministry staff to a Northern Assessment Task Force. The basic premises upon which the Northern Assessment Task Force was based included a desire to maximise interministerial co-ordination and interagency and interprofessional co-operation at the level of the individual case. Although the Northern Assessment Task Force initially was comprised of Ministry of Community and Social Services and Ministry of Education staff, it was recognised that the involvement of the Ministry of Health was required and some of their staff members were added to the group. The first concrete result of the inter-ministerial efforts of the Northern Assessment Task Force was the creation of an interministerial protocol that clearly specified each ministry's responsibilities regarding assessment services for children, and that set the stage for later developments.

The Northern Assessment Task Force operated from 1980 to 1987, accomplishing many important tasks including a survey of Northern Ontario-based children's services providers and a pilot test of a co-ordinated assessment programme in the Timiskaming District. The lessons learned from this Task Force eventually lead to the creation and approval of the Northern Initiatives Policy in early 1988. The major outcome of this new policy was the approval, by the Ontario Cabinet, of annual funding for implementation of a new children's services programme which became known as Integrated Services for Northern Children (ISNC). The ISNC Programme represented a systematic and ongoing response by the Ontario government to the need for services integration identified by the work of the Northern Assessment Task Force. The integrated service delivery and management models selected for implementation in the ISNC programme were chosen carefully through a review of "best practice". The new funding approved for the ongoing operation of the ISNC Programme was specifically dedicated to the delivery of services for children and their families in rural/remote regions of Northern Ontario. The result of these developments was the creation of a system of integrated services (i.e. assessments, interventions and consultations concerning children's mental health, physical rehabilitation and special education) for children who resided in the rural/remote areas of Northern Ontario.

Process

The Integrated Services for Northern Children Programme, which has been in operation across rural/remote Northern Ontario since early 1990, is a working model for interagency and interministerial collaboration. It is intended to improve service access in remote and underserviced areas, using a network of satellite workers who are based in rural/remote communities and who are linked to urban-based Resource Groups comprised of professionals from different disciplines (e.g. psychology, special education and physiotherapy). The rural/remote community-based satellite workers are the key to the ISNC Programme, serving as single entry-points for all referrals and as case managers for all children and families accepted by the ISNC Programme. The client groups consist of children at risk and their parents who are located in rural/remote communities in Northern Ontario. As noted earlier, those who live in the urban areas of Northern Ontario are not eligible for the services provided by the ISNC Programme. Many children have needs in special education, physical rehabilitation and mental health. The aims of the programme are to provide a more effective and fully integrated service for children with special needs. The result is the best chance for many children to reach their full potential. It is funded through the ministries of Community and Social Services, Health, and Education and Training. The service providers involved include: psychiatrists, psychologists and psychometrists (funded by Ministry of Community and Social Services); speech pathologists, physiotherapists and occupational therapists (funded by the Ministry of Health); and teacher diagnosticians (funded by the Ministry of Education and Training). All three ministries provide administrative support staff as well. Senior managers from each of the three ISNC-sponsoring ministries along with staff from the Ministry of Northern Development and

Mines also directly participate in the ISNC Programmes as members of interministerial management committees which are responsible for monitoring and evaluating the ongoing operations of the ISNC Programme. The programme has been running since 1990. More than 6 000 children have benefited from the programme since its inception.

Many factors impacted on the implementation of the Integrated Services for Northern Children Programme including the creation and empowerment of new inter-ministerial management structures; the requirement that programme implementation and operation be formally evaluated; the allocation of new financial resources to the programme; and the decision to fund each of the six sites equally despite major differences in rural/remote population sizes. Furthermore, an initial decision was made about which groups or organisations would be invited to participate in the new programme; it was decided that the new programme would serve rural/remote areas only; and, it was agreed that every effort would be made to advance politically mandated inter-ministerial co-ordination and integration.

Of the six Integrated Services for Northern Children sites, the Cochrane/Timiskaming site has produced the best outcomes according to the Project's evaluation criteria. The final report of ISNC programme implementation cited this site as the best overall example of ISNC Programme operations and observed that in many instances this site provided "benchmarks" against which other sites could be compared.

The Cochrane/Timiskaming area is mostly rural with a low population density. A few towns, varying in size between 400 and 7 000 inhabitants, are scattered along the major northern highway. Timmins is the largest town with a population of 45 000. Although the Cochrane/Timiskaming site headquarters are in Timmins, as noted earlier, the residents of this urban area are not eligible for ISNC services. The total number of inhabitants in Cochrane/Timiskaming is 100 000. This is the second largest rural/remote population in the programme with 20 per cent of the Ontario North Region's population. Another characteristic of this area is the relatively high percentage of French speaking inhabitants. Special cultural and language needs are an especially challenging aspect of assessment and service delivery in any underserved community.

This site operates as intended insofar as clear priority is given to children with multiple problems that require services from across ministry divisions. The Project's workers have been able to avoid competing with and duplicating already existing services. The team developed at this site is cohesive and well managed. The site level management committee has been able to do its intended job unfettered by over-involvement by agencies and micro-management. The service planning, assessment, consultation, and intervention services demonstrate both objectively evaluated and perceived value to this community.

Product

Three things are really unique about Integrated Services for Northern Children. One is the use of satellite (case management) workers who perform outreach, process all service requests, co-ordinate services, provide follow up, problem solve, and support involved professionals. Their role as actual community members allows them to be part of both natural and professional support systems. Another important and unique feature is the effective use of a management information system for case and programme monitoring. This system creates an electronic web that holds the programme together. Finally, along with the management information system, the benefit of having a continuous systematic programme evaluation plan built into the Project's activities has given a tangibility to the implementation of the project that has established a firm foundation for its philosophy and goals. Although the Cochrane/Timiskaming site exemplifies the most far-reaching achievement of the Project's goals, the ISNC Programme overall demonstrates the value and workability of full-scale integration of children's services.

The successful implementation of the innovative ISNC Programme at the Cochrane/Timiskaming site was the product of many influences including strong local leadership, dedicated staff, and useful information obtained from a thorough evaluation of programme implementation. This process has set the stage for additional developments at both the local and provincial levels in terms of improvements in the whole system of children's services. Information gained through the evaluation of the Integrated Services for Northern Children Programme has been incorporated by MCSS policy makers into the new Children's Services Policy Framework. The directions of enhanced services integration and co-ordinated access were strongly influenced by the success in implementing these policies within the Integrated Services for Northern Children Programme.

DISCUSSION AND CONCLUSION

Ontario committed itself to exploring the prospects and promise of primary prevention of children's problems experienced during the 1980s. The early models associated with this undertaking were derived from public health and social psychiatry. A shift to a more community and capacity-building focus has occurred in recent years. An emphasis on equity, or recognition that diversity is to be valued and that the mere existence of opportunities does not guarantee equal benefit, has become an important aspect in the development of public policy in Ontario. This inclusion has resulted from the consequences of world-wide economic adjustments, rapid demographic change, the call for alterations associated with feminist ideas, and a paradigm shift that has led to a renewed interest in conceptualising development as inseparable from context. The reframing of social policy associated with these considerations has had an impact not unlike the impact of ideas from ecology on trade and economic policy.

Several observations on services integration are suggested by the programmes reviewed. Services integration works among community services which face similar challenges that can be resolved better by their integration. Another facilitator of integration is a sharing of values, parallel understanding of practice issues, and similar perception of outcome priorities, among involved professionals. No evidence exists that services integration saves money in the short-term. Rather, it appears that the likelihood of services integration being achieved increases as a result of an increased supply of money and resources. Although these may be necessary conditions for services integration they are in and of themselves insufficient. Leadership is a vital aspect of successful services integration. Evident in the Cochrane/Timiskaming programme are examples of effective leadership based on traditional hierarchical authority. Highly rationalised formal relationships have been established between collaborating agencies. In contrast, in the Sudbury Project authority is charismatic and community-based.

If the integration of services is to contribute to the building of civil society and increase citizen participation, both forms of authority should be in place to provide political predictability and social solidarity. The collaboration of citizens needs to be transferred into the way public settings are operated. This only becomes possible when sufficient trust and goodwill are available to support networks of collaborating citizens and professionals.

REFERENCES

CHILD AND FAMILY SERVICES ACT (1995), Government of Ontario.

CONWAY, J.F. (1993), *The Canadian Family in Crisis*, James Lorimer and Company, Toronto.

ECONOMIC COUNCIL OF CANADA (1992), *Report on the Economic Consequences of Early School Leaving*, Ottawa, Ontario.

EDUCATION ACT (1980), Revised Statutes (1989), Queens Printer, Province of Ontario, Toronto, Ontario.

LEAVING SCHOOL STUDY (1992), *Stay-in-School Initiative*, Ottawa.

MALONEY, C. (1990), *Children First*, Ontario Ministry of Community and Social Services (COMSOC), Toronto

OFFORD, D. (1994), *Yours, Mine and Ours*, Premiers Council on Health, Well-Being and Social Justice, Toronto.

OFFORD, D. and BOYLE, M. (1987), *Ontario Child Health Survey*, Ontario Ministry of Community and Social Services, Toronto.

ONTARIO MINISTRY OF COMMUNITY AND SOCIAL SERVICES (1988), *Investing in Children*, Toronto, Ontario.

ONTARIO MINISTRY OF COMMUNITY AND SOCIAL SERVICES (1989), *Better Beginnings, Better Futures*, Queens Printer, Toronto.

ONTARIO MINISTRY OF SKILLS DEVELOPMENT (1992), *Yearly Report*, Queens Printer, Toronto.

REITSMAN-STREET, M. and ARNOLD, R. (1994), *Community-based Action Research in a Multi-site Prevention Project: Challenges and Resolutions*.

ROYAL COMMISSION ON LEARNING (1994), *For the Love of Learning*, Government of Ontario.

RYERSE, C. (1990), *Thursdays Child: Child Poverty in Canada*, National Youth in Care Network, Ottawa.

STATISTICS CANADA (1993), *Education in Canada: A Statistical Review for 1991-92*, Ottawa.

SWAN, W. and MORGAN, J. (1993), *Collaborating for Comprehensive Services for Young Children and their Families*, Brookes, Baltimore.

YOUNG OFFENDER'S ACT (1984), Government of Canada.

NEW BRUNSWICK

WORKING "SMARTER" THROUGH INTEGRATION

by

Peter Evans

INTRODUCTION

Background

The Canadian province of New Brunswick, whose capital is Fredericton, is on the eastern seaboard bordering on Nova Scotia, Quebec and the US state of Maine. It extends approximately 322 kilometres north to south and 242 kilometres east to west. It is rectangular in shape and is 73 437 square kilometres in area. The terrain is a mixture of mountains and plateaux with four main lakes. The principal industries are tourism, forestry, mining, fisheries and agriculture. The main manufacturing industries are food and beverages, paper, metal fabricating, transportation equipment, non-metallic mineral products and primary metal groups. New Brunswick is Canada's only officially bilingual province with 34 per cent of the population being French-speaking. In 1994, the total population was approximately 726 800 of whom 138 000 were of school age. The government structure is centralised and the local taxation system is limited to property taxes only.

Throughout New Brunswick there are eight school districts and seven regional health authorities. The education budget in 1994-95 was C$614.1 million. New Brunswick's mission statement for education is "to have each student develop the attributes needed to be a lifelong learner, to achieve personal fulfilment and to contribute to a productive, just and democratic society".

In New Brunswick, drop-out from school is the lowest in Canada. However, since 1985, as in the rest of the country, there has been concern over the growing numbers of children who live in poverty and who have health related problems associated with school readiness. These students are at risk of failing in school and of failing to obtain the qualifications necessary to make an effective transition to work.

Towards the end of the 1980s, several important developments took place. The governments of Canada and New Brunswick agreed to implement, between 1988 and 1991, a Youth Strategy, later extended to 1993 (for a review and evaluation of the earlier period see Rankine and Plummer, 1990). In 1990, a Stay-in-School initiative was also launched. The Youth Strategy provides a framework to enhance education and employment opportunities for youth in New Brunswick aged 15-24, and the Stay-in-School initiative is targeted at youth between the ages of 12 and 18 (Plummer, 1992). In 1995, a programme entitled the Youth Services Partnerships replaced the Youth Strategy/Stay-in-School initiative. Many of the programmes have continued under this new programme setting, with an increased focus on youth who are "severely at risk" of not being properly prepared to access regular employment and gain self-sufficiency.

In 1984, the Cabinet of New Brunswick accepted the need for reform in the way services were provided following an Office of Government Reform working paper which noted that:

> "The education system cannot depend solely on teachers to provide students with the best possible learning environment. Availability and access to a variety of professional support services are essential to teachers, administrators and parents in order to enhance students' learning process and to ensure a quality learning environment" (see New Brunswick, 1993).

Taking account of this conclusion and driven by considerations of economy and efficiency, and the scarcity of professional resources that meant that duplication of service provision had to be eliminated, the decision was taken to develop the concept of co-ordinated support services to education.

A mandate to investigate the means to implement support services to education, to be managed by Health and Community Services, began in 1986. This, in turn, led to new provisions being implemented, initially over the period 1988-93, which provided for a limited array of needed support services to be provided by the Department of Education, and a more extensive set by the Department of Health and Community Services. The two departments developed the services through joint planning, partly to avoid clashes in service delivery philosophy inherent in educational and clinical approaches, and to avoid similar services from different administrative areas being delivered to the same family or child. In 1994, efforts were focused on obtaining more resources for departments working together.

The strategic level

At the strategic level, the Student Services Branch of the Department of Education is responsible for all exceptional students and programmes intended to help them to be successful in school. These include stay-in-school programmes, counselling programmes, transition to work programmes, intergovernmental liaison and others covering curriculum development, professional development, student councils, extra-curricular activities, and assistive technology for students with special needs. The delivery of programmes and services requires collaboration and consultation among several provincial government departments including Health and Community Services; Human Resources Development, New Brunswick; Recreation and Sport; Advanced Education and Labour; Solicitor-General; Justice, Supply and Services and federal agencies such as Health and Welfare and Indian Affairs.

Although, at the central level, no staff members are co-located and there is no sharing of administrative resources, strong collaboration with the Support Services to Education (SSE), administered by Health and Community Services (HCS), and with post-secondary institutions has been established. Regular meetings take place with HCS, for instance, to develop Protocol. Ministers and senior government officials from different departments also meet regularly to review legislation and government policy.

These arrangements, which started in 1990, recognised that "resource allocation and service provision could most efficiently and effectively be provided to school children by the Department charged with the mandate to provide health and social services to the population as a whole". Specifically (New Brunswick, 1993), this arrangement would provide better co-ordination of health and social services and related resources, avoid service duplication, provide for the development of provincial standards for professional services, ensure the most effective use of professional staff, maintain professional and service linkage with the Health and Community Service network which might already be serving the child or its family, and reduce unnecessary competition between the two systems for scarce personnel. The services provided comprise nurses, occupational, therapists, physiotherapists, psychologists, social workers (see also the STAR pilot programme described later) and speech language pathologists. Their collaboration with schools is aimed at improving the students' capacity to function in the public school system. The arrangements operate under the amended New Brunswick Schools Act (1990) and the Family Services Act (1995). Services included are education, mental health, income assistance (STAR), teen mothers, alcohol and drug dependency, housing and recreation, and APSEA (Atlantic Provinces Special Education Authority).

Eleven principles guide the provision of these services. Briefly, they are to be community-based; delivered to the school and the home; accessible, flexible and bilingual; to consult parents and involve them in referral decisions; support students to enhance their learning with minimal disruption; reduce dependency; promote as normal a lifestyle as possible; avoid fragmentation and duplication; and be accountable through the determination of clear authority and responsibility lines.

In order to implement these arrangements, a Provincial Operating Planning (POP) Committee was established. Its purpose was formally noted, "to oversee the development and implementation of health and social services for children within the public school system". It comprises members from the

Department of Health and Community Services, the Department of Education, the Mental Health Commission and Human Resources Development, New Brunswick, and reports to the Assistant Deputy Minister of the Family and Community Social Services Division and the Solicitor-General's Office. This committee has the mandate to serve as an inter-departmental link in planning and co-ordinating the delivery of support services to education; to establish formal agreements between the two departments for the provision of support services; to establish priorities and guidelines; to establish mechanisms for long-term funding; and to resolve operational problems as they arise. In 1995, two new government departments, Human Resources Development, New Brunswick and the Solicitor-General's, were added to the POP Committee. The Committee was renamed the Omnibus Committee for Children and Youth in 1996.

To deliver these services a professional resource pool has been established. This consists of staff for the support services programme who respond exclusively to school referrals; the existing health and social services staff employed by the school districts who also respond exclusively to school referrals; and Family and Community Social Service (FCSS) inter-disciplinary teams, for special needs children, which will respond to school and FCSS referrals.

The pool is under the direction of an FCSS supervisor who is responsible for ensuring improved access for referred persons and the most effective use of scarce resources. Agreements have been reached concerning new reporting arrangements for professionals, and the implementation of a procedure to transfer financial resources from school districts to Health and Community Services in order to create additional positions exclusively for the support services programme. The POP committee also is responsible for ensuring that resources are appropriately allocated across the Province.

Responsibility for the detailed implementation of these arrangements has been given to Regional Operational Planning (ROP) Committees (now Regional Omnibus Committees) made up of representatives of interested parties but not including clients. This responsibility also covers planning the most effective utilisation of regional resources to meet student needs, the establishment of a referral procedure, the identification and resolution of problems, and the monitoring of service implementation.

Professionals providing these services are required to develop and keep an implementation plan. This must cover the identification of functional and measurable goals or objectives along with an account of the intervention method to be used and its time frame, including termination dates. A monitoring and evaluation procedure is also required along with a record keeping process which will note objectives achieved and progress made. This plan must also show evidence of collaboration with the family and/or the child, the school and other relevant professionals and must be focused on supporting the child's school functioning. It also needs to be realistic, taking full account of available resources. The intervention model used can be consultative, *via* monitoring programmes used by other professionals, or through direct treatment.

Respecting confidentiality is an important issue. Through the Family Services Act (1995) information can be shared with school staff without parental consent. However, formal parental agreement is required for schools to share information with support professionals. Electronic records will be kept on all persons receiving support services in the FCSS information system.

A recent evaluation of the working of the SSE showed that they served approximately 3 per cent of the school age population (Dilworth, Sanford *et al.*, 1994), and a further study provided evidence for their effectiveness, as perceived by themselves and students' teachers, in a wide range of school related competences, including academic progress, behaviour and attendance (Lapointe, 1994).

Implementation

The scheme, which is government focused and has not included the voluntary sector, was implemented through top-down instruction which, in hindsight, could have been better handled (Dingwall, 1994). For instance, communication with the services concerned could have been stronger and, over the first two years of implementation, there were some general misunderstandings. There were difficulties with school boards who were concerned that HCS could not deliver needed services, but the problem was eased by the introduction of additional and necessary resources for restructuring under, what was at the time, a generally increasing budget. Apart from the problems noted above, no other particular barriers were perceived, at least from a strategic level viewpoint. The perceived advantages, for instance, of consistent standards across the Province, the introduction of supervision of professionals, the reduction in the amount of duplication, and the clear delegation of responsibilities and accountability, all involving very little additional administration, suggest that a co-ordinated service should be less costly. No additional training budget was planned specifically to help with the implementation.

Other activities intended to help prevent or remediate problems faced by at risk students and families include the Early Childhood Initiatives, developments in school pedagogy and curriculum, transition to work and the STAR Programme for adolescents.

Early Childhood Initiatives

In response to the child health problems noted earlier, and to improve school readiness, the Early Childhood Initiatives were launched in New Brunswick in 1992 and targeted at 100 per cent of the at risk population who themselves comprise some 15 per cent of the total population (Department of Health and Community Services, 1993). They involve the collaborative efforts of Public Health and Medical Services Division and the Family and Community Services Division. Seven initiatives have been identified. Public health is responsible for enhanced pre-natal screening and intervention, including nutrition, enhanced post-natal screening and intervention, also including nutrition, and retargeted preschool health clinics. These are linked with four initiatives of the FCSS. They are home-based early intervention, integrated day care services, social work prevention services and home economics services, to help priority families develop skills in the areas of resource management and self-reliance. These services emphasize prevention and intervention practices, intended to promote healthy babies and families, particularly for those at risk. A risk assessment is made by a nurse during home visits which can lead to the provision of additional services which are aimed at 5 per cent of the population. The intention is to bring children to the kindergarten door who are as healthy as possible and ready to achieve their potential.

Schooling

Under the Stay-in-School initiative, methods to improve the emotional environment of schools for students and teachers through "alternative settings and strategies" have been developed. They include: implementing more individualised instruction via mentoring and tutoring programmes, summer enhancement programmes, co-operative strategies and other methods such as a work orientation programmes and computer assisted instruction. In addition, professional development programmes for teachers were initiated that stressed the development of counselling skills and general sensitisation to the problems faced by children at risk. Methods to improve basic educational skills such as literacy, for instance through peer tutoring (Plummer, 1993), were also encouraged. A feature of many of these innovative strategies was the involvement of other service providers and the use of mentors and others as facilitators between schools and other services.

Transition to work

Transition-to-work programmes were a feature of the Stay-in-School initiative between 1987 and 1994. Two main methods were developed and appear to be successful. Co-operative education, allowing students to receive organised instruction on the job and in school, and Work Orientation Workshop programmes, whereby students receive work experience and life skills training during the summer months, have been the most frequently used approaches (Rankine and Plummer, 1990).

In order to help young people in the transition to work further, New Brunswick has set up Access Centres in three cities. They are aimed at those at risk of criminality, defined as those in danger of dropping out of school, those with problems at home, and those who are already in trouble with the law. Youth between the ages of 16 and 19 were identified as most in need (there is no legislated support system for 16-18 year-olds) and the departments of Education, HCS, Mental Health, Welfare, Income Assistance and Justice, among others, were brought together to support the establishment of these centres. They are planned as drop-in centres to serve up to 200 students with the intention of helping them back into school. In 1995, the Access Centres discontinued operations and the majority of their programmes moved to Human Resources Development, New Brunswick locations.

Services Targeted to Adolescents at Risk (STAR)

The Services Targeted to Adolescents At Risk (STAR) pilot initiative operates under HCS in the three major urban areas of Fredericton, Moncton and Saint John (Department of Health and Community Services, 1994). It is mandated to reduce the chances of immediate harm occurring to 16-19 year-olds and to help to stabilise their lives so that they can stay in school, return there or participate in the labour force. STAR social workers respect the rights of the family and recognise that the responsibility for meeting the needs of youth are shared between the adolescent, the family, the community and the government. They respond first of all to those in crisis situations who are most in need and then to those with multiple problems which, without intervention, would prevent them from staying in school or completing a training programme and thus would impede their transition to work.

Concluding comment

Wide ranging reforms in services organisation have been carried out in New Brunswick following the recognition that those at risk of educational failure require a services structure which is holistic, covers the whole age range, is maximally responsive to clients' needs, and which at the same time avoids duplication of effort, inconsistencies and inefficiencies. This has been achieved through collaboration between many government departments, and with necessary changes in the legal framework.

SITE VISIT TO WOODSTOCK

Background and general arrangements

School District 12, Woodstock, was chosen by the Education Department for a more intensive visit. Woodstock covers 2 438 square kilometres and has a school population of approximately 5 000 students. The immediate hinterland is rural, with some industry. The population is mainly in the middle and lower income levels. Problems identified by respondents include poverty, transport, family break down and violence and low self-esteem. Dilworth et al. (1994), in a comparative study of the 18 school districts of New Brunswick covering cases being serviced by the SSE, placed District 12 in the middle range of districts. Thus, in these respects, Woodstock appears typical of the province of New Brunswick in general.

Problems presented by children and youth at risk have been identified through research studies carried out by the district itself. The research showed that students dropped out because they did not feel supported by the school. The main reason given for leaving school was the teacher. Other features related to drop-outs followed a familiar pattern (retention in grade, poor attendance, lack of interest shown by educators and parents, academic difficulty and pregnancy). However, on a positive note, it was found that communities, parents, schools and teachers could all make a difference in the lives of students and reduce school leaving. An analysis of school retention data to year 12 showed that the situation had been steadily improving between 1986 and 1991 (perhaps because of the successful implementation of the strategies noted in the Introduction of this report) and was substantially better than in the rest of Canada (Woodstock, 1991). Discussions with professionals in the education service identified the wide range of problems associated with teaching children at risk, including the problems of co-ordinating provision and communication with other agencies (Woodstock, 1992).

The set of available student services in Woodstock is shown in Figure 1. In 1992-93, these services comprised a team of 14 plus a director, being the equivalent of 13.5 full-time staff. There are four groups. The education team of four professionals providing services to schools covers special needs, the transition to work and school psychometric work. The APSEA staff, made up of three itinerant

Figure I. *Community level map of services integration for students*

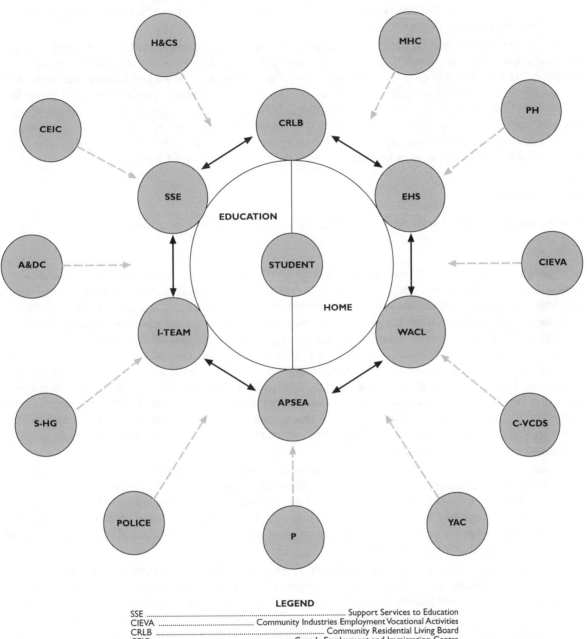

LEGEND

SSE	Support Services to Education
CIEVA	Community Industries Employment Vocational Activities
CRLB	Community Residential Living Board
CEIC	Canada Employment and Immigration Centre
YAC	Youth Access Centre
EHS	Extramural Hospital Services
I-Team	Interdisciplinary Team
C-VCDS	Carelton-Victoria Child Development Services
APSEA	Atlantic Provinces Special Education Authority
WACL	Woodstock Association for Community Living
P	Probation
PH	Public Health
MHC	Mental Health Centre
S-HG	Department of the Solicitor-General
A&DC	Alcohol and Drug Dependency Commission

teachers, covers the visually and hearing impaired. A team of two, working within the Stay-in-School Programme, serve at risk students from school, classroom and community perspectives. These professionals are supported by the SSE team of 1.5 social workers, two speech and language pathologists and a half-time occupational therapist.

In practice, in Woodstock, there is a seamless continuity of services provided for those who are at risk and those who are disabled. In the text which follows, a summary of information provided by professionals and others is given which emphasizes the provision made for children at risk. Because of the co-ordinated nature of services, an overview of Family and Community Social Services is given first. This is then followed by summaries of information received from the education workers of the student services staff, the Department of Health and Community Services support services to education, a school and a parent. Subsequently, information supplied on the Early Childhood Initiative, the Youth Access Centre and the probation service is summarised and conclusions are drawn.

Student services

Family and Community Social Services (FCSS) in Woodstock: operational level

Context and input

There are seven health regions in New Brunswick which are not co-terminous with school districts. Region 3 includes Woodstock and serves some 55 000 people. The major issues covered include sexual and physical abuse, family violence, lack of parenting skills and poor socialisation skills. FCSS is a division of HCS and provides both statutory and non-statutory services with an annual budget of C$6 200 000. Statutory services cover child and adult protection and guardianship for children in care, usually in foster homes. Non-statutory services include adoption, special needs children's services (*e.g.* respite care and transportation), support services to education (*e.g.* social work, psychological services and speech language pathology), early intervention services (similar to support services to education but for preschool children), day care services for 3.5-5-year-olds, services for youth at risk (transition to work services which are only in three regions on a trial basis), social assessments to establish if young people are eligible for income assistance, services to seniors, services to disabled adults and emergency social services.

These services work together depending on needs. The services generally started as government programmes from various departments and over the years have gradually become more centralised in HCS or Education. Private organisations have also developed to provide assistance. The key partners in the planning of integrated services are FCSS, District 12, Public Health, Mental Health, Early Intervention (a private, non-profit organisation), the Department of Income Assistance and the Federal Department of Human Resources Development.

The need for integration became evident in the mid-1980s when family problems began to encroach on schools and the need for a holistic approach was recognised. Political support was given to the concept and there was leadership and co-operation among government departments. Funding and human resources were also provided. Initially the integrated approach was planned by Education, HCS and the local education officials. Two social work and speech pathology positions were made available but there was a lack of nursing services.

Process

Decision making and the planning of integrated services are currently undertaken by the FCSS site manager (as part of the local Operational Planning Committee), by the Superintendents of Districts 12 and 13 (delegated to the Director of Student Services), by the Nursing Supervisor, and by the Manager of the Mental Health Clinic.

The SSE staff are co-located with education support staff in District 12's office complex. SSE staff work in the schools with teachers, using a consultative approach, to enhance the classroom teachers ability to address the needs of children in their charge. Methods and Resource (M and R) teachers play a key role. These teachers have special responsibility for the educational support of disadvantaged and special needs students in a particular school. SSE staff, working with the School Board support staff, as a team, has been the key element for success. This is true to such an extent that vacancies in the SSE roster are given priority. SSE staff have also gained credibility in schools by giving classroom relevant in-service education of teachers (INSET).

Obstacles to the smooth development of the co-ordinated service have been insufficient resources and insufficient knowledge and understanding on the part of educators. This has led, in some cases, to grudging acceptance or even open opposition to these new, and officially sanctioned, service arrangements.

Day-to-day direction of the SSE staff is provided by the Regional Director of HCS who works in close collaboration with the Director of Student Services in District 12. The FCSS management recognises the benefits of the close collaboration between these two groups of staff and the collaboration will carry on while the benefits continue to be recognised. The working relationship is strong and effective.

Product

The benefits of services integration have been a quicker response time, more effective targeting of resources, more effective case planning and intervention, and better support felt by teachers and parents. As for problems, the question of ownership has sometimes emerged in the context of who is the employer of the SSE staff.

Data is regularly entered into a data base administered by HCS. Services are provided to education under a formal agreement, with a joint intake form and inter-professional planning of programme delivery at this level. There is a planning and management committee at the district level which focuses on children's services issues, and data is shared on a "need to know" basis. Confidentiality problems are addressed through parent consent.

FCSS staff get resources from education such as space, computer equipment and supplies, and FCSS sometimes makes a financial contribution.

The average monthly case-loads in the Province according to the RPSS Data System (1992-93) were as follows (Family and Community Social Services Programme Statistics, 1992-93):

– Child protection	1 936
– Temporary status children	337
– Children in care	896
– Special needs children	643
– Subsidised children	95
– Young offenders in open custody	105

Family and Community Social Services (FCSS) in Woodstock: field level

As noted above, schools are supported by the 15 person Student Services Team. The professionals meet regularly. Student services consultants work out of a district office to support teachers in the schools. Their work involves managing and co-ordinating support for students by supporting teachers (in particular M and R teachers), planning individual teaching programmes for students, acting as tutors and mentors, carrying out INSET and liaising with other agencies.

In the next sections, more detailed perspectives are supplied based on information provided by a wide range of field level professionals.

The education professionals of the student services team

Context and input

Working with other services began in 1985 following the decision to integrate all disabled pupils into mainstream schools (Bill 85, an act to amend the Schools Act*). The benefits of integrated services, established with that group, have been spread to meet a wider range of special educational needs, including those of at risk students. Before the integration of services process was established each professional worked separately and in isolation. Following the development of a collaborative approach, service providers now meet regularly to discuss and solve problems, and parents and students are more directly involved.

Key partners identified were parents and students as well as health and community services, early intervention services, local associations for community living, teachers, public health, administrators, probation officers, mental health, the police, and the community suicide committee. The leadership of the Districts Director of Student Services was also identified as a key factor. The service taking the lead co-ordinating role depends on the age of the child. For preschoolers, it is early intervention services, for school age children, the education authorities, and for older children, the various employment agencies, such as Community Industries Employment Vocational Activities (CIEVA).

Although government legislation concerning the integration of disabled students was frequently cited as the starting point of the process, the main driving forces for co-ordination were perceived to be local leadership emphasizing the need for a holistic approach and information sharing, the desire to reduce parents' workload by developing one stop shops, improvements in efficiency, and government initiatives in other departments (*e.g.* SSE). The provision of a better service for students and their families was a clear objective.

These education professionals also noted that pressure for a more integrated approach came from a number of sources who all shared the same vision. Parents were active in lobbying for better and more inclusive services, especially for disabled students, and their concerns were shared by local administrators. In addition, central government spending cuts also provided pressure for reform. Despite these cuts the professionals also noted that funding was made available for M and R teachers, teacher assistants, INSET and materials. No inputs were perceived to be lacking.

Process

The process of operating the services was described as broad-based collaboration and co-ordination, with anyone who wanted to be involved being given access. However, the involvement of parents and students was not as good as some would have liked. The strategies used to develop the process were identified as leadership, the use of a problem-solving style to enable short, efficient and effective meetings, the development of a team approach and the formation of partnerships in the community, the use of funds from a variety of sources, training, the development of the M and R teachers' role and comprehensive guidance programme, building on existing initiatives, and the constant monitoring of the system and the process. The formative nature of the evaluation process was seen to lead to an ever-evolving system with more and more inter-dependence between the professionals involved. Developing a common vision was noted as important, as was the development of a positive school climate for success. The placement of the SSE at the school district office was also identified as an important development.

Obstacles to change were noted as insufficient time to meet, the lack of feedback, people trying to hang on to traditional roles and the maintenance of stereotypes. Fear of change, the need for more training and the lack of common vision were also cited.

These professionals noted that they worked through collaboration and teamwork using a problem-solving model involving constant review and development of the process. The interactive style with

* "Bill 85" is now found in the New Brunswick Schools Act (1973) in sections 1; 52; and 53. It was incorporated in 1987.

clients is forward-looking and holistic with the involvement of the client in decision-making being an important objective. The community, too, is an important contributor to overall success.

Product

The advantages of integration were associated with more creative approaches, more support and the benefit of a team spirit, which is exciting and rewarding and which meets the needs of clients better and more quickly. There is less duplication of service provision and time wasting and more can be achieved with fewer educational specialists. The quality of life for clients is also improved. In the future, budget cuts are predicted to increase the need for community involvement. This would bring more community members into the school and lead to more students learning in environments outside the school, which together would have the effect of uniting the school and community more tightly.

Problems associated with integration were noted as the difficulty in co-ordinating meetings and the large number of people that needed to be contacted. At first, there is a great deal of work to do with planning meetings and so on. There is also concern about confidentiality and, although in reality this has not proved to be a big problem, some professional groups are more cautious than others. A mind set is needed to see problems as constructive challenges leading to "smarter" working practices.

Records mainly are kept in schools and are concerned with programmes and interventions, meetings and recommendations for action. Some are kept on paper and some as computer files. Information is shared as appropriate.

Outcomes for clients were described as "great". They develop better self-esteem, stay in the school, and become integrated into the community.

The social work professionals of the student services team

Context

The educational professionals, noted above, are also supported by a team of social workers, co-located at the school district office, who support students at risk, their families and the school personnel. The services they provide include general parenting skills, specific behaviour management, suicide intervention, skills in conflict resolution, information on native education issues, community projects (*e.g.* community tutoring and family counselling), teacher education and awareness, liaison with other community agencies, school planning for at risk students (both social and academic), and direct service counselling for students and their families. These services are delivered in the home, school or other community settings.

The team has been working in this way since 1988 when the first school social worker position was created. The role of the school social worker has widened since 1988. A great deal of thought was given to a new delivery model which would balance direct service to clients with system issues affecting school climate and the successful education of all students. School social workers have been included as part of the district-based student services team to ensure that they do not operate independently in providing direct services to clients (the traditional model). This has achieved acceptance and a better preventive/reactive balance in service provision.

The three social workers agreed that education and health services are key partners, along with other community agencies. They confirmed that the student services take the lead in ensuring that the process of collaboration happens and is focused on the issue at hand. However, depending on the action agreed, different individuals will take the lead at any particular time. Co-operation was stimulated by the general recognition amongst the student services team that a collaborative approach was a better way to work to meet student needs. The objectives of this approach were noted as holistic care, more efficient and effective service delivery, and the achievement of change in students and systems.

Input

Support for an integrated approach was given by Bill 85. In addition, local philosophies were positive. Social workers are also given the flexibility, in their terms of service, to work in a way that they regard as best for clients – who themselves confirm that they feel better served by this approach. The community has also largely welcomed the involvement. Support came from both political and operational levels. From the latter it came as moral support and direction, training, physical use of facilities, manpower through this membership, and public awareness activities.

Planning was initially done by the health and education services as well as the regional planning committee. To achieve the new way of working planning meetings were arranged and some training provided. Office space and equipment were also supplied by the local school district. At the outset, not surprisingly, there was some professional rivalry.

Process

As indicated above, a wide range of services were identified as being involved. They pointed to the supportive policies of the School Board as being effective in implementing integrated approaches, along with a common vision, a problem-solving approach, and ability of the SSE to include others as partners.

Obstacles identified included an unwillingness on the part of some professionals to change to the new approach, communication difficulties with other members of the team, too little support given to staff to implement change in their work practices, and a failure to give people sufficient ownership of problems and, at the same time, guide them through the process of decision making by giving them sufficient information. The lack of time for people to reflect on their work practices and their effectiveness was also noted as an obstacle.

The relationship between the partners was described as one of "equality". There is a free sharing of information, a common knowledge base that crosses professional boundaries but which recognises relevant expertise. This leads to an approach to client care which is collaborative and based on a problem-solving model which, when necessary, will involve outside resources such as those available in the community. Clients views are sought and included in the case plan.

Product

Increased efficiency and improved professional relationships, change in systems and clients, a more supportive work environment, an understanding that a common set of strategies is effective in meeting a variety of client needs, and better services, were all identified as benefits. In addition, more efficient services and less staff turnover and burn out were seen as potential future advantages. The goal is to work "smarter" and not harder.

The main negative or unanticipated consequences identified concerned difficulties in communication and personal management. For example, finding the time to communicate and plan co-operatively, with the stress that this brings, and dealing with difficult people and confronting issues, rather than hiding from them, were all noted as challenges.

Recorded information kept included actions agreed, case demographics, case plans and conferences, and meeting and progress notes. Records are kept in the central files of the school board and in computer student files. The data is shared with others if the client agrees. Confidentiality is not a serious problem.

The outcomes for students include better general skills, problem-solving abilities and communication skills. A different social experience was also identified, with other students showing a more positive acceptance of challenged students, resulting in less alienation, isolation and drop-out.

Speech and language pathologists in the student services team

Context

Speech and language pathologists, from HCS, form part of the SSE. They assess, evaluate and provide front-line services (both consultative and direct) for students with communication needs. The students worked with are in grades 1-5. But some services for preschoolers and those in grades 6-12 are also given. These services take the form of consultation and planning with teachers and parents, direct work with students with communication needs, and preventive actions such as ongoing education with teachers and parents. Most of the work is carried out in schools, often in collaboration with teachers and SSE special services. For those students with sensory impairments, public health nurses, occupational therapists and physiotherapists are involved when necessary. The speech and language pathologists' work is now more co-ordinated than it was before. The key school-based partners are the M and R teachers who take the lead for more complex problems. But the speech language pathologist will liaise between the teacher and the home for less severe cases.

In January 1997, the speech language pathologists will move from the SSE administration to HCS regions administered by Regional Hospital Corporations. The long-term objective is the establishment of an integrated community pool and re-habilitation services, including occupational therapy, physio-therapy and speech language pathology. Consultation and collaboration will continue to be part of the inter-disciplinary management of the services provided directly to children in the public school system.

Involving all required professionals in a child's life is seen as a key intervention approach to address the needs of the child holistically and create a consistency of method in and out of school. The aim is to make the therapy, as far as possible, a natural part of the child's day.

Input

There was top-down pressure for partnerships that came from the DHCS as well as from the school board. Support in the form of professional development which emphasized collaboration was provided.

Process

Cases are co-ordinated, goals are identified and meetings held at the school. In some schools the emphasis on collaborative consultation has helped to develop internal expertise. The lack of time for co-ordination has proved to be an obstacle.

Methods of working vary according to need. Programmes planned with parents, teachers and students are developed and they can be specific or general. There is little community involvement.

Product

The outcomes of integrated services have been much more realistic, real and functional pro-grammes which can help to generalise learning. Records kept include case notes and assessment and termination information. These are stored on computer and paper at the district office and also for individual programmes in the schools. Copies are sent to parents and shared with other services. Confidentiality is an important issue although information is often shared informally.

Woodstock Junior High: a view from a school

Context

The schools catchment area is one of relatively low income in an agricultural community. The case study focused around a particular male student. Apart from teachers, he receives support from a Methods and Resource (M and R) teacher, a teacher assistant, a counsellor, a co-op education co-ordinator, a school mentor and a work site supervisor. The last two provide friendship and support. While they have different roles to play, all support the view that they work together and with other services including the district office personnel. They stressed that this is a different style of working

CO-ORDINATING SERVICES FOR CHILDREN AND YOUTH AT RISK

from previous arrangements which were more oriented to individual services. Individualisation of teaching has also become common practice in contrast to the earlier model where all students followed the same programme.

The informants represented a wide range of services: a work site supervisor from HCS; a mentor funded by the native Indian programme; a guidance counsellor, a co-operative education co-ordinator; a teacher assistant; a Methods and Resource teacher; and a teacher (all supported from the education budget). This group of professionals along with others such as social workers, and with the school taking the lead, work and plan together to provide the best holistic support for students, giving attention to educational, personal, social and motivational progress as well as prospects for work.

Input

All of the informants confirmed that support had come from many individuals and agencies – politicians, administrators, professionals, businesses and the community. Additional resources were provided in the form of support personnel, in-service education of teachers (INSET), funding and information systems. Resource constraints were seen as a problem leading to a fear that M and R teachers might be withdrawn. Vocational services also acted as a useful link between businesses and schools, and helped to reduce initial confusion over requests for work placements.

Process

In terms of process it is clear that innovations have been put in place through negotiation and the wide involvement of agencies and the community. A lack of funding and traditional mind sets are reported as obstacles. M and R teachers are a success. For success, clients need to be involved and treated as individuals. The model started as a top-down initiative but has evolved to take on a wider range of pupils as INSET and resources have been put in place. Community agencies have also become more aware of it.

Product

The benefits of integration were generally seen as a better knowledge of services and the roles of others, and better communication. Improved educational outcomes and self-esteem amongst clients were also noted, and confirmed by external evaluation (Lapointe, 1994), as well as improved efficiency. It was generally anticipated that improvements will continue with better life prospects for clients. Some respondents identified increased personal satisfaction. It was hoped that information flows would improve to avoid time wasting in gathering information. Various records were kept according to need and level of formality. Some were personal, others concerning individual programmes and pupil progress were kept on computer diskettes. Most were shared when necessary, given that permission was agreed. Confidentiality was identified as an obstacle but not a serious one.

The transition to work was noted as a problem. Work experience gave employers knowledge of the students and this could be an advantage. But if support stopped after school, skills would decline and this led to difficulties in finding a job. The community was often not as advanced as the school.

Some negative outcomes were identified, such as increased strain between professionals and increased time needed for preparation for at risk students. However, in general it was noted that the outcomes were good and they were more positive than negative.

A parental perspective

A parent provided another perspective. She noted the wide range of services that she called upon, as represented above, and commented that the new arrangements had led to more collaboration and more sharing of information. She also pointed out that she initiated many inter-disciplinary meetings. But she had also been fully consulted in the planning of the services and had undertaken much training. She found the professionals helpful and understanding. She was involved in decision making in the school but not with social services. This process has led this parent to have good knowledge of the availability of services and how to contact them. Access to social workers was noted as difficult because of their work load, as was the lack of initial information provided by social services to foster parents when children start in the foster home. More government resources were seen as needed to improve the system. These should be aimed at increasing personnel and providing more counselling for both foster parents and foster children.

Concluding comment

The various professionals that make up the student services team have worked together and with schools to develop a coherent support system that involves parents and students and appears to be highly effective. Positive outcomes include a reduction in school drop out, increasing standards and improved self-esteem. In developing this new approach, the holistic needs of students and families, in the context of educational success, are paramount. Problems in developing a new working style have been largely overcome and the issue of confidentiality, for instance, is not seen as preventing co-ordination. Although time for the increased number of planning meetings is hard to find, all the professionals agree that there is widespread support for the new services structure from local and national administrators and politicians. Furthermore, they argue that an integrated approach provides a more intelligent *modus operandi* than earlier fragmented models. It is instructive to note that these changes have developed in the context of reforms intended to integrate disabled children into mainstream schools with no evident disjunction between the approaches taken for disabled and at risk students and their families.

Early childhood services

Early Childhood Initiative and student health

Context and input

The public health (PH) services are organised as a community agency concerned with health promotion and disease prevention. There is a staff of 14 housed in three public health offices in Woodstock, Perth and Plaster Rock. A wide range of services are provided that act to maintain public health, but special consideration is given to the Early Childhood Initiative (ECI), the school health programme, well child clinics and communicable disease follow up.

The ECI is concerned with prenatal health, home visits for mothers and babies, and health clinics for 3.5 year-old toddlers, and it works on a more organised basis than was the case for the previous services. The key partners are public health nursing, nutrition, mental health, FCSS, early intervention, maternity units of hospitals, integrated day care, physicians, speech pathology, income assistance and school districts 12 and 13. ECI was initiated by managers, nurses and nutrition professionals to improve children's readiness for kindergarten, and its implementation was supported by politicians and managers. The last two groups supported programme developments and provided in-service training and some equipment.

Process

Managers, administrators and professionals are currently the main groups involved in decision making and planning, but it was felt that staff nurses and clients should have more involvement, even though clients were involved in decisions about their treatment. Training, the implementation of the Regional ECI Advisory Committee (which meets regularly to discuss progress on implementation and to assist in collaboration among agencies), and the development of better screening mechanisms, have all enabled the nurses to recognise children with high priority health concerns more accurately and make better referrals. Training and improved communication were identified as effective planning strategies in implementing an integrated approach. Obstacles identified were a lack of human resources and poor communication. The partnership takes the form of individual meetings and joint committees.

The school health programme operates through a School District 12 School Health Committee which monitors all health needs in schools. It provides a typical nursing service (teaching, counselling and consulting) to students and teachers who are referred to it. "Well child clinics" provide immunisation and health teaching, and assure the healthy growth and development of children from 0-16 years of age. As part of communicable disease follow up, contract training and health teaching are provided to individuals with sexually transmitted or other communicable diseases.

Product

The benefits of the integration of services have been earlier identification and referral, better services (*e.g.* nutrition and earlier intervention), improved communication and sharing among professionals, and a better database. Improved social and health outcomes are seen as future benefits for clients with ever improving databases and shared knowledge among professionals. Some problems, however, were identified including the increased stress level amongst staff because of the additional work load with no increase in human resources.

Assessment forms for all children are kept. At 3.5 years of age a student health profile form is completed for all children and is passed on to the school before entry into kindergarten. The data is stored both on computer files and manually and is shared with consent. Confidentiality is an issue and information is only shared without consent if neglect or abuse is suspected.

"The benefits that the client wanted to achieve" was given as the main outcome for clients by the public health nurses.

Early Intervention Programme

In support of the ECI is the Carelton Victoria Child Development Services Incorporated (CVCDSI) Early Intervention Programme. It is a non-statutory and community-based service which stresses child development from a family-centred perspective. It is mainly preventive but also has a remedial aspect *via* help to families. It operates through home visits, needs assessment, and the formulation in conjunction with the family and other service providers of an Individual Family Service Plan (IFSP). Regular home visits allow the provision of support, the development of appropriate family dynamics and interactions, the building up of advocacy skills, administration of follow-up screenings, updating of the IFSP, progress reports, and assistance with the transition to integrated day care settings or schools. At the family's request, team meetings can be held if they feel there is a need to bring together the team members to ensure co-ordination.

The service is an external service agency of the HCS, and is funded by it at the rate of C$3 000 per family. Other agencies are involved if the necessity for them is agreed with the family, but programmes that are the joint responsibility of several agencies are not delivered.

Co-operation with other agencies in the field of training is developing. All families are registered by the public health nurses since they are the case managers for families receiving early intervention. All referrals are processed through this route using the PH assessment forms.

Nurses consult the schools for which they have responsibility and make arrangements for visits and attendance at school staff conferences to explain the role of PH. Although, in the Woodstock area, staff of PH, Mental Health, Income Assistance and FCSS are located in the same building they were not described as co-located. Only occasionally has PH provided professional development for other agencies in schools, Mental Health, FCSS and Income Assistance.

There is no shared intake form, but some statistics are available on the ECI work. However, since the implementation of ECI, in December 1993, there have been regular meetings with other agencies involved with referring people to PH. PH also refers clients to other agencies. There is, for example, a regional ECI advisory group comprising representatives of various agencies that works in this way. PH is the single access point for children's services (excluding child abuse and neglect) and, under ECI, it has the responsibility for case managing each child and family. There are established policies for referral and feedback to other agencies and case planning. Follow up conferences with other agencies have just started. However, no single agency acts as an umbrella for children's services and there are no plans at present for further amalgamation.

Concluding comment

The preschool and health services co-ordinate their activities with other agencies including education in order to improve children's readiness for schooling. Although there have been difficulties to overcome and increased workloads, the results of co-ordination are seen as beneficial for clients.

Other services

Transition to work

Context

The Woodstock Access Centre is a small community-based agency specialising in youth employment and career counselling services which has been operational since 1989. This service is primarily remedial, focusing on individual barriers to employment such as education level, training or work experience. The Centre provides personal employment/careers counselling and a range of specialised assessment services, such as vocational, intellectual, educational, personality and occupational testing. It is a voluntary service and counsellors develop case plans to help young people. They often act as case managers and will refer clients to a wide range of federal and provincial programmes and services as well as community-based ones. There is a co-ordinator and four counsellors, one of the posts being federally funded. The clientele are aged between 15 and 24 and are either out of school, under-employed or unemployed. Usually they have not completed high school. The clients have changed over the past few years. Previously they were younger and had only completed grade 9. Client needs are wide-ranging. Those at risk tend to have poor family support and a history of deviancy. Often there are drug and alcohol problems. The Centre tries to provide a place for friendship and support, and focuses on education and personal development needs and the need for an alternative to school for at risk students. Services are provided on a drop-in or appointment basis.

In 1995, the joint federal-provincial Youth Strategy agreement, referred to in the following section, reached closure. The employees in Access Centres were moved to either federal or provincial Human Resources Development offices. The Youth Strategy agreement was replaced by a Youth Services Partnership in an endeavour to continue collaborative efforts to provide youth with support in their transition to the labour market. Through a new Youth Futures Initiative, funded by the Province, youth between the ages of 15 and 24 who are "puzzled about their future" are invited to contact their local office of Human Resources Development, New Brunswick. Case managers at these offices assist youth in accessing federal and provincial programmes and services. While the federal funding for school-based programmes also ended in 1995, provincial funding through Youth Futures has enabled school districts to maintain some of their Stay-in-School initiatives.

Since 1989, the Centre has networked with other services. Previously these services were provided by partner departments as part of their regular operation but were not well used by clients. The key partners are Canada Employment and Immigration (CEI) (Human Resources Development Canada) and the New Brunswick Department of Advanced Education and Labour (AE and L) (Colleges). Others comprise the New Brunswick Department of Education, New Brunswick Department of Income Assistance (Human Resources Development, New Brunswick) and the New Brunswick Department of the Solicitor-General. Others involved, but to a lesser extent, include HCS and Intergovernmental Affairs. The co-operation is driven by the Canada/New Brunswick Youth Strategy Agreement and by the labour force development needs of the lead departments. The objectives were to provide an enhanced service to youth who were out of school and work. Later the Stay-in-School initiative was added to the partnership. The objective was to help young people secure the education, training and work experience needed to gain entry into the labour force.

The Access Centre is jointly funded by federal and provincial governments and has recently been the target of severe cuts (over 50 per cent on the federal programmes/services budget with a smaller cut in the local programmes budget). In 1994, the total budget was C$740 000. There are other programme budgets which go to partner departments such as Education, Income Assistance and the Solicitor-General.

The agency often initiates consultation with other agencies in preparing service delivery plans, both at programme development level and individual case level, in order to improve the service. Review meetings involving all of the agencies are held. In addition, counsellors will negotiate with staff in other agencies to secure resources to assist in the implementation of case plans, and vice-versa. The Access Centres have, for example, purchased places in community colleges which are reserved for Access Centre clients. There is also an employment exposure programme that will provide weeks of paid employment. For cases where youth are clients of more than one agency, there will be case conferences to determine the best way forward. Some training input is provided to other agencies as well as to local colleges or training courses.

The Centre contributes to the provincial youth services computer records in Fredericton. There are also hard copy referral forms, the information from which is entered into the data base by the receiving agency. The intake form is for the Centre only. Forms from other agencies are used at the time of referral.

The Centre operates with an inter-departmental committee, the Local Delivery Management Committee (LDMC), which is co-chaired by the managers of the local Canada Employment Centre and the principal of the Community College. The rest of the committee is made up of the managers of the partner departments. The Centre's staff do not meet regularly with professionals from other agencies, only on an "as needed" basis with relevant individuals.

The Access Centre was designed as a single point of entry for youth with difficulties in the transition to work. However, there are differences in practice in different areas. The reasons stressed included conflicting leadership and management styles and lack of resources. The larger centres were more integrated, the rural ones less so. In Woodstock, the process of inter-agency collaboration or a consultative approach has never reached the level intended in the Youth Strategy Agreement. The imbalance of funding and management styles have been the main obstacles to a single access point for multiple services for youth at risk.

The Access Centres were encouraged to be innovative, flexible and non-bureaucratic. This has been interpreted to mean informal, consequently there are few formalised inter-agency agreements. In Woodstock, existing agreements have been followed in preference to the development of new ones and of new means of serving clients.

The Youth Strategy Programme and the Access Centre services are managed jointly by federal and provincial departments. Programme delivery is usually funded federally and managed provincially, but more collaboration is needed.

Transportation allowances also come from several different sources and departments and the Centre's operational budget is shared between federal and provincial sources. Other joint funding is spent on hiring of programme and support staff.

Input

There was political support for an integrated approach from the Federal Secretary for Youth and the Premier of New Brunswick. Support from other departments came with the extra funding derived from the Youth Strategy Programme. Subsequent to the implementation of this programme others followed, such as Career Exploration or Development for Employment. It provided for life skills training, career planning and academic upgrading supported through federal Youth Strategy training programme funds. In Woodstock, the academic component was not covered by federal funds. The Solicitor-General's Department received funds for prisoners, and the Education Department for in-school support workers. Now HCS, the native counsellor services, youth drug and alcohol counselling services and Stay-in-School programmes are included.

Process

A great deal of planning takes place in the lead departments and at central and regional offices. At the local level, committee structures are in place to review proposals prepared by management groups or teams of workers. The decision regarding funding rests with the agency who receives the budget.

There is a need for greater involvement of the private, non-profit youth organisations and front-line workers in the decision making process. There is a perception that management is not adequately tuned into the needs of youth as represented by professionals at the front line.

Implementation strategies have included a very wide variety of approaches from public consultation to the use of case records to illustrate need. The service has been reviewed and evaluated and changes have been recommended. These are on hold until the Youth Strategy Programme has been restructured.

The most effective strategies for developing integrated service approaches have been consultations with stakeholders, requests for funding outside the Youth Strategy Programme for services not otherwise provided, advocacy at the central and regional levels for the Youth Strategy Programme, and sharing experience of good practice at the local management group level.

Obstacles include traditional styles of management, fear of loss of control of decision making, turf protection, differences in mandates, and differences in attitude about the importance of education for youth employment.

Counsellors work with youth to simplify the way forward for them and to encourage them. They gain from sharing knowledge with other professionals and from the development of case plans.

The local community and private sector is sympathetic but there is little in the way of financial support. Most support comes in the form of employment placements and hands on training programmes, for which there is often financial reimbursement for client wages.

Product

The benefits of integrated services have been that youth needs are becoming well known, services have been upgraded, and more educational supports have been put in place. There is generally a better understanding of the various departments responsibilities and inputs and some new approaches have been tried which are now in place. Expected benefits are wide-ranging. They include: improved efficiency and effectiveness in programme delivery; the development of a continuity of services for clients between school and work; appreciation of the case management model of counselling; and a single entry point. It is also hoped that assessment of needs will lead the delivery of programmes for the client, that labour market information will be good enough to help in the guidance and development of training, that fewer people will fall through the cracks, that more youth will stay in school, and that more careers counselling will be provided to youth in and out of school. There have been few negative outcomes.

Client information is extensive. The more personal is kept confidential and only in writing, while other information goes on to computer records as part of a management information system accessible to central and regional directors. Statistical information is provided regularly to the management group (LDMC). Confidentiality is an issue for counselling services, and while sharing of information is part of the Youth Strategy Agreement, often this does not happen.

Client outcomes are varied. Over the last five years there has been a change from a high level of academic upgrading activity and a low level of training and employment services to an increased number of trained clients needing employment services. Thus it would seem that many youth are obtaining the education, career planning and occupational training needed for employment. However, the actual employment outcomes are low since there are inadequate employment assistance services in Woodstock to help youth access the job market. Nevertheless, youth remain the biggest referral source for new clients and this is probably indicative of the success the Centre is having in serving them.

Probation service

The probation service is a provincial, statutory and community-based agency which is generally remedial in focus. It is based in the town of Woodstock. The Woodstock service constitutes 6 per cent of the total provincial service with an annual budget of C$180 000. The probation office provides a service to the Court through investigations, written reports and the enforcement of court orders. Counselling and supervision of clients are also provided and can be at the clients homes.

Consultations take place with HCS, the Mental Health Clinic, schools, foster homes and the Access Centre in response to Court orders or to make recommendations for sentencing purposes. For these reasons, the probation service takes the lead role. There is little interaction with other services in the areas of training and sharing of information. Periodically meetings take place with other service providers such as the Access Centres. Also HCS is contracted to provide foster homes for open custody placements with the social workers who support these placements. Clients often receive services from other agencies, especially the Mental Health Clinic, schools, HCS and Access Centres. Other resources are not shared but additional professional resources are used when the need arises. Planning and follow-up conferences are held on an *ad hoc* basis.

Meetings and more open communication have helped to facilitate integrated services. However problems with managers who do not wish to provide services for offenders, especially in the Mental Health Clinic, have led to the suggestion that this service should be duplicated. But, when agencies have co-operated, improvement has been noted in the areas of client services, communications and relations among professionals, and knowledge sharing and efficiency.

Confidentiality problems have been encountered but they are not insuperable. However, some agencies are strongly territorial which does, at times, create conflict.

Client records are kept in paper files and include information on family history, medical background, education, employment, intoxicant use, financial situation and criminal background. This is shared as needed.

Clients placed on probation seem to do well, although no statistical information is available. The informants personal view was that most do not re-offend.

OVERALL CONCLUSIONS

The Canadian Province of New Brunswick has recognised that the challenges to educational success presented by students and families at risk cannot be met by the education authorities working alone. A holistic approach has been agreed which brings together many actors, especially education, health, social welfare, income assistance and labour, as well as local and federal resources, in a concerted attack on the problem covering preschool, school and transition to work periods.

In Woodstock, at least, this has had the effect of changing the way services are working, by encouraging a more responsive approach to student and family needs. This approach is generally agreed, by administrators, professionals, parents and students alike, to have been very successful. However, it is also clear that more remains to be done especially in terms of involving the community more fully – particularly in creating work opportunities. What has emerged are skilled services that support schools, teachers, students and families through a problem-solving model in which information and skills are shared in achieving agreed goals.

It is clear that comprehensive and effective reforms of this sort need the commitment of all – from law makers and strategic level policy makers to field level professionals and community agencies – and over the long-term. The fact that this approach is also commensurate with the successful integration of disabled students commends it for serious general application in the struggle against social exclusion.

REFERENCES

DILWORTH, C., SANFORD, S., CHRISTIE, M. and QUIGG, D. (1994), *Support Services to Education (SSE) Evaluation Project*, Phase I, Section II: Case Count, Planning and Evaluation Division, Department of Health and Community Services, Province of New Brunswick, Canada.

DEPARTMENT OF HEALTH AND COMMUNITY SERVICES (1993), *Early Childhood Initiatives – An Overview. A collaborative strategy of the public health and medical services division and the Family and Community Social Services Division,* Department of Health and Community Services, Province of New Brunswick, Canada.

DEPARTMENT OF HEALTH AND COMMUNITY SERVICES (1994), "Services targeted to adolescents at risk (STAR)", Draft FCSS Standards, Family and Community Services Division of the Department of Health and Community Services, Province of New Brunswick, Canada, mimeo.

DINGWALL, A. (1994), Personal communication.

FAMILY SERVICES ACT (1973), Consolidated in 1995, R.S.N.B, New Brunswick, Canada.

LAPOINTE, R. (1994), *Support Services to Education (SSE) Evaluation Project*, Phase II: Perception of Effectiveness, Planning and Evaluation Division, Department of Health and Community Services, Province of New Brunswick, Canada.

NEW BRUNSWICK (1984), "Working paper on support services to education. Office of Government Reform", Province of New Brunswick, Canada (quoted in New Brunswick, 1993).

NEW BRUNSWICK (1993), *Support Services to Education – Programme Service Standards*, Department of Education/ Department of Health and Community Services, Student Services Branch (Anglophone), Province of New Brunswick, Canada, September.

NEW BRUNSWICK SCHOOLS ACT, THE (1973), R.S.N.B, New Brunswick, Canada.

PLUMMER, G. (1992), "Youth strategy/stay-in-school review", Department of Education (Anglophone Division), Province of New Brunswick, Canada, mimeo.

PLUMMER, G. (1993), "Peer tutoring programmes – an overview", Province of New Brunswick, Canada, mimeo.

RANKINE, F. and PLUMMER, G. (1990), "Youth strategy activities", Department of Education (English Division), Province of New Brunswick, Canada, mimeo.

RPSS – Data System (1992/93), Family and Community Social Services Programme Statistics.

WOODSTOCK (1991), "Weighing the options: students at risk and school success. School Districts 28 and 29 drop-out research study", Woodstock, New Brunswick, Canada, mimeo.

WOODSTOCK (1992), "Schooling and at risk youth: Strategies and actions", Summary report on recommendations from six seminars on the educational issues related to students at risk, School Districts 28 and 29, Woodstock and School Districts 30 and 31 Perth-Andover, Woodstock, New Brunswick, Canada, mimeo.

3

FINLAND

A "SAFETY NET" APPROACH
TO INTEGRATED SERVICES PROVISION

by

Philippa Hurrell, Josette Combes, Jennifer Evans, Peter Evans,
Mary Lewis, Lucienne Roussel and Richard Volpe

INTRODUCTION

Finland, like other Nordic countries, is renowned for its strong tradition of social welfare. Generous government spending on education, health and social services is supported by a policy of high taxation. The outcome is a population characterised by high educational achievement, good health (particularly amongst infants), low poverty levels, and limited social marginalisation. However, in the last few years the global recession – which has hit the Finnish economy particularly hard – has signalled a change both in the government's philosophy regarding services provision, and in the nature and size of the client population. The government is looking for ways to make services more cost-effective, and also more successful in meeting the needs of clients; the client population is becoming more varied and larger as youth unemployment, social problems amongst youth such as substance and alcohol abuse, and the country's refugee population, continue to rise.

It is within this context that the present report will discuss government and local initiatives in Finland to provide "integrated" education, health and social services for children and youth at risk and their families. Many OECD countries see "integration", or increased co-operation, co-ordination and collaboration between services, as a means through which better services can be provided more cost-effectively. As a government policy, its significance is heightened in many of these countries by high rates of school failure and youth unemployment which increases the number of children and youth "at risk" of social marginalisation in their adult life.

Central questions which will be addressed in the report include: What kind of support for an integrated approach to services provision is provided at the government and local level? How are policies promoting integration put into practice by service providers? And how effective is integration as a means to improve outcomes? These issues will be addressed by considering, at a general level, Finnish legislation and policies concerning integrated services and, at a more concrete level, by describing three case studies of examples of "best" practice in integrated services, carried out by a team of OECD experts.

THE SOCIO-ECONOMIC CONTEXT

Covering 338 000 square kilometres, Finland is marginally smaller than the unified Germany (356 900 square kilometres) but has a population that is less than one tenth (5 029 000 in 1991) that of Germany's (79 819 000 in 1991) (OECD, 1993). The average population density is 14.9 people per square kilometre, but the majority of the population lives in the south, especially in and around Helsinki where population densities are highest. The age structure of Finland's population mirrors that of many other OECD countries with a relatively small proportion of the population under the age of 15 (19.2 per cent in 1991) and a large proportion over 65 years of age (13.6 per cent in 1991). Hence it shares with other Member states the specific economic problems associated with an ageing population.

Finland is characterised by its ethnic homogeneity although it has a small population (6 per cent) of Swedes who speak Swedish as their first language. The predominant religion in the country is Lutheran.

Of the total population, 2 559 000 people (1991) are active members of the labour force, and almost one half of these are women. Of all females aged 15-64, 71.8 per cent are employed, a percentage which among OECD countries is only surpassed by Denmark, Iceland and Sweden. What is more, almost 90 per cent are in full-time as opposed to part-time employment. This high level of female participation in the labour force has been facilitated by a relatively equitable perception of the sexual division of labour and generous state childcare provision.

Less than one tenth of its work force (8.5 per cent) are employed in agriculture, forestry and fishing, around a third (29.2 per cent) in industry, and almost two thirds (62.3 per cent) in services. Hence Finland's economy is more service oriented than its traditional "forestry and fishing" reputation would suggest.

During the 1980s, Finland's economy grew rapidly at a rate of around 3 per cent per annum. However since 1990, with the collapse of trade with Russia following democratisation and increased global competition, its GNP has declined by 15 per cent. It is now facing an economic crisis. This is reflected in an ailing banking system requiring government subsidy, and an unemployment rate of around 20 per cent. High and rising unemployment is a relatively new problem in Finland since as recently as 1991 it was below 8 per cent. A special feature is the extent to which it has hit young people: so far they have borne the brunt of the recession with unemployment amongst under 25-year-olds as high as 25 per cent.

However, for all citizens, including those in "risk" situations, Finland provides a "safety net" of services which are generously financed. Of the country's total GDP, 5.9 per cent are spent on education, 5.3 per cent on health, and 4.0 per cent on social security and welfare. Finland ranks in the top four OECD countries – for which data is available – on each of these measures. High spending on human services has been supported by central government and municipal taxes which together constitute a high tax regime. This is reflected in the disposable income of the average production worker as a percentage of gross pay: Finland is ranked only 17th out of all OECD countries (OECD, 1993).

With high unemployment, however, Finland's tax base has shrunk and cuts in human services have been a necessary response, albeit one that threatens the quality of support for children and youth at risk and their families.

FINLAND'S ADMINISTRATION

Finland is a parliamentary republic, the supreme authorities being the President, a Parliament with 200 members, and the government. In central government the two ministries responsible for human services are Social Affairs and Health, and Education. Their main role is to draft laws and regulations, plan resource allocation policy in their sectors, and supervise social welfare, health and education provision. Supporting the Ministry of Social Affairs and Health is the National Research and Development Centre for Welfare and Health, which carries out and disseminates research to inform planning and decision-making. The Ministry of Education also has a supporting body, the National Board of Education, which is responsible for developing educational objectives, methods and content for primary, secondary, vocational and adult education.

At the regional level, Finland has twelve provincial administrations each of which have several departments, including Social Affairs and Health, and Education. Departments of Social Affairs and Health control and supervise the implementation of social and health policies, approve the statutory activities of the municipalities, and are responsible for the payment of government subsidies. Departments of Education are responsible for the regional administration of general and vocational education.

At the base of Finland's three-tiered administration are its 455 municipalities which, in accordance with a policy of decentralisation, enjoy a large amount of autonomy in relation to central and provincial government. Financial independence is the outcome of the right to levy local taxes. Municipalities are responsible for the provision of basic services including welfare and education. However, they do not provide all public services themselves; for example, in 1993 around 60 per cent of social welfare services were bought from private organisations. The cost of running local services is shared with the central government which provides special state grants and subsidies. The government's average contribution is 50 per cent, although it is higher in poorer municipalities.

CHILDREN AND YOUTH AT RISK

Like most OECD countries, problems of definition and lack of statistics make it difficult for Finland to identify the proportion of children and youth nation-wide who are at risk of failure in school and in the transition to work. Recent estimates have been based on the number of children and youth who use psycho-social services, which means that those who are at risk but have not received professional support are not included.

In 1988, 58 395 children and youth aged 0-17 years, or 5 per cent of the total population in this age-group, were provided with psycho-social support: 20 539 received child welfare services; 21 635 received child guidance and family counselling; and 16 221 were provided with psychiatric help (National Board of Education and National Research and Development Centre for Welfare and Health, 1994). These figures are likely to increase as high unemployment, which is known to impact on children's well-being, persists.

Since OECD countries use different criteria for defining their at risk populations, the percentage figures they provide are not directly comparable. However, it is interesting to compare Finnish estimates with those for Japan and the Netherlands which are at opposite ends of the spectrum. Japan, defines at risk children as those who are likely to be school refusers or to drop out, and reports that in 1987 the rate of school refusal was 0.54 per cent and that of drop out, 2.1 per cent (OECD, 1995). In contrast, the Netherlands regards almost half (47 per cent) of its primary school aged population as "at risk", on the basis that additional resources are allocated to schools for these children.

One of the most significant risk factors for Finland's youth is alcohol abuse, with around 17 per cent of boys and 11 per cent of girls aged 16 consuming alcohol weekly. Also threatening to young people's successful participation in society is the high rate of youth unemployment which is emerging as an important cause of alienation and social marginalisation.

In terms of ethnic groupings in Finland, it is the children of the small Romany population who are considered to be most at risk. There are believed to be around 6 000 Gypsies in Finland, although the exact number is unknown because they cannot be registered by race. It is estimated that more than 70 per cent of these children drop out of school before they reach the age of 14.

SOCIAL WELFARE AND HEALTH SERVICES

Finland provides universal social welfare and health care from cradle to grave.

During pregnancy, almost 100 per cent of expectant mothers attend Maternity and Child Health Centres which are part of communal health centres. In these centres, the mother's health and the development of the foetus are carefully monitored, and the family is helped to prepare for child birth and child care. Expectant mothers and foetuses at particular risk are also identified.

Upon the birth of a child – which almost always takes place in hospital – the parents are entitled to Maternity, Paternity or Parents' Leave. During this time they receive a daily allowance amounting to 67 per cent of their normal salary, or a minimum allowance if they had no previous income. In addition, mothers are entitled to a Maternity Benefit either paid in cash, or in the form of a maternity pack (including baby clothes) worth twice the amount of the cash benefit. However, to receive this they must contact their local health centre or a doctor before the end of the fourth month of their pregnancy. Parents also receive a Child Allowance for every child they have between the ages of 0 and 17.

New mothers and infants (until the age of 6) are entitled to a variety of services, including health and psychological care, from their local Maternity and Child Health Centre. These centres monitor children's health and development, provide expert advice on child health and care, and provide necessary vaccinations. Before a child starts school, they also conduct a "school entry check-up". Relevant information is then shared with the educational authorities.

Child guidance and family counselling is available in Family Counselling Offices which help families to solve any problems that they may experience in child upbringing or general family life. Staffing these offices are multi-professional teams, including child psychiatrists, psychologists and social workers.

Extensive child care services are available to both preschool and school children. Once parental leave has ended, every child under the age of 3 is legally entitled to a Municipal Day Care place. Alternatively, if the parents wish to continue caring for their child at home, they are entitled to claim a Home Care Allowance. Parents of children under 3 can also claim a partial allowance if they reduce the number of hours they work each week in order to care for their child. In 1993, around 85 000 children under the age of 3 were provided for by the Home Care Allowance system. Parents can also receive compensation for loss of earnings resulting from the care of sick or convalescent children. Of all Nordic countries, Finland's home care allowance system is the most comprehensive.

Day care in Finland takes a variety of forms including Day Care Centres for preschool children, Day Care Centres for school children, Family Day Care, and Special Day Care. In addition, there are Open Day Care Centres for children and adults, Roving Day Care Centres in sparsely populated areas, 24 Hour Day Care Centres, and Day Care Centres open during extended hours. Around 48 per cent of all children under school age have a Municipal Day Care place of some kind. Most of these are full-time although there are a small number of part-time places for school children. These are paid for by the family according to its size and income.

Of those children who have a Municipal Day Care place, 58 per cent attend Day Care Centres. A total of 2 000 Municipal Day Care Centres exist in Finland and all are state subsidised. Working alongside them are Private Day Care Centres which are also subsidised by the state and function in a similar way. The other 42 per cent of children with Municipal Day Care places are cared for by Municipal Family Day Care. Parents can choose where they want to send their child.

The Finnish day care system also provides voluntary preschool education for 6-year-olds. In sparsely populated areas this is attached to comprehensive schools. In 1992, a total of 52 per cent of eligible children received a preschool education, either within the day care system or within the education system.

EDUCATION

Compulsory state education starts comparatively late in Finland: children are not required to attend school until they are 7. The first six years of compulsory schooling constitute the primary phase (7-13 years) and the last three years, the lower secondary phase (14-16 years). For both phases, students attend the same "comprehensive" school. A special feature of the comprehensive system is that all aspects of schooling, from textbooks to school meals and transportation, are free. In 1992-93, it provided for 591 655 children.

Post-compulsory education is provided in general upper secondary schools and vocational institutions. Finnish vocational education is mainly institution-based, although most programmes provide some practical training in industry. Some of those studying in vocational institutions participate in apprenticeship schemes; however, the number is small (3-4 per cent each year).

In accordance with stated national policy, participation in post-compulsory education is almost universal. Of comprehensive school leavers, 54 per cent continue their education in general upper secondary schools, and 40 per cent enter vocational institutions. The remaining 6 per cent either choose to do an optional tenth class, or try to secure work. However, with minimal educational qualifications, this group is at high risk of unemployment.

The majority (54 per cent) of Finland's vocational institutions are locally run, usually by a consortium of two or three municipalities. A further 34 per cent are owned by the state, and 12 per cent are private, although many state owned institutions are expected to be turned over to the municipalities in the near future. Courses are provided in three main areas: technical industries, service industries and primary production. Students with vocational qualifications at the upper secondary level are eligible for further studies at polytechnics or higher vocational colleges. For university education, general upper secondary qualifications are normally required. Of all Finnish students, 30 per cent win places on university courses each year.

Finland has a range of provision for special educational needs students who wish to follow vocational courses. These include special vocational institutions (mainly for disabled students), special classes, and integrated education in ordinary vocational institutions. Teachers of special classes frequently have a qualification in special education from one of two vocational teacher education universities in Finland (in Hämeenlinna and Jyväskylä).

Finland's special vocational institutions presently are threatened with an uncertain financial future. In contrast, special classes in ordinary vocational institutions became well established in the 1980s, and continue to be well funded (although recently there have been some cuts). While these classes can offer only a limited range of courses, they are well adapted to opportunities in local industries, and are especially tailored to meet individual needs.

A range of other specialist services can also be found in Finland's schools. Health care is provided by school doctors and nurses who, in addition to their day-to-day responsibilities, provide twice yearly medical check-ups. Psycho-social care is provided by school psychologists and social workers, and personal careers advice is offered by student counsellors.

Educational provision in Finland is, and historically has been, generous; however, schools are now preparing to tighten their belts as the government starts to implement planned cuts. In addition to budgetary changes, new education legislation concerning comprehensive, upper secondary, vocational and adult education is currently being developed by the Ministry of Education. This will lead to significant changes in the way in which education is organised and delivered. An important example in this respect is the transfer of responsibility for the curriculum from the National Board of Education to local comprehensive schools with the goal of allowing greater teacher, parent and pupil input into curriculum development.

THE ORIGINS OF GOVERNMENT SUPPORT FOR THE INTEGRATION OF SERVICES

Support for human services integration was a reaction to the proliferation of health and social services in the 1970s and 1980s, precipitated by the National Health Act of 1972 and the Social Welfare Act of 1984. This expansion was accompanied by an increase in professional specialisation. As the service system became more complex, service-users found it necessary to contact different professionals for different problems. Often no one professional or agency had overall responsibility for co-ordinating treatment. Professionals tended to focus upon a specific aspect of an individual's problem without considering their whole situation, or linkages with other service efforts. Although increased professionalism meant that more expertise was available, the service delivery system became less understandable and more complicated to use.

The need for greater integration in human services was recognised by many different groups including administrators, professionals and clients and was enthusiastically embraced by the government as a way to provide better services more cost-effectively. In the early 1990s, in a climate of high unemployment where growing numbers of children were at risk and public funds were limited, improvements in the quality of service provision and reductions in spending were both viewed as high priorities.

POLICIES SUPPORTING THE INTEGRATION OF SERVICES

In the late 1980s and early 1990s, several government laws and policies impacted on the ability of services to co-ordinate their activities. Five of the major pieces of legislation which have favoured integration are outlined below:

- Since the 1970s and 1980s, the maintenance of consistency in social welfare and health values and activities has been a guiding principle in order to facilitate the integration of human services. The 1992 Planning and State Subsidies for Welfare Act sets out common rules for the planning and funding of social welfare and health services to achieve this goal.

- In 1993, aiming to improve the accessibility of human services, Parliament passed the Integrated Customer Services Act which removed obstacles preventing public authorities from providing integrated services in joint "front-line offices".

- Implemented in early 1993, State Subsidy Reform has given municipalities greater control over central government funding. The state now provides each municipality with a lump sum – based on total population, age structure and local tax revenues – which they can allocate for social and health services as they choose. While they are bound by legislation to provide basic services, money can be used flexibly to purchase services from various agencies according to different funding arrangements. This means that there is more potential to finance integrated service programmes.

- A very strict obligation to observe secrecy concerning client information is characteristic of social welfare and health legislation. This is in contrast to the general principle of openness which prevails in social welfare and health services provision, and the extensive rights of individuals to access personal information which is kept by the state. However, in the last few years legislation on confidentiality has been eased in order to facilitate discussion between professionals concerning shared clients.

- Following a successful piloting programme between 1989 and 1992, a policy of Local Population Responsibility (LPR) has been adopted state-wide. According to this principle, a multi-professional team of social welfare and health professionals is given responsibility for a small geographically defined area containing 2 000 to 4 000 people. The aim is to improve the co-ordination, functioning and accessibility of services to better meet the needs of service users. Important focuses of this policy are family-centred approaches, community care and prevention. The National Research and Development Centre for Welfare and Health provides training teams and materials to support the LPR process and is assessing its outcome.

POLICY ASSESSMENT: LOCAL POPULATION RESPONSIBILITY

An assessment of the potential of Local Population Responsibility (LPR) has been made by Mäkelä *et al.* (1993). They consider the likely outcomes of Local Population Responsibility for health and social welfare services, although they are at pains to emphasise that it may be four to eight years before the real effects of this policy can be seen. They argue that one advantage of LPR is the clear designation of responsibility to provide basic health and social welfare services to a targeted group of citizens whom the staff can get to know. This potentially can lead to quicker and friendlier service, improved continuity of care, and higher visibility of service results. Team members can determine locally appropriate service plans with more versatility, and the number of services can be increased without employing extra staff. Staff can also identify local service needs, and develop solutions through multi-sectoral co-operation. Mixed participation in service planning can help to prevent unnecessary mistakes.

Mäkelä *et al.* also believe that LPR holds possibilities for fostering creative local experiments involving multi-professional and non-hierarchical teams. Successful team development can lead to greater commitment, efficiency and consensus about values and goals. Furthermore, the shift in approach from patients to populations is likely to re-focus operational efforts on preventive goals.

Many workers who already have participated in LPR have expressed satisfaction with their enhanced independence and the more varied content of their work. There have also been signs of improved satisfaction among clients.

On the negative side, LPR may mean that staff turnover will be problematic. The attempt by professionals to meet all types of client needs may reduce excellence in specialist areas. The elimination of strict professional borders may create the illusion that everyone can do any job, and arouse resistance amongst those who feel that important principles are being overlooked. In addition, too much familiarity with clients' situations could result in diminishing professional distance from clients which, in turn, could lead to infringements upon clients' privacy.

Mäkelä *et al.* conclude that Finland's current economic situation, which has led to decreases in human services staff and other resources, will motivate many municipalities to try LPR.

THE RESEARCH SITES

The locations for the case studies were Helsinki, on the south coast of Finland, Jyväskylä, in central Finland, and Hämeenlinna, 100 kilometres north of Helsinki. In Helsinki the focus was on preschool children, in Jyväskylä, school children, and in Hämeenlinna, youth in the transition to work. These towns were carefully selected as models of excellence in respect of their integrated services provision. The following provides a brief description of the socio-economic environment in each town.

Helsinki: Established in 1550, Helsinki is the capital of Finland with a population of around half a million people. Its major industries include metallurgy, ship building and engineering. The unemployment rate in Helsinki has rocketed over the last four years: in 1990 it was below 2 per cent; by 1994 it had reached 18 per cent. The population is relatively homogeneous. However, there are small immigrant communities from Scandanavia, western Europe, Africa, Asia, Estonia and Russia.

Jyväskylä: With a population of around 71 000, Jyväskylä is the fourth largest town in Finland. It is also the capital of the Province of Central Finland. It is an important educational centre, as the location of the University of Jyväskylä and other learning institutions, and is frequently referred to as the "Athens of Finland". It is also a commercial and industrial centre with significant pulp and paper, paper-making machinery, nuclear, and high technology industries. In 1993, the unemployment rate stood at 25 per cent of the work force.

Hämeenlinna: Hämeenlinna was founded in 1639 as the first inland town in Finland. Today it is a small settlement of 44 000 people. It serves as the capital of Häme Province, and as such is an important centre of administration and education. Situated on the main railway line from Helsinki to Lapland, it is also an important travel and tourist centre. After the service sector, the second largest industry is manufacturing, in which both steel-making and vehicle production are important. Hämeenlinna's population has traditionally been relatively prosperous; however, the economic recession has led to high youth unemployment. The town is ethnically homogenous with only a small immigrant community – approximately 300 – of whom around one half are refugees from countries such as Iran, Iraq and Somalia.

INTEGRATED SERVICES FOR PRESCHOOL CHILDREN IN THE CITY OF HELSINKI

The Helsinki case study focused on three different institutions providing preschool services: the Myllypuro Maternity and Child Health Centre, the Käpylä Home for Small Children, and the Oulunkylä Mother-Child Home. The Myllypuro Maternity and Child Health Centre is an example of a state-wide, public sector service which provides universal health care for mothers and their children. The Kapylä Home for Small Children is a municipal service which is targeted at young children in crisis situations. The Oulunkylä Mother-Child Home is also a targeted service – for mothers who have problems with intoxicants – but is run by a voluntary organisation. Each of these institutions has its own unique network of partners with whom it collaborates. However they also share many partners in common and frequently co-operate directly with each other.

The following provides a brief description of each institution, and then goes on to consider for all of them the nature of political support for collaboration, the resources and training made available, the process of services provision, factors promoting and inhibiting collaboration, and the results of collaborative efforts. The section will also endeavour to draw out the character of collaboration at each institution, and the nature of the relationships between them.

The institutions

The Myllypuro Maternity and Child Health Centre: The city of Helsinki is served by seven health districts and seven social welfare districts which cover identical geographical areas. Each of the districts provides an array of municipal human services. These include maternity and child health care, general health care, hospital care, mental health provision, day care, family counselling, home help, and social security support. In one of the districts is Myllypuro, a small community of around 9 400 Finns which is located on the east side of Helsinki. The incidence in the community of unemployment, dependency on welfare benefits, one-parent families, and poor educational attainment is higher than the national average; hence many families are considered to be at risk. The Myllypuro Maternity and Child Health Centre is one of the health services that operates in the area, providing universal health and social services for mothers and young children aged 0 to 6 years.

The Käpylä Home for Small Children: This is a reception home for children up to 4 years of age who are in crisis situations. It is run by the Social Welfare Board in Helsinki. The Home can accommodate up to 21 children (nine babies and twelve preschool children), and cares for between 70 and 80 children annually. The majority of these children are taken into care because of intoxicant abuse by their parents (62 per cent of cases) or because of parents' mental health problems (24 per cent of cases). They are cared for by the Home's 35 staff, of whom 27 are care workers. Most of these have backgrounds in nursing, and have formal training qualifications. The Home also has one social worker who liaises closely with the local social welfare centre.

The Oulunkylä Mother-Child Home: This home was opened recently (1990), and is part of a five-year experimental programme funded by the Federation of Mother-Child Homes and Centres, a voluntary organisation. It provides accommodation and care for (up to six) pregnant or new mothers who have problems with alcohol or other intoxicants. Clients range in age from 16 to 40 years old and come from a variety of social backgrounds, including middle class families. The main aim of the Home is to give mothers support to abstain from intoxicant use, and to become successful parents. Ten staff, including a director, welfare worker and eight counsellors, are involved in this task.

Political and other support for collaboration

According to respondents from the Myllypuro Maternity and Child Health Centre, collaboration between municipal services in the district was greatly facilitated by an organisational change, orchestrated at the administrative level, which gave health and social welfare professionals responsibility for a shared geographical area. Previously, in the early 1980s, professionals had tended to work in different service sectors, such as schools.

Staff shared the view that while this organisational change had made collaboration possible, one of the main impetuses behind it had been the realisation amongst professionals that they had common concerns. Their perception of collaboration as a grassroots initiative is reflected in the assertion that it was "our choice (...) our decision". It also manifested itself in comments which referred to the inability of top-down "commands" to force collaboration at the field level.

At the Käpylä Home for Small Children collaboration is articulated by staff as one of their central objectives. Part of the philosophy which underpins their activities is that crisis management should be performed in co-operation with families, and that co-operation with other service partners should be high. This perspective is supported and implemented by all staff who work in the Home.

Support for the setting up of the Oulunkylä Mother-Child Home arose from influential research by Dr. Erja Halmesmaki which highlighted the significant dangers of alcohol abuse in pregnancy. The research alerted local hospitals to the benefits that could be gained from collaborating with a specialised residential institution which could address the specific needs of mothers with alcohol problems. Staff in the Home, practice both intra-institutional and inter-institutional collaboration.

Resources and training

The Myllypuro Maternity and Child Health Centre receives its funding from the municipal health department. Staff reported that financial support to implement an integrated approach has been adequate. However, they have not been allocated sufficient time for collaborative meetings, and have not received any specific training in collaborative work practices. Support for collaboration was felt to be more forthcoming at the administrative level than at the operational level.

Funding for the Käpylä Home for Small Children comes from the municipal social welfare department. Care workers reported that they receive some joint training with nurses from other institutions which serve young children. However, they have not received any multi-disciplinary training.

The Oulunkylä Mother-Child Home is funded by the Federation of Mother-Child Homes and Centres, the Association of Slot Machine Charities, and the municipal social welfare department. The latter "buys" services from the Home, providing a set amount for each client served. The Home's staff received joint training for one month prior to its opening, and continue to receive it on a regular basis. The Home is considering whether they might in the future negotiate a contract with the municipality of Helsinki to take over the establishment's funding; however, there is some concern over loss of autonomy.

The collaborative process

Collaboration between health and social welfare professionals in the Myllypuro Maternity and Child Health Centre takes various forms which range in their degree of formality. Most formal are the six weekly general meetings which are convened to discuss policy matters. These grew out of joint lunches arranged by staff for social purposes. Senior managers recommended larger joint meetings but this advice was rejected. Slightly less formal are staff case conferences which can be arranged as the need arises. These are supplemented by informal bilateral contacts which often take the form of telephone conversations. While several professionals frequently co-operate to meet the needs of a particular client, they always designate one person as a case manager. In this way the client's family has a single, and therefore clearly defined, point of contact.

Much of the collaboration practised by Myllypuro's staff is based on close personal or professional relationships. A typical example is provided by a nurse and a social worker who, because they had developed a "good relationship", decided to work as a team in meeting the needs of multi-problem families in a particular street in Myllypuro. Coffee meetings, lunches and other informal meetings have played an important role in nurturing these kinds of arrangements.

At the Käpylä Home for Small Children, the involvement of the family in services provision is given a high priority. Once a child has been admitted, the Home convenes a meeting to which the family is invited to discuss the aims of the placement. These goals are recorded on an evaluation form, and the family is then asked at regular intervals to grade (between one and ten) the current status of its position in relation to them. The form serves as a contract with the family, helping them to articulate, remember, and work towards their goals. It is also used to decide the nature of the support that they require. The first meeting is followed by regular meetings with parents and other professionals who may be involved. In some cases, intensive support for the child is provided over a period of two months in the family home; the level of co-operation required between professionals and parents is then particularly high.

The Home's staff also work in close co-operation with other public sector services. For example, if a social worker from the local social welfare services is already involved in a case they will continue their involvement after the child has entered the Home. However, when there has been no history of social welfare involvement, the Home's own social worker takes responsibility. Staff also work closely with the child's local maternity and child health centre and, if the child has been hospitalised, with the hospital. The Home implements any health advice that it receives from these institutions.

Collaboration is not confined to other public services, and targeted, voluntary services may be approached if they are able to meet a specific need. A typical example is the referral of mother and child pairs whom the Home feels should remain together to the Oulunkylä Mother-Child Home. Other forms of external collaboration – aside from those centring primarily on the child – relate to the educational and employment needs of parents. In this respect the Home frequently liaises with educational institutions and employment authorities.

At the hub of these various kinds of collaborative activities is the Home's social worker. She regularly liaises with staff from the local social welfare centre, and is a key link person between them and the Home's nurses. She also negotiates and attends meetings, often with other members of the Home's staff, with various agencies. The local A-clinic – for people with alcohol problems – is a typical example.

At the Oulunkylä Mother-Child Home collaboration with the client is given a high priority. The decision of a client to receive treatment at the Home has to be voluntary. Once this decision has been made, clients are asked to sign an "agreement" with the Home indicating their willingness to receive help. Each client is allocated a personal counsellor who works closely with them. The client is an active partner in decision-making, and is required to sign a mutually agreed treatment plan which is evaluated every two months. The structure of activities in the Home is based on a community model where everyone works together and shares daily tasks. When the client leaves the Home she is not immediately "dropped" by the community but continues to receive professional support for around six months, and to be invited to social functions for up to two years.

The idea of community also extends beyond the Home with the client's family and friends also being regarded as an important part of the support system. Partners and the wider family are encouraged to visit clients in the Home and to participate in various social activities. Even so, some partners feel excluded from the treatment process, and reportedly this has been the cause of some "trouble".

The key professional partners in the treatment of clients are the Home's welfare worker and counsellors. However, there is also extensive collaboration with outside agencies. For example, the Home works closely with referring institutions such as health centres, hospital clinics and child welfare agencies, and also with agencies for adult intoxicant abuse such as the Helsinki hospital drug withdrawal unit and A-clinics. It also uses the services of the Käpylä Home for Small Children, typically in cases where it is felt that the baby should be separated from its mother at birth. It is at present common practice to take endangered babies into care very early on, so that at the earliest possible moment they can be placed with a foster family.

Co-operation with outside agencies is particularly intense when the mother leaves the Home. At this stage, for example, child care workers from the local child welfare services are normally invited by the Home to discuss the kind of external supports that the mother will need. The agency also liaises as necessary with other kinds of agencies who are able to provide support, such as the Housing Agency and A-clinics. Every effort is made to ensure that the mother receives adequate "post-treatment" care and guidance.

Promoting and inhibiting factors

The Myllypuro Maternity and Child Health Centre's health and social welfare professionals regard responsibility for a shared geographical area as one of the key supports to their collaborative efforts, since by definition they have the same clients. However, they also believe that there are some important obstacles to be overcome such as deeply-ingrained professional prejudices, and the lack of time available for collaborative work. The setting up of joint training programmes, and an increase in the time allowed for joint meetings, are seen by them as important solutions.

Staff at the Käpylä Home for Small Children have met with some resistance in their efforts to collaborate with outside agencies, particularly from those serving adult groups. This seems to stem from the fact that these agencies do not always perceive a need for child welfare services involvement. Furthermore there is sometimes a difference in perspective with respect to client treatment. For example, the local hospital prefers to keep families together when treating parents' mental health problems, whereas the Home is more inclined to take children into care – particularly when they are perceived to be at high risk. However, over the last two years through working together relations with other agencies have improved, and they have a better understanding of each other's perspective.

The Oulunkylä Mother-Child Home experienced a certain amount of hostility in its early collaborative efforts. This largely related to the view shared by agencies for intoxicant abusers that the Home was a child welfare facility with limited expertise in adult problems. However, with time these agencies have become more open, and now work closely with the Home.

Outcomes

Staff at the Myllypuro Maternity and Child Health Centre emphasised the difficulty in accurately and appropriately evaluating the outcomes of their collaborative efforts but were able to identify several areas in which there were apparent improvements. These include: increased speed in the allocation of professional help to clients; better continuity in professional-client contact; more consistency in the information and advice given to clients; and increased professional satisfaction and support. They also felt that by nominating a single case manager for each client, they were able to avoid multiple visits by different professionals to clients' homes.

The staff at the Käpylä Home for Small Children have seen a drop from 66 in 1991, to 29 in 1993, in the number of placements at the home. They felt that these figures could be interpreted in two ways: either preventive services have become more effective, or services have become less inclined to place children in institutional care. They also reported a decline between 1991 and 1993 from 66 per cent to 52 per cent in the proportion of children who were returned to their own homes. This was accompanied by a rise from 13 per cent to 24 per cent in the proportion referred to other institutions. In contrast to the earlier figures, this actually suggests a greater inclination by the authorities to place young children in care. Staff felt that, with figures such as these, it was very difficult to establish whether the Home had become more effective or not.

At the Oulunkylä Mother-Child Home staff estimated that about one third of their clients are successful in leading a normal life after they have left the Home: they stop drinking excessively and take good care of their children. On the other hand around one quarter of their clients continue to have serious problems: many have their babies taken into care and become pregnant again. No information was given on the other clients who had received treatment.

New directions in services provision in Helsinki

As of 1994, health and social welfare workers in Helsinki were no longer responsible for a specific age-group in their local area, but instead assumed responsibility for the primary health care of the whole population. According to senior managers, the purpose of this re-organisation was to improve the efficiency and effectiveness of services by reducing specialist services and increasing preventive efforts. However, the plan met with some resistance from professional workers who felt that as a result, they would lose many of their specialist skills and competences.

A second development is the general trend away from the institutional care of clients to open care in the community. However, there is a concern amongst senior managers that because of the recession fewer resources will be available to fund professional salaries for community provision. They believe that this will lead to a transfer of care responsibilities from the municipality to families, a pattern already distinguishable in the care of the elderly.

We were also informed that, in April 1994, Local Population Responsibility will be brought to Helsinki with the opening of a joint health and social welfare centre in Pihlajamäki. The professionals at the centre will be divided into four mixed teams which will each serve a population of around 3 000 people. The teams will consist of one or two doctors, three or four nurses, one or two social workers, between five and seven home helps, and a small number of auxiliary workers. Over a two-year development period prior to its opening, much consideration has been given to the training of these professionals for collaborative tasks. In Helsinki, as elsewhere, this kind of emphasis is quite new.

Future directions in Helsinki's human services are hard to predict. Present levels of government and professional support for integrated services suggest that efforts to increase collaboration amongst the city's services will continue. However, professionals indicated that future reductions in funding might hinder collaboration in two important ways: by increasing competition between services, and by reducing their ability to introduce integrated approaches.

Summary and discussion

Collaboration amongst human services for preschool children in Helsinki has been very well supported by government and local policies. Initiatives which have encouraged joint responsibility for geographic areas, a reduction in professional specialism, professional team work, and open care in the community, have created an environment in which collaboration can flourish. The professional will to collaborate in preschool services is high, and these initiatives have enabled field level workers to react to the multiple needs of clients in the way they see best.

However, collaboration has to some extent been hindered by a lack of support at the operational level. Special resources, such as time for joint activities, have not always been made available, and training programmes to promote collaborative work have been few. However, some of these shortfalls have been addressed in newer initiatives such as the joint health and social welfare centre at Pihlajamäki.

The process of collaboration amongst Helsinki's services for preschool children is many faceted. Professionals work together in both formal and informal ways, sometimes basing their collaboration on personal relationships that they have developed through social activities. The involvement of the client and their family in the planning and implementation of treatment is given a high priority, and strong efforts are made to help clients in the transition back to a normal way of life. Universal and targeted services, and public and voluntary services, work together in a mixed network to meet clients' needs. While not being truly integrated, a high level of co-operation exists between them and they exploit each other's resources as and when they are required.

Co-operation is not without its difficulties however. Service providers for adults have sometimes viewed the involvement of children's services as ineffective or unnecessary. At other times services have disagreed about how clients can best be served. These problems have tended to disappear as the services through experience have come to understand each other.

While co-operation had been a characteristic of Helsinki's preschool services for a number of years, it is difficult to pin-point the level of success that has been achieved in improving client outcomes. This is because very little evaluation work seems to have been carried out. Certainly this is an area which could be usefully developed in future integrated services initiatives in Helsinki.

INTEGRATED SERVICES FOR SCHOOL CHILDREN IN THE TOWN OF JYVÄSKYLÄ

In Jyväskylä, the OECD case study focused on three contrasting human services sectors, each of which have adopted integrated strategies and working methods to meet the needs of school children. Universal, public sector services were represented by the Huhtasuo Social and Health Centre and the Huhtaharju Comprehensive School. Also included in this category was the Nenäinniemi Elementary School and Day Care Centre which is a model programme that is likely to be replicated elsewhere. The Jyväskylä Town Youth Workshop and the Hovila Youth Home were introduced as examples of targeted, public sector services, and voluntary services were represented by the Mannerheim League for Child Welfare, and the Finnish Gypsy Foundation. As in Helsinki's preschool services, these services operate as a complex network in which within service and between service co-operation and collaboration are commonplace. The following account of these institutions will address the same kind of issues discussed in respect of the Helsinki example, but will also endeavour to draw out the characteristics of the Jyväskylä human services network which make it "special".

Universal public sector institutions

The Huhtasuo Social and Health Centre: The Huhtasuo Social and Health Centre illustrates Jyväskylä's approach to Local Population Responsibility, combining health and social welfare services at one neighbourhood site. The Centre, which was set up five years ago, serves around 9 365 people who live in a socio-economically disadvantaged area. It is located next door to the local comprehensive school, and also to a special school for children with cerebral palsy and motor disabilities. It is run by a combined Municipal Social Services and Health Board which grew out of the merging of separate social welfare and health administrations in 1993. Services provided by the Centre include health counselling, medical care, home nursing, school health care, day care, social welfare support and home help.

Nenäinniemi Elementary School and Day Care Centre: Nenäinniemi is a new residential area with a socio-economically mixed population including a number of families with serious problems. The Nenäinniemi Elementary School and Day Care Centre provides day care services and primary school education to children between 1 and 8 years of age at one site; the standard pattern in Finland is to provide these services separately. The Centre has two administrators, one in charge of day care personnel, and the other in charge of a pedagogical team of four teachers. In 1993, the day care programme provided for 97 children, and the education programme for 70 children.

The Huhtaharju Comprehensive School: The Huhtaharju Comprehensive School is a typical Finnish comprehensive school providing compulsory education for children from 7 to 16 years of age. Like most large comprehensive schools it has its own Student Welfare Group. This is a mixed professional team – including the headmaster, teachers, a school counsellor, a health visitor, a social worker and a family clinic representative – that addresses student and school problems. The Student Welfare Group was chosen as the main focus of the study visit.

Political support and objectives

The provision of combined services at the Huhtasuo Social and Health Centre was the outcome of the government's policy to promote joint social welfare and health services at single-sites; a policy that was facilitated by the unification of the separate national social welfare and health administrations into one Ministry of Social Affairs and Health. At the provincial and municipal levels unification of a similar kind was made optional – but in Jyväskylä both levels of administration decided to embrace it. The municipal administration is still in the early stages of the merger; planning, development and research functions have already been combined while the unification of administrative functions has yet to take place. The municipality's goal is to co-locate and merge the functions of both sectors in neighbourhoods throughout the city, the Huhtasuo Centre being an early example of this objective.

While national government policy was a major impetus for municipal reorganisation, Jyväskylä's decision to integrate its health and social welfare services was also a response to a perceived need on the ground. Administrators and managers from the different services recognised that they were often serving the same clients. Unification was seen as an effective way to provide clients with better, more co-ordinated services. They also appreciated that it could help to reduce costs.

The concept of combined day care and primary schooling, exemplified by the Nenäinniemi Elementary School and Day Care Centre, is not recent. It has frequently been discussed at the national level, particularly in relation to the Parliamentary debate on lowering the starting age for compulsory education from 7 to 6. In Nenäinniemi, initial support for the implementation of the concept came from a group of key individuals in the municipal education and social services departments who succeeded in securing support and financing to set up a combined centre. Their efforts were helped by the fact that Nenäinniemi was a new residential area in which education and day care facilities were much needed.

Community support for the initiative was gauged by sending out a questionnaire in early 1993, prior to the commencement of building in the summer. Inhabitants were asked about their expectations of the project and about their willingness to participate in it on a voluntary basis. The project also has been buoyed by the enthusiasm of the education administrator, who decided to work in Nenäinniemi because of the new approach, and is a strong proponent of introducing it nation-wide.

One of the main purposes of providing day care and education on the same site is to integrate the educational content of the day care programme and the school curriculum. Other expectations are that children's learning problems will be identified earlier, and that the transition from day care to school will be much less difficult (as children effectively stay in the same place). Furthermore school children will be able to benefit from on-site after-school care which will be much more convenient for parents.

Multi-professional Student Welfare Groups such as the one at the Huhtaharju Comprehensive School first emerged as a concept in the early 1970s. The idea was popular and received widespread support. It is now national policy that the services of a Student Welfare Group should be available to pupils in every school.

Financial and other inputs

Funding for the Huhtasuo Social and Health Centre comes from the Municipal Social Service and Health Board. The various professionals working at the centre receive ongoing in-service training around special topics such as violence and responsibility for citizens' welfare. In the future the Centre may benefit from in-service initiatives being developed at the provincial and municipal levels to improve social workers' (and teachers') networking skills.

Nenäinniemi Elementary School and Day Care Centre is funded by the municipal education and social services departments. Both the School and the Centre have their own separate budgets. Joint staff training was provided prior to the opening of the facility with the specific aim of familiarising staff with the perspectives and approaches of their colleagues.

The Huhtaharju Comprehensive School receives its funding from the municipal education department. The different professionals attending the Student Welfare Group are paid for by their own services. No mention was made of special training to facilitate collaboration.

Collaboration in practice

The Huhtasuo Social and Health Centre's professional staff are organised into four mixed teams, each of which serves a population of around 3 000 people in the Huhtasuo area. Co-operation with local schools is high. One of the Centre's eight social workers participates in Student Welfare Groups which meet every other week in Jyväskylä's schools. Similarly, one of the Centre's health visitors is responsible for comprehensive school pupils' health care. The Centre also invites teachers to its general monthly meetings.

At the Nenäinniemi Elementary School and Day Care Centre, considerable emphasis is placed on collaboration with parents and the community. Parents are seen as equal partners who can play an important role in the early development of their child. Therefore the Centre tries to get to know them; to find out about their personal interests and their goals for their children. Parents are also invited to attend regular child assessments at the Centre which take place at least once each year. At a more general level, their involvement is encouraged by making the facility available for community meetings. It is, for example, the location of a weekly meeting of mothers who wish to get to know other women in the area.

The Centre also provides a number of other "community" services beyond its basic day care and education functions: a day care worker is available to parents of sick children (who have already used up their three day entitlement to parental sick leave); a nurse is available on site once every two weeks; a local social worker is available to families in crises; and a meal service is provided to elderly residents. The Centre is also involved in co-operative programmes with some of the neighbourhood's churches, and collaborates with the local library to provide children with books.

The mixed Student Welfare Group in Huhtaharju Comprehensive School aims to prevent and solve pupil problems, including violence, unsociable behaviour, and drug abuse. The Group meets on a regular basis to discuss these kinds of issue and to decide strategies for dealing with them. In addition to planned meetings, a group of three to four members will meet whenever a crisis situation arises. The services of the Social Welfare Group are in theory available to all pupils in the school; however, in practice only a small percentage of pupils – those most at risk – receive its support.

Obstacles to collaboration

Early on in their collaboration the Huhtasuo Centre's staff were very aware of differences in professional values and principles, although with time they have found a common base from which to work. Most difficult was unification at the municipal administrative level where competition for resources with other departments led to certain tensions.

Day care and teaching staff at the Nenäinniemi Elementary School and Day Care Centre acknowledged differences in the way that they conceptualise their work, and in their aims for young children. Day care staff view children in the context of their social, cultural and family environments, and aim to achieve educational goals through play and project work. In contrast, the teaching staff are more child-(rather than family-) centred and work towards educational goals through a structured curriculum. They did not refer to the extent to which this had created difficulties.

No obstacles to collaboration in the Huhtaharju Comprehensive School's Social Welfare Group were recorded.

The results of collaboration

The Huhtasuo Social and Health Centre's staff were very positive about the outcomes of professional teamwork, in terms of the benefits to clients and their own satisfaction. They have reached a better understanding of the roles of other professionals, and have established more effective working relationships to prevent crises. A typical example was provided by one of the social workers. A family was referred to her because of inadequate child care. She made a home visit and assessed the mother as being mentally ill. Immediately she was able to arrange for a doctor to make a second home visit with her where a medical evaluation confirmed her diagnosis. Consequently a supportive plan for the mother and family was arranged before a serious crisis could occur. The Centre's professionals are also able to get together to devise special programmes for prevention – in areas such as antenatal training for parents. Clients benefit from being able to access these services from one location.

In terms of meeting professional workers' needs, one of the main benefits of collaboration is the network of professional support that is available in the Centre. Staff are able to share with their colleagues the responsibility, and sometimes the burden, of working with multi-problem families.

Staff perceptions of the success of collaboration in the Centre are borne out by evaluation studies. These have shown that in areas which have unified health and social welfare services hospital admissions are lower, fewer personnel and night shifts are required, and clients are more satisfied.

In Nenäinniemi, since both the Elementary School and the Day Care Centre use the same facilities, the municipality judges that efficient and economical use of the new building has been made. No information was provided on client outcomes.

At the Huhtaharju Comprehensive School, the regular meetings of the Social Welfare Group allow pupils' problems to be addressed before they reach crisis point. The mixed nature of the Group means that these problems can be examined from a variety of perspectives. In this way the Group is better able to meet pupils' various and often complex needs.

Targeted public sector institutions

Institutional backgrounds and objectives

The Jyväskylä Town Youth Workshop and the Hovila Youth Home: The Jyväskylä Town Youth Workshop and the Hovila Youth Home are both targeted at youth who are unable to adjust to or refuse to go to school. The Finnish term for this group is "youth with school allergy". Both institutions aim either to keep youth in the education system or to help them make progress towards vocational goals. The development of these kinds of institutions was spurred by a law which required municipalities to provide youth with further education or employment after compulsory schooling. However, the severe economic recession in Finland has necessitated the suspension of this legislation because of the lack of available jobs.

The Jyväskylä Town Youth Workshop grew out of extensive co-operation between many of the town's administrative services, and now operates under the supervision of the Town Office for the Co-ordination of Recreational Activities. It primarily serves young people who have completed compulsory education but are unemployed, although it also takes a small number of school aged youth. In 1990, the Youth Workshop provided employment opportunities for 133 young people, and in the first half of 1993, for 80 more. It has a total of nine staff.

The Hovila Youth Home was founded as a residential Home in the 1960s, but has recently been transformed into a facility for youth with severe emotional disturbances who cannot, or will not, live at home, and who have difficulties at school. The Home provides accommodation, social care and education to a maximum of six young people aged between 14 and 18 years. Many have a history of drug abuse, violence, criminal behaviour or mental problems. Six care workers are on its staff.

The process of collaboration

A co-operative arrangement with the Keskikatu Comprehensive School provides the opportunity for young people at the Jyväskylä Town Youth Workshop to complete their compulsory education or to achieve higher grades. Vocational experience is acquired through carrying out work consignments received from the municipality, private businesses, and individuals. Opportunities are available in areas such as weaving, textile processing, upholstering, wood and metal work, and car repairs. Young people also benefit from cheap meals, group activities, excursions and, occasionally, lodging. In addition, social services are available if and when they are needed.

A working principle at the Workshop is to find solutions to problems based on new and unprejudiced ways of thinking. For example, it gave young people who had been involved in car theft the chance to work in car-related activities. The Workshop has been supported in this kind of approach by the Niilo Mäki Institute at the University of Jyväskylä which designs special rehabilitation programmes for it.

At the Hovila Youth Home, initial referrals from the social services or local schools are followed by individual and family assessments. On this basis, staff decide appropriate treatment and learning objectives, often in collaboration with social services personnel. Parents are informed about treatment plans and meet with staff on a weekly basis. However, intensive work with families is rare because of the lack of resources, time and professional abilities. Treatment plans are implemented in co-operation with other community services.

All residents at the Home are registered as students at the Keskikatu Comprehensive School, like their contemporaries as the Town Youth Workshop. For three days of the week they follow an individualised curriculum which is designed in co-operation with a special teacher. This normally covers the school's core subjects and a range of social skills. Theoretical subjects are taught by special teachers while other subjects are taught by care workers. The other two days of each week are spent on a work placement. This arrangement reflects the Home's strong emphasis on "learning by doing".

Each young person is designated their own care worker, who functions as a social worker and teacher, and provides assistance in decision-making and tasks related to daily life. Youth-care worker pairs are decided on the basis of knowledge of previous family dynamics and gender role issues. Care workers are non-resident but take turns in providing over-night supervision and support.

Youth usually live in the Home for the duration of the school year, and then return to their families during the summer holidays. Once they have left the Home for good, monthly follow-up visits are arranged to provide continuing support.

Results

Through the activities of the Jyväskylä Town Youth Workshop, participants receive information about and experience of many different occupations, providing the opportunity to discover new interests and sources of motivation. By mixing with older workers and receiving supervision from section foremen they develop an understanding of the norms of the workplace. They also earn a wage and gain experience that can help them to obtain employment in the regular economy. However, according to the Director, the Workshop's provision is insufficient as there are many young people who are still not receiving the support that they need. These individuals are at high risk of alienation and social marginalisation.

No information was provided on outcomes for young people who had left the Hovila Youth Home.

Voluntary institutions

As a result of State Subsidy Reform, government policies favouring privatisation, and the difficult economic situation of municipalities, some service providers have anticipated a shift away from public service provision towards private and voluntary provision. However, others believe that the heralded expansion in the private sector may be more rhetoric than reality, arguing that public sector budget cuts often have been passed on to the (publicly funded) voluntary sector first. Two voluntary organisations which continue to work successfully in partnership with public sector institutions are the Mannerheim League for Child Welfare, and the Finnish Gypsy Foundation.

Institutional backgrounds

The Mannerheim League for Child Welfare: The Mannerheim League for Child Welfare was founded in 1920 to safeguard the rights of children and to promote the interests of families. It initiated many of Finland's public human services, starting with voluntary provision and then advocating government "take-overs" to make services available nation-wide. It is a powerful organisation with 63 000 members and 480 local organisations. Many of its initiatives have a preventive bias.

The Finnish Gypsy Foundation: The Finnish Gypsy Foundation sponsors projects for the benefit of Finland's small and culturally distinct Romany population.

Programmes involving collaborative and co-operative activities

The Mannerheim League for Child Welfare provided three examples of programmes under its control which involve inter-agency collaboration or co-operation. These are typical of the way in which the League operates.

The League's 21-year-old Peer Counselling Programme provides support for students throughout Finland. A total of 500 volunteer peer counsellors who are especially trained by the League aim to make classrooms more secure and comfortable, to address the problem of violence, to provide friendship and hospitality, and to offer voluntary help to staff. In Jyväskylä, teams of two to four peer counsellors can be found in each class in 90 per cent of schools. For the last four years the League has supplemented this programme with short training courses in social skills for students and parents. Group learning, case studies and role-playing are important teaching components.

One year younger, having spanned one fifth of a century, is the League's Home Help Programme which serves to supplement municipal provision in this area. In Jyväskylä, the League has a team of around 80 volunteers who were chosen selectively, and received special training on a 40 hour-course provided by the League. Some of the volunteers are people who have become unemployed because of the recession. The main kind of service that they provide is day care which is available to parents around the clock for a small hourly fee. The Programme does not ask questions about why help is requested, trusting parents' judgement of the validity of their needs. Typically they find that services are requested by working parents with sick children, parents with babies who are getting insufficient sleep, parents needing advice on child care, and parents who just need a few hours to relax together.

The League's Telephone Counselling Service was established in 1980. It provides help and guidance to individuals in crisis in eleven of Finland's twelve provinces. Each province has one full-time worker and a team of between ten and 40 volunteers who are especially trained to provide neutral and confidential help. Anyone can dial the national number, paying the price of a local call only. Callers are encouraged to act independently and to find their own solutions to their problems. They are frequently referred to other services for this purpose. A total of 40 000 calls are received each year of which 60 per cent come from children aged between 8 and 16 years.

One of the Finnish Gypsy Foundation's activities is a four-year project to improve the educational achievement of Romany children by addressing problems such as non-attendance and school drop out. The project is being carried out with the support of the Provincial Government of Central Finland, and with additional financial backing from the Association of Slot Machine Charities. The high priority it has been given is reflected in the provincial government's decision to set up a special guiding council which meets twice yearly. This includes representatives from different provincial government departments, and academics in education, teacher training and sociology from the University of Jyväskylä.

The project's Director and all of the staff are themselves Romany. Most of the work is done by the Director who arranges meetings with educational personnel and other professionals to disseminate knowledge about the Romany culture, and makes home visits to parents of Romany children. This work is supported by voluntary guiding groups in five of the province's municipalities. Future plans include providing trained tutors for Romany children and teachers who can give classes in the Romany language.

Summary and discussion

Support for integrated services in Jyväskylä had come from administrative, professional and community levels. Government policy advocating Local Population Responsibility – with the consensus of provincial and municipal administrators and professionals – has led to the implementation of a successful approach for the care of the population's social welfare and health needs. This success appears to be the product of a policy of integrating social welfare and health services at all levels in the service hierarchy from the very top down. National policy concerning Student Welfare Groups has ensured that these groups are present, and co-operating with each other, in all of Jyväskylä's schools. As a result of these initiatives client access to services and the ability of services to address community needs are good.

Support for combined day care and education services, such as those provided at the Nenäinniemi Elementary School and Day Care Centre, has come mainly from the municipal level. This Centre has much in common with grassroots initiatives because it has made efforts to involve community people in its work. Other services in Finland, which are backed by legislation, are perhaps less inclined to make positive efforts to win community support, and to view community people as equal participants in services provision. In providing day care and schooling on one site, this Centre has the potential to provide very large benefits for funders, parents and children. Funders reap the rewards of lower costs since buildings and resources are shared; parents save time through being able to obtain two services from one site; and children benefit from an easy and non-traumatic transition from day care to school. This service might be improved through increased collaboration at the administrative level – perhaps in relation to funding – to match the higher level of integration found on the ground.

In Jyväskylä, targeted public sector care plays an important role in preventing young people from falling through the gap between compulsory education and work. Strong links with schools and local businesses ensure that young people can either continue with their general education or obtain valuable vocational experience. The multi-faceted role of care-workers guarantees that they are able to get adequate social skills training, advice and support. The importance attached to parental involvement at this stage is fairly insignificant. However, this is perhaps appropriate at a time when they are moving from childhood to adult life.

While the quality of Jyväskylä's services for youth at risk is high, they are under increasing strain as a result of record-breaking youth unemployment. While previously they were able to provide for the majority of young people in danger of failing in the transition to work, this is no longer possible. It would appear that the main focus in addressing this issue should be on Finland's long-term economic "health" since this, rather than poor services provision, is the main problem.

The role of the Mannerheim League in providing services in Jyväskylä – and indeed in Finland as a whole – is striking. It has succeeded systematically in developing small-scale human services projects and then persuading the Finnish government to implement them nation-wide. This is a powerful example of the way in which voluntary organisations can succeed in influencing government policy, and of the way in which national governments can take a positive, open and supportive stance to non-governmental initiatives which work. The League is also interesting in terms of the variety of different roles it has invented for itself. In the Peer Counselling Programme it has entered into symbiotic relationships with school "hosts" in which it takes advantage of pupil-power and other school resources to provide pupils with a peer support service; in the Home Help Programme it has adopted an independent, supplementary approach where it works alongside the municipal social services to meet any shortfalls in public provision; and in the Telephone Counselling Service it has taken on the role of a "mediator" or "facilitator", putting individuals in contact with other available services.

The experiences of both the Mannerheim League and the Finnish Gypsy Foundation suggest that the government in Jyväskylä is open and supportive of voluntary initiatives to complement existing forms of public sector provision.

INTEGRATED SERVICES FOR YOUTH IN THE TRANSITION TO WORK IN HÄMEENLINNA

In the Hämeenlinna case study, research focused on the nature of support for integration at the provincial and municipal government levels and the way in which integrated approaches had been put into practice in a variety of public, private, universal and targeted services for youth in the transition to work. These included the Hämeenlinna Vocational Institute, the Employment Office, the Hämeenlinna Community Home, the Vanaja Reform School, and the Kiipula Institute. As in Helsinki and Jyväskylä, Hämeenlinna has a highly organised and cohesive range of services in which integration takes on a variety of meanings.

The administration

Häme Provincial Office: The Häme Provincial Office is one of twelve provincial offices throughout Finland. It is divided into seven units, two of which focus on services for children and youth. These are the departments of Education and Culture, and Social Affairs and Health. As a result of decentralisation, the Provincial Office has lost many of its responsibilities to the municipalities. However, it still plays an important role in drafting plans, co-ordinating municipal activities, and advancing new initiatives.

Hämeenlinna Municipal Office: The Hämeenlinna Municipal Office is one of Finland's 455 municipal bodies. It has a number of important features: it has been rationalised through a radical decrease in boards and committees; decision-making powers have been delegated from political bodies to civic administrators so that clients have better access to decision-makers; it encourages co-operation between citizens, municipal officials, boards and committees; and it has delegated economic responsibility downwards to Result-Responsible Units. These units are empowered to set their own priorities and run their own budgets, and are responsible for achieving their objectives and "getting results" (hence the name). Departments of the provincial office, municipal boards, and even individuals – such as headmasters and education officers – may be given these powers. Three departments in the administration provide services for children and youth. These are the Education Department, the Youth Department, and the Social Welfare Department. The municipality also provides a range of "special services" for intoxicant abusers, from which one – the Youth Detoxification Centre – was taken as an example.

Hämeenlinna Region Federation for Public Health: While each municipality in Finland runs it own Education, Youth and Social Welfare departments, health services are organised by groups or "federations" of municipalities. Hämeenlinna, for example, provides these services in partnership with the municipalities of Hattula, Hauho, Kalvola and Renko (total population: 62 834 in 1992). Health services provided by the federation include: health guidance, health education (in co-operation with education and youth services), maternity and child care (in special clinics), school health care, student health care, family planning instruction, dental care, occupational health care, out-patient care, hospital care, and medical rehabilitation and support. These are provided in separate units but together they are conceptualised as a "health centre".

Administrative and professional support for integration

The Häme Provincial Office plays an important role in developing and supporting co-operative projects that involve municipal departments and other public and private sector bodies. Sometimes the initiation of these projects is a response to special requests from government ministries. A typical example is the Project on the Prevention of Intoxicant Abuse by Youth. This was initiated by the Ministry of Social Affairs and Health through special memos sent to the provincial and municipal authorities which specified the need for inter-agency co-operation. In response, the Provincial Office set up a joint planning group including representatives from the Education and Culture, Social Affairs and Health, Police and Youth departments, and field level workers. This group has arranged several meetings and seminars to raise people's awareness of intoxicant abuse, and to encourage the development of local networks for prevention. The Provincial Office has encouraged the involvement of many service providers, including the municipal departments, the church, the military, employment agencies, mental health clinics, family counselling clinics, the Red Cross, A-clinics, drug prevention institutions and civic organisations.

While leadership from the Provincial Office has played an important role in stimulating co-operation between Hämeenlinna's municipal departments, the motivation to collaborate has also come from within. Since the late 1980s, municipal service managers increasingly have realised that collaborative working practices can better meet clients' needs while at the same time making field workers' jobs much easier. They have also been influenced by a number of studies which have argued that services for young people are like a dense "jungle" of separate bodies in which it is very easy for clients to get lost (hence pointing to the need for integrated services with a single gate-keeper to facilitate client access). An additional factor motivating co-operation has been the ongoing struggle to maintain separate services with limited resources. Integrated services are seen as a more cost-effective solution.

Municipal employees working at the field level have also lent their support, at least implicitly, to an integrated approach to services provision. Many regard it as the most effective and cost-efficient way to address clients' problems.

Resources and training for collaboration

Inputs to support collaborative working methods have been limited. The Provincial Office has received a small amount of money from the national government to fund evaluation work and in-service training. However, no financial support for collaborative working methods was reported at the municipal level.

Collaboration in practice

Much of the co-operation by the Municipal Education Department takes place within its schools. Typically they are offered as a site in which other services can operate. For example the Municipal Youth Department uses school premises to run after-school clubs; the local health services use school offices to provide pupil health care; and church priests visit schools to provide social support and spiritual teaching. Occasionally, the Department co-operates with other services on their turf. A typical example here would be the funding of a special teacher to work on the central hospital's psychiatric ward.

Additional to these arrangements are the co-operative roles played by the Education Department's two social workers and the multi-professional school Social Welfare Groups (in which the social workers participate).

The two social workers are attached to the Central School Office, but spend around half of their time in school-based offices shared with medical staff. They are responsible for referrals to outside agencies – such as the child guidance clinic and the municipal social welfare department – and for involving parents and children as fully as possible in the treatment process. They are involved in collaborative initiatives both inside and outside of school boundaries. Inside, they co-operate with various professionals in Student Welfare Groups, and also with individual teachers on a case-by-case basis. Outside, they co-operate with many different agencies, a typical example being their contribution to the manning of the Hämeenlinna Community Home's "crisis" telephone service.

The co-operative activities of the Youth and Social Welfare Departments cannot be separated completely from those of the Education Department, and as such have already received some attention. However, they also participate in additional activities and projects with other public and (some) private sector partners. The Youth Department articulated its co-operative work mainly in terms of special projects, while the Social Welfare Department referred both to ongoing activities and special projects.

The Youth Department runs a whole range of projects, many of which are aimed at youth at risk of school drop out or unemployment. Community input into these projects is provided through community meetings in which individuals are invited to make suggestions for new activities, and through a network of trained volunteers who work for the department.

One of the Youth Department's projects is an apprenticeship training programme for youth instructors which it runs in co-operation with the Children's Home and a neighbouring Municipal Youth Department. This is designed for youth who have a particular interest in working with young people, or who are unable to secure other forms of training or employment. Currently it has three participants although more have been involved in the past.

The Department has also set up a Youth Summer Project which provides workshops and training activities in local schools and other institutions for youth who fail to get summer jobs. This is funded by both the provincial and the municipal administrations, and involves the co-operation of many institutions (i.e. the Vocational Institute, the Technical Institute, the Data-processing and Economic Institute, the Vocational Adult Education Centre, the Häme Summer University, the Evo Forestry Institute, the Lepaa Horticultural Institute, the Tammela Handicrafts and Industrial Arts Institute, the Employment Office and the Hame Centre of Commerce). In 1993, the participation of 621 youths in this project proved it to be a success.

The Youth Department is currently preparing to extend co-operation between authorities in preventive work even further. It is, for example, planning a Link Project to develop "links" between services to prevent youth alienation. This will include the setting up of innovative summer camps, and a House of Youth, providing activities, services, crisis help and a safe haven for young people. The Department's intention is that this project should be novel and visionary; indeed, it cites "creative madness" as an essential element in its planning. Co-operative partners will include the Häme Provincial Office, the Hattula Municipal Youth Department, the Municipal Boards of Hämeenlinna, the Employment Office, the Health Education Institute, the Social Education Institute, the Association of Slot Machine Charities, the State Alcohol Monopoly and private companies. Trained volunteers will staff it.

The Social Welfare Department, as part of an ongoing service, provides assistance and advice to unemployed young people on housing and employment. Co-operative partners in this scheme include the Employment Office, the housing department and the criminal support service. It also recently experimented with two projects for children and youth at risk. The Unemployed Youth Project (1988-89) targeted unemployed or temporarily employed youth. Its main aims were to assess individual's life situations, help them develop plans for employment or education, and to monitor outcomes. Co-operative partners in this work included the local employment office, the social security office, the A-clinic and a youth psychologist. The Parents and Youth Group Experiment (1990) targeted five families who between them had six children in special education. These children had problems at school and at home, and some had been involved in criminal activities. The objective of the Experiment was to encourage group discussion so that parents and youth could help and support each other. The parents' group was led by a social worker, and the youth group, by a youth worker from the Municipal Youth Department.

The Youth Detoxification Centre (Municipal Special Services) works in collaboration with the Municipal Youth Department, health and social services, schools, the police, youth homes and the church, to prevent intoxication problems amongst Hämeenlinna's young people. The Centre is based in the police headquarters. A mixed team including a social worker and a nurse patrol the streets for intoxicated youth, who they take home, or to the police station, to dry out. Other forms of co-operation include agreed protocols with other agencies for client treatment, inter-agency referrals, and liaison with schools to provide preventive education. These arrangements are a response to national legislation which requires services dealing with intoxicant abuse to collaborate.

The Municipal Federation for Public Health's main partner in providing health care for children of school age is the Education Department. Schools provide medical teams, including a school doctor (part-time) and nurse (full-time), with on-site offices or "clinics" in which they can work. In addition to regular inspections and health care, their main function is to monitor the progress of children at risk, and to identify health factors which may be significant for students' career choices. This is done in co-operation with pupils, parents, school student counsellors and vocational counsellors from the Employment Office. Health professionals also co-operate with other professionals in school Student Welfare Groups. Furthermore, when necessary they may seek the involvement of other health staff, such as psychologists, physiotherapists and speech therapists.

As in Helsinki and Jyväskylä, out-of-school co-operation is facilitated by the creation of shared geographical areas in which both health and social services, and in some cases other services operate. Health care workers' most regular co-operative partners in these areas are social workers, psychologists, youth workers and employment officers.

Barriers to collaboration

Administrators and managers in the municipal government have experienced several obstacles to successful collaboration. These have included the disparate standpoints and objectives of different departments; communication barriers between professional staff; the lack of professional will to co-operate with other professionals and clients; the resistant attitudes of teachers to change; and the lack of time available for joint meetings. The traditional attitudes of teachers and a lack of time were also echoed as problems by field level workers. Medical personnel additionally referred to confidentiality issues.

Outcomes

At the provincial level two of the main benefits of collaboration have been improvements in the quality of inter-departmental relations and in the level of information sharing. At the municipal level financial savings and the sharing of professional knowledge and experience were seen as an important benefits. In respect of the financial advantage, the Finnish motto, "the Mark is the best consultant", was quoted as an important principle. Field level workers were also positive about collaboration. They referred to increased efficiency, the opportunity to discuss different professional viewpoints, a sense of security in sharing difficult decisions, a reduction in work pressure, and even basic "survival", as important gains.

The downside of collaboration for municipal managers has been the difficulty in reaching joint decisions with other departments, and the extraordinary amount of work that intensive collaboration can generate. A good example of the latter is provided by the Chief Officer in the Youth Department who, in order to maintain a dense network of collaborative partners, frequently is required to work a 60-hour week. Aside from occasional friction caused by professional differences regarding preferred treatment approaches, few disadvantages were reported by field level workers.

Universal services for youth in the transition to work

Both the Hämeenlinna Vocational Institute and the Employment Office are examples of universal services to facilitate the transition to work. However, they also provide specialised services to meet the needs of youth who are at particular risk of school failure and unemployment.

Hämeenlinna Vocational Institute: The Hämeenlinna Vocational Institute is owned and maintained by a consortium of eleven municipalities which supply two-thirds of its funding; the last third comes from the state. It provides vocational education for youth aged 16 to 19 years and an increasing amount of adult education. As one of the biggest institutions of its kind in Finland it offers almost 30 vocational courses to 1 085 students from around 100 municipalities. It has its own student dormitory which provides accommodation for around 160 students.

As well as standard post-comprehensive vocational training, the Institute also offers higher level courses for students who already have an upper secondary education, and special classes for students with special educational needs. The main branches of training available include mechanical, electrical or chemical engineering, construction, catering, dress-making, hairdressing, heating and plumbing, and surveying. However, the development by the National Board of Education of a new curriculum framework for vocational institutions is likely to lead to changes in what is taught.

The Institute provides a range of special services for its pupils, with two social workers, two special teachers, a doctor (part-time) and a nurse (full-time) on its staff. It also has three student counsellors who play an instrumental role in advising students on further studies and careers, and providing a link with employment agencies and the business community. These professionals co-operate in the Institute's Student Welfare Group, which is also attended by the two vice principals. There is some concern that some special services functions, such as those carried out by special teachers, will be reduced as a result of education funding reductions.

Aside from the Institute's student counsellors, the transition to work is also facilitated by vocational inspectors who visit the Institute on a regular basis. They negotiate apprenticeship programmes with employers and come to the Institute to give vocational advice and interview students for apprenticeship positions. Potential employers offer very little in the way of financial support to the Institute, although they do offer small gifts to pupils who have successfully completed their courses. They are also represented on Vocational Advisory Committees.

The Institute has two work-oriented special classes for low achievers or comprehensive school drop-outs: one provides training in mechanical and electrical engineering, and the other in catering. In addition, it has a one-year car repair course which is attached to the Harviala Reform School. The aim of these courses is to provide students with a marketable vocational competence. Partners who help facilitate the transition to work of special class students include local employers who offer students opportunities for work practice, and employment agencies who have special funding to employ youth at risk.

A recent innovation at the Institute has been the provision of a preparatory course for vocational education, designed mainly for students with learning difficulties and under-achievers. The purpose of this course, which provides the opportunity to study in any one of four vocational areas, is to facilitate the transition from comprehensive to vocational education. Partners in its implementation include comprehensive schools, student counsellors, teachers, and employers who offer placements for work practice. On successful completion of the course, students may apply to join one of the Institute's standard courses.

The Institute assesses the employment success of its students through a questionnaire sent out for completion six months after they have left. Many male students go straight into the Army to complete their National Service and therefore are not available for work. In 1993, of students who were available, 30 per cent gained employment, a lower percentage than normal. The Institute has noticed that youth unemployment has begun to impact in a negative way on students' attitudes towards vocational education. They can no longer see a guaranteed job at the end of it and therefore question its worth.

There has been a decline in the rate of drop-out from 15.0 per cent in 1989-90 to 6.7 per cent in 1992-93. However, it is still a significant problem amongst students at risk: in 1992-93, 35.1 per cent dropped out. The Institute's social workers try their best to put these young people in contact with the local employment office.

The Employment Office: The Hämeenlinna Employment Office is a multi-service centre providing information, employment and vocational guidance services. Specialist provision for youth at risk is available through both the employment and vocational guidance services: the employment service has a special unit for unskilled youth; and the vocational guidance service has a specialist psychologist for youth with special educational needs. These services are regarded as playing an important role in preventing youth problems.

Since schools now employ student counsellors to provide vocational advice, the role of the Employment Office's vocational counsellors in schools has been reduced (although student counsellors frequently co-operate with their Employment Office counterparts). Vocational counsellors' involvement with youth at risk is greatest when they are in the process of dropping out of school or when they have already left.

The Employment Office has co-operated in a number of special projects targeted at youth at risk. These include the Youth Summer Project which it has helped to fund, and the Vocational Institute's preparatory training course for which it has played an active role in selecting participants. As guided by national policy, it also co-operates with various professional groups on a case-by-case basis. For example, it works closely with health and social welfare personnel to help to find employment opportunities for individual youth as part of their therapeutic treatment or rehabilitation. In the future new forms of co-operation are likely to emerge as a response to the worsening job situation.

Targeted services for youth in the transition to work

National policies favouring community care, prevention, and the privatisation of some services are reflected in recent developments in the Hämeenlinna Community Home and the Vanaja Reform School. The Kiipula Institute is representative of the partnership between government and voluntary services.

Hämeenlinna Community Home: The Home, which was founded in 1983, receives its funding from the Municipality of Hämeenlinna, and operates under the supervision of the Municipal Social Welfare Department. It is divided into three sections: an eight place community home; a four place dormitory (plus an apartment) for young people in the transition to an independent life; and a refuge home for people threatened by family violence. The Home's ten regular staff include a director, a social worker, six social educators, a cook and a helper. They collaborate with a wide variety of outside partners including, in addition to the Municipal Social Welfare Department, the Mental Health Office, the psychiatric clinic, the A-clinic, the Family Guidance Centre, local schools and the police. One example of collaboration is provided by the new telephone "crisis service" which is manned by pairs of social workers. Characteristically, one is from the Home and the other from the Municipal Social Welfare Department.

Clients, ranging in age from 13 to 18 years, are referred to the Home by the Municipal Social Welfare Board. Commonly they have family or school problems, or require protection. As an open institution all children at the Home attend ordinary schools or have jobs. Most stay for between six months and several years during which time they are treated within a family-centred frame of reference. By the end of their stay, the Home aims to return them to normal society as self-reliant, active and responsible individuals.

The Home was due to be converted, in January 1994, into a Home Unit and Open Unit. This change was underpinned by the pervading view in Finland that non-institutional care is preferable to institutional care, and was also stimulated by recent budget cuts. While the Home Unit still will provide institutional care, the new Open Unit will address children's problems in the context of their family environment, and will focus on prevention.

The Vanaja Reform School: This school is one of ten state-owned reform schools in Finland. It provides accommodation in three housing units (16 places), and also has its own upper level comprehensive school. Only four places were taken in autumn 1993. Its staff of 20 includes a director, teacher, social worker and several social educators (care assistants) who provide 24 hour support. The services of other professionals, including a nurse, doctor, psychiatrist and personnel consultant, are bought from outside.

The school caters for children, aged 13-18 years, with severe behavioural problems. Many are truants and a large number have learning difficulties. Alcohol abuse, drug and substance abuse, car-stealing and shop-lifting are other common problems. Youth are either invited to join the school, or are referred by the Municipal Social Welfare Department. On average they stay for one and a half years.

Special features of the school are its family-centred approach, which includes family involvement in the planning, implementation and follow-up of treatment, and a scheme whereby pupils are allocated social educators who support them in every day life and are involved in the planning and implementation of treatment.

Co-operative efforts in the school centre around the social worker. For example, she liaises with the nurse on health issues, the police on student crime, and the teacher, parents and the child for meetings and twice yearly case conferences. While students are present at these conferences they do not play a role in decision-making. Co-operation within the Home is balanced by a general isolation from other institutions.

The results of the school's approach to student education and care have been mixed. Most youth achieve a comprehensive school qualification, and stable social relationships. Of all leaving students, 28 per cent have applied for places in secondary education, 7 per cent have applied for jobs, and the rest have become unemployed. The majority of students who have attended post-comprehensive institutions have dropped out.

In providing treatment rather than punishment, Finland's ten reform schools provide an important alternative to prison for many criminal youths. However, in the 1980s the state ceased to provide close to 100 per cent funding for these schools and instead gave municipalities a lump sum for education as a whole. The outcome of this policy, in an environment of municipal cost cutting, has been a reduction in the number of youth sent to reform schools for treatment. A second reason for the decline is the unpopularity in Finland of institutional approaches to care. The social services prefer to treat children in their families and local communities.

Of concern to many professionals is the Ministry of Social Affairs and Health's recent plans to close one reform school, convert two (including Vanaja) into youth prisons, and pass the control of the other seven to a foundation. This worry is heightened by the fact that a similar privatisation policy in Sweden was a failure, resulting in the return of reform schools to state control in 1993.

The Kiipula Institute: The Kiipula Foundation is a private trust which owns and maintains four educational institutions: a horticultural institute, a vocational institute, a commercial institute and an adult education centre. These offer a comprehensive range of student welfare, psychological, health and social rehabilitation services, many of which are not available in state education establishments.

While these institutions are privately owned, the state funds them in the same way as other vocational institutions. Additional funding comes from the home municipalities of attending students. The Foundation also receives some financial support from the National Pensions Agency and insurance companies for disabled students and rehabilitation activities.

Summary and discussion

Hämeenlinna provides a good example of a top-down approach to integration where co-operative initiatives often are instigated at the national or provincial level and are implemented at the field level. This method has succeeded because professionals on the ground are themselves highly appreciative of the advantages of teamwork. Solid political support has not been matched with new resource inputs and funding mechanisms; managers and professionals have been required to adopt co-operative approaches largely within the existing framework.

For school-aged young people, the school is at the hub of services activity: it is the location of a very full range of services, from social welfare and health care to special teaching and vocational guidance. School Student Welfare Groups are an important component in the co-operative activities of these services. In spite of the importance of schools for co-operation it is interesting to note that the traditional attitudes of teachers are seen by many professionals as an important barrier to effective teamwork.

As elsewhere in Finland, national policy promoting an area-focused approach to services provision has stimulated social welfare and health services to co-operate outside – as well as inside – the school environment. The motivation to co-operate among these two professional groups appears to be much greater than that among teachers. The current plans of the local Vocational Teacher Education University to set up a joint training course for teachers and social workers may help to change the outlook of some of them.

The Youth Department in Hämeenlinna is an anomaly because of its unusual inventiveness and dynamism. It has shown a high degree of imagination, perhaps largely emanating from the chief youth officer, in creating a broad array of projects which have involved many different partners from the Evo Forestry Institute to the State Alcohol Monopoly. "Creative madness" in a positive sense is a term that can be applied not only to the department's Link Project but also to its activities more generally. Furthermore, the Department has not drawn the line for co-operation at public and private organisations but has also looked to the community, taking into account its views and drawing on its voluntary manpower. This level of networking and community involvement is less characteristic of other public services in Hämeenlinna. However, the maintenance of such high levels of co-operation evidently requires a very large amount of time and commitment.

The presence in Hämeenlinna of the Youth Detoxification Centre, and many other similar institutions addressing alcohol abuse, is indicative of the significance of the problem in Finland as a whole. National policy requiring collaboration with other services ensures that these institutions are implanted in a wide network in which they give and receive advice and support.

Hämeenlinna's Vocational Institute and Employment Office function as an efficient partnership in preventing young people from making an undesired and potentially harmful exit from the education and work systems. The transition of under-achievers from comprehensive to vocational education is facilitated by the provision of a preparatory course for vocational education. Once in the Institute a wide range of special education courses and special services are provided to help keep students there. When they have completed their courses, student counsellors, vocational inspectors and vocational counsellors from the Employment Office are available to help students find jobs. Established contacts with local businesses, mainly through work placements, make this task easier. However, it is important to note that high youth unemployment is putting this highly developed system under increasing pressure, and it is no longer able to prevent the vast majority of children from "dropping by the wayside".

In contrast to universal services in Hämeenlinna in which changes appear to be gradual, targeted services are being more fundamentally altered. The Hämeenlinna Community Home is abandoning an institutional and crisis-centred approach to care and instead is moving towards open-care and prevention. The Vanaja Reform School is likely to be required to drop its remedial approach to youth care when plans for it to be turned into a youth prison are implemented. In other areas of Finland, reform schools face the prospect of privatisation. These changes appear to be linked to a policy of cutting back targeted services to reduce public sector costs, a policy which also extends to specialised provision within universal services. In some cases, private targeted services, such as the Kiipula Institute, appear to be faring better, receiving high levels of government funding to supplement their own resource inputs.

At the provincial and municipal levels the outcomes of co-operation largely were described in qualitative and anecdotal terms. The evidence was very positive, but little reference was made to evaluation studies which quantified the effects of co-operative arrangements. Both the Vocational Institute and the Vanaja Reform School recorded the educational and employment outcomes of their students. However, their data does not clearly specify the influence of co-operative work in achieving these outcomes.

CONCLUSION

Finnish human services and initiatives for integration

Finnish education, health and social services constitute a very dense and inter-connected network which – at least until recently – has protected and provided opportunities for the vast majority of Finnish citizens. State involvement in human services provision is at a high level although voluntary services play a significant role. Private sector participation is encouraged but appears to have been hampered by municipal funding cuts which have been passed on to publicly-funded, voluntary agencies first. The relationship between education, social welfare and health care providers from all sectors is generally harmonious, with little evidence of competitive tensions. Long established voluntary organisations such as the Mannerheim League work in a very close and symbiotic partnership with public services.

Human services for children and youth at risk in Finland are of a high standard. However, recently they have been submitted to intense economic pressures to which they have been forced to adapt to maintain standards. Services integration is an important component in the present government's strategy to respond to this new economic reality.

Education, health and social services in Finland show a high level of co-operation. Key features of integration in the national system can be summarised in the following way:

- The predominant approach to implementing integrated working methods is "top-down". In other words, government policy initiatives are used to influence the working practices of field workers. This government-led approach seems to have been relatively successful because of widespread support for co-operative methods at all levels in the services hierarchy.

- The level of co-operation between social welfare and health professionals is high. This is the result of fundamental administrative changes – of which the most significant is the merging of social affairs and health departments – and policy initiatives such as LPR (Local Population Responsibility). This contrasts with education services, which in funding terms are more isolated and whose professional body has been slower to embrace teamwork.

- Community involvement in service planning and implementation is seen as important. However, there appear to be few instances where programmes are initiated or run by community people to meet local needs. This may be a limitation, but equally may indicate that existing public services are sufficient.

- Business plays an important role in providing work placements for children in ordinary vocational institutions, and also for youth at risk in special vocational institutions. However, it offers few apprenticeships, and does not play a significant role in the funding of education (except through indirect means such as corporate income tax payments).

- The voluntary sector generally is well supported by the Finnish government. Many private institutions receive government funding which is attached to clients (although recently there have been reports of cuts in funding to publicly financed voluntary institutions). The Mannerheim League, which has initiated and "handed over" the control of a number of services to the government, is a major player in services provision.

- Overall, change towards integration in Finland's human services has been gradual, perhaps partly because they are complex, dense, and have a long established tradition.

- The emphasis placed on the evaluation of integrated approaches has not been significant. However, assessment of outcomes has been given priority in newer initiatives, such as LPR, where effects are predicted to be fundamental.

Evaluation of initiatives for integration

The number of formal evaluations of programmes which integrate services in Finland appears to be quite small, although the LPR assessments will be an important step forward. Using available data, the outcomes of integration can be gauged in two different ways: by considering the experiences and perspectives of administrators, professionals and clients; and, at a more general level, by referring to health, social, education and employment indicators. With respect to the first measure, the OECD case studies pointed to a number of advantages of co-operative working methods in Finland, as well as some problems. The reported advantages of co-operation were:

For *administrators and/or professionals*

- improved professional support;
- better understanding of the roles of other professionals;
- improved understanding of other professional perspectives;
- greater information sharing;
- improved relations between professionals and departments;
- reduced work pressure;
- reduced costs; and
- increased professional satisfaction.

For *clients*

- increased speed in allocating help to clients;
- increased ability to prevent crisis situations through multi-professional help;
- improved care by looking at client problems from different perspectives;
- greater continuity in professional-client contact;
- more consistency in advice given to clients;
- greater convenience for clients in providing one-stop services;
- avoidance of multiple visits to client homes; and
- greater client satisfaction .

The difficulties experienced in co-operative efforts were:

- ingrained professional prejudices;
- lack of professional will to co-operate;
- differences in professional values and principles;
- differences in perspectives on treatment;
- difficulties in reaching joint decisions;
- lack of understanding of the functions of other agencies;
- communication barriers;
- competition for resources;
- confidentiality issues; and
- lack of time to co-operate.

Examining national health, social, education and employment indicators is more problematic since they cannot be shown conclusively to be the outcome of between or within service co-operation. However, at the very least they are able to tell us something about the quality of the Finnish human services system as a whole. International studies by the OECD have shown that Finland has one of the lowest rates of infant mortality in the world, exceptionally high levels of educational achievement and participation, and until recently low levels of unemployment. These indicators suggest that the Finnish human services system is one which has been highly effective. However, present levels of unemployment of around 20 per cent are severely testing it.

Historical, political and economic impacts on integration

Finland has a long tradition of state welfare provision. Central government is accepted as an important and benign power which protects and provides for the whole population. Public services are comprehensive and well developed. While these features undoubtedly are positive they can at the same time make change more difficult. Finland is in no sense a "green field site" in which new approaches to services provision can be easily implanted. New approaches to working practices have to be imposed on existing structures with long (and successful) traditions. As a result moves towards integration generally have been gradual, avoiding major overhauls, and allowing time for agencies and professionals to adapt to new methods.

The attitude of policy-makers towards integration has been positive, and a wide variety of government initiatives have indirectly or directly made co-operation between services easier. Perhaps the most important of these is Local Population Responsibility which has significantly increased co-operation between the country's social welfare and health services through professional teamwork, co-location and the sharing of clients. The motivation behind government support for integration clearly is double-faceted: to provide better services, and to provide them more cheaply. Perhaps because of the fact that integration is seen as a way of reducing costs, the provision of appropriate professional training, and funding for collaborative work, has been less forthcoming.

The impact of the economic environment on Finland's human services system should not be under-estimated: unemployment has with a single blow significantly reduced the tax base and pushed a very large proportion of the population into "risk" situations. Hence there is less money to spend on more people in need. This has pushed Finland into a situation which contrasts deeply with that of the 1970s and 1980s when funding for human services was generous and few individuals experienced social marginalisation. Services – and especially special services – are being cut, and only time will tell if compensating initiatives, such as integration, will be sufficient to maintain standards.

Future trends

Efforts to increase the level of services integration are set to continue. However, this policy is only one of a battery of policies aimed at improving the quality and efficiency of Finnish human services. These policies form a national "package" that reflects similar thinking in other Member countries. The central components of this package are:

- decentralisation, involving a shift in power and funding responsibilities from the national and provincial levels to the municipal level;
- rationalisation, involving a reduction in the number of provincial boards and committees;
- community care, with a move away from institutional care towards open care;
- family-centred approaches to care, in which the client is treated within the context of his/her close;
- family;
- preventive care, involving an increase in primary care to reduce the need for specialist care and crisis management; and
- privatisation, to increase private sector involvement in the provision of human services.

Along with initiatives favouring integration, these are the policies that are most likely to shape the character of human services in Finland over the next decade.

Recommendations

Government initiatives to increase the level of co-operation between human services have been well supported at all levels in the service hierarchy and have achieved positive outcomes. On this basis, further progress towards an integrated system, involving increased use of joint planning and joint funding mechanisms, is recommended. However, higher levels of integration must be supported by necessary resource inputs, and in this respect funding for professional working time to co-operate, and joint professional training, seems crucial. In addition, new initiatives might benefit from the systematic inclusion of evaluation components to assess effectiveness.

The process of integration may be enriched further by encouraging a greater number of local, community initiatives to complement those of the government. These kinds of initiative are frequently characterised by their innovativeness, dynamism and appropriateness in relation to local needs, and can be a breeding ground for ideas which may have the potential for replication at the national level. Furthermore, high youth unemployment points to the need to explore new ways of strengthening links between schools and businesses, and to assess the requirement for additional training and work experience programmes for unemployed youth.

Closing comments

Human services provision in Finland for preschool children, school children and youth in the transition to work appears to compare favourably with other OECD Member countries. Adequate welfare benefits have prevented the existence of serious poverty amongst all but a few. High quality universal and targeted services have been successful in ensuring that the vast majority of young people – even those at risk – become active members of society. In this respect, a national philosophy that emphasises sharing and inclusion undoubtedly has played an important role.

These services must now find ways to adapt to the new, and harsher, social and economic environment, not only to preserve existing standards of provision but also to improve them.

REFERENCES

AALTO, V.L. (1991), Esiopetuksen järjestämisestä. Sosiaalinen Aikakauskirja, Vol. 6, 32.

JAUHIAINEN, A. (1993), School, Student Welfare and the Welfare State. The Formation of the Student Welfare System in the Finnish Compulsory Education System and its Network of Experts from the Late 1800s to 1990s, publications of the University of Turku, C 98, University of Turku, Turku.

KAUPPINEN, M. and SARJANOJA, M. (1991), Erilainen lapsi päivähoidossa, WSOY, Porvoo.

LIIMATAINEN-LAMBERG, A.E. (1993), Changes in Student Smoking Habits at the Vocational Institutions and Senior Secondary Schools and Health Education, Studies in Sport, Physical Education and Health 30, University of Jyväskylä, Jyväskylä.

LINNO, T. (1990a), Ketkä kompastuvat koulun kynnykseen? Koulun, päiväkodin ja neuvolan mahdollisuudet ennaltaehkäistä lieviä oppimisvaikeuksia Vantaalla. Koulutuksen Palvelukeskuksen julkaisuja 1990, Vol. 1, Vantaan kaupunki.

LINNO, T. (1990b), Jotta koulun kynnykseen ei kompastuttaisi. Koulutuksen Palvelukeskuksen julkaisuja 1990, Vol. 2, Vantaan kaupunki.

MÄKELÄ, M., WINTER-HEIKKILA, M., ASTROM, M. and ROKKA, S. (1993), "Local population responsibility – old wine in new barrels?, Dialogue", Journal of the National Research and Development Centre for Welfare and Health, pp. 11-13.

NATIONAL BOARD OF EDUCATION AND NATIONAL RESEARCH AND DEVELOPMENT CENTRE FOR WELFARE AND HEALTH (1994), "Services integration for children and youth at risk and their families", Unpublished report.

NIEMI, A. (1992), Neuvolatyö muuttuvassa terveydenhuollossa, Lapsen maailma, Vol. 3.

OECD (1993), OECD in Figures, Paris.

OECD (1995), Our Children at Risk, Paris.

OJALA, M. (1989), "Early childhood training, care and education in Finland", in P.P. Olmsted and D.P. Weikart (eds.), How Nations Serve Young Children: Profiles of Child Care and Education in 14 Countries, The High Scope Press, Ypsilanti, Michigan, pp. 87-118.

SYVÄNIEMI, U. (1994), "Review of the literature on integrated services for children and youth at risk and their families in Finland", Unpublished report.

TAKALA, M. (1992), "Kouluallergia – yksilön ja yhteiskunnan ongelma", Acta Universitatis Tamperensis ser. A, Vol. 335, Tampereen yliopisto, Tampere.

TARPILA, J. (1992), Neuvola ja sosiaalityö – yhdessä lapsen hyväksi, Lapsen maailma Vol. 3.

TERHO, P. and VAKKILAINEN, E.L. (1993), Kouluterveydenhuollon tukiaineisto, STAKES, Helsinki.

TIKKANEN, T. (1993), "Respecting and listening to children – Organisational and economical aspects", Koulupsykologi, pp. 14-16.

VALDE, E. (1993), The Role of Student Counselling in Senior Secondary School in Orientation towards Working Life and Vocational Choice, Publications of the University of Turku C 94, University of Turku, Turku.

4

GERMANY

THE HUMAN SERVICES UNDERPINNING OF EUROPE'S ECONOMIC GIANT

by

Karin Haubrich, Hermann Rademacker, Josette Combes, Jennifer Evans, Peter Evans, Philippa Hurrell, Mary Lewis, Lucienne Roussel and Richard Volpe

ECONOMIC DEVELOPMENT AND PUBLIC SECTOR SPENDING

The present situation in Germany is characterised by two challenges:

– German unification; and

– world-wide economic change led by new technologies and new ways of organising labour within business.

Both challenges until now have stimulated positive new developments as well as creating obvious symptoms of crisis. Establishing the basic structures of a democratic society, modernising the economy, the public services and administration, and starting to repair serious ecological damage in eastern Germany, are on the positive side of the balance – along with visible signs of economic recovery in western Germany. An unemployment rate unprecedented in German post-war history, which is even higher in the new *Länder* despite enormous amounts of money spent on promoting economic growth, counterbalances these positive developments. Severe cut-backs in social welfare over several years endanger the traditionally high standards in this field.

Tight public budgets at all governmental levels are another characteristic of the present situation. The financial position of almost all communities, which bear most of the burden of social welfare in Germany, often limits efforts to deal with the consequences of social change. Such change has had a significant effect on the situation of children and youth and their families. For example, it has led to an increasing demand for day care, and not only among single-parent and double-income families.

Day care is no longer subject to political and ideological controversies in Germany (related to the role of the mother in the family) as it was up until the early 1980s. Currently, the continuing political controversy regarding rather restrictive legislation on abortion has created additional political pressure for expanding day care facilities, especially for preschool children. But nevertheless the reality is a remarkable discrepancy between supply and demand because of the existing budgetary restrictions. And in the new *Länder*, the formerly exhaustive supply of day care has been reduced even below the decreasing demand because of a dramatically reduced birth rate and extreme rates of women's unemployment.

Ranking the three biographical phases that our case studies refer to in terms of socio-political priorities (as measured by the number of young people being served), the promotion of the vocational integration of disadvantaged youth comes first. The Disadvantaged Youth Programme (*Benachteiligtenprogramm*) is financed by the Federal Labour Administration under the Labour Promotion Act (*Arbeitsförderungsgesetz*), and is carried out by a broad variety of bodies responsible for youth work, and other public and non-governmental agencies. It was established in 1980 as a subsidiary structure to the dual system. It offers supportive training and social services for apprentices experiencing difficulties in meeting the demands of vocational training, as well as additional apprenticeships mainly in regions with severe shortages of training places offered through the dual system. At present, shortages are particularly common in the new *Länder*. While, in 1980, less than 500 apprenticeships were offered through the programme, in September 1994, 32 655 young people held programme apprenticeships. The number of young people in regular vocational training in the dual system who made use of supportive training and services increased from 15 956 in 1987 to 65 371 in September 1994.

DEMOGRAPHIC DEVELOPMENTS IN THE UNIFIED GERMANY

As a consequence of unification in October 1990, Germany has become the country with the largest population in the European Union. According to the *Statistical Yearbook* for 1994, the population in 1992 was 80.1 million including 6.5 million (8.0 per cent) foreigners. In the new *Länder* including East Berlin (the former GDR) we find 15.7 million (19.4 per cent) of the German population.

This population lives in an area of almost 357 000 square kilometres so that the overall population density is 227 people per square kilometre. There are important regional differences. In general, we find regions of low population density in the northern parts of the country in the coastal and rural areas of Lower Saxony, Mecklenburg-Vorpommern and Brandenburg. Remarkable differences between the old *Länder*, the area of the Federal Republic including West Berlin (263 people per square kilometre) and the new *Länder* (145 people per square kilometre) are increased by migration. Although since unification migration from western Germany to eastern Germany has increased (111 000 in 1992), the migration from east to west (199 000) is higher.

The foreign population largely is made up of Turks (1.9 million or 28.6 per cent of the foreign population) and immigrants from the former Yugoslavia (1.0 million or 15.7 per cent). No other single nationality (*e.g.* Italians, Greeks and Poles) makes up as much as 10 per cent of the foreign population. The foreign population from countries which belonged to the European Union in 1992 was 1.5 million (23.2 per cent).

The age diagram of Germany's population shows the typical characteristics of modern industrialised societies. The last 30 years or so have been characterised by a declining birth rate which for about 20 years has been stable at a low level of between 800 000 and one million births per year. These overall national data do not reveal the dramatic change in the eastern Germany's birth rate following unification: between 1988 and 1992 it decreased from almost 216 000 births per year to little more than 88 000. This was accompanied by a similar reduction in the number of marriages (137 000 to 48 000 per year).

Developments in the new *Länder* created by German unification have been partnered by social changes which have affected families. Around 34 per cent of German households are single occupancy, and in some big cities like Munich this share goes up to about 60 per cent. Almost half (42 per cent) of the remaining households of two or more persons are without children and those with two or more children constitute less than 20 per cent of households with two or more persons. Taking into account the remarkable regional differences in the distribution of households and family sizes in Germany, this means that an increasing share of children have no sisters or brothers in their families and are unable to find peers in their neighbourhoods.

The decreasing number of people living together in one household has led to a reduced capacity in families to take care of their children for the whole day. Together with the increased participation of women in the labour market these developments have resulted in an increased demand for day care facilities for children of all age groups. While Germany has seen increasing rates of female participation in the labour market (56.1 per cent in 1992), the participation rate for women with children is even higher (57.0 per cent). This means that 54.8 per cent of all children growing up in Germany have mothers participating in the labour market.

These data characterise the actual situation in the unified Germany in 1992 and are very similar to those in the Federal Republic before unification. The situation in GDR was totally different. As a result of the general shortage of labour together with the societal concept of labour as the central activity of society and individuals, the participation of women in the labour force was almost as high as that of men (around 90 per cent). Day care facilities, crèches, kindergartens and day homes for school children were available for 0-10 year-olds. They offered extensive care from early in the morning until late at night so that mothers could bring their children before they started working and could take them home after they had finished.

MAIN AT RISK GROUPS

The term "at risk" as used in the OECD project refers to "pupils from disadvantaged backgrounds who fail to become integrated into a normally accepted pattern of responsibility, particularly with regard to work and family life" (OECD, 1995). The German research on failure and success regarding integration into the workforce shows that the resources mobilised by families are crucial for most young people. Severe deficits regarding social background often result in school failure and, as a result, social disadvantage often is reproduced over generations. Also, for those who face serious problems in the transition from school to work, we often find that lacking social support for vocational orientation and for meeting the challenges of this transition is not counterbalanced by effective intervention by schools or other social services such as vocational guidance. This does not mean that schools and other services are ineffective with respect to supporting social and vocational integration but their effect becomes visible mainly when young people succeed in improving their educational and vocational status as compared to their family. The important difference seems to be whether or not young people and their families are able to make use of these institutions and services according to their own needs and interests.

The main factors related to increased risk of failure regarding social and vocational integration are: *i*) school failure – which in Germany mainly means leaving school after completing compulsory education (nine or ten years) with no certificate and often after mastering only grade seven or eight; *ii*) disadvantaged social background; and *iii*) belonging to an ethnic minority group. The risk of failure for those belonging to any one of these groups is dramatically increased if they have to bear additional burdens such as living in a broken home.

SOCIAL WELFARE

The social welfare system was introduced by establishing a national system of social insurance at the end of the 19th century (compulsory health insurance scheme: 1883, accident insurance: 1884, pension insurance: 1889). Unemployment insurance became established as a compulsory public institution in 1919.

One of the latest extensions of the German social welfare system, which is of particular interest for the vocational integration of youth, was public financial assistance for students and pupils. It was established by Federal Law in 1970 and was intended to become an effective means to create equal opportunities for educational participation.

As it was initiated in the context of broad educational reform during the 1960s and early 1970s, political support for the further development of this instrument declined. Therefore the originally intended provision of assistance independent of the financial situation of the parents was never achieved and neither was the expansion of this benefit to those in vocational education in the dual system (*e.g.* for financial assistance to live apart from the family). Instead, we had limited increases in the maximum support given, restrictions to the conditions of entitlement, and a lessening of the kind of support being given to those eligible for benefits (*i.e.* loans instead of subsistence allowances).

The social services administration in Germany is characterised by the division of its social services departments into welfare services, health services, and youth offices. The establishment of a youth welfare and youth service office and *Land* youth offices became compulsory by law after World War II. The function of the *Land* youth offices is to co-ordinate and promote the work of the local youth welfare offices. Implementation of legally required youth welfare tasks and administrative organisation is part of local self-government. This legislation also strengthened the principle of subsidiarity and codified the priority of the voluntary sector over the statutory sector (Jordan and Sengling, 1992, pp. 211 *ff.*).

Subsidiarity in the social services field in Germany means that smaller units (families, relatives and neighbourhoods) should provide help and care prior to statutory agencies and governmental organisations (Schäfers, 1981, p. 88; Schäfer, 1988, p. 19 *ff*). It also means that private welfare organisations, regardless of their size, have priority over services run by the community.

German unification has resulted in the transfer of the western German social welfare system to the new *Länder*. The Children and Youth Services Act (*Kinder- und Jugendhilfegesetz*, KJHG) was even put into force there three months earlier than in the old *Länder*. But the establishment of child and youth welfare structures and agencies has taken place against a background of totally different traditions of social services provision (Hoffmann, 1981; Deutsches Jugendinstitut, 1990). Youth welfare in the former GDR mainly concentrated on the needs of endangered youth which is – according to the tradition of the Youth Welfare Law in the old *Länder* – part of welfare work for the young (*Jugendfürsorge*). Youth care was, in contrast to the principle of subsidiarity in the old *Länder*, nearly exclusively the task of public authorities. Efforts were focused on the stationary part of youth welfare, especially residential care for children and youth (Backhaus-Maul and Olk, 1992, p. 94). Moreover, as a consequence of this difference in orientation, the vocational education of social workers in the former GDR had another profile. There were no special courses of study for social pedagogues at universities, and a great part of social work was done by unpaid honorary workers (Backhaus-Maul and Olk, 1992, p. 95).

COMPULSORY AND VOCATIONAL EDUCATION

Compulsory education in Germany was established at the turn of the 19th century through establishing the *Volksschule* (people's school) for the lower classes. It differed from traditional higher education which led to university, and this difference is apparent in the German school system today. Only during the Weimar Republic was the *Grundschule* (primary school for children aged 6-10) established as a compulsory school for all children. Prior to that, there existed expensive special private schools which prepared children for the *Gymnasium*. While the constitution of the Weimar Republic decreed they were to be cancelled, some survived until 1933.

The most important and persistent political controversy in the history of education policy in Germany dealt with the question of participation in higher education (*i.e.* schools leading to a certificate, the *Abitur*, which allows for university entrance). As the *Gymnasium* has remained within the structure of the public education system, the elite have not opted for private schools. They do not need to use expensive private schools to reproduce and legitimise their elite status as in many other OECD Member countries. But this also means that the changes in the educational system aimed at equalising opportunities interfere to a greater extent with the interests of social elites in Germany than in other countries. It also explains the strong selectivity of the German education system which decides for the vast majority of children at the age of ten which branch of a vertically differentiated secondary school system they will attend.

After putting an end to the Nazi regime in 1945, the occupying powers, wishing to encourage the development of a democratic society in Germany, supported educational reform efforts aimed at achieving more comprehensiveness in the educational system. In the western zones the political issue was to expand the *Grundschule* for another two years of common schooling for all children. This change only survived in Berlin (western part). In the Soviet occupation zone an integrated school system was established comprising grades one to eight, at the time the total period of compulsory general education.

The division between an integrated school system in the GDR and a differentiated system with strongly developed streaming in the western Federal Republic survived until German unification. The main change that occurred in the West was that, as a result of reform efforts during the 1960s and early 1970s, the comprehensive school in some of the *Länder* became established as a fourth branch of secondary school – in addition to the general secondary school (*Hauptschule*), the intermediate school (*Realschule*), and the grammar school (*Gymnasium*). In the East, the integrated structure called polytechnical high school (*Polytechnische Oberschule*, POS) was expanded for ten years and existed as long as the GDR did. The only differentiation that occurred was linked to the establishment of schools for special education (*Hilfsschulen*) for about 5 per cent of pupils, and extended high schools (*Erweiterte Oberschule*, EOS) comprising grades 11 and 12. Fifteen per cent of children who qualified for university went to extended high schools.

After German unification a differentiated school system also was established in the eastern part, with some modifications regarding the relationship between general secondary and intermediate school. The rates of participation in the different types of secondary education quickly approximated those realised in western Germany after almost 40 years of development. This means that almost one third of children are attending grammar school, another third intermediate school and the remaining third secondary general school. These quotas change by region. In big cities, the quota in *Gymnasia* often goes up to 50 per cent while the share in secondary general schools often is below 20 per cent. But this increased participation in higher education does not meet the educational aspirations of parents. As polls every two years show, only 10 per cent of parents want their children to attend secondary general schools while more than 50 per cent prefer grammar schools.

VOCATIONAL EDUCATION AND TRAINING

The basic structure of vocational education and training in Germany is the dual system. Its fundamental elements of practical training in companies and additional education in schools also were maintained in the GDR. The main differences were that companies were not private and schools – because of their close relationship with companies – not really public. More important still for developments since unification are differences which resulted from different levels of economic development in both Germanies. Specifically, there was a remarkable lack of modernisation in the production and service sectors in the East. These differences were reflected in the nature of the qualifications being taught and made modernisation necessary for vocational education and training.

With the dramatic decline of the eastern Germany's economy, many training facilities closed down. The reconstructed economy has yet to create the number of jobs needed or an adequate number of apprenticeships within companies. Since vocational education and training in Germany is seen as a public responsibility, in eastern Germany especially, a great number of apprenticeships are created outside of companies with public money.

ORIGINS AND DEVELOPMENT OF INTEREST IN INTEGRATED SERVICES

The discussion on integration of social services started at the end of the 1960s, following a period of re-establishing those structures and organisations of social welfare created during the Weimar Republic. The most intensive period of discussion was during the 1970s, in the context of a debate on the reorganisation of community social services.

Substantial new orientations started with the anti-authoritarian and student movement in the late 1960s. The critical social sciences urged a change of direction and step by step social work practices changed. The needs of clients were now analysed in a social context. Critical social work, it was felt, should not only help individuals but contribute to the development of society. During this period, reformative efforts aimed to encourage more client participation and less hierarchy (Barth, 1993, p. 115). This change in the philosophy of social work impacted theories and methods of social work as well as organisational and institutional structures.

Economic prosperity and a political open-mindedness towards social reforms during the 1970s facilitated the promotion of model projects. In many municipalities, projects to reorganise social services were initiated. In the history of German social work those projects can be regarded as important initiatives to integrate social services.

Since the 1980s, approaches to the integration of services have been concentrated on specific programmes. New impulses were created by German reunification and the new Children and Youth Services Act.

MANDATING LEVEL

The general structure of the *Reichsjugendwohlfahrtsgesetz* (RJWG, enacted in 1922) supplemented and reformed by the Youth Welfare Law (*Jugendwohlfahrtsgesetz*, JWG) in 1961, formed the basis of youth work and youth welfare services until 1990, when the new Children and Youth Services Act (KJHG) was enacted (Kreft, 1993, p. 323).

Political and professional discussions as well as official youth reports (presented to the German parliament by the Federal Government in each legislative period) contributed to the development of youth services (Der Bundesminister, 1990). In the late 1980s, there was an intensive discussion about youth welfare legislation that came to an end with the passing of the Children and Youth Services Act. This new law, in force since October 3, 1990 in the new *Länder* and since January 1, 1991 in the old *Länder* reflects the recent development of ideas about youth services and gives a new importance to service co-operation and integration.

The KJHG includes several sections that support the idea of services integration.

Section 4 makes public service agencies liable to co-operate with free agencies that offer youth services. In cases where educational support has to be given over a longer period of time, youth welfare agencies are bound to elaborate a support plan. To prevent one-sided views on problems and to be able to find programmes most suited to solve problems, this plan ought to be worked out by representatives of all agencies that will (or might) be involved in service delivery (section 36.2, KJHG). If necessary, professionals from different disciplines of social work and welfare should work together in order to find the best solution and the most adequate form of support or therapy (section 72.1, KJHG).

Section 78 summons public youth services agencies to establish working groups with free agencies. These working groups should aim to reconcile measures and programmes and to organise them so that they complement one another. To support co-operation between public and free agencies, the latter ought to be involved in the process of planning youth welfare that has to be done by public agencies (section 80.3, KJHG). In order to meet the expectations of pro-active youth services, the youth welfare agencies are required to co-operate with organisations like schools, training agencies and the public health sector (section 81, KJHG). This commitment traditionally has no equivalent on the other side. Only the latest changes in legislation for schools require corresponding commitment.

Although the idea of services integration is promoted in the Children and Youth Services Act, for the most part it is not legally required. On the one hand, most sections that refer to services integration include "ought-tos" or even "shoulds" and can be interpreted by every youth welfare agency according to its own ideas. On the other hand, these regulations are addressed to public agencies only, with free agencies being under no obligation whatsoever to work towards services integration.

RESEARCH SITES

Bremen: Bremen is a Free Hanseatic city, which, along with Bremerhaven, operates as a State within the western system. It is the smallest state in western Germany with a population of 680 000. It is formed by the two cities of Bremen (population 522 000) and Bremerhaven (132 000), both located on the Weser river close to the North Sea coast, with some 30 miles of Lower Saxony between them. Bremen has a strong republican and secular tradition. It was originally governed by liberal merchants from the city. So there is a strong tradition of autonomy and a strong identification with and pride in the city among its inhabitants. The effects of recession hit Bremen later than most other western Germany's regions but more intensely. In 1994, it had the highest unemployment rate among the old *Länder*, with the most important reason for this being the structural crisis in old industries like shipbuilding, steel, food, tobacco, and radio and television production.

Leipzig: Leipzig is in the *Land* of Saxony which has a population of 500 000 people. A total of 170 000 of them are children and youth. In Saxony there are about 100 youth-related non-profit organisations, many of which are local indigenous organisations. Leipzig alone has 150 free associations in the field of social services. Facing an enormous economic crisis, major concerns for Leipzig are to re-establish viable commerce and industry, to create jobs, to ameliorate the housing situation, and to improve opportunities for youth between the ages of 10 and 18.

Duisburg: Duisburg is part of the state of Northrhine-Westphalia. This state produces 25 per cent of western Germany's gross domestic product and 30 per cent of its exports. The industrial strength of this region is due to the 150-year development of the coal rich area around the River Ruhr, the growth of Germany's steel industry, and the associated evolution of manufacturing and commerce. Duisburg is one of the world's largest inland ports. Its current importance has its origin in the late 19th century when the city became one of Europe's principal iron, steel, and coal mining centres. But the demand for steel and coal has fallen rapidly, causing increasing unemployment. Duisburg now is in a process of economic restructuring, moving away from heavy industry and expanding the service sector.

INTEGRATION OF SERVICES FOR PRESCHOOL CHILDREN IN BREMEN

Institutions and key partners

The organisation of youth and social welfare services in Bremen is different from that in other parts of Germany. In other areas, youth and social welfare services are located in separate offices as a result of legislation which recommends that they should be provided separately. This type of organisation was criticised in the 1970s by academics and others. Therefore Bremen attempted to change its organisation of services along the lines indicated as useful by the research. In 1974, the Department of Social Affairs in Bremen financed evaluation research about the structure and work of social services in Bremen. The result of this study showed the necessity of improvement. And in 1982 they started a pilot project in the southern area funded by the Ministry of Youth, Family and Health up to the amount of DM 650 000.

There was an important need for a system of organisation which would take responsibility for a population regardless of whether or not any particular individual had a problem. This is an "integration-ist" or "inclusive" approach, which attempts to serve the whole community and not to marginalise or separate certain groups as "problematic". Orientation to the citizen as a consumer and receiver of services is a key requirement.

There are two aims which are at the centre of the reorganisation of social services in Bremen (Dolls and Hammetter, 1987, 1988). First, a "target group orientation" which implies an integrative "concept of acting" (*Handlungskonzep*) that aims at different demographic groups. In other words, the needs of clients must be diagnosed in the context of the stage of life they are at and help must be "holistic" (*ganzheitlich*). The new approach is to have professional competence in work with different demographic groups and to try to avoid gaps in population coverage.

The second central principle is neighbourhood or regional orientation which implies the diagnosis of needs in local contexts. Moreover it implies that regionally located agencies of social services should be working together in order to re-integrate clients into regional structures and living space (Dolls and Hammetter, 1988). This is an attempt to create a community.

These two principles structure the organisation of social services in Bremen and describe the two dimensions of the innovative "matrix organisation" of social services.

The organisational structure which represents the principle of target group orientation is the division of the four regional departments of social services (south, east, north and middle west) into so called *Bezirkssozialdienste* (for children and their families, youth and their families, adults without under-age children, and elderly people). For each demographic group there is one *Bezirkssozialdienst* which is responsible for all necessary statutory tasks. Additionally, there are special *Bezirkssozialdienste* focusing on specific problems which are not dependent on demographic factors and which require a specific professional knowledge (in economic social and youth welfare, guardianship exercised by the local authority, counselling for children, youth and their families, and socio-psychiatric care).

The second principle is represented by the regional division of social services. The office for Health, Youth, and Social Welfare in Bremen has four regional departments for the four areas of Bremen – North, South, East and Middle-west. Each of these has 100 000 to 150 000 inhabitants. Within each of these areas are smaller districts of between 20 000 and 40 000 inhabitants. With the exception of guardianship exercised by the local authority, all *Bezirkssozialdienste* are divided into small groups or responsible persons for each of the districts. Within each district there are smaller neighbourhoods of between 5 000 and 10 000 inhabitants.

The communal office of social services administers finance and monitors and controls the work of voluntary agencies. The area office delivers services and is responsible for their quality.

The reorganisation of social services on an area and district level is exemplified by the district of Huchting in South Bremen, where the site visits took place. It is one of the disadvantaged areas of Bremen, a result of the way planning and building was carried out in the 1960s. Now 25 per cent of families receive benefits.

Several different committees co-ordinate the different local organisations and institutions. There is one area committee in which all directors of the *Bezirkssozialdienste* and the director of the area office participate. At the district level, there is a committee consisting of social pedagogues (from the welfare office) who are responsible for the district, and one expert from each welfare organisation in the district (*i.e.* from kindergartens, youth clubs and institutions, playgrounds, the City Farm, the Local Council, the Social Centre, school psychological services, non-profit organisations and health services).

A central function of the district committee is to get all providers of social services around the table and thereby establish a forum for discussion and co-operation. Such co-ordination serves to identify needs in Huchting and to create a better living environment. Although the committee only has an advisory role towards the Council and the State Ministry it has become very influential. It also provides links between the community and the hierarchy by relating emerging issues within the agencies concerned back to management.

A co-ordinator was appointed to liaise between the local and central levels of administration, through supporting co-operation and creating and building networks. He attends the public sessions of the local council and its subcommittees, especially the social affairs committee, which enables contact between the local council and other staff, local politicians and other professionals who work in Huchting. The co-ordinator has to act as a social agent. He must have an overview of the whole district and the problems in particular neighbourhoods. This holistic approach to the planning of services is an innovative way of working.

This organisational structure not only builds links between the administration of Bremen and local activities, but also promotes co-operative practices among the local welfare organisations. During the site visit in Huchting some local organisations were visited and others were introduced at a meeting at the Social Services Centre in Huchting. The key partners in the social services network in Huchting will be described in the following section.

Mothers' Centre (Mütterzentrum Huchting)

The *Mütterzentrum* is run by, and for, women. It is a self-help project initiated in 1987 by a group of women with the aid of social workers and the support of the Ministry of Health, Youth and Social Affairs. The target groups are women and their families regardless of age, nationality and religion. In the Huchting area there is a high proportion of women with a low level of schooling who have never worked or are unemployed. So they are confined to their homes, often feeling depressed because of isolation and difficult living conditions. The philosophy behind the project is that the mother's well-being has positive effects on children's well-being. In order to help mothers to cope with emotional and other stress and with domestic isolation, the *Mütterzentrum* offers different opportunities for women to get into contact with other women and their children. It also helps them to find a training or job opportunity. To avoid stress, mothers can come in when they want and join in any activity. Another important aim is to encourage women to share their skills and experience. As the focus is on voluntary activities, however, experts only have a counselling function. All of the services at the Centre (breakfast, lunch courses, after school activities) are provided by the mothers. They receive a small payment through the welfare support fund. As women's work is often unpaid in society the *Mütterzentrum* tries to pay for all the different jobs and duties performed by women.

The *Mütterzentrum* co-operates with all the associations in the Social Services Centre in Huchting, who in turn, send clients to the Centre. They offer their rooms for activities and staff consult with professional counsellors in order to get help for their own work. There are also close collaborative activities with other institutions. Health guidance for mothers with babies is provided, a paediatrician from the child guidance clinic comes in to talk with mothers, and a specialist in handicapped children offers guidance to staff on ways to improve children's functioning.

Regional Department of Social Services – South: team of social workers for children and their families (Amt für Soziale Dienste – Süd: Sozialdienst Kinder und deren Familien)

The *Sozialdienst Kinder und deren Familien* (social service for children and their families) is one of the *Bezirkssozialdienste* in the matrix organisation described above. Although their central office is not in Huchting they have a small office in the centre of Huchting which they use two days a week. The target groups are families with children younger than 12 years of age, single parent, step and foreign families as well as families living on social welfare. They offer counselling and special help for children and their families when needed. A specific approach is used to provide professional help to families in crisis. A qualified professional assists families in their homes on a part-time basis and deals with educational problems, household management, budgeting, etc. This person may act as a surrogate parent and try to support and stabilise the family system. The focus of this approach is on counselling and enhancing the abilities of the families concerned in coping with their problems on a day-to-day basis. A different type of assistance is offered to families having to cope with parents absent due to illness, addiction and imprisonment. In this case, a qualified housekeeper will go into the home to take the parents' place. Both types of intervention are seen as preventative, and as an instrument for avoiding taking the children into care or placing them in a foster home.

They co-operate with all organisations and associations working with the same target group. For example, they co-operate with school and preschool workers to analyse problems and also with other agencies to support families.

Family House (Haus der Familie)

The Family House is part of the Social Services Department. There are ten staff working at the house (three are social workers and the rest are educators working on a sessional basis). The focus of their activities is educational. They organise projects like weekend activities, and educational seminars, and provide further training opportunities. They take a classical self-help approach and try to initiate activities. The target groups are parents with children in socially deprived areas, preschool and school children in need of socialisation, foreign children, girls and women, single parents, and women living in bad social and financial conditions. They offer 20 group activities in closed groups and have about 120 participants. They try to co-operate with other associations if they see problems arising and in order to establish new activities. The main objective is to help people to improve themselves through solving problems of isolation, by gaining communication skills, and exploring training and job strategies whilst at the same time coping with their family responsibilities. The key word for them is autonomy, for both children and adults, which allows the building of strong family relationships.

The main partners of the Family House are the central office and kindergartens near a housing complex built for migrant families from the former Soviet Union. In the Family House, a co-ordinator is allocated for ten hours a week to contribute to the Huchting Committee. And DM 10 000 per year for three years have been provided for co-operation work across all services for children in Huchting.

Child guidance

Five professionals, psychologists, family therapists and behaviour therapists, work in child guidance in the southern region of Bremen. The target groups are families, parents, youth and children who have difficulties concerning education, problems due to conflicts, or behavioural disturbance. Counselling can last from several months to several years. Moreover they support children by using remedial teaching or therapeutic methods. The service is confidential, free of charge and families attend voluntarily. They do preventative work as well as working with families with severe problems. Due to a holistic approach the psychologists co-operate with social workers, teachers and doctors. It was reported that co-operation with schools and doctors was very good.

Child and youth health services

The service is organised into 13 district teams, consisting of a paediatrician, one nurse and one medical doctor. The team has a "demographic approach" and works with the total child population up to the age of 18 years in a specific area. In this case it is the area of Huchting and one other area in the southern part of Bremen. This holistic approach was introduced in 1981. They work closely with the social services team, which is an important resource for information. They are included in the Huchting Committee and have good relations with other services. They also go into schools, nurseries and kindergartens and talk to parents as part of preventative medicine. They also are involved in co-operation through case conferences and have regular meetings with child guidance staff.

City Farm

The City Farm, initiated by a teacher from a local school, is a voluntary body. More than 100 children are involved in the farm and they can come whenever they like. The aim is to give space to children to enable them to build up social structures and to take responsibility. It gives them a feeling of being important.

Day care (preschool and school)

The city, as well as churches and other voluntary organisations, runs day care centres. Some are also run by self help initiatives set up by parents. In the whole city there are 71 centres for children from 3-12 years of age (with a focus on 3-6 year-olds) run by the community of Bremen. And there are 16 communal day care centres in the southern region which serve 1 990 children. Because of the disadvantaged situation in Huchting, the day care centres visited by the OECD experts have to deal with a high level of social deprivation. Many families live on social welfare and often both parents are unemployed.

Day care centre for preschool and school children – Dietrich Bonhoefer: This day care centre, part of the Protestant Church, started in 1970 with four groups. They additionally used an apartment to provide day care for school children. In 1980, they started out on a project developing day care for handicapped and non handicapped children. When this "first generation of integrated education" reached school-age, the centre and the parents were successful in developing a continuation of the project in school. Thus Huchting was the first place to provide regular primary school in Bremen offering an education integrating children with severe mental and physical handicaps. Now there are more than one hundred children attending this centre.

State funded day care centre – Kindergarten Höhpost: A total of 50 per cent of parents using the centre receive social welfare benefits. Staff cater for two age groups: preschool and school children. Their approach with the children is to emphasize the teaching of social skills and to enrich play activities. They also provide speech therapy and there are training staff to provide psycho-motor and sensory content to their work with children. It is hoped that this will increase staff competence in structuring activities for children. This is also an integrative approach aimed at avoiding social exclusion of disadvantaged children.

Co-operation between day care and other institutions also exists and is important. Staff from child guidance work in the kindergarten to avoid stigmatising children. There is also co-operation with the social services office in such matters as deciding whether a family helper is needed. Moreover, a close relationship exists with the Family House, the paediatrician, and school. Co-operation with school exists in two main areas: case conferences are held on the problems of individual children and staff try to influence what goes on at school.

Political support and funding

Maintaining an extensive network of social provision in Bremen requires important financial support. As public budgets are rather tight, western Germany has become more reluctant to fund this level of provision and is asking Bremen to lower its standards.

Funding of the organisations involved in the area-based network in Huchting comes from various institutions. The Mütterzentrum, for example, receives financial support from the social welfare budget, lottery funds, and a fund for supporting self-help projects. For regular groups of children of preschool or school age, money is received from the Office for Social Services, and the "Senat" Department of Youth and Social Affairs contributes money for projects. One early childhood professional worker is paid by the ministry which also pays for equipment, materials and food. The Family Affairs Department has given moral and financial support. They have provided access to funds which would not have been available otherwise. The budget of the Family House comes from the city. It is a free service and no fees are charged. The Dietrich Bonhoefer day care centre is funded and managed by the local church and the church is also the employer of the staff. The Kindergarten Höhpost is state funded.

A totally different form of funding was given to the City Farm which was set up in 1991. It was built within three days thanks to a TV programme, "Now or Never", which claimed to be able to realise specific projects within a short time, by finding sponsors of all kinds to give money and do the labour. The local authorities gave the land. The house and other buildings were paid for by the European Social Fund. Now the project is run by a local initiative and the funding of running costs is shared by the Education and Social Services Departments, although they also rely on sponsorship and donations.

Facilitating and inhibiting factors

The origins of reorganising the structure of social services in Bremen are to be seen in the context of the period of reformative efforts in Germany in the 1970s. It is not clear whether the stimulus for change was from the top or from the field. These reforms were generated at a strategic level but important impulses for initiating such reforms came from professionals. Many of the ideas came from professionals in the field. Pilot projects, based on these ideas, were then implemented.

A facilitating factor is the very short line of communication between the strategic and political levels as well as good links between field workers and operational managers. The long-term benefits of the system are that staff gain experience in dealing with new forms of co-operation and co-ordination.

On the local level, co-operation received an enormous push from a workshop on Kind-Sein in Huchting in 1991. This workshop was initiated by professionals (especially the directors of preschools) in order to analyse the problems of children in Huchting on the basis of all available data about children and families. The analysis showed that there were gaps in service delivery, with 50 per cent of needs linked to problems which needed a co-ordinated approach. The planning group considers all aspects of provision for children in Huchting and keeps an overview of who is doing what, which demands are being met and whether there are many gaps in provision. The partners in this group are directors of nurseries, paediatric, child guidance, social welfare and school psychology services. While they meet regularly, attendance is voluntary, and continuity might therefore be affected.

A fundamental problem to overcome is negative competition between institutions who offer similar services. As the example of day care shows it was an important step towards co-operation to get away from competitive thinking. As reported, strength and influence comes from the fact that partners cannot be divided as far as their work is concerned. They share the same knowledge and the same information. The planning group for children in Huchting also can contribute to avoiding situations of competition between different initiatives because they have an overview of different activities.

A factor promoting co-operation is the co-location of services in one social complex, the Social Services Centre. This appears to be efficient and to facilitate good personal relationships between the professionals.

But there are also some obstacles towards co-operation. Some problems show up in co-operation between schools and day care centres. They have different expectations of each other. Schools expect help with children's academic problems. The centres focus on the development of social skills as an precondition for solving academic problems. But this requires a different role of teachers. Different professions with different working fields have to find ways of accepting each other's work and complementing one another.

On the whole, personal relationships with colleagues and open-mindedness help collaboration. Bureaucracy, rigidity, and an unwillingness among people who consider the process time consuming and stressful, hinder collaboration.

Outcomes

The network of services in Huchting has developed through the co-operation team. Professionals have personal contacts with colleagues in other institutions, and gaps between the services have narrowed. But more time and involvement is required. Nevertheless it seems to be worthwhile, as the different institutions can profit from each other's experiences in solving problems and as the group is rather powerful.

In the Family House, it was reported that work is more interesting and pleasant because high quality is more likely to be achieved. Developments cannot be planned or achieved without co-operation with other services. New developments can be thought of as projects, rather than as single answers to problems. Moreover in terms of personal benefits, contact with other professionals makes the routine more interesting and enlarges professionals' field of knowledge and practice. And it alleviates some of the stress, linked to having responsibility for the poorest in society.

Of course there are also benefits for clients because there are less gaps in the net of social services, and the regional and target group principles have improved access to social services.

The main benefits for mothers attending the Mütterzentrum appear to be encouragement, contact, equality between members, diversity in training and work, and collaboration with professional (which helps to improve knowledge and self-esteem). Mothers in the Mütterzentrum nevertheless feel that they need professional counselling. They meet resistance from social workers, however, who do not believe in this type of activity. The only activity which seems to gain recognition is child care. Another important restraint is the pressure which men put on their wives. Men seem to be afraid of emancipation and some would not allow their wives to participate. There also appeared to be a need for better links with formal training and better access to outside labour opportunities.

Discussion

The reorganisation of social services in Bremen has produced many positive experiences. The target group orientation prevents the exclusion of certain age groups from social services. Moreover, social pedagogues develop more professional competence in their field of work and the needs of target groups become more transparent. Last but not least, organisation according to this principle makes co-operation easier. On the whole the reorganisation of social services in Bremen made a broad and complex network of integrated services possible.

As mentioned above, the long-term benefits of the system are that the partners involved gain experience in dealing with new forms of co-operation and co-ordination. In many innovative projects promoting services integration, funding ends at a time when good co-operative links and structures are just starting to emerge. This is a serious problem of short-term funding.

At the regional level, the Huchting Committee has been instrumental in bringing about an integrated approach. It perceives itself as a powerful pressure group for improving service delivery in the area according to the principles of target groups and regionality. At the strategic level, the efficiency in solving problems is emphasized. Co-operative social work at the local level is seen as a powerful force for staff development, as well as a means to achieve more effective provision for clients. The effectiveness of the Committee is believed to be enhanced by the co-ordinator, who keeps open channels of communication between local services, and between the local services and the strategic level.

At the strategic level it seems to be more difficult to achieve co-operation between ministries. Nevertheless informal networks across departments do exist, because the importance of developing links to work more effectively has been recognised.

A problematic feature seems to be competition between similar services. Communication and discussion can reduce this negative effect on co-operation, although the threat of budget cuts might increase the danger of competition. There will always be some overlap in the programmes offered by different agencies. For example, there are some similarities in the work of the Family House and the Mothers' Centre (*Mütterzentrum*) in terms of target groups and objectives, but there are also important differences. Neither one could cover all the different needs and constellations of problems found in the community. Maintaining the existing co-operative structure and good links between different services seems to be a key requirement for effective provision for clients.

At the present time there is a discussion about the splitting of responsibilities. Some ask whether the responsibility for managing budgets should be transferred from the state level to the area level. But, with more responsibility, areas would have to make difficult decisions about priorities. In the context of shrinking communal budgets this is a problematic task. Nevertheless there are good reasons for local control of funding.

INTEGRATION OF SERVICES FOR SCHOOL CHILDREN IN LEIPZIG

Context

In eastern Germany, children, youth and their families face many uncertainties due to the rapid changes in society since the revolution in 1989 and German unification in October 1990. Law in western Germany was transferred to the new *Länder* and new democratic institutions had to be established. Major changes are occurring within families and between individuals and societal institutions and the resulting problems have been exacerbated by the economic crisis.

The major focus of the study visit in Leipzig was therefore the forging of links among the newly emerging and changing services for children, youth, and families following the collapse of the GDR. A drastic shift has been taking place, from an authoritarian, paternalistic state that had no role for the voluntary sector to a democratic system of governance and public administration which values a prominent role for free associations under the subsidiarity principle.

Since services for school children were the focus of the visit to Leipzig, it is relevant to mention that a very selective new school system has been developed in Saxony which is similar to the one in Bavaria. Teachers are no longer responsible for after school care. There are insufficient leisure time and day care programmes for school children and youth. Unemployment and housing problems threaten family life, while juvenile delinquency and violence are increasing and combating xenophobia is a challenge.

The following provides a brief description of the involved partners and institutions visited in Leipzig as well as the nature of political support for collaboration. The process of services provision, factors promoting and inhibiting collaboration, and the results and outcomes for the clients will be discussed.

Institutions and key partners

The Leipzig case study focused on the activities of the *Regionale Arbeitsstellen zur Förderung ausländis-cher Kinder und Jugendlicher* (Regional Centre to Support Foreign Children and Young People, RAA). The RAA in Leipzig, which opened in 1993, is a local unit of the national voluntary organisation. This voluntary community organisation combines an international education support service, a community education support centre and a field agent organisation. It was founded in 1980 as a Freudenberg Foundation initiative in the big cities of the Ruhr region which were suffering from the collapse of the steel and mining industry.

Today there are regional centres in 18 cities in western Germany and in eleven cities in eastern Germany. This organisation supports foreign children and youth, fights discrimination, and develops and/or provides community based work with alienated youth or those who fear foreigners. One objective is to decrease violence against foreigners and immigrants. A second objective is to work with German youth who hate foreigners or are becoming alienated from mainstream society. The RAA opened in Leipzig in 1993. At first, the RAA functioned in conjunction with the Town's Education Department. They have since been given more autonomy.

In Leipzig, there are about 15 000 foreigners (3 per cent of the population). This is little compared to 8 per cent for western Germany and minimal compared to western German cities with 10 per cent or more. This number includes only 200 foreign children, and they can be found in attendance primarily at six different schools. Leipzig has the highest percentage of foreigners in eastern Germany. Most of them are eastern Europeans, and none are Turks. Most of the foreigners in Leipzig were never guest workers, but people who came to study at the University of Leipzig or for other personal reasons. There are not many refugees seeking political asylum, who must live in poorly equipped hostels or camps before they either get asylum or their application for asylum is refused. But there is a contradiction between the low rate of foreigners in eastern Germany and the high level of hostility against them, which is even greater than in western Germany.

As foreign youth and their families are vulnerable and endangered in so many respects, the services of multiple agencies are required to protect them from societal exclusion. But, in order to provide effective help, different services have to be co-ordinated. It is the aim of the RAA to promote interagency co-operation and to overcome the barriers created between organisations.

The RAA co-operates with the Local Government in many different ways; for example, on a project called "Schools without Violence" in middle schools in the eastern part of the city. The city works with the RAA to address the problems of immigrants, and to find solutions against discrimination and violence. Another initiative led by the School Office is called "Schools will be open for free associations to offer services for pupils". The Youth Office and the Office of Culture worked together to form this initiative. The RAA is a major partner in facilitating the process of bringing together schools with free associations. There is also a permanent collaborative arrangement between the Office for Foreigners and the RAA. If a problem arises with a foreigner in school, this office seeks advice from the RAA as well as from school officials, about how to solve it.

The RAA has a rather small staff of three in Leipzig to cover its different activities. The reason for this lies in the role of the RAA as a kind of catalyst. They try to encourage and create activities in other institutions. They want to motivate others, suggest ideas, provide information, and engage people from agencies and free associations to create the necessary support.

Political support and funding

The financial resources provided by all government levels can be used to nurture innovative social services in Leipzig.

As advance planning is of importance for maximising the chances of getting state money, Leipzig has successfully elaborated a comprehensive youth plan covering all fields of youth work, planning and evaluation which is enforced by the new Children and Youth Services Act but not yet realised by all cities and communities. There still exist some difficulties with the procedures for obtaining federal or state funding. Therefore better planning, budgeting, organisation and co-ordination at local level is recommended. Another problem is that Land money is distributed through two ministries, Social Affairs and Education, with different rules regarding grants to towns.

An important input was provided by a particular programme of the Ministry of Labour starting after reunification that gave financial assistance to employ staff and purchase equipment. But this programme ended in 1993.

Although it was assumed to be difficult to get funding to address all youth problems, the Town Council was said to have provided a good amount of money. The Town's financing has increased for the last years, amounting to DM 2.9 million in 1992, DM 3.1 million in 1993 and DM 4.7 million in 1994. The

Department of Youth, School and Education got DM 80 million (out of DM 330 million) for the reconstruction of buildings and equipment.

Financial support for the RAA is provided by the Town Government, the Freudenberg Foundation, the Federal Conference of Ministries of Culture and Education, and the Saxony Ministry of Education.

Integrated practices

The manner in which the RAA attempts to innovate includes several different steps. Its method of work is to first establish contact with the authorities who are responsible for schools, to develop an understanding of the problems of the students, to identify the schools that have foreigners and the ones famous for violence and truancy. Then a few schools are identified as a focus for developing working relationships. Negotiations take place to convince the teachers that engagement in collaboration will be positive. Incentives, support, and reassurance must be provided for employees to take risks incurred through the development of horizontal relationships. The function of the innovator is to identify and develop the common concepts and basis for work between professions and organisations and nurture these through in-service training. The innovative agency provides advice and support for co-operation and co-ordination, and takes new initiatives.

Teamwork with schools can be planned on a short-term or a long-term basis. In the last case, the RAA seeks other partners in Leipzig, such as free associations, who can develop leisure time activities. For example, they develop leisure time activities for small groups of boys aged 8-10 whose school attendance has dropped and who view teachers as enemies. They allow the boys to develop their own programmes and activities, using the school grounds or facilities. Or a theatre project is started to get in contact with girls in the school. The idea is to get young people involved in something that they enjoy in their free time near school, to modify their attitudes, and eventually become more involved in school life again.

In some cases co-operation was initiated by schools. Some schools requested workshops relating to foreigners, some asked for training in how to deal with conflicts and others needed help relating to the difficult circumstances under which they work. The school system was changed following reunification and there were a lot of problems connected with establishing new types of school. In some cases, renovation projects organised by the students themselves were promoted by the RAA.

The RAA also uses network approaches to achieve goals related to foreigners as well as those related to German youth. The aim is to develop an organisational network, including representatives of the public and voluntary organisations that have programmes in the same neighbourhood, in order to co-ordinate their activities. Such a network exists for example in Grunau, a residential quarter on the edge of Leipzig without a social infrastructure like shops or parks. Besides aiming to bring together all resources, and to encourage co-operation in concrete projects and the exchange of experiences, this network also has the goal of developing ways of working with youth that will counteract the development of xenophobic gangs.

The RAA also co-operates with organisations like the Young Men's Christian Association (YMCA). And in order to arrange urban activities concerning culture and art they collaborate with the town library. They organise meetings with writers or sponsor an annual literary autumn festival or show.

Facilitating and inhibiting factors

Imposing the law and administrative and political regulations of western Germany upon eastern Germany led to a lot of difficulties with establishing new political, economical and social structures. But on the other hand, the process of transformation provided a good opportunity to create effective new partnerships because authorities were less rigid as everything was new. It was reported that effective co-operation between different departments in the local government has been achieved.

A serious problem faced during the process of establishing new structures of social welfare in a period of rapid social transformation was that decisions had to be made very rapidly. While forming teams, the work had to be done. Moreover it was a challenge to get people affected by problems to talk about them because under the GDR they had become used to accepting decisions without getting explanations. Therefore activities must be initiated by social services personnel, although obstructive bureaucracy is already expanding.

Another inhibiting factor resulting from the transformation process is the problem of clarifying the ownership of property. Properties confiscated under the GDR government can be reclaimed and, until the ownership is settled, they cannot be used. Also, uncertainties concerning planning and budgeting are higher than usual. For example, the rapidly declining birth-rate has affected the planning of preschool and educational programmes.

Besides general problems induced by unification, there are factors inhibiting co-operation between schools and social services. Although teachers in schools are in a good position to help children, there are traditionally few links between schools and social services in the tradition of western Germany. Also a lack of mutual understanding between teachers and social services personnel as well as competition between both groups are inhibiting co-operation. The distance between schools and free associations is also a relevant factor now in the new *Länder*. Additionally there are traditions inherited from the former GDR to be considered.

Under the GDR, schools organised the whole range of youth activities during the day. But the totality of the grip that schools held upon the minds and bodies of children, and the pressure upon families refusing to allow their children to become members of Young Pioneers and the Free German Youth, did not remain uncriticised. Therefore there is a special challenge to create new ways to involve youth in constructive leisure time activities that give them and their parents choices.

In the GDR, there were no social work professionals. Therefore the people now performing social work inevitably do not have the kind of professional background found in western Germany.

For the RAA's work on integrated services for school children, it proved to be important that the headmaster of the school really wanted to co-operate, and that co-operation was based on a voluntary decision.

The principle of subsidiarity enhanced the innovative power of free associations. Community development, organisation and networking contribute to services integration activities.

Discussion

The transformation process in the new *Länder* created enormous challenges for developing a new youth service network through democratic processes. The local actors in Leipzig show competence and creativity in coping with the city's problems. Working within a western German framework provides guidance as well as obstacles. But financial resources can be used to nurture innovations within the western democratic tradition. And there could be benefits resulting from the exchange of experiences not only between western and eastern German projects, but also internationally.

INTEGRATED SERVICES AND THE CHALLENGE OF YOUTH UNEMPLOYMENT IN THE CITY OF DUISBURG

Context

The focus of the Duisburg study visit was on the transition from school to work and on a successful initiative to adapt the German apprenticeship system to current socio-economic demands through increased services integration.

Diversification in the economic sector and innovation in business and manufacturing in Duisburg made it necessary to train young and retrain older workers. This created enormous challenges for vocational education and employment services. But on the whole Duisburg has been unusually successful in combating youth unemployment and retraining youth, even those at high risk, in a variety of training programmes. An important factor helping this process was the integration of social, educational, and health services to facilitate the transition of youth from school to work.

Institutions and key partners

In Duisburg, strengthened attempts to combat youth unemployment and provide a broad supply of vocational training started in the early 1980s, when youth unemployment increased and the gap between the supply and demand of apprenticeships widened. This was due primarily to demographic changes and economic recession. Falling demand for steel and coal also contributed to emerging problems. Therefore youth unemployment was made a top priority and a Youth Unemployment Committee was established by the City Council to deal with it. As they could not cope with the problem alone, another committee called the Vocational Help Group for Young People was founded. Representatives from the Catholic and Protestant churches, the worker's welfare association, trade unions, the Employment Office, and Chambers joined this committee. Moreover a co-ordinating committee was formed to integrate efforts and advise the Town Council's Youth Unemployment Committee.

In order to reduce youth unemployment and support youth in the transition from school to work, extensive co-operation between the institutions and organisations involved in this process is required. To show how co-operation and integration works in Duisburg, some central institutions were visited. The Youth Office and the Employment Office are key partners in the city-wide network because of their codified responsibilities in the field of social services (Youth Office), and vocational counselling and training (Employment Office). Another central organisation contributing to the integration of services is the RAA, an arm of the Ministry of Education that provides an interface between education and social services. As important examples of vocational education for young people the Vocational Training Centre (*Kupferhütte des Verein für Jugendberufshilfe*) and the Berthold Brecht Vocational School were visited.

Youth Office, Department of Education: The Youth Office has a special status within the Municipal Government. It works closely with politicians, city administrators, and private groups. It has won its status partly because it is an administrative unit with political and private representations. Under the Children and Youth Services Act, the Youth Office is the community's umbrella organisation for youth services. It is responsible for dealing with children at risk, child protection, special needs children, child abuse, substance abuse among youth, and the transition from school to work by financing and co-ordinating local services. The Youth Office regularly communicates and plans its activities with other youth serving stakeholders. All municipal employees such as teachers and counsellors can be involved in its initiatives. The Employment Office was identified as the main partner of the Youth Office. Intensive interaction is needed to interpret the legislative mandate associated with youth schemes. In order to determine schools needing special attention and help for youth at risk, the Youth Office works with the RAA. Since changes in the primary labour market affect training programmes, the Youth Office also seeks the co-operation of companies.

Employment Office: The Employment Office is an agency of the Federal Ministry of Labour and Social Affairs. It is one of 184 branches of the Federal Labour Administration that is charged by the Labour Promotion Act to implement Federal social and economic policy. The current declared objective is "to reach and maintain a high level of employment, constantly improve the structure of employment, and thereby promote economic growth". The Federal Labour Administration is responsible for vocational advice, job placement, vocational training, job maintenance and creation, unemployment payments, child allowances, handicap payments, and labour market and vocational research. The Employment Office works closely together with all other stake holding agencies through both formal and informal agreements. Although joint programmes are undertaken, most of the operations and policies of the Employment Office are independent. The Employment Office co-operates with the Youth Office as both are highly interdependent, largely because educational problems are intertwined with social problems. And intense co-operation exists between this Office and free associations which provide help for youth in the transition from school to work. The Employment Office helps to co-ordinate programmes and when needed tries to ensure the coherence of what is provided.

RAA (Regional Centre to Support Foreign Children and Young People): In 1980, the first RAAs were implemented in five cities in Northrhine-Westphalia, including Duisburg. Since 1987, they have become regular facilities. At the moment there are 16 RAAs in Northrhine-Westphalia. As mentioned earlier, the RAA's aim is to reduce intergroup hostility and provide special services for youth both in and out of school. Although the RAA in Duisburg developed as a response to the needs of foreign students, it became so proficient at connecting services, establishing communication links, and solving community problems that it has become a major resource in dealing with the issue of youth unemployment. The RAA provides a bridge between educational and social services through its emphasis on integrated planning and the extensive employment of social educators. It employs a community development approach to tackling social problems and closing the gap between home, school, and support and employment agencies. For youth in the transition to work, the RAA provides remedial and preventive counselling services, acts on signs that students may be at risk of dropping out, and insures that after a student leaves school, needed services are continued. The RAA meets regularly with other stakeholders for both service planning and case management. Co-operation also takes place around the use and maintenance of a local data base, specialised work groups, and specific issues. The relationship with the Vocational Counselling Service is particularly co-operative. The RAA employs teachers and social educators due to co-operation with the Vocational Counselling Service and Ministry of Labour, but overlapping functions sometimes cause problems when they work in the same school.

Berthold Brecht Vocational School: This vocational school provides part-time professional studies for those students who are apprenticing in companies. The innovative aspect of the Berthold Brecht Vocational School is its *Kollegschule* (an institute preparing students for the higher education matriculation certificate). This school not only offers part-time professional education, but also full-time vocational education for students who could not obtain an apprenticeship. As a result, students can study for general education certificates. Thus this school integrates general and vocational education. The school has 1 700 students and 65 staff. Courses include engineering, telecommunications, computing, data technology, and car mechanics. The school's major partners are the Chambers, companies, universities, the Youth Committee and the Youth Unemployment Committee.

Vocational Training Centre (*Kupferhütte des Verein für Jugendberufshilfe*): The Training Centre was established in 1980. It provides vocational education leading to the same certificate as obtained at the end of a regular apprenticeship according to the standards specified by the Chamber of Commerce. It provides extra training places and gives its target group – students with special needs and personal or social problems – a special chance. The Centre serves students between the ages of 17 and 25, who are from the lower secondary level of education or special schools. During their vocational training they rotate between training school, vocational school and the work situation. Also included are social skills programmes that are not provided by either vocational or secondary schools. The Chair and other members of its governing board belong to the City Council. The head of the City's Department of Education and members of the Youth Unemployment Committee serve on the Board. The Training Centre co-operates with vocational schools in the dual system to provide theoretical training, with companies that provide practical training, with other similar training programmes and the Employment Office.

Political support and funding

As mentioned earlier, high youth unemployment and a lack of apprenticeships, resulting from the crisis in the steel industry and restructuring of the economic sector, made strengthened and co-ordinated activities necessary. The City Council of Duisburg gave first priority to these problems and initiated Communal Committees to develop co-ordinated strategies.

It is difficult to describe the funding of a broad and comprehensive network of co-operating agencies like the one in Duisburg. Funding is received from the public and private sectors. The Employment Office finances the majority of training schemes for youth and also helps to ensure accountability. With a budget of about DM 5 million, it supports vocational training, social skills training, and some specialised treatment services. The Youth Office finances different kinds of social services, including the services of private non-profit agencies, such as the parochial and other welfare organisations. The RAA is a municipal agency financed by all three levels of government. The Training Centre is funded by central government, regional government, municipal funds, and private donations. For the

Berthold Brecht Vocational School, the Community covers the costs of administering, equipping, and servicing the facility, and the State pays the teaching staff.

The Statistics Office also forms part of the network in Duisburg. This Office is an administrative authority of the City of Duisburg which produces an annual report about the situation of youth in the transition from school to work and is financed by the City of Duisburg.

Integrated practices

The different Communal Committees described above played a central role in creating and co-ordinating activities in Duisburg. An important basis for evaluating processes in the educational system and on the labour market is the annual report produced by the Statistics Office. Co-operation between all of the stakeholders takes place around the use and maintenance of this database. Beside the co-ordinating function of the Communal Committees and several "round tables" concerning special problems (*e.g.* integration of young woman, dealing with youth at risk), there are multiple bi- or multi-lateral co-operative activities involving Local Government, the Employment Office, free associations providing social services, companies and schools.

The Youth Office, according to its codified duty, is the umbrella organisation for youth services and has to finance and co-ordinate local services. Thus, when the Youth Aids Committee passes resolutions the actual work and effort in finding funding is done by the Youth Office.

In order to prevent school drop-out and help young people to get an apprenticeship, the Youth Office contacts the RAA to determine which schools need special attention. The job of the RAA and the Youth Office is to insure that all children in lower secondary schools get in contact with the vocational counselling department of the Ministry of Labour. The RAA remains in contact for a year with students who leave school without a certificate. Those that do not find work are looked after by the MAGS (Advisory Offices of the Ministry of Labour, Health, and Social Affairs). The RAA and MAGS work together to avoid overlapping activities.

As there are not enough apprenticeships available through the dual system the supply of voca-tional education has to be enlarged and special supports for disadvantaged youth are required. Students who are at risk need a type of schooling that provides more social care. According to the principle of subsidiarity, private groups like welfare associations and church agencies are supported in their efforts to help young people. Co-operation between these groups and the Employment Office is intense. The Employment Office helps to co-ordinate programmes and tries to ensure the coherence of provided courses.

In order to provide vocational training for disadvantaged youth, like that at the Training Centre, regular vocational teachers and social educators are employed. In addition, consultative services are provided for the teachers in vocational schools. Social educators and vocational teachers meet regu-larly. They see themselves as having a welfare mission in relation to students that is not reflected in the roles of regular teachers. They provide a bridge between school, the workplace and the families of students, as they know about students' needs, and have contact with vocational teachers and employers.

Other aspects of co-operation include the development of new training schemes and finding employment for youth after vocational education. Here co-operation with companies is an important factor. Therefore the Youth Office works with companies and groups proposing schemes to introduce the right programmes to take advantage of market developments. There are also good contacts between the Berthold Brecht Vocational School and companies. If companies want new or modified courses the school considers them and, in return, the school encourages companies to hire graduates and support its training schemes.

Facilitating and inhibiting factors

The level of integrated services achieved is high. This is because the efforts of all stakeholders were focused on a specific goal. Youth are seen as the hope of the future and there is wide support for solving the problem of unemployment. Another facilitating factor was the very difficult situation in Duisburg (as compared to other cities) for young people entering the labour market. It had the highest percentage of youth leaving school without a proper qualification from lower secondary school. The unemployment rate was high and jobs particularly hard to find. Moreover, the creation of a regional data base, that used the statistics of co-operating institutions and organisations, furthered communication between the actors involved. Although in the beginning there was scepticism to be overcome, and different interpretations of the situation of disadvantaged youth, this process resulted in a rather good co-operation.

But the success of concrete projects depends on more specific facilitating and inhibiting factors. The key role of the RAA in the process of integration of school and external social services has been possible not least because it employs teachers. Therefore there is more understanding amongst teachers at schools when problems and possible solutions are discussed. The insulation of teachers in their defined role, and the competing professional attitudes of teachers and social pedagogues, are normally obstacles to integration. But nevertheless there is some friction between the RAA and the Vocational Counselling Department of the Labour Office because of their overlapping functions. To avoid conflicts of interest, the RAA employs teachers and social educators through co-operation with the Ministry of Labour and Vocational Counselling.

Integration of services as developed by the Training Centre is another example. The success of this Centre depends on covering the individual needs of students as well as meeting the qualification standards of the labour market. This aim is achieved by employing teachers as well as social educators, giving social pedagogical training to the teachers, guaranteeing regular meetings between both groups of employees, and entrusting social educators with the regular vocational training of students. But even more is done. Teachers who want to work at the Training Centre are selected on the basis of their personality and ability to work with disadvantaged youth. So the staff have good qualifications for building the bridge between youth and their families, regular vocational school, and the workplace. Moreover the Head of the Training Centre sees his main job as creating a positive atmosphere in the school. He accepts criticism from students and communicates directly with them. Training fields have to be adapted to the labour market. But unfortunately, new areas of training depend on what moneys are available and are the outcome of slow discussion among stakeholders. Thus new programmes may come into being after they are needed and too late to provide employment opportunities.

Outcomes

An evaluation study concerning a European Country (EC) test project in Oberhausen, Moers and Duisburg, which started in 1983 and aimed to improve the transition of young people from school to work, found Duisburg to be the most successful city. It appears that one reason why Duisburg did well in the EC study was because its problems were so serious that it had to develop novel solutions and put aside professional rivalries to work as a unified community.

An important product of activities concerning the transition of youth into employment is the differentiated report on the situation and needs of youth in Duisburg. The production of this report not only furthered co-operation between the institutions involved, it also helps to determine groups of young people who are at risk and conceptualise adequate programmes.

The development of vocational counselling by the RAA has also been a positive outcome. Previously there was only co-operation between schools and the Vocational Counselling Service. Thus students who dropped out before receiving regular counselling were at particular risk. Prior to the RAA Programme neither schools nor the Vocational Counselling Service were aware of the needs of this group. Many early school-leavers are children of immigrants. Early school leavers, who are most at risk of unemployment, often are tired of school. Therefore special schemes were developed to help motivate them to stay in school. Moreover the RAA tries to identify pupils at risk through an early warning system, provides assistance for a continuous period of time, and helps them to find employment. Its success is evident in the reduced number of students leaving school early. The programmes developed meanwhile have gone beyond direct service in attempting to influence legislation to support youth at risk.

Specific outcomes for disadvantaged youth who get a vocational training at the Training Centre are extra care, a friendlier atmosphere, and more support than in regular schools. These are seen by students as a positive resource. So this programme helps to create a structure that keeps students on the right track.

However, for females the only expansion of training opportunities appears to be outside of the dual system in full-time vocational training in the health and public services. And, still, students leave school without certificates. So there remain challenges for further activities.

On the whole co-operation between all those who are concerned with youth unemployment is advantageous. Co-operation between stakeholding groups is the basis of the success of programmes developed in Duisburg. In this context the pilot project of the EC revealed the important role of counselling teachers and social educators in identifying young people at risk and taking steps to help them. Moreover the various schemes in Duisburg are highly differentiated. They include promotional programmes for those not mature enough to start training; vocational counselling; courses in basic social skills; and vocational training programmes. As a result, the multiple needs of youth at risk are covered.

But although good results have been achieved it should not be forgotten that it will become harder for poorly qualified people to get a job, as there is an increasing demand for higher qualifications. The City already has recognised that training alone is not enough if there are no jobs. If the situation worsens, the City will offer substitute training to keep youth occupied. This will involve the development of a secondary labour pool for whom jobs are subsidised by public funding. Nevertheless, the active and flexible work of the different programmes improves the life chances of youth.

GENERAL CONCLUSIONS

The case studies described in this report deal with a wide variety of initiatives and projects to link, co-ordinate and integrate services for children and youth at risk and their families. The political and administrative contexts of the three case studies (on social services for preschool children and their families in Bremen, on services for school-age children in Leipzig and on services for young people in the transition from school to work in Duisburg) are remarkably different.

The structure of social services in Bremen is the result of a continuing political process initiated by the administration with increasing and often controversial participation from field level professionals and independent youth services. Services for preschool children and their families are part of this general reorganisation of social services.

The situation in Leipzig is totally different. After replacing the political and administrative structures of the GDR with those of West Germany, administrators faced a situation where three years afterwards there was still no improvement. The main challenge for social services under these conditions was to deal with the obvious difficulties and deficiencies which resulted from the dramatic changes. School-age children mainly needed compensation for:

- the end of the "holistic" role of schools and teachers, many of whom were happy to see their responsibilities reduced;

- the reduction in day care facilities, especially for primary school children; and

- the almost total cancellation of extra curricular activities such as clubs and common interest groups, offered mainly to secondary school students by schools or by the socialist youth organisation, Free German Youth.

This is not an appropriate situation in which to aim at realising "ambitious" concepts of integrated services, but it is an obvious challenge for improving the situation of at risk groups, by trying to offer compensation for what has been lost, by building co-operation especially with schools, and by attempting to link activities and resources.

The situation in Duisburg is characterised by the fact that it is particularly difficult for young people to find their way into the labour market as a consequence of the declining steel and mining industries. As a result, an especially high political priority has been given to vocational education and training. Since the promotion of vocational qualifications for disadvantaged youth attracts little controversy in Germany, the general political context is favourable to the aims pursued in Duisburg. On the other hand, the transition from school to work is one of the most complex fields of social action, and the integration of services can be realised only in a narrow sense. Co-ordination, co-operation and problem-related discussion among agencies are probably the most that reasonably might be undertaken when applying the concept of integrated services to this field. Agencies involved in the transition period include business institutions (chambers of crafts, industry, and commerce), the labour administration, youth services and public schools.

In all three regions, services integration is linked to two shared aspirations:

- instead of modelling the legislative structure, developing an organisation of social services which meets the needs of people; and

- instead of approaching single clients, taking responsibility for a whole community regardless of age, problems and so on.

Factors facilitating and inhibiting services integration vary. On the basis of the case studies, it appears that the following generalisations can be made:

- Short lines of communication between the political and strategic levels as well as between the field and strategic levels are regarded by field level experts as favourable for programmes.

- Groups of field level experts should work together over a longer period of time with support from the strategic level for planning and funding to create integrated approaches (Bremen).

- When co-ordinated action amongst many agencies with different and perhaps conflicting interests is necessary (such as in the transition from school to work period), groups or committees which negotiate on different levels are needed. These might bring together the city government, business, welfare organisations, the unions, the labour administration, political parties, and other bodies that are able to contribute to the improvement of young peoples' chances (Duisburg, Bremen).

- Surveys which describe social support needs in the community and identify existing resources (outlining by whom and to what degree they are used and for whom and to what extent they are effective) are seen as helpful for initiating change towards integration (e.g. Bremen, Duisburg). Such surveys form a good basis for analysing deficits in service delivery and future planning.

- Co-ordination of action across a broad variety of different agencies, sometimes with different or even conflicting interests, requires concentration on a clear and specific aim (such as vocational education and training for all youth) and a consensus on values (such as seeing youth as the hope for the future).

A key role in integrating services at the field level is performed by the professionals involved in service delivery. Social services which aim towards the successful integration of children and youth at risk in "regular" institutions (such as kindergarten, school, vocational education and training) and towards improving their chances of participation in society (for example, in labour, culture and politics) need professionals (notably teachers and social workers) who are able to build bridges between institutions (such as schools and the workplace) and children's families. It is also necessary to provide support for the successful realisation of transitions between consecutive institutions such as kindergartens and schools or vocational training schools and companies, by preparing young people for the different demands of the coming phase and getting professionals they know already (transition tutors) to accompany them into their new environment.

In general, the co-ordination and integration of services result in broader and more intensive co-operation between social, educational and other professions. Co-operation has to be taught. One necessary constituent of training is to learn to understand and respect the standards of related professions, in order to avoid misunderstandings and dysfunctional conflicts. Co-operation between social workers and teachers in Germany often suffers from the transmission of one's own professional standards to the other profession. A broadening of the professional profiles of interacting groups seems necessary in many cases where integration is a goal.

Nevertheless, the improvement of services for children and youth at risk is clearly linked to economic and political circumstances. This is especially obvious in relation to the transition from school to work (Duisburg), although the preschool case study (Bremen) also points to the importance of political conditions. Efforts to integrate and co-ordinate services – if they are effective – may lead to increased bureaucratisation. The same internally generated growth processes that facilitate front-line co-operation and agency co-ordination may thus create complexities that interfere with the communication (Duisburg).

REFERENCES

ADLER, H., GÜNTHER K., LAMBACH, R. and VÖLKER, U. (1993), "Aufbau von Jugendhilfestrukturen in den neuen Bundesländern. Einige Informationen zur Lage der Jugendämter", *Jugendhilfe*, 31, pp. 129-134.

ALFF, J. and KUNKEL, P-C. (1989), *Jugend und Familie als Herausforderungen kommunaler Politik*, Köln.

BACKHAUS-MAUL, H. and OLK, T. (1992), "Die Konstitution kommunaler Sozialpolitik; Probleme des Aufbaus sozialer Versorgungsstrukturen in den neuen Bundesländern", in C. Rühl (ed.), *Probleme der Einheit. Band 5: Institutionelle Reorganisation in den neuen Bundesländern*, Marburg, pp. 83-112.

BALLAUF, H. (1994), "Scheitern in Beruf und Lehre verhindern. Wie Jugendlichen am Übergang Schule – Arbeitswelt zu helfen ist, Ein Projekt der Münchner Volkshochschule", Munich.

BARTH, K. (1993), "Aspekte der Organisationsberatung in der Sozialarbeit/Sozialpädagogik", in E.J. Brunner and W. Schöning (eds.), *Organisationen beraten: Impulse für Theorie und Praxis*, Freiburg im Breisgau, pp. 111-124.

BARTHE, S. (1994), "Sprung ins kalte Wasser. Erziehungsberatung in Ostdeutschland", *DJI-Bulletin*, p. 6.

BAUM, J. (1987), "Die Bedeutung der Organisationsentwicklung für eine integrative kommunale Sozialpolitik", *Zeitschrift für Sozialreform*, 33, pp. 449-471.

BOCK T. (1991), "Wie können wir von einander profitieren? Rahmenbedingungen und pädagogische Konzepte in Kindertageseinrichtungen der Deutschen Demokratischen Republik und der Bundesrepublik Deutschland ", *Die soziale Arbeit in den 90er Jahren. Neue Herausforderungen bei offenen Grenzen in Europa*, Gesamtbericht über den 72, Deutschen Fürsorgetag 1990 in Hannover, Frankfurt am Main, pp. 805-814.

BÖLLERT, K. (1989), "Soziale Arbeit als aktive Gestaltung von Lebensweisen", in K. Böllert and H.-U. Otto (eds.), *Soziale Arbeit auf der Suche nach Zukunft*, Bielefeld, pp. 213-223.

BÖLLERT, K. and OTTO, H.-U. (1993), "Soziale Arbeit in einer neuen Republik. Kritische Texte", *Sozialarbeit, Sozialpädagogik, Sozialpolitik*, Bielefeld.

BRAUN, F., LEX, T., SCHÄFER, H. and ZINK, G. (1993), "Öffentliche Jugendhilfe und Jugendberufshilfe – Ergebnisse aus der wissenschaftlichen Begleitung des Bundesjugendplan- Modellprogramms, Arbeitsweltbezogene Jugendsozialarbeit", *Jugend Beruf Gesellschaft*, 44, pp. 182-187.

BRONKE, K. and WENZEL, G. (1980), "Neuorganisation – staatliches Handeln in der Krise?", *Sozialarbeit als Sozialbürokratie? Zur Neuorganisation sozialer Dienste, Neue Praxis*, Sonderheft, 10, pp. 121-132.

BUNDESARBEITSGEMEINSCHAFT DER LANDESJUGENDÄMTER (1993), "Empfehlungen zum Thema 'Jugendhilfe und Schule'".

COLBERG-SCHRADER, H. (1993), "Kindertageseinrichtungen – soziales Kinderleben in einer arrangierten Kinderwelt", in Arbeitsgemeinschaft für Jugendhilfe (AGJ), *Kinderwelten – Kinderrechte – Angebot für Kinder*, 2, Bonn, pp. 45-57.

DAS NEUE KINDER- UND JUGENDHILFEGESETZ (1990), *Einführung und Materialien, Berichte und Materialien aus der sozialen und kulturellen Arbeit*, Vol. 4, Nürnberg.

DER BUNDESMINISTER FÜR JUGEND, FAMILIE, FRAUEN UND GESUNDHEIT (1990), *Achter Jugendbericht. Bericht über Bestrebungen und Leistungen der Jugendhilfe*, Bonn.

DEUTSCHER VEREIN FÜR ÖFFENTLICHE UND PRIVATE FÜRSORGE (1993), *Fachlexikon der sozialen Arbeit*, Köln.

DEUTSCHES JUGENDINSTITUT (ed.) (1990), *Entwicklungsbedingungen und perspektiven der Jugendhilfe in der früheren DDR*, Munich.

DITTRICH, G. (1989), *Kooperationsformen zur Unterstützung von Regeleinrichtungen bei Einzelintegration*, Eine Dokumentation von Praxisbeispielen, Munich.

DITTRICH, G. (1990), "Entwicklungen von Einzelintegration in einzelnen Bundesländern und Erfahrungen mit Kooperationen zwischen Regelkindergarten und Fachleuten der Behindertenhilfe", *Gemeinsam Leben*, 25, pp. 7-12.

DJI Projekt, "Orte für Kinder" (1991), *Workshop: Alternative Formen der Kinderbetreuung – Weiterentwicklung von Kinderbetreuungsmodellen in Selbsthilfe und Institutionen,* Munich.

DJI Projekt, "Orte für Kinder" (1993), *Gemeinsam planen. Ergebnisse aus Einrichtungsanalyse und Elternbefragung,* Munich.

DOLLS, M. and HAMMETTER, V. (1987), "Innovation durch Neuorganisation behördlicher sozialer Dienste", in B. Maelicke (ed.), *Soziale Arbeit als soziale Innovation. Veränderungsbedarf und Innovationsstrategien,* Weinheim and Munich, pp. 165-179.

DOLLS, M. and HAMMETER, V. (1988), *Zielgruppen- und stadtteilorientierte soziale Arbeit,* Neuorganisation der Sozialen Dienste in Bremen-Süd, Frankfurt am Main.

FRAUENINITIATIVE QUIRL E.V. (1993), *Fünf Jahre Modellversuch und mehr. Ein Bericht,* Bremen.

FRIESENHAHN, G. (1993), "Lebensweltorientierung als Leitmotiv sozialer Arbeit?", *Jugendhilfe,* 31, pp. 208-212.

FROMANN, A., KEHRER, H. and LIEBAU, E. (1987), *Erfahrungen mit der Schulsozialarbeit. Möglichkeiten der Zusammenarbeit von Sozialpädagogik und Schule,* Weinheim und Munich.

FUNK, H. (1980), "Neuorganisation und Planung – zwei Seiten einer Medaille?", *Sozialarbeit als Sozialbürokratie? Zur Neuorganisation sozialer Dienste, Neue Praxis,* Sonderheft, 10, pp. 225-238.

GLANZER, W. (1993), "Schulsozialarbeit in den neuen Ländern – Schlagwort oder zukunftsweisende strukturelle Manahme", *Jugendhilfe,* 31, pp. 19-22.

HAASE-SCHUR, I. (1980), "Realisierungschancen von Neuorganisationen sozialer Dienste", *Sozialarbeit als Sozialbürokratie? Zur Neuorganisation sozialer Dienste, Neue Praxis,* Sonderheft, 10, pp. 208-216.

HABERKORN, R., HAGEMANN U. and SEEHAUSEN, H. (1988), *Kindergarten und soziale Dienste,* Freiburg im Breisgau.

HABERMAS, J. (1981), *Theorie des kommunikativen Handelns,* 2 volumes, Frankfurt.

HEBENSTREIT-MÜLLER, S. and PETTINGER, R. (1991a), *Organisation, Förderung und Vernetzung von Familienselbsthilfe. Erfahrungen aus einem Modellversuch mit Familien und Nachbarschaftszentren,* Vol. 14, Bielefeld.

HEBENSTREIT-MÜLLER, S. and PETTINGER, R. (1991b), *Miteinander lernen, leben, engagieren – Neue soziale Netze für Familien. Ergebnisse der wissenschaftlichen Begleitforschung von Familien- und Nachbarschaftszentren,* Vol. 15, Bielefeld.

HINTE, W. (1991), "Stadtteilbezogene soziale Arbeit und soziale Dienste", *Sozialarbeit deutsch-deutsch,* Neuwied, Kriftel and Berlin, pp. 59-65.

HOFFMANN, J. (1981), *Jugendhilfe in der DDR. Grundlagen, Funktionen und Strukturen,* Munich.

HOYER, H-D. (1993), "Sozialpädagogische Familienhilfe nun auch in den neuen Bundesländern – einige Erkenntnisse, Erfahrungen und Problemstellungen", *Jugendhilfe,* 31, pp. 26-31.

JAPP, K-P. and OLK, T. (1981), "Zur Neuorganisation sozialer Dienste", in Projektgruppe Soziale Berufe (ed.), *Sozialarbeit. Problemwandel und Institutionen. Expertisen II,* Munich, p. 82-115.

JORDAN, E. and SENGLING, D. (1992), *Jugendhilfe. Einführung in Geschichte und Handlungsfelder, Organisationsformen und gesellschaftliche Problemlagen,* Weinheim and Munich.

JUGENDHILFE IM VERBUND (1992a), *Jugendhilfe,* 30/2, pp. 76-77.

JUGENDHILFE IM VERBUND (1992b), *Jugendhilfe,* 30/3, pp. 121-129.

KREFT, D. (1993), "Erziehungshilfe Auf der Grundlage des KJHG. Geschichte – Stand – Ausblick", *Jugendhilfe,* 31, pp. 321-328.

KREFT, D., LUKAS, H. et. al (1990), *Perspektivenwandel der Jugendhilfe. Forschungsmaterialien und eine umfassende Bibliographie zu neuen Handlungsfeldern in der Jugendhilfe sowie Ergebnisse einer Totalerhebung (Daten/Fakten/Analysen) zur aktuellen Aufgabenwahrnehmung der Jugendämter* (Vol. 1), Nürnberg.

KÜHN, D. (1980), "Historisch-systematische Darstellung von Neuorganisationsmodellen der kommunalen Sozialverwaltung", *Sozialarbeit als Sozialbürokratie? Zur Neuorganisation sozialer Dienste, Neue Praxis,* Sonderheft, 10, pp. 90-106.

KUNKEL, P-C. (1990), *Jugendhilfe und Schule. Zum Verhältnis beider Institutionen nach dem neuen Jugendhilferecht,* Kehl.

LAMBACH, R. (1993), "Aufbau von Jugendhilfestrukturen in den neuen Bundesländern. Vom Start eines neuen Beratungsprojektes", *Jugendhilfe,* 31, pp. 70-73.

LEPPIN, H. and TERSTEEGEN, G. (1980), "Die Neuorganisation sozialer Dienste in Bremen. Zur Entwicklung eines Reformprojektes", *Sozialarbeit als Sozialbürokratie? Zur Neuorganisation sozialer Dienste, Neue Praxis,* Sonderheft, 10, pp. 132-139.

MAAS, U. (1991), *Aufgaben sozialer Arbeit nach dem KJHG. Systematische Einführung für Studium und Praxis*, Weinheim and Munich.

MERCHEL, J. (1993), "Pluralität sozialer Hilfen? Probleme bei der Übertragung 'westlicher' Trägerstrukturen auf die östlichen Bundesländer", in K. Böllert and H.-U. Otto (eds.), *Soziale Arbeit in einer neuen Republik. Anpassung oder Fortschritt*, Bielefeld, pp. 188-205.

MIELENZ, I. (no date), "Jugendhilfeplanung – Mit welchen Zielen, für wen, mit wem wie, was, wo?", in Arbeitsgemeinschaft für Jugendhilfe (AGJ), *Reader Jugendhilfe*, Bonn, pp. 37-48.

MOLLENHAUER, K. (1992), "Jugendhilfe. Modernitätsanforderungen und Traditionsbestände für die sozialpädagogische Zukunft", in T. Rauschenbach and H. Gängler (eds.), *Soziale Arbeit und Erziehung in der Risikogesellschaft*, Neuwied, Kriftel and Berlin, pp. 101-117.

MÜNDER, J. et. al. (1993), *Frankfurter Lehr- und Praxiskommentar zum KJHG*, Münster.

OECD (1995), *Our Children at Risk*, Paris.

OLK, T. (1986), "Die professionelle Zukunft sozialer Arbeit", in H. Oppl and A. Tomaschek (eds.), *Soziale Arbeit 2000. Modernisierungskrise und soziale Dienste*, Freiburg im Breisgau, pp. 107-136.

OTTO, H-U. (1991), *Sozialarbeit zwischen Routine und Innovation. Professionelles Handeln in Sozialadministrationen*, Berlin and New York.

RAAB, E. (1992), "Berufsausbildung und Arbeitsmarktchancen Jugendlicher in den alten Bundesländern", *Aus Politik und Zeitgeschichte*, 38, pp. 36-46.

RAAB, E. (1994), "Schulsozialarbeit – Perspektiven für die 90er Jahre", *Jugend Beruf Gesellschaft*, 44, p. 5.

RAAB, E. and RADEMACKER, H. (1994), "Schule und Jugendhilfe – Schulsozialarbeit", Unpublished manuscript, Munich.

RAAB, E., RADEMACKER, H. and WINZEN, G. (1987), *Handbuch Schulsozialarbeit. Konzeption und Praxis sozialpädagogischer Förderung von Schülern*, Munich.

REICHWEIN, A. and KIRCHHOFF, G. (1980), "Integration sozialer Dienste als Problem", *Sozialarbeit als Sozialbürokratie? Zur Neuorganisation sozialer Dienste*, Neue Praxis, Sonderheft, 10, pp. 132-139.

SACKS, P. (1993), "Die Qualifizierung benachteiligter Jugendlicher und junger Erwachsener als bildungspolitischer Auftrag", *Jugend Beruf Gesellschaft*, 44, 4, pp. 187-190.

SCHÄFER, H.M. (1988), "Das Subsidiaritätsprinzip. Anmerkungen zu seiner verfassungsrechtlichen, politikwissenschaftlichen und sozialwissenschaftlichen Einordnung", in O. Filtzinger, D. Häring, H. Schäfer and F.W. Seibel (eds.), *Soziale Dienste: öffentlich oder privat?*, Berlin, pp. 7-29.

SCHÄFER, P. (1980), "Der Beitrag der Neuorganisation der sozialen Dienste für eine bürgernahe kommunale Sozialpolitik", *Sozialarbeit als Sozialbürokratie? Zur Neuorganisation sozialer Dienste*, Neue Praxis, Sonderheft, 10, pp. 106-121.

SCHÄFERS, B. (1981), *Sozialstruktur und Wandel der Bundesrepublik Deutschland*, Stuttgart.

SCHEFOLD, W. (1992), "Lebensweltorientierte Jugendhilfepolitik", in Arbeitsgemeinschaft für Jugendhilfe (AGJ), *Lebenswelten – Lebenslagen. Veränderungen in der Praxis der Jugendhilfe?*, Bonn, pp. 16-23.

SCHMIDT, G.B. (1992), *Schülerhilfe Weinheim. Schulbezogene und auerschulische Sozialarbeit als Hilfe für sozial benachteiligte Jugendliche*, Weinheim.

SEIDENSTÜCKER, B. (1993), "Jugendhilfe im Übergang", in K. Böllert and H.-U. Otto (eds.), *Soziale Arbeit in einer neuen Republik. Anpassung oder Fortschritt*, Bielefeld, pp. 147-159.

SOZIALSTATIONEN IN MECKLENBURG-VORPOMMERN (1992), *Jugendhilfe*, 30, 5, pp. 224-225.

SPÄTH, K. (1992), "Das KJHG im Praxistest", in Arbeitsgemeinschaft für Jugendhilfe (AGJ), *Lebenswelten – Lebenslagen. Veränderungen in der Praxis der Jugendhilfe?*, Bonn, pp. 84-93.

THIERSCH, H. (1985), "Erziehungsberatung und Jugendhilfe", in H.-P. Klug and F. Specht (eds.), *Erziehungs- und Familienberatung. Aufgaben und Ziele*, Göttingen, pp. 24-40.

THIERSCH, H. (1992), "Lebensweltorientierte Jugendhilfe", in Arbeitsgemeinschaft für Jugendhilfe (AGJ), *Lebenswelten – Lebenslagen. Veränderungen in der Praxis der Jugendhilfe?*, Bonn, pp. 24-36.

THOLE, W. (1993), "Strae oder Jugendclub. Zur Reaktivierung der auerschulischen Kinder- und Jugendarbeit in den neuen Bundesländern", *Neue Praxis*, 23, 3, pp. 185-206.

WABNITZ, R.J. (1992), "Das Konzept 'Lebensweltorientierte Jugendhilfe' und die gesetzlichen Regelungen des KJHG", *Jugendhilfe*, 30, 5, pp. 210-214.

WENDT, W.R. (1986), "Das breite Felde der sozialen Arbeit. Historische Beweggründe für die ökologische Perspektive", in H. Oppl and A. Tomaschek (eds.), *Soziale Arbeit 2000. Soziale Probleme und Handlungsflexibilität,* Freiburg im Breisgau, pp. 43-79.

WINTER, H. (1993), "Jugendhilfestationen – Konzeptionelle Grundgedanken und erste praktische Erfahrungen", *Jugendhilfe,* 31, 6, pp. 260-263.

5

PORTUGAL

INTEGRATING SERVICES IN THE CONTEXT OF SOCIO-ECONOMIC CHANGE

by

Peter Evans, Josette Combes, Jennifer Evans, Philippa Hurrell, Mary Lewis,
Lucienne Roussel and Richard Volpe

INTRODUCTION

In 1992, Portugal had a population of 9.86 million people. With an area of 92 400 square kilometres the average population density was 106.7 inhabitants per square kilometre. However, much of this population is concentrated in the coastal areas and a few major urban centres. There continues to be a steady exodus from rural to urban areas which is associated with considerable poverty. The gross domestic product per capita is the third lowest in the OECD. A mixture of poverty, poor housing, health and nutrition, and child labour, has put many children at risk.

Demography

The distribution of age in the population is in the mid-range for OECD countries, with 19.1 per cent being under 15 (OECD range 15.5-35.1 per cent); 66.9 per cent between 15 and 64 (OECD range 60.5-69.7 per cent); and 14 per cent over 65 (OECD range 4.4-18.1 per cent). There was zero population growth between 1991 and 1992.

Employment

At 4.1 per cent overall (OECD range 1.2-18.1 per cent), the unemployment rate in Portugal remains relatively low. Even for young males under 25, with unemployment at 7.8 per cent (OECD range 4.6-29.6 per cent), this remains true.

Social trends

Portugal is facing challenges that are similar to those in most other OECD countries with smaller more widespread families, an increase in the divorce rate (132.9 per cent in the last ten years) and a growth in the number of single parent families. Nevertheless, compared with other European Union (EU) countries, it is ranked third for the proportion of families with more than five children (16.6 per cent), and has the highest number of families with three generations living together.

There has been a steady improvement in the educational qualifications of Portugal's work force. In 1989, 37.5 per cent of employees had completed the 2nd and 3rd cycles of basic education or secondary education. This contrasts with 28.6 per cent in 1984. Nevertheless, about one million Portuguese over the age of 10 are unable to read, 6.4 per cent of people in employment do not hold primary school leaving certificates, 51.7 per cent have only a primary certificate and 37.5 per cent a lower or upper secondary diploma.

Education services

Following the 1986 Education Act, the education system in Portugal comprises a balance of public and private sectors. There are optional preschool services for 3- to 6-year-olds, partly funded by the state, as well as compulsory basic education up to the age of 15. Pupils who have successfully completed a basic education may join any secondary education course, all of which take three years to complete.

In addition, there is an adult education sector which allows adults who have not had access to nine years of compulsory education to acquire a school leaving certificate by pursuing a curriculum which parallels that in force in schools.

While the state is compelled to provide sufficient resources to ensure that schools can perform their role effectively, Article 43 stipulates the necessity of establishing "interaction with the community thanks to the participation of teachers, pupils, families, local authorities and associations with a social, economic, cultural or scientific purpose".

The state education system is co-ordinated by the Ministry of Education. However, according to a policy of decentralisation, regional education boards have been set up to act as intermediaries between the central administration and local authorities and schools. Between 1982 and 1990, the Ministry increased expenditure on education as a percentage of GDP from 4.4 per cent to 4.9 per cent. Education has also benefited from financial assistance from the European Union, particularly in respect of funding for the development of infrastructure.

Vocational education is provided for those students who want it and who have completed their basic education. These programmes last for three years and lead to a professional qualification certificate as well as a secondary education diploma which gives access to higher education. Demand has increased significantly since 1983/84 when they were introduced. In 1990/91, some 32 000 people attended these programmes.

A recent innovation is a national apprenticeship scheme set up in 1986 by the Institute of Employment and Vocational Training. Apprenticeships are available to youth between the ages of 14 and 24 years who have completed compulsory schooling, and last for one to four years. Industrial sectors participating in the scheme range from agriculture to tourism. General and technological training is provided in vocational training centres, and practical training in various enterprises. While only 9 000 youth were involved in this scheme in 1989, a figure of 20 000 was targeted for 1993 (EURYDICE and CEDEFOP, 1991).

Social services

The objective of the social security network is to provide support for all citizens, and to protect workers and their families in situations where their working capacity is reduced, as well as in situations of involuntary unemployment, old age and death. It is financed through contributions from workers and employers, and transfers from the state budget. The system gives special priority to the underprivileged.

The system has two components, namely social security schemes and their institutions. Regional Social Security Centres (RSSCs) manage the schemes, granting benefits and providing social services. Benefits may be paid to the employed who make compulsory contributions and to those who are not covered through direct contributions. Social services provide protection through the provision of programmes and equipment for children and youth, the handicapped and the elderly. Access to social services is not, however, a right and is conditioned by the coverage of the network of services and financial limitations. The social system also includes "private social solidarity institutions" (IPPS).

Health services

There is a national health service in Portugal comprising primary health care services and hospitals which are open to the whole population regardless of their economic or social situation. The care is free of charge but complementary diagnostic and therapeutic examinations are chargeable, as is part of the cost of medicines which are considered non-essential or are for chronic conditions.

Main at risk groups

The main at risk groups in Portugal may be described as those children and adolescents:

– who come from large, low income families; and

– who come from minority groups.

Origins and development of interest in integrated services

Despite favourable economic growth during the 1980s, Portugal remains a country with a great deal of poverty; indeed the proportion of families who are classified as "poor" still stands at around 30 per cent (Vasconcelos, 1993). This high level of poverty as well as insufficiently developed social support has compromised the well being of children of all ages, from the very young to those negotiating the transition from school to work. The lack of child care facilities in Portugal is typified by the case of Lisbon. In 1988, for example, Ramirez *et al.* (1988) reported that less than 40 per cent of children between the ages of 3 and 6 in the city were attending public child care services even though the proportion of women who had jobs was very high.

According to Silva (1989), only 30 per cent of children start primary school following a preschool education and as a consequence a great number of them are entrusted to grand-parents and other forms of private care arrangements. A substantial group of children are simply left out on the streets, locked out of home. At the other end of the school period, recent work (Cardoso, 1993) has shown that in the poorest quarters of Lisbon, OPorto and Setubal over 50 per cent of youth ranging in age from 14-24 had failed to complete their compulsory basic education. Under these circumstances, it is difficult to find employment through vocational training arrangements, and children and youth can become exploited as cheap labour, compensating, through low wages for Portugal's lack of high technology (Silva, 1989).

As a result of Portugal's history, the country has only recently (since 1984) begun to develop a network of state child and family protection services in co-operation with other public and private organisations. The administration of these children's support services is divided between the ministries of Education, and Employment and Social Security. The first administers the public preschool education network while the last controls some children's centres and licences private institutions. The fact that all educational activities planned for children were integrated in the preschool education network and co-ordinated by the Ministry of Education led to great expectations about the quality of the services. However, although initially it was intended that the state should have direct responsibility for welfare services, latterly policy has switched to increasing the role of private initiatives. As a result, the RSSCs have not created more child centres but have transferred their management to the private social solidarity institutions (IPSS).

Growing out of this context has been a concern about school failure and a corresponding realisation that schools alone cannot compensate for the situations that many children find themselves in. This has led to a number of initiatives.

Inter-ministerial Programme for the Promotion of Educational Success (PIPSE)

This programme, was launched in December 1987 with the intention of reducing academic failure by giving priority to the first four years (the primary cycle) of basic education. Among other things, PIPSE was based on the idea of a clearly articulated, multi-sectoral method of intervention that could be implemented in all municipalities across Portugal. The ministries involved were Education; Planning and Territorial Administration; Agriculture, Fisheries and Food; Health; Employment and Social Security; and Youth. The whole was chaired by the Minister of Education and was jointly financed.

Ten components were identified for action:

– the strengthening of nutritional support;

– the provision of health care, including prevention and diagnosis;

– the extension of preschool education;

– the gradual spread of special education;

– support for families;

– leisure activities and sport;

– the provision of school transport;

– the supply of school materials;

– psychological, pedagogical and didactic support; and

– professional and pre-professional initiation.

PIPSE was planned as an experiment to terminate in 1991/92 for evaluation and consolidation. Although initial evaluations were promising (OECD, 1995) the final evaluation is still awaited. It was intended that the lessons learned would be transferred to the departments of the relevant ministries and to the regional and local levels.

Education Programme for All (PEPT 2000)

A recent innovation has superseded PIPSE. This is the Education Programme for All or PEPT 2000. This programme began in 1991 and is planned to extend to the year 2000. It is intended to lead to full compliance of the nine years of compulsory schooling and successful access to a further three years. It is aimed at combating school failure and drop-out and restructuring schools and teaching, to provide education for all and to promote educational success among all pupils.

Unlike PIPSE, the programme is mainly concerned with wide ranging school-based reforms including pedagogy, curriculum and organisational issues, while preserving and extending links with the local community.

Projecto Vida

A further collaborative programme involves the ministries of Health, Employment and Social Security in an attempt to provide effective services for the treatment of alcohol and drug abuse. Grants and equipment are provided to voluntary organisations for day centres and hostels.

Co-operation with the European Union

In an attempt to deal with the problem of street children, a project has been set up in Lisbon in co-operation with the European Poverty Programme. The project, which is described more fully later in this report, is a further example of an integrated service approach. In Lisbon, it is estimated that a significant number of children live on the streets – some throughout the full 24-hour period – in considerable poverty. The programme employs social workers and educators to work with the children and youth on the streets as well as other agencies, such as businesses and the police, in an attempt to reintegrate them into their families and society.

Conclusion

Portugal joined the EU in 1986 and has since that time been extending and developing its education (preschool, school age, post compulsory and adult), health and social support structures for children and families in line with those existing in many other countries of the Union. This has been carried out against a background of substantial adult illiteracy and poverty and includes a broad recognition that policies and practices must be developed on a wide front if substantial progress is to be made quickly. There has been a demonstrated commitment to the co-ordination of services in an attempt to meet these challenges. Although initial evaluations of PIPSE have proved positive, the final evaluations are still awaited. Other studies are still at the developmental stage and evaluations are yet to be carried out. In reality, perhaps inevitably, this approach was varied during the site visits to accommodate the different arrangements that were encountered. Brief accounts of the methods actually used in the sites visited now follows.

CASE STUDY RESEARCH

Visits to services for preschool children

The case study research took place over two days in Oporto in Northern Portugal and comprised a mixture of interviews and visits. A general outline of the situation in Oporto was provided by the Director of Social Services. Interviews were carried out with four social workers following visits to the Anti-poverty Trap Project in the old quarter of Sé and Saõ Nicolau and to the Casa do Caminho Association at Matosinhos in the suburbs of Oporto. Interviews also were conducted with other personnel at the operational and field levels.

Visits to services for school-aged children

Visits were made to a programme to help children on the streets, an SOS children's telephone service, and the intercultural school Quinta da Princesa in Amora, a Lisbon suburb.

During the visit to the street children's project interviews at all levels of interest were carried out during the course of a morning in a large group. Attempts to arrange individual interviews were not successful.

The information on the SOS centre was obtained during a small group meeting with some of the field level workers.

Information about the intercultural school was obtained at the field level from informal discussions during the visit to the school as well as from the school doctor for the Amora area. Further information on the "intercultural school programme" was obtained from the programme director at the State Secretariat as well as from the President of the Association of Portuguese Social Workers and the International Federation of Social Workers which is co-ordinating with the EU in this domain.

In addition, brief interviews were held with the Director General of Social Affairs (strategic level) and with the operational level manager of the adult education programme.

Visits to services for youth in the transition to work

The data pertaining to this visit were gathered mainly following individual interviews with the actors involved during the site visit.

The reports that follow reflect these different methodologies in the way they are reported. In an attempt to avoid repetition, the sources of the information are not always supplied except where contradictions were apparent.

INTEGRATED SERVICES FOR PRESCHOOL CHILDREN

The context

The study of integrated services provision for preschool children took place in the city of Oporto in the northern region of Portugal. Oporto is situated on the river Douro near to the coast and is the home of "port wine". The population is concentrated along the coast and the rural exodus has created a great cultural and economic divide between urban and rural areas. In Oporto, there is a considerable degree of poverty with high levels of unemployment. Although the cost of unemployment benefit has doubled over the past three years, only 65 per cent of unemployed people receive benefits. In the city, 53.8 per cent of the population live on the edge of poverty and apply to the social services for benefits. A quarter of those at work also need to claim special benefits. In addition, many children aged between 10 and 14 have black-market jobs or work at home.

Social services provide extra support in the form of cash, housing, services and equipment to clients with health needs or family problems, and to individuals who are marginalised, unemployed or handicapped. Fourteen per cent of the client group are aged between 0 and 5. At best only 26.8 per cent of 3- to 6-year-olds attend day care, and in the rural areas the proportion is much lower.

Between 1991 and 1992, the number of adopted children almost doubled. Growing numbers of parents do not wish to keep their children because of financial, alcohol, and drug-related difficulties. For those children who are at risk, two types of foster care exist: temporary care and care by relatives. Both of these are funded by the social services. Temporary arrangements are mainly provided by children's homes for children under 6. Between 1992 and 1993, the number of children requiring temporary care increased by about 84 per cent. The number of children at risk needing care by relatives increased over the same period by approximately 27 per cent.

A range of services are provided for young children by the RSSC including day care, kindergartens, play centres and children's homes, as well as childminder services. These are partly supported by parental contributions. In total, the RSSC provides services to around 20 650 children in the city.

Anti-poverty Trap Project 3

This project operates in the old parts of Oporto called Sé and Saõ Nicolau. These two areas have a population of some 14 000 people, many of whom live in poverty. There is a high population density as well as high levels of overcrowding, family break up, violence, school failure, prostitution and drug addiction.

A recent study on the quality of housing by the Centre for Community Information and Assistance (CIAC) revealed that about two-thirds of families were living in seriously dilapidated buildings with 75 per cent lacking a bathroom. A total of 50 per cent of young people leave school without completing the six years of compulsory schooling and 14 per cent of them attend for less than four years. Twenty-two per cent of the population are estimated to be totally illiterate. Abandonment of school is most often caused by the need to contribute to family finances with nearly 25 per cent starting work at the age of 14 or less. Of those families studied, 72 per cent have a monthly income below the minimum wage of approximately $300. A total of 40 per cent earn only half of this sum.

The Anti-poverty Trap Project is managed by the Foundation for the Development of Old Oporto. The management committee comprises representatives of the RSSC, local council and charitable organisations. Fifty-five per cent of the budget come from the European Social Fund (ESF) and the other 45 per cent from central and local government as well as other sources. The project seeks to rehabilitate urban areas and is an agency for social, educational and cultural development. There is a centre in Saõ Nicolau which caters for preschool children aged between three months and six years as well as providing other services for school-aged children and the elderly, thus covering a wide range of needs relating to housing, education, the transition to work and lifelong learning.

According to an evaluation reported in 1993, the main benefits of the programme were in the improvement of housing, the development of self-help and management skills in families, the improvement of income levels, the acquisition by clients of technical and vocational, social and work-related skills, and the enhancement of self-image.

The project has also led to a new dynamism in the local community as a result of the participation of local residents in the programme, and changes in traditional methods of social work. Respondents pointed out that the situation could be ameliorated further by improving relationships with schools, in which there is a traditional resistance to external influences.

The co-operation that has developed is based on developing synergies between the various agencies with the aim of:

– meeting all of the needs of clients; and

– full exploitation of resources (*e.g.* budgets, sites, buildings) through pooling and effective management of equipment and personnel.

In order to co-ordinate the services, analysis has revealed the need to:

– empower front-line workers by giving them a broad range of skills;

– organise regular meetings for consultation to ensure that people are working together and taking a cross-disciplinary approach;

– avoid traditional hierarchical lines in favour of functional relationships; and

– intervene at all levels concurrently to avoid over-burdening front-line workers (especially volunteers).

The training that has been developed to achieve such collaboration is based on real problems and not theoretical abstractions.

Staff reported on the advantages of collaboration. They agreed that it led to lower costs and better use of resources and gave the public a better understanding of services on offer because sources of information could be unified. It promotes a speedy and co-ordinated response to problems with activities being integrated and not compartmentalised.

For the system to work there needs to be a clear political will and a co-ordinator must be appointed to manage the partnership. This person has to promote links between the various players, to fight the tendency for hierarchies to nullify the effort, and to take a lead in negotiating and mediating to ensure the integration of activities. In practice, managers at the operational level have fulfilled this role.

Collaboration with other projects financed by the ESF was also seen as crucial whether they be in Portugal or other countries. The exchange of information fostered through collaboration was seen as invaluable.

There are also personal advantages for staff such as more satisfaction derived from more effective working practices and a sharper focus on the point of delivery because of the frequent contact with clients on the ground. Staff also commented on the pleasure and mutual enthusiasm which come from working within a supportive and committed team and the advantage of work which allows for growth and personal development and which gives the feeling that progress is being made.

La Casa do Caminho in Matosinhos

This programme focuses on abused children and was developed in a hospital by a number of voluntary workers. The centre opened following arrangements made between the RSSC and the town hall. It provides protection and accommodation for babies and toddlers as well as older children. The building has been refurbished and redecorated by gifts from local individuals and businesses. For the most part, the children that are in the home have been abandoned by their parents and are placed by the Children's Court or the RSSC. The centre has welcomed approximately 100 children over its first three years and is funded by the RSSC, the local council and business. It employs a paediatrician, a psychologist, a social worker, child workers and support staff. Each month there is a meeting between representatives of the home, the court, the adoption service and local offices of central government to review cases and plan the children's future.

An extension to the building is planned and will be jointly funded, by the same groups as before, as well as through various fund-raising activities.

It has signed service agreements with education, health and justice services which give it certain rights. The education service seconds a member of staff. It also has priority for medical visits and the supply of prescriptions and simpler reimbursement procedures.

In all of this work the RSSC has a central role. The Director manages a staff of 215 and co-ordinates services across the district. She pointed out that services often find themselves working together because of problems faced on the ground by workers. However, this was difficult to manage mainly because of a lack of tradition of partnership in Portugal. Involving education was especially difficult – health and social services co-operation is more natural. In addition, political commitment can vary substantially region to region and initiatives need to be developed. This view was widely supported by other social workers.

Recent national policy, as described in the introductory section, is leading to the privatisation of public services. From January 1994, the IPPSs will be managing projects.

The partnerships which are developing include the IPPSs, the health services, the local council, the employment and training agency, and education, and were initiated in 1988/89. These developments often have a bottom up nature because staff already know each other. Nevertheless, it takes five to six years for arrangements to become effective and to match up the services. At the senior management level, the process is very slow. There is little supportive legislation.

The Assistance to Children and Families Project was the first to be planned at a political level as a project to integrate services. There is an inter-departmental service agreement which sets aims and identifies resources. Specialists are seconded and training is given and there are exchanges with Belgium. Time is set aside for consultation and planning and evaluation is currently under way.

Client involvement does not flow of its own accord and strategies are required to encourage it.

The advantages were reported to be:

– more effective use of resources and an increase in financial flows;

– increased participation of the local community as witnessed by the dynamism of the voluntary sector;

– services are better adapted to needs and there is a fuller understanding of clients;

– there is enhanced transparency concerning outcomes allowing demonstrations of positive results, especially at social, cultural and educational levels; and

– personal development of members of the team and greater satisfaction related to more clearly identified outputs (which compensates for fatigue in the constant struggle against poverty).

Concerns were expressed about the control being passed to the voluntary sector and the extent to which integration efforts will be sacrificed to other more limited projects, thus losing synergy and dynamism.

Organised community action can increase the vulnerability of some groups such as Gypsies who can find themselves more exposed to intrusion from outside and not well prepared to defend their culture.

Partnership highlights gaps that exist between the expectations and conditions laid down by the authorities and the goals identified by the communities concerned. This often leads to difficult or impossible paradoxes to reconcile.

There is also a need to keep careful control of the distribution of power and avoid one solution creating another problem.

INTEGRATED SERVICES FOR SCHOOL CHILDREN

The sites concerned with integrating services for school children were located in Lisbon. There were three of them:

– a programme to help children on the streets;

– an SOS children's telephone service; and

– an intercultural school called Quinta da Princesa.

Although these were the programmes that were explored, it is important to note another parallel initiative, which perhaps has its roots in the completed PIPSE Programme. This is a protection commission which works locally, can be initiated by concerned citizens, and has the responsibility of protecting children from birth to nine years of age. When problems are identified, such as non-attendance at school, the commission can put groups of people together to try to solve them.

The Street Children Project

This project is run by the Institute for the Support of Children (IAC) which is an IPSS. The IAC was set up in 1983 within a multi-disciplinary context. Its main aim is to "contribute to the integrated development of children, to the protection and promotion of their rights" especially in areas not covered by other institutions. From the outset there was an insistence that there should be close co-operation with the community: "we must instigate active and widespread participation on the part of the community so that local institutions and organisations work together in a co-ordinated fashion".

The street children programme began in 1989 as part of a national programme to combat poverty in southern Portugal. It has been included, as a pilot programme, in the third anti-poverty programme of the EU.

Structure

The programme's headquarters, which also serve as a reception and emergency centre, have been provided by the Ministry of Employment and Social Security. The Ministry of Education has seconded teachers to work "on the streets" within the structure of the TEJO club, a street school which aims to facilitate children's social and educational integration. The IAC has signed agreements with a variety of ministries (*e.g.* Education, Health, Employment and Social Security, Justice and Youth), institutions (*e.g.* Casa Pia and Misericordia), enterprises (*e.g.* the zoo) and local authorities (*e.g.* the Townhall of Lisbon, the Prefecture and Junta de Frequesia). Thus at the strategic level the programme is well known and endorsed, and political support can be easily mobilised. The financial resources made available have been adequate and no complaints in this area were made by staff.

The group is staffed by social workers paid for by the Ministry of Employment and Social Security while the programme director, a pre-primary school teacher, is paid for by the Ministry of Education. Other staff include health care workers who may be called upon to work on a part-time basis.

Method

The project deals with children who have been abandoned or who have run away from home, who are exploited, who beg and who in one way or another have become, or are close to becoming, marginalised from society. The aim is to re-socialise these children by encouraging personal growth with the goal of persuading them to "re-insert" themselves.

There are four steps in the programme. The first is to gain children's trust and to make friends with them. Contact with their families is not made until the children are ready and desire it. The second is a period of transition, whereby the relationship between the social worker and the child is strengthened and other professionals such as educators and nurses are introduced. At weekends, for instance, an attempt is made to encourage them to live in a group and to develop a normal lifestyle.

The third step is to re-integrate them into some form of family life either with parents or relatives or in hostels or community homes. The fourth and final step is to develop participation in home, school or work as appropriate.

Clearly the arrangements just described provide great flexibility in method and this is encouraged. An example can be taken from work with the zoo. One of the street workers knew about the zoo and asked the authorities there if they wished to become involved with the street children – to which they agreed. The children benefit from educational and socialising experiences at the zoo. They do not work since this would be contrary to Portuguese law. The teachers in the zoo are veterinarians and they teach general zoo theory and skills but not basic educational skills. There is a plan to extend these arrangements by developing a course for zoo keepers, with help from the EU, which will be the same as school-based training. At the moment the zoo receives no government support for its work.

In the Street Children Programme there is an emphasis on teamwork between the social workers, street educators and others to ensure that contact is maintained with the children and to prevent recidivism. They meet regularly: each morning to plan priorities and twice a year for three or four days to evaluate progress. During these meetings representatives from other institutions are invited such as Misericordia and Casa Pia.

Problems and issues

Perhaps not surprisingly in a programme of this sort there are many difficulties to resolve. It was of significance that no complaints were received concerning funding and resources. However, the programme leaders stressed that it was crucial to have the support of decision-makers and what was required most of all was a change in attitudes, a view that was frequently expressed.

It was regarded as essential that those working at the grassroots level are kept informed and are willing to participate actively. The methods of work are new. As a result, it is often necessary to know how to interpret the regulations and lubricate the functioning of institutions often encumbered by red-tape and rigid hierarchies. This is particularly true, it would seem, of the ministries of Education and Health and certain IPPS such as Misericordia. Both structures and staff were seen to be at fault, with breakdowns in communication and a rigid application of rules cited as frequent problems. On the other hand, instances of improved efficiency in the very same structures or in others like them were reported, thanks to the flexibility and good will of the staff involved. This was especially true of the Ministry of Justice. This ministry was impressed by some of the working methods of the IAC – in particular its supportive rather than punitive approach – and is beginning to take them on board. This organisation also recognises the need for the training of managers in the "quartiers" to work with the Mayors. In addition there needs to be a case manager to co-ordinate actions. The police also are involved in helping to locate children.

Schools were seen as being especially resistant to change and innovation. They were often held to account when reasons for the marginalisation of children were sought. "School doesn't mean anything to them", we were told. In addition it was pointed out how difficult it is to "sensitise a standardised education system" to the importance of being understanding, open-minded and willing to adopt new methods when confronted by problematic situations. We were also told that at the outset there were difficulties with schools taking in children perceived to have problems in behaviour. Furthermore, teachers also were said to have difficulties adjusting to the methods needed for working on the streets.

On the positive side, the education department of Lisbon urban council was working with prevention in mind and had supplied good schools, transportation and meals with the intention of keeping children in school.

Representatives from the Ministry of Education were unavailable and so it is not possible to comment further on their view of the sources of their difficulties. For instance, it was pointed out that conflicts can arise because school buildings are controlled by the urban councils, but teachers by the Ministry – a point that at present cannot be elaborated further.

Health

Health issues are of importance too and we were told that hospitals would not always take in children who were not in their catchment area, although we were assured by senior government officers that this should not have been a problem.

There are several health centres that children can use in order to avoid some of the bureaucracy. Nurses teach the children how to use available resources. The children themselves are especially interested in sex education, contraception and AIDS. By contrast the IPSS, Misericordia, was said to be unused by children, despite welcoming them there, because of its bureaucratic and clinical structure. However, we were told of successes in the fight against drug use when the street method was used.

Training

At the outset, the IAC recognised the need for training and this has formed a central element in the development of its work. Not only have IAC staff been trained but also staff from other organisations, such as the RSSCs, Misericordia and school principals. Training based on discussions of evaluations of the programme was reported as being especially effective.

Outcomes

Evaluation work carried out by various internal and external agencies focuses in particular on methods, effects and impact on the participants. In general, the work appears to be well received by government agencies who particularly like the dynamic aspects of it. The press, police and shop-keepers also report being impressed by the effects of the programme, as witnessed by the apparent reduction of children wandering the streets of Lisbon. This impression was confirmed by evidence given to us by street children themselves and a parent.

The findings of the evaluations have led to proposed developments in the area of partnership, especially with enterprises, and further determination to improve harmonious working arrangements. This is in spite of the fact that "there are areas of public administration which are difficult to modify because they are so entrenched in an outdated organisational culture".

Other changes have led to the adoption of preventive strategies which include the planning of activities in schools and local communities, promoting parent associations, and improving co-operation between parents and teachers. These changes have been stimulated by reflection on how to develop the programme to meet clients' needs more effectively.

Conclusion

This community development programme has profited from a consensus at the decision-making level. The concern to win the support of all of the actors involved, including the target group of young people, has created a system which seems to be producing good results.

Despite these efforts, however, there is still resistance to be overcome. Staff of the official social assistance services do not necessarily approve of the methods used. Many are wary, for example, of having young non-professionals working in the programme.

Teachers are also disconcerted by an activity conducted on the streets that represents a pattern of working so different from the one they have been trained for and are accustomed to, and which requires them too change their whole way of working and their expectations. However, as noted above, teachers were unavailable for interview and the lack of their perspective is a serious omission.

There is quite a difference between the decision-makers who, being informed about and aware of problems, support the programme, and those working at grassroots level who sometimes grow weary of struggling to solve problems without always receiving the specific backing that is required. Unresponsive behaviour, reflected in long delays or an obsession with regulations, may well reflect the bitterness of "traditional" staff who feel they are being criticised or opposed by newcomers who often seem to lack the necessary qualifications but may well be asked to train them.

Friction may also result from political differences. The government and the local authorities do not belong to the same party.

The programme to help children on the streets is led by a dynamic team which has set up an entire system of interconnections. Above and beyond the functioning of the programme itself, it is the functioning of the administrative system – in the wide sense of the term – that is called into question, directly or indirectly, including the people who work within it. Those in charge admit this and, interestingly enough, find the issues the programme raises useful. Spurred on by the programme's call for community development, the official services and other institutions are now reviewing their methods.

SOS Children

Background

In its efforts to promote children's rights, the IAC is particularly concerned about child abuse, a serious problem in Portugal. It has already made various attempts to combat the problem (cf. Report on Violence presented to the Steering Committee of the Council of Europe).

In 1986, the IAC decided to set up a telephone service to help children and families at risk. The service can be reached during opening hours when staff are on duty. At other times, an answering machine registers calls. Not only children but also adults turn to SOS Children to signal emergencies or frequently to obtain information on a wide range of problems. The aim is not necessarily to find immediate solutions although this is quite often done. The overriding concern is to anticipate possible crises. To begin with, efforts are made to listen sympathetically to the people who phone in and put them at ease so that they feel able to explain clearly their problem. Only then does SOS Children seek appropriate answers. In order to sort out problems it often has to contact relevant services or institutions. It may have to persuade institutions to relax their regulations, to authorise delays, to push for quicker action, or to co-ordinate their time-tabling and procedures with other services. SOS Children acts as "ombudsman" between services and users.

Means

Among the staff of SOS Children are two social workers, a psychologist and a nursery school teacher. They are seconded from the IPPS Misericordia and from the various ministries that have drawn up an agreement with the IAC. Two staff members have attended training seminars held by associations such as the Red Cross in Paris.

The process of integration

The IAC launched the programme, contacted the appropriate specialists, formulated aims and organised the service. Now, however, SOS Children has a certain freedom of action. Despite this, there is no head of service as such, even though the psychologist seems to direct the operation.

When the agreement was first signed in 1990 by the relevant administrative units and institutions, the introduction of other programmes of a similar kind was foreseen. Preliminary plans were even made for a centre to receive children rejected by their families. It was intended, too, that each local RSSC would have a member of staff whose main task would be to manage educational activities in support of children in need. Unfortunately, it seems to have proved impossible to establish an efficient network among the various services so as to ensure that problems can be rapidly and inclusively solved. If anything, a certain disenchantment was expressed by those interviewed about the programme.

Yet again it was stressed that each institution has its own methods and ways of thinking, often deep-rooted and resistant to change. Unwieldy and bureaucratic machines often hamper progress.

Despite all the efforts and pressures, the desired breakthrough has yet to be fully achieved. For example, in order to create a stable and efficient network of activities it would have been necessary to have a designated person working within each service. Moreover, the people receiving calls from SOS Children are not always adequately informed or prepared to take appropriate steps. Their replies are sometimes unhelpful and fail to produce the desired results. At the same time, the various services still compete with one another. The SOS and IAC teams complain that the people they talk to lack multi-disciplinary skills and are often too specialised and limited in their range of activities to be of much use.

Conclusion

It appears that an evaluation of SOS Children is planned for next year but nothing definite has been arranged so far. Whatever the case, it is clear from the discussions and reports on the programme that services are still too closed and centralised. Again, mention was made of the need for a change in attitudes, so as to enable services to work together and ensure that the law is enforced objectively. Attention was drawn to the weight of a traditional, Latin culture that continues to confer great authority on the "pater familias" and sometimes overrides or contradicts children's interests.

The Intercultural School No. 5

Context

The Intercultural School No. 5, Quinta da Princesa, is situated in the Setubal district, on the opposite bank of the river from Lisbon. There is a significant proportion of children of foreign extraction living in the district (14.2 per cent); the highest after Lisbon (16.2 per cent). The children come from a variety of countries, particularly from former colonies, such as Cape Verde and Angola. There is also a high number of Gypsies (almost 10 per cent of minority groups).

The school is in a very disadvantaged area. It has 167 pupils, aged 6-11. Sixty one per cent are from abroad. They belong to at least five different nationalities and also include Gypsies. The school failure rate is high, that is, 27 per cent. The school principal is very dynamic. She has the spirit to improve the lives and learning of her pupils.

Means

In 1990, a programme on "multi-culturalism in schools" was launched in association with an American school that has a similar cross-section of pupils. One of the programme's objectives is to improve communication between families and the school so that parents co-operate more willingly and become more skilled at helping their children. The programme is intended to last five years. What advantages the school has gained from its pairing with the American school are difficult to ascertain.

The key problem is how to improve the children's school results by means of diverse activities. While fostering relations with the parents is important, it is also essential to improve facilities, watch over the children's health, ensure they are not under-nourished, and adopt measures to prevent violence and drug abuse.

The local council has released funds and authorised building repairs. In addition, a doctor and a nurse check the children's health. This is not exclusive to the school in question. All schools are supposed to provide this service but only during the first year. For the Quinta da Princesa to obtain more medical help, it must have sufficient means. We were told how difficult it is to persuade other services to co-operate, but no precise details were given.

The police work with the children in small groups, usually at the teachers' request. Policemen on the beat also establish contact with the parents.

There is no psychologist or social worker at the school. Those working there complain bitterly that they do not have enough funds to feed the children properly and to develop extra-curricular activities. More teaching-posts are also asked for, although the pupil-teacher ratio of 15:1 is favourable.

The children's parents started a parents' association at the beginning of the year but it has only two or three members.

Conclusion

It is very difficult to assess this programme as it was not formally presented to us. We could only try to understand it from short and isolated discussions held under difficult conditions. The meeting with the various partners failed to elicit much information, particularly since many of the participants were meeting together for the first time. Clearly, they do not yet share a common purpose with regard to how the school might interact with other institutions.

The programme leader is apparently a professor at a teacher training institution but he was absent during our visit. Despite the good will of the school staff and ministry officials, we were unable to obtain the kind of information we would have liked. The actors at the grassroots level, including the school principal herself, were tied up with their own particular work problems while the "education team" concentrate on the direction and pedagogical content of their activities.

Despite these setbacks, it was intriguing to observe at first-hand how little the partners were able to co-operate. Many seemed not to know what was expected of them, some wanted to pose questions, yet others were on the defensive.

Perhaps there are plans to integrate the various services so that the local community and, above all, the children can be better served. At first sight, however, it looks as if the work now under way and the resources obtained depend more on the principal's efforts to contact each partner than on a concerted effort by the services to work together. Indeed, the concept of synergy does not seem to exist at all in this programme, even though there is a strong need for it. Perhaps what is lacking is political will or an institutional leader?

It should be noted that, alongside this programme, another on "multicultural education" has been initiated by the EU. It covers two school sectors, each consisting of two primary schools and a lower secondary school. This programme shares the same aims as Quinta de Princesa but we could not review it since it has only just begun.

Overall conclusion

The integration of services was considered at different levels depending on the programme under review. Each of the three programmes focused on disadvantaged social groups but in different circumstances:

– a captive and designed audience – pupils;

– a "voluntary" group which has been given the means to establish contact if it so wishes (IAC); and

– an "absentee" group, liable to reject help, whom it is necessary to seek out and win over (IAC).

Integrating services for improved efficiency

The principal aim of the three programmes is to enhance the efficiency and use of services created to help disadvantaged children. Many potential clients do not know that these services exist, refuse, or are even afraid, to use them. The reasons for this are varied.

In the case of the IAC programmes, it is important that the different actors work together. The "children on the streets" programme cannot work effectively without a co-ordinated public service covering all areas of prevention and treatment. So important is this priority that several partners were persuaded to come to common decisions and to endorse and adopt new methods in order to tackle problems that none of them could cope with on their own. In this case, the services seem to accept the concept of integration and to have analysed in quite lucidly.

The need for services to co-operate and, above all, to set up a network is recognised and encouraged in the case of SOS Children but only, it would appear, by one of the partners involved, that is the IAC. As yet, little wider co-operation has been achieved.

Those engaged in the "intercultural school" project feel a profound need for backing and support so that all their efforts can prove more effective, but as yet no conception of co-operation among the services seems to exist.

The integration of services to answer new needs

It is because of new developments demanding urgent attention that decision-makers and those working at grassroots level alike have recognised the need to work differently. The large IPSS and administrative units, hampered by old and cumbersome structures, centralised procedures and rigid hierarchies, have difficulties in doing anything other than running business as usual. When innovations are necessary, external influences must be brought to bear, such as the IAC. At the same time, the support of the administrative hierarchy is required. This process further requires the added impetus of activities and training aimed at making the people affected realise just how serious are their needs and problems. They will then come to reassess working methods and accept innovations. Each one of them must feel directly involved. This is already happening in the case of the programme for children on the streets. SOS Children has not yet reached this stage.

Professional requirements

The integration of services may require a re-evaluation of professional requirements. Every profession has its own system of thinking and training. New needs demand that people re-adjust to working methods that are alien to their background training. This is true of teachers, for example, as well as social workers. They are often disoriented by the disappearance of familiar landmarks. Although not professionally trained to do so, teachers ought to adopt some of the aims and methods practised by social workers in order perform more effectively. But how far should they go? They are still teachers first and foremost.

In the same way, social workers feel professionally threatened when young and inexperienced people are asked to tackle a problem from a new angle (that is, to approach and win the trust of young drop-outs), as if to suggest that all their training was inadequate.

If services are to co-operate with one another, the staff have to learn to be open-minded and less defensive. They must be sufficiently sure of their identity and professional skills to accept this change of attitude without being afraid that they will no longer command respect or appreciation.

Sound professional training, together with careful interdisciplinary consideration of the issues at stake, would seem essential if co-operation between services is to increase efficiency without disrupting staff or undermining their sense of responsibility and professional worth.

In the case of the "children on the streets" programme, the IAC is bent on achieving this balance, even though training within the different administrative units lies beyond its control. The other two programmes would seem to require a similar approach, not yet sufficiently explored by the people promoting them.

Those working at the grassroots and the administrative levels must learn to see their specific programmes in a wider context. Only training and time will achieve such a shift in attitude. This is why it is crucial to know if the activities will continue to be financed when EU funding comes to an end.

INTEGRATED SERVICES FOR YOUTH IN THE TRANSITION TO WORK

In Portugal, the case study on integrated services for youth in the transition to work focused on Pina Manique, a semi-independent, vocational school for children aged 9-18 years, many of whom are disadvantaged. The school is one of a group of seven institutions for children at risk of all ages, collectively called Casa Pia de Lisboa. Casa Pia caters for some 3 000 students of both sexes between three and 18 years of age. In addition, visually and hearing impaired children are also provided for.

Pina Manique has a long tradition (since 1776) of educating Lisbon's poor and underprivileged children, with some success it would appear, since the school's walls are covered with plaques of former students who have excelled as artists, scholars or inventors. Pina Manique has a strong vocational training focus and remains forward looking with up-to-date equipment in auto-mechanics and information technology.

Vocational training is provided at three levels. At Levels I and II, the equivalents of the 2nd and 3rd cycles of basic (general) education, courses taught include dressmaking, upholstery, building construction, car painting, shoe-making and carpentry. Level III courses, the equivalent of general secondary education, are aimed towards skilled work: students can train, for example, to become car mechanics, electricians, administrators and graphic artists. While most pupils follow vocational courses in the 2nd and 3rd cycles, the option is available to continue with a general education which is the normal path to university.

Casa Pia places a strong emphasis on links with business and the community, and has co-operation agreements to formalise these relationships with the following companies and institutions:

- Swiss Watch Maker's Federation;

- Portuguese-German Chamber of Commerce;

- Ford;

- Graphic Arts;

- Confederation of Commerce;

- Institute of Employment and Vocational Training; and

- Santa Casa da Misericordia (an important social institution in Lisbon).

These agreements symbolise Casa Pia's philosophy of combining modern technologies, ideas and approaches with a tradition of which it is proud.

Funding for Casa Pia is mixed. Three-quarters comes from the Ministry of Employment and Social Security, and most of the rest from its own patrimonial resources (from the renting of land and property, and commercial interests). Some funding also comes from the European Union (EU): for example, the EU is supporting an extensive building renovation programme at Pina Manique. As "an official institute in the ward of the Ministry of Employment and Social Security" Casa Pia is not representative of the state education system as a whole. This special status confers upon it a greater degree of independence from central government than that enjoyed by normal state schools. Pina Manique, for example, was functioning as a vocational school long before the government initiative to set up a national network of vocational schools in 1989. Furthermore the school provides a much higher level of social support and care for its students – with three social workers and three psychologists on its staff – than is required by government legislation.

Casa Pia is very much a model institution; it is the exception rather than the rule. Its special status, funding arrangements, buildings, educational facilities, social care provision and relations with business, together act to provide opportunities for its pupils unequalled in other parts of the Portuguese education system.

The clientele

Of the 1 400 students at Pina Manique, 99 per cent could be considered at risk according to the Vice-Principal. The majority come from the poor disadvantaged regions of Lisbon (including the "barrios"). However, there are some from more privileged families, often with learning difficulties. There is also a residential facility in the school for children with emotional and behavioural difficulties. Some children have attendance problems which the school's social workers address through home-school liaison.

The interviewees

In constructing this report, data based on interviews with a wide range of actors was used. At the strategic and operational levels the Principal and Vice-Principal of Casa Pia were interviewed. Internal to Pina Manique, a clinical psychologist, five social workers (one from Pina Manique and four from Casa Pia), two co-ordinators (teachers) and a "patron" (an ex-student who had become a junior teacher) were spoken to. External workers interviewed included a child psychiatrist from a mental health centre in a local hospital, two social workers from the local social services and a representative from a local trade union.

The link between the school and employers also allowed for information to be gathered from two managers at Legrand, the French electrical company.

Strategic and operational level professionals in the school

The Principal and Vice-Principal

In a joint interview with the Principal and Vice-Principal of Casa Pia we were informed that the school has links with a wide variety of institutions and agencies ranging from government ministries to local and international businesses. The school co-operates, as laid down in national policy, with many government services including the courts, social services and health services. Since the school has a residential home for children with acute problems it regularly liaises with local hospitals. As well as referring children for special treatment to hospitals, it also accepts children from hospitals for care.

The two ministries with which the school has the strongest links are the Ministry of Employment and Social Security and the Ministry of Education. The relationship with the Ministry of Employment and Social Security is largely a financial one since the school depends on it for the majority of its funding. The relationship with the Ministry of Education is more symbiotic: while the Ministry provides help in the development of new courses in Pina Manique, it also follows teaching approaches in the school with a view to adopting them elsewhere. This is indicative of Pina Manique's status as a "model school".

The school has a range of links with the business world. The Principal has signed a number of co-operation agreements or protocols with companies (see above), although these are not fixed as seen in the cancellation of one protocol by Bosch. The school's protocol with Ford is typical, and was signed by the Director General of Casa Pia and a Director of Ford following an approach made by Ford. As part of the agreement the company provides technical support to the school and input for courses. Similar support is provided by a number of other companies which collaborate with Pina Manique. Along with the Ministry of Education, the Institute of Employment, the unions and representatives from Casa Pia, companies are also involved in examining courses. However, some companies' demands for payment for this work have made co-operation problematic.

As well as receiving outside input into its courses, the school also has courses which are run by outside agencies. The administration course is organised by the German and Portuguese Chambers of Commerce, and as part of their special relationship the school provides them with classrooms free of charge.

The school's links with business result in improved job opportunities for its students. Pupils studying administration, commerce and mechanics courses regularly work for companies with which the school has protocols during the school holidays. Once they have graduated from school these companies often offer them full-time jobs. While firms may approach the school when they are looking to fill a position, the relationship is two-way, and school co-ordinators frequently approach them. Indeed this is one of the co-ordinators' stated responsibilities.

The relationship with the union representatives in the school, in their function as monitors and examiners of vocational courses, is ambiguous. While the officials are reportedly positive about the quality of preparation of the school's pupils for work, they will not sign their exam certificates, which evidently would have implications for students' ability to find work. The problematic nature of co-operation between the unions and the school was linked by the Principal and Vice-Principal to some form of resentment, resulting from the widening gap in terms of educational qualifications and familiarity with modern technologies between newly qualified students and older workers.

Casa Pia also has links with educational establishments in Denmark and Spain, and is involved in teacher training and a youth project; however, there was insufficient time to discuss these in detail.

The Principal's and Vice-Principal's overall view was that Casa Pia was "not closed" as an institution, and had good relations with most of the outside agencies they worked with. However, at the same time reference was made to outsider dissatisfaction concerning the institution's special status. This is something they are trying to appease.

Field level professionals in the school

Five social workers

We interviewed a senior social worker in Pina Manique, and a social worker who is a former employee of the school (but is now working in another Casa Pia institution). Later we spoke to another three social workers who also work in Casa Pia schools.

The first two social workers informed us that children are referred to the school's residential home by an outside agency and are then assessed by a special intake team including social workers and psychologists. When the team accepts a child, the school takes over responsibility for them. Resident social workers help them to adjust to their new "home" and act as a point of liaison with outside social services, the juvenile court and the child's family.

Normally, Pina Manique is only asked to become involved in a particular case after local social services have failed. At this point local services take a back seat, although they may co-operate with the school during the transition from school to home or to work. Pina Manique occasionally provides follow-up care; however, this is seldom offered by local services because they are overburdened. For children opting for higher education, the school sometimes offers accommodation and other kinds of support.

Pina Manique does not have responsibility for the case management of children living at home. This rests with the local social services whose social workers form the bridge between home and school.

The three social workers employed by other Casa Pia institutions informed us that their relations with local social services and other outside agencies are on a case by case basis, and are largely informal. Connections between professionals in Casa Pia institutions are similar. Recently, tension has been created between Casa Pia and outside agencies because of problems with a child cared for by Pina Manique. In addition, there are internal tensions within the school between resident social workers and teachers.

A psychologist

We interviewed one of three psychologists working in Pina Manique. All three psychologists have offices located in the same area of the school, along with the school's three professional social workers.

The psychologist we spoke to said that within the school she works most closely with the teachers and the social workers, although she also liaises with the school doctor and the school director. Once or twice each month she has meetings with the school's class teachers where they discuss children's problems and strategies for coping with them. The social workers also attend whenever they are available. She regarded these meetings as important since the teachers are often the first to know when a child has a problem and therefore can provide her with important information. In addition, her view was that with guidance teachers can play an instrumental role in addressing students' problems. In order to cope with the large number of pupils who are her responsibility, she has adopted a strategy whereby she transfers her specialist knowledge and skills to teachers so that they are able to address problems at the "front-line". As a result, the direct contact she has with pupils presenting problems is very limited. However, this gives her time to liaise with other professionals to find solutions for the most acute cases. She felt that this method of working was effective and that it should be extended by offering teachers formal training.

Both parents and children are involved in any decisions she makes regarding treatment, although normally only the parents attend decision-making meetings. However, in general her contact with parents is limited and they are mainly referred to the social workers. The reason for this was not clear but may be connected to the stigma attached to psychological treatment.

Outside of Pina Manique she has meetings with professionals from other Casa Pia institutions on a regular basis. The twelve psychologists in Casa Pia meet once a month to discuss problem cases and to plan common projects. They also organise joint workshops on a variety of themes. As a result they know each other well, and are used to working together towards common goals. She also meets teachers, social workers and psychologists from her own and other Casa Pia institutions as part of her responsibility as a career planner. They meet twice each month to discuss student's career options, and also have joint training seminars on "Planning Careers". Furthermore, she is responsible for giving talks on careers options to classes and liaising with companies to arrange visits. Her secondary role as a career planner means that she has an important opportunity to collaborate with other professionals on matters in addition to those which relate directly to children's problems.

She also works closely with a professional team, including a psychiatrist, psychologist, social worker and nurse, in a Mental Health Centre which is part of the local hospital. Children are referred to the Mental Health Centre when they have very severe problems, such as personality disorders and incontinence, which cannot be treated in the school. At the beginning of each school year the team meets to discuss the new school intake, and in addition they meet once every three months to discuss particular cases. Sometimes the latter will be attended by a school teacher or social worker who is knowledgeable about one of the children being discussed. In addition to these joint meetings, the psychologist also has separate discussions with the psychiatrist so that they can talk in more depth about individual cases and strategies for dealing with them. The psychologist was very positive about these one-to-one meetings in contrast to the joint meetings which she felt were too large, with too much variety in the professional backgrounds represented. In her view, other professionals could sometimes be "difficult to work with" because of their different approaches. On the other hand, she described her separate discussions with the psychiatrist as "intimate", and this was indicative of her perception of their meetings as an important and valuable opportunity to communicate within a shared framework.

The psychologist explained her method of work as an adaptation to her responsibility for a large number of children (around 200). Since she did not have the time to deal with cases herself, it was essential for her to co-operate with other professionals and agencies who could take them on. This meant in some instances passing her expertise on to ordinary classroom teachers, and in others referring cases to specialists. Her view was that she simply had to work in collaboration with others because it would be "impossible" to work in any other way.

However, she said that collaboration was not without its problems, the main ones being time and distance. Thus, paradoxically, while she used collaborative meetings as a time saving device (*i.e.* to reduce her case workload), a barrier to these meetings was the time involved in attending them. Another apparent paradox was that while she regarded the multi-professional meetings at the Mental Health Centre as too large and mixed in terms of professional perspectives, she also expressed the view that in addressing children's problems it was better to share ideas, and to work with "several minds" and "different visions". These contradictions are indicative of the existence of costs as well as benefits in a collaborative approach.

Two teachers

We interviewed two teachers in the school: one was the co-ordinator of administration courses for students at Levels II and III (Teacher A), and the other was the co-ordinator for metal mechanics (Teacher B). The focus of the second interview, which was spontaneous and therefore short, was the co-ordinator's special links with the Mental Health Centre.

Teacher A, a young woman in her late 20's, informed us that she has a very good relationship with the school's social workers and psychologists, and frequently co-operates with them.

To illustrate this co-operation, she told us that if one of her pupils has a problem, she informs either a social worker or psychologist, and sometimes sends them to the social worker's office. In addition, she liaises directly with the social worker and/or psychologist to discuss what the child's problems are and what strategies they can use to address them. In serious cases, the social worker or psychologist will take the responsibility for involving the child's parents by contacting them and inviting them to the school. She felt that in these ways the school's social workers and psychologists provide her with vital support and advice.

While co-operating closely with other professionals in Pina Manique, Teacher A reported little formal contact with those working outside of the school. Occasionally she discusses courses with a teacher from another school but she emphasized that this contact is informal and personal.

However, the contact she has with local businesses is quite strong. She initially developed school-business links by writing letters to appropriate companies listed in a telephone directory. While this particular approach was her own initiative, working closely with businesses in helping students to find employment is one of her formally stated responsibilities. She said that companies are much less active in approaching the school to establish links, and that company visits and presentations to the school are quite uncommon. This she linked to the fact that school visits are not part of company managers' normal routine, and the fact that, in their outlook towards schools, some managers can be "closed" and "disinterested".

One of the main reasons for developing links with business is to assist students in gaining employment. Each year she writes to local companies to ask them if they can provide summer placements for her students, and, frequently, if a student successfully completes a placement, they are later offered a full-time job. Furthermore, she also makes inquiries about full-time jobs for any graduating student who requests it. This is often done by phone – in her spare time – and results in almost 100 per cent employment amongst students leaving her course. Occasionally, companies take the initiative by phoning the school to inquire if they have any good students. She said that this occurs because of Pina Manique's strong reputation for vocational training.

In addition to employment, she also liaises with local companies on course content. For example, occasionally a company will find that a placement student does not have a particular skill which they require, and the school will respond to their needs by adding the relevant training into the curriculum. Equally, if the school is not happy with the experience a placement student is getting in a company, they will discuss it and reach a mutually satisfactory solution.

The teacher felt that the school benefited greatly from its links with business, particularly with respect to employment for its students and the development of courses which are relevant to working life. However, she felt that the situation would be improved if companies played a more active role in the relationship and were willing to visit and give presentations in the school. Asked if school-business links were strong in other schools, she said that they were not and that Pina Manique was fortunate in having a reputation which made it more interesting than other schools to companies.

Teacher B had worked for several years as an occupational therapist and teacher in the Mental Health Centre but gave up his position to work as the metal mechanics co-ordinator in Pina Manique. However, in spite of this change in career, he still has a strong interest in psychology and psychoanalytic theory. Therefore in his new job he has chosen to maintain his links with the Centre and, along with other professionals, is involved in the referral of cases to the Centre, and also in receiving cases who have been referred to the school from it. In connection with this work, he has occasional meetings with the Centre 's psychiatrist to discuss individual cases.

Teacher B spends a sizeable portion of his time addressing pupil's emotional and behavioural problems, and the school has been very flexible in this respect. Significantly we saw no evidence of competitiveness or resentment from the social workers or psychologists; indeed, they seemed very happy to work side by side.

Clients at the field level

We interviewed two mothers who had children with learning difficulties in the school, one senior student who was evidently a model pupil, and a patron who had recently been a star student at the school but was now working temporarily as a teacher. His nickname was "Einstein".

Both parents appeared to be middle class although their occupations and those of their husbands were not known. The son of the first mother had come to school because he was academically weak and was struggling in his original school. His mother felt that in Pina Manique he could follow more practical courses and could successfully gain qualifications in vocational subjects. The daughter of the second mother had failed her exams twice in her old school and the mother had turned to Pina Manique for the special kind of education and support it could provide.

Prior to her son's arrival at the school, the first mother met with a school psychologist, a social worker and a teacher. However, since her son has been at the school, additional meetings have been unnecessary as her son has settled in well. In contrast, the daughter of the second mother had experienced some difficulties, and therefore the mother has been invited to meetings with both the class teacher and the psychologist to try to find a way to solve them. She emphasized that she was very appreciative of the opportunity to discuss her child's problems, and added that in her daughter's last school, internal professional help and advice had not been available. The patron and the senior student both said that they had never seen the school's psychologists and social workers simply because they had never needed to. Furthermore, they said that even when students do have problems they seldom choose to seek professional help. They often do not know where to go for assistance, and in addition think that psychologists and social workers are for "crazy people".

All of the informants agreed that aside from weekly family meetings with class teachers, meetings with the school's professionals only take place when there is a problem to be solved. A social worker (who was translating) explained this in terms of the limited number of professional staff in the school which means that their approach has to be one of treatment rather than prevention.

It was generally felt that the school had very good links with business. The second mother told us that her daughter was on a catering course run by Gertal, a local company, and that many of the students got jobs there afterwards. The student said that companies regularly approached the school, and was very positive about the prospects of finding employment. The patron reported that with the help of his teacher he had obtained a vacation job in electrical repairs. The teacher had asked him if he wanted work and then had talked with an employer who was also a friend. However, he said that normally it is up to students to approach their course co-ordinators if they are looking for work. Once asked, the co-ordinators make every effort to provide assistance; however, students who do not request help frequently do not get it.

All four interviewees believed that while school-business links were good, they could be improved. The patron suggested that the school should advertise itself to a greater extent as it is not well enough known in the business community. Both of the mothers believed that companies should be coming to the school to find employees rather than vice-versa. These views were clearly related to a shared perception of Pina Manique as a quality school which had something valuable to offer.

Operational level professionals external to the school

Two business managers

We spoke with two managers at Legrand, a French company which makes electrical components. They told us that the firm had developed contacts with Pina Manique following an invitation from the school to visit it. During their visit they had met the Principal, course co-ordinators and pupils and had been "amazed" by the courses and facilities which were available. Following this visit, the course co-ordinators made a return visit to Legrand, and eventually an agreement was signed committing both sides to a co-operative relationship.

Pina Manique was chosen by the company as a partner largely because they believed that its students were well prepared. However, the relationship was clearly strengthened by the fact that one of the managers was an ex-student of the school with a declared "affection" for it. In addition, the same manager had close personal relationships with the school's watch repair co-ordinator and another former co-ordinator; in other words, he had important informal links.

Despite the agreement, co-operation and contact between the company and the school are quite limited. This was blamed on current restructuring in the company which means that they are unable to provide student placements. The only evidence of co-operative action by the company was the donation of electrical appliances to the school free of charge and the recruitment of one or two Pina Manique students each year through the former co-ordinator. They also have a member of staff in their Technical Department who is responsible for liaising with technical and vocational schools and who as part of his responsibilities arranges a school challenge each year. However, his contact with Pina Manique appeared to be quite limited.

Pina Manique's mechanics co-ordinator, who was also present at the interview, made the point that in contrast with other companies, the school had no technical exchanges or consultations about course content with Legrand. The managers blamed this on lack of time. However, shortly afterwards they said that links with the school should be improved, and suggested that monthly or bi-monthly meetings and student visits to the company might help in this regard. We hoped that this proposal might be implemented in the aftermath of our visit.

Field level professionals external to the school

A psychiatrist

We were fortunate to have the opportunity to interview the psychiatrist with whom both the psychologist and Teacher B liaise.

We were informed that in the Mental Health Centre, the psychiatrist works in a multi-professional team, including psychologists, social workers, teachers and a nurse, which meets twice weekly to discuss follow-up treatments and new cases. The team works together very closely, and frequently several professionals will collaborate on one case. Children are normally referred to the Centre by their doctor, teacher, psychologist or family. Following the first interview, which always includes the psychiatrist, the child and his family, there is a general meeting where the team makes a joint decision on how the child's problems should be addressed. Collaboration, communication and harmony within the group is promoted by joint training once a week.

However, collaboration is not simply an internal feature of the Centre. The psychiatrist regularly visits Pina Manique's residential centre and discusses cases with the school's psychologists, social workers and teachers. The school's psychologist and Teacher B frequently visit him in the Centre as well. Contact between the two institutions is constant and there is a intermittent flow of cases in both directions.

Despite government legislation in 1992,* which integrated Juvenile and Youth Mental Health Centres into hospitals thereby inhibiting community work, the psychiatrist's philosophy was that it is essential to work with families and schools in order to prevent and treat children's mental problems. Therefore he makes special efforts to maintain and build community links. The psychiatrist felt that the main advantages of this approach were the opportunity to observe the functioning of the child in different contexts and to have the benefit of different professional viewpoints. Furthermore, he felt that by working with families and schools it was much easier to promote children's social integration. The persistence with which he maintained school and family links in the face of hostile government legislation (and limited financial and staff resources) was testimony to his belief in the importance of an integrated approach. In his view, working together posed few problems and was "a very positive experience".

Two social workers

We spoke to two social workers from the local social services. They informed us that they saw Casa Pia as a place to refer children in need of protection. They liaise with Casa Pia on a case by case basis, working most closely when a child is in residence. Occasionally, the institution's social educators and teachers contact the local services if a child or his parents complain about their treatment. Relations between Casa Pia and the local social services are professional and friendly, and there is little overlap in the services they provide.

---

* This legislation is laid down in Diario da Republica No. 190/91, II serie, 17 May 1992 and Diario da Republica No. 193, I serie A, Law edict 319/91, 23 August 1992.

While co-operation is good at the field level, it is based on informal relations. Casa Pia does not co-ordinate its activities with other agencies; nor do they with Casa Pia (or with each other for that matter). In other words, according to these informants, co-ordination of agency activities at the strategic level is limited.

A union representative

The union representative works with the Ministry of Employment and Social Security in overseeing the examination of students.

He said that the standard of training at Pina Manique is higher than average – to the extent that some workers see the school's students as a threat. In fact, he felt that the union's hostility towards the school was a factor in preventing it from becoming a true collaborative partner. The reason why the union is interested in maintaining contacts with the school is to protect professional standards and because students are highly skilled potential members.

Conclusion

What can we learn from these accounts of services provision in Pina Manique? In this respect, three sets of questions seem relevant. First, what practices exist in the school that involve or facilitate collaborative work? Second, what prevents professionals from collaborating with each other, and why is this? Third, what are the perceived benefits of an integrated approach and according to professionals what negative impacts does it have?

With respect to child welfare and health, many practices associated with a collaborative model of work are evident in Pina Manique. The social workers and psychologists work in the same corridor, hence providing many opportunities for (informal) discussion, in addition to the regular meetings they have together. Teachers are also involved to a large extent in discussions concerning their pupils, and are frequently offered strategies by the psychologists and social workers for addressing children's problems in the classroom. Furthermore, it is normal practice to involve both parents and their child in any decision-making regarding the child's welfare.

The school's professionals also co-operate with professionals from outside the school, including other Casa Pia employees and the professionals of the Mental Health Centre. Within the Mental Health Centre there exists a second group of collaborating partners which is linked to the group in Pina Manique by the psychologists and Teacher B. Collaboration within the Centre, which includes joint decision-making and training, was reported to be high.

Many of these examples of collaboration are commonly found in integrated services. However, two or three of them were felt to be "special". The first of these is the method of work adopted by the psychologist whereby she shares her expertise with class teachers by instructing them about appropriate strategies to address their pupils' problems. In this way she delegates aspects of her role, and is thus able to cope with a large clientele. However, perhaps more important, her approach has a large potential for prevention: with the appropriate knowledge, teachers can work toward solving problems amongst their pupils before they require additional professional attention. As the psychologist suggested, a method of further developing this model of work would be to offer teachers formal training in psychology and social welfare. Multi-skilling of this kind would enable teachers to play a variety of roles, thus enhancing and contributing to the work of professional specialists.

Also impressive at Pina Manique is the apparent flexibility of the school with respect to independent collaborative initiatives. This is exemplified in the freedom given to Teacher B to work closely on cases and projects with the Mental Health Centre. Grass roots initiatives which, as in Teacher B's case are often founded on informal ties, clearly have a place alongside top-down approaches to integrated services. We were also struck by the extent to which conviction in the viability of a collaborative approach can help sustain it. Despite legislation inhibiting community work, the Centre continues to find the resources to work closely with schools and families. This demonstrates that, with sufficient professional belief in collaboration, it is possible to overcome some of the obstacles which can act to prevent it.

Collaboration between Pina Manique and local businesses exists in a variety of forms. Perhaps, most important are the protocols or co-operation agreements between them which, amongst other things, give the school access to companies' technical expertise. However, the strength of the relationship signified by these agreements seems to be variable – certainly that with Legrand was quite limited in a practical sense. Also important are the courses in Pina Manique which are run by outside institutions, such as the German and Portuguese Chambers of Commerce and the food company Gertal. These bring outside expertise into the school, and since pupils are often employed by the companies afterwards, improve prospects for work.

In addition to running their own courses, companies also influence the content of courses organised by the school. Teacher A, for example, explained how Pina Manique responds to the needs of companies by changing and modernising course content, while at the same time companies adapted their placements to accommodate the school's requirements. Hence both sides are willing to listen to each other, and to meet each other's needs.

Particularly innovative at Pina Manique is the responsibility given to course co-ordinators to contact companies to arrange short-term placements and jobs for the school's students. This occurs through regularly liaisons with companies who have previously co-operated with the school and initiates links with new companies. The high rate of employment amongst leaving students is testimony to the benefits of this strategy.

However Pina Manique does not always have to take the initiative: the school is regularly contacted by companies who are seeking suitably trained job applicants. In this sense Pina Manique has a special status since other schools are seldom approached in this way. There appear to be several reasons for this. The school has a long tradition of vocational education and an unusually rich source of funding which allows it to buy high quality equipment for training. Both of these enhance its reputation. In addition, the school is persistent in updating courses and making them relevant to working life.

While collaboration between the school's professionals, and with outside business is strong, there are some aspects of a truly integrated approach which are less in evidence. In particular, there is little apparent vertical collaboration (except for that with the school's director). The professionals in Pina Manique told us that they are under-represented at a senior level and that their communication with the school's administrators is quite limited. Also little in evidence are links with outside agencies (other than informal ones with the Mental Health Centre and local social services). Certainly they were hardly ever mentioned as key partners. This may be because the school belongs to the larger institution of Casa Pia – hence its natural partners are other professionals in the institution rather than government agencies. Finally, treatment rather than prevention was the focus of most collaborative efforts. While the importance of prevention was acknowledged by the school's professionals, one of the social workers said that they felt that they were too small in number to do other than address existing problems.

Several perceived obstacles to integrated working practices were mentioned by the staff in Pina Manique. One of these was money. According to the Principal and Vice-Principal demands for payment from some businesses to examine courses had made co-operation problematic. Clearly, they felt that their co-operation was not something they could provide free of charge. Another perceived barrier to co-operation was a certain amount of envy. According to the Principal and Vice Principal, union officials' envy of new students' qualifications explained in part why they would not sign pupils' exam certificates. Time also emerged as a problem. Both the managers at Legrand and the psychologist said that lack of time prevented them from meeting with other professionals. However, the psychologist implied that the time once taken was well spent, and indeed saved time in the long run. Another perceived obstacle to collaboration was a lack of interest by the actors potentially involved. Teacher A, for example, explained that businesses seldom visit Pina Manique to give presentations because their managers are not sufficiently open in their outlook. The two parents, taking the view that the school had much to offer to companies, both suggested advertising as a means of tackling this problem. Finally, some of the government's legislation was seen as a barrier to integration. The psychiatrist mentioned that legislation passed in 1992 has inhibited community work, making it more difficult for professionals to work with children in their family and school contexts. However, he was hopeful that this would change.

In a slightly different vein, we also discovered obstacles which prevented children's access to professional care in the school. The patron and the student said that often children do not know who to go to for help, and frequently will not seek advice because of the stigma attached to it. The provision of information on sources of health and social care, and efforts to de-stigmatise professional support would help address these problems.

Whether or not professionals are motivated to overcome obstacles to collaboration will depend on its perceived advantages. The psychologist implied that collaboration was an important time-saving strategy. For example, she said that by working closely with the Mental Health Centre she was able to refer difficult cases which she would not have time to treat in school. She also regarded collaboration as valuable insofar as it allowed children's problems to be analysed and discussed from a variety of perspectives, a view shared by the psychiatrist in the Mental Health Centre. With respect to working in the local community, the psychiatrist saw two further advantages of collaboration. He felt that it provided the opportunity to observe children's social functioning in different contexts and that it was also important for devising successful strategies for social integration.

Few perceived disadvantages to integrated practices were mentioned. However, the psychologist found the amount of time required for meetings with other professionals problematic, and also felt that too much of a mix of professional viewpoints could be counter-productive. She also found on occasion that it was difficult to work with other professionals because they did not share her (psychological) perspective.

Overall, however, Pina Manique is a school which seems convinced that the benefits of collaboration outweigh its disadvantages, and this is demonstrated in many of its daily practices. Perhaps most impressive is its activity in reaching out to local businesses and in building relationships with them. As a result, close to 100 per cent of the students in the school – most of them at risk – are able to gain skilled employment when they have completed their education. This is an important step towards social integration and financial security in their adult life, and is a mechanism through which cycles of disadvantage can be broken.

GENERAL CONCLUSIONS

Portugal is a country which is undergoing structural change – a process which has accelerated since joining the EU in 1986. Education, as well as health and social services are expanding, with goals being the provision of 15 years of education for those able to benefit, and more complete health and social coverage. Many services are being privatised.

Families are changing even though the traditional "pater familias", in which children's rights can be overridden or contradicted, are still in existence.

Many children and families live in poverty. The government has recognised the importance of stimulating a holistic developmental approach if improvements in health, nutrition, education and general social circumstances are to take place.

This report has described some initiatives to co-ordinate services for children and their families across a wide age range. They are at different stages of development. For instance, the transition to work programme is well established, the street children programme is in an intermediate stage while the intercultural school programme is at the beginning. All of the programmes described in the earlier sections are used in drawing conclusions here. Since the issues identified in the report appear essentially the same, no matter what age level is described, the particular programmes are not named in this section.

Aims

The aims of co-operation were noted to be:

- to enhance the efficiency and utilisation of services to meet the needs of all clients; and

- to fully exploit resources *via* pooling and the effective management of equipment and personnel.

These aims have been derived from a recognition, by many of the public services concerned, that they alone cannot tackle effectively those problems they are responsible for solving.

In order to achieve these aims, certain necessary pre-conditions have been identified. There needs to be a clear political will and a co-ordinator to manage co-operation by promoting links between various players. This person must fight the tendency of hierarchies to nullify efforts and must take a lead in negotiating and mediating to ensure the integration of activities.

To co-ordinate the various players it is necessary to:

- empower front-line workers by giving them a broad range of skills;

- organise regular meetings for consultation to ensure that people are working together and using a cross-disciplinary approach;

- avoid traditional hierarchical lines in favour of functional relationships; and

- intervene at all levels concurrently to avoid over-burdening front-line workers, especially volunteers.

Advantages

Because sources of information can be unified, collaboration can lead to lower costs and better use of resources and give the public a fuller understanding of the services on offer. Collaboration also promotes a speedy and co-ordinated response to problems. Other advantages are listed below:

- More effective use of resources and an increase in financial flows.

- Increased participation of the local community as witnessed by the dynamism of the voluntary sector.

- Services become better adapted to needs and reach a fuller understanding of clients.

- Personal development of team members, with greater satisfaction related to more clearly identified outputs, compensating for fatigue in the struggle against poverty; and

- Benefits for staff resulting from more effective working practices and a sharper focus at the point of delivery because of frequent contact with clients on the ground. In addition pleasure and mutual enthusiasm are derived from a supportive team and framework which leads to growth, personal development and a sense that progress is being made.

Collaboration can also lead to skill development within schools which can be made available to parents and children. This comes from an approach which enables others to become more effective with the additional potential for developing a preventive role at the level of the classroom. "Multi-skilling" enables teachers to play a variety of roles, which enhance and contribute to the work of specialists. This process, of itself, can support and even encourage collaborative initiatives. Furthermore, it has the advantage of helping children overcome the stigmatising effect of being "treated" by professionals.

Negative outcomes

Some dangers of co-ordinated community action were reported which may expose certain minority groups to an intrusion from outside which could threatening their cultures.

Obstacles

A number of obstacles to success were identified and are listed below:

- A lack of political will and an appropriate management structure.
- Difficulties in collaboration between social service projects and education. These were less evident in the case of social services and health.
- Institutions were often seen as being encumbered by red-tape and rigid hierarchies. Both staff and structures were reported as being at fault, with breakdowns in communication, rigid application of rules and an unwillingness to change being common causes for complaint.
- Time was seen as a crucial factor at various levels.
- It takes five to six years for arrangements to become effective for services to match needs. At a strategic level, the process is very slow and there is little supportive legislation. In fact counter-productive legislation was identified.
- Time for consultation and planning had to be allowed for. Time is also needed for effective collaboration and meetings and there has to be a perceived advantage.
- Partners experienced problems in co-operating in programmes at an early stage of development. They did not always know what was expected of them. Some of the partners became defensive, possibly because of a lack of leadership.
- Services to support fundamental needs, such as nutrition, were seen to be lacking, as well as services to support extra-curricular activities.
- There is a need to change methods to work with clients on the streets. This caused particular difficulties for teachers whose working practices were not developed for this approach. However, success in using this method to overcome drug addiction was reported.
- Certain tensions were also apparent. Grassroots workers often felt unsupported by decision-makers in their difficult work.
- Concern was also expressed that the policy of privatising services at the point of delivery could undermine the dynamism and synergy that had developed.
- The SOS service found itself acting as an "ombudsman" between services and their users, while also helping to co-ordinate actions.

Evaluation

Evaluation was viewed as an important component of the developmental process, serving not only to justify methods but also acting as a useful formative training tool.

Training

Training was often identified as a key component of success. It was needed for multi-skilling of the various professionals involved as well as for creating understanding between them. Teachers for example need to adopt some of the aims and methods practised by social workers without, of course, forgetting that they are first and foremost teachers.

Training needs to be based on real problems and not theoretical abstractions. As noted above, it was especially effective when built into an evaluation exercise.

Training needs to go beyond the professionals directly involved and should also include managers, such as those in the "quartiers" who must liaise with Mayors.

External collaboration

Collaboration with other groups outside of the regular service system should be encouraged. For example one group found links with another country, where similar problems were being tackled, especially helpful.

In the transition to work period collaboration with businesses to exchange ideas, develop a greater understanding of each other's needs, and formulate new curricula and training methods, as well as the opportunity afforded for donations of expensive training equipment, were a clear advantage.

Closing comments

It is clear from the reports that changes are beginning to happen in certain places. Some ministries, in collaboration with workers from different disciplines, appear to be changing their working methods to meet client needs more appropriately. This development could well represent a first step towards institutionalisation of the process.

It is interesting to note that in the school situation, a multi-service model for children at risk was apparently effective in finding after school work for pupils. This method does, however, require a greater concentration of support staff in the school than is normal for Portugal.

If services are to co-operate with each other, staff must learn to be more open-minded and less defensive. They need to be sufficiently sure of their identity and professional skills to accept this change of attitude without being afraid that they will no longer command respect or appreciation. Training is obviously a key issue in the development of the required openness of mind.

It is the common recognition of problems that demand urgent attention that has led decision-makers and grassroots workers to change their practices, often as a result of the interventions of external agencies. It is important that all administrations and players are supported through these changes as they come to realise the significance of the problems they face and the corresponding need to change methods and to create more effective plans of action.

REFERENCES

CARDOSO, A. (1993), *A Outra Face da Cidade – Pobreza em Bairros Degradado,* CML, Lisbon.

EURYDICE and CEDEFOP (1991), *Structures of the Education and Initial Training Systems in the Member States of the European Community,* Commission of the European Communities, Brussels.

MINISTRY OF EDUCATION AND CULTURE PLANNING AND RESEARCH BUREAU (1987), *Comprehensive Law on the Education System: Law 46/86,* MECPRB, Portugal.

MINISTRY OF EDUCATION PLANNING AND RESEARCH BUREAU (1992), *Portuguese Education System: Current Situation and Trends 1990,* MEPRB, Lisbon.

OECD (1995), *Our Children at Risk,* Paris.

RAMIREZ, M.E. et al. (1988), *Criança Portuguesa: que Acolhimento?,* Rede da Comissão Europeia de Acolhimento de Crianças/Instituto de Apoio à Criança, Lisbon.

SILVA, M. (1989), *A Pobreza Infantil em Portugal,* UNICEF, Lisbon.

VASCONCELOS, L. (1993), "Pobreza em Portugal – variação de medidas de pobreza a partir de orçamentos familiares de 1980/81 e 1989/90", Working papers, CISEP, No. 2.

6

THE UNITED STATES

The following case studies describe examples of best practice in integrated services in Missouri, New York City and California. The focus is on programmes for children at risk which are being implemented at the local level.

The United States is interesting because the federal government, state government and community organisations all are active in the development of integrated programmes. Since the American case studies consider integrated services within different states and municipalities, the over-arching role of the federal government receives less attention. This is addressed separately in *Successful Services for our Children and Families at Risk* (OECD, 1996). However, a brief description of federal policies promoting integrated services for children at risk will be provided here to set state and local initiatives in the broader national context.

The federal government has been implementing policies which directly or indirectly promote services integration for over 30 years. In the last few years, several major programmes have been introduced which encourage integration in the (increasingly autonomous) American states. The Empowerment Zone and Enterprise Community Programme, for example, was introduced in 1993 to revitalise communities by creating jobs. To qualify for programme funding, communities must submit a plan to improve local social and economic conditions which involves a wide array of agencies and individuals, including state and local governments, business and financial institutions, neighbourhood groups and residents. Money allocated to selected Empowerment Zones and Enterprise Communities (around $1 million in total) may be spent on the prevention and treatment of drug and alcohol abuse, training and employment for adults, schemes to promote home ownership, and non-school services provided by community-based organisations.

Also in 1993, the federal government introduced the Family Preservation and Family Support Legislation with the goal of inciting and enabling states to create, expand or operate services that encourage and assist families at risk or in crisis to stay together. A package worth $900 million over five years has been offered. However, the Department of Health and Human Services has promised to provide additional discretionary funding to states and communities which include services for maternity, child and mental health in their planning for family support and preservation, thus promoting services integration.

In 1994, Goals 2000 legislation was enacted, setting out for the first time voluntary national standards for curriculum content and educational performance. Goals 2000 has promoted integration through the requirement that State School Improvement Plans must be developed, and that these must be formulated by a broad-based panel, including the Governor and chief state school officer, education personnel at all levels, parents and community representatives, and state and local officials responsible for health, social and other services. In addition, the Improvement Plans must describe mechanisms for co-ordinating school reform with school-to-work and vocational programmes as well as strategies to increase community involvement.

Finally, the School-to-Work Act, enacted in 1994 and administered jointly by the departments of Education and Labour, aims to promote partnerships between schools, employers and other institutions to facilitate the transition to work. At the state level, the Governor, the chief state school officer, and state agency officials responsible for job training, employment, economic development, post-secondary education and other relevant areas, are required to collaborate in the planning and development of a school-to-work system.

In the case studies which follow some aspects of federal legislation (including the above) will be referred to, although all references will be planted firmly in the context of state or municipal activities.

MISSOURI

INTEGRATING SERVICES THROUGH PUBLIC-PRIVATE SECTOR PARTNERSHIP

by

Philippa Hurrell and Richard Volpe

INTRODUCTION

The United States is a liberal democracy with a popular ideology dominated by notions of limited government regulation, individual freedom and self-sufficiency. This particular brand of liberalism has impacted profoundly on the character of American institutions, and has played an important role in defining American human services provision. More specifically, it has led to services characterised by low federal and state government involvement and significant participation by private sector agencies. American liberal individualism has also created a society in which opportunity and "success" exist alongside alienation and "failure". Under these conditions, as in the rest of the world, there is a considerable and growing gap between the rich and the poor. In 1990, over 20 per cent of all American children were living in poverty. Today, a very large number of these children continue to live in "risk" situations, threatened by problems ranging from under-nutrition to gang violence and drug abuse.

It is within this context that the present report will discuss government and local initiatives in the state of Missouri to provide "integrated" education, health and social services for children and youth at risk and their families. Integration is seen by many OECD countries as the most effective strategy to meet children's needs, while at the same time reducing costs. Key objectives in the report will be to explore how examples of best practice in integrated services operate, what kind of barriers exist to effective collaboration, and how efforts to integrate services are translated into outcomes. Its focus will be on state level initiatives and local programmes in which collaboration with other agencies, businesses or the community is an important feature.

STATE INITIATIVES

At the forefront of Missouri's efforts to promote services integration is the Family Investment Trust which is the main conduit for system reform.

Created by the Governor's Executive Order in 1993, the Family Investment Trust is a public-private partnership of state officials and private sector leaders charged with establishing community-based human services systems that achieve positive measurable results for Missouri families and children. The Governor established the trust outside of the state government to ensure that it would withstand changes of political leadership. Members of the trust board include four top state officials – the directors of the departments of Elementary and Secondary Education, Health, Mental Health and Social Services – as well as a group of business and civic leaders. By involving important state officials, the trust hopes to facilitate cross-agency service delivery as well as financing strategies that meet community needs.

The mission of the trust is to work towards three types of change:

– change in the way agencies respond to families by promoting the use of family-focused and preventive services;

– change in the way decisions are made by promoting a participatory decision-making process at the local involving collaboration between the public and private sectors;

– change in the way money is spent by promoting the use of "flexible dollars" to improve family outcomes reducing the red-tape linked to government funding.

The trust is currently developing a strategic plan for its operations across the state, and an implementation plan for the federal Family Preservation and Family Support legislation. A key goal is to establish a policy framework that will improve outcomes for families, identify and promote collaborative operating strategies, and develop capacity at the community level.

Four foundations have contributed nearly $1 million over two years to launch the trust. Although a state level entity, the trust will work through community-based planning and decision-making bodies.

The Family Investment Trust is one of the main catalysts of change at the state level. However, dynamic action to improve human services in Missouri also exists at the municipal and local levels. Kansas City is perhaps the most important example of municipal level activity. Over the last five years it has been pushing hard, through various initiatives, towards its stated goal of "reinventing government".

MUNICIPAL INITIATIVES: KANSAS CITY

LINC

In Kansas City, the main engine for human services reform is the Local Investment Commission (LINC). This is a collaborative group of business and civic leaders, social service professionals, service participants and private citizens which has been charged by the Missouri Department of Social Services to oversee the reform of the city's social services system. Appointed in November 1992, the Commission (or governing committee) is composed of 23 lay persons from diverse backgrounds. It is supported by a 15 member professional Cabinet which provides technical expertise in all aspects of the services system. The Commission has established seven working committees which have been given the responsibility to plan reform in the areas of Children and Families, Health Care, Welfare Reform, School-linked Services, Housing and Safety, Business and Economic Development, and Ageing.

LINC's vision is to create a community that provides meaningful opportunities for children and families to achieve self-sufficiency, attain their potential, and contribute to the public good. LINC regards its role as to provide leadership, and to engage the Kansas City community in creating the "best system" to support children and families, "holding the system accountable", and "changing public attitudes to the system" (Missouri Department of Social Services, 1994a, p. 1). It believes that a desirable system is one that is both integrated and locally governed. The system that LINC envisages for Kansas City includes the following:

– a wide array of accessible preventive, remedial and support services which are delivered under a administrative structure with a common case management and eligibility system;

– methods to ensure that appropriate services are received and adjusted to meet the changing needs of and families;

– a focus on whole families as participants, resources and allies of the system;

– efforts to empower families within an atmosphere of mutual respect;

– an emphasis on the needs of participants, community values and achieving measurable improvements in for children and families; and

– flexible funding mechanisms that enable resources to be used to meet the needs of participants.

LINC has been given the authority to work towards these goals by the Director of the Missouri Department of Social Services, Scott Best (pseudonym), who has made the Commission an "agent of the state". To achieve its objectives, LINC primarily uses a collaborative strategy in which community partners are brought together to establish common goals, jointly plan and implement services, evaluate new services and procedures, pool resources to support innovation and address joint problems, and delegate individual responsibility for the outcomes of their joint efforts.

The Commission has established broad principles to guide the work of its committees. These bodies are charged with developing specific recommendations for service delivery reform. The present objectives of the committees are as follows:

- *Children and families*: To develop a professional, integrated, and effectively delivered child welfare system through effective local leadership, addressing resource issues, and establishing an effective structure for services delivery.

- *Health care*: To complete an assessment of the current health care delivery system in order to identify unserved populations and barriers to service delivery, and to design an effective system of health care delivery for the poor and "near poor" populations.

- *Welfare reform*: To develop a model for self-sufficiency which can be expanded, to work towards taking the proven successes of FUTURES and FUTURES CONNECTION to scale, and to maximise opportunities presented by the 21st Century Communities initiative (see below for a description of the FUTURES and 21st Century Communities Programmes).

- *School-linked social services*: To complete an assessment of needs to form a basis for the design of social and medical services which can be delivered to children and families in an efficient and accessible manner through the existing school system.

- *Housing and safety*: To develop strategies for increasing the supply of liveable, affordable, and safe housing; to improve the safety and security of neighbourhoods; and to support the development of the housing component of the 21st Century Communities initiative.

- *Business and economic development*: To identify businesses willing to create jobs and to develop career opportunities within 21st Century neighbourhoods.

- *Ageing*: To develop a system to support old people in the community and, when necessary, to provide quality care in nursing homes; and to support families and neighbourhoods in providing a caring and safe environment for the elderly.

While collaboration is a defining feature of LINC, charismatic leadership played an important role in its creation, and continues to be significant for its success. The two key figures in the development of LINC have been the Director of Social Services, Scott Best, and a prominent Kansas City businessman, Harry Hamilton (pseudonym). Harry Hamilton came up with the LINC concept, Scott Best gave it an official mandate to initiate reform, and both men have actively supported and promoted it. They have been the real driving forces behind LINC, without whom radical reform may not have been initiated in Kansas City. Both have wielded their considerable powers to initiate change for the better.

The rhetoric which has partnered the development of LINC has been dramatic and exciting. The literature on LINC refers to "a quiet but startling revolution in the administration of social services", "a ground-breaking recognition that the capacity to solve the problems of a major city may lie in the city itself", and "a new era in which government resources are a catalyst for fundamental, forward-looking change" (Missouri Department of Social Services, 1994*b*, p. 1). This dynamic outlook has succeeded in energising and motivating social services administrators, service providers and the community itself.

21st Century Communities

One of LINC's key responsibilities is to manage the 21st Century Communities initiative, which is a ten-year comprehensive approach to the development of low-income, urban communities. A planning group composed of representatives from three LINC committees (Welfare Reform, Housing and Safety, and Business and Economic Development) has been given the task of developing the programme.

Kansas City is the first pilot site for the initiative. It will be implemented through partnerships with government, the private sector, and local community organisations. Programmes with a proven track record, such as Head Start, FUTURES and FUTURES CONNECTION, and child support enforcement, will be brought together in new initiatives in the areas of job creation, wage supplementation, work skills, learning readiness for children, and family and neighbourhood support.

In order to implement the 21st Century Community initiative, a special application for a federal waiver was submitted to the Department of Health and Human Services. The waiver request was made in order to:

- allow Aid to Families with Dependent Children (AFDC) grants to be used to supplement wages for up four years;
- allow participants receiving wage supplements to accumulate assets of up to $10 000 during the four year for certain uses, such as college education or to start a business;
- allow participants receiving wage supplements to remain eligible for non-wage benefits, such as Medicaid and child care, for up to four years. (This was seen as important for individuals in jobs not providing cover.); and
- allow parents to receive child support payments and get maximum support benefits while they are in supplemented employment.

The granting of this special waiver by the federal government has been vital to the goal of rejuvenating economically disadvantaged communities. It is significant that the waiver was won through the (necessarily) determined efforts of the Director of Social Services, Scott Best.

The proposed activities of the initiative relate to the following broad areas.

- *Job creation*: The initiative aims to create new jobs by recruiting businesses – that might otherwise have gone abroad – to establish community-based enterprises. An attraction will be a wage supplementation scheme whereby employers receive a cash welfare grant to supplement the wage "they would pay overseas" to provide an acceptable salary for employees. Employees benefit by continuing to receive government health and child care benefits which are normally lost on taking up employment. To counteract potential exploitation by employers of state subsidised wages, wage supplemented employment will be tied to guarantees of non-subsidised jobs that pay adequate incomes. In this respect, it needs to be emphasised that, because minimum wages are so low in the United States, many people who have full-time jobs live in poverty. The initiative also aims to provide entrepreneurial training and business management mentoring to community people to encourage and support them in setting up their own businesses.
- *Skills training*: The initiative aims to provide education and work skills training as a preparation for employment. These activities will be co-ordinated with existing programmes such as those offered by FUTURES and through the Job Training Partnership Act.
- *Education*: The initiative will establish a comprehensive strategy to ensure that all children are ready to learn when they enter school. This will be achieved by focusing on preventable causes of diminished learning capacity – such as low birth weight, prenatal exposure to drugs or alcohol, and inadequate nutrition – and on preventive health screenings and immunisations. The initiative will also ensure that comprehensive case management is available to secure the provision of a range of services for families with multiple needs. Furthermore it will determine that local schools, Head Start Programmes, and the Parents as Teachers initiative, form an integrated network to provide comprehensive child development services for preschool and school children.

A strong evaluation component will be built into the 21st Century Communities Programme to ascertain the magnitude of its effect. An independent third party will assess its impact on residents, businesses, and the community infrastructure, and will conduct a cost-benefit analysis from the perspective of the participant, community, government and taxpayer. This evaluation will be longitudinal.

Kansas City FUTURES Advisory Committee

Efforts to "reinvent" government in Kansas City began, in fact, as far back as July 1989 when a group of concerned citizens and local agency representatives, under the auspices of the Heart of America United Way, developed recommendations for the implementation of the welfare reform provisions of the Family Support Act of 1988. A couple of years later, in January 1991, the Missouri Department of

Social Services vested ownership of reform in the Kansas City FUTURES Advisory Committee. This committee was asked to design and oversee the implementation of the federal Job Opportunities and Basic Skills (JOBS) training programme – which was established by the Family Support Act – in the three counties surrounding Kansas City. Effectively, FUTURES is Missouri's JOBS initiative, its basic aim being to help individuals to achieve economic self-sufficiency.

Significantly, it was the success of the FUTURES Advisory Committee which led the Director of the Department of Social Services, Scott Best, to believe that a larger organisation committed to public and private sector collaboration could work. Hence the creation of LINC which embodies many of the Advisory Committee's principles and working methods. Once LINC was created, the role of the Advisory Committee was expanded into LINC's Welfare Reform Committee (which also works on 21st Century Communities). LINC is, in effect, the fully grown "baby" which has grown from the "embryo" of the FUTURES Advisory Committee.

The exclusive clients of the FUTURES Programme are adult members of families who receive Aid to Families with Dependent Children (AFDC). The programme provides education and job training to help its clients to prepare for employment. This is achieved through the co-ordination of various state agencies – representing social welfare, elementary and secondary education, labour and industrial relations, economic development, and mental health – who administer the different programme components. Typical opportunities on offer include Adult Basic Education, English as a Second Language, Post-Secondary Education, Job Skill Training, Job Readiness Training, Job Search Assistance, On-the-Job Training, Community Work Experience, and Alternative Work Experience. To remove barriers which prevent programme involvement, participants are eligible to receive basic assistance, including child care, transportation, training related expenses and Medicaid.

Kansas City's FUTURES Programme is one of many JOBS initiatives which have been implemented throughout the United States. However, it has its own special character, and indeed describes itself as a "departure from the way state government has run federally mandated human service programmes". The distinguishing features of the programme are set out below.

Community involvement: Unlike many other FUTURES Programmes, the programme is committed to local community and private sector involvement. It is "locally driven" and has been characterised as "a grassroots response to government and a government response to grassroots" (Missouri Department of Social Services, 1994c, p. 1). In other words, it represents community commitment to the government's goals, and the government's willingness to delegate power to the community. The programme was designed by six sub-committees. These were chaired by Advisory Committee members but also included representatives from the public and private sectors who could provide special expertise.

Approach to services provision: The programme implements special principles in the provision of its social services. These values have been communicated to the Division of Family Services (Department of Social Services) staff who operate the programme, and who are an important state partner in providing services. Case managers are referred to as "advocates" and recipients of services as "participants". This makes the language of welfare provision less pejorative and more acceptable, in a national climate where welfare support is regarded negatively. The programme also uses a special case management system, devised by the University of Kansas, which is referred to as the "strengths Model". This focuses on the strengths and goals of participants in all areas of their lives. Services are provided in local, user-friendly settings which are accessible to participants. This removes the need for visits to distant (and often intimidating) bureaucrats' offices.

Collaboration: The Kansas City's FUTURES Programme emphasises collaboration with public and private sector partners. Special partnerships have been established with the Full Employment Council, Adult Basic Education (in four districts), Employment Security, the Career Exploration and Assessment Centre (Penn Valley Community College), and the Women's Employment Network. These agencies, through their participation in a special sub-committee, were involved in the original design of the programme, and continue to be involved in its ongoing enhancement. The programme tries to use their services rather than to duplicate them, and to fill any gaps in their provision. A typical example, is the augmentation of Adult Basic Education classes with workshops on parenting, life skills, career exploration and consumer education.

Private sector involvement: The private sector is well represented on the Advisory Committee and its subcommittees. Additional private sector involvement was encouraged, and indeed necessitated, by a decision by the Missouri General Assembly to contract out new services rather than to expand existing ones. As a result, the Advisory Committee issued Requests for Proposals and awarded contracts to run "complete FUTURES Programmes" to five private agencies. This was done in order to try out the "privatisation" of a state programme. Payment to these agencies is based on outcomes, and their performance will be compared to the state administered programme.

Outcome driven and accountable: In addition to outcome measures mandated by the federal government, including participation rates and types of person served, Kansas City has set additional measures of its own. These include levels of educational achievement, rates of training completion, rates of pay for those gaining employment, and job retention levels. In 1994, the government of Missouri commissioned a statistical analysis of the outcomes for FUTURES participants (Missouri Department of Social Services, 1994*d*). This research found that participation in the FUTURES Programme increased individual's chances of coming off AFDC and remaining of it for at least twelve months. The Advisory Committee has also commissioned a process evaluation to determine how the programme can be improved.

The widely perceived success of Kansas City's approach to its FUTURES Programme is reflected in the replication of many of its innovations throughout the state. This is indicative of the state government's willingness to utilise lessons learnt at the local level, and to implant "good ideas" elsewhere.

The Partnership for Children

In contrast to LINC, 21st Century Communities and FUTURES, which are in essence public sector initiatives with heavy private sector involvement, the Partnership for Children is first and foremost a private sector initiative. Developed by the Heart of America United Way and the Greater Kansas City Community Foundation, this ten-year programme, set up in 1991, aims "to improve conditions for children by mobilising powerful new voices in the community to work on their behalf" (Partnership for Children, 1993, p. 1). The Steering Committee for the Partnership for Children is drawn from the boards of directors of its two parent organisations, as well as community representatives.

Each year, in order to stimulate community action, the Partnership produces a Report Card on the status of children in Greater Kansas City. In 1993-94, the Report Card gave Kansas a grade of D+ ("seriously deficient") – the same as in 1992. However, it was also able to report powerful community action in response to the 1992 Report Card, bringing about improvements in certain key areas such as immunisation, child care and child poverty.

One of the most important products of the yearly Report Cards is the summary table of Greater Kansas City's performance in each of four benchmark areas: safety and security, health, education, and teen years. In addition to providing the 1992 and 1993-94 grades in each of these areas, it looks at trends over the last five years, performance compared to the national average, and achievement in relation to Year 2000 goals (when available). Table 1 provides "at a glance" information, and as such is well designed for its intended purpose: "to educate fellow citizens about the needs of children".

By collecting this kind of detailed data on the children of Greater Kansas City, the Partnership for Children has succeeded in leveraging a significant amount of community support. It is important to emphasise that this task has been made easier by the strong and rather striking sense of community and public responsibility which exists in Kansas City, in spite of its urban nature.

Table 1. **Greater Kansas City Children's benchmark chart
(Partnership for Children, 1993, p. 12)**

Category	Five-year trend	National average	Percentage of Year 2000 goal
Safety and security			
Violent crime	Worsening	Worse	N/A
Child abuse and neglect	Incomplete	Worse	N/A
Aid to families with dependent children	Incomplete	N/A	N/A
Health			
Early prenatal care	Improving	Better	Within 10 per cent
Low birth weight	Stabilising	Worse	Within 25-49 per cent
Infant mortality	Improving	Better	Within 25-49 per cent
Immunisations	Incomplete	Worse	Within 50-74 per cent
Women, infants and children programme	Incomplete	N/A	N/A
Education			
School readiness	Incomplete	N/A	Incomplete
Achievement scores	Improving	Better	N/A
High school completion	Worsening	Better	Within 11-24 per cent
Post-graduate success	Incomplete	N/A	N/A
Teen years			
Teen births	Worsening	Worse	Within 25-49 per cent
Alcohol and other drug use	Improving	Worse	More than 74 per cent
Teen homicides	Worsening	N/A	N/A

Note: N/A = data not available for the United States or Year 2000 goal.
Incomplete = data not available for metropolitan area.

MUNICIPAL INITIATIVES: ST LOUIS

Municipal level efforts to integrate human services are far less well developed in St Louis than in Kansas City. Indeed, none were brought to our attention. One informant put this down to the more conservative nature of St Louis, and the weaker interest amongst its business people in public sector social services involvement.

The administration of integrated services

In order to explore the nature of strategic processes in Missouri, the case study focused on LINC, which is the dominant force behind the organisation of human services in Kansas City. It is also perhaps the best example in Missouri of public and private sector collaboration to meet the needs of children and families at risk. While the broad structure and goals of LINC were outlined earlier, the following provides more detail, particularly in relation to the processes which have allowed LINC to function successfully.

The establishment of LINC

LINC was established through the collaboration of two important community leaders: Scott Best from the public sector, and Harry Hamilton from the business world. During the initial stages both men pushed hard to promote the concept of LINC and to win private sector participation.

Scott Best came from the perspective that public social services should play a central role in co-ordinating, and also financially supporting, private social services. He also took the view that the community had a role to play in strategic level decision-making. These beliefs underpinned his commitment to collaboration between the public and private sectors. In trying to establish LINC, he placed considerable emphasis on business involvement, believing that if he initially won companies' time and support "money would follow". As a means to this end, he rang businesses "cold" and was met with a general willingness to co-operate. A major coup was to persuade the owners of a powerful local company to be involved. They were regarded as "having clout with the elite" and as "providing good leadership". The process of establishing LINC was not easy. To achieve his goals Scott had to be very political, able to take "lots of bruises", and willing to accept the legal consequences of actions he believed in. He also encouraged others to share his commitment, with convincing rhetorical statements and descriptions of his perception of what LINC should be. One informant, for example, reported that Scott had urged that "our challenge is to be bold enough; our challenge is to take risks". The same informant, referring to Scott's leadership skills, commented that he was "good at tossing people together", "did the vision thing very well", and "is where the puck will be".

Harry Hamilton, a septuagenarian, is chairman of his own company. He had the original vision of community involvement in the organisation of social services and, like Scott, played a strong leadership role in the development of LINC. To attract business involvement, he was able to take advantage of the fact that he was well established and respected in the community, and had helped a few people out; hence he was able to "call the chits in" (ask for favours to be returned). He approached companies by giving presentations on LINC. As a result, several business people now serve on agency boards and are very committed to their work. Harry views their involvement as true altruism: "they don't think about what's in it for them, but what's in it for the community". He also sees this kind of commitment in ethical terms: "you need to be a step above" and "to do what is morally right".

One of Harry's main concerns was to build good relations with other agencies; he did not want LINC to be seen as an unwelcome "new kid on the block". Therefore he also gave presentations to various agencies – including the powerful United Way Organisation – emphasising that LINC was interested in collaborating with them, would not set up new agencies, and should not be seen as a competitor. As a result LINC was almost immediately accepted, but as Harry said, this was because he had done his "homework". He also approached community groups to encourage their involvement in LINC. A typical example is Kansas City's Hispanic community which was at first rather surprised to be approached by him. Significantly one member said "after all these years of not talking, why are you talking now?" Harry managed to overcome this initial scepticism, and the Hispanic community is now represented on the Commission.

Resources

LINC oversees a budget including both federal and state moneys of $273 million. This money comes from many different sources with different spending requirements attached. However, LINC has been pushing for increased flexibility in the way it can allocate funding, which should be reflected in the 1995 budget. LINC's considerable financial resources are supplemented by the voluntary involvement of many community people on its committees.

LINC structure and processes

LINC's organisational structure is informally referred to as the "Centipede". The Commission, which sits at the top of the hierarchy, is made up of various community representatives. Intentionally, none of the Commissioners are political figures. This prevents disruption connected with changes in political power, and decision-making based on the needs of particular constituencies. Working closely with the Commission is a Cabinet of professional experts who are regularly consulted. As one informant put it, "to some degree lay people don't really understand how the system works"; as a result they need expert advice to guide their decisions. However, maintaining the Commission as a strictly non-professional group is regarded as essential since it avoids the rivalry that is associated with vested professional interests.

Work in specific areas is divided among seven main committees. From the start, these were given complete freedom to "do something different", and as quickly as they liked. While this amount of liberty required some "difficult mental adjustment", a few of the committees "took off like lightening" and others have made significant progress.

Factors facilitating collaboration

Collaboration has been facilitated by the fact that many social services staff in LINC have worked together for 15 or 20 years. While Kansas City is very much an urban centre, job mobility in many sectors is comparatively low. The result in social services is that professional relations approach those of an extended family.

Outcomes

According to Harry Hamilton, the achievements of LINC have been significant: social services staff have "spread their wings", "the shackles have been taken off", and "they have been released". The political aspects of services organisation have been removed, and "true community governance" has taken hold. Other states are taking a strong interest in the LINC approach, and it is due to be replicated in Kansas City, Kansas in the near future.

To date, no formal outcome measures to assess the achievements of LINC have been developed, although a need in this area is recognised. On the basis of informal conversations it was clear, however, that LINC had succeeded in motivating and enthusing the management of state social services.

INTEGRATED SERVICES FOR PRESCHOOL CHILDREN

New Start (Kansas City)

The background

New Start was developed by the Child Development Corporation (KCMC) which is the Head Start grantee in Kansas City. In contrast to normal Head Start Programmes which provide half-day services, New Start offers all-day, year-round child care. In partnership with other agencies, such as FUTURES and the Full Employment Council, it also provides educational and employment services for parents. Low income families who are working, in education, or in a job training programme, are eligible for this programme. Its main aim is to help families to achieve self-sufficiency through adequate employment.

Funding sources

Initial funding for New Start came from a variety of federal, state and private sources, including the United States Office of Human Development Services, the Missouri Department of Social Services, KCMC, the Greater Kansas City Community Foundation, and the Hall Family Foundation. Private funding was used to train staff, hire a family advocate to help families, and upgrade a children's learning centre with state of the art equipment. On-going funding is provided by Head Start, the Department of Social Services and parents.

The process of service delivery

One of the organisations providing New Start services is the Goppert Child Development Centre in Kansas City. This centre provides high quality child care and education to children between the hours of 06.30 and 18.00 (although children can only be left at the centre for a maximum of ten hours a day). Breakfast, lunch and afternoon snacks are provided to all children free of charge. Extensive health, dental and mental health services – including health screenings, immunisations and special services – are also available. The educational curriculum includes visits to museums, theatres and zoos. Parents are encouraged to be involved in the programme's educational activities as much as possible. They are also invited to provide input into programme planning through monthly parents' meetings. A family advocate, with a social work background, is available to help families with practical problems and, where necessary, to direct them to appropriate services. The advocate also has a small budget to buy minor items which can improve families situations; for example, an alarm clock so that a parent can get to work on time, or some laundry soap so that a mother can wash her child's school clothes.

Goppert has 100 New Start places to offer to disadvantaged children. For those who have taken up places, the centre is required to meet or exceed an attendance rate of 85 per cent. One informant reported that, to date, attendance has been very good and that the programme has been popular with parents who frequently provide voluntary help.

Adult education, organised by the federally funded FUTURES Programme, is available for those parents claiming ADFC (welfare). Most work through self-study, guided by an adult education teacher, towards their GED (General Educational Development, the equivalent of a high school diploma). Parents who study for more than 20 hours a week are entitled to a weekly payment of $25. On average 15 or 16 parents attend the programme each day, or whom around nine or ten have children attending New Start. Many of these parents provide occasional help to the staff who care for their children downstairs.

FUTURES also collaborates with the Full Employment Council to provide parents with relevant job training and employment counselling. Each parent is provided with a FUTURES advocate who meets with them weekly to discuss problems and to provide advice. Like the New Start family advocate, the FUTURES advocates have social work backgrounds. They also have training in the "Strengths Model" referred to earlier.

Like the New Start Programme, FUTURES is extremely popular, with many parents on its waiting list. Collaboration between New Start and FUTURES means that parents are free to study, and to achieve their GED, while their children are occupied elsewhere. The testimonies of two FUTURES participants, reproduced below, highlight the advantages, and also the disadvantages, of participating in this joint venture.

Anita and Thomas (pseudonyms): Anita, 24, is a single black mother with three children aged 16 months, 4 years and 5 years. Thomas, the 4-year-old, attends New Start, the eldest child lives in another district, and the youngest is cared for by a grandmother. Anita failed to get her GED after dropping out of school at 15, and is unemployed. With the help of FUTURES, she is trying to get her GED so that she is better qualified to find work. She is very uncomfortable with the fact that she is on welfare and wants to get off it as quickly as she can. Her son, Thomas, has speech difficulties which require treatment.

Anita now regularly attends the FUTURES Programme. She also contributes to the New Start Programme through attendance at parent meetings and helping out with educational trips. Through New Start, Thomas is receiving treatment from a speech pathologist.

Anita is very positive about the joint arrangement whereby she is able to learn in one part of the building while Thomas is being cared for in another. She finds it very convenient, although she believes that it could be improved by providing child care for infants like her youngest child who has to be looked after elsewhere. Her advocate has helped her considerably, particularly in planning the future and in helping her to regain her self-esteem. Thomas is also very happy at the centre.

Carla and Naomi (pseudonyms): Carla, 25, is also a single, black mother with three children who are aged 2, 3 and 7. The 3-year-old, Naomi, attends New Start. Carla left school at 18 due to pregnancy, has no GED, and is currently unemployed. However, through FUTURES she wants to try to get her GED so that she can train as a nurse.

Unlike Anita, Carla seldom sees her advocate and has received very little advice. However, she appreciates the child care, and feels that her daughter is happy and has benefited. She is less satisfied with her GED course which she feels is too long.

Programme assessment

An evaluation of the first three years of the New Start Programme, completed in 1993, found "compelling evidence of New Start's impact as a provider of high quality developmentally appropriate child care designed to prepare children for school while offering comprehensive services to support families". The evaluation discovered that, because of the full-time day care provided by the pro-gramme, parents experienced increased job productivity, could work longer hours, and took home higher incomes.

Parents as Teachers (St Louis)

Background

Parents as Teachers (PAT) is a "home-school-community partnership" which is designed to provide expectant parents, as well as parents whose children are aged 5 or younger, with the information and support they need to give their children the best possible start in life (Parents as Teachers National Centre, 1993a, p. 2). The programme, which originated in Missouri in 1981, is based on the belief that a child's early years are critical in laying the foundations for educational success, and that parents, as children's first teachers, can play a vital role in their development. It is often a component of larger preschool programmes, such as Head Start, or part of a broader array of family support services.

The programme relies on voluntary participation, and is available to parents from all social groups. This is, in part, to avoid the stigma which is often attached to services which are targeted at a particular sector of the population. A recent survey showed that of all PAT participants, 36 per cent were families with limited incomes, and 14 per cent were teenage parents (Parents as Teachers National Centre, 1993b).

The main goals of Parents as Teachers are to empower parents to educate their children so that they can be successful in school, to increase parents' sense of confidence in what they can do for their child, and to improve parent-child interactions and family relationships. The programme operates state-wide in Missouri although its national centre is in St Louis.

Funding and training

Funding for Parents as Teachers comes from a very wide array of sources, including federal and state governments, foundations and business. Funders include:

- *The Danforth Foundation*: This has funded Ready to Learn collaboration grants for eleven PAT Programmes. The funding is used for projects which address inter-disciplinary collaboration and effective programming.

- *The Nancy Reagan Foundation*: This has provided a grant to revise, field test and distribute a guide entitled "Teen Parent Supplement of the Parents as Teachers Programme Planning and Implementation Guide".

- *The Missouri Department of Education*: This has allocated federal funds for the prevention of drug-related problems to a training scheme which helps parent educators to understand the needs of families affected by substance abuse.

- *The Missouri Department of Social Services*: This has provided a block grant for in-service training of child care providers in Hollister, Missouri by the PAT National Centre.

- *The Unites States Department of Education (National Diffusion Network)*: This has provided federal money for the development of a system to gather data from PAT "adoption sites" on programme quality.

- *The federal government*: This provides grants for family support under Family Preservation and Family Support Legislation. These grants are administered by state child welfare agencies, but provide PAT with the opportunity for collaboration in providing family support services. Federal funding is also available under the Goals 2000 Act.

The main organ for training, research and curriculum development is the Parents as Teachers National Centre in St Louis, Missouri. The centre is responsible, amongst other things, for certification of parent educators, technical assistance, national conferences, curriculum and materials development, and adaptation to other agencies and states. Training is provided at Parents as Teachers Institutes throughout the United States and abroad, and is underpinned by a 600-page PAT Programme Planning and Implementation Guide. This includes information on a broad spectrum of topics including programme organisation, home visit plans, group meeting plans, parent educator resources, suggested programme record keeping and evaluation forms, and parent handouts. Special training is provided for parent educators working with adolescent parents and other high needs groups.

How the programme operates

The four components of the Parents as Teachers Programme are personal visits, group meetings, developmental screenings and a resource network.

Parent educators, who are specially trained by PAT in child development and home visiting skills, meet on a regular basis with parent and child, normally in the context of their own home. These visits vary in frequency according to the family's needs and wishes, and may be weekly, bi-weekly or monthly. The parent educators provide parents with individualised information and advice about child development and rearing which is designed to be relevant to the child's specific stage of development. Parents are helped to understand what can be expected from their child at different ages, and are taught appropriate parent-child learning activities.

Group meetings are held during out-of-work hours to create opportunities for parents to share successes and common concerns about their children's development and behaviour, and to receive additional guidance from PAT staff and outside speakers. Parent-child activities also form a part of these meetings to reinforce family interaction. Some meeting sites, including schools and Parent Resource Centres, have the capacity to add a "drop in and play" component, which provides parents with the opportunity to use the site facilities, and to meet other parents and parent educators informally.

Developmental screenings are conducted annually, starting at the age of 1, to reassure parents that their child is developing normally, and to identify problems for timely intervention. Parents are also encouraged to monitor their child's development on an ongoing basis.

Parents as Teachers also helps parents to access other services in the community – which are referred to as "resource networks" – including education, health and social services.

Collaborative activities

PAT collaborates with many different agencies who wish to adopt its approach to family support. In partnership with the National Centre for Family Literacy, it provides home visits and services for children up to age 3, according to the Bureau of Indian Affairs Family and Child Education Programme. PAT now operates in over 20 Indian reservations. The parent educators, who are all Native Americans, are encouraged to make appropriate cultural adaptations to the PAT curriculum and materials. PAT also provides training and teaching materials to child care centres who wish to use the PAT model; and funding from the AT&T Foundation has allowed PAT to provide on-site technical assistance and structured telephone consultations at five different child care sites. A further example of successful collaboration is demonstrated by the partnership between PAT and the Missouri Department of Elementary and Secondary Education which led to the setting up, in response to parents' demand, of the three- to five-year-old component of PAT. PAT is also integrated with the FUTURES Programme which gives special credits to parents who are involved in PAT.

Through Ready to Learn collaboration grants, funded since 1992 by the Danforth Foundation, PAT hopes to increase the level of collaboration between itself and other agencies. In the original proposals for these grants it was clear that few applicants knew what "collaboration" meant:

"The complete set of original proposals gave evidence that many applicants were not familiar with the concept of 'collaboration' as it is currently used in the field of social science. Many of the proposals described 'outreach' or 'co-operation' efforts rather than true collaboration. It was determined that awarding grants to promising projects and then providing technical assistance during the year-long development process would provide an opportunity to educate the grantees on the topic. As a result of this process, several projects increased their efforts to attain the goal of more comprehensive collaboration."

Successful grant applicants have been asked to write reports on their collaborative activities. These will provide detailed descriptions of the different models of co-operation and collaboration between PAT Programmes and community agencies.

Evaluation

In 1985, an independent evaluation of a pilot programme involving 350 Missouri families found that, at the age of three, PAT children were significantly more advanced in language, social development, problem-solving and other intellectual abilities than children who had not benefited from PAT. The evaluation also discovered that their parents had more positive attitudes towards their local school district.

A follow-up study of the pilot programme, completed in 1989, showed that PAT children in the first grade achieved significantly higher standardised reading and maths scores than a comparison group. Furthermore, a significantly higher proportion of PAT than non-PAT parents initiated contacts with school teachers and took an active role in their child's schooling. An additional evaluation conducted in 1991, produced similar findings.

Since Parents as Teacher's only significant expense is its part-time parent educators, it is low cost as well as being effective. As a result it has received significant federal, state and private support, allowing it to expand from four pilot sites in Missouri to over 1 500 local programmes in 43 states and Washington DC. The approach has also been implemented as far away as St Lucia (West Indies), the United Kingdom, Australia and New Zealand. While it is low-cost, insufficient funding in the face of high demand means that waiting lists for PAT services exist in most states.

The St Louis Crisis Nursery (St Louis)

Background

The St Louis Crisis Nursery was opened in 1986 with the primary goal of preventing abuse and neglect of children by their parents. It is a temporary service for children (aged 0 to 8) of families who are experiencing a crisis, such as the hospitalisation of a parent, homelessness, or domestic violence. It provides care for children at risk for up to three days, and is open 24 hours a day, seven days a week. Nine places are available. The most frequent demand for the nursery's services is from single-parent, low-income families.

The nursery fills an identified gap in children's services, and is the only facility in the St Louis area where parents can voluntarily leave their child in care. More recently, the nursery has opened two other facilities, also in the St Louis area. Like the original nursery, the two new nurseries are located in local hospitals.

The nursery presently employs 36 people, who have backgrounds in social work, counselling, early childhood education and special education. It is governed by a 23 member Board of Directors, which includes both professionals and community members. It also has a Parent Advisory Committee made up of five families who have used its services.

Funding and training

Funding for the nursery is mixed. In addition to federal grant money and support from the United Way, it receives solicited funding from various foundations and individuals. It also asks the parents of children who attend the nursery for a donation of $5 per day, although in practice this is seldom paid. Significant non-financial support is provided by the Deaconess Hospital which provides rooms, medical services and food free of charge. The nursery also benefits from the voluntary services of trainee nurses from the local nursing college.

Specialist training for staff, in areas such as crisis intervention, housing and domestic violence, is provided by other agencies. In addition, the nursery sometimes forms partnerships with other agencies to organise joint training sessions.

Services provision

The nursery provides a wide range of services, including 24 hour care, physical examinations, developmental assessments, crisis intervention, counselling, referrals to other services, parent education, and follow-up support.

Parents are usually referred to the nursery by other services. Frequently, referrals come from the hospital's emergency department which has to solve the urgent child care needs of admitted patients. The nursery will not accept a child until it has the parent's signature agreeing to place the child in voluntary care. Occasionally this causes problems when the hospital urgently wishes to obtain child care but finds that the nursery has strict rules about parental consultation prior to accepting the child. Sometimes, social workers from the social services come up against the same problem: when they try to liaise with the nursery to place a child, they find that the nursery wishes to work with the parents instead. These rules are strictly upheld to preserve the rights of the parents.

Meetings with parents are used as an opportunity to fill out a family objectives plan, to discuss problems and to suggest solutions. Parents are frequently referred to other agencies that can provide appropriate services. In this respect, the United Way Services Directory is an important "Bible" providing detailed information on available provision.

Collaboration with the hospital to provide services for children in the nursery is generally good. However, there is sometimes reluctance on the part of doctors to visit the nursery to provide medical support because they are not reimbursed for their services. Outside of the hospital, the nursery co-operates both with agencies which are already serving clients, and with agencies which are required by clients. Staff also visit other agencies to publicise the nursery's services. At a more strategic level, co-ordination with other agencies is promoted through participation in different inter-agency committees, including the state-wide Committee for the Implementation of the Family Preservation Support Services Act, the State Crisis Nursery Planning Committee, and the Child Care Committee of the Penrose Family Support Centre (see below).

Outcomes

Around 75 per cent of parents who have used the nursery's services are successfully contacted to gather follow-up information. Of these, approximately 60 per cent have been in touch with other services for ongoing support. Even so, many of the staff at the nursery feel concerned about what happens to the children when they return home. About 40 per cent of families who ask for the nursery's support have used it previously. While there is a rule that parents can use the nursery no more than once every six months, in exceptional circumstances this is broken. One of the nursery's funders, the United Way, is encouraging the management to carry out a detailed evaluation study, but this has yet to be undertaken.

INTEGRATED SERVICES FOR SCHOOL CHILDREN

The William Herron Health Clinic, South-east Health Professions Magnet High School (Kansas City)

The context

One of LINC's first service delivery initiatives was to create ten health clinics in schools in the Kansas City area, the aim being to address the high rate of preventable health problems amongst Kansas City's children. At present, two clinics are functioning, one of which is located at South-east High School.

South-east High School is a health professions magnet school situated in a low income area of Kansas City. Many of the children who attend the school can be defined as at risk. A large number come from ethnic minority, low income or single parent families, amongst whom the incidence of drug and alcohol abuse is high. Many of these families have no medical insurance. The rate of teenage pregnancy and parenthood is also high: at the time of the research visit, 70 out of the total school population of 550 were young mothers. Many pupils with parental responsibilities drop out. Over 90 per cent of pupils are "bussed" in from other areas to meet the target 70:30 black-white ratio. While this has reduced the effects of segregation, it also means that the school is unable to function as a "community school". Most pupils and their families live too far away.

The social problems of the school's pupils has put increasing pressure on its teachers. One informant suggested that teachers were close to being at the end of their tether: "they can't cope" and "don't know what to do". The prison-like appearance of the school, the locked doors, the metal detector at the entrance, and the school police patrolling the corridors, all are evidence of the increasing levels of violence both by pupils in the school and by outside gangs who try to break in. Under these conditions, teachers have realised that a high quality curriculum and teaching materials are not enough, and that deep-seated social and health problems have to be solved before children can be ready to learn.

Funding sources

The clinic's original funding has been exhausted. Therefore LINC has developed a new funding partnership, with the Missouri Department of Social Services, the Kansas City School District, and the Community Funding Partners (a group of foundations), to keep the clinic operational and to prevent it from closing. With these partners, LINC has set up a School-based Health Centre Transition Committee to oversee the operation of the health clinic and to develop a long-term solution for both funding and governance. The Swope Parkway Health Centre has been operating the clinic – as a "satellite" facility – and is negotiating with the School-based Health Centre Transition Committee for reimbursement.

As a result of a federal government waiver, and a recent state Health Bill, federal money for health care has been made available to the Kansas City School District to provide health services in schools. This will be achieved through the creation of eight more school clinics, in addition to the two which already exist.

Services provision

The health clinic delivers services through a multi-disciplinary team including a nurse, medical assistant, social worker and intake worker. The services of a physician, substance abuse counsellor, nutritionist, and health information co-ordinator, are also available through co-operation with the Swope Parkway Health Centre. The main services provided by the clinic are health assessments, laboratory screenings, treatment, and counselling in several areas including nutrition, family, peer and educational problems, sexuality, pregnancy and drug abuse.

To become a member of the clinic, pupils' parents are required to complete, at a cost of $5, a special consent form which states that they agree to their child receiving health care on the school premises. Some parents are unwilling to sign these forms because of a deep-seated distrust of government intervention which they feel impinges on their right to freedom. Others feel that the health clinic will distract their children from attending school classes.

To address children's problems, the clinic's staff work as a team: the nurse and social worker regularly liaise with each other, with the school's teachers, and with the staff of Swope Parkway Health Centre. Co-operation with the latter has sometimes been problematic because of funding. More specifically, Swope Parkway feels that it should not have to provide and fund services for children who live outside of the local district for which it is responsible. Many children fall into this category because they have been bussed in from other districts.

The results

About 70 per cent of pupils have become members of the health clinic. The school's Head reported that the clinic is responsible for lower rates of absenteeism because pupils can be treated for ailments in school. He also reported lower suicide rates. However, pregnancy rates have remained similar.

INTEGRATED SERVICES FOR YOUTH IN THE TRANSITION TO WORK

The Women's Employment Network (Kansas City)

Background

The Women's Employment Network (WEN) was founded in 1986 by two women from Kansas City's wealthy elite, described by one informant as "pillars of the community", dedicated to improving local conditions. It is a private organisation and, as such, has been selected to run a "privatised" FUTURES Programme, parallel to the main state-organised programme. The main aim of WEN is to "assist low-income women to achieve self-sufficiency, personal dignity and independence through gainful employment" (Women's Employment Network, 1993, p. 1). Each year, it serves between 200 and 250 women who are at risk.

Most of the women who come to WEN are in their late 20s or early 30s. The majority come from disadvantaged backgrounds, and many are second generation welfare dependants. However, around one quarter are from middle class families. In total, 74 per cent are African-American and 70 per cent are single parents with dependent children. One informant emphasises that many of these women have "a good work history but something has gone wrong in their lives", divorce being a typical example.

Funding sources and training activities

The funding for WEN is mixed. Federal and state grants are provided by the Full Employment Council, the Missouri Department of Social Services, Kansas Private Industry Council, the Missouri Department of Economic Development, and the Missouri Council on Women's Economic Development and Training. The grant from the Full Employment Council is money allocated according to the federal Job Training Partnership Act. Funding from the Missouri Department of Social Services includes a federal grant for the state's FUTURES Programme, which is being implemented by WEN. These public sector resources are supplemented by significant financial contributions from over 15 private foundations, including the Hallmark Corporate Foundation (Hallmark cards). WEN also receives non-financial support from the Department of Employment Security, which has located one of its employees in WEN's offices, and from the Missouri School District which "lends" WEN one of its Adult Basic Education Instructors. The Department of Employment Security employee has a computer, which is linked to the Department's Job Bank, and can be used by WEN participants for job searches.

A small group of foundations and charitable organisations also provide funding for a special project which has been set up by WEN, called the Extended Support Pilot Project. This aims to create, operate and test evaluation, tracking and research activities, and to provide longer term support for WEN graduates.

Staff training at WEN is done in conjunction with other programmes and agencies, including the Full Employment Council, FUTURES and the Missouri School District.

WEN services

WEN provides a five-week long programme to all participants. This begins with a week of testing and orientation, followed by a three-week Job Readiness class, and ending with a week's intensive job search. The Job Readiness class emphasises basic life skills including assertiveness, improving self-esteem, grooming, budgeting, goal setting, decision-making, and conflict resolution. It also teaches job-related skills such as identifying interests and marketable skills, writing a curriculum vitae, filling in job application forms, interview techniques, and job search methods. WEN also provides services to help women overcome obstacles that can prevent them from attending classes or job interviews, such as child care, transport, and clothing. Furthermore, in co-operation with the Kansas City School District, WEN provides opportunities for participants to prepare for their GED.

After graduation, WEN tracks all participants for up to two years to assess their progress. It also offers additional services, including counselling, emergency assistance and a support network (the WEN

Sisterhood) to graduates who are considered to be at particular risk. These services constitute the Extended Support Component of the WEN Programme.

Collaborative activities

WEN front-line staff work in a co-ordinated team and, as one informant put it, "move freely between each other". They also liaise with other professionals – including FUTURES workers, School District staff, and Full Employment Council personnel – through regular case planning and committee meetings. In addition, they are knowledgeable about other services that participants may wish to use and, in the words of another informant, are generally "well plugged in". At a more strategic level, WEN board members serve on the boards of a wide range of other programmes including 21st Century Communities, LINC, FUTURES, the Women's Foundation, Boys' and Girls' Clubs, Empowerment Zones and First Steps. Furthermore, inter-agency agreements exist with the Full Employment Council, FUTURES, the Department of Elementary and Secondary Education, Kansas City, the Missouri School District and the Department of Employment Security.

WEN's contacts with local employers are quite strong; indeed, one informant described it as having an "excellent working relationship with the business community". Human resources personnel from local businesses visit WEN to give mock interviews which form part of the training, and frequently contact WEN when they have vacancies to fill. The informant emphasised that "employers are very comfortable working with WEN because they know WEN women are well prepared and that they can contact WEN staff regarding any problems".

Programme evaluation

Many of the grants that WEN applies for require an evaluation component. In 1991, WEN began a three-year assessment of its Extended Support Pilot Project. The evaluation report for fiscal year two (1992-93) was encouraging. The average class Economic Self-sufficiency Scores (ESS) – which take into account education and employment, and access to basic resources such as housing, transportation and child care – increased by as much as 49 per cent in the three months following the Job Readiness class, and 112 per cent after six months. The evaluation also reported improvements in self-efficacy, a measure of familiarity with employment related skills and confidence in performing them. While classes beginning the programme registered average scores ranging from 5.98 to 7.73, post-class averages ranged from 8.21 to 9.56.

Efforts to track WEN graduates over a two-year period also proved to be relatively successful, with 72 per cent of graduates in one group of classes returning at least one quarterly questionnaire on Economic Self-sufficiency. A few women sent notes which show how WEN can successfully help (some but not all) women to solve their problems. Typical comments are quoted below:

"Currently on SOC SSI benefits, but not forever. I thank God for women like yourself and others reaching out to those that want more. I can make it. I am enough".

"I feel great since WEN and I have a good job. Back in school and my life is fine. Thank you all for your help in getting me back on my feet".

"I was unable to pay my taxes last year and now this year's are due. What am I to do?"(Women's Employment Network, 1993, p. 12).

The failure to respond to the questionnaire by some graduates is blamed on high levels of mobility, embarrassment when success has not been achieved, and a tendency amongst some women to regard WEN as "part of the system" and therefore untrustworthy.

The case of Cynthia (pseudonym): A face was given to WEN's overall success in helping women to achieve self-sufficiency through an interview with a graduate called Cynthia. While she is undoubtedly a "star", in many respects she represents the average participant. In 1991, she was a mother of two children living on welfare. She could not apply for a job because she had no child care. She heard about FUTURES through a friend and joined the programme. As a result she received help with child care and transportation. She was then directed towards WEN's training course which she took. Later, she went to

Penn Valley Community College to take a microcomputers course, and is now employed as a computer operator at FUTURES. She feels that her self-esteem has improved and that she is "on the way to becoming a success story"; she is hoping in the future to set up a small computer business. She is very positive about WEN's contribution to her success: "they never let you lose site of your goals", "the doors are never shut", "once a graduate, always a graduate". She is still very involved in WEN and frequently acts as a spokesperson.

St Charles Employment Office (St Louis)

The context

The St Charles Employment Office is situated in one of 15 service delivery districts which receive Job Training Partnership Act (JTPA) funding from the federal Department of Labour. This Act, passed in 1982, aims to "establish programmes to prepare youth and unskilled adults for entry into the labour force and to afford job training to those economically disadvantaged individuals and other individuals facing serious barriers to employment who are in special need of such training to obtain productive employment" (Missouri Division of Job Development and Training, 1994, p. 1). The use of JTPA funding has been strongly influenced by the Missouri Governor's Co-ordination and Special Services Plan which, amongst other things, sets the goal "to assure co-ordination of Missouri's employment and training activities through public/private partnerships so that services are provided in an efficient and cost-effective manner".

At the state level, the Governor has appointed a Training and Employment Council for Missouri (MTEC) to provide advice on ways to enhance the job development and training system. This is made up of representatives from Missouri's business community, industry, labour, education, state and local governments, and the general public. The Governor has given responsibility for the administration of JTPA funding to the Missouri Division of Job Development and Training (JDT), which is also responsible for the evaluation of job training programmes.

At the local level, each of the 15 districts referred to earlier appoints a Private Industry Council (PIC) to identify training needs, and to design programmes to meet those needs. Private Industry Councils select the organisation that will administer services in their area – which in the case of Service Delivery Area 14 is the St Charles Employment Office.

The stated mission of the Office is "to build partnerships between business, industry and public agencies that will benefit our ability to provide service to our target groups" (Private Industry Council 1992, p. 3) . This is facilitated by the co-location at the Office of JTPA staff, and representatives of the Division of Family Services, FUTURES, the Division of Employment Security, Adult Basic Education, and St Charles County Community College. Hence it functions as a "one stop shop" through which residents can access the services of several, co-ordinated agencies in one trip.

It is important to emphasise that the Employment Office's Director arranged the building of the multi-service centre before federal money became available and, as one informant explained, "took a risk and made enemies" in doing so. The same informant added that the Director "got it done and decided to sort out the aftermath later". This implies that he had to go against the grain in Missouri's employment services.

Inputs

The St Charles Employment Office receives a federal JTPA grant of $3.2 million, and some FUTURES money.

Along with Employment Security and FUTURES staff, JTPA staff receive training at the Missouri Training Institute. The Employment Office also offers locally developed training courses, and in the past has brought in a consultant to help local agencies to better co-ordinate their services.

Co-ordinated activities

St Charles Employment Office is involved in a very wide range of collaborative activities, of which three major examples will be focused upon here.

Co-operation with the Division of Employment Security has led to its representation on the Private Industry Council, and the assignation of staff to St Charles Employment Office programmes. More specifically, one member of staff participates with the St Charles Employment Office in meetings to co-ordinate a response to mass layoffs in local industries, and another is located in the Employment Office to provide special employment services. A similar relationship with the Division of Family Services has led to the location of an Income Maintenance Worker and a FUTURES case manager in the Employment Office. These workers co-ordinate their activities with JTPA Programmes through regular meetings to provide a holistic service to clients with multiple needs. The Employment Office also collaborates with many local businesses who provide subsidised placements for the Office's on-the-job training programmes.

Day-to-day co-operation between the agencies located in the Employment Office is at a high level. Case management by JTPA and FUTURES is co-ordinated (although not by formal arrangement) so that they can agree on who is to take the leading role in client support, and how the supporting agency can provide appropriate, non-duplicative back up. JTPA also refers clients to FUTURES for required services – such as child care and transportation – when it is unable to provide them itself, and FUTURES uses JTPA in the same way. They accept many agencies' assessment forms and are currently working on a joint intake document. Administrative resources and information are shared by all agencies – including JTPA and FUTURES – located in the Office. They are presently discussing the usage and sharing of an automated data system with the Division of Employment Security and the Department of Social Services.

Co-operation between the different agencies has not been problem free. Different funding sources, administrative hierarchies, application forms, and time sheets have all caused difficulties. However, in some cases staff have developed strategies to overcome them; for example, they copy participants' details from one agency's application form to another's to avoid asking the same questions twice.

Outcomes

The Employment Office tracks participants, monitors outcomes, and sets yearly goals. Quantitative data shows that over 60 per cent of participants who complete the JTPA Programme find jobs. In a qualitative sense, staff reported that "we can do more together than we could alone", that "co-operation allows us to reach more people", and that "we can stretch the dollar, and our resources, because we can tap into what everybody has". This clearly points to an important synergy, as well as increased cost-effectiveness.

The success of the Employment Office has been recognised through many state government honours, including several Governor's Awards, and a series of awards presented to the Office's Director.

INTEGRATED SERVICES FOR FAMILIES

Family Focus Centre (Kansas City)

Background

The Family Focus Centre aims to promote "confident and competent parenting" by providing a facility where parents can come together for educational courses and group support (Project Early, 1994, p. 1). The Centre provides comfortable and well-equipped adult classrooms as well as vital support services such as assistance with transportation, nutritious snacks and child care. It is presently located in an old school (although this arrangement is temporary), and is staffed by a Programme Manager, a Director of Child Care, a Programme Specialist and 22 part-time child care workers.

At the beginning, the Centre's classes were available exclusively to participants in Project Early (see below). However, the Centre is now available to all families in the neighbourhood – not just Project

Early families. The majority of the local population are Spanish-speaking Hispanics, of whom many are recent and sometimes illegal immigrants from Mexico. The neighbourhood has many of the problems associated with low-income, disadvantaged areas, including drug abuse, gang violence and a high rate of teenage pregnancy.

Project Early is a programme offering continuous case-management and other support to a targeted group of families in the area with children aged between 0 and 6. Project Early case managers are referred to as "investment managers" to communicate the concept of investing in families to promote educational success and self-sufficiency. These case managers provide holistic support to targeted families through regular liaison with appropriate government and community services.

Funding

Project Early funding is provided by the Kauffman Foundation which has pledged a five-year commitment. The Foundation also funds the Westside Cabot Clinic – which collaborates with Project Early – as part of a "systems approach" to addressing community problems.

Services provision

The Centre provides educational, social and community programmes. As part of the education component, it offers classes in child development and parenting skills in both English and Spanish, as well as English as a Second Language (ESL) courses. Social activities include birthday celebrations, cultural visits and family field trips. Parents also have the opportunity to socialise during breaks in classes (specially arranged for this purpose) or, at other times of the day, in a "drop-in" lounge area. Community activities have included collaboration with parents and other agencies to improve local park areas, and special sessions to address the issue of gang involvement and associated violence.

Child care, for new-born infants to adolescents, is provided whenever adults are attending classes or group sessions. Five different child care rooms allow for adequate space and segregation according to developmental level. Since the child care provision is classified as "temporary sporadic care" it is exempt from licensing standards, although in fact it meets or exceeds most of them. The bilingual child care staff speak to each child in their own native language.

Collaboration

Parents are involved in programme planning through a Parent Advisory Committee which meets bi-monthly. This group provides feedback on specific class presentations and the programme in general. They also identify topics for future presentations – indeed, around 90 per cent of the classes offered at the Centre were originally suggested by the Advisory Committee. This group is also instrumental in planning and implementing social activities.

The Centre also collaborates with many other programmes and agencies in the community, with the goal of providing better services and promoting the Centre's visibility and permanence. The Parents as Teachers (PAT) Programme helps the Centre to identify appropriate class topics, and provides parent educators to present child development and other parenting classes. The Centre and PAT are also planning joint social events and field trips. The neighbouring Guadelupe Centre is sharing its ESL curriculum and instructions with the Centre, conducting two classes a week. In addition, some parenting classes have been provided by the Guadelupe Centre's staff. The Mattie Rhodes Counselling and Arts Centre is currently conducting two of its groups – the Young Mom's Group and the Hispanic Women's Group – at the Centre, while the Westside Cabot Clinic is helping to present prenatal and childbirth classes.

While the Centre's official aim is "to build upon these collaborations in order to increase and better co-ordinate community services to families" (Project Early, 1994, p. 3), the Programme Manager emphasised that collaboration was far from being easy. Indeed, he referred to it as "fraught with pitfalls", "hard, hard work" and a "pain in the butt". By way of explanation, he alluded to "territorial attitudes" and "parochial approaches" connected with each agency having its own separate programmes, funding and clientele. He also referred to agency rivalries, claiming that Kauffman funded programmes like his were seen as "new kids on the block" with a "big, fat plastic spoon in their mouths". This even led him to speculate whether their programmes should be developed through existing rather than new agencies. A typical example is the Guadelupe Centre which regards the Centre as a unwelcome competitor for funding for the provision of child care.

While the Programme Manager felt that collaboration was very time intensive (estimating that he spent 50 per cent of his time working with other agencies), and weakened institutions identities to the point where they felt threatened, he described it as "where we're all at". In these circumstances, he felt that one could not afford to have a "big ego", and that skill in "schmoozing" (networking) was vital.

Evaluation

Evaluation research is currently being carried out by the University of Missouri, but no data is yet available. On an anecdotal level, parents have said that their children have improved. Parents are also doing more with their children and are interacting to a greater extent with other families.

Grace Hill Neighbourhood Services (St Louis)

History and context

Grace Hill, which is part of the Settlement House movement, first began providing services to communities in the early 1900s. It states its mission as threefold: "to provide direct services cost-effectively within the self-help traditions of the Settlement House movement through neighbourhood organisation; to work for social change within society to foster greater support and understanding of the disadvantaged; and to work in disadvantaged neighbourhoods creating strong, healthy, helping communities by encouraging and supporting neighbours helping neighbours" (Missouri Department of Social Services, 1994e).

Grace Hill is a multiple-service agency serving around 42 000 disadvantaged people in eleven neighbourhoods in the City of St Louis, and St Louis and St Charles Counties. Of these, 35 per cent are classified as "poor" or "near poor" according to the poverty index, and many live in insecure or dangerous circumstances. Many programme participants are single parents, welfare dependants or elderly people, who require a wide range of services.

The President of Grace Hill stressed that one of the main aims of Grace Hill is to "get out of the business of providing services" through the promotion of "self-help" and "self-healing". He takes the perspective that people with problems are essentially "good people" whose difficulties are caused by external factors and that is these factors, rather than the individuals affected by them, that need addressing. Furthermore, he takes a negative view of professional help, believing that it leads to dependency, and feels that it should only be used as a last resort. His aim is to create a complete "system" of support incorporating linkage ("connecting people up"), direct services (to provide help where it is needed), and a neighbourhood college (to train people to provide services).

Input

Grace Hill's main source of funding is the United Way. However, it also receives financial support from the federal government, a typical example being support from the United States Public Health Service to provide health services. In addition, it runs various funding campaigns and activities – often in collaboration with programme participants – to raise its own money.

Services

Services provided by Grace Hill fall into four categories. The first is neighbourhood organisation involving a Member Organised Resource Exchange (MORE) model in which neighbours exchange resources and abilities in order to help each other. Key features of neighbourhood organisation include a computerised service credit exchange, voluntary services, emergency services, employment services, counselling, youth programmes, services for the elderly, wellness programmes, and education services. The latter are offered by a neighbourhood college which provides training in areas such as parenting and health that can be used to help others in the community. Other services provided by Grace Hill include health care (*e.g.* primary health care and dental care); support for children (*e.g.* child care, prevention of child abuse, and parent and child counselling); and housing (*e.g.* subsidised apartments and a transitional family shelter).

Collaborative activities

In general, Grace Hill is not keen to co-operate with agencies who adopt a more traditional approach to services provision in which they provide outside, "professional" support to help "clients". For example, one agency had a large grant for drug prevention which it wanted to use to provide services in a Grace Hill neighbourhood. However, since it insisted on employing its own staff rather than local people and, in addition, did not want to co-operate with Grace Hill, the latter refused to give the agency entry.

However, Grace Hill is more interested in co-operating with agencies in the field of employment. For example, it has three careers centres in which it has allowed the FUTURES Programme to operate, and in which registration services are provided on a regular basis by an outside employment officer. It also works closely with local businesses, which provide mock interviews at the careers centres, and telephone them when they have positions to fill.

Results

All of Grace Hill's programmes have specific goals, a monitoring group and an evaluation component.

An evaluation report of MORE, submitted in 1988, found that the effects of the MORE system were generally positive. Key findings were that MORE members felt that they had an improved understanding of the needs of others, and that their participation in activities to help others had increased; that members felt more confident and better able to solve their problems; that around one third of Neighbourhood Services employees were previously MORE members; and that levels of resident involvement were stable or increasing. These positive findings were confirmed during our site visit when informants said that MORE led to an increased sense of pride and self-esteem, works well, and that "the neighbours love it". On the negative side, the evaluation discovered that there had been little increase in the exchange of services through the computerised resource bank. The report also listed a number of barriers to the successful implementation of MORE, of which the most significant was changing budget resources resulting in fluctuating staff levels and neighbourhood boundaries.

The Grace Hill "neighbours helping neighbours" approach has been well documented, and has been the subject of considerable interest from other states and countries. In response to this interest, Grace Hill recently set up the Jones International Training Centre which was established to disseminate the Grace Hill approach. In 1993, 26 community leaders visited the Centre from several states in the United States as well as Germany, Japan, Uruguay and the Czech Republic.

The Penrose Family Support Centre

Context

The Penrose Family Support Centre was set up after Scott Best persuaded St Louis Hospitals to buy and donate an old hospital – which would be renovated with Civic Progress funds – to the Missouri Department of Social Services. The Department wanted to create a "one stop shop" providing services which worked with each other. With this goal in mind, the Department invited various community people, including a Catholic priest, a member of a foundation, businessmen and local residents, to set up an Advisory Committee with a free rein to plan the development of the Centre. The Committee was encouraged and energised by Scott Best who urged, "You've got to help me fight this through; it's a battle". Reflecting this spirit, the Committee has been willing to "break the mould" to provide "something very different" for a community that wanted change. In doing this, the members of the Committee have shown remarkably high levels of commitment, often connected with feelings of moral duty.

The local population is predominantly black and low-income. The area in which they live is notable for its lack of services of any kind, including local shops. This is a product of local violence connected with gang membership and drugs, and ultimately with poverty and despair, which makes it difficult for businesses to operate securely and profitably in the area.

Input

The Centre is run by the Department of Social Services, although each of the agencies which are housed in it have their own funding sources.

Services and barriers to collaboration

The Advisory Committee has identified a range of services, including employment, community and health care services, which it would like to attract to the Centre. So far the Centre is part full but, according to one informant, services are queuing up to join. One of the main principles of the Centre is to provide services in pleasant and welcoming surroundings. To this end, its offices are comfortable and modern, and staff at its reception desk provide a friendly welcome. According to another informant, this is part of a conscious effort to avoid making clients feel like "parasites" in the way that other over-burdened and bureaucratic state services often can.

While the Director of the Centre was keen to encourage collaboration between agencies, she saw different funding sources, different rules and contrasting attitudes as significant obstacles.

Evaluation

It is too early for a proper evaluation. The Centre's main goal at present is to win the trust of the local community so that they are willing to take advantage of its services.

Caring Communities

Context

The Walbridge area of St Louis is, at first glance, a leafy neighbourhood with detached, pleasant looking housing. However, on closer inspection one realises that the houses are very poorly maintained and that some are boarded up. Walbridge is, in fact, a "war zone" where two gangs, the Crips and the Bloods, are involved in an ongoing and bloody battle for "territory" (or, rather, street corners), and drug pushers have set up numerous "crack houses" in dilapidated accommodations. Gang presence is marked by graffiti made up of symbols and signs known only to them; drug pushers relax openly on their front verandas. The homicide rate here is one of the highest in the United States, and apparently it is not uncommon for locals to spend nights on the floor, or in their baths, to shelter from gun-fire. In these conditions, a very high proportion of children and families are at risk, not only of social deprivation, but also of serious injury or death. The Walbridge Caring Communities Programme, based at the Walbridge Elementary School in St Louis, was established in 1989 to serve the very serious needs of this area.

The Danforth Foundation acted as the catalyst to create the programme, bringing together various agencies, including the St Louis Public School District, and the state departments of Mental Health, Elementary and Secondary Education, Health and Social Services (all members of the Family Investment Trust). They worked together to set up a locally organised programme tailored to meet community needs. At the time, this was regarded as a "visionary" concept. One informant explained that "they realised that the people in Jefferson City (the state capital) cannot know the problems and come up with the answers". The same informant emphasised that, in contrast to Missouri, other states have not been "as bold" in delegating responsibility and resources.

From its inception, the Caring Communities Programme has been a collaborative effort to integrate home- and school-based services to effectively meet the needs of children at risk and their families. It provides a blend of locally developed prevention and intervention strategies aimed at family preservation and community empowerment. Its main objectives are to keep children in school, safely in their homes (avoiding out-of-home placements), and out of trouble with the juvenile authorities. In addition, it aims to establish a renewed sense of hope and pride in a community touched by despair and alienation, and by a strong sense that government is not working "for them".

To achieve these goals, Caring Communities is attempting to establish a viable family and neighbourhood support system with "school at the hub". The programme strongly emphasises a wide variety of collaborative strategies. These include sharing resources, power and information; building collaborative relationships with agencies and individuals at all levels, including parents; providing services when families want them and on "their own turf"; and building professional teams which communicate with each other. The Director emphasised that "when agencies aren't integrated, people aren't talking, and it's the families who suffer". However, while collaboration is seen as important, he stressed that "the ultimate goal is not to collaborate but to improve services".

Another key feature of the programme is its cultural sensitivity. Since the majority of the local population are African-Americans, the programme promotes the concept of Afrocentricity, according to which racial differences are acknowledged in a positive way, and self-identity and purpose are emphasised. It also promotes a set of seven principles, the "Nguzo Saba", which are traditionally celebrated during the week-long African-American Festivities known as "Kwanzaa". The programme Director is himself an African-American who is charismatic, highly intelligent, and very committed to the local community. He is supported in his work by an Advisory Board made up of neighbourhood residents, parents, school personnel, community, civic and religious leaders and agency representatives, who are equally committed to developing creative solutions to local problems.

Funding and training

Initial funding for the Caring Communities Programme came from the Danforth Foundation, and the state departments of Mental Health, Elementary and Secondary Education, Health and Social Services. More recently, financial, political and public support has been provided by the St Louis Public School District, the Department of Public Safety, Drug-free Schools and Civic Progress. The Public School District also has provided school facilities free of charge. At times, inflexible funding rules have led Caring Communities to ask state departments to "cut the red tape" and, where necessary, the programme has found "creative" (and sometimes rule-breaking) ways to make sure that funding is available for the families who need it.

Staff are specially trained in collaborative techniques, and efforts are made to recruit professionals who have diverse backgrounds and a demonstrated aptitude for teamwork.

Services

The services offered by Caring Communities aim to remove the social, educational, psychological and health problems which prevent children from succeeding in school and families from achieving their goals. Preventive services include after-school tutoring, cultural classroom presentations, drug-free recreation, a latchkey programme, pre-employment counselling and job placement, teen leadership development, a teen drop-in centre, and a "respite night" programme (whereby children can spend up to four nights per year at school to give their parents a break). Remedial services include an anti-drug and anti-gang task force, a case management programme, day treatment services, drug and alcohol counselling, a Families First (family preservation) Programme, and health fairs, outreach and screening. Anti-violence initiatives include "protection" of witnesses of crimes, and of children walking home from school (some of whom have been caught in gun-fire).

Referrals to Caring Communities Programme are made by staff at the Walbridge Elementary School or by outside agencies such as the Division of Family Services or the juvenile courts. Parents are involved right from the start. They are invited to a Parent Conference where an initial needs assessment is made, and where they are asked if they are willing to accept the intervention. The child's family is then allocated one or more services depending on its particular needs. Cases are discussed at Team Treatment Meetings, involving all of the staff involved in services provision and, later, teachers and parents are asked to evaluate the programme's efficacy.

While most Caring Communities services have been welcomed by the local community, its anti-violence and anti-drug street campaigns have met with some resistance. Gang members and drug pushers have intimidated those involved with verbal threats and fire-bomb attacks. At times this has necessitated community action, led by Caring Communities, to protect individuals. The programme's Director, is actively involved in the street marches and has remained at the front-line of services provision in spite of personal danger. He feels strongly that "you need to be there to know what's needed".

Barriers to collaboration

While the School District has been very supportive in allowing Caring Communities to use school facilities, school administrators have not always been so. One of the principals had some misgivings regarding possible interference with regular classroom instruction due to his lack of familiarity with the programme. However, once collaboration began, these concerns disappeared.

Other obstacles to collaboration have been the lack of time to hold meetings; different professional languages and terminologies; personality differences; confidentiality laws and fear of related law suits; and negative attitudes towards other collaborators. Of the various actors, drug dealers, individuals critical of the Afrocentric model, and teachers, were reported to be the most unsupportive. According to one informant, some teachers tended to operate according to an old-fashioned paradigm in which school is seen as an "ivory tower" that should function independently of other professionals, and social problems are seen as being of little relevance to education.

The Director also voiced concerns about the recent move of the Caring Communities administration to the more distant Penrose Family Support Centre which he believed would create barriers to co-operation with the community. He felt that he might "lose a sense of what's going on". Since Caring Communities does not actively co-operate with other agencies in this "one stop shop", it has, perhaps, gained only a limited amount from the move.

Outcomes

Preliminary evaluation results for Caring Communities show large and consistent improvements in academic performance among children at Walbridge who received Families First or case management services. Other children at Walbridge have also shown academic improvements that are generally greater than those of students in a control school; and the improvements are more substantial amongst the children who have been served the longest. On an anecdotal level, the Director felt that the programme had "led to a change in teachers' perceptions"; that they felt that children were more disposed to learn, and that parents were more willing to get involved. He also felt that, because of the programme's innovative approach, staff were more motivated and "energised".

The success of the Walbridge Caring Communities initiative has led to its expansion into another elementary school and a middle school in the same area. In addition, three more St Louis schools are planning their own Caring Communities Programmes, and the possibility of a state-wide programme is being considered. However, the Department of Social Services is uncertain as to how expansion can best be achieved. While the Caring Communities Director would like to develop the programme by creating his own programme administration, the Department is concerned about creating a second bureaucracy (and locus of power) in addition to its own. Also problematic from the Department's perspective is the tendency for Caring Communities to reject the services of other state agencies, leading to some duplication of services. Presumably this is because Caring Communities regards these agencies as too traditional in their methods. A final question mark centres around the viability of Caring Communities Programmes which lack the powerful and charismatic leadership of the present Director.

He has without doubt played a vital role in the success of the original programme. However, promisingly, the new sites are functioning successfully with different leadership.

CONCLUSIONS

The climate in which services operate

Missouri (and the United States in general) is distinctive in terms of the nature of its problems and the attitudes of its client population. Teenage pregnancy, gang violence, drug abuse, and poverty amongst full-time workers are present at levels which surpass those in many other OECD countries. At the same time the population is characterised by a strong belief in self-sufficiency, a negative attitude towards state welfare provision, and a distrust of government intervention. In these conditions, many families are forced into dependency on state (and private) services which they accept with reluctance and even shame.

Key features of human services

Significant features of human services provision in Missouri include:
- very strong private sector involvement including many large and influential organisations, such as the United Way;
- important business participation in the planning and implementation of services;
- a high level of community involvement linked to state and programme level emphasis on local;
- limited government involvement in the provision of social services (although its strategic role is important);
- mixed funding of programmes including various federal, state and private grants; and
- dynamic, innovative and bold leadership which is prepared to break inflexible rules.

The nature of integration

The strong rhetoric on integration in Missouri is linked to considerable action at the state and programme levels. Public-private sector partnership is significant, as is collaboration with local businesses and the community. Since there are a very large number of agencies in Missouri – often operating on a small scale – there is an important need to collaborate in order to provide comprehensive services. While services provision is often of a very high quality, its coverage is frequently limited: some neighbourhoods benefit from an impressive array of services, while others receive very little. However, state involvement in private sector social services in Missouri has helped to ensure that the population is served in a more coherent way.

Barriers to integration

The main barriers to collaboration reported by programme staff were:
- a lack of time for joint meetings;
- old-fashioned attitudes, especially among teachers;
- personality;
- the varying terminologies of different professional groups;
- confidentiality;
- differing eligibility (and other) rules;
- concerns about payment for services;
- separate funding sources;
- fears of weakened agency identity; and
- agency rivalries.

Programme evaluation

Private funders of human services programmes often require an evaluation component. As a result, very few programmes in Missouri go unassessed. Of the programmes visited, all reported positive outcomes although it is unclear what role collaborative activities had in achieving them. Programmes which are effective are often well publicised, and sometimes have the capacity to disseminate their activities, both nationally and internationally. Replication of successful programmes is commonplace.

Trends in services provision

Increasing emphasis in Missouri is being placed on the following:
- preventive approaches;
- family-focused care;
- privatisation of state programmes;
- decentralisation; and
- integration.

Concluding remarks

The state of Missouri provides an excellent example of integration in practice. The Department of Social Services is not only an impressive and successful collaborator, but also an efficient promoter of collaborative methods. This is reflected in the high level of professional and inter-agency co-operation on the ground.

REFERENCES

MISSOURI DEPARTMENT OF SOCIAL SERVICES (1994a), *Local Investment Commission Summary*, Jefferson City, MO.

MISSOURI DEPARTMENT OF SOCIAL SERVICES (1994b), *Kansas City Social Services Project*, Jefferson City, MO.

MISSOURI DEPARTMENT OF SOCIAL SERVICES (1994c), *Kansas City Futures Advisory and Welfare Reform Committee*, Jefferson City, MO.

MISSOURI DEPARTMENT OF SOCIAL SERVICES (1994d), *Outcome Measures Report*, Jefferson City, MO, October.

MISSOURI DEPARTMENT OF SOCIAL SERVICES (1994e), *Grace Hill*, Jefferson City, MO.

MISSOURI DIVISION OF JOB DEVELOPMENT AND TRAINING (1994), *A Guide to the Missouri Job Training System*, Jefferson City, MO.

PARENTS AS TEACHERS NATIONAL CENTER, INC. (1993a), *Parents as Teachers: Investing in Good Beginnings for Children*, St Louis, MO.

PARENTS AS TEACHERS NATIONAL CENTER, INC. (1993b), *1993 Annual Report*, Parents as Teachers National Center, Inc., St Louis, MO.

PARTNERSHIP FOR CHILDREN (1993), *Report Card and Data Briefing Book: The Status of Children in Metro Kansas City, 1993/94*, Kansas City, MO.

PRIVATE INDUSTRY COUNCIL (1992), *PY 1992 Annual Report to the Governor: Service Delivery Area 14*, Private Industry Council, St Charles County, MO.

PROJECT EARLY (1994), *Family Focus Center*, 1829 Madison, Kansas City, MO.

WOMEN'S EMPLOYMENT NETWORK (1993), *Extended Support Pilot Project: Annual Progress Report to Community Funders, Fiscal Year 2, July 1, 1992 to June 30*, Kansas City, MO.

NEW YORK CITY

CO-ORDINATING SERVICES IN A MULTI-ETHNIC METROPOLIS

by

Jennifer Evans and Josette Combes

INTRODUCTION

In the city of New York, one in seven of the total population, or one million children, go to school every day. Of these, around 130 000 children have special educational needs requiring extra support. Twenty years ago, the child population was declining, and as a result many school premises were closed down or converted for other purposes. However, the recent increase in number of children has led to a shortage of school places. Many children now are sent to schools which are some distance from their homes. Recent efforts to build local "community schools" have been hampered by this trend.

In the last three years, 138 000 new students have enrolled in the municipality's schools. Most of these are recent immigrants or refugees. This pattern of intake has led the creation of an ethnically diverse school population with around 50 different languages being spoken. The teaching population currently does not reflect this diversity; however, many recognise the need to recruit teachers from minority groups.

More than half of the children in New York City live in poverty, and many reside in neighbourhoods where ethnic tensions and other social problems are rife. As a result, the city's schools are unable to meet adequately the social needs of their pupils. Only a few schools offer an extended day (opening early in the morning and again in the evening). Only half of the children eligible for preschool services receive them. Less than one third of students are actively engaged in schooling during the summer months.

There is widespread debate about why the school system is failing. Lack of adequate funding is seen as a crucial factor. Education is funded 48 per cent by local taxes, 45 per cent by the State and 7 per cent by the Federal government. Unfortunately, the tax base in most American cities is falling.

The mainly white middle classes are deserting the public school system in large numbers. Public schools are seen as institutions for "other people's children", and less than 25 per cent of families have children studying in them.

There are three levels of governance within the school system: the State, the City of New York and the local school districts. Educational provision is formally democratic but, informally, there is separation on the basis of socio-economic status and race. Failure is seen as the responsibility of students, not schools. The relationship between standards, assessment and instruction is unclear, and accountability is mainly procedural rather than outcome-based.

There is a significant input into educational provision from voluntary organisations: over 1 000 organisations work with schools in some way. Voluntary organisations were involved in all of the research sites we visited.

SITES VISITED

Visits were made to the following five sites:

- Community Schools IS 218 and PS 5, Washington Heights;
- The Door;
- Project Highroad, IS 183, The Bronx;
- The Decatur-Clearpool School, Brooklyn; and
- Camp Clearpool, Carmel, New York.

No preschool sites were included in the itinerary. PS 5 is an elementary school (for 6-10 year-olds) and IS 218, IS 183 and the Decatur-Clearpool School are intermediate schools (for 11-14 year-olds). PS 5 has a Head Start preschool project located in the school, but it did not form part of our visit. We did not visit any High Schools or Community Colleges. The only site which was involved in transition-to-work programmes was the Door, although the Intermediate Schools were offering work experience to their older pupils (13- and 14-year-olds).

There was very little opportunity to interview people. We interviewed formally the Principal and the Head of the Community Programme in IS 218, and the Principal and the Superintendent of the School District in the Decatur-Clearpool School. We received no completed questionnaires. This report is written mainly from published material supplied by the schools and voluntary organisations (including evaluation reports), supplemented by notes taken during the visits.

COMMUNITY SCHOOLS IS 218 AND PS 5

Context (strategic, operational and field levels)

Characteristics of the research sites

IS 218 and PS 5 are located in Washington Heights, an extremely deprived area in the north of Manhattan:

- The community has the highest poverty rate in the city. Around 40 per cent of its families have incomes below $10 000 per year.
- Washington Heights-Inwood, the 34th police precinct, has the highest levels of drug addiction and crime, including murder, of all city precincts.
- Teenage pregnancy is common. Two out of three babies born in the community have mothers between 15 and 19.
- Washington Heights has the largest youth population in Manhattan, and school utilisation is the highest in the city, leading to over-crowding in local schools.
- A total of 86 per cent of students in School District 6 are Latino. The great majority are recent from the Dominican Republic. As a result, the district had the highest number of students with limited English proficiency of any in New York State. The district is ranked last amongst New York City's 32 school districts for students' reading ability.
- None of the city's traditional youth organisations have a presence in Washington Heights-Inwood (Koerner, 1993).

The role of the Children's Aid Society of New York City

In the late 1980s, the Children's Aid Society (CAS) decided that its next neighbourhood centre should be in the Washington Heights-Inwood area. The Society has a long history of providing neighbourhood centres in deprived areas. However, they experienced some difficulty in finding a suitable building. Eventually, they found a building which seemed suitable, but discovered that it was due to be demolished and that a new school was to be built on the same site. The CAS then approached the Schools Chancellor, Richard Green, and District 6 Superintendent, Anthony Amato, and proposed a joint venture, in which the Board of Education, the Board of Community School District 6 and the CAS would be full partners. The newly formed New York City School Construction Authority was about to embark on a major school building programme which would include several new schools in the Washington Heights District. It was agreed that three of these schools would be purpose-built as community schools. The idea was to use the school buildings out of school hours to provide a full range of recreational, educational, medical and mental health services for children and adults, and to open them six days a week, 15 hours per day, all the year round.

The three partners agreed to work in "full partnership" and to liaise over all aspects of school life and community provision. School District 6 already had an administration that was committed to community involvement, having introduced several community focused programmes. All three partners were highly committed to the partnership and to a collaborative approach to working with the community.

Both sides perceived advantages in the arrangement. The Board of Education believed that children would be more eager to attend school and better prepared to learn; teachers would be able to concentrate on teaching rather than on children's family or health problems; and that the schools would become centres of community life.

For the CAS, the arrangement provided an opportunity to integrate its programmes and philosophy into the life of the neighbourhood. Furthermore, it was seen as cost-efficient since the large sums of money which would have been required to build a community centre could be devoted to the provision of programmes. The CAS also appreciated that the partnership with the School Board would provide a core of staff (from amongst school teachers) to run programmes, and equipment such as computers, books and musical instruments.

Three schools were eventually chosen for the partnership:

- IS 218: to serve 1 200 6th-8th graders (12-14 year-olds), and to open in March 1992;

- PS 5: to serve 1 150 children K-5th grade (6-11 year-olds), and to open in February 1993; and

- IS 90: to serve 1 800 6th-8th graders, and to open in 1995.

The building of IS 218 was too far advanced for the CAS to have any substantial input into the design process. However, for the two other schools, the ideas and suggestions of the CAS were incorporated into the design, including space for health and dental clinics, and areas suitable for parent gatherings and community events.

Input (strategic, operational and field levels)

Preparatory work

During the two years when IS 218 was being built, the CAS began to work with the Washington Heights Community. The CAS medical/dental van visited Head Start centres and public schools in the community three or four days per week. One hundred children from the area were taken each year to a CAS summer camp, and local physically disabled children were taken for a vacation to another summer camp specially equipped for their needs. The CAS also made contact and worked closely with local groups such as the Association of Progressive Dominicans (to learn about the community's need for English classes and high school diploma equivalents) and the Alianza Dominicana (to set up an after-school programme in another school in Washington Heights).

Gaining the support of the community

Strategies to involve the community were set up and implemented during the planning period. Members of the community (parents and other adults) were taken to see other CAS centres in the City. CAS staff addressed meetings of local groups and explained the project to them, stressing that the CAS's only agenda was the welfare of local children and their families. They were impressed by the support received from local people who were generally ambitious, hard-working, and keenly focused on their children's futures.

Financial input

The new programmes were to be financed 50 per cent by the government and 50 per cent by funds raised by the CAS from private sources, so an intense fund-raising drive was initiated. A grant of $1 million was given by the Charles Hayden foundation and $500 000 by the Clark foundation. However, there is an awareness that fund-raising needs to be ongoing in order for the programmes to expand and continue. Financial support from government sources – municipal, state and federal – has been slower to develop than the CAS originally projected. However, the CAS is confident that the community schools initiative will demonstrate that it is more cost-effective than providing outreach programmes and facilities that are under-utilised.

Recruitment of staff

Staff were seen as a key input for the new school. The prospective Principal and Assistant Principals met to decide what the model of governance for the school should be. They came to an agreement that teachers should be given a great deal of autonomy, time to plan and scope for development, and that they should operate in teams. Teachers were brought into the school mainly through transfers from other schools, the Principal having only a limited ability to select them. However, it was made clear to candidates that the school was not going to be traditional and that a different approach would be required of them. The senior management of the school invested (and continues to invest) a lot of time and effort in staff development and in empowering teachers to be innovative.

Process (operational and field levels)

The school

IS 218, formally named Salomé Urena Middle Academies after a nineteenth century Dominican educator and poet, opened in March 1992 with 650 pupils. The full intake of 1 200 entered in September 1992. The building design was the result of a competition and does not resemble the traditional design of a school. It is built on five floors, with wide curving corridors which provide space for exhibitions of students' work. Each of the four upper floors is the base for one of its four "academies" – Business Studies, Community Service, Expressive Arts, and Maths, Science and Technology – into which the student body is divided. Students, therefore, have most of their classes on the same floor. Parts of the school can be closed off when the after-school and weekend classes are being run. Special community rooms are provided for the use of parents and other community groups.

Each academy has its own Assistant Principal and staff, and each offers the courses taught in all intermediate schools including English, Maths and Science. In addition, each academy offers courses unique to itself; for example, the Business Studies Academy is the only one to offer business courses. Incoming students are invited to choose which academy they wish to join. On the day of our visit, a group of prospective students was being entertained by the Expressive Arts Academy.

The division of the student body into these smaller units is perceived to have several advantages: it creates a sense of community amongst the students and staff in each unit; teachers and students get to know each other very well; and teachers can come together with children on a regular basis to work on mutually agreed projects. Examples of project activities include the dissemination of information on immigrants' rights and campaigning for improved subway lighting. These projects link the children and the school with the community and allow students to have some control over their activities and learning.

The Extended Day Programme

An Extended Day Programme is organised and financed by the CAS. It offers a wide range of programmes for children, teenagers and adults. Initially, the 07.00 to 09.00 programme was called the Preschool Programme and the 15.00 to 18.00 programme was called the After-school Programme. Later both became part of what now is called the Extended Day Programme to encourage the concept of a seamless day. Dr. Kavarsky (the School Principal) views the collaboration "as providing not so much an after-school programme as a continuation; it's part and parcel of what we do during the day". For example, if a child is having difficulties with Maths, the teacher will inform the CAS staff so that when that child comes to register for the Extended Day Programme he or she will be encouraged to take a Maths tutorial.

The CAS has its own administrative office in the school, staffed by personnel brought in from other centres and programmes or recruited from the local community. Regular meetings are held between the school and CAS staff. All aspects of the Extended Day Programme, the Family Resource Centre and the Medical Centre are discussed.

The teaching staff for the Extended Day Programme are chosen and paid for by the CAS. They consist of teachers from the school, staff from other CAS centres, parents and other members of the community with particular skills to offer. The teachers' union at the school – The United Federation of Teachers – has been very supportive. Some courses are extensions of what is offered during the school day. Project Advance provides basic English courses, and there are tutorial sessions in academic subjects for children who need special help. Each academy provides its own activities; for instance, the Maths, Science and Technology Academy offers computer games and the Expressive Arts Academy, puppetry. Sports and musical activities are also available.

Around half of the school's 1 200 students register for extended day activities.

Business courses

Business courses are an important additional component of the extended day. A Business Continuity Course designed by the National Foundation for Teaching Entrepreneurship (NFTE) is available to all students. This has led to some students setting up their own businesses with "seed money" provided by the CAS. In some cases, parents are also involved. There are also three student-run corporations which operate in extended day hours as CAS-sponsored extensions of the Business Academy curriculum. These are: a catering company; a T-shirt company; and the SUMA store, an in-school shop.

The SUMA store is located in a room originally intended to be a lounge for school aides, but the Principal allowed the students to use it. The CAS obtained a grant to finance the store. It is run by 8th grade students from the extended day business course.

These examples illustrate the close working partnership between the school and the CAS. Staff from the two organisations work and plan together. The collaboration enhances both what can be offered as part of the school's education programme and what can be offered by the CAS during the extended day. The orientation of many of the programmes is towards vocational activities, thus providing useful "transition to work" experiences for younger pupils.

The Saturday Programme

In addition to the extended day, the CAS offers a Saturday Programme. This is open to all of the children in the community, not just to IS 218 students. It runs from 10.00 to 15.00 every Saturday of the school year, and offers gym and computer proficiency classes, and day trips.

The Summer Programme

The school's Summer Programme is made up of two components: a summer school for children who would not pass on to the next grade without extra classes, and a CAS programme which runs throughout the vacation from 10 a.m. to 6 p.m. This includes school-based activities such as reading, writing, computer and art classes, and trips to the beach, swimming pools and museums. There have been two special CAS programmes based at IS 218: in 1992, a two-week business course and, in 1993, a six-week dance and creative writing course. The latter was open to children across the city and a total of 25 IS 218 students participated in it.

The Teen Programme

The school also has a Teen Programme for 14-18 year-olds. It offers activities two evenings per week. The programme includes basketball and other sports, arts and craft classes, and workshops on AIDS, violence, sex education and pregnancy prevention. It is expected that the numbers who attend will grow as former students of IS 218 return to the school to participate.

The Medical Centre

There are very few medical facilities in Washington Heights. Children requiring treatment used to be taken to the emergency room of the only hospital in the area. This usually meant a long wait and treatment by a doctor who had no knowledge of the child's medical history.

The original design of IS 218 did not include a full health centre but, after the CAS became involved and it was decided to develop the school as a community school, rooms were made available for medical and dental care. The facility comprises a medical clinic, a dental clinic, and a reception and records room. The medical clinic is staffed on alternate days by a paediatric nurse practitioner (PNP) and a registered nurse. There are also regular visits from a faculty member, and student PNPs, from the Columbia University School of Nursing. Recently, the CAS has negotiated an agreement with the Visiting Nurse Service of New York to provide a PNP every school day. The dental clinic is staffed by a dentist three days a week and a dental hygienist on the other two. Volunteers – mainly mothers of IS 218 students – act as receptionists and do much of the record keeping. They have also been trained to do sight and hearing screenings.

Both clinics are equipped for diagnosis and basic primary care. Those children requiring more complex medical treatment are sent to the local hospital, not to the emergency room as before but directly to the relevant department. Children requiring complicated dental treatment are sent to the School of Dental and Oral Surgery.

Thus a collaborative network has been set up which offers access to a full range of medical and dental treatments which were not available before the CAS began to operate in the school. The network consists of the school's medical and dental staff, parent volunteers, and personnel from the Visiting Nurse Service, hospital and dental school.

The school also houses a Family Resource Centre and a Social Services Unit. These provide a CAS mental health programme. The mental health team includes a full-time social worker, a part-time social worker, two doctoral students in psychology, a drug prevention counsellor and five social work masters interns. Children are referred to the programme by any of the agencies working in the school.

From the point of view of the professional staff in the school, a major advantage of their location is the opportunity for follow up. Often, in paediatrics, there is no continuity of treatment because the children are not brought back.

Services for parents and other adults in the community

The CAS has initiated within the school an extensive range of classes, workshops, services and self-help groups for the adults of Washington-Heights. These mostly take place in the evenings and at weekends and are co-ordinated by the Family Resource Centre, located just inside the school's main entrance. It is open from 08.30 to 20.30. The services and classes offered are largely a response to community demands. The CAS's community director conducted research amongst parents and other adults living locally to see what they would like the Centre to provide. In the course of the day, hundreds of parents and other adults use the school. Since many of the adults are recent immigrants who do not speak English, one of the most popular classes is English as a Second Language (ESL). Recently over 400 adults applied for the 275 places offered on ESL courses. Many other classes, such as computer proficiency, were heavily over-subscribed. There is also a strong demand for the General Educational Development (GED) equivalency course, which provides an opening to university or college.

In addition to the CAS, many other community groups use the school's facilities (such as the gym and auditorium). The school is seen by the Principal not just as an educational facility, but as the hub of community life.

Payment for classes

All classes in the Extended Day, Summer, Saturday, and Adult Programmes are subject to a nominal fee. The CAS believes that this engenders a sense of ownership among the participants and gives them more power to make demands regarding course content.

Initial problems and their solutions

The problems and unforeseen consequences of collaboration are quickly identified because the scheme is constantly monitored and evaluated by an evaluation team commissioned by the CAS. As a result, any initial or ongoing problems are tackled before they become a threat to the collaborative effort.

There was a process of mutual adjustment to the different professional languages and cultures of CAS staff. For example, the procedure for the recruitment of staff for the Extended Day Programme was aligned with normal teacher recruitment practice.

A major initial impediment to collaboration was the way in which social workers traditionally operate in schools. They are seen (and see themselves) as an auxiliary service. Their role was viewed by the teachers as within the Extended Day Programme, and not as an integral part of the normal 09.00 to 15.00 school day. The Medical Centre and Family Resource Centre were not fully operational in the early stages and their contribution was not fully realised. Thus, instead of creating a culture where social service providers and educators worked together, the CAS and the teachers were operating within two distinct work cultures.

The decision was taken to tackle this problem as soon as it became evident. The On-site Director, the Principal, a group of teachers, the head of the Parents' Association and the Associate Executive Director of the CAS worked together to restructure the After-school Programme. They decided to base it within the four academies around which the school was already structured and to create a ninth and tenth period in the school day. They believed that this would foster more continuity between normal school hours and the After-school Programme. It was also decided that teachers and CAS staff would work together in teams to develop the programmes to be offered, and that students would be guided by their teachers towards programmes that were felt to be suitable for them. Thus the CAS and teaching staff began to work as a unit and to develop a shared language and culture.

A positive outcome of this arrangement has been that staff working in the ninth and tenth periods have access to the whole school building, while being able to use their own classroom as a base. This maximises the use of the building and its facilities.

There were some initial problems concerning the rate of referrals of children and families for mental health services. The guidance teacher who handled the referrals was sending more children than the staff could cope with. A revised referral process has been instituted, which involves greater consultation between the guidance teacher and the CAS office. Also, an additional social worker has been employed so that more families can be seen.

Confidentiality is another problem which is currently being addressed. The aim is to develop procedures to ensure confidentiality while permitting the sharing of information necessary for team-work and joint decision-making.

Key elements which support collaboration

These are taken from the Interim Evaluative Report (Robison, 1993).

- community-wide planning process;
- indigenously generated;

- strong leadership;
- broad citizen and parent involvement;
- focus on accountability;
- step by step approach to collaboration;
- an extremely talented and motivated staff (especially key staff);
- staff who can cope with some uncertainty and disorganisation;
- leadership focused on the collaboration; and
- strong support from the sponsoring agency.

Product (strategic, operational and field levels)

Financial benefits

The model provides the most economic use of the community's financial resources. There is no need for two separate school and community buildings, each standing empty for a proportion of the day. Combining the two means that 90 cents of every dollar are spent on programmes, a much higher proportion than in free-standing community centres. The incremental cost of additional programmes is relatively small, given the benefits to the school and the community. The annual cost of a child in a District 6 school is around $6 000. The additional cost per child of the CAS programmes is $1 000. About half of this will be provided from government funds, and the rest raised by the CAS, primarily from private sources.

Benefits for children

The children benefit from on-site medical, dental and social care. Many children have never before seen a dentist. Around 20 children a day visit the medical centre for first aid treatment. Sight and hearing screenings have been established. A referral procedure with the Columbia Presbyterian Medical Centre has been set up.

Educationally, the school has recorded the highest attendance level in the district, and a higher than expected academic rating given its student intake. Almost half of its students enrolled in the Extended Day Programme during its first year of operation.

Initially, the mental health services were receiving more referrals than they could handle. However, with a new referral procedure and more staff, they are now providing ongoing counselling for 39 families.

Benefits for staff

Teachers at the school are enthusiastic about the scheme. Many of them offer their services in the Extended Day Programme and work long hours in the school (for which they are remunerated). Thirty-five of the 48 staff working in the Extended Day Programme are teachers.

Another benefit is that teachers know that there are staff in the school equipped to deal with children's health and emotional problems, allowing them to concentrate their efforts on teaching. The Extended Day Programme also encourages teachers to relate to their students in a more holistic way as they do leisure activities with them too.

The ongoing opportunities for staff development ensure that teachers feel supported and enabled to develop their professional competences.

Benefits for the community

Parents are enthusiastic about what is offered for their children and supportive of the school. Many of them work within the school as volunteers, and some as paid staff. Adults from the community use the school extensively for educational, recreational and community activities. The school appears to have become the hub of the community, which was one of the primary goals of the collaboration between the CAS, the School District and the Board of Education.

THE DOOR

Context (field level)

The Door is an open access centre for young people. It offers a range of educational, recreational and medical facilities. It was started by a group of professionals, including street-workers, dancers and artists, who were working with young people. The model was developed in 1971 and operated for two and a half years without funding. The Door's founders (all of whom were volunteers) brought together the professional expertise of a wide range of disciplines (mental health, the law, education, the arts and health). Their goal was to create more comprehensive and more accessible services for youth.

Input (field level)

Currently the Door occupies four floors of a six-storey condominium building and has a paid staff of 145, and over 100 volunteers. Thirty per cent of the paid staff have advanced degrees in areas such as medicine, public health, business, social work, public administration, nursing and education. The Door provides a health clinic, library, crèche, cookery room, art and pottery studios, gymnasium and a central meeting place.

Funding comes from a variety of sources, including nine government bodies (city, state and federal), 78 foundations and corporate funders, and a number of individual donors. The total annual funding is currently $6.7 million, most of which comes from the foundations.

Process (operational and field levels)

The Door serves young people between the ages of 12 and 21. It aims to offer a programme that helps them to side-step the fragmentation and bureaucratic red-tape of the human services system. The Door now provides over 30 preventive, remedial and enrichment programmes on a single site, all co-ordinated around the developmental needs of youth.

Services offered fall into four broad categories:

- health services (medical care, preventive health, sexual health/family planning, HIV testing, nutrition advice and prenatal care);

- education services (basic skills, GED test preparation, tutoring, careers counselling and job);

- placement (college preparation, youth apprenticeships, leadership training and computer training);

- human services (legal counselling, social support, drug prevention, parenting and HIV counselling); and

- creative and physical arts (music, drama, dance, basketball, weight-lifting, aerobics, art and pottery).

The Door is open in the afternoons and evenings up until 21.30, Monday to Friday. An average of 250 young people visit the centre each day, and around 6 000 use it each year. People who want to use the Door's facilities have to become members. Membership is free, but implies certain responsibilities and commitment. Most new members learn about The Door from their peers, but schools, clinics and community programmes also refer young people.

Currently 39 per cent of the members come from Brooklyn and 32 per cent from Manhattan. 57 per cent are African-American, 30 per cent Latino, 6 per cent White and 7 per cent Asian. The average age of members is 17. Around two thirds attend school and 17 per cent are employed.

Education and transition to work programmes

There are a number of programmes at the Door which focus on education, careers counselling and the transition to higher education or work. The Door's educational approach is geared towards the needs of students who have not succeeded in traditional learning environments. Co-operative, small-group learning is supplemented by individual instruction. A number of work-readiness programmes are designed to bridge the gap between school and work. Services include:

- basic skills training in English and Maths;
- English for Speakers of Other Languages (ESOL);
- high school equivalency (GED) preparation (75 young people achieved a GED in 1993);
- computer training;
- homework help;
- employability skills training, which helps young people to develop their social abilities;
- career exploration, which offers opportunities for job shadowing, voluntary work and entrepreneurial work within the Door;
- work support, a workshop which helps young people already working to identify personal issues affecting their work performance;
- college preparation, which aims to increase young people's awareness of the post-secondary options open to them. It offers assistance with applications and financial aid as well as tutoring upgrade academic skills. In 1993, 70 participants enrolled in college;
- youth development, which is a scheme to offer young people opportunities to develop leadership and organisational skills by becoming involved in community service and other of the Door's activities; and
- youth apprenticeship, a scheme which uses volunteer work sites to provide members with training and hands-on experience of the business world.

Other services

The Door also offers a range of medical and social services, and recreational activities. In 1993, almost 2 300 young people were seen at the Adolescent Health Centre. Services are confidential and are provided free of charge by experts in adolescent health care. There is a laboratory and a pharmacy on-site, which means that most immediate health needs can be met in a single visit (young people are often reluctant to return for follow-up). In addition to primary health care, there is a range of prenatal services for expectant mothers as well as advice on contraception and sexual health. Nutritional health education is also provided.

The young people who come to the Door often arrive in a state of crisis. They need immediate welfare services: food, shelter or legal help. The Door offers a variety of services through its Counselling Centre. These include: legal services (offered by on-staff lawyers and a team of volunteer attorneys); substance abuse prevention and treatment; support for young parents; support for young people with physical handicaps; HIV services; various support groups; and individual counselling for people with mental health problems.

Product (field level)

Aside from the positive outcomes mentioned earlier regarding employability, staff perceive another benefit of collaboration to be that it provides a holistic approach to meeting young people's needs. Young people do not refer themselves easily across systems but, at The Door, all of the services they need are under one roof. However, staff have realised that it is not enough to co-locate services, and that a team approach is needed. Therefore they have developed a shared in-take system and set of forms. They also have generated a simplified language and a common culture to make themselves more accessible. They aim to become like parents to young people, getting to know them in a holistic way and helping them to cope with their lives.

The model of The Door has been replicated in a number of towns and cities in the United States and elsewhere. The staff have acted as consultants to new centres in several other countries, including the United Kingdom, Australia, Finland and Mexico.

PROJECT HIGHROAD IS 183

Context (strategic level)

This project is sponsored by the Fund for New York Public Education and the United Way of New York City. The Fund was set up in 1989 in order to channel money into the public school system. It supports a range of projects in New York City schools, of which Project Highroad is one. Funding comes mainly from foundations (66.6 per cent), government (9.8 per cent), corporations (12.3 per cent) and individuals (7 per cent). The Fund's budget in 1993 was $9.7 million.

Context (operational and field levels)

Project Highroad is a drugs prevention programme which is currently operating in three schools in New York City. We visited IS 183 in the Mott Haven section of South Bronx. Mott Haven is the poorest congressional district in the United States. It is a high crime area with a thriving drugs market. It accounts for 10 per cent of New York city's population, but 17 per cent of drug-related arrests, 18 per cent of drug-related deaths, and 19 per cent of AIDS deaths related to intravenous drug use.

IS 183 currently serves 660 students in grades 6-8 and has a poverty index of 80 per cent. The student population is 56 per cent Hispanic, 44 per cent Black and less than 1 per cent White. A total of 61 per cent of the students are eligible for free lunches based on family income and 60 per cent are eligible for Chapter One services. Approximately 7 per cent of the students are recent immigrants from nine different countries. A total of 13 per cent have limited English, nearly all of whom are native speakers of Spanish. The school's mobility rate is 28 per cent. Its "damage index", and the number of inexperienced or uncertified teachers, are higher than the city average. Its attendance rate, at 87.2 per cent, is one percentage point higher than average, but the Maths and English attainment of its students is below average.

Input (strategic and operational levels)

There are a number of factors which appear to explain the success of the United Way and the Fund for New York Public Education (the "central partners") in their work:

- They conducted extensive research into prevention models and synthesised these into a model to guide planning and implementation at the local level.

- The model has been tested in three different communities, allowing the stakeholders to evaluate what does and does not work.

- The central partners share a strong interest and commitment to evaluation and feedback.

- The central partnership is a model of collaboration: the Fund has educational research and programme development expertise and the United Way, expertise in working with community organisations. The creative tension generated by two organisations with different approaches and constituencies demonstrated to the local communities that new ways of collaborative working could be developed.

- The two partners' reputation for effectiveness enabled them to stimulate collaboration and formal agreements between senior managers in housing, education and community associations.

– The partners have fund-raising capabilities and access to grant-makers that smaller organisations do not. They also can provide "credibility" and guarantees of monitoring and accountability for their projects.

An evaluation of Project Highroad made the following observations about the United Way and the Fund for New York Public Education:

"Organisations that do not implement programmes directly may be well-positioned to assist educators and service providers to move programme and service planning for youth to a more strategic level. Similarly, these types of organisations are well-positioned to translate the lessons learned from local communities into refined models that will enable other neighbourhoods to follow suit, and to advocate for policy and legislative reform that will enhance programme development and co-ordination on a larger scale" (Mirand Research Associates, 1993).

Input (operational and field levels)

The design of Project Highroad required the involvement of a community-based organisation (CBO) near each target school. This was entrusted to select project staff and establish a local advisory committee comprising representatives from the school, housing management, parents' association, tenants' association, police and other CBOs. The local advisory committees assess community needs and plan programmes and services designed "to reduce risk and increase resilience" amongst middle school youth and their families. The central partners (The Fund for New York Public Education and the United Way) assist all of the local advisory committees in their programme planning by providing them with research findings and information about programmes which have been successful in other locations.

The central partners have developed ten guiding principles for the Highroad model which the advisory committees are asked to follow when devising their plans:

– a memorandum of understanding between the school, the lead CBO and other partners;

– a clear mechanism to ensure that programme activities are co-ordinated;

– training for key participants to establish a common understanding of programme goals;

– parent, student and community involvement in programme design and activities;

– a process for referring and dealing with students and families who have substance abuse and problems;

– a curriculum which offers information about the effects of drug abuse and strategies to help resist peer pressure;

– skill-building exercises which focus on social and life skills;

– a clear message from the school, housing authority and community organisations that substance abuse will not be tolerated;

– activities which do not label, stigmatise or segregate participants;

– a mix of activities which treat a 24 hour-a-day problem within and outside the school day.

Within these guidelines, the local advisory committees have considerable flexibility to create that they feel will meet community needs. The committees meet monthly and are chaired by their site co-ordinators and school principals.

Process (operational and field levels)

Certain programme features are common to all of the sites, as would be expected given the principles outlined above. The common features appear to be:

– after-school programming (offering a range of activities from 15.00 to 17.00, four days per week);

– summer programming (offering a range of sports and arts-based activities);

– field trips (to provide cultural and recreational activities outside the local area);

- counselling and/or case management services;
- a conflict resolution and peer mediation programme (through project STOP which has trained a core group of students and parents and which is now developing school-wide programmes); and
- youth leadership (which has encouraged the formation of a student council and related system).

A number of initiatives developed in IS 183 are unique to the site. There are drug and alcohol prevention workshops in every class and seminars for 8th grade students on AIDS awareness. There have been staff development workshops to train teachers in using value clarification techniques with their students. Highroad staff at IS 183 have developed a referral procedure to link students and their families to the services they need. Two Highroad staff currently offer counselling and case-management services. A total of 75 students and their families were supported in 1991-92. A student council has been set up with representatives from each class in the school. This is involved in planning events and community service activities, such as a recycling campaign and the development of a school-based store.

The project sponsors a Youth Leadership Programme for approximately 35 8th-grade students per year. Students are selected through a rigorous application and interview process. Selected students receive training and orientation to the "World of Work" in a series of after-school workshops. They are then placed in part-time supervised internships with local business and non-profit organisations. The project provides a weekly stipend of $30 and the students meet once a week to discuss their work experiences.

Project Highroad sponsors an after-school programme at IS 183. It operates from 15h to 17h. In 1992-93, approximately 160 students participated. As well as recreational activities, tutoring in basic school subjects is offered. Pupils whose grades are unsatisfactory are required to enrol in tutorial classes as well as recreational classes.

The Project also offers weekend activities and a summer programme. Approximately 70 young people participate in the summer programme, which is held in the school each year.

Other programmes are designed to involve parents and the wider community. These include the Mott Haven Restoration Project which works to improve the quality of life in the area. This involves community policing to rid the area of drug traffickers. A number of parents in the Mott Haven community have become actively involved in Project Highroad.

Product (strategic and operational levels)

The central partners have been involved in disseminating the Highroad model and its implementation strategies. They have provided assistance with the development of New York City's Beacon Schools Initiative. This has used the model in making the school the focal point of a network of community programmes and services.

They have produced a video, "Project Highroad: Blueprint for the Future", and a newsletter, "Highroad News", as part of the dissemination effort. They have also been invited to present their model at a number of conferences concerned with drug abuse prevention.

Product (operational and field levels)

The following outcomes were referred to by Project Highroad staff:
- Parents and students have played an active part in designing the programmes to meet their needs. However, the number of students involved in after-school programmes is small (159).
- The Student Council has provided a means for the development of leadership skills in young. This has involved 20 students.
- The World of Work Programme is helping students to develop the skills and attitudes needed for.
- A group of parents actively participate in the programme and advocate for its continuation.
- There has been networking with other collaborative efforts in the community.

The evaluation team from Mirand Research Associates has identified the following factors as being associated with successful implementation:

- substantial, widespread agreement about the need for change and the actions needed to bring it;
- observable and sustainable change in the structure of the school or organisation;
- widespread participation in efforts to bring about change;
- leadership which encourages contributions from others and offers them the chance to take on roles;
- time to develop new types of funding mechanisms which cut across existing agency boundaries.

There has been a tension between the approaches and perspectives of education and health/human services. In general, it has been used creatively to promote system-wide change. In some instances though, to avoid conflict and turmoil, there has been "tinkering around the edges" rather than real development. A number of programmes have been school-focused with limited community involvement. Most activities for the community have been focused on providing meeting space, and co-sponsoring activities and special events such as street fairs.

IS 183 has decided to become a Magnet School specialising in health careers and has set up links with the local hospital. This means that it will now select pupils from a wide area rather than just from the local community. It is likely that this initiative will cut across the activities promoted by Project Highroad, which was essentially set up to serve and involve local people.

As yet, there has been no evaluation of the success of Project Highroad in preventing drug abuse. The evaluation so far has concentrated on how to improve collaboration between the partners. However, one needs to ask whether co-operation should be seen as an end in itself, or as the means to achieving some other goal. If the latter point of view is accepted, then the following questions need to be addressed: would the young people involved in the project (often relatively stable and well-motivated students) have been successful anyway; and has the project had any impact on the students who are in real danger of being sucked into the drug culture? Some base-line data gathered by the evaluation team indicate that Project Highroad participants at IS 183 have a higher attendance rate than non-participants, and higher scores in Reading and Maths. Around 60 per cent of all students in Highroad Programmes across the three sites claim that they have not been involved in drug or alcohol use. By following these students over time, the effectiveness of the intervention can be more rigorously assessed.

THE DECATUR-CLEARPOOL SCHOOL AND CAMP CLEARPOOL

Context (strategic and operational levels)

From 1901 to 1990, Camp Clearpool (in Carmel) operated as a non-profit residential summer camp for children from New York City. In 1990, Camp Clearpool and the Edwin Gould Foundation started working together to create a new approach to provide for the educational and social needs of New York City children. In partnership with Community School District 16, they began to design a new model for urban public education. This model would provide year-round education on two campuses: the Decatur-Clearpool School and Camp Clearpool. The school would cover the age range pre-kindergarten to grade 8, and would offer an extended day, a Saturday programme and a summer programme.

The school opened in September 1992 with 300 students, kindergarten to 5th grade. By 1995, the school plans to be enrolling 600 students (from pre-kindergarten to 8th grade) a year.

Context (field level)

The Decatur-Clearpool School (PS 35) is located in Community School District 16, in Bedford-Stuyvesant. The community has many of the features of a typical urban area: a large proportion of the children are from low income families; many parents are unemployed and under-educated; and crime, violence, drug and alcohol abuse, homelessness, and health problems (including AIDS and TB) are major concerns. The population is predominantly African-American.

Input (strategic and operational levels)

The site chosen for the school was an existing Junior High School which had numerous problems. The students were transferred to other schools and the existing staff was given the opportunity to apply for positions in the new school. A year was spent designing the school's programme and organisational structure. This process involved parents, teachers, administrators, academics and members of the business community. Dr. James Comer, of Yale University, provided the support of the School Development Programme (SDP). The SDP became involved in the design of the school's structure and governance system, agreed to carry out a three-year evaluation, and provided training for staff and key educational leaders in the community.

A wide range of organisations are involved as active partners in the provision of services and resources to the school. In addition to the original founders of the school and the SDP, contributing institutions include the Bethany Baptist Church, the Brooklyn Hospital Centre, and large companies, such as SEGA and Pfizer Inc.

The "Clearpool model", which was articulated during the design stage, provided guidelines for the development of the school. These guidelines are based on the following premises:

- Quality twelve-month education is more effective than conventional nine-month education.
- Families have a greater stake in the school if they have chosen it and are involved in it.
- Academic achievement and high self-esteem are inextricably linked. Rather than seeing the of self-esteem as a discrete goal, it needs to be fully integrated into the curriculum school culture.
- Constructive channelling of peer pressure is a powerful way to engage children in the process. The development of a school culture where children value achievement is a goal.
- Experiential learning is more enduring and effective than traditional, text-based methods.
- Developing constructive relationships between parents, educators and school supporters shared perspectives, allowing adults to make co-ordinated decisions that best suit needs of children.

The financial support provided by the sponsors is estimated to be around $2 000-$2 500 per pupil. This is over and above the $600 which is the average cost per pupil of elementary students in New York City. This extra input provides the extended day, the family and health centres, and the campus at Camp Clearpool. This is currently being renovated, at a cost of $3 million, by the Edwin Gould Foundation.

Process (operational and field levels)

The management structure of the Decatur-Clearpool School is based on the need to involve all stake-holders in its organisation. As a new type of school (operating ten hours per day, all the year round and on two different campuses), new forms of management and governance were needed. The school houses a family centre and a health centre and involves parents, the local community and teachers in its collaborative efforts.

The structures described below are those recommended by the SDP. They have been adapted to the needs of the school, but follow the basic principles of the SDP model:

- *The School Planning and Management Team*: This is the chief policy-making body of the school. It includes representatives of all of the partners in the school community: parents, teachers, administrators, paraprofessionals, unions, health centre and family centre staff, extended day staff, Sponsors for Educational Opportunity (SEO) personnel and custodial staff. It meets once every two weeks and addresses every aspect of school policy.
- *The Mental Health Team*: This co-ordinates and integrates the work of all mental and physical health personnel within the school. It consists of guidance staff, special education staff, profes-

sionals from the health and family centres, school administrators, and developmental staff from the Brooklyn Hospital Centre. It meets once every two weeks.

– *The Parent Programme*: There are a number of aspects to this. There is a Parent Teacher Association (PTA) which is the parents' main governing body. There are also Parent Class Representatives – two per class – who provide lines of communication between the parents and the school decision-making bodies.

– *The Leadership Team*: Its role is to ensure that the school's policies, as determined by the School Planning and Management Team, are upheld. They act as an executive, ensuring co-ordination between the agencies working within the school and those from outside. The Team consists of the school principal, the director of education, the assistant principal, director of the family centre and director of the extended day programme. The Team meets weekly, and monthly with the PTA.

– *School Committees*: There are a number of committees within the school, some concerned with school-based issues and some with outside partners. The committees are Curriculum, Professional Development, Hiring, Bankers Trust and Communications.

A number of mechanisms have been set up to ensure that the structures described above are supported in achieving the goal of maximum collaboration and communication between all of the partners in the school. These mechanisms are:

– *The Comprehensive School Plan*: This is used to guide the school's activities and as a method of evaluating successes and ensuring accountability. It is revised annually.

– *Internal Assessment and Modification*: The school constantly monitors and modifies the provisions made through its various teams.

– *External Assessment*: This is being provided by a team from Dr. Comer's School Development Programme. Its purpose is to provide feedback to the management teams and key staff, to assist the school in refining the model, and to encourage replication by other schools.

– *Comer's Guiding Principles*: These are a no-fault approach to making decisions; decisions made by consensus; collaborative decision making.

– *Meeting Format*: All meetings follow a consistent agenda. Every meeting is facilitated and recorded, with the responsibility for these tasks rotating between team members. The meeting always ends with 15 minutes reflection on the meeting process.

– *School Schedule*: This has been revamped five times since the school opened. The aim was to ensure that in each of the three sections (or mini-schools) all staff have time to work together for up to 80 minutes per day. This supports collaborative approaches and allows time to plan professional development, curriculum and assessment plans.

– *Residential Programming*: Once the Clearpool Summer Camp is opened – it was in the course of being renovated in 1994, during our visit, and was due to open in the summer of 1994 – it will be used to provide residential programmes for students, staff and parents. Already the school has held two two-week residential programmes, which served to build strong social bonds between the partners.

– *Retreats*: These are held for staff to develop team-work, discuss roles and responsibilities and to develop curricula and professional development plans. There have been five retreats in the course of the school's first 18 months of operation.

Problems encountered in implementation

The implementation of a collaborative model which attempts to break down traditional structures and ways of working has not been without problems. The complexity of a decision-making process set up to involve all partners has created the need for substantial communication. Decision-making cannot be undertaken by one or two administrators but requires negotiation with all those affected. This places a great burden on the system. The challenge to professionals of working outside their traditional boundaries causes stress, and requires ongoing support and professional development which, again, is a demand on the system. The school has to find new ways of carrying out these tasks, as well as coping with the primary task of meeting the needs of children and their families.

The school's experiential approach to teaching and learning is innovative. Therefore attracting professionals with expertise in working in inner-city schools, and a commitment to new approaches, was problematic. Often, hiring decisions were made at short notice without full consultation as the school philosophy demands. Some of the school personnel have job descriptions mandated by the city and state government which inhibit their full participation in the school's programmes and management structure.

There are also challenges from the external environment. The Decatur-Clearpool School is attempting to work with an innovative model which cuts across existing agencies and bureaucracies. In order to promote the model and to counter resistance from the wider community, the school has to be involved in outreach and dissemination work. This, in itself, deflects time and energy away from its primary task, creating dilemmas for staff.

Product (operational and field levels)

The school has been open for a relatively short time, so the availability of measured outcomes is somewhat limited. However, the following information is available:

- Attendance at the school is 93 per cent. This places the school in the top 3 per cent for attendance in New York City.

- In standardised tests, the students showed a 23 per cent improvement in Maths and a 4 per cent increase in reading attainment between 1991 and 1992.

- Outcomes noted by teachers and parents include an increased desire to learn, an ability and a willingness to be challenged. We were impressed by three students aged 9 or 10 acted as "diplomats" during our visit and talked to and questioned us with confidence and intelligence.

- The Decatur-Clearpool School has become a Beacon School, part of a city-wide initiative to create model community schools which work in partnership with local community organisations. The original funding for the Beacons Initiative was provided primarily by the Mayor of New York's Safe Streets, Safe City Programme. More recently, private foundations have contributed to a number of Beacon Schools. There is now one Beacon School in each of New York City's Community School Districts.

THE NEW YORK CITY BEACON SCHOOLS INITIATIVE

This initiative currently involves 37 schools. The funding comes from the City as part of a crime prevention initiative. Beacons are described as "school-based community centres" and are located in the most deprived neighbourhoods in the City's five boroughs. The aim is to open these centres to children and adults 365 days per year. Currently, most New York City school buildings are open 1 180 hours per year while the Beacon centres are open around 3 500 hours per year.

Beacon centres are operated by non-profit community-based organisations which work with the community school board, the school principal and their own community advisory council made up of the school principal, teachers, parents, youth, community residents, neighbourhood service providers, community police officers and the district's city council member. Beacon centres operate with the support and co-operation of the New York City Board of Education and the Community School Districts.

The initial start-up funding of $5 million came from the Mayor of New York's crime prevention budget. The New York City Department of Youth Services currently provides $450 000 from several funding sources to each centre to pay for managers and programme staff and to provide recreational, cultural and educational activities for adults and children. Space and maintenance costs for the use of schools are paid centrally by the Department. Department funds are also used by many Beacons projects to match state and federal grants in order to maximise social services provision. The Beacons project also receives funding from private foundations. Thus, it provides an example of integrated funding from a number of sources – city, state, federal and private – to offer a range of services in an integrated way on one site. These include recreational, educational and vocational activities for young people. Parents and other community members are also encouraged to use the Beacon centres for meetings and forums. They are also used for social activities and the organisation of community programmes, such as the creation of drug-free zones. The Beacons initiative is an example of the way in which a local government department can act as a catalyst to bring providers together to generate an integrated response to multiple social problems.

OVERVIEW AND SUMMARY

The collaborative projects we saw in New York City were primarily based in schools (with the exception of The Door). The movement towards using schools as a catalyst to develop support for deprived communities appears to be a growing trend. A report on the Beacons Initiative describes the problems faced by American society as follows:

"Unlike the relatively recent past of 20 years ago, there are major missing personal and social linkages for large numbers of young people today. Significant changes in family composition and greater stresses on family life resulting from economic demands, crime, poverty, substance abuse, and homelessness have weakened traditional family supports. Religious groups have fewer contacts with youth, and neighbourhoods have become less safe, less cohesive, and weaker as venues for transmitting values and standards of behaviour to children and adolescents" (Cahill *et al.*, 1993).

One approach to tackling these problems is to encourage the use of school buildings for community purposes both within and outside school hours, and to promote extensive collaborative networks of educators, community leaders, parents and paraprofessionals. The examples given above illustrate some variations on this approach.

Common features of the three schools we visited were:

– an after-school programme (in two of the schools renamed an "extended day") which provided and recreational classes related to school work;

– a summer programme, which in two of the schools was designed to provide year-round education;

– health and mental health services on the school premises to support children and their families;

– extensive involvement of parents, as participants in evening programmes, as volunteer and paid workers in the school, and as key decision-makers;

– extensive financial and advisory input from private foundations with wide experience of working with schools or communities;

– a clearly defined model of collaboration which was actively promoted;

– training and professional development of staff as an ongoing activity;

– committed and effective leadership in both the school and the community;

– support from key administrators within the public school system;

– support from other local government departments, such as Youth Services;

– support for community policing from the Police Department;

– a commitment to ongoing evaluation and adaptation;

– involvement of community leaders in the development of programmes.

REFERENCES

CAHILL, M., PERRY, J., WRIGHT, M. and RICE, A. (1993), *A Documentation Report on the New York City Beacons Initiative,* Fund for the City of New York, New York.

KOERNER, E. (1993), *A Unique Partnership: The Story of a Community School,* The Children's Aid Society, New York.

MIRAND RESEARCH ASSOCIATES, INC. (1993), *Project Highroad Programmatic and Policy Evaluation. Interim Report on Implementation Progress,* Mirand Research Associates, Inc., New York.

ROSE, P.B., KNOWLES, T.F.C. and ARNOLD, E.M. (1992), *The Clearpool School Concept Paper,* Clearpool Inc., New York.

ROBISON, E. (1993), *An Interim Evaluative Report Concerning a Collaboration between the Children's Aid Society, New York City Board of Education, Community School District 6 and IS 218 Salom Ure-a de Henriquez School,* Fordham University.

CALIFORNIA

MOVING TOWARDS INTEGRATION IN AMERICA'S "HONEYPOT" STATE

by

Mary Lewis and Lucienne Roussel

INTRODUCTION

The state of California has created exemplary initiatives to promote interagency multi-disciplinary collaboration to provide more co-ordinated and effective services for children and families.

This case study highlights state and local initiatives to provide school-linked integrated services. Appointments during the study visit in Sacramento, the state's capitol, focused on two major developments. One is a unique formal partnership between private foundations and State Government to promote and support school-linked integrated services. The second is California's Healthy Start Programme and related policies that provide state incentives to counties. There were brief contacts with one expert on early child care and one on transition from school to work programmes, but information obtained about these was insufficient to provide equally rich description and analysis.

San Diego County was the site of operational and field level visits. It was one of the first places in the nation to undertake school-linked integrated services. Its New Beginnings (NB) model has achieved national recognition (Levy and Shepardson, 1992; Melaville and Blank, 1993). NB leaders have provided national technical assistance through presentations at workshops, conferences and consultations. They have advised the United States House of Representatives about shaping re-authorisation of the Elementary and Secondary Education Act. Tom Payzant, former County Superintendent of Education, and a founder of NB, is now the Assistant Secretary for Elementary and Secondary Education in the United States Department of Education.

SALIENT CHARACTERISTICS OF THE STATE AND POPULATION

The population challenges

California is the most populous and the third largest state in the United States, containing 158 693 square miles. Admitted to the Union in 1850, its population now includes 30 867 000 people, about one-ninth of the nation's population. Its economy has strong manufacturing, agricultural and trading components. However, the state has experienced a sharp recession for several years. Since 1990, about 836 000 jobs have been lost in defence industry layoffs, military base closures, and other business and industry down-sizing (Lewis, 1994).

The State Legislature described vulnerable children in California in a recent act:

"The condition of California's children is in sharp decline. In 1991, 1.8 million of, or 22.3 per cent of California's children, lived in poverty, 200 000 more than in 1988. Over the past four years, the birth rate for teenage mothers has risen by 25 per cent. Child abuse and neglect reports rose from 63.5 to 70.2 per 1 000 children between 1988 and 1991. In 1992, 10 per thousand children were separated from their parents and were living in foster care. Homicides among youth rose from 456 in 1987 to 702 in 1990. California's performance was worse than national data on 83 per cent of measures of children's welfare included on a 1992 state-wide 'report card'. The current service delivery system for children and families, based on a multitude of uncoordinated, separately funded, narrowly targeted categorical programmes emphasizes short-term crisis management over prevention, and typically fails to address the broader needs of the child or family (...). Not only does current funding prevent families from receiving appropriate services, but administrative requirements often use up to 25 per cent of programme funds and bury local agencies in duplicative paperwork" (California Legislature, AB 1741, 1993).

California has been the leading state of intended residence of the country's legal immigrants in every year since 1976. Thirty-five per cent of all immigrants who were granted lawful permanent resident status in the United States in 1992, a total of 336 663 people, came to California. There were 6.1 million "legal foreign born" residents in California in 1993. In addition, about 40 per cent of the country's illegal immigrants reside in California (Lewis, 1994).

Political factors impacting on services integration

It is important to note that the structure and relationship of state and local governments vary widely among the 50 American states. In California, there are 58 counties and they are viewed as the providers of state government services as well as those common to all local governments such as police, fire, safety, sanitation, libraries, parks and recreation. In other words, there is a long-standing pattern of local government involvement in the provision of state government services. Nevertheless, there are many structural complications. As in most states, the education and human services sectors are very separate. Unlike most states, the Governor has no direct control over the education budget. There is an independently elected State Superintendent of Education who is authorised by the state constitution to go directly to the legislature to seek funding. This separation of the education function from other state functions goes down all the way to the county level. There are over 1 000 school districts in California with independently elected school boards and superintendents. Money appropriated by the State Legislature for education goes directly to school districts. In contrast, budgets for state human service agencies are included in the budget submitted to the Legislature by the Governor. Each Department then allocates money to achieve its goals to its respective unit at the county level. California's heavy emphasis on county control and governance has made county administration a natural place to promote collaboration. Without county involvement in services integration efforts, it would be impossible to change the system of services for children and families because the pending policy reforms that affect services are county-based or county-channelled, especially health reform/managed care, welfare reform, de-categorisation and outcome-driven funding.

Economic and fiscal issues impacting services integration

California's fiscal crisis rose to an unprecedented level in 1991. Revenue shortfalls experienced by local and state governments resulted in service reductions and staff layoffs. At the same time, the economic downturn increased demands for public assistance. These developments impacted on human services in drastic ways and the measures taken to deal with them have affected services integration efforts. Major structural changes that occurred in the relationship between counties and the state have been labelled realignment. Realignment legislation transferred approximately $2.1 billion of funding and programme responsibility for health, mental health and social service programmes to counties. Ten realignment principles were set relating to minimum standards, assuring the maintenance of efforts by counties, and providing for greater county flexibility in deciding how money is spent and the way services are provided. Although some new state taxes were created to raise the needed revenue, the major ones are regressive taxes that have a disproportionate impact on poor families. There is doubt about whether there will be sufficient funds for services and the situation is likely to precipitate competition among local children's programmes and with the claims of ageing and other adult constituent groups. County collaboratives focused upon children and family services could advocate solutions to these needs (Chang et al., 1991). DeLapp (1994a) reported, however, that the repeated state budget cuts affecting human service programmes have dampened the motivation to share or blend funds among agencies. More budget cuts are expected this year, some of which will be triggered by a legislative requirement that goes into effect if the Federal Government does not provide reimbursement for the costs of illegal aliens. There is no expectation that Congress will voluntarily provide more than token reimbursement. The state has requested $2.3 billion, but in the past Congress has voluntarily provided only about $550 million. California's governor has joined the governors of a few other states to sue the Federal Government to get reimbursement for the costs of illegal immigrants.

During difficult economic times, such as now, the intensity of public feeling about the costs of illegal immigrants escalates. Proposition 187 emerged from a petition at the ground level reflecting these feelings and was placed on the state's ballot in the November, 1994 election. It passed by a large majority, calling to make illegal immigrants ineligible for any welfare or medical benefits except emergency aid. Also, it required schools to check students' citizenship status and exclude illegal immigrant children. Police and schools were required to report children and parents suspected of being illegal residents. However, as soon as possible after the election results were announced, the San Diego Unified School District and other concerned organisations serving children filed a suit in the federal courts to stop implementation of the proposition while its constitutionality is being tested. Although agency personnel have been notified that they should function as before, many immigrants do not know or understand this and are keeping their children at home and/or not seeking needed health care. Existing federal law, stemming from a United States Supreme Court decision, requires all children residing in the United States to be educated regardless of the legal residence status of their parents. In addition, previous federal rulings have prohibited officials from asking about the immigrant status of children entering schools. Under previous law, emergency medical assistance is available to everyone, and women who are illegal residents are entitled to maternity care, and to the services of the Women, Infants and Children's Programme (WIC), a supplemental nutrition scheme for the disadvantaged. The electorate's response to Proposition 187 has complicated the atmosphere for collaboration in California (Jehl, 1994).

An estimated $2.2 billion were spent in California in 1992 by Federal, State, and local governments on education, Medicaid, Aid to Families with Dependent Children (AFDC), state prisons, and the Food Stamp Programme for illegal aliens and their citizen children (US General Accounting Office, 1993). The California Department of Finance estimated that about 392 260 of California's 5.3 million children in public schools in the 1994-95 school year will be illegal immigrants and that it will cost the state $1.65 billion to educate them (Stewart, 1994).

Most of the cost-benefit studies on immigrants' fiscal impact have concluded that immigrants generally have contributed more in federal tax revenues than they have taken from the Federal Government in services. However, most services are provided at the state and local levels where immigrants often receive more services than they contribute in tax revenues (Lewis, 1994). Before 1978, 55 per cent of elementary and high school funding in the state were raised locally, primarily from property taxes, and were dispensed by local boards of education. But in 1978, California voters enacted Proposition 13 which reduced and capped property taxes and placed limitations on the possibility of raising some other taxes. Since then California's spending per public school pupil has dropped from the top five in the nation to the bottom ten, about $1 000 less than the national average. By the 1990s, less than one-third of public school funding was local, more than 60 per cent being from the state, and 7 per cent from the Federal Government. Before Proposition 13, California was ranked amongst the top five states for achievement in grades kindergarten through 12. Since then it has steadily dropped into the bottom ten states. Average classroom size, now 29 in elementary school, escalated to second in the nation. Half of school libraries were closed, giving the state a current student/librarian ratio of 8 512 to 1, compared to a national average of 826 to 1. On the other hand, California's teachers are still amongst the highest paid in the nation (Reeves, 1994).

STATE (STRATEGIC)-LEVEL INITIATIVES TO LINK SERVICES TO SCHOOLS

The Foundation Consortium for School-linked Services

The Foundation Consortium for School-linked Services was founded in 1992. It includes 17 California-based foundation grant-makers amongst whom are the California Wellness Foundation, the Walter S. Johnson Foundation, the Henry J. Kaiser Family Foundation, the Marin Community

Foundation, the San Francisco Foundation, the Sierra Foundation, the Stuart Foundations and the Zellerbach Family Fund. Some are national or regional in scope but the majority are smaller foundations who limit their contributions to specific areas in California. The motivation for uniting efforts was mutual interest in improving outcomes for California's children and families. They shared a conviction that comprehensive, integrated, school-linked services had a better chance of impacting favourably on children and families than the existing systems of service provision. They believed that by pooling and sharing resources they could impact relevant systems more strongly and therefore produce more positive change than they could by individual grant-making activities. They believed that effective systems change would require strong connections with mainstream rather than small, isolated programmes and that a partnership with state government was essential. The Consortium players believe that the biggest barrier to effective services integration is not money but the "stovepipe" system of separate state agencies that function according to hierarchical dynamics in ways that fragment services for children and families. The fundamental issue is how to design service systems at the local level to bring these "stovepipe" agencies together to serve families and children holistically. If this can be discovered, the next issue is how to change the administrative systems at state and county levels to support them (Chynoweth, 1994).

The Partnership

The Partnership between the State of California and the Foundation Consortium for School-linked Services is a nationally unique formal agreement between the public and private sectors. It was established in January, 1992 with three objectives: 1) to create and support models of comprehensive school-linked services; 2) to create stable financing mechanisms so that comprehensive models can continue when foundation grant money ends; and 3) to create significant, sustained, state-wide changes in systems that serve children and families through school-linked services, cutting across a range of disciplines and agencies.

The Agreement in Principle signed by the State and the Foundation Consortium set forth the commitments of each. The Consortium's contribution to the Partnership includes:

- at least $1.75 million per year for three years, subject to available funds;

- technical planning, start-up, and evaluation assistance to the state and to local programme sites;

- consultancy services at the state or local level to provide detailed expertise on a variety of issues, such as the design of needed federal waivers;

- support for state staff needed to fulfil the goals of the programme statement;

- independent evaluation of the programme; and

- active participation in the Principals Group (defined below).

The State Government's commitment to the Partnership includes:

- The provision of in-kind personnel and equipment up to the value of $1.025 million per year for three years to develop, implement, and monitor a state-wide comprehensive school-based/school-linked service system subject to available appropriations in the budget.

- Agreement to request an annual appropriation of $20 million under the Healthy Start Act subject to passage in the annual Budget Act.

- Commitment to return funds generated from federal financial participation to school districts for use towards preventive children's support services. The Principals Group will provide oversight to assure that a mechanism is in place to return moneys to districts for school-based/school-linked children's support services and determine policy related to the distribution of reimbursements.

- Pursuit of required federal approval and waivers needed to obtain federal financial participation from Medicaid and other programmes for state and locally funded school-based/school-linked services.

- Development of a minimum data set to collect uniform information on clients and their needs, services, outcomes and costs.
- Participation in and administration of the Principals Group.

The state-level governance structure of the Partnership rests with three primary groups: the Principals Group, the Advisory Group, and the Implementers Group. The Principals Group includes the State Superintendent of Public Instruction, the Secretary of Health and Welfare, the Secretary of Child Development and Education, the Directors of the departments of Health Services, Mental Health, Social Services, and Drug and Alcohol Programmes, the Director of the State-wide Office of Health Planning, and representatives of the Foundation Consortium for School-linked Services. The Principals Group has as its goal the development of a strategic state-wide comprehensive school-linked service system. It also provides policy direction on administrative, legal, and legislative issues, directs staff and projects, and provides advocacy. It meets monthly. Its agenda is set by the Deputy Directors of participating State Departments who meet weekly (Kelley, 1994).

The Advisory Group includes senior state staff to the Principals, field representatives, foundation partners, and all those deemed necessary by the Principals Group. The Advisory Group provides staff work and recommendations to the Principals Group related to the strategic plan, state policies and state issues. It also provides support to implement and evaluate sponsored activities.

There are three implementation sub-committees. The Evaluation Work Group focuses primarily on developing criteria to evaluate systems change as well as student and family outcomes. There is a Technical Assistance Work Group, and a Medi-Cal Billing Option Work Group which will also focus on other refinancing strategies to create more flexibility in categorical funds and better use of existing funding streams, including the blending of funding sources.

Healthy Start

California's Healthy Start (HS) Programme is the linchpin strategy to achieve the first objective of developing school-linked services. It is California's first comprehensive effort to bring social, health, mental health, and educational support services together at the school site. Some state general funds have been made available to provide annual vision, hearing, and scoliosis screening, and for assessments of eligibility for special education. HS was enacted by Californian legislation in 1991 (SB 620) to promote expansion of all types of services linked to schools under the auspices of local collaboratives of public and voluntary organisations working together. It authorises the Superintendent of Public Instruction to award planning grants ($50 000) and three-year operational grants ($300 000 plus $100 000 for start-up costs) to collaboratives composed of local government, schools, parents and community organisations to provide school-based, school-linked integrated health, mental health, social, educational, and other support services for children and their families. It is a discretionary grant programme administered by the California Department of Education. Solak (1994) characterised the funds as "glue money" intended to bring a school-linked collaborative into existence, based upon a conviction that school is the place where the community should meet. HS programmes must include shared governance and resource allocation among all partners; also, involvement of parents, teachers and community groups in programme planning, design and operation. Counties that already have existing interagency children's councils and networks are urged to use them as the basis for developing HS collaboratives, where feasible and effective, rather than creating new and possibly duplicative bodies.

During the first two years, 1991-93, 65 operational grants serving 210 schools and 163 planning grants serving 485 schools in 52 counties were awarded (California Legislature, 1994). Additionally, 47 operational grants and 44 planning grants were awarded for the 1993-94 fiscal year (California Department of Education, 1994). HS collaboratives must provide local matching funds to a value of 25 per cent of the grants in cash, services, or other resources. Non-education entitlement and categorical programme funds may be used as matching funds, such as United States Maternal and Child Health or Child Welfare Service funds, private funds or in-kind contributions. HS collaboratives are expected to develop stable long-term financing to continue their programmes when the grants expire.

Collaborating schools must exhibit high levels of need defined as high poverty levels and high percentages of students whose primary language is not English in order to be eligible for grants. The guidelines also require the programmes funded to be integrated, family and outcome focused, both school-linked and linked to state school reform efforts, prevention-oriented, and locally controlled and governed. Key components described by the State Department of Education include culturally appropriate systems, case-managed service delivery, and one-stop shopping for some services. Also, they must meet the needs of students and families in a holistic rather than a categorical fashion. The term, integrated, as used in HS, means that services are offered in holistic rather than categorical ways (DeLapp, 1994a and b). Each collaborative must provide a minimum of four support services to students and their families. One official document provided a non-exhaustive list of services that could be offered:

- health services including immunisations, vision and hearing testing and services, dental services, physical examinations, diagnostic and referral services, and prenatal care;
- mental health services, including primary prevention and crisis intervention, assessments, and treatment referrals;
- substance abuse prevention and treatment services;
- family support and parenting education, including child abuse prevention and teen parenting programmes;
- parent education, in areas such as job search skills, family dynamics and decision-making, language development, and family and individual health;
- academic support, including tutoring and mentoring;
- school/community safety programmes;
- youth development services, including employment development, recreation, and community service internships;
- counselling, including family counselling, suicide prevention and counselling for children who experience violence in their communities;
- nutrition services, including nutrition assessment, nutrition counselling services, nutrition education programmes, and provision of nutritious foods;
- provision of on-site workers who determine eligibility for Medi-Cal, social services, probation, mental health, and other services; and
- other services such as transportation, early childhood care and development, probation, or services for foster children (California Department of Education, 1993).

Other services not named can be included as long as they are based on identified needs.

The state funds a field office for the Healthy Start Programme located at the College of Education, University of California at Davis. It provides technical assistance, state-wide workshops, and is a clearing house for written information on HS programmes. Also, the law required the Superintendent of Public Instruction to commission a three-year evaluation of collaborative processes and outcomes. This evaluation is being funded by the Foundation Consortium for School-linked Services.

An interim evaluation (Wagner et al., 1994) was based upon the 40 sites funded during the first year. These sites involve 124 schools, with 23 sites or a majority operating at single schools. Most of the others operate in groups of two to five schools, and three programmes are district- or country-wide, involving more than ten schools each. Elementary schools comprise the majority (75 per cent) of participating schools. This is congruent with the intent that HS should be a preventive programme that focuses on younger children. Fourteen per cent of affiliated schools are high schools and 8 per cent are intermediate schools. A few sites involve alternative school settings such as special education and juvenile court facilities. Enrolment sizes of affiliated schools range from a rural one-school district with 19 students, that is part of a county-wide programme, to an urban high school with 3 263 students. Forty-two per cent are suburban schools, 29 per cent are urban institutions, and the rest are rural. Students attending HS schools had diverse ethnic backgrounds. Fifty-one (51 per cent) of the schools had student bodies in which the majority were children of colour. Twenty-one (21 per cent) were comprised almost entirely of children of colour. Latinos were the predominant minority group.

Almost half of the 1992 grants were awarded to partnerships that either had no prior history of collaboration (12 per cent) or who had come together in the preceding year, presumably often in response to the availability of HS funds. The intent of the legislation to provide "glue money" to encourage new partnerships succeeded. Of those with previous collaborative histories, 10 per cent had worked together for more than five years. For about one-third of the collaboratives with previous experiences, entering the HS programme represented the first school-linked service activity. In about one-fourth of the experienced collaboratives, HS became an umbrella programme under which other school-linked service activities were organised. HS was an add-on or expansion of an existing programme for the rest. Private or non-profit community organisations comprised 44 per cent of the collaborative members, education organisations 26 per cent, and the rest were county and city public sector agencies. Collaborative size ranged from five to 69 members with an average of 17 members. Education and county agencies were more likely to hold leadership positions than community organisations.

The HS programme is not a defined set of services. It does not envisage or prescribe one model of services. The philosophy behind it is that each community must tailor programme design to respond to its citizens' needs and expectations and to build upon local strengths. The first year's interim evaluation revealed four basic service delivery patterns:

- *School-site family resource centres* (N = 16) had an identified space at an operating school to which families could come for a variety of services on their own initiative or by referral from teachers, other service providers, or a service co-ordination team.
- *Satellite family service centres* (N = 4) involved service centres not located at operating schools. Two of these emphasized identification of family needs and referral to community resources. Two provided more direct services.
- *Family service co-ordination teams* (N = 12) did not base services around a physical location. Instead they featured teams of service professionals who assessed the goals and needs of students or families who had been identified as at risk and developed service strategies to address them. These programmes tended to involve more school personnel as project staff than other types.
- *Youth service programmes* (N = 8) addressed the health, education, and social needs of adolescents. Five organised themselves around a school-based or school-linked health clinic. Three were organised to make a broad array of services available to adolescents (Wagner *et al.*, 1994, p. 9).

This evaluation described noticeable differences in the patterns of services provided and benefits to clients among these four types of programmes.

School-site family resource centres were associated with:

- providing the broadest array of services to meet the diverse needs of the family units that were the focus of their work;
- significant reductions in families' "unmet" basic needs;
- significant improvements in clients' use of health care for illness or injury and reductions in health care access problems or in "lack of a medical home"; and
- significant improvements in clients' mental health, such as reductions in reported depression and thoughts of suicide.

Satellite service centres were associated with:

- serving the fewest clients, delivering the fewest services, and providing those services with the least intensity. However, these programmes were the most active in providing basic needs assistance;
- significant reductions in families' "unmet" basic needs;
- significant increases in access to dental care. No other significant health benefits had been noted;

- significant improvements in clients' mental health, such as reductions in reported depression and problems with anger or hostility.

Service co-ordination teams were associated with:

- A greater emphasis on academic services and school-related counselling than other programmes and significant gains in students' educational performance, the only type of programme to have affected academic performance thus far;
- Significant increases in access to dental care and physical examinations. No other significant health benefits had been noted.

Youth service programmes were associated with:

- the strongest emphasis on health screenings and medical services, consistent with the many school-based or school-linked health clinics included in this type of programme;
- significant improvements in clients' employment status, with a significant proportion of teens acquiring part-time jobs;
- significant reductions in health care access problems or in "lack of a medical home" (Wagner et al., 1994, p. 9).

The evaluators concluded that no Healthy Start model could be labelled the best one at this early stage. Overall the preliminary results for the first year of HS were encouraging.

STATE (STRATEGIC)-LEVEL INITIATIVES TO ESTABLISH COUNTY COLLABORATIVES AND FLEXIBLE FUNDING

The Medicaid Billing Option

School districts in California are commonly referred to as Local Education Agencies (LEAs). The LEA's "billing option" is one strategy for achieving the Partnership's objective of creating stable financing mechanisms to provide ongoing financial support for these collaborative programmes when the HS grants end. The billing option allows LEAs to identify medical services already being provided by schools whose costs could be reimbursed through Medicaid. In California, the Medicaid Programme is renamed Medi-Cal. California ranks last among the 50 states in per capita Medicaid funding (California Institute for Mental Health, no date). In 1992, the Federal Government approved the concept that school districts could be designated as official Medicaid providers. The necessary operational regulations and procedures made it possible for LEAs to sign up for the option in June, 1993. For simplicity of billing, the following nine LEA health service categories were established: health and mental health evaluations, physical therapy, occupational therapy, speech and language therapy, psychology and counselling services, nursing services, school health aide services, medical transportation services, and relevant mileage. Enrolment in the billing option is required of LEAs with Healthy Start grants. Actual submission of claims is elective (California, Department of Education, Department of Health Services, 1993).

Medicaid is the Federal Government's medical assistance programme for very poor individuals, in particular, those who qualify for two means-tested programmes, Aid to Families with Dependent Children (AFDC) and Supplemental Security Income (SSI). In California, eligibility for Medicaid is determined by the county social services department. It reimburses designated providers for specified medical and support services after the services have been provided. This is referred to as a fee-for-service (FFS) system of payment. By billing these services to Medicaid it is possible to draw down additional federal dollars to California because Medicaid is funded through a federal-state matching formula in which the Federal and State Government each pay 50 per cent of the costs. It is important to note that the billing option requires school districts to reinvest additional federal dollars obtained in developing and providing additional or expanded "Healthy Start like" services needed by children and their families. Another requirement is that expanded services must be decided upon through collaborative rather than unilateral decision-making. The initial implementation of the California billing option is through pilot tests with a limited number of LEAs. Training sessions for pilot LEAs and school staff regarding billing and administrative procedures began in 1993 and actual billing under the option began during 1994.

An estimate of the amount of additional federal funding that could be captured during the first year of full implementation was $40 to $60 million (Foundation Consortium for School-linked Services, 1993). If implemented properly, the billing option has potential for increasing the number of local collaborations beyond what could be funded through HS. However, DeLapp (1994*b*) reported that the billing option is not yet being heavily utilised by LEAs. State officials are concerned because some HS sites now entering into their third year have not begun billing, yet they have established no other plan for funding their programmes when the HS grants end.

Another state law, Senate Bill 910, allows school districts to claim reimbursement for administrative costs associated with these Medicaid-financed services. The requirement to use this money to develop new or to expand existing services was not included in SB 910. Chynoweth (1994) noted that many school districts used the money recaptured through SB 910 to offset deficits during the recent financial crisis rather than to expand services.

The Foundation Consortium spent over $300 000 to contract Peat Marwick to assist the Californian Department of Health to design the billing option. It also spent $99 840 for two positions whose sole function has been to support the creation of the option and to train LEAs to become providers. It will continue to fund developments in quality assurance and training for programmatic and technical areas.

Many states have designed Medicaid billing options related to recovering special education costs required of school districts. California's billing option is different from other states because it is constructed to promote systems change. Accomplishing this required extensive collaboration between state departments and bureaus within departments that have quite different cultures and little history of working together (Chynoweth, 1994).

Redeployment of funds

Chynoweth (1994) pointed out that the billing option alone does not meet the need for ongoing stable funding for comprehensive, integrated, school-linked services. In fact, implementation of the billing option is complicated by the fact that the State Government has decided to require counties to provide managed health care for all recipients of Aid to Families with Dependent Children. Over the past twelve years, enrolment in Medi-Cal climbed by 79 per cent and the cost of the programme more than tripled. Despite this, access to primary health care is limited for Medi-Cal beneficiaries. The Health Department believes that a viable alternative to the fee-for-service system is managed health care which means placing a pre-paid cap or limit upon the amount of money spent on each person. Managed care systems or health maintenance organisations (HMOs) provide beneficiaries access to a stable, continuing relationship with a primary care physician and should result in an assessment of health care needs, followed by planning and service co-ordination in a timely manner. The State Health Department has contracted several models of managed health care in which over 700 000 Medi-Cal beneficiaries are enrolled (Foundation Consortium for School-linked Services, 1994).

School children who are enrolled in a pre-paid managed health care plan may not be eligible for LEA provided health services. This poses a challenge to serving them through the billing option. Specific methods of doing this are being developed. It is not the billing itself that poses a threat to school-linked services but the fact that so many health care options further fragment the health care delivery system and complicate the effort to achieve comprehensive school-linked services. HMOs represent large groups of vested interests not necessarily focused upon comprehensive services integration. They might fear that involvement with school-linked services would result in a reduction in their funds. However, if a way can be found to involve the managed health care systems in collaborations with schools, this could result in redeployment of funds to support school-linked services integration.

The Foundation Consortium for School-linked Services is addressing this dilemma by funding three pilot projects to develop and implement specific strategies that can be used to integrate Medi-Cal managed care and school-linked/school-based services. Three incentive grants of $50 000 have been awarded beginning in July, 1994, and ending in June, 1995. The projects are located in geographic areas with operating Medi-Cal managed care projects (either county organised health systems, county-sponsored HMOs, or commercial health plans) which are committed to working closely with existing family-focused, school-linked services and are also involved in mental health managed care planning efforts. The expectation is to learn much that will be transferable to other situations. The Foundation Consortium created an Integration Advisory Group (IAG) to provide guidance and feedback to the pilot projects. The IAG will meet quarterly with the pilot projects to discuss successful concepts, barriers and general progress.

Interagency children's collaboratives

There were legislative efforts to promote county co-ordination of children's services predating the Healthy Start Act. The Presley-Brown Interagency Children's Services Act of 1989 (SB 997) authorised counties to establish Interagency Children and Youth Service Councils to take responsibility for local co-ordination of children's services. The law prescribed that the councils must include but are not limited to:

- the presiding juvenile court judge;

- the County Superintendent of Education; and

- the county staff persons who manage 1) alcohol and drug programmes, 2) children's services, 3) housing and redevelopment, 4) mental health services, 5) public health services, and 6) welfare programmes;

- a city or county prosecuting attorney for health;

- a non-profit representative;

- a member of the board of supervisors;

- a law enforcement representative; and

- a local child abuse council representative.

The statute allows counties who meet the requirements to obtain waivers of state regulations that inhibit co-ordination of children's services. In order to qualify there must be an interagency council authorised by the Board of Supervisors and a three-year plan for establishing a system of co-ordinated children's services that includes a description of how programme success will be measured.

Chang et al. (1991) examined county level collaboratives in 25 counties, encompassing 83 per cent of all California children. In this study a county collaborative was defined as a council, network or consortium that focused on improving services for children and families by engaging in cross-agency policy making, service co-ordination, programme planning and/or fund raising, and was designed to effect system change at the county level. The authors discovered fourteen collaboratives within twelve counties that were discussing implementation of SB 997. Some of them had come into existence in response to SB 997. However, some counties had not found this legislation to be particularly helpful. One concern was that the mandated members of the councils were not always the appropriate people to include in co-ordinating service efforts. Others felt that implementation of SB 997 had been stymied for lack of a clear process for working with the various state agencies that could authorise waivers. A chief officer of the Family and Children's Policy Bureau in the State Health and Welfare Agency was cited as saying that the biggest hurdle to SB 997 implementation was the requirement that counties must submit three-year plans with clear objectives for improving service co-ordination. At the time this study was published, not a single waiver had been obtained. Only one county had met the eligibility criteria for a waiver. DeLapp (1994b) reported that one county had requested a waiver under this legislation.

Another state official expressed the view that the biggest impediment to SB 997 implementation was that neither the Governor, the legislature, nor the agencies designated sufficient resources to oversee the waiver. She recommended that the state designate and fund agency contact people who could provide technical assistance to counties as they develop their county plans and help them to obtain waivers (Chang et al., 1991).

In 1991, the State Legislature enacted SB 786 in an effort to eliminate some of the delays and ambiguities hampering implementation of SB 997 (California Legislature, 1991). It permits counties with "997 Councils" to enter into "negotiated contracts" with the state to reallocate or combine existing resources from participating agencies for purposes described in the contract. For example, a council might request combined funding from social services, child abuse, mental health, child care and special education to fund a parent-child centre for preschool children. The bill required state agencies to respond to a proposed contract within 60 days of its receipt. This bill clarified application procedures but did not specify how state-level agencies would co-ordinate their responses or what types of waivers would be allowed (Chang *et al.*, 1991). DeLapp (1994*b*) reported that no county has yet applied to reallocate or combine funding from different agencies under this legislation.

Blended funding

AB 1741 permits up to five counties selected by the Governor to combine a portion of state funds for child and family services, for five years, starting in 1995. The first five counties selected were Alameda, Contra Costa, Marin, Placer, and San Diego. Participating counties must combine funding for at least four of the following services: adoption, child abuse prevention, child welfare, delinquency prevention, drug and alcohol, eligibility determination, employment and training, foster care, health care, juvenile, mental health, housing, youth development and others. Local education agencies, cities and non-project agencies may also contribute to this blended fund. The blended funds, which will be freed from state categorical restrictions, must be used for comprehensive, integrated services for low-income, multi-problem children and families. Only counties with demonstrated records of successful interagency collaboration and services integration are eligible for the programme.

Participating counties must appoint broadly representative child and family interagency co-ordinating councils to plan, implement and evaluate the programme. County strategic plans must describe the population and geographic area to be served; how funds will be used; and an evaluation process to measure base-line and annual outcomes for children and families served by the blended funding. Pilot programmes will be deemed successful if the outcomes show improvement over base-line performance. The Health and Welfare Agency, as the Governor's designee, is responsible for state interagency co-ordination, technical assistance, assistance with federal waivers, and monitoring county pilots.

STATE (STRATEGIC)-LEVEL CAPACITY BUILDING FOR SYSTEM CHANGE

The Partnership recognises that state legislation and funding options to promote interagency and multi-disciplinary collaboration at the county level are not sufficient to overcome the customary ways in which services have been delivered in the past. Serious obstacles exist to achieving the intended goals due to established patterns of agency operations, leadership styles, professional development, confidentiality regulations, ambivalent attitudes about sharing financial resources, and difficulties spanning organisational boundaries to form new team-building and service delivery capacities.

The Partnership addressed this challenge through a strategy named the Policy Academy. This is an approach that helps people to create collaborative teams and engages them in, and provides support for, a planning process as well as a conceptual framework. The sponsors provide experts and facilitator-coaches who work with the teams at intensive retreats and in their communities. The Foundation Consortium hired and worked with the contractor who developed and ran the process in California. Chynoweth (1994) was a key player. She had developed the Policy Academy Process utilised nationally under the auspices of the Council of Governors' Policy Advisors that is affiliated with the National Governors' Association. The application in California brought together top level decision makers in counties and leaders of the state's human service agencies. An Academy is viewed as a twelve-month process that includes two three-day work sessions held off-site for county collaborative teams. The initiative began with eight counties that had previous experience with collaboratives that had been successful. They were chosen by a competitive application process. The Request for Applications (RFA) for the Academy invited counties to indicate whether they intended to apply for funding under AB 1741. If selected, such counties would be expected to select goals and outcome measures which would provide the basis for the blended funding. The RFA also designated important elements of systems change towards which the Academy is working and which could be useful to any group attempting to improve service outcomes for children and families:

- the new system is customer-drive; the old system is agency-focused;

- in the new system, the family is the customer (family-centred); in the old system, the individual (or child/student) is the client;

- the new system is outcome-driven; the old system in input-driven;

- the new system emphasizes a balance between prevention and intervention; the old system is heavily crisis-oriented;

- the new system is decentralised; the old system is centralised;

- the new system provides services through public and non-profit agencies, private vendors, and informal supports; the old system uses primarily formal service delivery systems;

- the new system provides integrated or co-ordinated services; the old system provides categorical services;

- the new system is evaluated for its effectiveness; the old system is monitored for compliance with rules and regulations;

- the new system is more community-based; the old system sees clients in agency offices;

- the new system delivers services through teams of professionals, non-professionals, and parents; the old team delivers services primarily through credentialed professionals;

- the new system seeks institutional change at scale; the old system funds isolated projects.

Each county chosen designated two teams. One consisted of a core group of eight to twelve members who attended the three-day retreats. The second was a larger group of people, viewed as stakeholders in the collaborative process in the community, who were considered to be essential in implementing the county's strategic collaborative plan. Team membership included people who had the breadth of involvement and level of decision-making authority to allocate resources, such as elected and/or appointed county and school district leaders; staff from key county, city, and non-profit agencies involved with children and families, schools, businesses, community-based organisations and co-ordinating groups (reflective of the diversity of the county); employees who deliver services directly to children and families; parents; and major funders. Each county designated a team leader, and they attended at least two pre-Academy orientation sessions and two follow-up meetings after the Academy retreats. Money was provided to help the teams defray expenses for the off-site training sessions. The responsibilities of each county team were:

- to secure support from a broadly based, diverse set of partners needed for programme success;

- to assure participation of the county's and school district's senior policy officials;

- to commit to reinvest any refinanced federal funds, achieved as a result of the Academy, in expanded services for children and families;

- to identify ongoing policy and budget initiatives that reflect the capacity of the county to address issues affecting children and families; and

- to prepare to implement the strategic plan developed during the Academy process.

The State's responsibilities were:

- to involve senior state agency officials in the year-long effort;

- to enable the reinvestment of refinanced or redirected funding in expanded services for children and families;

- to help develop alternative funding approaches; and

– to work to remove state and federal regulatory and administrative barriers to providing more comprehensive services to children and families in priority areas.

During the retreats, each county's team met intensively with experts to develop their own unique goals and objectives. It was anticipated that they could then serve as resources for other counties who had not attended the Academy. An example was provided by the San Diego County teams who developed a county-wide strategic plan to improve outcomes for children ages 0-6, shifting toward prevention rather than crisis-oriented programmes and not basing efforts upon categorical programme demands. The first priority was for the safety and security of children, reflecting great concern about the high risk of physical and emotional harm in the lives of too many San Diego children. This priority referred primarily to economic security without which no community programmes can be very effective. A second priority chosen was health and well-being. The third was community and organisational capacity building, a goal that addressed the existing state of fragmentation and programme-driven accountability. Implied in this aim was a determination to invest in infrastructure that makes programmes work, to train staff and thereby improve the ability of professionals and non-professionals to work as accountable teams, and to build upon the diversity of neighbourhoods and cultures in the county.

In addition to staffing the Policy Academies, the Foundation Consortium has provided technical assistance to more than ten counties who did not attend them. The Consortium is also undertaking a project to help county governments to integrate data systems across various "stovepipe" agencies. There are many incongruities in county data systems; ethnicity, for example, is defined in different ways. The state partners have not indicated how they will participate in this project.

STATE (STRATEGIC)-LEVEL MEASURES TO ADDRESS CONFIDENTIALITY ISSUES

An important principle in ethical human services provision is maintaining the confidentiality of information provided by clients. The importance of respecting the privacy of people is embedded in the ethical codes of most human service professions. Numerous federal and state laws specify confidentiality requirements relating to records, such as medical, educational, juvenile court and child welfare. Confidentiality regulations facilitate the development of trusting relationships with clients. They prevent embarrassment and humiliation, avoid exposure of inherently inflammatory allegations such as abuse or mental instability, protect personal and family security, and reduce the likelihood of prejudicial or stereotyped responses. However, it is often necessary for service providers to share information about individuals and families in order to conduct comprehensive child and family assessments, to provide them with all necessary services, to co-ordinate, monitor and avoid duplication of services, to make services family-focused, to secure full reimbursement for services from federal and other sources, to conduct research on community needs and programme effectiveness, and to promote public safety. Soler *et al.* (1993) reviewed the privacy and confidentiality restrictions in federal and state laws, regulations and practices and in professional standards. They concluded that confidentiality restrictions are not absolute, but instead balance individual interests in privacy against agency interests in providing effective services. Usual agency practice has been to obtain adult or parental consent to release confidential information or records from one agency to another.

Because of the practical difficulties in developing cross-agency information sharing and management, the Healthy Start Field Office is providing technical assistance to help HS programmes make important distinctions between what is or is not confidential, and to establish how to facilitate exchange of information while respecting clients' rights.

The California Legislature took steps to make the sharing of information easier between agencies for certain purposes. One purpose enunciated in SB 997, discussed above, is to facilitate the integration of children's services at the local level. In this context, a multi-disciplinary service team was defined as two or more persons trained and qualified to provide the services offered by an integrated children's services programme. AB 2184 (1991) permits them to share information that is relevant to services for a child if they have received signed consent from the parents or legal guardian. All members of such a team who receive information are subject to the same obligations and penalties as the person providing the information.

A special law (AB 3688, 1992) applicable only to San Diego County was enacted that permits team members, without obtaining signed consent, to disclose information to each other and to view records on a child or family if this is deemed necessary to formulate and deliver an integrated services plan. Exceptions to this rule are that signed consent must be obtained to release information concerning the child's mental or physical health and for drug or alcohol records. San Diego County officials requested this specific legislation in order to facilitate their services integration efforts described below. Additional legislation extended these principles throughout the state (Roberts, 1994).

Existing law also permits members of a multi-disciplinary personnel team that is engaged in the prevention, identification, and treatment of child abuse or neglect to disclose and exchange relevant, confidential information. AB 3491 (1992) expanded the potential for pooling such information by authorising counties to establish a computerised data base system that could contain specified information relating to child abuse and neglect from at least the following entities: schools, law enforcement, probation, social, children's health and mental services. The law allowed each county to define families "at risk of neglect or abuse" who could be included in the system. It also designated who could have access to the information and in what circumstances.

SB 931 (1993) authorised the exchange of information between the housing and public assistance agencies about persons applying for services without notifying them in advance. The purpose of this law was to increase the availability of housing and services to those who needed them. Only information that is necessary for determining eligibility for services sought by the client can be exchanged. The housing or welfare department must notify people that these information exchanges may occur and allow those who request it to review information that has been exchanged.

SUMMARY AND DISCUSSION OF STATE (STRATEGIC)-LEVEL INITIATIVES

The Presley-Brown Interagency Children's Services Act of 1989 (SB 997) and its 1991 sequel, SB 786, appear not to have stimulated as much county-level inter-agency collaboration as envisioned. AB 1741 appears to be pushing inter-agency collaboration further as counties have developed plans for blended funding.

The shapers of the HS programme attempted to incorporate lessons learned from previously existing collaborations throughout California. The Partnership between the Foundation Consortium and the State Government (to promote HS, and to provide technical assistance, capacity building and evaluation) mobilises powerful resources in the effort to build and sustain school-linked services integration.

Formal evaluations have provided information about achievements and barriers yet to be overcome. The first year interim state-wide evaluation of HS programmes (Wagner et al., 1994) summarised positive child and family outcomes as follows:

- Basic needs: HS activities seem particularly effective in meeting the fairly immediate needs of families, such as food or clothing.

- Health care experiences: Smaller, but significant positive impacts on some aspects of health care use were noted, particularly an increase in participation in early childhood health screening, diagnosis, and treatment, and a reduction in health care use for illness or injury, and also effective linkage with dental care providers.

- Emotional health: Indicators of emotional health also show significant improvement, with a reduced incidence of depression, suicidal thoughts, and problems with hostility and anger, and less serious existing problems.

- Youth behaviours: Programmes that have the goal of reducing teen pregnancy have achieved significant reductions in the age at which youth become sexually active, and a significant increase in reliable contraceptive use among sexually active teens.

- *School performance*: Students' grades and classroom behaviour were marginally, though significantly, improved, particularly amongst students who were performing least well before participating in HS.

- *Complex behaviours*: More complex behaviours associated with family functioning or the participation of youth in several high-risk activities appear less amenable to short-term impact through HS (pp. 6-31).

The evaluation revealed broad community involvement and support for school-linked, multi-disciplinary, collaborative efforts. Lack of staff time was the most frequently mentioned (95 per cent) barrier to collaboration. Most of the difficulties presented by local policies, procedures, relationships, and interfacing with other collaboratives, were partially resolved. Difficulties with federal and state policies and with categorical funding were less amenable to resolution as they cannot be dealt with at the local level. Another evaluation of HS sites in seven counties (Carreon and Jameson, 1993) agreed that many obstacles to system-wide change require legislative directives at the state and federal levels, such as synchronising eligibility requirements or otherwise reducing eligibility burdens, blending funding streams, and coping with the separate nature of school and county governance. Various officials interviewed referred to the phases involved in developing integrated services portrayed in Figure 1. It was frequently stated that collaboratives continually come up against the need for changes in regulations before system changes can occur.

Chynoweth (1994) believes that the Consortium is more interested in and committed to state-wide system change than the state partners. She noted that the Consortium and the State have different cultures, time-frames, and objectives. Also, the state agencies reel from continual budget cuts. She has found the state partners to be committed to implementing the HS initiative, to developing the billing option, to providing technical assistance, and to obtaining competent evaluations of HS. The enactment of AB 1741 represents the extent of other formal state government commitments to services integration. It has the potential to change how services are funded and delivered.

Kelley (1994) provided the perspective of a state agency representative on the Partnership's Advisory Committee. She said that the weekly meetings of the Deputy Directors' group started with

Figure 1. ***Phases in inter-agency collaboration***

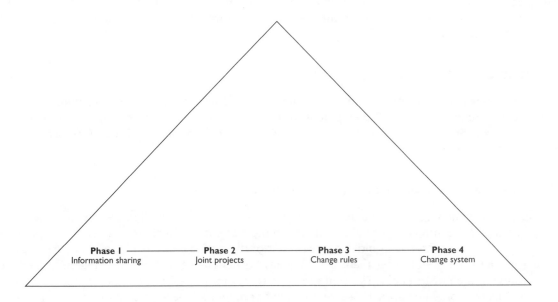

Source: Authors.

discussions about implementing HS and school-linked services. Now they are expanding discussions to include the concept of services integration outside of schools. She acknowledged that the state agencies are in a formative process around collaborative planning for integrated services, sharing information more than undertaking joint projects. Each agency has some money to utilise on behalf of children and families. The Mental Health Department is working on a system of care to keep emotionally disturbed children out of residential care and in the community and family. The Health Department is planning a system of managed health care. The State's Alcohol and Drugs Programme receives federal funds that should target drug-using mothers and their children. Kelley is interested in how abused children can access these programmes, and how all of the agencies can complement each other to target high-risk groups. Very young children are a focus of her Division of Children and Family Services as over half of foster children are under the age of 7. Although she values the possibilities of school-based services, she favours a "softer" type of collaboration in which the education sector is an active partner, but not always the base or location for integrated service provision. She believes that other groups who are not yet fully involved need to be included at the planning table, such as juvenile probation and housing services, and representatives of business (who can become involved in job creation to address high unemployment and economic insecurity). In view of the detrimental environmental conditions confronting many high-risk children and families, she deplores the fact that none of the money available can be spent on neighbourhood development.

She believes that most innovative budgeting actions to facilitate services integration are taking place at the county level, such as those stemming from AB 1741. The state officials are hoping to receive feedback from these localities about what types of state-level legislative or administrative action would be helpful. In an effort to promote collaborative, community-based decision-making, her agency decided to allow the County Boards of Supervisors, instead of the County Child Welfare Agencies, to decide how to spend the $100 million made available by the Federal Government for Family Preservation and Support Services over the next five years. This decision antagonised many county child welfare directors. The Family Preservation guidelines permit the first year's allocation of funds to be spent on planning, training, and building collaboratives and teams. A similar decision was made regarding available resources for Greater Avenues of Independence (GAIN), an employment programme.

When asked what she saw as the biggest barriers to services integration, she noted that staff may be open to new ideas but often feel overwhelmed by a perceived lack of personnel and resources. The amount of work required to make tangible gains is enormous. The federal system of categorical funding poses serious barriers to the design of new service systems. Another obstacle to change is the time required for collaborative discussions at the state level to permeate the whole organisation and impact action at the field level.

SAN DIEGO COUNTY (OPERATIONAL) LEVEL

San Diego was the site of visits at the operational and field levels. Kathleen Armogida, Deputy Director of Planning, Policy and Development for the County Department of Health, and Jeanne Jehl, Administrator on Special Assignments Related to Services integration, San Diego City Schools, were hostesses for the visit.

Salient characteristics of the county and its population

The county, spanning 4 200 square miles and containing over 2.5 million people, has the second largest urban and the fifth largest rural population in the state. It has 18 cities and many migrant worker camps. The county includes just under one per cent of the nation's population and has more people crossing its United States border than any other in the nation. As an economic region, government entities employ the most people. The United States Navy and the superior natural harbour of the city have been major economic forces. However, the number of military personnel in the county reached its highest point in the last ten years in 1990 and has declined steadily ever since. Small businesses containing less than 23 employees comprise 98 per cent of the private sector employment base. The county does not have a large industrial or corporate base. This makes it difficult for the county and its cities to form partnerships with business interests.

San Diego is behind the rest of the state in recovering from the recession and the whole state is behind the rest of the nation, so the future direction of the local economy is uncertain. The population has recently lost some of its white, middle class residents. Wages are lower here than in other major United States cities such as Los Angeles, San Francisco and New York. Yet the cost of living in the county is six per cent higher than the national average. Housing is particularly expensive compared to the nation as a whole. At least 50 per cent of the total income of low-income families is commonly spent on housing and there is a five-year waiting list for public housing. The county's population under the age of 18 comprises 24.5 per cent of the total. This is the second largest child population among the state's 58 counties. More than 16 per cent of them live below the poverty level and more than 18 per cent receive AFDC.

San Diego residents have the second highest utility rates in the country. Public transport is limited and insurance premiums far exceed national averages. The county suffers from inequitable state financing for its public services. For example, San Francisco City and County receive the same state budget for public health service as San Diego County. Yet the latter contains four times more people. The county is the primary provider of health and social services and is responsible for probation and jails. The county contains 43 school districts, each having an independent school board. School construction has not kept pace with the needs of the student population. In order to alleviate crowding, many schools have converted to multi-track, year-round schedules. Per pupil spending approximates the state average; however, California's ranking for education spending among the 50 states is expected to fall. Despite limitations, the county's school drop-out rate has steadily declined from 24.9 per cent in 1986 to 11.4 per cent in 1991 (Armogida, 1994; Jehl, 1994; New Beginnings, 1990; San Diego County, 1992; United Way, 1992).

The San Diego City School District is the nation's eighth largest urban district with an enrolment of 125 000 students in 1992-93. Approximately 34 per cent are white, 30 per cent Hispanic, 20 per cent Asian (predominantly Indochinese and Filipino), and 16 per cent African-American. More than 60 different home languages are spoken (Jehl, 1993). Most live in mixed neighbourhoods. There are 158 schools in this district. Some elementary schools serve over 1 000 children. Sixty per cent of the children in this district live below the poverty line and there are 23 schools with more than 90 per cent of their children living in poverty (Jehl, 1994).

New Beginnings: A skilfully crafted planning phase

The collaborators who initiated New Beginnings in 1988 were the Director of the San Diego County Department of Social Services and the Superintendent of the San Diego City Schools who recognised that children who do not succeed in school often live in families receiving social services and that closer collaboration on their behalf was needed. The City of San Diego Government and the San Diego Community College District joined them to form a nucleus to deliver services to children and families that would overcome the uncoordinated, inconsistent, often wasteful, crisis-oriented, and duplicative existing system. Later the University of California at San Diego Medical School, the Children's Hospital, and the San Diego Housing Commission, became key partners.

The original partners all have elected boards. A conscious decision was made to keep them informed but not directly involved. The reason was to avoid politicising the effort because if it became an elected official's pet project, it could arouse opposition from rivals. Politicians became directly involved when they approved the collaborative's governance agreement and its statement of philosophy. Staff from the partner agencies keep their elected officials apprised but ongoing meetings of the collaborative involve agency staff only. Under California's open meetings law, inviting public officials means opening meetings to the press. Jehl believes that staying out of the limelight gave the group time to plan, freedom to act, and to seriously address policy and funding issues (Melaville and Blank, 1993, p. 28).

In the beginning, top managers of 26 public agencies pledged to meet monthly to seek collaborative ways to remain involved in what later became the NB Council. Initially they focused their attention on several areas of mutual concern such as school attendance, teenage pregnancy, and the health needs of young children in City Heights, a densely populated, multi-ethnic area with high rates of poverty, crime, and child abuse. They compiled extensive information about services being provided to children and families there and none felt that they were having a sufficiently positive overall impact. Then they focused on the neighbourhood of Hamilton Elementary School as a possible site for a demonstration project because it had an extraordinarily high rate of student mobility which is associated with low academic achievement. The area has the highest density of housing in San Diego dominated by low-income apartments, the highest crime rate, and the second highest child abuse rate. The school enrols 1 300 students in grades kindergarten through five in a year round, four-track schedule. Forty per cent of the children are Hispanic, 30 per cent Indochinese, 20 per cent African-American, and 10 per cent from other ethnic backgrounds (Jehl, 1993).

A detailed six-month feasibility study, funded with $45 000 from the Stuart Foundation and in-kind contributions of $217 000 from partners, was undertaken to determine the need for school-linked integrated services and the resources that each participating agency could provide. It consisted of six different elements portrayed in Box 1 and may be the most detailed feasibility study completed in the nation by a public service collaborative (Barfield et al., 1994, p. 2). Enrolment data from Hamilton School was matched electronically with case-load data from several programmes of the Department of Social Services, such as AFDC, food stamps and Medi-Cal. This revealed the number of families served by several programmes and showed that the Department of Social Services spent $5 7000 000 in 1989, including administrative costs, for families of children at Hamilton. The study revealed that over 60 per cent of the families of Hamilton School students were served by at least one partner's programme and 10 per cent were known to four or more programmes. Agency staff and the school tended to work with individuals as though no other agency were involved, and were not family-focused. The NB feasibility study supported the view that families needed help to access the existing fragmented service systems. Families indicated that they trusted the school as a place to get help (New Beginnings, 1990, p. vi). Following the study, a decision was made to develop an implementation plan based upon a set of principles developed and agreed to by the collaborative.

Box 1. The New Beginnings feasibility study

In 1989 and 1990, the New Beginnings collaborative engaged in a detailed study of many aspects of the needs of families and the service delivery system. This study included:

- *Focus groups of agency workers*: Nine focus groups of 77 agency line workers to explore their perspectives on the needs of families and children, the barriers to service, the available and helpful services, and family-agency communication.

- *Case management study*: Placement of an out-stationed social worker at Hamilton Elementary School to provide case management services to 20 high risk families, documenting their needs and their barriers to service.

- *Family interviews*: Interviews with 32 Hamilton families to understand their needs for services, their barriers to service, to identify helpful and accessible services, and communication issues.

- *Agency liaison network*: Creation of agency liaisons to expedite referrals, and share information with the Hamilton school staff in order to increase access of staff and families to agency services.

- *Data match*: Determine the extent of multiple service use by families by using the data bases of three agencies to explore which of those families are served by more than one of them and the total resources of these agencies used by these families.

- *Migration study*: Determine the patterns and extent of family and student mobility in and out of the Hamilton area (Barfield et al., 1994, p. 3).

This feasibility study utilised a bottom-up approach to get the perspectives of agency line workers, and interviews with family members. Commendations across the nation have extolled the usefulness of this approach. In contrast, a collaborative in Savannah, Georgia, used a top-down planning process and a team of professional planners were the primary shapers of the service delivery plan. People who were expected to implement the plan, such as principals, teachers, and agency line workers, were barely involved in its development. The Director of this collaborative later concluded that the first year of implementation effectively was lost due to the haste to get started without attending to the perspectives of the direct service workers and families, and without developing commitment, clear lines of communication, and broad interagency agreements (Melaville and Blank, 1993, pp. 114-115).

Before beginning service operations, the collaborating agencies developed a governance agreement in the spring of 1991, that defined the rationale, organisational structure, purpose, and responsibilities of each agency.

The Executive Committee was designated the co-ordinating committee for the endeavour and included the following people: the City Manager, the County Chief Administrative Officer, the Commission Executive Director, the Community College District Chancellor, the Unified School District Superintendent, and Directors of the County Health Services, Social Services, Housing, and Probation Offices. They meet monthly to review system-level and policy issues, leaving the day-to-day decisions about service delivery to the New Beginnings Council which consists of middle and upper level managers from the partner agencies. The Council identifies staff and community issues to address through collaboration; frames broader issues of institutional change from what is learned at demonstration sites; develops solutions to site issues that have system-wide applications; creates communication links with other collaboratives concerning structures, roles, governance and responsibilities; and defines operational barriers and makes recommendations to the Executive Committee for removing them.

Purposes and objectives of New Beginnings

– To develop an integrated services approach based on a shared philosophy, a collaborative leadership structure, and more effective use of the expertise of agency staff.

– To develop a centre at or near Hamilton Elementary School to provide multiple levels of support to children and families that enable agencies' staff, through increased authority, to solve problems and promote deeper involvement with families.

– To develop a cross-agency training institute that can build commitment to the shared philosophy and provide technical skills training to managers and staff

– To develop an information management system that facilitates information sharing, referral and feedback, data collection, outcome measurement and evaluation recognising current legal restrictions on records' confidentiality (IEL Policy Exchange, 1994, p. 13).

The basic principles adopted by the collaborative were:

– To make collaboration school-linked, but not necessarily school-governed.

– To focus the system of services on the family, not on any single member of the family.

– To shift as many resources as possible to prevention, instead of waiting for intervention after serious problems have arisen.

– To fund the new system of services to the greatest extent possible with existing funding streams, rather than becoming dependent on short-term funding.

– To adapt the application of these principles to different communities and available resources (Jehl, 1993).

The collaborative intended to influence the whole service delivery system rather than to operate a single demonstration project. They identified desired outcomes at three system levels. They are portrayed in Box 2. Desired outcomes for children and families are portrayed in Box 3. They emphasized the financial and social well-being, and health, of families, and the school performance of children.

Box 2.   **Changing the system through New Beginnings: the desired outcomes**

At the executive level:

- shared collaborative philosophy;

- common eligibility screening/requirements;

- more flexible funding;

- more flexible service area boundaries;

- data sharing;

- promoting the spread of New Beginnings.

At the service level:

- a focus on families, not individuals;

- case management, featuring worker autonomy, generalist workers, shared responsibility;

- a focus on prevention or early intervention;

- easy entry to and exit from the system.

At the family level:

- increased awareness of services;

- perception that the system responds to their needs;

- perception that they are respected and valued by service providers (Barfield *et al.*, 1994, p. 5).

The New Beginnings Centre at Hamilton Elementary School

After two years of planning, a demonstration centre at Hamilton Elementary School opened in September, 1991, in three portable classrooms donated by the school district and remodelled with funding from the County Health Services and local foundations. Funding for the first year of operation included $225 260 from grants and $347 980 from institutional funding. The goal was to replace all grant contributions with money from the agencies' regular funding sources (Melaville and Blank, 1993, p. 109).

Each agency was asked to provide adequate staff, furniture, supplies and equipment for the new Centre as no new funds for operational expenses were available. Also, each agency was expected to provide dedicated support staff in the home agency base to back up their personnel in the Centre. These people were designated as the "extended team". San Diego City Schools became the fiscal agent for NB. IBM contributed to the development of the management information system.

Links with the school

Teachers receive intensive training on problem identification, supportive techniques in the classroom, the roles and services of other agency staff, and referral processes. There is a task force including NB staff members, parents, designated Hamilton School teachers and staff that meets twice per month to facilitate co-ordination and communication. Quite specific guidelines for making referrals to NB were developed. NB and the school together created a Family School, a one-night a week, five-week set of sessions designed to orient parents to what the school will expect from their children and how they can support their progress. Parents are taught skills such as creating a time and place for their children to do homework and helping them with it. Attendance has been high.

Box 3.   **Helping children and families through New Beginnings: the desired outcomes**

Improvements in financial and social well-being among families:
- basic needs met;
- employment;
- less time on AFDC;
- fewer reopened cases with social service agencies;
- less deep and lasting involvement in the foster care system.

Improved health indicators including:
- a regular source of medical care;
- regular receipt of check-ups, screenings, immunisations;
- fewer school absences due to illness;
- fewer hospitalisations due to lack of prompt medical care;
- fewer undiagnosed conditions in need of care.

Improvements in school indicators including:
- attendance;
- promotion;
- reduced suspension;
- improved performance;
- increased parental involvement (Barfield *et al.*, 1994, p. 6).

Staffing and services now include:
- A Director, Administrative Assistant, and secretary.
- Four Family Services Advocates (case managers) who identify family needs, set goals with them, and help them to obtain services. They are employees of the partner agencies who are reassigned to the Centre.
- A full-time nurse who performs physical examinations, provides immunisations, treats minor ill-nesses and injuries, and assists each family in finding a "medical home" outside the centre.
- A part-time Licensed Visiting Nurse, two community health workers, and a physician half a day per week.
- One full-time and one part-time worker from Greater Avenues for Independence (GAIN), the federally funded job training programme for welfare recipients.
- Mental health services for children provided by the Union of Pan-Asian Communities through a contract with the County Department of Health.
- Eligibility assistance so that families can find out what programmes might be available to assist them.
- Parent education/adult education programmes, with child care available for preschool children.
- School registration is expanded to the Centre so that from the beginning every family of children entering Hamilton becomes familiar with the Centre and its services. Also, all NB staff participate in pre-registration for kindergarten.
- Community outreach workers to provide ongoing child development and health education, targeted at parents of preschool children in the community. The Parents as Teachers home-based Programme, originated in Missouri, is a major outreach programme targeted on individual children and families. It offers a planned age- and culture-appropriate curriculum, training in positive reinforcement techniques, and help with accessing agency services.
- Two community development workers to nurture community leadership.
- Multi-lingual staff who speak the major languages spoken in clients' homes.
- Additional assistance from partner and other community-based organisations provided by an "extended team" of designated agency-based workers who work with the centre (Jehl, 1993, 1994; Barfield *et al.*, 1994).

A family focus

Generally, the targeting of families for services proceeds in the following way. On school registration days, all families learn about NB, are provided with a list of available support services in the community, and are offered an initial assessment of their service needs. The most extensive case management services are targeted upon 250 plus students who are deemed at risk according to the school district's academic criteria and who are known by at least three agency programmes. There is less intensive assessment, and referral where necessary to the agency-based extended teams, for the 600-800 students/families who are known only to AFDC, Medi-Cal and/or the free-and-reduced-price lunch programmes (New Beginnings, 1990). Families who live in the neighbourhood of Hamilton School, whose children attend other schools, may also receive services. Efforts are being made to develop the continuity of services for clients who move to other neighbourhoods.

Simplifying eligibility determination and data management

One of the biggest barriers to providing co-ordinated, family-oriented service systems is the differing eligibility requirements for federal and state-financed programmes. The feasibility study identified and analysed the multiple forms, interview formats, and unique programme eligibility criteria of different agencies that frustrate and discourage families. A common screening form is being utilised by some services but many do not yet co-operate in simplifying eligibility.

Much effort has been expended to develop a user-friendly Management Information System (MIS) that provides on-line access to information on parent agency programmes, clients, and eligibility; protects the privacy of clients; generates forms; and provides reliable, comprehensive data for planning, providing and evaluating services. Another goal was to organise it so as to facilitate steps in the case management process and billing.

The extended team concept

Achieving the goal of making the big bureaucracies family-centred would require a reduction in the number of different people one family must ask for help. Originally, NB partners had hoped that all of the work required for programme eligibility determination could be accomplished in the Centre by the re-assigned agency workers. This proved to be impossible, but screening for probable eligibility has made the process easier for families. Another goal of the NB partners therefore was to assign small units of agency-based workers to specific neighbourhoods to collaborate with field-based personnel on eligibility determination and service provision. However, large-scale implementation of this concept requires detailed interagency agreements designating workers' roles and the information that they are allowed to share. The Department of Social Services took the position that it was important to work through the issues required to implement the extended team concept for at least a whole department of the agency, such as Income Maintenance, and not just at one site. Now the Income Maintenance Section determines eligibility for welfare benefits for the majority of welfare cases associated with Hamilton School through a unit of seven workers who report to one supervisor. Previously such cases may have been referred to any one of 250-300 eligibility workers in the agency (Melaville and Blank, 1993, p. 110). Two of these eligibility workers are out-stationed at the New Beginnings Centre, although sometimes they need to go to the district office. Having worked through the issues that would need to be settled through interagency agreements, the Social Service Department concluded that selective criteria must be used to apply the extended team method, and that it could not be utilised throughout the county. Office space could be a barrier at some locations, for example. Staff productivity measures utilised by the agency requires case-loads of a certain size, an issue that affects the appropriateness of using the extended team concept in some areas of the county (New Beginnings, 1990; Roberts, 1994).

Confidentiality

Confidentiality issues were addressed from the beginning through an extensive study of the requirements of the law and of partner agencies (San Diego County Department of Social Services,

1991). Over time, policies and procedures have been developed that balance the privacy rights of families and the importance of exchange of information between agencies. As discussed above, San Diego County obtained a state legislative act, applicable only to itself, to facilitate the pilot testing of these policies. Since then, additional state legislation has extended these principles throughout the state (Roberts, 1994).

Capacity building

The NB Executive Committee established the Institute for Collaborative Management (ICM) in April, 1991, and charged it "to institutionalise collaboration among the partner agencies and make it our operational norm through an ongoing training process" (Barfield *et al.*, 1994, p. 11). A training conference for 123 upper level executives and directors from health, education, social services, law enforcement and other agencies in the county was held in 1993. It was viewed as very successful (Jehl, 1994; Carlisle, 1994). Plans are being made to have a second training conference for middle managers. Following the first conference, the ICM made recommendations to the NB Executive Committee for future development.

Expanding the New Beginnings model: Going to scale

The United States Department of Health and Human Services gave a two-year grant of $400 000 to the San Diego County Department of Social Services to facilitate the expansion of NB to Vista, El Cajon, and National City, three very different communities within San Diego County. Expansion of NB involved senior personnel associated with the original programme who advised key players in the new communities to facilitate consensus building and planning. Each community formed an Executive Committee of key agency executives and a council of middle managers to develop its own principles, vision, and concepts to guide its endeavour. Each community also conducted its own feasibility study and designed a service delivery model. National City, a relatively homogeneous poor area of eight square miles and 50 000 people, is now phasing in a school-linked service site and is considering a mobile unit to provide services throughout the area. This partnership includes a greater variety of agencies than at the San Diego site. The other two communities contain conservative religious factions who oppose the delivery of any school-linked health services. One is still in the community assessment stage. The other has decided not to provide any case management services, but to use a community organisation and development approach to reduce violence and provide more safety and security. An office has been opened at a downtown recreation centre near a park and the plan is to work with recreation leagues and neighbourhood watch groups. The Sheriff is a key player. Every step in the expansion process has taken longer than anticipated (Carlisle, 1994).

Hoover High School receives many children who attended Hamilton Elementary School, after their middle school years. NB leaders facilitated the development of a health and social service centre which received a HS grant. The Centre provides physical examinations and acute health care. Also, several community agencies have relocated workers at Hoover to provide case management and counselling services.

The Executive Committee and Council of NB have actively lobbied state legislators and administrators to promote system support for family-focused, community-based, interagency collaborations. Healthy Start legislation was influenced by the NB model. NB is co-ordinating the Healthy Start grants in San Diego County, and is providing technical assistance and quarterly meetings for all school-linked integrated service collaboratives in the county.

NB also co-ordinated the county's application to be one of the five counties chosen for implementation of AB 1741, discussed above. Jehl (1994) believes that the county's collaboration processes during the development of the 1741 proposal developed further momentum for interagency collaboration within the county.

Summary and discussion of the San Diego County initiatives

San Diego's New Beginnings Programme is an exemplary collaboration led by public sector agencies that bear heavy responsibilities for educationally and socially disadvantaged children, youth, and families. The evaluation of NB (Barfield *et al.*, 1994) reported positive results in achieving objectives. NB has achieved the goal of developing an integrated services approach based on a shared philosophy across many agencies and a collaborative leadership structure that can be replicated in other communities. The approach, philosophy, and leadership structures in different areas result in different types of service delivery models adapted to different neighbourhoods or communities. NB's second goal of developing the Centre at Hamilton Elementary School to provide multiple levels of service has also been accomplished. There is agreement that it makes more effective use of agencies' shared resources while providing family-centred services. Its third goal of developing a cross-agency training institute has been achieved. Its fourth goal addressed the need for a management information system. Enormous effort has gone into understanding and simplifying the varying eligibility requirements for services in partner agencies and resolving dilemmas related to confidentiality requirements so that different agencies' data bases can be shared in one MIS. Eligibility has been streamlined for free/reduced-price meals, housing, and some health services for families. The lessons learned have been documented and disseminated for wider use. The existing system facilitates family-focused case management, but the goal of being able to determine eligibility for major programmes on site could not be accomplished due to complicated federal and state regulations. However, the agency-based, extended teams provide a communication and support structure that partially reduces the fragmentation. San Diego County has taken advantage of nearly every type of support offered by the state to develop interagency collaboratives to serve disadvantaged children and families. On the other hand, the county implemented new models and shared experiences with state and federal officials that stimulated state-wide policy developments.

SUMMARY AND CONCLUSION

This study has highlighted major policies in California to promote services integration for educationally disadvantaged children and youth. There have been state legislative efforts to promote county-level co-ordination of children and youth services since 1989. In California the decentralisation of responsibility for delivering public health and welfare services to the county level has proceeded far more intensely than in most states.

The Foundation Consortium for School-linked Services provides a striking example of co-operation in the voluntary sector, combining foundation resources to reach the shared goal of developing comprehensive school-linked services. The Partnership with the state is a model for combining public and private efforts and resources. It enables the voluntary sector to have a direct influence on both public policy formulation and implementation processes. Targeting private money on evaluations, consultants and support mechanisms enhances service delivery and public accountability. The governance structure of the partnership brings executives of the major public child-serving agencies into regular dialogue with executives of the foundations that contribute private money to children's causes.

The Healthy Start Programme, a product of this partnership, embodies key principles that seem essential to promote organisational partnerships to create interagency, multi-disciplinary services. Planning grants make additional resources available to support the extra demands on personnel that are essential to establish coalitions, mutual goals and trusting relationships. Viable interagency commitments cannot be attained without taking these steps which lay the foundation for successful outcomes. The operational grants, characterised as "glue money", can sustain the effort until a collaborative is able to rearrange customary ways of organising and financing services. As a discretionary programme, the approach is not forced upon localities that do not want it. The money is targeted at schools and neighbourhoods with high levels of poverty and many linguistic minority groups. Required programme elements are specified to promote successful collaboration to achieve school-linked services. These include agencies sharing resources and governance, parent involvement, and family- and outcome-focused delivery of services. Although a minimum of four services must be included in an HS programme, localities have freedom to decide which ones. Periodic external evaluations are required. Preliminary results from these have already provided information that could guide future efforts.

Related fiscal policies, such as the Medicaid billing option and allowing waivers of categorical restrictions, are being devised to create sufficient permanent funding for school-linked services after the HS grants end. Many sources cited barriers to maintaining programme innovations, such as categorical funding policies, resistance by organisations to sharing fiscal resources, other vested interests, and bureaucratic delays and red tape, that inhibit localities from using more flexible funding mechanisms. Since HS programmes were launched, fiscal resources in the public sector have been slashed continuously. More reductions are expected. This reality generates a self-preservation dynamic in agencies that may discourage collaborative efforts.

The Partnership Principals recognise that permissive legislation and funding options are insufficient incentives to promote the degree of interagency and multi-disciplinary collaboration that they envisioned. The strategy of the Policy Academy exemplifies their effort to develop attitudes, knowledge, skills, and other needed collaborative capacities, in key decision-makers at the county level. Additional issues addressed include confidentiality regulations and the need for technical assistance in automated information management.

The New Beginnings case study graphically illustrates some of the collaborative processes, pitfalls, and successes at the local level, that can be expected in a sustained attempt to achieve interagency service provision. Many of NB's collaborative goals have been achieved according to external evaluations. Both HS and NB are examples of a community-based model of planning and developing services integration. This model has the potential to produce system change. It mobilises key local constituencies to develop and sustain change in the way agencies organise and deliver services, particularly in the public sector. Other models of services integration do not have this explicit goal of system change. For example, the well-known federal Head Start Programme provides educational, social and health services to low-income, preschool children and their families through one initiative. A case management model is used by several public agencies to attempt services integration at the client level without expecting to change the basic way in which services are organised.

This case study provides a picture of the stresses and strains resulting from pressure from federal and state levels on local governments to assume more responsibility for health, education and welfare services. It contributes examples of co-ordinated policies and programmes, supported by public and private partnerships at both state and county levels, which marshall available resources to promote more family-focused, culturally sensitive, effective, integrated services for children and families. The people encountered during the site visits are committed to sustaining the dynamic processes that have emerged despite intermittent political and economic setbacks.

REFERENCES

ARMOGIDA, K. (1994), Deputy Director, Planning, Policy, and Development, Department of Health Services, County of San Diego, Personal interview.

BARFIELD, D., BRINDIS, C., GUTHRIE, L., MCDONALD, W. and PHILLIBER, S. (1994), "The evaluation of New Beginnings", Mimeo.

CALIFORNIA, DEPARTMENT OF EDUCATION (1993), "SB 620/Healthy Start grant application materials", Mimeo, 1st November.

CALIFORNIA, DEPARTMENT OF EDUCATION (1994), Memorandum from Jane Henderson to SB 620 Healthy Start Principals and Senior Staff, 3rd May.

CALIFORNIA, DEPARTMENT OF EDUCATION, DEPARTMENT OF HEALTH SERVICES (1993), "Overview of the LEA Medi-Cal billing option", Mimeo.

CALIFORNIA INSTITUTE FOR MENTAL HEALTH (no date), *The California Managed Mental Health Medi-Cal Plan*, Mimeo.

CALIFORNIA LEGISLATURE (1991), SB 620, Chapter 759, *Statutes of 1991*.

CALIFORNIA LEGISLATURE (1991), SB 786, Chapter 994, *Statutes of 1991*.

CALIFORNIA LEGISLATURE (1992), AB 3688, Chapter 477, *Statutes of 1992*.

CALIFORNIA LEGISLATURE (1993), AB 1741, Chapter 951, *Statutes of 1993*.

CALIFORNIA LEGISLATURE (1993), SB 931, Chapter 985, *Statutes of 1993*.

CALIFORNIA LEGISLATURE, ASSEMBLY OFFICE OF RESEARCH (1994), Memorandum prepared by Lynn DeLapp.

CARLISLE, P. (1994), New Beginnings Collaboration Manager, Department of Social Services, County of San Diego, CA, Personal Telephone Interview, 5 December.

CARREON, V. and JAMESON, W. (1993), *School-linked Service Integration in Action: Lessons from Seven California Communities*, California Research Institute, San Francisco State University, San Francisco.

CHANG, H.N., GARDNER, S.L., WATAHARA, A., BROWN, C.G. and ROBLES, R. (1991), *Fighting Fragmentation: Collaborative Efforts to Serve Children and Families in California's Counties*, California Tomorrow and the Children and Youth Policy Project, San Francisco.

CHYNOWETH, J. (1994), Director, Foundation Consortium for School-Linked Services, Sacramento, California, personal interview, 17 May.

DELAPP, L.R. (1994a), California Legislature Assembly, Office of Research, 27 September, Telephone interview.

DELAPP, L.R. (1994b), California Legislature Assembly, Office of Research, 24 October, Personal communication.

FOUNDATION CONSORTIUM FOR SCHOOL-LINKED SERVICES (1993), Annual report, July 1 1992-June 30 1993.

FOUNDATION CONSORTIUM FOR SCHOOL-LINKED SERVICES (1994), Background of Medi-Cal managed care, Mimeo.

IEL POLICY EXCHANGE (1994), *Information about New Beginnings*, Institute for Educational Leadership, Inc., Washington.

JEHL, J. (1993), *Testimony to the Subcommittee on Elementary, Secondary, and Vocational Education*, US House of Representatives.

JEHL, J. (1994), Administrator on Special Assignment, Office of the Superintendent, San Diego City Schools, Personal interview, 18 May, Telephone interview, 7 October.

KELLEY, M. (1994), Deputy Director, California Department of Social Services, Division of Children and Family Services, Personal interview, 17 May.

LEVY, J.E. and SHEPARDSON, W. (1992), "A look at current school-linked service efforts", *The Future of Children*, 2(1), pp. 44-55.

LEWIS, J.R. (1994), *Summary Report Assembly Select Committee on State-wide Immigration Impact*, Assembly Publications Office, Sacramento, CA.

MELAVILLE, A.I. and BLANK, M.J. (1993), *Together We Can*, US Government Printing Office, Washington.

MITCHELL, T. (1994), Deputy Director for Health Information and Strategic Planning, California Department of Health, Personal interview, 17 May.

NEW BEGINNINGS (1990), *A Feasibility Study of Integrated Services for Children and Families: Final Report*, New Beginnings, San Diego, CA.

REEVES, R. (1994), "The tax revolt that wrecked California", *Money*, pp. 90-103.

ROBERTS, C. (1994), Deputy Director, San Diego County Department of Social Services, Telephone interview, 5 December.

SAN DIEGO COUNTY DEPARTMENT OF SOCIAL SERVICES (1991), *Tackling the Confidentiality Barrier: A Practical Guide for Integrated Family Services*, San Diego County Department of Social Services, San Diego, CA.

SAN DIEGO COUNTY OFFICE OF EDUCATION (1992), San Diego County Condition of Children.

STEWART, S.A. (1994), "California may try to 'save state' from illegal entries", *USA Today*, p. 6A.

SOLAK, J. (1994), Evaluation and Research Consultant, California Department of Education, Personal interview, 17 May.

SOLER, M.I., SHOTTON, A.C. and BELL, J.R. (1993), *Glass Walls: Confidentiality Provisions and Interagency Collaborations*, Youth Law Centre, San Francisco, CA.

UNITED WAY (1992), *San Diego County Children's Future Scan*, United Way of San Diego County, San Diego, CA.

US GENERAL ACCOUNTING OFFICE (1993), *Benefits for Illegal Aliens*, General Accounting Office, Washington.

WAGNER, M., GOLAN, S., SHAVER, D., NEWMAN, L., WECHSLER, M. and KELLEY, F. (1994), *A Healthy Start for California's Children and Families: Early findings from a state-wide evaluation of school-linked services*, SRI International, Menlo Park, CA.

Part II

CASE STUDIES CARRIED OUT BY FINLAND AND THE NETHERLANDS

7

FINLAND

EXPERIMENTAL EFFORTS TO INTEGRATE HUMAN SERVICES

INTEGRATION OF HEALTH CARE AND SOCIAL SERVICES IN THE CITY OF HELSINKI

by

Tuula Vesanen

THE LATOKARTANO HEALTH AND SOCIAL SERVICES CENTRE

The Latokartano health and social services centre opened in spring 1994. It is an experiment unique in Helsinki since it is, so far as is known, the most far-reaching project to date in the integration of health and social services functions. It involves physical, functional and administrative integration.

This paper presents the objectives of the Latokartano project, the anticipated benefits and the problems encountered. It roughly observes the interview framework and headings employed in the OECD/CERI case studies on the integration of services. The paper does not concentrate solely on services targeted at children at risk, and instead adopts a general perspective. It is a compilation of the materials produced during the five years of the project.

AREA AND POPULATION

The Helsinki North-east (NE) major district

The city of Helsinki is geographically divided into seven major districts and 33 districts. At the end of 1993 the city had a total population of 509 000.

The NE major district is the fourth biggest in size, with around 82 000 residents as of January 1st, 1994, and takes in the districts of Latokartano, Malmi, Pukinmäki, Suutarila, Puistola and Jakomäki.

The population of this major district has risen steadily as new suburbs have been built. Some 60 per cent of the dwellings were built in the 1970s, 1980s and 1990s. The population will continue to grow in the 1990s and in the first decade of the new millennium with the completion of the new Malmi housing estates, and the Viikinmäki and Viikki-Latokartano residential areas.

More than a quarter of the residents live in council apartments, the highest proportion in any of the major districts.

The proportion (82 per cent) of the population living in families is also higher than in any of the other major districts, and the average family size is largest. Around 65 per cent of the families have children, again the highest percentage in the city. The proportion of singles (32 per cent) is, correspondingly, the lowest of the major districts.

The population of the NE district will, it is expected, continue to be dominated by children, young people, and families with children, though there will be some changes in the age structure. Of all the children aged 0-7 and 7-16 in the entire Helsinki area in the 1990s, nearly one-fourth live in the NE district, accounting for 11 per cent of both age groups in 1994. The proportion of young children is expected to fall slightly over the years ahead, and that of the youth-aged population to grow.

The proportion of old-age pensioners (8 per cent) was the lowest in the city in 1994, but is expected to take an upward turn in the 1990s.

The level of education in the NE district is below the average for the city; around half the population has received no more than a basic education. Living in the area are large numbers of people employed in services, manufacturing and transport. The income level is below the city average for all of the districts, the mean income (*i.e.* the income per capita) being the lowest of all the major districts. The employment situation varied in 1994 from one residential area in the major district to another; the unemployment rate was higher in Jakomäki, Malmi, Pihlajamäki and Pukinmäki than the city average (18 per cent) but lower in Tapanila, Tapaninvainio, Suutarila, Tapulikaupunki and Heikinlaakso.

The public services in the major district have been improving since the 1980s, but many schools, for example, still suffer from a shortage of space, and a waiting list accumulated for places in children's day care in 1994. There are far fewer private welfare and health services in the area than there are in the city as a whole.

The Malmi shopping and cultural centre is the focal point of the area and houses the main private and public services: a shopping centre, a large social and health services centre, a hospital, Malmi congregation premises and facilities, the Malmi labour exchange, a post office, swimming baths, and the Malmitalo cultural centre.

The associations and societies are lively in the area. The local residents and City administrations have, under the leadership of teams of City officials in the region, got together to develop projects in Jakomäki and Pihlajisto.

Of great significance in creating a feeling of affinity in the major district has been the local newspaper, MaTaPuPu, which has been exemplary in publishing articles describing the social welfare and health care in the area.

The Latokartano district

Growth periods in the Latokartano district were the 1960s, when the suburb of Pihlajamäki was built, and the 1970s, which saw the construction of the Pihlajisto estate. The district now has a population of around 12 000. The next growth period is expected at the turn of the millennium, if the plans for the Viikinmäki and Viikki housing estates materialise. The population of the district is relatively older than in other parts of the NE major district, and the education and income levels are below the district average. The social situation of the population could be described as inferior to that of the district or the city on average.

The district has long had a residents' association known as the Pihlajamäki Association. A new form of resident activity emerged in the district in the first half of the 1990s, stimulated by the residents' concern about the problems of intoxicant abuse and unemployment and a desire to enhance their own living environment.

All kinds of activities have been started in the Pihlajisto area on the initiative of the Pihlajisto Young and Old Association: the surroundings have been cleaned up and repaired, an adventure park has been built for children, and an activities centre called The Old Fox has been established. Pihlajisto is also one of the suburbs chosen for a refurbishment programme (1992-1996) being run by the National Research and Development Centre for Welfare and Health (STAKES) and the Ministry of the Environment.

In autumn 1994, a local Health for All by the Year 2000 project was launched in Pihlajamäki. The aim was to bring about an improvement in people's health, through co-operation between the local residents and organisations. The background organisation is the Finnish Council for Health Education.

SERVICES PROVIDED

Social and health services in the major district

In their organisation, the various administrations providing services in Helsinki, such as the Social Services Department, the Health Department, the Youth Department and the Workers' Institute, are divided into the same major districts. The local social services are the responsibility of seven social services centres, the health services that of seven health centres. Responsible for institutional care and other centralised services are the Social Services Department's joint service division and the hospital division of the Health Department.

The NE Health Centre is responsible for the health services in its area. Each of the six districts in the major district has its own health centre. There are eight dental units. The area also has a hospital, Malmi Hospital, with a unit for emergency and primary treatment. Also within the same hospital are surgical and internal medicine units providing specialised medical care. The whole area is served by the NE mental health unit.

Responsible for the social services in the area is the NE social services centre. Community care, child welfare and income security services are provided by three local social services offices, the Malmi and Tapuli social services offices, and the Latokartano health and social services centre. Social services for the disabled and elderly are organised centrally for the whole area, and children's day care likewise has its own organisation. The NE family counselling office and a special clinic for the care of intoxicant abusers serve the entire area.

Services of the Latokartano health and social services centre

The new Latokartano health and social services centre was opened at Pihlajamäki on April 11, 1994. It houses the Pihlajisto health centre, the Pihlajamäki maternity and child health centre, the Pihlajamäki dental unit, community care services, welfare services for intoxicant abusers, and income security services previously handled by the Malmi Social Services Office. A total of 45 members of staff transferred from health care and 34 from social services.

The Latokartano district is divided into four areas called Pihlajisto, Johtokivi, Pihlajamäki and Aarnikka, each with its own team of workers. The staff consultation rooms and working facilities are located in the building according to the area division.

Each team consists of one or two doctors, public health nurses, nurses, social workers, office clerks and community care personnel. Within its area each team provides child health, maternity and nursing services, community care, district nursing, child welfare support, welfare support for intoxicant abusers, and income security services. The aim is to achieve true team work and to widen workers' job descriptions in each of the professions. Detailed job targets are included in the experiment plan for 1995-1996.

The health and social services centre is a joint unit for the NE social services and health centres and has its own joint budget and administration. The director in 1995 is the district's chief physician, with the head social worker as deputy.

In the same building as the Centre is a dental unit, a laboratory and a consultant psychologist's room. These do not, however, belong to the Centre.

THE SERVICES INTEGRATION PROJECT

Services before the integration project

Before the start of the project aiming at the integration of social services and health care, the Latokartano district mainly observed a sectoral mode of operation. In autumn 1991, only one social worker and the head social worker for the area were engaged in integrated social work, taking in income security and child welfare work. The health centre doctors were responsible for specific areas in accordance with the personal doctor system, but the work of the other health workers was not tied to this area division. The public health nurses specialised in areas such as maternity or child health, school health, and non-institutional care. Community care and home treatment were separate functions.

Stage 1: Basic investigation and planning (autumn 1989 – spring 1992)

Work on planning the premises began in 1989, when separate plans were approved for the establishment of a health centre and a social services office. The integration programme only really began when an integrated establishment plan was drawn up on the initiative of the Deputy Mayor for social affairs and public health. This plan was approved by the City Council in November 1990.

The building project went into action in early spring 1991. In the same year it nevertheless proved necessary (for financial reasons) to reduce the space plan by 30 per cent. This was duly approved by the City Council in January 1992. The second plan eliminated the psychiatric team consulting rooms, physiotherapy premises, and other consulting and meeting rooms. In debating the project, the City Council approved a petition made by Councillor Hiltunen (Social Democrat) concerning the implementation of a multi-professional, population-responsible working procedure.

The functional development project got under way in spring 1991, when the NE social and health services committee approved the project plan for the formation of the Latokartano primary service district.

The practical implementation of the project was the responsibility of the project leader and project team. Over the years the project team had four different line-ups. In the final years it included representatives of all the occupations that would be operating at the Centre. The project was led by two chief health centre physicians, two chief nurses and the present chief district physician. All the development work was carried out in addition to the team members' normal work and there were no project staff. Since the Centre opened, the responsibility for development has been entrusted to the Centre's management team.

In the course of 1991, the integration areas were agreed on, training of many kinds was provided, and the project team in particular was briefed on similar development projects in other parts of Finland.

In November 1991, a client inquiry was held into the combined use of welfare and health services, the results of which were published in 1993 in the publications series of the Helsinki Social Services Department.

Stage 2: Building and development of the operational model (spring 1992 – spring 1994)

Work began in spring 1992 on the development of an integrated, multi-professional working procedure, the emphasis being on the creation of a joint operating model for the social services and health care using work study methods. The consultant was a researcher from the Functional Health Centre project, Riitta Simoila, Chief Nurse. The development work was based on an analysis of conflicts and tensions in the existing procedures and an historical analysis of services. The first reports on the team procedures were completed just before the Centre opened.

The goal of the team procedure is to seek compatibility between the demand for services in the area and the available resources. It is based on an assessment of the need for services in a residential area, the social and health problems manifest in the population, and the community's resources for solving these problems. It then defines the tasks of the team workers, the jointly approved division of labour, the principles of co-operation, and the team organisation.

Each team determined the number of children and families with children in its area, the number of social services and health care clients, and the services offered to families with children in the area. Each team defined as the central target for co-operation families in which the parents have not, because of their use of intoxicants or for some other reason, been able to care sufficiently for their children. The aim is more systematic co-operation and faster assistance in times of crisis. Another objective is to intensify co-operation with others working with children and young people in the same residential area, such as day nurseries, schools, youth centres and resident associations.

Stage 3: Regularisation of the administrative experiment and procedure (spring 1994 – autumn 1996)

Now that the building plan and the functional model were complete, it was time to create an administrative model suitable for integrated operations. On May 18, 1994 the Helsinki City Council approved experimental regulations for an integrated NE social services and health centre for the period June 1, 1994 to December 31, 1996.

The NE Social and Health Services Committee decided to establish the Latokartano health and social services centre as of October 15, 1994. Since January 1, 1995 the unit has received joint funds for social services and health, determined according to the size of the population. The head of the unit until the end of 1995 was the chief physician, with the chief social worker as deputy. The practical running of the unit was in the hands of a management team consisting of the head, the deputy head, the chief nurse and the community care officer.

A plan is to be approved for the experiment and monitored by a team of representatives of the local residents, City departments, centres, unit staff, and the main contracting parties.

THE GOALS OF SERVICES INTEGRATION

The goals for the development of the district services and the integration of social and health services have been defined more closely at each of the three stages in the course of the project.

In 1991, the objective set for the Latokartano project was to create an independent social services and health care centre with the functional, economic and administrative prerequisites for providing the local residents with primary welfare and health services.

The development project was then entrusted with the task of:

- creating a joint population-responsible multi-professional working procedure for the social services and health care;
- agreeing on joint operating areas for the social services and health care;
- investigating and developing administrative and economic solutions for the primary service district;
- furthering co-operation between local residents, organisations and other administrations in planning services; and
- developing an integrated computerised client information system.

At the second stage, in 1992-1994, the objectives were specified more closely using the concepts developed in the designation of the new working model:

- the work was aimed at the entire population of the district and sought to establish dialogue with the population and new co-operation practices;
- the Centre would take possession of new facilities in the form of the health and social services centre building, equipment for examining and treating patients, a joint client information system, a joint operating model and work orientation, and new quality assessment methods;
- the work would be carried out by teams representing many social services and health care professions;
- the working community would serve as the teams' network;
- the division of labour would be developed by creating flexible, complementary job descriptions;
- the aim would be to assure the Centre functional and economic autonomy.

At the third administrative experiment stage, the purpose and scope of the Latokartano health and social services centre were defined in conjunction with the decision to establish a Social and Health Services Committee. The purpose of the experiment involving the Latokartano health and social services centre is to provide and develop welfare and health care services according to the needs of clients. The experiment will combine the social services and health care activities and resources of the district in one single unit. The aim is to investigate the advantages and disadvantages of integrating services.

The Latokartano health and social services centre will be jointly accountable for welfare and health care with responsibility for providing the welfare and health care services required by the local residents according to their needs. The Centre's own operations will consist of local out-patient welfare and health care and non-institutional services. In the opening stages these will consist of community care, home treatment, social work connected with income security, welfare for intoxicant abusers and child welfare, consultation for out-patients, health counselling and school health.

The unit will provide the client services itself or purchase them from other providers.

The experiment plan states objectives for outcomes related to:

- service;

- effectiveness; and

- cost-efficiency.

In order to achieve the objectives, the unit will develop a population-responsible, multi-professional team procedure. A model based on team work will be developed and evaluated.

According to the experiment regulations, the Committee will appoint a head for the health and social centre for a set period. The management tasks are also experimental. Multi-professional team work has been emphasized throughout the experiment and was very much to the fore when the regulations were debated by the City's various administrative organs. The regulations stated, among other things, that the project cannot proceed according to its objectives unless the prerequisites exist for a management and decision-making system in keeping with the principle of team thinking.

During the experimental period it is necessary for a manager from both the social services centre and the health centre to gain experience of the management of the unit. The integration of activities will thus observe the principle of equality at the management level.

There will be no separate post for the head of the joint health and social services centre. Instead, the head of the unit will manage the unit in addition to his or her normal work. A member of the management team will therefore be appointed head of the unit. The operations of the entire unit will be based on four population-responsible local teams, who will provide their local residents with services. The managers will work in these teams, one in each.

The head of the health and social services centre will act as the general manager of the unit. The responsibility for professional work supervision (for nursing, medical, social, and community care) will continue to lie with the present managers. The professional and administrative management may be split in the team structure.

INPUT

Political support for services integration

Issues connected with the Latokartano project have been discussed or decided by city committees, such as the NE Social and Health Services Committee, the Social Service Committee, the Health Committee, the City Board and the City Council. The entire project was in fact initiated by one of the Deputy Mayors.

The personnel committees of both centres have issued statements on the building and development plans.

The handling of the plans has observed the normal municipal administration procedure, with two exceptions. In January 1992, the City Council voted in favour of a petition (discussed in connection with the reduction in space plan) on the development of a multi-professional working procedure that read as follows: "In approving the amendment to the establishment plan, the City Council stipulates that the multi-professional, population-responsible work procedure aimed at by the project be implemented on as wide a scale as possible, and that further development be carried out jointly by all sections of the staff".

In debating the experiment regulations for 1995-1996 the Social Service Committee, the Health Committee and, later, the City Board decided to limit the application of the experiment to the Latokartano Centre. Originally, the NE Health and Social Services Committee had proposed the formulation of looser experiment regulations that would later have permitted the establishment of similar integrated health and social services centres in other major districts.

In Helsinki it was decided in 1993 that integrated health and social services will be the responsibility of two different departments. The Latokartano health and social services centre is so far the only administratively integrated unit spanning two departments. The decision on the experiment regulations proved that integration is to be confined to this experiment only, the results of which will be followed with great interest at all levels of the administration.

Support

The Latokartano project has over the years won the support of politicians, leading civil servants, experts, local residents' associations (such as the Pihlajamäki Association) and clients, who have been favourably disposed towards the integration of services.

The managements of the social and health services centres have been committed to the project, monitoring and supervising its progress. The staff have been given space and time to adapt, while flexible modification of the goals and implementation have been possible as the project has proceeded.

Outside the major district the experiment has had a mixed reception, as indicated by the decision on the experiment regulations, for example.

Resources

The Latokartano project has been carried out mainly as the staff's own work. The chief responsibility for the period 1991-1994 was assumed by the project team and its leader. No special project or other extra staff were available. The working procedure was developed by an expert experienced in work study methods. Workers have been given a lot of training, but only a few outside experts have been used as trainers. Assistance and computer software were given by an expert from the City of Helsinki Information Management Centre in analysing the client survey.

The project has been financed out of the funds awarded for the NE social services centre and the NE health centre, with minor financial support from the departments' central training units.

No additional members of staff have been taken on for the new centre.

The new premises and facilities have been the only material additions. The building, which cost about Mk 18.3 million, was built by a property company owned entirely by the city of Helsinki, from which the social and health services centres rent premises. The sum of Mk 5.5 million was reserved for basic supplies, but the actual costs of fitting out the building have been about Mk 4 million.

EVALUATION OF THE NEED FOR AND ADVANTAGES OF INTEGRATION

Since the integration has only just got under way, the benefits have not yet been measured or evaluated.

The need for integration has, however, been debated throughout the project, and various attempts to investigate and argue the need have been made.

Client survey

In order to investigate the need for an integrated welfare and health system, a client survey on the subject was carried out in November 1991 in the Latokartano district and three therapy and treatment units belonging to the major district. The aim was to investigate, by area of provision, the number of clients using both welfare and health services, with the idea being to estimate the proportion of clients making extensive use of services in different client categories, and to compare the use of other services by regular and occasional clients of a specific unit.

The investigation was conducted as a client survey in 11 areas of provision simultaneously. Clients were asked to state whether they had used any of 17 welfare and health services at district and major district level over the preceding 12 months. Replies were received from 952 clients. The majority of the respondents were, with the exception of the A-clinic, women.

The services of the health centre doctor and public health nurse were the ones used most by the clients of other services. Three out of four home treatment, community care, child welfare, income security and mental health clients had consulted a doctor, and a slightly smaller proportion a public health nurse. In contrast, 50 per cent of A-clinic and family counselling office clients had done so. The doctor and health nurse considered that few of their patients were also social services clients. Of the doctor's regular patients, one-third were community care clients, and around one-fifth were income security clients. Social services clients visited the doctor only in exceptional cases.

Community care and home treatment constituted a tight-knit service entity, since over half the clients used both. Apart from the services of the doctor, the community care and home treatment clients used very few other services.

The A-clinic, family counselling office clinic and mental health office had fewer clients in common than was expected. The family counselling clients used other services for families with children, whereas the A-clinic and mental health clients made quite frequent use of the income security, health centre doctor's and other services.

The income security and child welfare clients were multiple clients who also made fairly extensive use of the doctor's, duty doctor's, A-clinic, family counselling office and mental health services.

Certain differences were observed between regular and occasional users in the use of other welfare and health services. To begin with, the regular clients used the other services mentioned more than the occasional clients. This was revealed in the case of the doctor's and the A-clinic's clients, for example. The regular and occasional clients also used services of different types, as manifest in the community care clientele.

As found in previous investigations, the majority of the social services clients in the Latokartano district also used health care services, but only a small percentage of the health care clients also used social services. Although the expectations of integration may differ considerably for this reason, the all-round care of joint clients is nevertheless a demanding challenge for the primary welfare and health service teams. Joint clients represent only a fraction of the population, but they consume a large part of the welfare and health services and constitute a large clientele for the various professions.

The clients used many services more than the population of the major district or district. The client groups taking part in the survey used more public services. They had, for example, visited a doctor as often as the population on average (70 per cent), but their visits were to a health care doctor.

Analysis of the present operational problems

The grounds for integration were also examined at the beginning of the stage aiming at renewal of the operating procedure. The work study began in May 1992 with a basic survey directed at the welfare and health personnel in the Latokartano district and aims to produce a tentative scheme for social services and health care as a whole. It is important, with a view to future joint development, for the views and personal experiences of persons employed in different occupations and at different points to be sought and documented right at the outset. This method differs from the accustomed practice, since the goal is not to establish middle-of-the-road opinions but to form a tentative overall picture made up of many different views and opinions on the state of the district.

In the basic survey, workers answered a series of questions used in the Functional Health Centre project and modified for the project in hand by Riitta Simoila. The replies of the workers were collected from the social and health services centres separately under theme headings in the order used in the basic survey framework. This revealed the ideas of the staffs of the social services centre and the health centre on their operating system.

The tensions in the social services centre were identified as follows:

- The sectoral approach to work has led to a diffuse, slack administration at the social services centre. The administration and management lack an overall perspective, while the individual worker does not have a clear image of the entity to which he belongs.
- The population is seen as fragmented in relation to the worker's own sector. The sectoral approach has led to a protection of one's own territory both at the administrative level and at the level of individual workers. Unofficial groups within the sector are important.
- The client-oriented objectives set by the worker for his/her work conflict with the rules and regulations of the organisation (*e.g.* savings measures), causing distress in the worker. The workers work as individuals, with their own problems, experiencing the conflict in private.

The tensions in the health centre were identified as follows:

- The perception of the target group is fragmented and lacks an overall concept. Each professional group performs its own role but information is not transferred from one professional group to another, and this is reflected in the perception of the target group.
- The strict job designations and sectorised division of labour prevent the transfer of information acquired within one profession to another because the only division of labour is that within the professional groups. This causes conflicts in the work community.
- There is an absence of dialogue between the management and workers of the health centre. The management simply informs and issues instructions, and the staff feel their opinions are sought and listened to merely as a formality.

Compilation of a history of the social services and health care

Work began in December 1992 on histories of the social services and health care. The two separate histories were completed in April-May 1993. The material is so extensive that no joint history has yet been compiled within the confines of the project. Both presentations gave a lively picture of the development of social and health services in the district up to the beginning of the 1990s. The trend has clearly been towards the sectorised provision of services greatly influenced by legislation and other administrative measures.

ANTICIPATED BENEFITS OF SERVICES INTEGRATION

The anticipated benefits of services integration are written into the objectives set at the various stages of the project.

Improved services

The health and social services centre operates on the principle of regional population responsibility; the needs of the population are thus examined as a whole and the resources for each team are correctly allocated. Identification of the resources and problems of the community and exploitation of the community's potential are means of supporting the population's own self-support and life management capabilities.

The results of the district's client survey were in line with those of other surveys of the use of social and health services and can be used as a basis for determining areas for co-operation:

- The clients needing integrated services represent only a small section of the population but they consume a large share of the social and health services and constitute a major client group for the various professions. Concentrating on the care of these large users of services is a core area for integration and can be used to achieve both functional and economic benefits.

– The health care and social workers have a different attitude to integration: according to the doctor and the health nurse there are relatively few shared clients, whereas the other workers think quite the opposite. The number of shared clients has grown in the past few years as the situation in society has deteriorated; more people are, for example, signing on for income security and welfare for intoxicant abusers as a result of unemployment. The crucial issue is to find the clients that would benefit from integrated services.

– Community care and home treatment constitute an entity. The joint clients are the ones who have received most assistance, since a good two thirds of the (mainly old) clients receiving weekly help were clients of both social services and health care. Services can be intensified by organising – in teams – community care as a single entity.

– Welfare for intoxicant abusers requires closer co-operation between the doctor, the social worker, the specialised medical units and institutions. The A-clinic clients, among others, made great use of the doctor's, duty doctor's and income security services. The goal is a new, flexible practice for referring patients for treatment and more active preventive work in the district.

– The child welfare and income security clients are multiple clients; in working with them, the potential for making flexible use of the entire service network is extremely important. The services for these clients pose a challenge for the whole team. While the individual client should on the one hand have dealings with fewer workers, the ability of the entire team to spot and handle their serious problems should on the other hand be improved. The aim is to increase clients' independence and control of life by means of a systematic, comprehensive approach.

Updating the working procedure

The new working procedure for the social services and health care is one of team work involving a number of different specialists. There are four basic teams working in the district: in Pihlajisto, Johtokivi, Pihlajamäki and Aarnikka. These teams aim to pool their expertise, to assume joint responsibility for services, and to give matters the quick, flexible treatment made possible by physical proximity. Expert skills and know-how are, however, the cornerstones of operations.

Judging from the analysis of the old procedure, the following problems need to be solved in developing the work of the social services and health centre:

– The sectoral division of social services and the fragmentation of health care into different professions were revealed to be factors causing tensions in the working community and disuniting the administration. The aim is to create a shared view of the object of the team's work, to structure the service chain as a meaningful entity dictated by clients' needs.

– Differentiation of the expert groups and sectors, breaks in communication and the defence of personal territory were sometimes manifest in occasionally amusing ways (such as coffee-break habits). The challenge is to mould the centre and the teams into a working community in which there is communication and interaction between the groups of experts.

– The working procedures should be made democratic. Tension was noted between the workers and rules in both the health centre and the social services centre: limits, rules and the procedures were felt to be either undemocratic (health centre) or oppressive (social services centre). The aim of the experiment is to give workers more influence and to determine how a team of experts in different fields could act as a new channel for influence.

Development of the administration and management

Judging from the basic analysis, it is extremely important to develop the centre's management. A style of management should be found that is better than the one criticised by the workers as being authoritarian or regarded by the social services centre as lacking an overall grasp.

The management of the health and social services centre is likewise an experiment. Multiprofessional team work has been stressed throughout the experiment and was very much to the fore in debating the regulations. The project cannot proceed according to its objectives unless it has the prerequisites for a management and decision-making process operating according to a team principle. The fact that the unit has a single manager appointed for a set period is new. The teams are organised so that each of the four management team members acts as the leader of one team. The most senior representative of each profession continues to act as the professional supervisor.

The goal is thus a management system that crosses professional and sector borders. The way in which the compatibility of professional and administrative supervision is solved will become clear as the experiment proceeds.

Administratively, the health and social services centre falls between two departments. In practice this means operating within the confines of two different control systems. How well the centre can adapt itself to two departments and two control systems will become clear during the two-year experiment period. Valuable experience will in the meantime be gained of how the integrated client responsibility and economic responsibility entrusted to the unit actually works in practice.

PROBLEMS OF SERVICES INTEGRATION AND FACTORS CRITICAL TO ITS IMPLEMENTATION

No evaluations or other studies of the implementation of the project have yet been made. The following is a brief outline of problems and factors that have arisen during the project and that should be allowed for in the integration of services.

Integrating services

- Lasting change can only be achieved by sustained work. Changing habits is a slow process, because the attitudes, methods and customs of the old, sectorised procedure are strong. Workers must be given time and liberty to examine and adapt their way of thinking and working. The opposition and regression arising in the course of change must be given time to be dealt with. During the project, each new move elicits opposition and suspicion, and in order to deal with these, the basic criteria of the project must if necessary be re-examined.

- Success is possible with a clear development approach and any expert aid that may prove necessary, under the leadership of a consultant, for example. In the early stages of this project, the project team became aware that neither experience nor methods exist for the planning of integrated population-responsible work or team work involving experts in different fields. The solution was found in work study, the application of which proved to be a laborious but appropriate choice. Procedures were created for the teams. This would not have been possible using conventional methods.

- Integrating development work and client work creates tensions. Having to do this on top of their normal work is a strain on the whole staff. Although the management is favourably disposed towards the project, there is strong pressure to let the service remain as before. Output as an indication of activity should be accrued, regardless of the time spent on development. On the other hand, people have great expectations of being able to achieve quick results by means of development work.

- It is difficult for the social and health services to find a common philosophy and language. This is manifest at all levels of the organisation. Study of the past and the handling of manifest problems also revealed how little the various professions knew about what others did, with less being known about social workers than any other group. An understanding of others' views and a common attitude can only be achieved by working together so that problems are used as a means of learning, and different approaches to solving them are discussed.

- Apart from the development of a procedure and co-operation, there is a need for continuing vocational education in order to form new, broader job descriptions. The new professionalism and a new attitude to co-operation go hand in hand.

- Physical and functional solutions are significant in practical integration. An arrangement by which the members of a team actually work in adjacent offices has proved that staff location can enhance co-operation. This was proved first of all in the co-operation between community care and home treatment. Clients, too, have approached the social workers in a new way.

Management of the project

- The commitment of the managers of both sectors to the principles of the project and its implementation is extremely important in bringing about change. The staff developing the new activities need a guarantee of continuity and protection against the outside staff rejecting new activities. In the course of a project lasting years, the management should clearly steer it towards the common objectives and be ready to set an example of personal commitment.

- Different control systems prevent co-operation between several administrations and the working community. Until the new centre was opened, the staff worked at five different points under two different departments. The social services and health departments had different control systems, rules and other working practices which constantly emphasized their differences. The social services centre and the health centre sometimes handled the same task in very different ways. These differences of procedure may cause confusion and even amusement among the staff. Now that the new centre is in operation, the different procedures are having to be reconciled daily.

- Reassuring management that grants equality for all is a basic prerequisite for an integration project of this type. An ability to manage both things and people is essential.

- Changes in project management make objectives more difficult to achieve. So far the project has had five leaders and the project team four different line-ups. On the other hand this indicates that the project organisation has always been modified as necessary and that the new people have managed to handle their tasks, because the project has proceeded according to the objectives and schedule. Progress has, however, been extremely laborious because initiating the new people has used up some of the meagre resources.

Relation to other development work

- The attitude to other development work in the area is problematic. The staff have a favourable regard for the other projects under way, but when their own development work has been at its most demanding, they have had no opportunity to engage in broad co-operation with other administrations or resident movements. They cannot begin to think of co-operating until the new working procedure has been established.

- Links with other corresponding development projects are important and rewarding from the staff's point of view. If the staff are to remain motivated and active, it is important for them to have a chance for interaction, for obtaining and passing on ideas.

Evaluation and reporting

- Regular evaluation and rest periods are needed in carrying out a project. People should from time to time have a chance to stop and take a deep breath, to look back over what has been achieved and to make a realistic assessment of what lies ahead. A halt was therefore called at Latokartano after the centre was opened and the new management team began to get organised and to assume responsibility for the project.

- Careful documentation is vital in a project lasting years and involving many stages. In accordance with the chosen development strategy, the workers must themselves produce the written material, such as descriptions of the team working procedure. This is demanding when it has to be done on top of one's normal work, and workers' skills also vary in this respect. The writing of fuller accounts and research reports calls for a professional, a researcher, a planner or a separate project worker.

CHILDREN AT RISK IN KORSO:

A DEVELOPMENT PROJECT IN CHILD WELFARE AND CHILD PSYCHIATRY

by

Johanna Mäenpää, Merja-Maaria Turunen and Satu Siikander

INTRODUCTION

Children account for 24 per cent of the Finnish population. Although the status of children in Finland is, by global comparison, good, there are still some groups of children living in conditions which constitute a threat to their health and development. The focus in the studies of these risk factors is shifting more and more clearly from somatic health problems to psycho-social risk factors. According to one Finnish epidemiological study, 15 per cent of children are in need of psychiatric evaluation and/or treatment.

The mental health and child welfare services for children and young people are in the process of change and face new challenges. The reform of the state subsidy system in 1993 put an end to centralised governmental control and gave the local authorities greater power to decide on the provision of services. One of the criteria in carrying out the reform was that the basic level of municipal services would not alter. This principle has not, however, been easy to observe in view of the economic recession.

The recession and unemployment are having an impact on children. The need for strict economies has forced the local authorities to cut their expenditure and to place their services in some order of priority. In this prioritisation contest, services for children have only too often been the losers. Of the preventive services, the first to be hit have been the well baby and maternity clinics and school health care. Many family guidance clinics have been closed. In communities and families there is less money available for positive, supportive hobbies and cultural services outside the home. Club activities are being reduced, and other school support measures are being curtailed. The tighter economic conditions of life in the family are being reflected in human relations within the family, often in a way that is negative.

The social worker's time is being taken up more and more by clients needing financial support. Since, under the principle of integrated social welfare, the same worker is responsible for income support, welfare for substance abusers and child welfare, the growing need for income support has necessitated cutbacks in other fields of social work.

The problems facing the family in need of child welfare are becoming more and more complex and numerous. A few modes of operation are no longer sufficient in child welfare to meet the multiple needs of the child and the family. Child welfare therefore requires diverse services and modes of operation in order to meet the various problems encountered. Child welfare services should be conceived of as special services and various activities developed to meet the needs of the individual family. Family assistance is, however, provided by a highly competent, determined band of social and health workers which, consisting mainly of women, has long been accustomed to assuming responsibility for two working fields, one inside and one outside the home, according to the financial resources available at the time.

The worst victims of the pressure of work on the professional helper are families that are neither motivated nor willing to receive assistance from the authorities. Often they are, however, the ones in greatest need of assistance and support. In order to identify and help such families, it is important to increase and develop intersectoral co-operation. Crossing the professional boundaries may seem difficult, but positive results can be achieved by combining resources and directing them at families.

The status of children in Finland has also received publicity in, for example, the Charter on the Rights of the Child and a government report. The slow but steady stream of research findings (*e.g.* the government report on child policy) is helping to develop and to allocate services to children too.

BACKGROUND TO THE PROJECT

In August 1991 a five-year project aimed at the development of child welfare and child psychiatry was launched at the Korso-Rekola Social Welfare and Health Centre in Vantaa. Its goal was to reduce the number of disadvantaged persons and to bring more families with children at risk within the confines of child welfare. Resources and different professional skills are accordingly being pooled in an attempt to discover new ways of handling difficult child welfare cases.

The decentralisation of services has rapidly forced the local authorities to develop means of adapting the services provided locally, under the principle of small area resident responsibility to meet the needs of children and families who have so far been particularly difficult to help. The advantage of the patch work model is that the services are close to the clients, and the worker gets to know both the area and the other agencies operating within it. One problem in patch work may be the broad range of the case work and the fact that the worker is very much alone in handling difficult cases, unless a special network is created to provide support. By working as a team, the workers can better make use of their combined experience and know-how and are not left to deal with cases alone. Paying greater attention to the needs and rights of children and working with children directly will in the future be necessary new developments in social welfare and health care.

The project aims to establish a rational procedure for integrating broad, patch social work and one specialist field of health care, child psychiatry. Both professions encounter situations requiring broad and deep expertise simultaneously. This means that problems can be solved at an earlier stage (*e.g.* when a client applies for income support), and permits the social worker to allow for children in services traditionally targeted at adults.

Vantaa and Korso

The city of Vantaa had a population of about 159 200 as of January 1 1993, and was divided into five district centres for social welfare and health. The Korso-Rekola Social Welfare and Health Centre served a population of about 38 600 and the experiment was also being conducted in the district of Korso, with a population of around 22 400. According to the forecasts, the population of the district will continue to grow, with an expected increase of 10 000 over the next ten years.

Korso has a large proportion of young people and families with children, and the families are larger than average for the city. More children are born in this district than in other parts of Vantaa, and there has been marked migration to the district. The district has traditionally consisted of detached houses, but since the 1970s, urban estates of blocks of flats have been built, and it is here that most of the city's council houses are situated. There is thus a high proportion of rented housing and the tenants are often selected on social grounds.

The people in the Korso-Rekola district have, on average, more problems than those elsewhere in Vantaa. The impact of the economic recession is, furthermore, pronounced in the area, which is the most vulnerable of the Vantaa districts in terms of other socio-economic indicators, too. In view of the socio-economic structure of the district, there is a higher than average demand for social assistance and welfare, and the number of social welfare clients is the city's highest in proportion to the population. The sum paid out in income support is over a third higher than the average for the city as a whole. As a result of the recession, there have been radical cuts in public spending and society's safety nets have become so thin that people are increasingly being left to their own resources. The main primary services are, due to the structure of the population, children's day care, primary health care (including well baby clinics), and schools.

To summarise, Korso may be described as an efficiently built urban area with a high population density, a large number of families with children and many of the problems related to an urban way of life in concentrated form. On the other hand the area is, because of its growing population and the large proportion of families with children, a dynamic region posing challenges for the development of services.

Child welfare in the Korso district

The social work (child welfare, welfare for substance abusers and income support) in the Korso-Rekola district is done by two offices, the Korso office being included in the project. Patch social work is now in its fourth year in the Korso district. Before this, the area had two child welfare workers, but now all the social workers do child welfare work. In addition to providing welfare services for children and substance abusers, each social worker has about 120 income support clients. The handling of income support has been rationalised by using written applications, decisions covering longer periods, and assigning some of the work to clerical assistants.

One of the advantages of small area social work (patch work) is that by working in pairs, workers are subjected to less pressure than if they are working alone. On the other hand, the social workers doing area work are so overworked that they do not always have time to concentrate sufficiently on their cases. There is nevertheless agreement that the area work model should continue in the Korso district. Co-operation with child psychiatry would, it is believed, relieve some of the pressure of work.

Taking a child into care is usually a last resort in order to solve problems of parenting in the home and to ensure the conditions for the healthy development of the child. In the Korso-Rekola district these children are as a rule from young families in which the foundation for an ordinary life has given way after a long fight.

Half the children taken into care in Vantaa are from the Korso-Rekola district. In this respect the district differs considerably from the other parts of the city. In 1993, 41 children were taken into care and there were 120 families in receipt of child welfare. The number of children taken into care and other child welfare cases doubled between 1990 and 1993. Child welfare has been able to handle only the most serious cases. The rise in the number of children taken into care does, however, appear to have levelled off. The number of clients has not, however, fallen, but families are now served increasingly by community care.

Apart from the recession, one reason for the rise in the number of child welfare cases in Korso is thought to be the introduction of patch social work, which has revealed previously hidden cases in need of child welfare. The demand for child welfare work in Korso does in fact greatly exceed the capacity. Faced with a growing need for child welfare, the social workers need support in their work. The focus in child welfare work is now on situations where there is often no alternative but to take a child into care. There has, for example, been little opportunity for preventive work. The emphasis will continue to be on corrective measures, though every attempt will be made to intervene as early as possible, thereby necessitating lesser support measures.

The main causes of the need for child welfare are substance abuse and mental health problems in the parents, and behaviour harmful to the development of young people. The aim in child welfare is to improve working methods so as to recognise the situations that may constitute a risk to the child's development, to come into contact with children and to meet the parents with special problems in parenting.

The Peijas child psychiatry clinic

In child psychiatry, the economic recession and the reduction in primary care resources are causing pressures on specialised medical care, because the problems are getting more and more complex. There are also many new challenges facing the population-based services in child psychiatry. In 1992, the outpatient clinic examined and treated 214 children/families, 95 of whom were new patients.

If the working procedure by which services are provided is fit only for children and parents well motivated to seek examination and treatment, children at risk are left without any mental health support. The project therefore aims to seek out the families and children previously excluded from mental health services. It also focuses on helping client families in which family problems are observed as the cause of symptoms in the children.

There is a pressing need to develop working methods for helping children and their families with multiple problems, while at the same time supporting and monitoring parenthood by means of child welfare.

OBJECTIVES OF THE PROJECT

The objectives of the project are as follows:

- To develop a procedure for integrating social work and child psychiatry so that specialised child psychiatric care based on small area responsibility is co-ordinated with patch social work to provide services for families with children at risk. Child welfare work calls for a multiprofessional approach and methodological studies. The project aims to overcome the obstacles that have traditionally stood in the way of co-operation between social welfare and health services.

- To prevent children getting taken into care by providing earlier, more effective support and by improving work methods. This also will make it easier for children to return to their homes after placement. A well discussed and well timed placement respecting the needs of the child supports the future development of the child.

- To enhance the social workers' ability to recognise children at risk even in work directed primarily at adults. When a family seeks income support or care for substance abuse, the social workers are supported to rehabilitate the whole family in a comprehensive way. Workers are required to deal with a number of tasks requiring different types of expertise. Acquiring and maintaining the professional skills required in child welfare work calls for additional training and support. Regular interaction with workers dealing specifically with children and families with children is one form of education and support.

- To develop a model for area child psychiatry work that is more comprehensively equipped to ensure that children at risk will receive care. The project is therefore developing methods that can help a child even though the parents are not initially convinced of the need for assistance. The child as an individual also has a right to treatment. The project also aims to promote greater understanding of the problems encountered by parents living in difficult conditions. The experts are being made more aware of the significance to parenthood of social structures and intervention by the authorities. Workers are being helped to develop ways of supporting parents in a way that does not imply blame.

- To ensure that all children needing a placement outside the home receive the necessary psychiatric support. This psychiatric care must, should the need arise, be continued while the child is an institution or a foster family.

- To arrange joint primary health care and social welfare training events to integrate the project with the basic services in the district and to ensure that the experience gained of new methods is put into widespread use in the area. The training should study in depth the risks threatening the development and mental health of the child, and ways of identifying and rectifying them.

- To support, with the help of a family worker used to observing children, parents who, through lack of experience, substance abuse or mental illness, have difficulty in coping with the everyday running of the home and parenting their children.

- To seek ways of helping poorly motivated families and to find practices approved by the families themselves.

- To prevent families prematurely withdrawing from services, especially at the stage when the family moves or is transferred to another working team or another office.

METHODS FOR ACHIEVING THE PROJECT OBJECTIVES

- Regular, systematic work done together week by week aiming to assist the resources and coping skills of families with children at risk. The aim is for the families to be present at the case conferences.

- Psychiatric examination and treatment for children at risk provided at as early a stage as possible.

- Psychiatric assistance for all children who have to be taken into care. This psychiatric care must, should the need arise, be continued while the child is in an institution or a foster family.

- The workers involved in the project enter the child's network: the day nursery, clinic and school. A child-oriented family worker also helps the family in the concrete task of parenting.

- Sustained, intensive commitment to the job and its objectives, making expedient and flexible use of home visits as a method of intensive rehabilitation and care.

- Joint training sessions for social welfare, primary care and specialised health care personnel as a means of integrating the project with the other services in the area and to ensure that the experience gained of new methods is widely shared in the area. The training should provide in depth knowledge of the risks threatening the development and mental health of the child, and ways of identifying and rectifying them, respecting the knowledge and skills of each member of the multiprofessional team. So far training has been arranged for all workers in the areas of post-natal depression, early interaction with the child, substance abuse and the mental health problems of parents. More than a hundred workers have attended each of the seminars.

EXECUTORS OF THE PROJECT

The Korso-Rekola Social Welfare and Health Centre

Social work (child welfare, income support and welfare for substance abusers) comes under the Korso and Rekola district offices. The project is being carried out in collaboration with the Korso office.

At the start of the project the working team consisted of nine social workers, two head social workers and a social services secretary. In 1994, there were twelve social workers. The social workers operate according to the integrated social welfare model; specifically each worker is responsible with a partner for all the work within the team's responsibility.

The Peijas Hospital child psychiatry clinic

The child psychiatric outpatient clinic, opened at the beginning of 1991, is responsible for Vantaa and Kerava, which have a combined population of over 40 000 children and young people aged 0-16. The clinic is primarily responsible for providing specialised child psychiatric care within the Peijas medical district. Patients are referred to the clinic for examination and treatment by a physician. The majority of the referrals come from school health care, the paediatric clinic and child welfare.

The clinic specialises in providing family-oriented, flexible and quick service in times of crisis in collaboration with the family guidance clinics, day care, schools and child welfare authorities in the district. It co-ordinates the referrals to the university hospital, engages in consultations, examines children and families, and provides the necessary treatment. The fact that the paediatric clinic is situated next door means that long-term child patients can be given all-round treatment including both medical and psychiatric care. Child welfare families with multiple problems constitute a major category of the clinic's clients.

At the start of the project the working team consisted of a chief physician, a specialist nurse, a social worker and a psychologist. A psychology trainee also took an active part in the project. In 1994, the clinic had a second specialist in child psychiatry and a second psychologist.

The family worker

There were plans right at the start of the project for including a family worker, but the necessary funds were not available until 1992, and then only for one year. The family worker's salary was paid by a charitable foundation (*Kotisisaropiston kannatusyhdistys*), which thus supported the project. When the year was up, the contribution of the family worker was considered to be so important that the city of Vantaa decided to provide the necessary funds to continue the work. The family worker is a trained childminder from a day-care centre.

The family worker first meets the family at a joint case conference and later on a home visit with a social worker. The worker from the Peijas child psychiatric team and the social worker also make a joint home visit if necessary. The family is asked what the family worker could do to help. The type of assistance requested varies considerably. Forms of assistance which the family consider necessary are then sought.

The help requested by a family may involve filling in applications, a father or mother may simply wish to talk about his/her child, or a single father may need advice on cooking. Sometimes the family worker may take the children out for a few hours so that the parents can rest. The emphasis is on the meaning of play with parents. This way the parents also get to know their children better. The most important thing is, however, for the family worker to make sure that all is well with the child, and that he or she is being well cared for. The work is not, therefore, an extended form of family work but first and foremost a working practice dictated by the needs and interests of the child.

The most common problem encountered in families is that the parents are in some way "at a loss". It is thus the job of the family worker to encourage the parents in their parenthood and to make them understand that they are the dearest and most important people to their children.

Families usually have a very realistic view of their situation, but they often see no hope of any change taking place. Outside help is then necessary to overcome their despair and feeling of powerlessness. The work of the family worker differs from that of the community carer in that he/she does not act for the family but tries to get the parents to help themselves and their children. The work of the family worker is only one part of family assistance. The parents may, for example, be receiving treatment at the A-clinic for their substance abuse or the mental health clinic, or the social worker may do follow up work in case the children should need protective measures.

The family worker has a wide network of partners. She should be ready for various kinds of partnerships, since she occupies an important role in building bridges both between the family and agencies and between different agencies. She in fact operates in a delicate border zone between different organisations and systems, yet at the same time on private territory, in the home.

The family worker has about ten cases at a time. She may meet some families a couple of times a week, some much less frequently. The work is hard and subject to pressure from many sources. Regular supervision is necessary. A team partner would in many cases be a help and support, even if the partner did not accompany her on home visits. Discussing and sharing difficult cases with a colleague employed in the same field would undoubtedly ease the mental strain of the job. At its best, the work of the family worker is, however, rewarding and gratifying. The results are most clearly visible when taking a child into care can be avoided or a crisis has been resolved and the family embarks on a new life.

Partners

The need for regular, systematic co-operation with other helpers in society has been observed. Co-operation does indeed exist, for example, with the family guidance clinic, the A-clinic and day care. The municipal agency for fostering is a crucial partner in child welfare and is always present at conferences discussing and preparing child placements.

The project meetings have been attended by such partners as day care, the family guidance clinic, the child welfare lawyer, foster child welfare workers, the directors of children's homes and workers from the refugee centre. A new form of co-operation has also been instigated with adult psychiatric care;

workers from this agency also need to leave the conventional mental health office and go out into the field with the social workers and child psychiatrists. Creating and maintaining co-operation channels makes various crises outside the project easier to handle.

In autumn 1993 two pupils in the upper level of comprehensive school (13-16 age group) committed suicide in Korso. Because co-operation channels had already been established, the authorities were able to react quickly. On the project's initiative, the subject was discussed at school with the victims' schoolmates in an attempt to alleviate their anxiety. Also present were a school guidance counsellor and a youth worker. These joint meetings assessed whether there were any other youngsters at risk, and ways of preventing further suicides were discussed with the adolescents and their parents.

OPERATION OF THE PROJECT

All the people involved in the project have embarked on systematic work drawing on the expertise of both professional fields. Instead of trying to establish a common theory, the project has consciously decided that practical work should be carried out together.

Both agencies – child welfare and child psychiatry – have respect for and a desire to support the expertise of the other. Working together on the same families has forced both agencies to analyse their own approach and helped them to establish criteria for their own working practices. As a result of working together, both agencies have learnt more and broadened their scope. There is also greater commitment to working with the client and less of a "it's not my problem" attitude. Setting the limits for individual jobs is also easier as the workers learn to justify their actions better.

Children and families at risk benefit from having access to the expertise of several professions simultaneously. Despite working together, taking sides with different members of the family has not led to workers blaming each other. The family also benefits from the fact that the workers are able to voice any differences of opinion at the earliest possible stage. Setting up common goals and respecting and trusting another's expertise make helping more efficient and effective.

The users of services no longer have to seek assistance for the same problem at different places but can receive all the assistance they need in one place. Parents with small children thus no longer have to travel from place to place, which is in practice very laborious. The workers' analysis of the criteria for their own work, respect for the work of others and tolerance of different theoretical ideas is also reflected in a growing respect for the autonomy of the client. The workers learn to explain to their clients, too, the reasons for their decisions, and the result is more open dialogue. Tolerance of difference increases.

It is now easier for families to seek the services of the child psychiatry clinic or child welfare more flexibly, and the transition is more successful since both agencies are committed to co-operation. Monitoring is also more efficient; matters do not get overlooked. The conventional case conference does not guarantee that the family gets drawn into the co-operation.

The shift in focus in psychiatric services towards non-institutional care has increased the demand for the closer evaluation of children's needs. Withdrawn parents who are suspicious of outsiders because of their own disappointments require sustained effort before the development of the child can be assessed and supported. The joint home visits made by child welfare and child psychiatric workers have already proved extremely useful in the project. It is then possible to assess the children in their own environment and at the same time to grasp the reality within the family. Empathic forms of support are easier to accept. It is therefore important to make time for demanding and effective forms of work such as home visits.

The presence of child psychiatry also permits the making of a flexible, all-round assessment of the child. The paediatric clinic, or sometimes even the child psychiatry ward, may be part of the network of support the child needs. The social worker knows the situation in the child welfare institutions and can if necessary make a reservation if a placement appears to be the best solution.

In addition to the fact that project workers enter the child's networks, the family worker helps the family with the concrete running of the home and pays special attention to the needs of the children.

The emotional aspect of parenthood is stressed by pointing out how important it is for parents to play with their children. Doing something together in a way that gives pleasure and satisfaction reinforces self-assurance and creates a favourable self-image in parents and children alike.

Joint consultations

Achieving the objectives calls for regular weekly meetings. Due to the growing pressure of work, the meetings have had to be reduced to three a month.

To begin with, the meetings concentrated on the planning of client work, agreeing on the division of labour and seeking new ways of solving problems. Later on, the working teams began to discuss cases they wished to be taken up by the co-operation project. Ideas were sought on the best way to approach each case. If, for example, a child in need of psychiatric treatment has been brought to a worker's attention because the parents have applied for income support, ways are sought of motivating the family to seek help.

Work with a family begins by evaluating the family's motivation for co-operation. Few families refuse to co-operate, whether the suggestion comes from a worker at the psychiatric clinic or a social worker at the social welfare and health centre. Next the social workers and the Peijas child psychiatry team hold a conference with the family to hear its views on the subject. The family also helps to decide what needs to be done. The feeling of powerlessness is reduced if the family has a chance to influence its own affairs.

The joint conferences show families that it is possible to discuss matters and to reach an agreement that is acceptable to all. Once families have been made clearly aware of the changes required to safeguard the child's development, they are willing to take part in the work. The basic premise is that all parents love their children and want to be good parents, even though they are not always able to act in the child's best interests.

Thanks to this co-operation, it is possible to offer families more than just understanding and discussion. If, for example, a family is in financial difficulty, the project team decides which member will address this. Therapy, too, is more successful once the family's subsistence and housing problems have been solved.

Working in close collaboration also has its problems. Sometimes it may be difficult for a worker to retain his own specific role and to decide the precise limits of his responsibility, yet an awareness of these is important if the co-operation is to continue for some time. Constant clarification of the worker's own field of responsibility is important for all taking part in the work. Co-operation leads to a reassessment and changing of working procedures in both of the project agencies. Project work cannot replace the unit's natural mode of operation; new procedures must be adapted to its normal work. Development work also needs the approval of the broader support networks and administrative leaders of the operating units.

Home visits

The common practice in child welfare work has been that once all the various means have been tried and it looks as if a child will have to be taken into care, then a home visit is planned. Such visits have not even been considered in mental health work. A home visit has thus been resorted to only as an extreme measure for resolving a family crisis.

The procedure should begin much earlier. A home visit should be made as soon as a client seeks assistance, because it yields valuable information on the family that might not otherwise come to light. A home visit also gives the worker a better, more concrete understanding of the situation in the family. From the point of view of the child, it is also useful to see the conditions in which the child lives and grows up. Not every child necessarily has such things as a bed of his or her own, toys, and a place in which to do homework.

The home visit does not need to take the form of an inspection or a fact-finding event; it may be one way of working on the family's home ground, within its own territory, and with respect for this. It may provide a means of establishing mutual trust and placing both parties on a more equal footing. It should not stress a hierarchical client-helper relationship; nor should the worker become firmly ensconced behind an office desk.

Home visits are a demanding form of work calling for special delicacy and tact in the worker. Sometimes a home visit may seem to be a time-consuming way of working, even though it is surprisingly fruitful. A home visit may also save the family the laborious process of having to visit various offices, or it may provide the worker with an opportunity to encourage poorly motivated families loath to visit an office.

EVALUATION OF THE PROJECT

No reduction seems likely in the number of children taken into care, since the state of society (with the high unemployment rate) is greatly adding to the burden of families with children living in worrying situations. Closer co-operation is also bringing to light a lot of latent need for help in families with problems.

Cases of abuse of children are being revealed in greater numbers than before, and the cases are becoming more serious. The number of refugees and foreigners has increased and these groups are demanding new types of know-how from the professionals in the area.

Some of the custody cases can be prevented by intensified working methods. The new practice can prevent families from withdrawing, because they remain in contact with one or both of the project agencies, even though the contact has at times been on the verge of breaking.

The teams involved are eager to develop and modify their work. One problem is, however, sometimes the sense of chaos as work piles up, leaving insufficient resources for planning reforms. The establishment of new working procedures takes time and strength. There is a danger that a future benefit will seem too far away to motivate work in the present if in the initial stages it involves more work than the traditional method. On the other hand the workers themselves determine the quality of their work and are able to change in spite of growing pressures.

The commitment to the development project varies in a working team even of this size. A special ability is needed to listen to workers with very different approaches to problems and their personal styles. Some of the workers see no need to change their working methods.

The fact that almost all of the members of both working teams have changed in the course of the project has been an obstacle to continuity and has meant that new workers have had to be initiated into the project.

We workers nevertheless have firm faith in our knowledge and skills and the importance of our work. People, not principles, change an era.

A CASE EXAMPLE

The child welfare office is informed of a suspected case of child sexual abuse. A meeting is held the same day to discuss the matter, and it is decided that the family should be referred to the family guidance clinic and the child for somatic investigations to the health centre doctor dealing with incest. A worker from the family guidance clinic, the health centre doctor and a city lawyer are invited to the next meeting. Each has made his or her own investigations, but together they agree how the parents could be persuaded to report the offence, as this is considered essential.

It is the job of the social worker in this case to counsel and support the family, that of the project team to liaise and act as experts. Responsibility for further measures is transferred by agreement to the family guidance clinic.

This jointly agreed procedure reduces the volume of work, unnecessary investigations and duplication in the early stages of the case. It is also easy to check that all the necessary measures have been taken. The workers clearly suffer less anxiety since the case is viewed jointly from many angles, and no one worker has to assume sole responsibility for the entire case.

WORKING TOGETHER ACROSS BORDERS

by

Marika Vilen and Riitta Kauppinen*

"Preschooling takes into account the child's own individuality. All children, including those who require special care and education as well as those who are especially gifted, are ensured growth and learning according to their own requirements. A learning environment which stresses quality teamwork is suitable for most children. Every child has the right to their own language and culture." [Initiatives for the planning of preschool education, Joint Policy of the National Board of Education and the National Research and Development Centre for Welfare and Health (STAKES), 31.12.1994.]

INTRODUCTION

The OECD/CERI study on "services integration for children and youth at risk and their families" (1993-95) was inspired by concern about the growing numbers of people excluded from society and a desire to provide assistance by combining resources at all levels. Finland's contribution to the study is the responsibility of the National Board of Education and the National Research and Development Centre for Welfare and Health (STAKES).

In this report, the term "at risk" refers to a wide range of unfavourable social conditions and children whose development is endangered because of these conditions. The development of at risk groups can be attributed to socio-economic factors.

"Services integration" is taken to mean modes of working together which vary in degree (namely, co-operation, co-ordination and collaboration). It concerns the amalgamation of the know-how and resources of two or more services.

The target population consists of groups at risk from birth to independence. The focus is on four groups in the juvenile and adult population:

- children under school age (0-6 years);
- school children;
- school leavers;
- youth at risk and their families.

The present report is part of the case study component of the OECD project and examines the lives of children under school age and their parents within the confines of public preschool education. The aim is to describe a few experiments and development projects carried out in preschool education that are trying, by integrating services, to improve the learning and quality of life of children at risk and their families.

As case examples, we have chosen experiments that represent a new trend and philosophy in preschool education. We try to describe each project and development programme, its problems and achievements, as accurately as possible in the light of existing material. Some of the projects are still in

* Further information is available from STAKES, P.O. Box 220, Fin-00531, Helsinki.

the early stages and so far there has been little monitoring and evaluation of outcomes. We do, however, wish to present the development work already begun as there have been few experiments in Finland in profound multi-professional co-operation. The present authors have no knowledge of any broader regional projects aiming to integrate services.

THE SITUATION IN FINLAND

Paragraph 18 of the International Charter on the Rights of the Child states that signatory states shall be obliged to help parents and other providers in their task of up-bringing in order to implement the rights of the child. This could be reframed by saying that the signatory states, Finland included, are obliged to develop preventive child welfare work (The Central Union for Child Welfare, 1991). One of the objectives of the Finnish Child Welfare Act in recent years has been to develop this. Previously, child welfare failed to succeed in ensuring that sufficient attention was paid to its needs in the planning and building of society, and therefore was not able to influence the reasons for problems or offer solutions.

Services integration aiming at preventive care for children at risk and their families is still relatively rare in Finnish preschool education. There has been little scope for timely integrated intervention to meet the needs of children under school age. Services have concentrated chiefly on school welfare work.

The problems caused by the state of the national economy and the economic recession have raised the importance of preventive action. More effective integrated means are now being sought in an attempt to improve the situation of families suffering from the recession. The lives of families with children are being impoverished by financial difficulties and unemployment. The situation is particularly serious in families where managing life is difficult anyway. Children suffer the most during crises in society.

Families' disposable income has decreased due not only to unemployment but also to higher taxes and charges. The savings necessitated by the decline in the national and municipal economies have affected social security in particular. In the biggest social services sector, children's day care, the cuts have been appreciable, and families with children and, above all, families with multiple problems, have suffered the most. The cuts have specifically affected those who are poor advocates of their own affairs and have few advocates to defend them (Publications on social welfare and health, 3/1994).

Child guidance services

The integration of child guidance services is not new in Finland. This report takes a look at integration carried out in public preschool education. In Finland, most early education is provided in day care centres (kindergartens) and consists of preschool education, family day care and play activities. Day care aims to support the up-bringing provided in the home (Act on Children's Day Care, 1973/36). The primary responsibility of parents to bring up their children gives them the right to participate in the development of day care. The quality of services and the parent perspective have been enhanced in recent years and ways of increasing user-democracy are being sought in the day care field. Opportunities for children and parents to participate and influence are being widely developed and researched.

Co-operation has in recent years been increased between the various forms of day care – day nursery, family day care and play activities – by, among other things, integrated staff training. Children both within and outside the municipal day care system also attend play groups run by the local churches. Co-operation between municipal day care and the church play groups is particularly important in rural areas, where most of the day care is provided in a home-like environment.

Schools and day care systems have together been developing the quality of preschool education ever since the first kindergartens were founded. Preschool education has been provided for 6-year-olds ever since the 1960s and children in Finland begin their compulsory education at the age of 7. The day care system and preschool are administered by the Ministry of Social Affairs and Health; compulsory education and preschool for 6-year-olds are provided by the Ministry of Education. A report (STAKES oppaita 24/1995) published at the beginning of 1994 by the National Board of Education and STAKES on the basic premises for the planning of preschool education lays the foundations for child-oriented education. The report stresses active learning for children and co-operation between all of the agencies involved in order to construct environments conducive to learning. The renewable criteria for the planning of education for children of preschool and comprehensive school age guarantee an unbroken lifelong learning process. The prerequisites for integrated childhood education services thus exist already and the day care and comprehensive school staff have in numerous municipalities drawn up joint curricula for preschool and primary education.

The legislation demands little multi-professional expertise in children's day care. At the crossover points in growing and learning the child has the right to receive special guidance or education. The Act on Children's Day Care (1973/36) states that a plan must be made in order to integrate the rehabilitation of a child in need of special care and guidance, and that the child's parents and, if necessary, the local welfare, health care and education authorities must be consulted.

Children at risk have equal access and rights to day care and education. Under the Act on Children's Day Care (1973/239) priority is given in awarding day care places to children in need of it for social or educational reasons. Day care aims to support the favourable growth and development of the child and thereby prevent social and educational problems within the family. In practice, day care's potential for multi-professional, preventive activity seems to depend on the state of the local economy. Socio-economic "uncertainty" factors should be reflected in the quality and intensity of co-operation with families.

Other co-operation with day care

There has long been services integration between day care, child health clinics, child welfare, and various organisations. Multi-professional work to develop the services and expertise supporting the needs of the child and the family is in the early stages. In most cases, development is the responsibility of one or a few persons who have set out to update the service philosophy in day nurseries and preschool education. The impetus for development in the workplace has to some extent been provided by the greater autonomy which local authorities now enjoy to plan their services from the perspective of the client – the child and the family. Social welfare, health care, the municipal administration and other services have displayed a varying degree of enthusiasm for the experiment. The local authorities have in certain cases proved regrettably disinclined to try out new ideas. Most of the integration experiments encountered in making the present survey have been initiated by people with a passionate desire to defend the status of the child.

ENCOURAGING SOLUTIONS

The account of each of the experiments or development projects outlined here is based on available material. Most of the interviews were conducted using the OECD questionnaires. Some visits were also made in conjunction with the interviews and telephone discussions were held with various spokesmen. Each project is concisely described from the angles: what, why and how? Further information is available from the contact persons.

Preschool somersault and day care network

A national day care development project called the Somersault Ride Project for Early Childhood (Kuperkeikka) co-ordinated by STAKES was launched in 1992 and focuses on the child's perspective. Field workers in children's early learning and education formed networks around specific themes. The project is looking at subjectively experienced quality, which is the basis for the creation of a dynamic learning environment. The aim of the project is to renew working procedures so that children can be seen and heard and so that the staff can learn to plan their work with children.

Countless network nodes are being formed at the development centres and numerous centres of excellence. In order to acquire greater expertise, research and development is being integrated with basic early education and teaching services. The centres are locally anchored in each individual municipality but they have a nationwide operating radius and an international orientation. The emergence of innovative co-operation networks is being monitored and they are being modelled as operating strategies in the social welfare and health services.

The Somersault Ride project is described in the report *"Esiopetuksen kuperkeikka – käyntikortteja lapsipedagogiikasta"* (Kauppinen *et al.*, 1994).

The Kokkola development centre is applying the principles of new co-operative action to day care, Tampere is furthering the links between preschool education, nature and sustainable development, Toijala is applying methods developed at the Reggio Emilia day care centres to Finnish conditions, Imatra is innovating early learning projects, Sipoo is developing instruction in the natural sciences and nature in preschool education, and Kempele is promoting the use of information technology in linking preschool educators at home located far from one another. The following is an account of childhood services integration as approached by two development centres in the Somersault Ride project.

The Kirkkonummi centre – co-operative learning

The municipality of Kirkkonummi has, for some years now, been building bridges between various forms of day care and school in order to improve children's growth and learning potential. In 1991-92, it conducted a project called Etsikko (Searching) in collaboration with the National Agency for Welfare and Health (nowadays STAKES) (Riihelä, 1993). Taking part in the project were the day nursery, family day care, school workers and parents, who all got together to seek ways of achieving a more child-oriented form of preschool education. Since 1992, Kirkkonummi has had a development centre for co-operative learning which, by drawing preschool and primary education closer to one another, is updating teaching methods and developing schooling for the youngest pupils. The principles of co-operative learning are being applied in the everyday day care and school environment to ensure that transferring from one growth milieu to another is an enriching experience for the child. One concrete pedagogical bridge between preschool and primary education is the learning portfolio in which the children themselves report what they have learnt, what they can do, and what they need to know. The development centre has also been establishing contacts with other early learning developers in the municipality, training and research establishments, and international co-operative learning networks. Co-operative learning environments for children aged 1-9 are being developed at the Huuhkajavaara Day Nursery school in Kajaani. In both Kirkkonummi and Kajaani, municipal teaching plans have been drawn up by a multi-professional team.

The Mikkeli, Uusikaupungi and Pyhäsalmi multi-professional co-operation centre

Mikkeli, Uusikaupunki and Pyhäsalmi together constitute a multi-professional co-operation centre. By means of joint training and multi-professional co-operation they are developing preschool education chiefly for children at risk. The development centres began their own and the joint work at the beginning of 1994. Among the joint forms of activity are monitoring of their own projects, documentation, public relations and joint training events.

Mikkeli: The day care personnel in the Mikkeli region have for some years now been actively working to improve the quality of day care. Day care is being repeatedly faced with new challenges, yet the resources have decreased. The day care people sometimes feel ill-equipped to attack the new reforms; their time and resources seem to go in handling day-to-day routines.

Issues to be faced are refugees, returning emigrants, children in need of special education, organising preschool education, the use of information technology in teaching and administration, growing co-operation with parents and schools, unemployment, and parents' right to demand quality day care.

The Province of Mikkeli has no full-time personnel for planning and developing day care. It does, however, have a large number of day care workers and children in preschool education and day care. The networking project taking in Mikkeli, Ristiina, Juva, Anttola and Pertunmaa is one answer to solving the problem of planning, training, co-operation and communications.

In the networking project (Figure 1), a modular network is being formed in which each module consists of one or more day nurseries from different municipalities, family day care, or day care units from different municipalities. Each combination – or centre of excellence – is developing and experimenting with a theme of its choice:

- The private Marski Day Nursery in Mikkeli is developing an educational culture that will guarantee the individual welfare of the child in confidential interaction with families. The different needs of each family are taken into consideration and each family has its own person responsible for it.

- The Finnish language instruction for returning emigrant and refugee children provided by the Ristiina Day Nursery is a form of preventive work. The children are at the same time being taught mathematical skills with the help of computers.

Figure 1. **The network scheme**

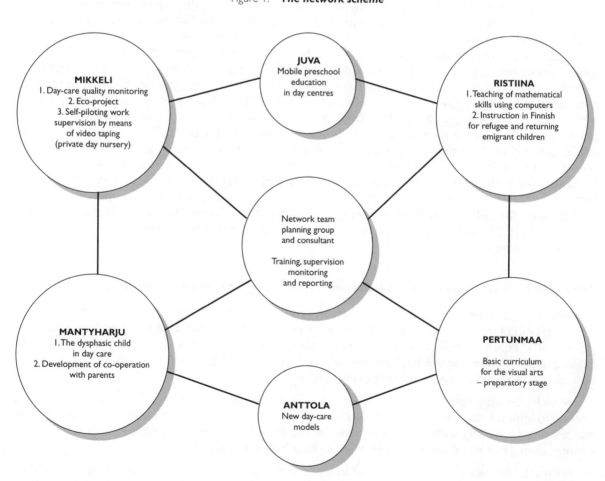

Source: Authors.

- The project at the Muksula Day Nursery in Mäntyharju is developing co-operation between the parents and day care personnel and improving the quality of the dialogue on education. The day nursery staff are also engaging in professional co-operation with social workers, psychologists, clinic nurses, the health centre and central hospital.
- The Keinula Day Nursery in Pertunmaa is developing preventive child welfare work in the municipality. It has drawn up a curriculum for preschool education and a basic curriculum for visual arts.
- The Anttola Day Nursery is planning new models for education and teaching.
- The Juva Mobile Day Nursery is developing preschool education for children in rural areas. The mobile day nursery is trying to make allowance for the special needs of these children as a preventive measure.

The primary aim in developing day care in the Mikkeli region is to focus on the status and welfare of children. In doing this, the region is trying to get as many children as possible involved in the development work. Within the modules, long-term programmes are being devised to address objectives, progress, and the need for consultants and training. The development centre's planning group assembles the programmes and provides the necessary training and consultant services.

The idea for the project was stimulated by the need of day care personnel working in the field to develop their own work with children and families. Assistance was obtained in launching the project from experts and county officials. One of the biggest problems so far has been the lack of financial support, and especially the absence of funds to employ a consultant.

Numerous agencies have taken part in the project. Each unit has its own co-operating institutions and persons, and the component projects are, furthermore, under obligation to inform the others of the evaluation of their own work. People from the development centre are co-operating with other development centres, especially those in Pyhäsalmi and Uusikaupunki, and the co-ordinator, STAKES.

The project is still at such an early stage that it is difficult to estimate any negative or positive results. So far the day care personnel have welcomed the increase in support, information and relations. They no longer have to deal with problems alone and can share them with others. The only disadvantage has been the extra work involved.

Uusikaupunki: Every attempt has been made to keep the quality of day care in Uusikaupunki as high as possible by means of well-qualified staff and progressive growth. The unemployment brought by the economic recession has been a major problem in the town of Uusikaupunki, which relies on the motor industry. Growing unemployment has meant a reduction in day care places. The staff have had to face new challenges. Civil servants are being trained for new types of work. More flexible transfer from one job to another is being facilitated by equipping workers with supplementary skills and know-how.

Various models for internal training have been developed in Uusikaupunki:

- staff transferring to new jobs are briefed and qualified in, for example, caring and cleaning, through training provided by the employer under apprenticeship schemes;
- self-piloting training in education (*i.e* the application of the staff's know-how in a training network).

The project aims to combine the expertise and experience of persons interested in the same development item at joint training sessions. Communications are intensified by improving contacts and co-operation between workers. The objective is to improve services and to develop the quality of education, its appropriateness and general standard. This calls for the correct use of the capacities of a large working community.

Training is mostly provided according to an apprenticeship and further education principle. Training is purchased from outside the municipality on a reciprocal exchange basis.

Under the KAIKU project, goal-oriented training and activities were introduced in 1994 in fields such as the environment, arts, traditional culture and music education. Co-operation between social work and day care and the curriculum for preschool education have also been developed. There is ongoing development of new training fields such as health, work and international education and co-operation across municipal borders. Some contacts have been made on a small scale with colleagues in Japan.

Training is regarded in Uusikaupunki as being of primary importance in the development of progressive modes of operation. The ability to satisfy the needs of children at risk and interest in services integration are increasing all the time. One of the aims of the project was, after all, to increase co-operation between local officials. Learning to use the same concepts and approaches takes time.

The training has been financed out of the local authorities' own resources and has not therefore required any great investment, considering its extent. The development centre receives funds from the administration's joint training funds. The Uusikaupunki development centre organises training at minimum cost. The economic benefit has also been reflected in the growing multi-professionalism of local officials. Job transfers and efficient work organisation are now possible.

Pyhäsalmi: Within the few years since an initiative was started by the social services department, Pyhäsalmi has developed municipal services from the point of view of preventive social work. The aim is to create a service organisation that better corresponds to the needs of child welfare. In spring 1994, as part of the Somersault Ride project, the Pyhäsalmi development centre began training aimed at a number of professional groups, and some new services were introduced. Work on the Somersault Ride project continues, focusing on the needs of young children.

The Pyhäsalmi development centre has the following goals:

– To develop and improve the capabilities of social welfare workers for multi-professional networking. The focus is on the development of day care services for family rehabilitation and the prevention of problems in children and families.

– To continue breaking down the borders between different forms of day care according to the principle of integrated, goal-oriented action. The work of day care leaders is being developed so that the Pyhäsalmi district day care centres co-operate with parents and other professionals involved in preschool education with a view to constantly developing of the contents of day care.

– Together with the Oulu County Administration and other nearby municipalities, to develop regional co-operation in order to provide preschool education that is both flexible and what families need in both urban and rural areas. Regional conferences are accordingly held and the development centre sends out written bulletins.

In order to develop its co-operation capabilities, Pyhäsalmi has begun providing multi-professional continuing education. Services development and training have gone hand in hand so that learning serves work, and work serves learning. As far as possible, the training is inter-sectoral. The participants have included people working in the social services, children's day care, primary schools, and clinics.

One of the most successful ventures achieved through training so far has been the Mental Health Centre. This provides services previously supplied by the mental health office, the A-clinic, the family guidance clinic, and the health care centre. It is staffed by a health centre psychologist, a psychiatric nurse, a mental health nurse, a social therapist, a psychiatrist (one day a week), and a doctor (two days a week). The services of the mental health centre are open to all, from children to the elderly. The centre adjoins the health centre and also collaborates with the welfare office and school health services.

The Veitikka Club project (1993-94) was an experiment planned and executed on a voluntary basis by officials and workers from three administrations. It aimed to improve the learning capabilities of children found to have learning problems when examined at the clinic at the age of 5. The 6-year-old members of the club had already undergone closer examination at the Oulu University Central Hospital. Children not otherwise in day care were given priority. The club also sought to increase inter-sectoral co-operation. It is now taking over preschool education in Pyhäsalmi designed to include all children of preschool age.

In its day care, Pyhäsalmi has tried to increase co-operation in training, and in planning the mode and content of preschool education. Its partners have been children's clinics, schools, welfare for the handicapped, community care, the local church, the Mannerheim League for Child Welfare and other voluntary organisations. The social welfare management team, including the officer in charge of day care, meets regularly. The network also has a child welfare support team including a day care worker. The members of the Board and senior officials hold joint development meetings a few times a year. Working groups are convened by the partners as the need arises. The joint working and development projects cover both planning and monitoring, the emphasis being on the prevention of social problems.

Welfare for the elderly and community care have in Pyhäsalmi been combined to form one single service. Human resources have been transferred from community care to child welfare. Community care now covers people of all ages and, like day care, services co-operate widely with the various administrations and voluntary organisations.

Pyhäsalmi has also scrutinised its costs in the course of reorganisation. Services are being integrated, both to improve quality and to reduce costs. As a result, welfare expenditure and costs have decreased. Efficiency has at the same time improved, and so have the level of service and service relations. Economy has proceeded hand in hand with better results.

Integration is expected to continue creating a more effective level of service. Preventive work is regarded as being of primary importance. The only negative consequence of the development work has been the increase in work load, especially at the initial stage, but this has been outweighed by greater job satisfaction.

Family group experiments

The Ristikivi Day Nursery in Jyväskylä and the Mustikkamäki Day Nursery in Lahti have been experimenting with family groups extending beyond the conventional day care borders. The participants did not know one another at the start of the experiment. In both day nurseries, the idea was initially put forward by the head of the day nursery in an attempt to solve on humanitarian grounds the numerous problems encountered by families living in the area.

Jyväskylä – Ristikivi Day Nursery

An experiment of a new kind was launched at the Ristikivi Day Nursery in Jyväskylä at the beginning of 1994. This has aimed to develop group support for parenthood and bringing up children. Ideas are also being sought for promoting the learning, growth and development of the child. The activities of the group have been in the hands of two workers, one a kindergarten teacher and the other a childminder. They have been backed by a support group consisting of the head of the day nursery, a social worker, and a psychologist from the family guidance clinic. The experiment is part of a child welfare development project being carried out by the Jyväskylä social services department.

Concern about the way families suffering from unemployment or other forms of social exclusion are managing in their task of bringing up their children served as a challenge to develop activities together with families. The aim has been to act as a preventive support for families at risk and to help all members of the family to live in their own home environment. In supporting parenthood, the experiment particularly wishes to emphasize the importance of teaching everyday things, of adopting a positive attitude, of finding joy in work, and of gaining a command of life.

The aim of the family group experiment is, by working with other families and members of staff, to construct a social network for families in which they can learn to assume individual and joint responsibility. The group tries to supplement and to some extent replace social welfare services. This reduces the duplicate use of welfare or health services but on the other hand encourages families to seek help as necessary. The family group experiment has tried to prevent the necessity for "weighty" measures.

The idea for the experiment was proposed by one of the workers at the Ristikivi Day Nursery. It was then approved by the management and the assistance of an expert was sought. The family group was invited to meet in the recreation office adjoining the day nursery. A kindergarten teacher was hired out of substitute funds and a childminder was transferred from elsewhere. There have been no other expenses.

The families have mostly been advised of the group by the social workers and the clinic. The workers also have contacts outside the day nursery with the local psychologist and community care. The workers receive work supervision once a week.

The family group meets daily and arranges activities for both children and families. It was originally planned to consist of five to eight families but began with four. The group has a systematic weekly programme in which the growth and learning of the child are promoted in many ways. The parents do whatever interests them according to their own personal skills.

According to interviews carried out by developmental psychology students from the University of Jyväskylä (Juvonen and Tuikkanen 1994), both the workers and the mothers feel the experiment has been successful and that positive results have been achieved. Co-operation with clients and other partners has been relatively smooth. The day nursery appreciates the new "upbringing culture" in which, instead of concentrating on the child alone, the focus has now shifted to the entire family as an important element in society. The family group workers would like more training, especially in the participation of the family in the joint task of upbringing.

The City of Jyväskylä has extended the length of the Ristikivi family group experiment.

Lahti – Mustikkamäki Day Nursery

A report entitled "Learning Together" (in Finnish, *Yhdessä oppien arkeen*) has been published on the work and results of the Mustikkamäki Day Nursery. It was written by Marjaana Seppänen and published by the City of Lahti Social Welfare and Health Department. The information given in the present report is based on this publication.

There are a number of families in need of support living in the Liipola district of Lahti. Children are referred to the day nursery for social and educational reasons. The day nursery nevertheless felt there was little it could do to influence these children's lives. There was thus a clear need to develop new ways of helping families in need.

When one day nursery group was closed, the opportunity presented itself to launch a family group experiment using existing resources. By participating in the group and applying the working methods of day care, the families in need of help receive support and supervision in handling everyday situations.

On the initiative of the head of the day nursery, the City's Chief Welfare Officer asked the head of the child welfare department to form a team to plan a family group procedure. Also invited to join the team were a representative of the family guidance clinic, a municipal home maker, and the head of the local welfare centre. The experiment was to last for eleven months beginning on February 1st, 1993, but the length was later extended. The families were selected by the child welfare or clinic authorities. To begin with there were four, and there have been ten in all.

As in Jyväskylä, Lahti approached the project as an experiment in preventive child welfare. The idea has been for parents to learn a new mode of action, to receive support in living with their children, and to develop positive emotional ties with their children. The daily routines and working procedures have been the same as in Jyväskylä.

In Lahti, too, the families and workers have on the whole been satisfied with the family group and its results. Its members have enjoyed working together, and the group gave rhythm and meaning to everyday life. It has also fostered co-operation between officers.

Naarajärvi – family-oriented work

Naarajärvi has been trying to integrate its day care, school, health care and welfare systems since 1991. It has great respect for the family. Families are ill-equipped to succeed in bringing up their children in today's society. Problems are difficult to solve alone. For many, the threshold for seeking help is high and help is not sought until real problems have emerged: the child is truly ill at ease, the family is already or in danger of breaking up. The day care workers best equipped to create trusting relations with parents are the ones with the best potential for getting through to the family and its problems in time. Workers should be given a chance to act as case workers supporting families and as a channel for co-operation with other official helpers.

These were some of the ideas behind the suggestion made by the Naarajärvi day care personnel to its various partners with a view to closer co-operation. In autumn 1992, three development centres, in Mikkeli, Savonlinna and Pieksämäki, were set up following a seminar arranged by Mikkeli County Administration. The Pieksämäki development centre embraces Pieksämäki Rural District, the town of Pieksämäki and Kangasniemi. The Siili Day Nursery at Naarajärvi belongs to the development unit of Pieksämäki Rural District.

Meetings started to be held at the Pieksämäki development centre in autumn 1993 and have continued as necessary. They have agreed on development needs, and have discussed the expectations and projects in each municipality. As its joint development project, the centre has chosen "family-oriented work in co-operation with other partners". Each municipality is developing its operations as it sees fit. At the joint meetings information and experiences are exchanged and ways of co-operating, such as in training, are sought.

The aim in developing co-operation is:

– to try to eliminate the duplication of services and unnecessary forwarding of clients from one expert to another;
– to increase confidential communication between the partners, with the client's permission;
– to intensify the support for child upbringing by families all through childhood and youth; and
– to influence the attitudes of the local communities to encourage joint responsibility, and to introduce more humane values.

Pieksämäki town and rural districts have developed a joint preschool curriculum. After a training event to be held in autumn 1994, this will be developed in collaboration with the school authorities.

The development of co-operation between health care and other social welfare services has been slower. Numerous ideas have been put forward, but working on them and their practical application have been slow. Co-operation has, however, been increased at the individual case level.

Many ideas have also been proposed for experiments in co-operation between other social welfare and day care services, but these too still need processing. It has been considered important for welfare and day care personnel to get to know one another, and to gradually formulate uniform concepts and working procedures.

Ideas for experiments have sprung from initiatives made at the grassroots level. An active role has been played by day care workers, who have long been talking among themselves about the need to develop day care in a direction that would better support the upbringing provided in the home. Some training and guidance has been provided with the assistance of the management, other officials, and experts. More support is, however, needed, and news of the experience of other municipalities or similar projects would be welcome.

Since the development work is still in its early stages, the benefits and drawbacks are so far difficult to assess. Problems have included persuading partners to commit themselves to continuing development, poor internalisation of goals and needs in co-operation groups, and the increase in work. On the other hand, the people involved have been adamant in their wish to continue. Preventive work is regarded as important: it increases the efficiency of services and saves money over the long-term. The active participation and contribution of municipal managers is awaited.

Iisalmi – the active Lippuniemi residents' association

Services integration in the Lippuniemi district of Iisalmi was instigated by the work of the residents' association and community, at the grassroots level. Lippuniemi has just over 3 000 inhabitants and consists of blocks of flats, row and detached houses. There is a large number of council apartments. Many of the people living there are workers, unemployed, single parents or incapacitated for work in many ways. Services are scarce in the area. The nearest schools are close to three kilometres away.

Community work in Lippuniemi operates on the assumption that the immediate environment and community are of decisive significance in people's lives. The environment to some extent determines people's functional capacity, sense of security, physical and mental health, and interaction. It is also important to view the individual as a subject, a creative actor. Man moulds his own well-being by his own action.

The aim of the "development centre for basic capabilities and community growth" project planned by the residents' association is to transform Lippuniemi Day Nursery into a development centre for preschool education. The following are among the objectives:

- The project will be guided by the needs of children and by parents and other residents.

- Day care, the first class of primary school, and afternoon care for school children, will be combined to form a seamless entity providing the child with security, basic skills and a place in which to grow and learn. The experiment mainly concerns children aged 5-8 made eligible for full-day school by deviating where applicable from the normal day care selection criteria.

- The entire staff of the centre will participate in educational interaction on an equal footing, regardless of job designation. Pedagogical-didactic methods will include learning through play, the development of mental activities arising from the child's experiences, conscious awareness of personal learning, and the extension of learning to life and the environment as a form of community interaction.

- The aim is to execute the project with no additional costs, through voluntary work, the merging of functions and job transfers.

- The development centre activities are being initiated as a 5-year experiment in collaboration with and under the guidance of the Kajaani teachers' training department of the University of Oulu.

A study has been made at the University of Oulu of the social problems in the Lippuniemi district, the aim being to chart the need of risk groups for preventive intervention. A number of small-scale services have in fact already sprung up in Lippuniemi, for children, young people, the elderly and mental health patients. The aims of services integration have been the creation of a sense of shared responsibility, the growth of independent initiative, the rational use of resources, the prevention, amalgamation and all-round treatment of social and other problems, and the awakening of residents' interest in being of influence in society.

Residents, the residents' association, local officials, municipal boards and even private enterprise have all become involved in developing the Lippuniemi services. Although politicians have been slow to offer their support and have been prejudiced against the project, the residents have been provided with integrated services for a couple of years already.

Although the project has been in operation for only a short time, it is already possible to list some of the benefits. Services have been made more economical and more efficient. People's knowledge has increased and attitudes (*e.g.* to deviation) have become more positive. The prejudice of politicians and the somewhat more strained service relationships have proved to be unexpected negative consequences.

Karkkila – strength from family holidays

The Rajakatu Day Nursery in Karkkila has made a major contribution to preventive child welfare work in the town. On the initiative of its Principal it has taken part in a number of experiments run by the Mannerheim League for Child Welfare. In addition to family holidays, it has organised playground activities, afternoon care for school children, training in supervisory education for parents and workers, a "kids club" meeting place for parents, and open days for young people.

Family holidays have been arranged in Karkkila since 1989. The organisers of active family holidays try to satisfy parents' expectations of holiday activities and parent education. The families have been selected in collaboration with the social welfare authorities, child welfare, community care and the child guidance clinic. The system draws in families that have not had a chance to experience a favourable sense of family togetherness on holiday. These families usually have a history of problems which they have difficulty in solving without help from outside.

In summer 1992, the Uusimaa district of the Mannerheim League for Child Welfare arranged four active family holidays, two in collaboration with the social workers' trade union, one with the City of Helsinki Social Services Department, and one with the Karkkila Social Services Department. The Rajakatu Day Nursery in Karkkila has proved to be an active leader in this two-year process.

During the seven-day family holidays activities are arranged for the children and adults, both together and separately. The parents meet daily to discuss questions of upbringing and human relations. The aim of these discussions is to give the parents greater confidence in themselves as educators and people and to learn to find new ways of relating to and solving everyday problems. At the same time the discussions give them an opportunity to meet families in similar life situations. The children's activities are biased towards education in the arts and nature exploration. The children gain new experiences and a sense of achievement. Families are drawn together during the camp. In the afternoons the families work together.

Continuing to work together after the holiday is an important part of the experiment. The parents meet at regular intervals and continue their joint holidays at family camps. Karkkila has established relations with the twin town of Tûr in Estonia. Families from the two towns have met and got to know one another and exchanged views on various issues, upbringing included. The project has continued for the planned two years and in autumn 1994 the families will meet for the last time within this context.

The Rajakatu Day Nursery has tried to serve as a centre which families living in the town can get advice on bringing up their children. The idea of developing the day nursery into a support centre for children and families came about from practical needs. Support for various projects has been obtained mainly from experts, with very little from politicians and managers. The day nursery has allocated some of its general funds for the special projects. Support has been obtained for the family holidays from the Association of the Slot Machine Charities (RAY), the Mannerheim League for Child Welfare, and to some extent, from preventive welfare provided by the social services.

Services integration and an increase in multi-professionalism in the day nursery have been regarded as favourable developments. Databases have improved, likewise service relations, and there have been some economic advantages. Children and adults have learnt to value divergence. More attention will in the future be paid to questions of equality and the results are expected to improve even further. The difficulties staff have in adapting to the new issues have been the only problem in the development work.

The Rajakatu Day Nursery is continuing its development work. In autumn 1994, the day nursery was made into a co-operative. It hopes to reinstate the potential curtailed by the recession for developing a broader service within the day nursery. The recession has hit both the local administration and ordinary families in Karkkila. The day nursery does not wish to stagnate but to try to make its own contribution to the town in the form of preventive social work.

Malmi – language teaching for refugee children

Numerous refugees, both adults and children, suffer from various psychic and psychosomatic symptoms. In addition to their general malaise, refugee children often wet themselves during the day and at night, have sleeping disorders, are afraid of falling asleep, and suffer headaches (Sosiaalihallituksen raporttisarja 14/1990).

In seeking services aimed at foreigners and in particular refugees, we were disappointed to find that Finland has very little knowledge of, skill with, or desire to deal with the mental problems facing refugees and their families. The basic material security which Finland has been able to offer does not guarantee that the refugee family will be able to adapt to its new life situation. The children of refugee families are at risk in just the same way as the children of, say, alcoholics. The transfer from a dangerous situation to a safe but completely alien culture is brutal. Finnish society is ill-equipped to deal with issues related to the refugee's native culture. Material welfare does not make tragic memories any easier to deal with and forget, nor does it help people to adapt to a new culture.

The Pekanraitti Day Nursery at Malmi in Helsinki has tried to rise to the multicultural challenge through language teaching. This began on the initiative of the National Board of Social Welfare to provide day care for the children of asylum seekers. Administratively, Pekanraitti belongs to the Unit for Foreigners of the Joint Service Division of the City of Helsinki Social Services Department.

Pekanraitti may provide a placement of relatively short duration for a child or a growth environment lasting a couple of years. There are children from babies up to the age of 8, and of numerous nationalities. An important role is played in developing activities by the staff, who already have experience of cultural adaptation issues.

Pekanraitti concentrates on language teaching. The children are immersed in Finnish from the day they enter the nursery. In the absence of a common language, the staff converse with parents through an interpreter. Finnish is spoken with the children from the very first moment. The aim of the day nursery is to act as a "soft landing" in the process of integration into the new society and culture.

Preserving the child's own culture and language is also considered important. The language spoken within the family is respected. There is no legal obligation in Finland to provide preschool education in the child's native language. Day care services are available in Finland only in Finnish, Swedish and Sami (Lapp).

The Pekanraitti Day Nursery keeps in touch with the child's subsequent placement in either a day nursery or school, and issues information on customs in different cultures. Consultant aid is also provided for others interested in and working in the area of preschool education and culture. There are in fact plans for temporarily releasing the present principal of the day nursery for full-time consultation. The know-how acquired by the day nursery is unique in Finland.

When it opened in 1986, the Pekanraitti Day Nursery was financed entirely out of state funds, but its budget now comes from the City of Helsinki Social Services Department. The achievements and significance of the work for the child's development are discussed with the Unit for Foreigners. Communications within the day nursery have so far been handled without any planned meeting or conference procedure. There have not been any monitoring projects.

CONCLUSION

A child-oriented philosophy and the social significance of the family are emphasized in the day care field. Single parenthood, and the inability of parents to bring up their children, have raised new questions and given new impetus to co-operation between professional educators and parents. The economic recession has also meant that it has been imperative to develop new forms of service. The fat years of the 1980s are a thing of the past.

The treatment of children and families at risk has often been affected by arguments between agencies over who is responsible for what. A child goes into day care, the mother is perhaps advised to seek social assistance, the father mental health services, and the family has little chance of growing together. Numerous questions have arisen in the development of services. Who deals with whom? Who has the right to intervene in a family crisis? Where is the place of the child? Who cares about people?

Multi-professionalism in training and integration in the organisation of work have been attempts to eliminate the conflict in social welfare and health policy. The conflict has become particularly pronounced as a result of the economic recession. The families which have difficulty managing their everyday lives and problems even in good times have suffered most from the recession. Children are affected most of all by the change for the worse. The social network of an unemployed parent becomes narrower, to say nothing of the child who, in many cases, remains beyond the confines of public preschool education. The child of unemployed parents has no real right to a place in day care and preschool education. In some municipalities, day care still primarily serves the needs of working and student parents.

Integrating services simply means a new division of labour. In the new division, there is flexible co-operation between different agencies. Traditional professional and sectoral thinking is being revised and practices that do not work are being abandoned. The alternative is collective responsibility and shared expertise. In preschool education, integration means co-operation between professional educators and with parents. Pedagogic material must be updated to allow for the uniqueness of the child as the nucleus of the family and society. Networking has yielded favourable experiences. There is strength in a network because people are in it of their own free will. New ideas are discovered together, and there is giving and receiving.

"Hidden in the power that moves a child's development onwards is his or her curiosity, the struggle to control things and the feeling of success and competence", says the document on initiatives for the planning of preschool education (STAKES oppaita 24/1994). In developing services for children central values should be an orientation towards children, and a perception of the child as a unique individual. The obligation to allow children to state their opinions on matters concerning them and to respect their experience lays the foundation for equality in adult-child encounters.

The idea of prevention in preschool education derives from a child orientation. Guaranteeing the growth potential of children and investing in child welfare work are solutions that have an impact now and lay the foundations for the welfare of society in the future. What is more, the new services integration models outlined here have – even though they have been in operation for only a short time – already begun to prove, to some extent, that integrated child welfare work is more economical than conventional social welfare and health services. Prevention operates at two levels: in the child's learning and development, and in the economy of the organisation. Could this be an idea for "saving municipalities"? Because public preschool education, day care and early learning are a normal service for the youngest members of society and their families, there is scope for the versatile development of its work to ensure the growth and welfare of all.

REFERENCES

CHARTER ON THE RIGHTS OF THE CHILD (1994), The Central Union for Child Welfare, Forssa, Auranen.

Esiopetuksen suunnittelun lähtökohtiä (The basic premises for planning preschool education), STAKES Report 24/1994, Jyväskylä, Gummerus.

JUVONEN, T. and TUIKKANEN, S. (1994), *Kuikka-perheryhmäkokelun osallistuneiden mielipiteitä ja kokemuksia* (The opinions and experiences of participants in the Kuikka family group experiment), Field assignment, University of Jyväskylä, Department of Psychology.

KAUPPINEN, R., RIIHELÄ, M. and VESANEN, R.M. (1994), *Esiopetuksen Kuperkeikka – käyntikortteja päivähoidosta* (Somersault Ride in preschool education – day care visiting cards), STAKES report 168.

Lastensuojelun kehittämisprojekti, väliraportti (Interim report on the child welfare development project), Publications on social welfare and health 3/1994, City of Espoo.

OECD (1996), *Successful Services for our Children and Families at Risk*, Paris.

Pakolaislapsi suomalaisessa päivähoidossa (The refugee child in Finnish day care), Report 14/1990 of the National Board of Social Welfare, Helsinki.

RÄTY, K. (1994), *Toiminnallinen perheloma osana vanhempainkasvatusta* (The active family holiday as part of parent education), Thesis, University of Helsinki, Faculty of Education.

RIIHELÄ, M. (1993), *Lapsipedagogiikalle siivet – yhteisen esi – ja alkuopetuksen jäljillä*, STAKES Report 117.

SEPPÄNEN, M. (1994), *Yhdessä oppien arkeen – raportti perheryhmäkokeilusta* (Learning together – a report on the family group experiment), City of Lahti Social Services and Health Department.

Sosiaalihallituksen raporttisarja 14/1990.

STAKES oppaita 24/1994.

STAKES oppaita 24/1995.

VUOLLE, A. (1994), *Pekanraitti on silta Suomi-tietoon. Lapsi päivähoidossa 4/1994* (Pekanraitti as a bridge to knowledge about Finland. The child in day care 4/1994), Discussion and information journal for parents and day care personnel, Vantaa, Suomalainen Lehtipaino Oy.

THE NETHERLANDS

THE QUEST FOR ECONOMY, EFFICIENCY AND EFFECTIVENESS

by

Ghiti Brinkman and Guido Walraven*

PREFACE

1994 saw the publication of the country report on the Netherlands which was written in the context of a long-term project on Services Integration for Children and Youth at Risk and their Families (Geelen *et al.*, 1994). The project was undertaken by the Member states of the OECD on the basis of a proposal from its Centre for Educational Research and Innovation (CERI). The country reports concluded the first phase of the project. They gave a general picture of the legislation and policies related to the provision of services as well as of the range of integrated services available.

Following on from the country reports, in the second phase of the project attention has been focused on some sites of good practice in integrated services. Although three periods in the life of children and youth at risk are studied in the project, in this report we restrict ourselves to the preschool and school phase. This is because the third period, the transition from school to work, in the case of the Netherlands, has been dealt with in an independent study carried out by the Institute for Sociological and Economic Research (ISEO) at the Erasmus University of Rotterdam. The results of the enquiry have been published separately (Veenman *et al.*, 1995).

In this chapter, the case study on the school phase was written by Ghiti Brinkman and that on the preschool phase by Guido Walraven. For the first case study, the information collected has been presented largely according to the agreed OECD/CERI model; this design has also been followed as far as possible in the other case study. Both authors contributed to the concluding section. The introduction was written by Guido Walraven, who was also responsible for the final form.

As was the case with the country report, the preparation of the case study report was partly made possible by a grant from the Ministry of Education, Culture and Science. Mr. Buis was the contact person of the Ministry; he commented on the design and elaboration of the study in the initial phase. At a later stage this role was taken over by Ms. Koole, who commented on the draft report.

We should like to thank all those interviewed (see the Annex) for their valuable information and for providing written material. We are also grateful to Berthilde Borreman, who collaborated on the interviews in Emmen and who in another context has described the general educational policy situation in Emmen. Finally we express our thanks to all those who were prepared to comment on earlier versions of this report, namely Pieter Appelhof (School Advisory Service, Utrecht), Yvonne Boxem (Municipality of Emmen), Jantien Kriens (FAO, Rotterdam), Tineke van Rossem (SARDES) and Josee van de Waarsenburg (Educational Priority Bureau, Emmen).

---

* English translation by Rachel van der Wilden-Fall. Abbreviations used in the text are defined in the Annex.

INTRODUCTION

The research

Purpose of research

The challenge before the OECD Children and Youth at Risk Study is the creation of case study reports that describe and evaluate some of the world's best efforts to integrate services. More modestly formulated it is a question of studying good practice in integrated services provision, or the way in which services are co-ordinating their work to meet the needs of children and youth at risk and their families.

According to the OECD, services integration should be manifest at two levels: the first refers to multidisciplinary co-ordination directed to the decisions concerning individual children and their families; and the second involves interagency co-ordination that focuses on decisions concerning entire programmes. Both forms of co-ordination require considerable co-operation and communication.

In this context the objective of the Dutch case studies can be formulated as the description and evaluation of some examples of good practice in the co-ordination of services for children and youth at risk, if possible at the various levels.

Cases – choice of sites and examples

In the OECD study, a distinction is made between three periods in the development of children at risk: preschool, school and the transition from school to work. In this context it was originally the intention in the Netherlands to study three cases of good practice, namely one for each period. In the country report three possible locations have already been mentioned.

However, in looking for financing for the case studies the possibility occurred of having a separate study carried out on the transition from school to work, in which more than one case of good practice could be analysed. As noted in the preface, such a study was completed by Veenman (1995), leaving the case studies to be presented in this report to focus on the preschool and school phase.

This did mean, however, that a choice had to be made from the three sites of good practice proposed in the country report. That was not easy, since it could be said of all three sites that they have years of experience with strong project management, that they are firmly committed to the principles of integration, co-operation and networking as well as to innovation, and that they play a major role in advancing knowledge and skills related to the Educational Priority Policy Programme. The choice was finally made of Emmen for the preschool phase and Rotterdam for the school phase. Through this decision there was a differentiation both in geographical location and also in the number of inhabitants of the sites: Rotterdam is one of the four largest cities in the Netherlands and is situated in the urban agglomeration of Western Holland, while Emmen is a medium-sized town in the northern province of Drenthe. The geographical situation and the size have partly led to a difference in the composition of the groups at risk in the two municipalities. As well as this both municipalities work on the problems around the integration of services with different organisational models. Moreover, it can be said, without undervaluing the importance of the third site, that particularly in Emmen there are good and interesting developments in the preschool field and particularly in Rotterdam with regard to primary and secondary education.

The national context in the Netherlands

In a number of respects the Netherlands is a small country. It measures 40.8 million square kilometres and has a population of more than 15 million. In other respects the Netherlands is not so small, in particular when it comes to the Dutch economy. With a GDP of over US$320 billion in 1992 and a balance of payments surplus of US$4.5 billion in the same year, the Netherlands is one of the wealthier western countries. The structure of its economy shows the typical characteristics of a post-industrial society. Of the working population of 7 133 million, 4 per cent are employed in agriculture and fishery, 24.6 per cent in industry, and 71.4 per cent in the services sector. In 1994 unemployment stood at 7.5 per cent. Incidentally, the labour participation of women in the Netherlands is low in comparison with other Western countries.

The population structure is as follows. In 1992, 68.7 per cent of the population were between 15 and 65 years old, but now the country is undergoing a process of ageing, with the proportion of people older than 65 (13 per cent in 1992) gradually increasing. With regard to origin, 5.5 per cent of the population belong to an ethnic minority group. The most important of these are the Surinamese (1.6 per cent), Turks (1.4 per cent) and Moroccans (1.1 per cent). If we include Moluccans, caravan dwellers, gypsies and refugees in the category of minority citizens, the total proportion comes to 6 per cent of the population.

The main groups that are at risk of educational, social and vocational failure are children and youth from families with a low socio-economic status (SES). This group is relatively large among ethnic minorities, such as Turks and Moroccans, many of whom were recruited as unskilled labourers. Until recently primary school pupils at risk of educational failure were defined by looking at the educational and occupational level of the parents on the one hand and ethnicity on the other. However, as this resulted in almost half of all pupils being designated "at risk", a discussion was started on narrowing down the criteria. The present criteria focus more strongly on the educational level of the parents. The aim is to arrive at a group of 20-25 per cent of all pupils who most need extra support. It is important to note that this is a larger group than the group considered to be at risk by the welfare policy sector, which identifies 15 per cent of all young people in the Netherlands as experiencing problems or disorders in their development requiring special attention. For 10 per cent of these it is necessary to take special preventive action, through mild forms of assistance and to offer extra attention, while the remaining 5 per cent need a more intensive type of assistance to solve their problems.

For the developments of the past few years in the various policy areas relevant to at-risk groups – such as social services, welfare and youth care, health, compulsory education and vocational education – we refer to the country report on the Netherlands (Geelen *et al.*, 1994). That report describes policies and legislation by the central government and deals with the origins and development of interest in integrated services, as well as a number of Dutch characteristics and traditions affecting attempts to co-ordinate and integrate provisions for at risk groups. In this sense the country report constitutes the background for the case studies described in the present report.

Since the completion of the country report (summer 1994), a new government has taken office, which apparently intends to speed up current developments relevant to the integration of services. The most relevant policy developments will be discussed in the following sections.

In the development of good practice, it is important to note the growing role of municipalities in a more coherent approach to disadvantaged groups, both in education and also in other policy fields.

Recent policy developments

Policies with regard to welfare and health care in the Netherlands were decentralised many years ago and were transferred from the central government to the provincial, and in particular to the municipal authorities. A more coherent approach to problems of deprivation within the framework of the policy programme of "social renewal" has also meant the delegation of many responsibilities to the local level. A number of proposed changes with regard to education will considerably widen and expand the scope of local policies.

The plans drawn up by the Ministry of Education are dealt with succinctly in the memorandum on Local Educational Policy (June 1995). Firstly, several measures will be taken during the next few years to give municipalities a central role in an integrated local approach in which all institutions and organisations involved co-operate. These measures also cover decentralisation of provisions for teaching Dutch as a Second Language, school advisory services and housing. It is also the intention that municipalities should develop a "deprivation plan" for a coherent allocation of all resources involved. The extra funds available for education for groups at risk, which the central authorities pay directly to the schools, must then be used in accordance with the said plan.

To some extent this allocation method seems to be at odds with the trend of giving schools (or rather school boards) more autonomy in the allocation of human and other resources to achieve their aims. However, the underlying supposition is that co-operation at the local level between schools, other local institutions and local government is necessary to achieve the objectives. Only co-operation can ensure an integrated approach to the problems of youth in disadvantaged situations. The responsibility for managing co-operation at the local level lies with the municipal authorities. The growing autonomy of schools means that schools are given more responsibility for the quality of their teaching and this requires new checks and balances. Hence the plea for a dialogue between the schools and their immediate environments (Netelenbos, 1995a). The paper of junior minister Netelenbos, which has the catching title The School as a Learning Organisation (Netelenbos, 1995b), deals extensively with the role of schools in a professional quality policy, i.e. with the question of how schools can become learning organisations which systematically and in close co-operation with their environment search for ways of doing their work better.

In addition, a plea is made for renewed attention to education for the young child. Three areas of concern are noted: language teaching, education in the junior department and dealing with differences between children. It is important for a municipality to follow these developments on account of the extra measures: setting up a specialised language teaching centre, setting up an action programme for the junior department and additional staff for the junior department. The junior department is a crucial factor in preventing educational disadvantages and diminishing the number of referrals to special education (see below).

When it is a question of children and youth at risk, there are several other developments which are of importance because they are directed to increasing the intake capacity and special needs provisions in education. For instance, changes in secondary education such as the introduction of a national core curriculum for everyone in the first two or three years of secondary school, and the relationship between pre-vocational education and junior general secondary education. Another development to be considered is the relationship between special education (directed to children with learning and upbringing problems) and mainstream education, whereby an attempt is made to deal with children as long and as well as possible in mainstream education, in primary education by means of the policy programme "Going to School Together". Here too the pursuit of co-operation and integration certainly plays a part. The Educational Priority Policy (OVB) and the policy programme "Going to School Together" are in fact complementary programmes for children at risk. The latter programme aims at improving provisions for children with special needs in ordinary schools.

Other departments also press for co-operation and integration. In this respect the Ministry of Health, Welfare and Sport (VWS) speaks of an integrated youth policy, concentrating on the reinforcement of co-operation between such sectors as education, primary health care, youth welfare work, job centres, the judicial authorities, the police and social services, in order to prevent drop-out.

In the past the policies of the Ministry of VWS have led to compartmentalisation and thus to discontinuity in care services. In order to break through this compartmentalisation, the provincial, and in particular the municipal authorities have been given a key role in youth policies. Within the national policy framework, it is the provinces and cities which must take action. In its report Youth Deserves a Future (November 1993), the department mapped a number of areas of common ground and co-operation and outlined the intersectoral youth policies of the years to come. The subsequent discussions included an increasingly wide policy area. This is also the reason why the government expressed its views in the white paper Direction in Youth Care, which was published (in July 1994) on behalf of the Ministries of VWS and Justice. This also focuses on the administrative division of tasks between the municipalities, the provinces and the central government. It was proposed that a development process be set in motion which is to lead to an integrated system of youth care.

The Ministry of VWS subsequently engaged in consultations with local administrators, partly because in its attempts to set up a guiding framework, the central government wished to operate as it wishes to see others operate: demand-oriented and on the basis of equality. The results were published in the policy paper Prospects for Youth: Opportunities for Municipalities (June 1995), which also elaborates on suggestions for municipal control. With regard to local preventive youth policies, the paper mentions the following trends: a shift from problem-solving to improving the prospects of the target groups, increasing interest in co-operation and network development, an emphasis on the lower age groups, and a move towards an approach at the neighbourhood level.

A step further was taken in the memorandum Preventive and Curative Youth Care (September 1995), in which three departments jointly outlined a policy framework for future policy. Apart from this important macro-framework for youth policy, VWS, Justice and OCW also promised in the memorandum to put in a considerable amount of extra money to stimulate co-operation in local preventive youth policy, and announce indirect financial linking between the volume of supply and demand (based on existing variants in the care on offer and on the political vision on taking on the responsibility to provide care). One of the spearheads is the creation of one reporting centre per region, where on the one hand the diagnosis and the indications are established, while on the other hand an adequate placement pathway is designed: the so-called "one counter model".

As far as the younger youth is concerned, the increasing interest is directed to the preschool and early school phase. In March 1994 the (Pre)School Education Committee published a report on the subject, whose recommendations were adopted in a joint policy reaction by OCW and VWS (April 1995). Extra funds are being made available to start up a number of innovative programmes, which are directed amongst other things to the attunement of preschool facilities to the primary school. In this connection programmes which have proved effective in the United States, such as Slavin's "Success for All" and Weikart's "High/Scope", will be closely followed.

For several years now, youth policies have also gained importance in terms of prevention of juvenile delinquency and the integration of youth in society. The Ministry of Justice feels increasingly responsible as a result of the upward trend of juvenile delinquency. The Ministry is focusing more and more on crime prevention, and considers it necessary to co-operate with the fields of education, welfare, the policy, and – with a view to job prospects – also with job centres.

Ministries of VWS and Justice also jointly published the National Youth Care Plan 1995-1998 (February 1995), the subtitle of which indicates the wish to move "towards a macro framework for youth care". A separate part of this plan deals with the promotion of coherence and co-operation, not only listing a number of pilot projects in youth care (an element that was missing from *Youth Deserves a Future*). The plan also gives a number of impulses for local preventive youth policies.

In the early 1990s the Ministries of VWS (then called WVC), Justice and Education published a white paper entitled Education and Youth Care, which helped draw attention to the need to improve co-operation between education and youth care. For example, national and regional conferences were organised where both policy-makers and practitioners explored problems and possibilities with respect to co-operation. Furthermore, examples of good practice were identified and disseminated on a large scale. In June 1995, the youth policy directorate of the Ministry of VWS made a grant available for a Youth Care – Education Information Exchange Agency (which is a continuation of the National Education – Youth Care Forum). The aim of the agency is to offer advice on policy, to develop methods and to provide information on good practice.

The Ministry of Internal Affairs is also concerned with youth problems, in particular where these are connected with aspects of public order and safety, such as crime and petty abuse. In June 1995 the report Safety Policy 1995-1998 was published, detailing proposals for an integrated safety policy. These proposals include offering youths a perspective in combination with a consistent and alert policy of keeping order, and also optimal use of the administrative scope for fighting aspects of petty abuse related to the use of drugs, and increasing the level of surveillance in the street. To achieve this, it is proposed to structurally increase the level of co-operation between all concerned. The focal point in this safety policy lies with the municipal councils, while the provincial and central authorities also play a role.

Summarising the policy developments, we may state that youth problems figure prominently on the political agenda. There is growing consensus that phenomena such as school drop-outs, children roaming the streets, and various forms of juvenile delinquency demand a joint effort by central, provincial and municipal government. A process of administrative renewal aims to improve co-ordination between the various layers of administration. Local government is expected to exert powerful control in this field. Co-operation between the institutions involved (such as schools, youth care, job centres and the police) is of great importance. Municipalities should investigate the possibilities of joining in with this development. Since the case studies are also concerned with the municipal level, we shall go into the role of the municipalities here in slightly more depth.

The role of municipalities in developing co-ordinated services for children at risk

The starting point of many of the recent policy developments is the view that responsibilities belong at the lowest possible level and that municipalities (and in some cases provinces) are the primary administrative level where the various services for children at risk must and can be integrated. The government is increasing the municipalities' scope for policy-making and is also considering upgrading the ability of municipalities to increase coherence and to take steps towards integration of services. Thus the *Memorandum on Local Educational Policy* contains examples of "good practice" and agreement has been reached with the Association of Netherlands Municipalities to support municipalities (and schools) in the further development of local educational policy. Further the Ministry of VWS has commissioned the drawing up of guidelines for integral municipal policy on deprivation with the aim of facilitating an ongoing line in services for groups at risk between 0 and 18 years of age (Kloprogge et al., 1995).

If cities are given more authority, it will be necessary to develop a specific policy. The new government puts the emphasis on "large city policy", an area for which a co-ordinating junior minister has been appointed. Using an integrated approach, involving almost all ministers, the government must develop solutions to the degeneration of the poorest areas, while at the same time reinforcing the city economy. Target areas are problem communities in the four major cities. These communities are characterised by an accumulation of social problems: unemployment, poverty, bad housing, poor health, low educational performance and low life expectancy.

In July 1995 a covenant was signed between the central government and the four large cities. The government provides Gld 2.7 billion to tackle the problems, while the cities commit themselves to achieving specifically described goals with respect to the number of school drop-outs, the number of young people who do complete their education, the number of young people who come into contact with the law and the number of crimes committed. The next step was a covenant with 15 medium-sized cities with major problems concerning children and youth at risk. The covenant was concluded in October 1995.

The role of the municipality is discussed in an advisory report drafted at the request of the four departments by Schuyt, Professor of Sociology, entitled Vulnerable Youths and their Future. In his report Schuyt states that the large number of policy lines and policy incentives issued by the central government confronts municipalities with the question of where integrated policies are most needed and how a coherent policy can be realised in practice. It is clear that, as a result of the various policy incentives issued by the central government, the municipalities are obliged to establish both a local preventive youth policy and a local education policy.

One of the ideas dealt with in more detail by Schuyt is that of a chain of responsibilities. At the municipal level this means that aldermen have their own control function and that it is their task to ensure, possibly in co-operation with a local steering or support group:

– that certain problems are exactly localised and well-defined;

– that it is made clear under whose authority these problems fall; and

– that adequate links are created and maintained between problem and responsibility on the one hand, and between the various responsible authorities on the other.

Particular care must be taken that the various problems are not claimed by either too many or too few agencies, and that, if necessary, responsibilities are shifted or combined accordingly.

Schuyt stresses the importance of an integrated and ongoing policy of care for youth at risk, which should be directed to the links between family, school, leisure, work and society. Transitions between these may reinforce problems in youth at risk. Schuyt argues the case for an intensification of out-of-school activities.

The ministers of the four departments who asked Schuyt's advice have shown that they were pleased with his proposals. These and other policy recommendations could have far-reaching consequences.

The increased cohesion between all the policy fields directed to children and youth and to the prevention of educational and social failure can lead to what is called an educational policy. As the responsible body for the local educational policy the municipality can fulfil the following management functions (Kloprogge *et al.*, 1995):

- *Middleman*: the municipality takes initiatives and stimulates the various interest groups to participate in the local educational policy. It is a question of consultations with school boards and institutions aimed at reaching agreement.
- *External management function*: the municipality steers the local educational policy. The municipality sees to the development of policy, in which schools, institutions and parents are actively involved. The municipal council decides on the educational plan.
- *Supervision of implementation*: the municipality sees to the implementation of the plan. To achieve this the municipality must have a qualitatively high-grade educational infrastructure, in which there is intensive co-operation. Further, quantitative and qualitative data must be available in order to chart the progress and quality of the implementation.
- *Own initiative*: on some points, such as compulsory education, the municipality has its own responsibilities. For relatively "new" items, such as catering for a wider range of educational needs in secondary education, violence at school, counselling children with traumas, the municipality will more than in the past have to take the initiative itself to develop a local plan of campaign.
- *Regional management*: for the problem of school drop-outs the municipalities have a reporting and co-ordinating function.
- *Internal management function*: integral policy at municipal level raises attunement questions. One of the aldermen must be made responsible for the definition of local problems, for bringing in the appropriate bodies, and for seeing to good linkage between policy and implementation. In this connection it is important that the municipality is well supplied with information on, for example, the results of enquiries, national and local developments, and the strong and weak points of institutions and organisations with whom they have to co-operate or from whom they want to obtain services.

The case studies of "good practice" in two municipalities to be presented in this report should be seen against the background of the recent policy developments outlined above. In view of the nature of these developments it is possible that the case studies are not only usable for the international OECD project, but also for the discussions in the Netherlands itself. Indeed, the latter would fit in very well with the attention which also exists on the part of the OECD for the national dissemination of the case study results on this project.

PRESCHOOL CASE STUDY: EMMEN

During the last few years work has been in progress in Emmen on a model for the development of policy and activities in the field of preschool education. The Dutch abbreviation of the model's name is MOVE; this was partly chosen because of the reference to the English verb "to move", and the abbreviation is pronounced as in English. The final model is explicitly intended to facilitate the movement towards more integration of services in the preschool phase in other municipalities. This is defined as attunement within the existing supply and more co-operation between institutions. This orientation to transferable results fits in very well with the result-oriented method, of which Emmen has already had experience for some time, especially in the field of Educational Priority Policy. Apart from this, due experience has been acquired of co-operation and co-ordination of services in so-called neighbourhood networks for youth care work. Moreover, the preschool period has for a long time received attention in the Educational Priority Policy in Emmen. All these factors make the MOVE Programme a suitable example of "good practice".

Case context: description of the research site

The case study was carried out in the municipality of Emmen, which is situated in the province of Drenthe in the north-east of the Netherlands. Emmen itself is a medium-sized town, which together with nine villages forms a municipality. The town has 54 000 inhabitants, the municipality a total of some 94 000. Emmen is thus the second largest municipality in the North of the Netherlands. Emmen has the greatest industrial concentration in the North: more than 2 200 enterprises, the most important sectors being plastics, electronics and the engineering industry. As well as this, cultivation under glass is also developing, witness the growing number of market-gardening enterprises and the service facilities for market-gardeners. Various training colleges are established in Emmen, in particular for senior secondary vocational education (MBO) and higher professional education (HBO). These institutions make Emmen the most important town in the province for education. Moreover, on account of its numerous facilities, Emmen is the care centre of south-east Drenthe (250 000 inhabitants).

In the field of tourism the Noorder Dierenpark (zoo) in Emmen scores particularly well with 1.7 million visitors per annum. Apart from this there are numerous possibilities for recreation in the countryside (of the total surface area of the municipality of 28 000 hectares, 1 325 hectares is woodland, 1 343 uncultivated ground and 20 076 agricultural land).

As far as children and youth at risk and their families are concerned in Emmen, the situation can broadly be described as follows. The educational priority area (OVG) is characterised by a higher concentration of children at risk and has twelve preschool playgroups with 568 infants and 23 participating primary schools with 2 628 pupils. Although there are also children at risk to be found outside these institutions which co-operate in the OVG, a rough indication of the size of the group at risk in the preschool phase can probably be given by the number of toddlers in the playgroups mentioned: some 9 per cent of the age group of 0-4 years.

The groups at risk in Emmen include many indigenous children whose parents have a low level of education. These groups also include a relatively large number of caravan dwellers. As a matter of fact the proportion of non-indigenous children in Emmen is relatively small. For example, of the children aged from 0-3 years some 3 per cent have a nationality other than Dutch, which can be contrasted to the total population where just under 2 per cent have another nationality.

Some indication of the number of families of children and youth at risk in Emmen can be gained from the number of those entitled to benefits – about 3 500 in 1994 and 1995 – and from the unemployment level, which in 1994 amounted on average to 5 853 persons, that is to say 15.5 per cent of the labour force (and double the national average).

Case input

Services provided

Historical background: In 1976 the departments of O&W and WVC took the initiative for an experimental social priority policy directed to children and youth at risk of educational, social and vocational failure. South-east Drenthe, where Emmen fulfils a regional function, was one of the areas designated for a social priority project. The problems in this traditionally fen community area were mainly connected with the low level of education of the parents. By no means everybody had completed primary school education and they were not overly concerned about school absenteeism by their own children. Thus the social priority project was principally directed to combating absenteeism and to activities for parents.

In 1986 the experimental social priority policy was replaced by regular Educational Priority Policy, whereby schools with many children at risk got additional staff and so-called educational priority areas were designated, in which the co-operation between schools and other services would be promoted.

South-east Drenthe then became just such an educational priority area (OVG). An OVG can be seen as a network of services for children at risk, in particular a network of schools (principally primary education, but also secondary education and to a lesser extent special education) and of welfare institutions.

Emmen was moreover one of the municipalities which from the end of the 1980s participated in the experiment on integrated municipal youth policy. One of the objectives was to try to achieve an integrated approach to the regular provision of support services for upbringing. For our case study the most important form in which that took place was in a neighbourhood network. In a neighbourhood network for youth care services clear-cut agreements are made for each district or neighbourhood on which facilities should fulfil which preventive functions. In Emmen that took place partly with reference to the problems in the situation of parents and children in disadvantaged neighbourhoods. For instance, preschool playgroups there were frequently confronted with children who were already developmentally delayed at preschool age. To eliminate such deprivation calls for a coherent approach from various disciplines. The neighbourhood network sees to efficient alignment of the supply to the questions and problems of the target group. For example, if the supply of social priority facilities of the playgroup does not match up adequately with what happens in the child's home situation, then that can be a reason to start a project for support services for upbringing (VNG, 1995).

Preschool policy: From the start of the experimental social priority policy in 1976, a discussion was cautiously set in motion in Emmen on the importance of the preschool period for educational opportunities for children. The educational priority area South-East Drenthe has from the very beginning in 1986 given priority to the preschool and early school period. Initially the emphasis was mainly put on making services more accessible for parents and children from disadvantaged backgrounds. In many villages and neighbourhoods, it has proved possible to considerably raise the participation percentage for preschool facilities. In a following period numerous activities were carried out which were directed to expanding the possibilities for toddlers to develop and to increasing the commitment of parents.

Since preschool activities are chiefly viewed from the perspective of educational disadvantage, with the attunement to education thus forming a core theme, there has been an ever increasing discussion about a coherent preschool and early school policy in the 1990s. That also occupies a central position in the OVB policy framework for Drenthe. The following two core themes have been included in the framework:

- the improvement of the starting conditions for the school careers of the OVB pupils through offering preschool programmes; and
- the stimulation and support of the parents in bringing up and guiding their children.

These themes are closely aligned to the National Educational Priority Policy Framework 1993-1997, which, with regard to the preschool and early school years aims to:

- stimulate the preschool development by means of family-oriented activation programmes and support for the parents in the upbringing and guidance of their children;
- promote participation in extra-curricular activities;
- stimulate reading;
- strengthen the function of the preschool playgroup; and
- organise preventive networks.

In the National Policy Framework, where it was a matter of combating educational deprivation, it thus became evident that the preschool phase was considered increasingly important. A female politician once graphically expressed this as: "the problems of disadvantage enter society with the toddlers". From the national evaluation of the OVB it appeared that many of the pupils at risk already suffered from a certain degree of developmental delay when they entered primary education, and that participation in preschool facilities can be one of the means of reducing such a disadvantage. Additionally, specific projects began to be developed during the late 1980s for children at risk in the preschool and early school years, such as *Instapje*, *Opstap* and *Boekenpret* ("Fun with Books") (for details of these projects see the country report, Geelen *et al.*, 1994). Emmen, for example, was one of the three development sites in the Netherlands for "Fun with Books".

In other respects as well, Emmen was active at the national level with regard to the preschool period and when, at the request of the National Consultative Body on Educational Priority, a Platform for the Prevention of Educational Disadvantage among Children from 0 to 6 was set up, Josee van de Waarsenburg of the Emmen Educational Priority Bureau became its chairman.

Services: In Emmen there are also a large number of facilities for children in the preschool period. An illustrated poster has recently been produced in the town giving an overview of these services; the most important information from the poster is summarised here in Table 1. On the one hand the poster and the table show the institutions which can be of importance for children, on the other hand they indicate the themes and subjects which will become relevant as children grow older. The illustrated poster deals with the age range from 0-12 years, which is divided into four phases; the themes remain the same for each phase (development, health, upbringing), but the subjects are adjusted to some extent for each theme. In the table only the subjects from the preschool period are shown. On the poster there are colour indications to show which subjects can play a role in information, advice, help and support, referral, or in activities such as courses, play and encounter groups. By affixing stickers interested parties can be directed to the nearest address of the institution in question.

The poster and the derived table in any case make two things clear:

– there are numerous institutions which deal with the preschool phase: eleven are mentioned in the table, although the list is not exhaustive, since some of the more broadly defined forms of activity are carried out by more than one body, for example socio-cultural work, and since the police, for example, is missing; and

– partly as a result of this there are on the other hand numerous institutions which concentrate on a specific subject: the subjects "nourishment" and "support with upbringing" have the highest scores with the mention of seven institutions each time.

The inescapable conclusion is that co-ordination or integration of preschool services deserves serious consideration. In Emmen such considerations led to the MOVE Programme.

Towards services integration

Before it was decided to use the MOVE Programme in Emmen, there had already been earlier initiatives for co-ordination and integration. These initiatives are discussed below: the educational priority area (OVG) and the neighbourhood networks, as well as the municipal role and organisation in that connection. Attention is also paid to the way in which Emmen sought to find a meaningful next step along the path to a more integrated supply of services.

OVG: When Drenthe became an educational priority area in 1986, the experience gained with social priority experiments led to the establishment of the Foundation for Educational Priority in South-East Drenthe. At that time the OVG comprised three municipalities. In September 1993 the OVG was extended to cover 71 municipalities, and the name was changed to the Foundation for Educational Priority in Drenthe. A foundation as an organisational form had by then already become more usual in that field. The present foundation comprises all the bodies concerned with compensatory policy. That is to say, delegates from the various school boards, welfare work and the various municipal authorities. The municipal councils of the "regional centres", Emmen and Hoogeveen, each have one delegate, the other 15 municipalities of the OVG Drenthe jointly share two seats on the board of the foundation. The representative of the Emmen municipal council (the alderman for education) has the function of independent chairman, with the other functions being allocated within the board. The office of secretary is fulfilled by a representative of one of the participating municipalities.

The foundation is advised by an OVB management group, in which policy workers participate from the ranks of special education, public-authority education, secondary education and welfare work.

A central position in the work organisation of the educational priority area is occupied by the Educational Priority Bureau, which formally comes under the Foundation for Educational Priority in Drenthe and which is established in Emmen. The development of the priority policy and the direction of the implementation takes place from this Bureau. Staff from the Bureau support schools and

Table 1. **Social facilities in Emmen**

| | Institutions | | | | | | | | | | |
Subject	Home care	Preschool playgroup 2-4 years	Child care facilities 0-12 years	Socio-cultural work	Play and meeting place "Playotheque"	Schools	Municipal medical service School doctor	Library	Social work	General practitioner	Dentist
Development											
Language development	X	X	X		X			X		X	
Physical development	X	X	X		X			X		X	
Socio-emotional development	X	X	X		X			X			
Mental development	X	X	X					X			
Playing/toys	X	X	X	X	X			X			
Reading/books	X	X	X		X			X			
Education/school								X			
Sexuality	X				X			X		X	
Health											
Chronic non-specific respiratory diseases	X	X	X		X			X		X	
Allergies	X	X	X		X			X		X	
Care	X	X	X		X			X		X	
Hygiene	X	X	X		X			X		X	X
Nourishment	X				X			X		X	
Toilet training	X				X			X		X	
Sleep	X							X			
Dental care	X							X			X
Safety in and around the house	X			X	X						
Illness	X									X	
Upbringing											
Striking behaviour: fear, teasing, cry babies	X	X	X		X			X		X	
Attachment/detachment	X	X	X		X			X			
Setting limits	X	X	X		X			X			
Independence		X	X		X			X			
Child care facilities		X	X	X	X			X			
Choice of school						X		X			
Family situation	X			X				X	X	X	
Watching TV	X			X	X			X			
Support in upbringing	X	X	X	X	X				X	X	
Help in upbringing	X								X		

Source: Illustrated poster "Goodness knows", Emmen (no year).

institutions in the implementation, but these institutions have to realise the implementation themselves. Bureau staff are also involved in renewal activities, such as evaluation, registration, policy advice and project development. The size of the Bureau has deliberately been kept small: the nuclear role is co-ordination and innovation. The Bureau strives to achieve a work style which is characterised by flexibility, speed, orientation to clients and solutions, jumping in where necessary and allowing people their own responsibilities.

Since the expansion of the OVG the Bureau has working relations with 17 municipalities. It is no easy task to bring all the participating municipalities into line; it often takes a "culture reversal" before the importance of integrated action really penetrates to the municipalities. As a regional centre, the municipality of Emmen has always played a pioneer role in this respect. Our case study is restricted to Emmen, since that is where the MOVE Programme is being carried out.

Neighbourhood networks: In about 1991 it was observed in Emmen that problems with raising children, resulting from a variety of social, economic and cultural circumstances, frequently occurred in two centres. The municipality concluded that the upbringing skills of these parents should be increased and that what was needed was the availability of support and guidance in upbringing and the formation of a neighbourhood network for youth care. These activities took place in the framework of a Local Integrated Youth Policy experiment, which was carried out from 1988 onwards in twelve Dutch municipalities and in which Emmen also participated.

The basis for the neighbourhood networks was developed through the experiment by the Council for Youth Affairs, a provincial community development body. The neighbourhood networks were set up by the local institutions for youth care services, youth health care and education, under the direction of the Foundation for Information on Play and Upbringing in Drenthe and the Educational Priority Foundation of Drenthe.

Core items in the neighbourhood networks are:

– signalling, advice, assistance, referral;

– co-operation between the identified problem spots, the peripatetic youth health care and youth care services, and where necessary (in connection with referral) the second-line services (Youth and Family Foundation, medical day nursery, etc.);

– an integral approach to problems in the development and upbringing of children aged from 0-12 years; and

– making a contribution to the realisation of a purposeful, coherent supply of preventive activities, both individual and collective.

In 1994, there were seven neighbourhood networks in Emmen. Broadly speaking these networks develop in a similar manner but at different tempos. In the initial phase of a network the emphasis is mainly on case discussions; in the following phase the tasks are expanded when, apart from case discussions, attention is also paid to information on the methods of second-line institutions; in the third phase, that of stabilisation, a start is made on the organisation of preventive activities. The seven neighbourhood networks are in different stages.

The composition of the neighbourhood networks varies, but the following institutions usually participate: police, general social work, community work, socio-cultural work, Boddaert Centre, municipal health service, child care, preschool playgroup, home help, primary school, general practitioner.

The network meets five to ten times in each school year. As the people from the network know each other and the neighbourhood well, contacts can also take place informally. If the need arises, outside meetings are held.

The community work mostly fulfils a co-ordinating function in a neighbourhood network. The community worker in question is employed by the Foundation for Socio-cultural Work Municipality of Emmen (SKGE). As of January 1st, 1995, this was incorporated into the welfare umbrella organisation *Stichting Opmaat*. In the framework of the OVB policy, the SKGE and Educational Priority Bureau entered into a contract whereby agreements were made on input, registration and quality.

The neighbourhood networks for youth care services in Emmen were set up in 1991-92. An interim evaluation in December 1993 showed, amongst other things, that the participants regarded having contacts (formal and also informal) as something positive. This gave the networkers a sense of support. Furthermore, consultations and better entry to other institutions at an earlier stage produce information, which enables earlier and more preventive action to be taken. The fact that representatives of the participating institutions must be sufficiently motivated, and thus regularly present at the consultations, poses a problem, which is not made any easier by the fact that some people work on call, as for example in home help. Another problem is that of privacy pertaining to information regarding clients – how to make adequate agreements about this and how to get people to keep to them. An attempt has been made to overcome this in part by a note recording the agreements made for the collaboration.

In order to further the professionalism, courses have been organised for (future) neighbourhood network co-ordinators and for preschool playgroup teachers.

Municipal organisation and policy: In the course of a recent reorganisation, the municipality of Emmen divided the machinery into several sections. In the period 1990-94 the two fields of welfare and education came under the same alderman (which promoted cohesion), and were also brought into one sector. This sector, "Learning and Care", includes the care for children and youth at risk. The following subsections come under the "Community Structure" department of the sector:

- education (including intensification of educational priority, specific attention for ethnic minorities and for catering for a wider range of educational needs);
- welfare (including child care and support in upbringing);
- employment (including the transition from school to work); and
- art and culture (including reading promotion).

This organisational form should facilitate the formation of a continuous line of policy from the preschool years to a basic qualification. The objective of the sector is: a one-third reduction in the number of people entitled to a benefit in the decade 1993-2003. Each subsection has to make its own contribution. Educational priorities include enabling the achievement of a primary vocational qualification and the combating of early school leaving. The attention to the preschool phase is fostered by the above-mentioned priority for prevention and for a continuous line in the school career. The fact that those working in the Learning and Care sector were housed close to one another after reorganisation (enabling a quicker exchange of information and facilitating informal consultations) was cited by those involved as leading to greater cohesion.

Emmen looks for the next step: The OVG was started up in 1986 and the neighbourhood networks some five years later. The OVG started out from the educational realm, and the networks predominantly from welfare work (including youth care services), before entering into greater co-operation with education. Partly because of differences in organisational development and policy culture, there was a great deal to be improved upon with regard to attunement and cohesion in the preschool field. Given this, an initiative was taken from the field to set up a Working Party on Support in Upbringing in 1991. Experts from various sectors personally participated in the Working Party, which had no formal status. Participants from the welfare sector came from the SKGE and the Child Care Foundation; health care was represented by the GGD and home care; the RIAGG, General Social Work, the Boddaert Centre and the Foundation for Information on Play and Upbringing represented the help organisations; from the education sector there were representatives from primary education and the Educational Priority Bureau (which also provided the chairman); and finally, varying experts from the municipality of Emmen also participated. The Working Party drew up a plan of action, in which it formulated the starting points and accents for a more coherent policy directed towards the target group aged from 0-12 years. The objective of the Working Party is to see how that coherence can be furthered and to what extent the supply is aligned to the wishes and needs of the target groups.

In January 1992, the Burgomaster and Aldermen of Emmen asked the Working Party on Support in Upbringing for advice on municipal policy to be pursued for the preschool period, making use of experience gained in the integrated youth policy. Separate mention was made with regard to requests for possible co-operation, development of networks and linkage between the informal and formal channels.

The Working Party dealt with the request for advice very seriously. By means of a questionnaire they first investigated which institutions devoted attention to which aspects of preschool policy. They established that what was on offer was somewhat fragmented and that it was not clear how and where attunement took place. There were also questions concerning bottlenecks and lacunae, and how these could be eliminated by means of further co-operation and alignment. On the basis of the information thus obtained, the Working Party made its recommendations in November 1992. It reported that there was need of a municipal policy framework. According to the Working Party, it was a question of both a good attunement of the supply to the demand, and of an efficient and coherent supply.

The central policy objective was formulated as: the realisation of an integrated set of measures, offering optimal chances of development for children from 0 to 6 years. Three subsidiary objectives were defined as:

– the stimulation and improvement of the development possibilities for young children by offering family-oriented and institution-oriented activities;

– the backing up and strengthening of the upbringing atmosphere in the family, in the neighbourhood and in the services; and

– the prevention and/or diminution of problems in the development and upbringing of young children.

Themes are given for each of the three objectives. These themes are then linked in a matrix to the inventory of the existing preschool supply from the institutions. Since this matrix (shown here in Table 2) also gives insight into overlapping services as well as lacunae, it forms a good starting point for future policy development.

With regard to future and renewal policy the Working Party stated that the municipality and also the institutions must be prepared to invest in these objectives. At the same time the concrete result of the method must be visible at the implementation level. It was therefore recommended that there be a two-year plan of action, directed on the one hand to improving the cohesion and co-operation in the existing supply and on the other hand to stimulating innovative, integral activities, which make a contribution to the central objective. It is desirable to have budget financing with the aid of contracts. There should also be retrospective assessment of results by means of an evaluation study.

The recommendations led to a plan of action for the years 1993 and 1994.

The municipality of Emmen had in the meantime, in June 1992, produced a memorandum entitled Preventive Youth Policy, which discussed the development of an accessible and coherent pattern of services for youth, particularly in the realm of housing, work, knowledge and welfare. The alignment of local care and services and the co-operation of institutions were mentioned as essential conditions for the development of a future-oriented local youth policy.

The Local Integrated Youth Policy experiment finished in December 1991. The results were so positive that both the municipality and the institutions involved wished to continue and further develop the integration and co-operation so far achieved. The municipality wanted to play an initiating, encouraging and stimulating role. An important part was destined for the Educational Priority Foundation, which was to continue the setting up, elaboration and broadening of a coherent youth policy. According to the memorandum the implementation of that policy was to be the responsibility of other institutions and organisations. The memorandum concluded with an action programme for youth policy, to be updated every two years and assessed on the implementation of the formulated items for action. For every action, item mention is made of who is ultimately responsible, which organisations are involved in the implementation, what the costs (or cost indication) may be and whether the implementation can be put in hand in the next two years or only prepared.

After February 1992 a draft of the municipal memorandum had been circulated with a request for comments from the bodies involved. It is therefore not surprising that the November 1992 recommendations of the Working Party for Support in Upbringing are so well attuned to the municipal

Table 2. **Objectives and preschool supply**

	Health care		Welfare			Counselling				Education
	Home care	GG and GD	Child care facility	Socio-cultural work	Library	AMW	Boddaert	RIAGG	S&O	Educational priority
	0-4 years	4-6 years	0-6 years	0-6 years	0-6 years		4-6 years			
Objective 1										
a. Total development	X	X	X	X			X		X	X
b. Promoting ability to plan			X	X					X	X
c. Language development			X	X	X		X		X	X
d. Informal instruction									X	X
Objective 2										
a. Information	X	X	X	X	X		X	X	X	X
b. Advice	X	X	X	X	X		X	X	X	X
c. Support	X	X	X	X	X				X	X
d. Courses	X	X	X							X
e. New facilities			X	X						X
f. Educational relationship	X	X	X	X		X	X	X	X	X
g. Social environment			X	X			X			
Objective 3										
a. Specific information and advice	X	X				X		X	X	X
b. Early recognition of developmental deficiencies	X	X	X			X		X		
c. Help close to home	X	X		X		X	X	X		X
d. Self-help/social support	X	X				X	X	X		
e. Vade mecum										
Strategy										
a. Preventive	X	X	X	X		X	X	X	X	X
b. Development of network	X	X	X	X		X	X	X	X	X
c. Co-operation	yes	yes	yes	yes	yes	yes	yes	yes	yes	yes

Source: Working Party on Support in Upbringing. Recommendations on policy for preschool period municipality of Emmen, November 1992.

memorandum. The most important added value of the recommendations consists of the Working Party's elaboration of plans for the preschool phase as requested.

The municipality of Emmen adopted the recommendations of the Working Party together with its own memorandum as directive for the municipal policy. In co-operation with the umbrella welfare foundation SKGE, and the Educational Priority Bureau, the municipality formulated an assignment to draw up a note, in which the preschool policy would be more thematically elaborated. This assignment was carried out by the policy and projects co-ordinator of the Educational Priority Bureau, Josee van de Waarsenburg, and the educational adviser (in particular for children aged 0-7 years) of the municipality of Emmen, Yvonne Boxem. Their report was published in January 1994: the project plan MOVE.

The process of implementing MOVE – chronology and content

January 1994 – the intention

The project plan MOVE: In January 1994, the municipality of Emmen and the Foundation for Educational Priority Drenthe presented a project plan for the Model for the Development of Policy and Activities in the field of preschool education (MOVE). This plan described the way in which these actors apply innovation in order to be able to give shape to the intended integrated policy, in particular in Emmen. The results of MOVE were to form the basis for the development and introduction of the preschool policy in other municipalities in the province. In view of the fact that the project plan is one of the most important documents about MOVE, its content is given here in some detail.

Project plan

New ways are being sought of using the available resources as efficiently and purposefully as possible, especially for the most vulnerable groups. Work development, policy stimulation, research and evaluation are considered necessary to achieve this. The process is geared to reach the following output, as formulated by the Educational Priority Foundation, by 1997:

- having 75 per cent of the OVB children participate in the preschool playgroup;

- having all preschool playgroups and schools affiliated to the OVB collect information on the course of the development of OVB children; and

- having 75 per cent of the OVB parents with a child aged from 3-12 years participate annually in activities which help them make an active contribution to the development and learning process of their children.

The efforts for the benefit of the preschool and early school years are related to the general basic assumption that the objective of the Educational Priority Policy is to attune the pupils' transfer qualifications to their capabilities and ambitions. This policy is directed to improving the educational opportunities of the most vulnerable groups, which very often means children whose parents have a low level of education. Specific attention is focused on children of caravan dwellers, immigrants, those seeking asylum and refugees, Moluccan children and children from isolated families. The preschool policy meshes here so well with the Educational Priority Policy that both policy developments can be integrated in a centrally directed approach.

It is true that during the last few years there has been an increase in the projects and programmes on offer for the 0- to 6-year-olds, but the critical comments made in the project plan included the following remarks:

- There is evidence of fragmentation and continuity is insufficiently guaranteed because: *a*) the services and activities are developed and/or offered by different bodies at the municipal, provincial and national level; *b*) the decision to launch certain programmes is to a great extent influenced by the possibilities of external financing; *c*) a programme is not fully worked out; and *d*) the policy emanates from an individual civil servant or institution).

– Activities are not aligned and do not reinforce each other to the benefit of the target group (for instance, institutions whose work is primarily family-oriented and services which are institution-oriented are insufficiently aware of what the other is doing).

– There is an evident degree of tension between supply and demand for reasons including the fact that *a*) experts formulate the supply, while it is often impossible to predict beforehand whether the supply will reach the intended target group; *b*) users have to be sought, which sometimes leads to stigmatisation which could have been avoided; *c*) as a rule the requirements of the target group itself receive too little attention.

However, the problems caused by the threatening spectre of educational deprivation call for a broad range of solutions. Children and their parents should be positively stimulated from various angles of approach in order to improve their chances. That requires co-operation between education and welfare in the broad sense (health care, help services, welfare work and child care). This co-operation must result in a clear and well-attuned supply of facilities for parents and children: on the one hand family-oriented programmes and on the other hand an accessible infrastructure of services, which calls on the parents to play an active role in the stimulation and guidance of the development of their children.

The "go-between mother"

The principal innovative element in the project plan is the figure of a "go-between mother". She establishes a relationship with the family and links the demands of the family to the existing supply. In other words, there is an investment in relations and trust as a basis for setting stimulation in motion. The introduction of this new function is geared at making possible a more demand-oriented way of working. At the same time it is a stepping stone towards the realisation of integrated policy.

The "go-between mother" fulfils a crucial function in attempting to link demand to a "made-to-measure" supply. As far as the intended made-to-measure supply is concerned, it is a question of the following forms:

– made-to-measure as regards the infrastructure, *i.e.* the reach, participation and explicit attention to intermediary functions between family and facility;

– made-to-measure as regards development-oriented activities for young children;

– made-to-measure as regards activities in support of upbringing; and

– made-to-measure as regards signalling and prevention.

The basis for the development of the innovative model is the integration of municipal policy and Educational Priority Policy. During the last few years, much has already been realised by means of that policy in accordance with the project plan. Knowledge and experience are now available, both in terms of policy development and work development. Work remains on the infrastructure – programmes and innovations need to be directly linked to the demand of the family, both child and parent. The "go-between mother" has had earlier equivalents, in particular the neighbourhood mothers in the *Opstap* project; the paraprofessionals in, for instance, the "Fun with Books" project; and with "confident parents" from both the welfare and educational sector.

The objective is formulated as follows: to enable the intended target group, on the basis of their individual requirements in the field of development stimulation and upbringing support, to make use of the existing supply with the aid of a "go-between mother".

The group of children to be served

The intended target group is defined as: children aged between 0 and 6 years, who are vulnerable in their development as a result of socio-economic and cultural circumstances, and their parents, who have a need in the field of "development stimulation and upbringing support" but who either cannot, or can, but only to a limited extent, make use of the existing supply. This target group is estimated at about 10 per cent of the OVB children.

The "go-between mother" visits the target group at home and tries to determine which facilities in the realm of "development stimulation and upbringing support" match up best with the needs of the family. She works on building up a relation with the family with the aid of resources (which at that time were still to be developed), such as a photo album, games or a questionnaire.

The two phases of project plan

The first project phase is concerned with the following activities. While receiving training, the "go-between mother" starts to set up a network. Use can be made here, for instance, of the position of the community worker at the site in question. The national Averroës Foundation, which is involved amongst other things in the development and realisation of preschool projects such as *Opstapje* and *Opstap*, has been asked to develop a profile and training model.

The "go-between mother" is guided and supported by a programme leader, who in the future will serve at the provincial level. The programme leader, also undergoing training, is acquainted with the supply of materials and service, and assists the "go-between mother" in determining which service is most suitable.

In the second phase the "go-between mother" approaches the families. This can be done direct through the network which she has already built up, or in co-operation with other entities with access to the family (thus making use of their network). The "go-between mother" builds up, and maintains contact with the family. She records their questions and guides them towards existing facilities.

In the second phase the programme leader gives the "go-between mother" both support and feedback. He/she also acts as intermediary between supply and demand, "customises" the existing facilities on offer, maintains contact with various bodies and takes care of the substantive work development.

Project Management

The town of Emmen was chosen to develop MOVE and a project management team was formed to steer and develop the innovation. It comprised a representative of the municipality of Emmen (process co-ordination/chairman), of SKGE (project implementation), the Educational Priority Drenthe Foundation (project and work development), and Home Care Drenthe. A project team was formed for the implementation, attached organisationally to the OVG.

The MOVE project can be said to have a two-track policy, with innovation and implementation reinforcing one another. Apart from the development of the methodology in the municipality of Emmen (innovation), the years 1994-97 also saw the start of the preschool and early school policy in the province of Drenthe (implementation). At the beginning each site was to be analyzed, after which a strategic plan for the period up to 1997 would be drawn up with the municipality and institutions. The contents of the plan would then be laid down in the policy plans of institutions and in an educational priority plan to be determined for each municipality. The responsibility for this work lay with the participating institutions and municipalities. The OVB Bureau for Drenthe is involved in this from the point of view of preparation, development and direction. Preparations are thus being made, which will, in due course, enable the model developed in Emmen to be implemented in the rest of Drenthe. In other words, MOVE Emmen can grow into MOVE Drenthe. It is not intended that the proposed development of the model be a restrictive blueprint, but that rather, it should give an overview of possibilities which can be used to make suitable choices according to the situation or site – a model with scope for local integrated policy to be filled in according to local needs.

The MOVE implementation plan

The MOVE project plan was presented to the alderman responsible for welfare in the municipality of Emmen at the beginning of 1994. On the basis of the plan the municipality decided on an experiment which would run from September 1994 up to and including July 1997. The preparatory work for the more integral preschool and early school policy as proposed in Emmen was put in hand in May 1994. The participants were the municipality, the SKGE, Home Care Drenthe and Educational Priority Foundation. These four bodies have concluded a covenant, in which the tasks and accountability are apportioned in broad lines. The MOVE project management provided for in the project plan was formed from representatives of these four bodies and officially installed by the municipality.

In November 1994, the project management produced a first draft implementation plan, MOVE Emmen of the project plan. Not only were a number of items further elaborated in the draft, but it also contained shifts of emphasis.

The most important shift was in the tasks of the "go-between mother", lightened to such an extent that now the function could only be called "contact mother". The task of the professional programme leader in the "link up" between the requirements of families and the services on offer had thus become heavier. It was now proposed that the programme leader be the first to make contact with the families, chosen in consultation with home care, preschool playgroup, welfare work and schools. The "contact mother" then visits the family at home and maintains the contact.

In elaborating the project organisation, a level for senior management consultation among the covenant partners was added above the project management, resulting in four organisational levels (see Figure 1). This framework called for a solid consultative structure, worked out on a hierarchical basis. While that might have seemed elaborate for the first pilot sites, the intention was that this would facilitate MOVE's expansion over the municipality of Emmen and later, over the province of Drenthe.

Figure 1 shows, moreover, that the function of contact mother can also be fulfilled by "neighbourhood mothers" who are already active in other projects, as for example *Opstap* or "Fun with Books".

Since the aim is to produce transmittable products, the implementation plan paid due attention to evaluation and research, an area in which the national Averroës Foundation, as well as the Science Shop of the State University of Groningen were to be involved.

It was already indicated in the project plan that a basic package of family-oriented and institution-oriented programmes relating to support for parents in the upbringing and guidance of the

Figure 1.   ***Framework of MOVE project organisation***

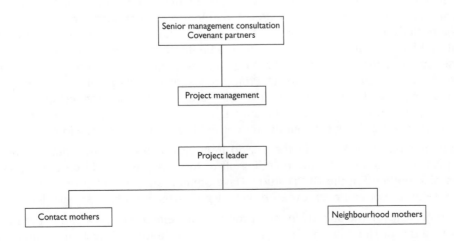

development of their children should be drawn up. There was consultation on the package with Averroës, which proposed the following criteria for programmes:

- the target group must be known;
- the definition of the objectives must be clear;
- the methodology must be specified;
- the programme must be described;
- evaluation data must be available; and
- from the evaluation it must be apparent whether the programme had a positive effect.

A new idea in the implementation plan was to set out pathways for individual children and parents, thus making it possible, with the use of the programmes from the package, to work step by step towards the intended results.

The number of pilot sites in Emmen were extended to three, namely: the Emmermeer and Angelslo districts and the village of Nieuw Dordrecht, which belongs to the municipality. For each site a description was first drawn up of the existing situation in terms of:

- structural supply of facilities, activities and programmes;
- age structure of 0-7 year-olds, with specification of ethnic origin;
- reach of the preschool playgroup;
- participation by the target group in other services/activities; and
- bottlenecks and blank spots in the supply as identified by professionals (in this context information from the neighbourhood network for youth services is also of importance).

In the implementation plan for each pilot site, consideration was given to more recent developments, and concrete expectations of results were formulated. These expectations specify the results formulated for the whole project (also in the project plan): an increase in 1997 in participation of children and parents in preschool and early school activities compared to 1994; and more clarity on which methods are the most successful.

As an example, we restrict ourselves here to the expected results in the village of Nieuw Dordrecht (chosen because it comes up for further discussion later). The objective is that all children should take part in a family-oriented programme before they go to the preschool playgroup, and that an active role for the parents be stimulated *via* the preschool playgroup, possibly in combination with a continued family-oriented programme.

The implementation of MOVE: The four organisational layers of the MOVE project organisation (from Figure 1) can be linked with the three levels which are distinguished in the OECD study. There is senior management consultation among the covenant partners at the strategic level. These consultations played a particularly important role in the first phase of the experiment, when, in connection with attunement problems, a number of decisions had to be lifted above the project management. After the initial phase, senior management consultation group involvement was more or less limited to being kept informed of the progress of the project. Project management was given a mandate for an increasing number of matters, so that it also functioned at the strategic level. The programme directors saw to the day-to-day progress and work at the operational level between project management and contact mothers. The latter were doing community work at field level as paraprofessionals.

The implementation of MOVE in the period from November 1994 (the date of the draft implementation plan) to October 1995 (the rounding off of this case study) will be described here on the three levels differentiated in the OECD study. Development and research work contracted out will be dealt with here on the operational level, because it produces input for strategic decisions.

At the strategic level, the already formed project management played a part in the substantive and managerial steering of the project. Amongst other things, it was a question of strategic decisions, engaging the programme directors and guiding them in their work, and of involvement at the field level, through, for example co-ordination, acquisition of supplementary funds, helping recruit staff. Also of importance was the contact with the Averroës Foundation, which was brought in for the development of the methodology, and for training staff. In January 1995 the project management drew up a note, in which they formulated the results as follows:

- structured methods enabling contact mothers to be brought into contact with families who need extra attention and help in choosing to participate in preschool and early school programmes. These methods could also assist the contact mothers in carrying out these programmes;
- appropriate training for the contact mothers and their supervisory programme leader; and
- an evaluation framework on the basis of which the added value of the use made of contact mothers can be established.

According to the report, the intended purpose of the contact mothers called for an active and integral network of professionals who make a pre-selection of families to be contacted and who gain entry to these families. This network could include district nurses, preschool playgroup leaders, primary school teachers or welfare workers. After the pre-selection and application of the families with the help of such key figures, the intention was that the first contact should be made by the programme leader and the contact mother together. The programme leader was to try and make an assessment of the questions or needs of the family, an assessment which can be directive for the subsequent contact of the contact mother.

An important event at the operational level was the appointment of programme leader Ellen Bos in December 1994. She received training at the beginning of 1995 (in particular in the field of preschool projects of Averroës) and did preliminary work for the implementation of the project by, for example, making contacts at neighbourhood level and drawing up a basic package of facilities. Discussions were held between Averroës and MOVE as to the number of programmes, and kind of programmes to include.

In the field of research and development the following activities were undertaken. The Science Shop of the State University of Groningen carried out research on the pre-implementation situation in the three pilot sites in Emmen by means of a questionnaire for preschool playgroups and district nurses.

Averroës was brought in to develop the methodology and accompanying training courses, as well as to advise on the basic package of facilities to be offered. In connection with this package efforts are being made to increase the flexibility of the use of (national) programmes, for example where it concerns the number of participating families. Preparatory contacts were made between January and April 1995, a contract was concluded in the summer and parts of the draft methodology were discussed in the autumn. In this connection a note was written about the implementation and procedure of the programme. For the first time mention was made of the function of "the intermediary". Contrary to the initial view, the people to be considered as possible "intermediaries" were not limited to professionals who work for groups at risk in the preschool and early school stage, such as district nurses, preschool playgroup leaders or teachers, but also included imams or parents. The role of intermediaries was to refer, to MOVE, those families where contact had been established. It was therefore essential that the intermediary be well acquainted with the possibilities of MOVE and also capable of recognising which families had (latent) need of extra attention for stimulating development and for support – by means of a programme or facility – in upbringing. If necessary, the intermediary could also accompany the programme leader and contact mother on the first visit to the target family.

The question naturally arose as to whether, with such a three-(wo)man strong visit, the risk of "intimidation" as expressed earlier in connection with the contact mother, was not even stronger. On the part of MOVE the following answer was given: the core role of the contact mother was to build up a relationship with the families based on mutual trust, to obtain a clear idea of their questions and needs, and to steer them to the services on offer. If, however, there were problems making contact with the families, and professional intermediaries had no time to help, a possible solution might be to call in other intermediaries. Consideration was to be given to a practicable strategy for each family, making for a varied approach; the expectation was that in practice a three-(wo)man visit would very rarely, if ever, take place.

Averroës has also produced a manual for the methodology of working with contact mothers, in which the whole process is fully described and accompanied by guidelines, tips, questionnaires, report forms and information material.

At field level it is a question of three pilot sites within the municipality of Emmen. The institutions concerned at the pilot sites were informed about the MOVE project in writing in December 1994. In March 1995 there was an information meeting at each of the sites. In general the reactions were positive, but it was indeed remarked that the contact mother's visit to a family could be experienced as intimidating. The contact mother's qualities, character and introduction to the family are therefore crucial.

The recruitment and selection of contact mothers was thus an important task. The programme leaders and project management decided on an maximum educational level of junior secondary vocational education and on paraprofessionals with the same (ethnic) background as the target group families. There were to be two native Dutch, one Surinamese and one Turkish contact or neighbourhood mother. The municipality then made a request, which was allocated, for four places in the government's so-called employment plan for neighbourhood mothers. These were functions for 16 hours, except at the Nieuw Dordrecht pilot site, where the intention was to have a combination function with 8 hours for MOVE. Candidates were recruited for these functions by various means.

The training of the selected contact mothers took place in September/October 1995, and the activities in the neighbourhoods started in November.

In May and June 1995, comprehensive information evenings about MOVE were held at neighbourhood level. A plan of action was drawn up for each site, all made according to the same design: characteristics of the site (current responsibility for preschool activities or projects); core theme and intended activities; elaboration for each activity in terms of objectives, reference points for time phasing, parties involved in reparation/implementation, resources, evaluation; annexes with descriptions of current projects and tasks of the MOVE contact mother. An important step in the implementation of the action plans was taken in November 1995 with the trial introduction of the methodology.

Analytical aspects of the case process

From the elaboration given by the OECD to the "process" element in the CIPP evaluative model of context, input, process and product (see Volpe, 1995), the following three aspects merit closer analysis:

- support and resources;
- obstacles;
- strategies in the co-operation process.

Support and resources: The Netherlands is sometimes called a consensus democracy, since each of the political parties is too small to form a government on its own and it is thus necessary to form a coalition. The same applies to local politics, which is why building up support and consensus, as well as maintaining it, is also important in Emmen.

At the political management level, the importance of Educational Priority Policy is never in dispute. There is a broad basis of support from the four largest parties in the municipal council for extra efforts for children and youth at risk. In connection with the maintenance and increase of support, the political element is also approached. For example, in the formation of opinion on preschool education, information evening are sometimes held before municipal council meetings, or the problems and possible decision making are talked through in other ways.

The civil service machinery and the institutions were also important in creating a broader base, for ultimately, all the actors have to back the policy. In Emmen a lot of energy has gone into this, which has resulted in the Educational Priority Foundation, in which all the actors participate as equals. It takes time before everyone realizes that co-operation is in the common interest, but the experience in Emmen shows that it helps if an attempt is made to work on the basis of the content, and to avoid questions of competence.

In the educational field there are good contacts between the different school denominations (Roman Catholic, Protestant and non-denominational). Everyone wants to keep it that way and the importance of attunement or co-operation for all concerned is often to be seen.

During the last few years efforts have been made in the welfare field to achieve one umbrella welfare foundation. That meant the sometimes difficult task of restructuring welfare work. However, the result is that there is now only one "producer" in that field, a situation which allows all types of organisations to work together. This is advantageous, since such a reorganisation can only succeed if there is a basis for integration.

At the implementation level and as concerns interaction with clients, the basis of support is also an important factor for success, as an unfortunate experience with the preschool *Opstap* project in Emmen clearly showed. The manner in which the plan was introduced, and the criteria used for the participation of indigenous Dutch families, were felt to be stigmatising by both the schools and local inhabitants involved.

In Emmen, many have remarked that with programmes such as MOVE it is not so much a question of new financial sources as of a shift in the flow of funds. It is quite clearly recognised that economic cuts call for increasing integration, and in budgetary matters too. Only if actors are prepared to co-operate with one another can they strengthen each other, which is necessary if as much as possible is to be achieved with limited resources. In other words, the money which is available should be used in a more efficient and effective way. This attitude calls for orientation toward prevention, since early intervention can mean savings later: for the prevention of developmental delay in the preschool phase can obviate the need for participation in truancy projects at secondary school.

In general, the Educational Priority Foundation looks after the budget for the funds which are contributed by the state and the participating municipalities in the framework of their partnership. In 1994, the Foundation's budget was Gld 2.3 million. This budget increased in the following years, since municipalities put their existing budgets into the integrated activities and more became available from the OCW budget. In some years, the municipal contribution in Emmen was bigger than that of the state, contrary to many municipalities. Emmen hereby showed that it was not only willing to invest, but that the steering possibilities were increased.

As regards the preschool phase, the funds from the welfare sector are especially important. In 1994, child care received about Gld 1.5 million, and preschool playgroup work about Gld 800 000. For specific projects in the preschool phase apart from MOVE, Gld 15 000 were allocated for infant plus projects. Additionally, a part of the funds for specific social renewal projects (up to 1994 about Gld 130 000) was spent in the preschool field.

With regard to MOVE, in 1995 financial resources were received from the municipality of Emmen (Gld 35 000), the Educational Priority Foundation (Gld 45 000) and the SKGE (Gld 15 000), making a total of Gld 105 000, in contrast to 1994 when there was only Gld 63 000 in the budget. The Ministry of VWS was asked for a contribution to the development of the model, which is after all intended to produce products usable elsewhere, thus fitting in well with the VWS strategy of developing nationally transmittable projects. Unfortunately, VWS was not able to provide the requested resources.

In the project plan, Gld 127 500 per annum was budgeted for the project development (for four "go-between mothers", one programme leader, one project secretary, activities and overheads).

In Emmen people believe that not only money matters, but certainly also people; in particular motivated and qualitatively good people. Indeed, the fact that a number of people are involved who really care about the preschool case and who have a great deal of experience is mentioned as one of the strong points of MOVE in Emmen. Against this background, there is attention in MOVE to courses and training for the programme leader and the contact mothers, and use is made of detailed profiles for these functions. The alignment to the experience of neighbourhood mothers from "Fun with Books" can also be seen in the same light.

Obstacles: Across the board a need is seen to: get rid of preconceived ideas, build up the willingness to learn from one another and achieve something together. That calls for a switch from a culture of compartmentalisation to a climate of mutual reinforcement.

For instance, it is often a question of "natural" competency disparities between education and welfare. Years ago there was also this sort of competency battle in Emmen (according to the alderman, for example). This was neutralised by the reorganisation of the municipal machinery, under which education and welfare came under one sector (and temporarily also under one alderman).

In education the implementation of a more coherent approach in school policy is a particular problem. That says something about the culture in education, about the management qualities of the school management teams and the training of teachers. It seems to be very difficult to make Educational Priority Policy into school policy. The purposeful and specific use of the OVB weighting of funds, for example, forms an obstacle, while the problems of disadvantaged indigenous Dutch pupils persist.

Obstacles to integration in the field of welfare exist both in material and institutional spheres. From the material point of view there is the weak position of child care and preschool playgroups: too many voluntary workers, too little money to make changes. From the institutional point of view, the interests and positions of the various foundations play a part. In Emmen an attempt has been made to deal with these obstacles by forming a welfare umbrella organisation, in which most of the preschool playgroups also participate.

As regards neighbourhood networks, the obstacles include the fact that many actors call for many consultations, that levels differ between the participants, and that delegates do not always have the same mandate from the management of their institution.

Strategies in the co-operation process: With MOVE, Emmen wants to achieve made-to-measure services for the preschool period, in which the so-called "go-between mother" or "contact mother" plays a central role. She sees to it that the families which belong to the target group participate in programmes or activities which best meet their specific problems.

A plan has been drawn up for MOVE in which the intended aims, methods and available financial resources are clearly described.

When MOVE spreads throughout Drenthe, a local deprivation plan will be drawn up for each municipality, in which there will be integral policy with regard to education and welfare.

The general strategy behind this working method is that of management by objectives. Efforts are being made to realise a change in the management and culture of all the institutions involved. The specific effort to achieve objectives defined in output terms can then also be striven after in the co-operation between institutions.

More particularly, a double strategy is followed in MOVE, whereby the basis of support is created at the implementation level, while legitimisation for the implementation is regulated at the management or executive level. This method has been applied in more programmes in Emmen, for example the working party for upbringing support, the neighbourhood networks for youth services, "Fun with Books" Emmen and the "Upbringing in the Picture" project.

The start is made at the strategic level. As a result of the good contacts between the Educational Priority Bureau and key figures in the municipal sector "Learning and Care", agreement was soon reached at policy level over working on the preschool phase, ultimately in the form of MOVE. From these bridgeheads, work on political embedment and support, and gaining co-operation from institutions was continued in the local network. This strategy led to the covenant on MOVE between the municipality, Educational Priority Foundation, Home Care Drenthe and SKGE.

At a later stage, use was also made of national networks, in particular the National Consultative Body on Educational Priority, ministries, NIZW and Averroës; national support was also found to be necessary. At the beginning WVC was not greatly in favour of MOVE, whereas Averroës was enthusiastic immediately.

The co-operation of the Ministry of WVC (later renamed VWS) and of Averroës was necessary, for example, to make the conditions for the *Opstap* programmes in the Drenthe OVG more flexible. Thus there is now no longer any question of an obligatory number of participating families, since this was difficult to reconcile with a flexible, target group-oriented supply of services.

On the basis of the agreement at policy and management level, the second part of the double strategy was then taken in hand, namely convincing those at the implementation level. Initially, the work for groups at risk in Emmen was mainly institution-oriented, but as of the last few years it has become more family- and demand-oriented – identifying exactly what the problems and needs are. In the solutions the emphasis was put on the role of the parents as upbringers of their children and the point was the empowerment of parents. This slight shift of emphasis led to MOVE making a flexible package, offering both family-oriented as well as institution-oriented activities. A strategic novelty here was working with paraprofessional contact mothers, who link demand and supply.

In the realisation of the double strategy (at management and implementation level) "tempt and demand" tactics were employed – parties were offered something on the one hand and on the other hand something was asked of them. In other words, it was shown that investment was favourable for all concerned and that a win-win situation could be created.

Children at risk and their families are those targeted by this strategy. Every effort is made to reach those families early on and also to locate those who are most disadvantaged. MOVE focuses especially on hard to reach families and preschool play-groups, which because they are natural meeting points for parents, prove to be useful venues. Nevertheless, between 20-30 per cent of disadvantaged families fall through the net.

Case product

Results

MOVE is a development project which has already been running for several years, but is not yet rounded off. Thus only provisional or interim results can be reported on here. These results will be viewed on the three levels which have been distinguished. Since the process has mainly been top-down, it is not very surprising that up to now the most results have been achieved at the strategic level and the least at field level. There seems to be a broad consensus on MOVE and also on the result-oriented method in developing the programme at all levels. The method comprises amongst other things: making plans (for MOVE, for the districts which are going to participate) which are well under-pinned substantively, clear and realistic objectives, clear phasing, well-defined division of tasks and concrete activities with the expectation of results.

The not insignificant results which have been achieved at the strategic level concern a covenant between the actors most involved and a basis of support with a broader political-administrative reach. Among the things this has led to a concentration of the flow of funds and the co-operation of the covenant partners in senior management consultations of MOVE. A project management team has also been installed, which meets monthly and both directs the progress of the project and creates the conditions for the implementation. If necessary, the project management initiates consultations with the senior management of the covenant partners.

Another result is that a contract has been concluded between the Educational Priority Foundation and the Averroës Foundation for the development of the content of the work and further adoption of the programme in Drenthe.

At the operational level a programme leader was appointed with effect from 1 January 1995, who looks after the co-ordination and practical implementation of the project.

At the field level three pilot sites have been chosen in Emmen, where the basis of support for the implementation of the project is formed by schools, preschool playgroups, welfare institutions, home care, educational priority and the programme leaders. The contact mothers or neighbourhood mothers are to function as the binding link between these interested parties and the families (parents and children). They were appointed with effect from 1 September and, after training, began their work in November 1995.

In the following paragraphs, more detail is provided at the "field level" through describing a preschool playgroup. Though at the time of our visit there was not yet a contact mother of MOVE involved, the playgroup leader has been functioning there so well for so long, that she served as a model for the figure of the "go-between mother". Her preschool playgroup can also serve as an example of good practice.

The fact that a preschool playgroup and its leader could act as an example for the MOVE development project may provoke critical questions with regard to the need for the project and for the "go-between mother" in particular. After all, doesn't a properly functioning preschool playgroup leader make a "go-between mother" superfluous? Following on from this, doesn't it make more sense to improve the functioning of preschool playgroups, primary schools, home care and neighbourhood networks, instead of creating new functions and structures?

Such questions are all the more cogent, since it has been found that the making and maintaining of contacts is a weak link in the entity. MOVE is a top-down design and has proved to be most difficult to realise at the base. First of all, there was to be a "go-between mother", who was however already replaced in the planning stage by a "contact mother" with a smaller task. In the elaboration of the methodology, the latter could, if necessary, be preceded by an "intermediary". The core of this function in different definitions is still: to enjoy the confidence of the target group, of the parents and children whom it is all about.

And does that not mean a core of professionals at field level in the preschool playgroup, primary school, home care, neighbourhood network, etc.? In Emmen people seem to have recognised this, since by "intermediaries" they explicitly mean professionals.

Practice may prove whether the comparatively long route, which is now used before families can actually participate in a programme, is really necessary, as well as whether a separate contact mother offers added value for the maintenance of contact with these families.

Be that as it may, Emmen has chosen to solve the existing problems along the MOVE pathway, and that pathway does not appear to lack perspective. The conclusion deals in more depth with the factors which have played a part in achieving the above-mentioned provisional results with regard to integrated work.

"Good practice" in a preschool playgroup

As an example of a product in the preschool phase we have made a closer study of a preschool playgroup by means of a visit and a group interview. The group discussion took place with Trijn Lambers, playgroup leader and also "Fun with Books" supervisor; Trijn de Graaf, board member of the preschool playgroup and parent of a preschool child; Jane Muskee and Ria Fijen, parents of toddlers who come to the playgroup.

The playgroup premises are in Nieuw Dordrecht, an "outskirts" village of about 800 inhabitants belonging to the municipality of Emmen. The educational level of the residents is not very high on average and, on the basis of the socio-economic scores of the OVB, the village primary school is one of the poorest schools of the Drenthe OVG. Although the educational attainment is below the national average, it is relatively good within the OVG.

The preschool playgroup in question is situated in the same building as the primary school. At the time of the interviews (November 1994) a total of 21 toddlers attend the playgroup. Two groups have been formed, each of which attends two mornings a week.

It quickly became evident how much the discussion partners cared about the playgroup and how happy they were to participate in the activities. For example, a parent told us how much she had missed the contact and activities of the playgroups when her elder child went to the primary school and how glad she was to rejoin now that her younger one was old enough for the playgroup. It also becomes clear how central a role is played by the playgroup leader. She seems to be a confidante for many of the parents, who not only come to her if it is something to do with their child, but also with all sorts of other problems.

In fact, it is easy to form the impression that the leader is idolised but that the playgroup is run jointly by the parents and leaders can be seen from the following paragraphs.

Parent involvement: Most of the parents are enthusiastic about the playgroup and all join in when collections are held, such as selling raffle tickets or the collection for *Jantje Beton* children at risk.

The involvement of the parents is also apparent from their participation in the various types of evenings which are organised. There are information evenings, when certain themes come up for discussion, including such serious matters as children with burns. Other evenings involve reading aloud, playing with children, or discovering games suitable for toddlers. Once a year there is a business meeting (with annual accounts and elections for the board), but this is combined with "something jolly", such as a video tape for the toddlers. The parents' involvement is also apparent from the fact that once a month and every holiday the parents clean the playroom and all the materials.

The playgroup has far-reaching effects, for example because it enables parents to make good contacts. Moreover, parents see how much their toddlers enjoy their visit to the playgroup.

The role of leader Trijn Lambers: Trijn Lambers has been working for ten years as the voluntary leader of the playgroup. Little by little she has taken numerous courses for this work. Her basic principle is that the playgroup must stimulate the development of the toddlers. An important aspect is the observation of the children as they are developing. A newsletter, which comes out about four times a year, includes sayings of the children, and remarks from parents along with more general information. She meets with parents not only at the playroom, for so-called "ten-minute" talks, but also at the family's home, to be able to speak with the father.

Drawings and handiwork and a few photos are collected from each toddler and stuck into a book, which is given to the child on transition from the playgroup to primary school. Each child also received a "hands towel", with imprints of the hands of all the children from the group. Ms. Lambers also discusses the children with the primary school teacher who will later be responsible for them which is very much appreciated. The teachers are very positive about the playgroup agreeing that it addresses "disadvantages which cannot fully be compensated any more at the primary school".

In the course of these ten years Ms. Lambers has become the confidante of many parents. If there's something wrong with, or problems with a child, the parents talk to her about it, with the aim being to work together towards a solution. Parents also come to her with other problems. She has had to learn how to set aside time for herself, as well as how, on occasion, to refer the parents elsewhere, or suggest that the parents deal with the matter themselves.

"Fun with Books": Following observations that the children's use of language was deteriorating, and in consultation with the board of the preschool playgroup and the Educational Priority Bureau, it was decided to participate in the "Fun with Books" project, then in the process of being developed. This is a reading promotion project for 0- to 6-year olds, directed in particular to stimulating literacy. The basic principle is that the process of literacy must be fed and stimulated through interaction and help from the social environment. The project is aimed at children from groups with a low educational level. This target group of non-indigenous and indigenous children is approached through parents and other educators, including staff from the institutions with which the child has contact.

Ms. Lambers became a "Fun with Books" supervisor, when Emmen became a pilot site, introducing and guiding the project in the participating families. For children from three months to two years use is made of a Book Bear (developed in Emmen), a bright cardboard bear with pockets on its tummy, in which there are various sorts of books and a cassette with baby songs. Reading aloud, looking at pictures, rhymes and music can lead to a child getting more enjoyment out of reading later on. The intention is that the parents spend a few moments every day, for example before bedtime, on this sort of activity, although they need to be encouraged to continue with it.

For 2- to 4-year-olds use is made of a Discovery Book, which the toddlers and their parents fill with drawings or cut and paste work. The idea is that the children regularly take the Discovery Book with them to the playgroup to show the leader what they have made. The aim of "Fun with Books" is that the children derive so much enjoyment from it that later on they will continue to read and enjoy books.

The neighbourhood network in Nieuw Dordrecht started up in 1992. It was Ms. Lambers who in consultation with the Educational Priority Bureau pointed out the need for such a network because the problems presented by children were becoming more difficult to handle and needed a more co-ordinated response.

The parents clearly welcomed the neighbourhood network, and felt that something similar should exist everywhere.

Problems: Despite the apparent success of the playgroup, there are concerns that it may not continue in its present form. First, there is a chance that professionalisation of the playgroups will change its leadership structure, and a second point of concern is that the incorporation of the foundation which now runs the preschool playgroup into a big welfare umbrella organisation, which would involve an increase in the parental contribution (from Gld 25 to 55 per month), would have a negative impact on 40 per cent of them, with the fear that the most needy would not be reached.

The future

It is clear that this is a flourishing playgroup with a dedicated leader whose contribution is strongly endorsed by parents. Furthermore, the MOVE project developed the idea of its "go-between mother" from this playgroup leader's style of working. The research on MOVE took place in 1995. The experiment was to run from 1994 to 1997. What were the effects of the programme found in the research study? The method of working with "contact mothers" or "neighbouring mothers" was tried out at more sites in Emmen in 1995 and 1996. A further step was taken towards wider implementation ("Move Drenthe"), as more municipalities began to show an interest in implementing the method. One of these municipalities is Hoogeveen, which has decided to implement the method following an analysis of its existing preschool situation.

As far as the results are concerned, the goals set for 1995-1997 were met to a reasonable degree. Of the OVB target group children, 80 per cent are now attending a preschool playgroup, which exceeds the set target of 75 per cent. Half of the playgroups and all primary schools now have a pupil monitoring system; this is a good result, even though the target figure of 100 per cent has not been reached. Also, the aim to have 75 per cent of the parents participate in annual activities has been largely attained. The biggest group of parents are now reached by the *Boekenpret* reading promotion project (90 per cent), because this project is now running in all playgroups and primary schools. Active families participate on average in 1.6 activities. However, not all families are active participants: of the 189 families reached, 130 participated in activities. Reasons why people did not participate were, for instance, that they could not combine participation in the activities with their work, or that they were unable to chose a suitable activity. The MOVE Programme has reached 189 families, which is about 30 per cent of the families with children aged 0-7 in the experimental sites. Of these families, about 75 per cent belong to the target group, *i.e.* have children at risk. Half of these are Dutch and half are ethnic minorities. This means that the programme reaches a high proportion of ethnic minority families, because Emmen has a relatively small immigrant population.

The experiment in Emmen has been extended by two years. During this period, the quality of the method is to be further improved and research is to be conducted to cast light on the relationship between participation in activities and children's achievement in school. In addition, a start has been made to make the experiences in Emmen and Drenthe transferable to other parts of the Netherlands. The Averroes Foundation intends to present the model nation-wide under the name *Move-Stap in* (step in). Incidentally, in the dissemination of MOVE, use is being made of a short video film that was included in the film "Children of Promise", which was made to help disseminate the entire OECD/CERI Integrated Services project, and which was premiered at the dissemination conference held in Toronto, Canada in the Autumn of 1996.

SCHOOL CASE STUDY: ROTTERDAM

Case context: the research site

Rotterdam is the second city of the Netherlands and with the world's busiest port, is a centre of industrial activity. The city itself covers an area of about 30 000 hectares. The centre, destroyed by bombing in the Second World War, has for the greater part been rebuilt and in the 1980s and 1990s considerable attention has been paid to renovation and new development in severely dilapidated city quarters. Furthermore Rotterdam is the socio-cultural centre for the Rijnmond region. There is a flourishing cultural life with numerous theatres, cinemas, concert halls, museums and libraries.

Rotterdam is a part of the largest conurbation of the Netherlands with more than 1 million inhabitants. In 1994 the city itself had almost 600 000 inhabitants (including about 140 000 children and young people aged between 0 and 20 years). It is anticipated that that number will increase to 650 000 by the year 2000.

About 20 per cent of the inhabitants are not of Dutch nationality. The largest groups come from Turkey, Morocco, the former Yugoslavia and Spain. The remainder is divided over 138 nationalities. Nationally the percentage of non-indigenous Dutch is much lower, at 5 per cent. Half of the immigrants live in the four cities of Amsterdam, Rotterdam, The Hague and Utrecht. In the coming ten years the number of migrants who do not possess Dutch nationality will amount to almost 30 per cent of the population of Rotterdam. Apart from this there are also migrants who do possess Dutch nationality (and are not included in the statistics as "migrants").

The diversity of the inhabitants of Rotterdam came about in the 1950s and 1960s, when a large number of Dutchmen from the former colonies returned to resettle in the Netherlands. Apart from this, as in most of the cities of Northern and Western Europe, unskilled labour from the Mediterranean area started to flow in. At the time, it was assumed that these peoples would return to their land of origin once the Netherlands was again able to provide its own labour. In the 1970s it became increasingly evident that it was not a question of a temporary stay and in the 1980s and 1990s family members of the "guest workers" also settled in the Netherlands in the framework of the family reunification. During the same period the number of non-indigenous Dutch rose, because young people wanting to start a family looked for a partner in their country of origin. Furthermore both the number and diversity of inhabitants with a non-Dutch ethnic background have risen through the influx of refugees and people seeking asylum from, for example, the former Yugoslavia and a large number of African and Asiatic countries. There is thus a great diversity in pupils' backgrounds, stemming not only from possible reasons for having come to the Netherlands, but also because of language and cultural differences.

In spite of the fact that Rotterdam is the largest port in the world and that there is great industrial activity, unemployment amounts to about 21 per cent of the working population. The national figure is 7.5 per cent (1994).

Of the Rotterdam pupils, 75 per cent have a low score on a scale to assess socio-economic status, which may be due in part to the low educational levels of the parents, and their low-paid menial jobs. This means that both Dutch as well as immigrant families are in deprived situations. Of the children in primary education 75 per cent are at risk, with little chance in education and poor future prospects. About half the pupils have a non-Dutch ethnic background, which means that either one or both of the parents was not born in the Netherlands.

Case input

Services provided

In the OECD case study in Rotterdam the co-operation between municipality, education and welfare in the municipal Fund for the Reduction of Educational Disadvantages (FAO) is of central importance. The FAO is a platform for the Educational Priority Policy in greater Rotterdam and is responsible for the preparation and determination of policy for the reduction of educational disadvantages. Both as regards content as well as funding, the forces of the municipality, the Rotterdam schools and welfare institutions, which are involved in Educational Priority Policy, are combined in the FAO. The FAO works both preventively and curatively, but the emphasis is more particularly on the preventive approach. However, the ultimate objective is to improve the performance level of education and thus have a curative effect on disadvantaged pupils.

At the strategic level, the FAO board develops policy and exercises control. Municipal council members, members of school governing bodies and members of the board of a welfare institution sit on the FAO board. The operational level consists of representatives from education and welfare. School management (members of school management teams), the senior management of the welfare institution, and co-ordinators of projects/project leaders put the policy into practice and create the conditions for co-operation between the various sectors. The field consists – as far as welfare and education are concerned – of the practical co-operation in various projects. These will be explained in more depth.

The main objective of the FAO is "the improvement of educational performance in the basic skills and school careers of pupils at risk". To achieve this a four-track policy has been mapped out consisting of:

- allocation of resources to schools;

- exchange of good practices;

- evaluation; and

- projects.

The first track – allocation of resources to schools: Schools receive extra resources, either in the form of extra staff or cash, so as to be able to work independently towards the realisation of the FAO objective. The criteria for receiving resources are based on the number of pupils from ethnic minorities, the number of pupils with socio-economic disadvantages and the total number of pupils in a school. In 1994, 132 of the 200 primary and 35 of the 53 schools for secondary education received such resources. This was guaranteed up to August 1995 on condition that schools participate in the local evaluation of pupil results in language and mathematics and that they formulate a plan on how they intended to reach the main goals. They could receive guidance with this from the school advisory service.

The second track – exchange of good practices: Information evenings are arranged to give schools ideas on how they can tackle the various issues that arise, and schools inform each other about what works and what does not. This takes place in small conferences, in a monthly magazine about educational practice, in brochures about worthwhile experiences in schools, etc. The welfare institutions are often involved here as well.

The third track – evaluation: An important part of the FAO strategy is evaluation, not only of pupils' results, but also of the school and the effectiveness of the policy and of the projects. In order to receive additional resources, schools are required to participate in evaluation and describe their plans in the school work plan.

The fourth track – projects: In order to achieve the objectives, the FAO finances and supports projects on a systematic policy basis. It is partly a question of already existing projects and partly of new projects, whereby in many cases there is co-operation between the school, welfare institutions and immigrant organisations. The central objective of a project is always to try to find answers in practice. The projects are grouped round five themes:

- preschool period;

- Dutch as second language and multi-lingualism;

- effective learning time;

- co-operation with parents; and

- reduction of early school leaving rates.

The projects where in practice there is an integrated approach by welfare and education are shown in Table 3. There are still more forms of successful co-operation, but then it is a question of co-operation between schools (thus co-operation within a sector and not an integrated approach) or of *ad hoc* co-operation or regular consultations. Such forms of co-operation are of importance for Rotterdam, but are less relevant to this case study. The projects included in Table 3 are explained in more detail. Moreover some of them are discussed in the paragraphs on the functioning (obstacles and results) of the integrated approach.

Table 3. **Projects with an integrated approach from education or welfare**

Theme	Project	Schools	Welfare
Care for newly arrived immigrant school entrants	• BOA: Out-of-School Care for non-Native Speakers • GIDS: Care for non-Dutch speaking Newcomers	3 4	10 1
Effective learning time	• Extended School Day	9	10
Effective relationship with parents	• Model of Project School Social Work • Projects of migrant organisations	10	5
School careers and moments at risk	• Learning outcomes and health (*Binnenboord*) • Reading for the examination list • Library in the class	5 3 5	6 1 6

Project theme 1 – care for newly arrived immigrant school entrants: A great deal is done at school on the theme "care for newly arrived immigrant school entrants", who are non-Dutch speakers. Thus there is a project for preschool children, "Multilingual care for preschool children", for the primary school there is *Prisma* and for secondary education *Ster*. In these projects, language instruction occupies the central position. There are also two projects in which both education and welfare participate: Out-of-School Care for non-Native Speakers (BOA) and Care for non-Dutch speaking Newcomers (GIDS).

The goal of the Out-of-School Care for non-Native Speakers (BOA) Project is to increase the development possibilities of Moroccan children. The activities are directed to improving the school career and the integration process of the children into Dutch society. Attention is also paid to Moroccan-Arab culture. The combination of a school and play approach appears to work very well. The children get homework on school concepts and themes such as housing, animals, parties and sport are discussed, but they also have tea together and do games. Both aspects are instrumental in increasing the oral command of the Moroccan and Dutch language. Moreover the children enjoy taking part in the project.

Since the activities concern both education and the school as well as leisure activities and the community centre (welfare), this project to some extent bridges the gulf between school and home for these Moroccan children.

The GIDS project has been predicated on the idea extending the care for newcomers to education social integration. Co-ordination has been achieved with *Prisma* and *Ster* school-based programmes for newcomers.

Just as with BOA, GIDS is indeed directed to improving educational performance, but the emphasis is on the children quickly getting to feel at home in their new living environment. Children can only do their best at school if their basic needs have been met. They must feel secure, be adequately acquainted with their surroundings, be able to find the way, be protected against climatic influences and come safely through day-to-day life. This is worked on in the GIDS Programme under the guidance of a voluntary guide and may take the form of visits in small groups to the fire brigade, the library, the market, the police station, the animal ambulance service, etc. Activities such as swimming, cycling and skating are also undertaken.

Project theme 2 – effective learning time: With the theme "effective learning time", a four-year experiment *Verlengde Schooldag* has been carried out in Rotterdam, Amsterdam, The Hague and Utrecht. This can be compared with the American model of the Extended School Day. The experiment has been evaluated and, as it did not sufficiently yield the desired results, the extra subsidy from the Ministry of Education will be stopped. Nevertheless, the project had considerable effect in Rotterdam and the concept so integrated into the participating schools and welfare institutions, that possibilities are being sought to finance the activities from the regular budget. On the basis of the experience with the Extended School Day the concept of *de Brede School* (the broad school) has been formulated. Further information will be given on the latter and on the Extended School Day.

The Extended School Day is a co-operative project of education and welfare for children and youth at schools who are educationally deprived. It is a question here of an activity programme which takes place in free time, but which should be seen as supplementing the regular curriculum: for example, art training, sport, technique, etc. A reading aloud afternoon is also part of the project. The activities are supervised by specialised teachers and take place partly in school and partly outside.

A child welfare worker, who is employed by a welfare body (*Stichting Welzijn Afrikaanderwijk*), has a development function in the framework of the Extended School Day Project. She forms the link between the specialist teachers who organise extra-mural activities and the children. In the school she has a bridging function between education and welfare. The project is in progress in Rotterdam at eight primary schools and one secondary school. That means that more than 1 000 pupils are involved in it, mainly in the age group 8-12 years.

The aim of the project is to optimise the development of the children. The learning achievement is a part of this, but attention is paid especially to the creative and societal development of children. As a representative of the project expressed it, "it is not only a question of your head, but also of your heart and your hands". People work on the assumption that socio-economic factors also play a role in educational disadvantages and that attention must be paid to the children's general education as well as to maths and language. A representative of a welfare institution considers that both the school and the community centre have an important function in teaching children fundamental skills and that they can complement each other in doing so.

Children who are hardly ever read aloud to at home, who have nothing to draw or paint with and who cannot become a member of a sports club (on account of social or financial impediments) can take part in such activities in the Extended School Day. The school has the trust of the parents and it is therefore a good thing for activities to be organised for children in their free time which can ultimately also influence their school results. Account is also taken of the fact that children are confronted with great differences in norms, values and customs at school, in the street and at home. Respect for different cultures is indeed one of the central points in the project.

The project ran until 1996, when the experimental subsidy from the Ministry of VWS (formerly WVC) expired. However, the co-operation was developed and is continuing in the form of the *de Brede School*. Already there are activities which are organised jointly by the school and by welfare in the framework of purposeful leisure interests. Thus the reading aloud club and the nature and environmental education from the community centre – financed from the regular budget – now already come under the denominator of the Extended School Day.

The experience gained with the Extended School Day has been worked into the concept for *de Brede School* and a framework has been outlined, on the basis of which each school can further elaborate and make concrete the ideas. The basic principle in the concept of *de Brede School* is that children's development progresses better if the differences between the influences and experiences at school, in the community and at home are not too divergent. There should be a large contribution from welfare institutions such as clubs and community work, but the school must form the core of the activities. The fact is that the school enjoys the trust of many of the people in deprived situations, has a societal responsibility which can no longer be fulfilled within the school walls and has moreover a relatively professional machinery at its disposal. Important though the co-operation with welfare work is, most of those involved consider that the ultimate responsibility for activities in the framework of educational priority must lie with education, particularly since it is educational funds which are involved.

Project theme 3 – effective relationship with parents: The theme of effective relationships with parents covers activities such as projects by migrant organisations and school social work.

In order to increase the involvement of immigrant parents in the education of their children, various projects have been started up in co-operation with diverse migrant organisations. The underlying idea is that people with the same background as the parents can more easily establish contact with them and gain their confidence. Thus the Cape Verdean community organises meetings for Cape Verdean parents about the education of their children and the association of Turkish teachers has developed a course for Turkish parents of children at the primary school. Moreover various migrant organisations arrange activities for the parents in co-operation with schools.

There are two different sorts of school social work in existence in Rotterdam: school-oriented and in-school work. Schools can themselves indicate which form of social work they prefer and which recognised institution for social work they wish to make use of. In school-oriented social work pupils and parents are referred to a social work institution with which the school has close contact. Here, however, there is still the barrier which many non-indigenous parents experience with this sort of institution. In in-school social work that is not the case as the social worker is present in school for a number of hours per week. He or she also takes part in the discussions on pupils. This situation can be compared with school advisory services. There is also a possibility for schools to refer pupils themselves by means of a social chart (an address file containing bodies in the field of counselling, social work, education, labour market guidance, etc.).

A concrete example of the activities of the social workers is the participation in multi-disciplinary teams. Once a month such teams meet at various schools to discuss the pupils with serious problems. Before a pupil is discussed in one of these teams, an internal pathway has been followed of counselling by teachers and school social work. The multidisciplinary team comprises internal and external experts representing: student counsellors, the school psychologist and a remedial teacher from the school and further youth health care (the school doctors from the GG and GD), youth social assistance (Rijnmond youth *aid*), school social work, the municipality (the compulsory education officer). The objective of the teams was to create an easily accessible advisory body without a deterrent effect. The initial resistance disappeared when positive concrete results were achieved.

Project theme 4 – school careers and moments at risk: Both within the school and also in integrated projects attempts are made to prevent early school leaving. The prevention project B*innenboord* is directed at optimising the internal measures and setting up a local network with the following participants: school, school doctors, youth welfare organisations and the compulsory education officer. The latter plays a central part. He or she not only has a checking function, but also acts as a student counsellor. Efforts are also made to build up co-operation with youth social assistance work. B*innenboord* made this co-operation possible for pre-vocational education. The relationship with youth social assistance work will be further expanded.

"Reading for the Examination List" and "Library in the Class" are projects in which schools co-operate with libraries in an attempt to encourage students to read more.

Services integration

History, background and present structure: Both national and local policies played a role in the realisation of the FAO. However, the most important stimulus came from actual practice: from people in education who realised that they could not solve the problems in the school by themselves. The need to look outside the school and to co-operate with welfare institutions could happen, however, when matters had been settled at the administrative level and an organisational structure had been developed. The clarity which emerged in the financial situation also formed a major stimulus for the developments.

To understand just how difficult it has been to achieve the co-operation between in particular municipality and education at the administrative (strategic) level, it is important to know that the school boards are financed directly by the Ministry of Education. There is thus no direct subsidy relationship between mainstream education and the local authority. The country report mentioned how difficult it often is for the local authority to commit education to joint local policy.

In the following paragraphs an outline will first be given of national educational policy (decentralisation, economy cuts, Educational Priority Policy and social renewal), the needs of the educational and welfare sectors and the final result of the negotiations of municipalities, education and welfare in the Rotterdam Fund for the Reduction of Educational Disadvantages (FAO).

Government policy: As described in the country report, the national decentralisation policy in the 1980s led to greater responsibility and autonomy in the development of policy by local authorities.

Prior to that, education was regulated centrally from the Ministry of Education and Science (now Education, Culture and Science). Welfare came under the responsibility of the Ministry of Welfare, Health and Cultural Affairs (now Health, Welfare and Sport). In Rotterdam, decentralisation resulted in responsibility being accorded to a level below that of the municipal level to eleven boroughs in which directly elected borough councils function with administrative competencies.

This made it very difficult to achieve the alignment of education and welfare. It was evidently necessary to find a model in which this could indeed be realised. There would have to be an umbrella organisation of welfare institutions from all the boroughs, which could see to the contacts between welfare and education. With that objective in mind, the welfare institution *Stichting de Meeuw* (the Seagull Foundation) was set up. It was not intended as an executive institution, but as a body with an intermediary function.

Apart from decentralisation, the financial cuts of the 1980s have had a great influence on local policy. The flow of government subsidies was cut short for many of the institutions which were connected with youth and young people in deprived situations. It is true that education still receives subsidies, but ever higher standards are being set with regard to effectiveness and efficiency. One of the results of all this is that the supply in the field of welfare *and* education must be better aligned to the demand.

In the country report, information is also given on the Educational Priority Policy (OVB). The OVB has also played an important part in the realisation of a specifically Rotterdam way of combating educational disadvantages.

For 200 Rotterdam primary schools this meant that they received about Gld 50 million per year extra, on top of a 1994 education budget of nearly Gld 499 million [the size of the amount is partly determined by the so-called "weighting regulation", in which children from a deprived situation can count for a per capita weighting of 1.25 to 1.90 (the norm being 1.0)]. Secondary education received about 8 million extra (in this case the size of the amount is calculated on the basis of the "regulation for extra facilities for schools with ethnic minority pupils"). In primary education that meant 800 extra teachers and in secondary education some 110 extra teachers.

The primary and secondary schools which are eligible for these extra facilities participate in an educational priority area, a partnership between schools and welfare institutions in which the problems are tackled jointly. The budget is made available to the educational priority areas for the realisation of the objectives.

A positive result was that schools and school boards, welfare bodies and school advisory services began to co-operate. The networks which were formed in that first period still play a part in Rotterdam. But from the organisational point of view, Educational Priority Policy did not seem able to function optimally. Rotterdam was in fact divided up into nine educational priority areas, each with its own area co-ordinator. These areas did not completely correspond with schools and districts which needed extra support, there was no alignment on content and a disproportionately large amount of money was spent on overhead costs. Furthermore, the activities undertaken were often not really concrete and especially not measurable. For the schools the situation was obscure. Administratively and practically speaking it was not efficient and had little effect on daily educational practice. Level of satisfaction decreased at both school board and school level, with many feeling unable to understand what was actually happening in the educational priority areas. Policy in the area of educational priority was difficult to grasp and this led to increased willingness to co-operate in the realisation of a central structure with a central policy.

In doing this, it rapidly became clear that it would be better to start developments from the point of view of content, which required, first of all, the establishment of a sound administrative base. It would only be possible to find schools willing to carry the developments substantively if they were firmly steered in that direction.

Apart from the Educational Priority Policy, the legislation in the field of social renewal has also provided an impulse for the development of the Rotterdam policy on educational deprivation. An important factor in the social renewal policy is the stimulation of an integrated approach to combating social deprivation situations. In order to promote the co-operation between schools, other institutions and the local authority, the legislation makes it possible to conclude local agreements, which under certain conditions might diverge from educational legislation. Moreover, it is possible to concentrate the financial resources of different partners in a local fund. Both aspects have been vitally important in the realisation of an effective structure to assault educational deprivation in Rotterdam: the Municipal Fund for the Reduction of Educational Disadvantages.

Local initiative: Government policy, as described in the previous section, has had a great influence on the realisation of the co-operative structure, but the real initiative was taken by the people in Rotterdam who were responsible for education in general and the reduction of educational disadvantages in particular: the municipality, the school boards, the schools themselves and the welfare institutions. It is important to know that in the Netherlands the responsibility for education rests with the school boards, which account directly to the subsidiser: the central government. It was therefore important to get the municipality and the school boards aligned.

The schools with a great diversity of ethnic groups are particularly important in this context. The 50 per cent of the children between 0 and 12 years with a non-Dutch ethnic background are not divided equally over the Rotterdam schools. Depending on the district in which the school is situated, or the type of education given, there are schools with mainly Dutch children (white schools) and schools where more than half the pupils are from ethnic minorities. Moreover, there are schools with almost exclusively non-indigenous pupils (black schools). Around 20 per cent of the primary schools have more than 70 per cent non-Dutch children and there are schools with more than 90 per cent non-indigenous pupils. In addition, some schools continually receive newcomers, including children from countries where war has broken out. It is therefore not simply a problem with the language, but also differences in education, as well as the unstable political situations in the countries of origin.

When the number of non-indigenous pupils began to grow, the schools first tried to solve the problems themselves. This was partly done through pupil counselling. However, it soon became evident that the problems in education were too closely tied up with problems at home which could not be solved by teachers. So gradually people became willing to look beyond the school boundaries and to call in the help of ousted institutions, with expertise in dealing with these same young people. At the same time there were welfare institutions which pointed out to the schools the need for co-operation. They too are confronted with children from disadvantaged backgrounds and realise that there are many children whom they are unable to reach directly. For welfare institutions such as community work, social work, art education and immigrant groups the school represents an important source.

Outside the realms of education and welfare, attempts have been made to solve the problem, for the most part by setting up experimental projects. From an analysis of the situation in 1989 it appears that these were useful and interesting, but that they did not produce lasting results. The problems must be tackled from the heart of the school. The existing projects must be integrated and given a central position in education. This was finally achieved in the FAO, whereby the municipality played a steering role.

Both the national government policy: decentralisation, economic measures, Educational Priority Policy and social renewal as well as local initiative formed incentives to achieve coherence and co-operation in Rotterdam policy on educational deprivation. Fragmentation and marginalisation played a part in this connection. Indeed, examples of fragmentation included not only the nine educational priority areas, each with their own co-ordinator, but also municipal policy and co-ordination groups. The multiplicity of activities in the framework of educational priority were, despite efforts to the contrary, marginal and not at the core of the struggle to reduce educational deprivation.

In 1989, a municipal policy group was formed with the aim of producing proposals for improvement of the situation. In 1990, this resulted in a working paper with the following proposals:

- to formulate a clear-cut joint objective;
- to develop an integral, coherent policy;

- to put the emphasis on the introduction of improvements in everyday practice; the basic principle should be: "the-school-as-unit-of-change"; and

- to realise a clear-cut, flexible and close-knit organisation for the Educational Priority Policy.

Subsequently in 1991 the municipal authorities and the school boards signed the "Fund for the Reduction of Educational Disadvantages" Order and the "Horizontal Covenant Concerning Social Renewal in Education" and the FAO came into being. The following paragraph gives details of its structure. It is characteristic of the development of the FAO that the municipality of Rotterdam decided not to enforce the policy by economic and/or legal means, but through trying to achieve a joint objective by means of communication and consultation with the different bodies accountable.

Fund for the reduction of educational disadvantages: At the end of the 1980s the municipality, education and welfare were in agreement that joint efforts were needed to tackle the problems. Those who were involved in educational deprivation situations were basically in agreement with one another as regards the content. The educational results formed the centre point and "the effective school" thus became the basic principle of the educational deprivation policy. Efforts would be made to improve the basic skills (arithmetic and language) and attention would also be paid to the social and emotional development of the children and to the relations between the different ethnic groups. Priority would, however, be given to the basic skills. During the last two to three years a shift has become evident to more attention to the latter in combination with arts education.

Apart from being in agreement on the main points of the content, those involved also agreed on the policy to be developed in the framework of the effective school. The basic principle was a bottom-up development with substantive changes taking place at the school itself. The view was shared that changes must take place in the school, and on the basis of practice, and that at the administrative level the conditions should be created to make these changes possible. Strong top-down support was needed – not only financially, but also administratively. According to one of the FAO board members, it should in some way be possible to compel the schools to co-operate. If it were to be too non-committal, then nothing would be brought about.

With regard to the organisational structure of the co-operation those involved had much more difficulty in reaching agreement. At the beginning both the municipalities as well as the schools and welfare institutions tried to defend their own interests as far as possible. The municipality was in favour of a municipal service. The schools wanted to set up an independent foundation. In the initial stage the outcome of the tough discussions was negative. There was disagreement on a number of points both on the part of the municipality *vis-à-vis* the representatives of education and also on the part of the schools amongst themselves. It was only after fierce controversy and a great deal of discussion that compromise was reached on the structure of the FAO a board with representatives of the municipality, the schools and a welfare institution, the De Meeuw foundation.

In August 1991, the agreements for the collaboration were fixed for four years in the "horizontal covenant for social renewal in education". The balance of power between municipality and education was laid down in the covenant in a pragmatic, workable manner. The municipal council has enacted a by-law for the City Board FAO, which gives the board freedom to determine policy, but requires it to render account to the municipal council of Rotterdam (and thereby as agreed also to the Ministry of Education). The steering is in the hands of a municipal committee, or rather the municipal council has transferred the competencies to this committee. Once a year account is given to the municipal council. Since all those involved are so aware of the importance of co-operation, in practice joint solutions are always found. Each party needs the other. The municipality could withdraw its own financial contribution from the FAO and the joint decision making, but that only represents a part of the FAO funds. Moreover, the major part of the educational funding from the Ministry of Education is directly at the disposal of the school boards. That applies both to the regular resources and also to the weighting funds.

In the relationship between education and welfare there is no question of an equivalent position, but through the pragmatic attitude of all those concerned, it does turn out to be workable. According to some people De Meeuw should not be represented on the board at all, for they feel that participation by the local authority, which provides the subsidy for the welfare institutions, should be sufficient. Welfare institutions could then be forced to co-operate in the central direction by making collaboration in educational deprivation programmes a condition for obtaining a subsidy. According to others the success of the FAO has indeed partly depended on the participation of De Meeuw, since it has acted as an intermediary between all the different welfare bodies. The different opinions and points of view over who should and should not participate in the FAO board is illustrative of the precarious balance of the construction. The same applies to the representation from the rank and file of welfare and education.

Rotterdam education – in so far as schools with disadvantaged pupils are concerned – is represented on the board directly or by mandate. The representation of welfare is rather more complicated. The De Meeuw foundation does indeed maintain good, practical contacts with the welfare institutions in the city, but there is no question of any representation by mandate. However, it is seen as such on the FAO board. The FAO assumes that De Meeuw represents the entire welfare field. According to the director of De Meeuw it works as well as it does because the situation is dealt with pragmatically. De Meeuw has been able to convince most of the welfare institutions of the importance of co-operation within the FAO construction. In this connection the fact that the client occupies the central position has above all played an important part. All those involved become increasingly convinced that it is better for the client if institutions consult and co-operate instead of defending their own territory. An example of this is that children and parents can be helped more quickly, because in a multi-disciplinary team the school can discuss the problems with experts in the field of counselling and assistance. They can then refer their clients to the most suitable institutions.

Since educational funds are concentrated in the FAO, it is generally considered that the voice of the educational sector is decisive. However, in practice things are settled by consensus, even though there is certainly not a balanced administrative situation. This is confirmed in the field. Representatives of the Extended School Day project do indeed realise that their project is financed in the framework of educational deprivation and that the educational sector has the most to say about the way in which the project takes shape. But at the community level, education and welfare feel jointly responsible for the children from disadvantaged backgrounds. The welfare body concerned does not view this imbalance as a risk factor.

To support and assist the board a small, high-powered bureau has been set up – the FAO City Bureau – which is under the direct control of the board. As the secretariat of the board, this bureau is responsible for the preparation of policy and the implementation of the decisions of the FAO City Board. As the budget controller, the bureau arranges the facilitation within the criteria set by the board. The bureau is also responsible for the policy of the projects carried out with the FAO funds. There are regular consultations with the project leaders involved and sometimes also with participating schools and institutions. The bureau thus has a good overview of the whole, can point out overlaps and organise and stimulate co-operation. Activities can be continually brought into line with the demands of practical experience (that is to say the school). The bureau is also well equipped to fulfil an information function. The bureau commissions the production of information material and makes an active contribution to the organisation of communications activities such as conferences, round table discussions, network meetings, etc. The FAO also makes links with institutions in the field of artistic education, with immigrant organisations and with institutions in other large towns, and sometimes also in the European context.

The De Meeuw Foundation: The welfare body which occupies an intermediary function between institutions has a central position. De Meeuw not only forms a link between policy and practice (vertically between strategic level on the FAO board and the field in the projects), but also between different schools and other institutions (horizontally, mainly at the operational level, that is to say, senior management of schools and welfare institutions).

The De Meeuw foundation, which is largely subsidised by FAO, came into being on the basis of the decision of the municipality of Rotterdam to place the welfare element of the Educational Priority Policy under the direction of one board.

The objective of the foundation is "to prevent, combat or reduce the educational disadvantages of children from 0 to 18 years, which are caused by social, cultural and economic factors and to increase their possibilities for development". Since the achievement of the objectives can, according to the foundation, be measured by the success of the children in their school career, education also occupies the central place for this welfare body.

The core function of De Meeuw is "innovation". Thus the foundation does not supplement the existing regular welfare work, but stimulates innovations and improvements in the work. Many of the projects which are described under the FAO activities have been developed by De Meeuw; a large part of these activities are directed by a project co-ordinator who is employed by the De Meeuw foundation. De Meeuw also plays an important role in the implementation of projects in the regular programme of the school or other institutions.

De Meeuw actually forms the link between schools and welfare institutions. From various discussions it is apparent that right from the beginning of the existence of the FAO De Meeuw has stimulated an integrated approach. Thus one of the core tasks is seen as: bringing about the inclusion of Educational Priority Policy in the institutional policy of institutions for regular welfare work. In the period 1991-94 schools only slowly began to realise that they needed the expertise of another sector.

Case process

Support and resources

As has become apparent in the description of the realisation of the co-operation between municipality, education and welfare, the idea of co-operation received broad support. That applies both to the substantive and policy aspects as well as to the financial consequences. Education and welfare both saw the need for co-operation as far as content was concerned. Each needed the expertise of the other to be able to help solve the problems of and with the children. The well-intended attempts at co-operation in the 1980s proved, however, not to be enough. The municipality then realised that a clear strategy must be plotted from above, in such a way that institutions would no longer be able to evade it. Thus the present alderman* for education believes that dissatisfaction led people to start looking for new possibilities of optimising all the efforts of teachers, parents and institutions. For initiatives which came from the bottom there was a need of central direction by the municipality.

The co-operation was made possible financially because the municipality and education and welfare (the latter in so far as educational priority funds were concerned) were prepared to combine monetary resources. On condition that a covenant should be concluded between all those involved (the municipality and the school boards), it was agreed that part of the area funds should be put into a central fund: the Fund for the Reduction of Educational Disadvantages (FAO). At the same time the participating schools expressed their commitment to the substantive use of the funds they had received in the framework of the weighting regulation.

The FAO has a budget of about Gld 20 million at its disposal. In addition, the separate schools have about Gld 40 million to dispose of. The municipality added further money to the educational priority budget from its own resources. This involves a sum of Gld 100 million, which is being used to work on the educational disadvantages in Rotterdam schools.

Thus the financial resources which are at the disposal of the FAO are not primarily intended for stimulating an integrated approach, but because education needs welfare in the educational deprivation policy, an integrated approach is the ultimate effect. So the municipality did not provide the financial stimuli to further the process of integration. There was, however, a financial impulse which had a positive influence on promoting integrated policy.

Apart from the municipal subsidy for the FAO, the municipality also finances De Meeuw. These are extra funds, since the regular subsidy for welfare comes under the responsibility of the boroughs. This

---

* Alderman is an elected local politician who has been given by the local Council a portfolio such as education.

extra funding was necessary to ensure that De Meeuw would conform, as regards content, to the point of view of the FAO board. For that matter, De Meeuw only agreed to this if the welfare budget was earmarked for welfare efforts.

There was no pilot project in preparation for the collaboration. Both at the administrative and the practical level it was clear that an integrated approach was needed to solve the problems and that central direction could achieve this more effectively than nine educational priority areas with their own little kingdoms.

Since all schools are represented on the FAO board either directly or *via* a mandate, the whole educational field in Rotterdam feels involved in the FAO activities. There is also great willingness on the part of welfare to make a positive contribution to FAO projects. The De Meeuw foundation feels adequately represented on the board – especially on account of the quality of the board members in question. Other welfare institutions wish to co-operate above all in the interests of their clients. A number of immigrant organisations, however, felt themselves excluded when the FAO was set up. They feel themselves highly involved in the problems at the schools, since the percentage of immigrant children at educational priority schools is considerably higher than at other schools. Originally these organisations also wanted to participate in the FAO board. The municipality and education areas concluded that immigrant organisations could not bear executive responsibility for the educational funds which have been put into the FAO. But they considered good co-operation and communication with immigrant organisations of eminent importance. In the beginning there were sharp, often politically troublesome discussions with a large number of platforms for foreigners, but in the course of the past three years there has been a change in the attitude of most of the immigrant organisations and they also support the present arrangements. There are now consultations every five weeks for the necessary exchange of information. Moreover, projects are jointly programmed and carried out. Usually financial resources from immigrant organisations are used as well as the FAO funds.

By the beginning of 1991, most schools gave the FAO the benefit of the doubt. Many schools were – in view of the experience with the educational priority areas – somewhat sceptical. This did not make it any easier to achieve good communication. The willingness to take part slowly increased. That is apparent, for example, from the growing number of participants in mini-conferences and projects and from the great improvement in the quality of school work plans, which people are increasingly inclined to take seriously.

Obstacles

In all the discussions the foremost comment on the question of possible impediments in the process of co-operation was to emphasize how well it is going. At the strategic level there is a clear-cut and sound structure, at the operational level the collaboration is well-managed and in the field the workers are getting to know and appreciate each other better. Nevertheless obstacles do occur at all three levels. Some of them are slowly but surely being solved, while others will play a role in the future. Problems in this context are financial obstacles, uncertainties about the organisational structure and the differences in culture between education and welfare.

At the administrative level the point is put forward that the differences in the flow of budget funds of education and welfare could be a problem in the near future. Though the De Meeuw construction was worked out, and in spite of the feasibility in practice, the formal construction is certainly not optimal. It remains a compromise.

In August 1995, the "horizontal covenant concerning social renewal" expired. New agreements were made for the functioning of the central direction. The coherence and central direction of the FAO have been found feasible and productive at all levels. The metropolitan themes in particular call for municipal direction.

A problem which is always being brought up, especially in the field (but also at operational and administrative level), is the great difference in culture between education and welfare. This is the case with co-operation in multidisciplinary teams, in projects such as the Extended School Day, care for newcomers and reading promotion projects. At the same time it is precisely in such cases that there are indications that a great deal has already altered in the past three years. Many prejudices have been removed, mutual understanding has greatly increased and is still increasing. Before people started working together, there was a considerable lack of familiarity with each other's work and ignorance of each other's methods. When welfare embarked on a field survey in the framework of co-operation with a school, education reacted suspiciously. There was a feeling that welfare was entering educational territory and posing a threat. Moreover, teachers (in particular at a technical school) considered that young people at school had to learn a subject and that was that. The welfare workers' suggestions that attention be paid to matters which were not directly connected with education were considered superfluous and insubstantial. Furthermore the teachers quite often had the feeling that the contribution of the welfare workers was rather too non-committal. On the other hand the welfare workers often thought that the children were not appreciated at their full value at school. Because the educational achievements were all that counted, the social and emotional development of the children was lost sight of.

In the meantime collaboration has helped to adjust the images of both parties, but at school this applies more particularly to the school management team. Removing the prejudices of teachers still requires a good deal of attention. Nevertheless a definite change can be observed. Some of the reasons for this will be shown in the next paragraph on strategies.

Strategies in the co-operation process

At the different levels (policy, management, implementation) strategies which enable the collaboration at that level to progress as effectively as possible are used. At the same time there is a lively exchange between the different levels. According to all those interviewed this is a necessity and works in a satisfactory manner.

Strategic level: The municipal strategy to further stimulate the co-operation is initiatory, directive and supervisory. The national political level provides impulses for the effective alignment of all the activities which are undertaken in the framework of combating disadvantages. The municipality creates the conditions for the work to be picked up and elaborated on in practice. According to the alderman for education the field workers are fortunately very willing to get on with the job. He maintains that as a policy maker you are unbelievably dependent on what happens at the base. At the administrative level you determine what should ultimately happen, but a basis of support must exist in practice. The municipality then checks whether the agreed action has actually been taken.

The most important strategy in the co-operation between education and welfare at the administrative level has been to include an umbrella representative of welfare institutions on the FAO board. In fact the money concentrated in the fund represents educational resources, but alignment and co-operation with welfare institutions was necessary on account of the nature of the clients. Partly because these institutions were not financed centrally by the city, but by the boroughs, it was impossible to get a grip on the situation. De Meeuw, which does not itself have an implementation task, but a development function and an intermediary role, did manage to do so. This foundation is financed centrally by the city and could therefore be included on the FAO board. All the plans of De Meeuw are presented to the FAO board for approval. This brings about a commitment from both education and welfare (where it is a question of development and making conditions). The fact that the whole of the welfare field is not involved, but only an umbrella organisation without a mandate, in no way detracts from the success which FAO enjoys thanks to the compromise model, in which De Meeuw fulfils a central role.

The agreements which are made by the FAO board cannot be regarded as non-committal for the rest. The municipality sees to it – and that really applies to the whole board – that the agreements and co-operation produce results.

Operational level: At the managerial level (school management teams and project co-ordinators) the strategy to promote co-operation has principally been directed to translating policy into practical possibilities and creating conditions for collaboration in the implementation.

The most significant aspect of the last three years has been securing the trust of the schools. After a distrustful start, the schools started to believe in the FAO construction. Initially the school management teams were afraid that a situation would arise similar to that in the nine educational priority areas, in which the schools had the feeling that matters were being arranged over their heads. However, the FAO bureau has very forcefully and successfully propagated and put into practice the basic principle of the FAO policy, namely to observe the wishes and needs of schools in the combating of educational disadvantages.

An important point in the success of the FAO has above all been the clarity and the financial certainty. Objectives were set with which everybody could work and schools knew that if they once got additional resources at their disposal, then these were guaranteed for four years. The obligation on the school to specify how they would spend the extra money also had a positive effect. Not only has the quality of these plans improved, but the schools are handling the extra funds for reducing educational disadvantages in an increasingly purposeful manner. The same applies to the obligation to co-operate in evaluation. One of the strategies which turned out to be fruitful was the action "schools for schools", financed by the FAO. With the professional support of the FAO bureau small conferences are organised where schools and welfare institutions show each other effective methods and exchange experiences.

There have also been model projects in the framework of social renewal, to allow institutions to discover by experience that collaboration yields results. In this connection, the FAO has organised an extensive communications network, so that everybody who could possibly be involved in this could get to know the positive experiences of co-operative projects. Working conferences were organised where a large number of schools and institutions could become acquainted with these experiences. This knowledge could then spread steadily over the city.

The school management teams have in particular used strategies to combat the mutual mistrust between education and welfare. Thus in the schools the basis of support for developments in the collaboration is enlarged by continually involving different teachers in the co-operative projects. Account is then taken of whether a teacher has a positive attitude to a project and whether he or she can actually achieve something with it. The enthusiasm of a teacher for a co-operative project can prove contagious for other staff at the school.

The school management has not only to create a broad basis of support, but must also establish the right conditions for the implementation. It was evident in the Extended School Day project that the pace of the developments was highly dependent on the commitment of the school management team. If a head teacher backs the co-operation, he can also make his team enthusiastic. It is therefore an important strategy – at the strategic level – to ensure that the operational level is enthusiastic about a particular development.

One of the initiatives, which was developed in the framework of the Extended School Day to bring education and welfare closer to one another, is the publication of a news sheet. Representatives from education and welfare use it to explain to one another what exactly their work involves.

Field: At the implementation level the strategies are also principally directed to combating mistrust of each other's methods. The field workers make use of strategies which are passed down to them from the operational level (for instance the distribution and discussion of the information sheet mentioned in the previous paragraph). Apart from this, they also introduce their own strategies on the shop floor. For instance, in the Extended School Day project the fact that people got to know one another personally was very effective.

Before the project got under way there were all sorts of prejudices on the part of education with regard to input from welfare workers. The welfare workers also had prejudices about the educational sector. They claimed that people in education had no sympathy for the methods of welfare workers because it was too non-committal and only reached a small proportion of the target group, that the educational system allowed the children insufficient scope for development, was too highly structured and that too little emanated from the children themselves. However, through co-operating in the project representatives of education and welfare got to know and appreciate each other's work much better. Progress has been made to the extent that, on the basis of educational and welfare principles, a new methodology can now be developed, which is oriented to the situation in the neighbourhood.

In eliminating preconceived ideas and developing understanding of welfare work on the part of the educational sector, the fact that a welfare worker was present every day in the school played an especially important role. Because teachers got to know a child welfare worker and saw him or her at work, they were able to show understanding and appreciation at least of that particular worker. Nevertheless, scepticism remained about welfare workers in general.

The following stage is that the school learns that this one person is not an exception, but that the preconceived ideas about welfare work do not tally. For instance, at the beginning of the project the school teachers were worried that the specialised teacher, who did drama with the children in the framework of the Extended School Day, was just letting them run about doing nothing in particular. Through talking it over the teachers came to realise that the children were not "just running around" – the specialised teacher had got the children enthusiastic and indeed had them under control.

An ever increasing number of joint activities are now being undertaken by teachers from mainstream education and the specialised teachers from the project. Thus activities are organised based on *one* theme and presentations are organised jointly for the parents. That too strengthens the mutual ties and understanding of each other's work.

The same things are experienced in multidisciplinary teams, in which the members discuss the children with one another at the practical level. Through explaining each other's methods the prejudices could gradually disappear.

To summarise, both at the administrative, managerial and implementation level people are conscious of the fact that co-operation involves difficult processes, which cannot be rounded off from one day to the next. All those involved have found that co-operation takes time and that above all patience is needed. But everyone also says that the co-operation between education and welfare in the framework of educational disadvantages is on the right road and that people are very willing to continue on the adopted course.

Case product: results

In the preceding paragraphs repeated mention has been made of the fact that the co-operation between education and welfare within the FAO construction has led to good results.

The results stemming from this can be divided into two parts: on the one hand improvement of the co-operation at the administrative level, and on the other, practical collaboration between the institutions responsible for implementation. The latter directly benefits above all the client – children, young people and their parents from disadvantaged backgrounds. The former has principally led to greater effectiveness in the use of the available resources. Examples of both aspects are described below.

Strategic level: At the administrative level no negative consequences resulting from the co-operation between education and welfare have been reported. According to the alderman for education the attunement between different sectors, the integrated approach between education and welfare in Rotterdam has been very successful. The participation of welfare on the FAO board has played an important role in this. However, the FAO has above all succeeded in bringing about co-operation between the schools and between education and municipality. The school boards which take part directly or by mandate in the FAO board are placing more and more emphasis on the importance of education – in particular of educational disadvantage – in Rotterdam as a whole. Both the boards and the local authority are positive about the FAO construction.

In spite of the fact that welfare's position on the board is less strong than that of education (two representatives as against twelve from the educational sector), the welfare contribution on the board is quite considerable. That is due to the pragmatic attitude of the De Meeuw foundation, which has to maintain the contacts with welfare institutions although it has no mandate from them. According to the director of De Meeuw that is also due to the quality of the board members who sit on the FAO board on behalf of the welfare sector. They make a particularly big contribution both qualitatively and quantitatively.

A concrete result of the co-operative process is that an effectively functioning bureau (the FAO bureau) has been set up for much less money than the co-ordination of the less well-functioning educational priority areas. In general the schools are also satisfied about what is done in and from the FAO bureau. An important reason for this is that *via* the board they can exert direct influence on the policy decisions which are taken. Thanks to the central direction, the funds which are destined for education also end up at the schools.

The alderman, a board member and members of school management teams all confirm that there is definitely a basis of support for FAO. That applies particularly for the school boards and school management teams. Teachers and welfare institutions do sometimes need to be convinced of the importance of central direction for the fleshing out of the educational disadvantages policy. Comments from various quarters indicate that the contribution from the FAO as regards educational content, steering and motivation is widely appreciated. The FAO construction has created a culture of jointly seeking solutions on the basis of dialogue and mutual trust. All those involved are indeed in favour of the continuation of the FAO.

Operational level: An important result of the efforts of the school management teams at the operational level was set in motion by the requirements which were attached to the facilitation by the FAO: namely, evaluation and the submission of a school work plan. However, the evaluation is principally concerned with the learning achievement of the pupils and is therefore not relevant to this case study. What is important, is the way in which FAO schools handle the drawing up of the school work plans. The school work plans describe what the school intends to do with the extra funds to reduce the educational disadvantages. The result is – apart from a more systematic, verifiable approach – that the funds do actually benefit children at risk. It was often a question of projects which were carried out in the framework of a partnership with a welfare institution, such as school social work, care for newcomers, library in the class, etc.

Another striking result of the co-operation at the operational level is that schools (in particular school management teams) are now much more inclined to take notice of one another. According to one of the school heads, schools feel more involved with each other and want to get to know each other's products and methods. "It is now less a matter of isolated thinking and more a feeling of pulling together. Both for the schools amongst themselves and also in the co-operation with welfare that is one of the great achievements."

One of the ways in which schools and welfare institutions can get to know each other is during practical conferences. They can exchange experiences and are thus able to learn from one another. Indeed the conferences are attracting an ever increasing number of participants. However, the information which school management teams collect on these occasions still does not trickle through sufficiently to the implementation level, the teachers and welfare workers.

Implementation: The results at the implementation level are to be found in the projects which are carried out in the framework of a partnership between education and welfare. For details see the overview in the paragraph "Services provided". Further it can be said in general that the mutual distrust between schools and welfare bodies – based on differences in culture – has greatly decreased. Because the people involved got to know each other and each other's methods, they not only became more understanding, but also more appreciative. Co-workers on projects realise that they need each other's expertise and qualities and that these can complement one another very well.

Another important point is that the educational disadvantages of many children are increasingly seen as a joint responsibility of education and welfare. Through getting to know each other's work, there can gradually be a division of tasks between school and welfare work. Then it becomes possible for each of them to use their own qualities to the full. The alignment of the activities of both sectors means that the children have a much better idea of where they stand and where they can get answers to which questions or problems.

The great advantage of attunement of activities is that *one* pedagogic line can be drawn and that at least at school and in part of the free time there are more or less the same norms and values.

The projects, which already existed before they were facilitated by the FAO, could start to function more effectively. An example of this is school social work. According to one of the FAO board members, school social work is indeed one of the clearest and most successful examples of an integrated approach. A number of schools had gained experience with school social work, but were confronted with an extremely divided field of welfare institutions which worked from different socio-political groups. Since the creation of the FAO, the contacts of welfare and education have become a good deal clearer and more workable. A large number of welfare institutions were found willing on certain conditions to provide social work for schools which were facilitated by the FAO. There was also a need for social work in schools which did not yet have it, but they could not make the funds available. With the present regulation, that is now possible.

Since the facilitation through the FAO, almost all schools with a high proportion of disadvantaged pupils now have some form of social work at their disposal. This was a classic example of the fact that attunement between education and welfare could only be achieved if everything could be brought under one umbrella – the central direction of the FAO.

For concrete results at the client level some examples are given from the Extended School Day project and GIDS. One of the concrete results of that project is, that from a first evaluation it appears that children acquire more self-confidence through the extra-curricular activities. Amongst other things they learn to co-operate better with each other and realise that they can be good at something, for example sport or drama, activities which get less chance in the regular curriculum. That does not produce better learning achievement in the direct sense, but teachers note that children, who were very shy in class, become a little less withdrawn through the activities in the extended school day. This means that teachers can ask more of these pupils, which in the long run can improve the learning performance.

It is accepted that children benefit from different forms of learning; ordinary learning at school, but alongside that the experience-oriented activities of the community centre. In the joint projects it has been found that both ways of learning are useful and that they can very well complement one another.

Thanks to the co-operation of education and welfare in the GIDS project, it was possible to devote attention not only to the learning achievement, but also to the social and emotional development of the children. As the results of the project in getting newcomers in the neighbourhood familiar with their own environment were positive, the objectives of the project have now been included in the care-for-newcomers project within the school. The aims are:

- to get children successfully settled down through specific orientation to their living environment and school environment; and
- to provide an adequate frame of reference so as to be able to produce optimal learning achievement.

The activities of the De Meeuw foundation can also be counted among the concrete results of the co-operation within the FAO. Without the intermediary function of De Meeuw a great many of the projects directed to children at risk and in which both schools and welfare institutions were involved, would not have got under way.

De Meeuw was able to arrange, for example, the starting of certain projects under central direction, though in principle these projects were financed by boroughs. This meant that more schools and thus more children benefited from the facilities. The same applies to projects where the Ministry had granted an extra subsidy. Through the intermediary function, central direction was translated into practice so that practical results could be obtained.

Update and the future

In the future the co-operation between education and welfare in Rotterdam will be expanded. Particularly with regard to content. All those involved agreed that this type of approach is necessary to tackle the problems which confront children at risk. The central direction for Rotterdam, which is so important for this, was to be continued in the form of an FAO.

Through the experience which has been gained with joint projects, but also on account of the social problems of pupils with which schools are confronted, the willingness and the need to tackle them jointly have become ever greater.

The alderman for education has made it known that in the next few years attempts will be made at the strategic level to bring about shifts between the various sectors. Instead of assistance on an *ad hoc* basis, the aim will be to tackle the problems in the school on a structural basis. Thus in the future the school can become the place where peripatetic help can be given. To achieve this the schools will have to co-operate with the school advisory service, school social work and youth social assistance.

But it is not intended that there should be *one* organisational unit, one counter where clients would come with questions and problems. The proposal is that more adequate use should be made of the network of institutions surrounding schools, such as welfare bodies, youth social assistance, youth health care, etc.

The idea that an integrated approach will have to be further elaborated is also in the mind of the FAO board and the FAO bureau. In the draft policy plan for 1995-99 two of the six core themes advocate an integrated approach:

– care for newcomers in relation with extra-mural activities, directed to developing a covering network of collaborating schools in a neighbourhood; and

– further development of the broad school.

A discussion is already in progress in the FAO board over the broadening of the FAO objectives. It is true that the emphasis will remain on the improvement of educational achievement, but an increasing number of board members consider that the formation of partnerships between schools and bordering institutions should be stimulated. The school will have to become the pivot in an infrastructure, which is also directed to the care aspects in a community.

In this connection it is obvious that the regular welfare work will play a more prominent role and that the co-operation with school social work, socio-cultural work, youth social assistance and immigrant organisations amongst others will have to be stimulated. In the following covenant period more attention will certainly be paid to this.

Schools also point out that the FAO priority system is too restricted – social and emotional problems, for instance, are not covered. In particular, schools for pre-vocational education (VBO) will in the future be more than merely a learning institute. Schools must look for partners who can help to realise this broader design, such as youth care, socio-cultural work, libraries, institutions for non-formal education in the cultural, artistic or sports realm, trade and industry, labour services and the police and the judicial authorities. There are various schools where this is already in progress in the form of projects and those concerned would like to see this included in mainstream education.

People at all levels (strategic, operational and implementation) are convinced of the necessity of cutting across the boundaries of their own sector and as far as content is concerned, they now know how to find one another.

FAO – What has happened since?

By the time the FAO convenant had to be renewed, a debate had commenced in the Netherlands about new laws and regulations governing local educational policies. Municipal authorities were to be given wider powers, including the task of drafting a local educational policy plan in consultation with the school boards. Up to that time, school boards had had to deal mainly with the Ministry of Education, while the main tasks of the municipal authorities had been to enforce compulsory school attendance and to allocate state funds to schools in accordance with national regulations. In this new political context, it was decided to introduce a number of administrative changes. FAO was not continued in its existing form. In its place, the Rotterdam Education Forum was established in the summer of 1996. In this new forum, all schools were represented, whereas in FAO only educational priority schools had participated. Also, in the past, funds had been controlled by the FAO board; now all finances were to be controlled by the municipal executive. As a consequence, the FAO bureau was closed down and its staff were transferred to the city's Education Department. In the past, schools had been closely involved in each step of the policy process (preparation, decision-making, implementation, evaluation); now, schools had to find a new position for themselves alongside the municipal executive. This re-orientation took quite some time. The work of FAO was continued along much the same lines: the attempt to alleviate the problems of children at risk by an integrated approach with a basis in educational practice was continued. The extended school day experiment was taken a step further and developed into the concept of the "broad school" (a school that offers a range of programmes outside school hours), which is now receiving much attention in Rotterdam. In 1995, a discussion paper about this concept was given the title of an African saying (used more often in an educational context): it takes a whole village to raise a child. Thus, co-operation between education and welfare was strengthened and extended to other sectors. As early as November 1995, a municipal project organisation was established to further the development of an integral youth policy. The broad school has also been given a place within this organisation. Other policy sectors have responded with enthusiasm to the initiatives that were taken in order to enhance the integration of various areas of policy. All sectors of municipal policy are now working together, in particular: education, health care, welfare, social affairs, employment and recreation. The concept of the broad school makes it possible for schools to develop into community centres offering a range of services besides traditional educational programmes. With hindsight one could say that FAO was a phase in a process leading towards an integral approach in policy and practice – a process that is still going on in Rotterdam.

CONCLUSION AND DISCUSSION

In this final section of this case study, we look back on the integrative efforts in Emmen and Rotterdam and evaluate them in a way which will enable other locations in the Netherlands and abroad to profit from their work. For this purpose, two lines of approach were presented in the introduction: 1) that of the case study methodology which is used in the OECD study; and 2) that of the management functions which can be fulfilled by a municipality. The first line of approach can be strengthened by combining it with success and failure factors from the evaluation literature. On the basis of findings in both cases, the second line of approach needs to be expanded to include the educational priority network, which alongside the municipality has been found to be of such great importance.

First line of approach: OECD methodology and factors for success and failure

The OECD study defines services integration in such a way that it can be seen from two aspects:
– multi-disciplinary co-operation directed to the decisions *concerning individual children and their families*; and
– inter-agency co-ordination that focuses on decisions concerning *entire programmes* (emphasis added).

In Emmen the second form of integrated services is practised. On the one hand the agencies, such as the municipality, Thuiszorg Drenthe, SKGE/Opmaat and the Educational Priority Foundation took a co-ordinated decision at the strategic level to opt for the MOVE Programme. On the other hand, with regard to the application of certain programmes for individual clients, co-ordination takes place at operational and field level *via* the contact mother and the programme leader of MOVE. However, the co-ordination is not of a multi-disciplinary nature: it is a question of "linking up" the demand and needs of clients and the existing programmes on offer. Indeed, in drawing up an integrated packet of services in the form of project/programmes there was only inter-agency co-ordination concerning programmes. Nevertheless, this does not alter the fact that ultimately one of the intentions of MOVE is to promote an individual approach *via* multidisciplinary co-operation between services such as schools, preschool playgroups, home help and socio-cultural work. In other words, the first form of integrated services will also be further developed. This already sometimes occurs, for instance when the content of the programme of a play class is determined and organised jointly by the preschool playgroup and primary education, or when there are multi-disciplinary discussions on individual cases in the neighbourhood networks for youth services.

In Rotterdam the second form of integrated services is to be found on the strategic level. The municipalities, the school boards and one welfare institution have formed the urban Fund for the Reduction of Educational Disadvantages (FAO), which as we have seen, has now a wider brief as the Rotterdam Education Forum. The board of FAO has been responsible for the educational deprivation policy and for combating educational disadvantage. Education occupied a more important position herein than welfare. On account of the good co-operation in practice, welfare had an important voice in the decision-making.

At the field level on the other hand it is a question of the first form of integrated services. In projects, representatives of schools and welfare institutions offer children and parents joint services. This applies in particular to the school social work and the Extended School Day project.

It was agreed that the OECD Study would be based on the CIPP Model (Context, Input, Process, Product) and that as well as looking at three organisational levels, the clients should also be subject to scrutiny. The model and the levels can be placed in a matrix, which makes it possible to judge the cases in summarised form. This judgement can be reinforced by making use of an assessment framework with elements which evaluation research has shown to be influential. In filling in the matrix for the two cases investigated, we have chosen to make use of success and failure factors from the literature. In the evaluation literature on attempts at co-operation, networking and integration, four groups of factors are described, which influence the extent to which these attempts are successful. These are: peripheral conditions, organisational, specifically institutional and specifically personal factors.

A recent Dutch study on intersectoral co-operation concerning youth offers an extensive check list of such success and failure factors (Research voor Beleid, 1994, p. 55), which we include here as Table 4.

We have used this list of factors especially to help us to highlight the strong, but also some of the weak aspects of our cases. Success factors can after all become failure factors if certain conditions either are not, or are not sufficiently, fulfilled. The result of the evaluation is summarised in Tables 5 and 6. In these tables we use the CIPP model and the levels, while we have arranged the text according to the four types of factors.

Emmen

The general conclusions on MOVE in Emmen are contained in the section on Emmen entitled "Case product". This shows the part played by success and failure factors in obtaining results. Following on from Table 5, it may be remarked that MOVE is in a number of respects still in the development stage and with regard to some others already in the implementation stage.

Peripheral conditions: New ideas often cost money, but experience in Emmen has shown that a great deal can alter by shifting financial resources. One must be prepared to take a critical look as to whether certain expenditure is still justified or whether different deployment would be of more benefit to the objectives in mind. In this way Emmen managed to achieve a concentration of funds.

The initiators in Emmen gave the impression that they were aware of factors such as network costs and excessive job loads, and that they took measures which could prevent such factors from leading to failure. There were no laws and regulations which hampered this co-operation.

Organisational factors: As regards organisation in MOVE, the results are positive. The co-ordination at the strategic level was in the hands of people who knew each other well and who already had a good work relationship. They were capable of involving other institutions in MOVE and of setting up and expanding a firm organisational structure for this project. This was also helped by the fact that the project had a good substantive foundation, and that a great deal of energy had gone into forming a broad basis. In the operational field the co-ordination was in the hands of a programme leader described as forceful, while work was carried out very systematically at all levels.

In comparison with the other organisational factors, the client protection and embedding in the participating institutions formed the weaker links in establishing and implementing the co-operation. Consequences stemming from a planned shift in task description for the contact mother will become

Table 4. **Success and failure factors: an overview**

Network stage	Type of factor	Success factors	Failure factors
Development stage	Peripheral conditions	• subsidy • co-operation within working hours	• network costs • legislation and regulations • co-operation outside working hours • too heavy job load for field worker
	Organisational	• co-ordinator • good substantive underpinning • clear, realistic objectives • clear-cut phasing • co-operation at implementation level	• ambiguous, non realistic objectives • co-operation at policy level
	Institutional	• readiness of institution to invest	• little readiness of institution to invest • institutional interests weigh heavily
	Personal	• well motivated field workers • readiness to invest by field workers • mutual respect • familiarity with other disciplines	• unmotivated field workers • little readiness to invest by field workers • personal antipathy • mistrust, lack of respect • different visions, opinions methods
Implementation stage	Peripheral conditions	• subsidy • co-operation within working hours	• network costs • legislation and regulations • co-operation outside working hours • too heavy job load for field workers
	Organisational	• co-ordinator • co-operation at field level, embedded in organisation • detailed plan of campaign • continuity; structural contact • clear-cut work agreements, good division of tasks • concrete activities	• no plan of campaign • no continuity • vague work agreement • client protection
	Institutional	• readiness to invest by institution	• little readiness to invest by institution • institutional interests weigh heavily
	Personal	• well motivated field workers • readiness to invest by field workers • mutual respect • familiarity with other disciplines • high expected added value	• unmotivated field workers • little readiness to invest by field workers • personal antipathy • mistrust, lack of respect • different visions, opinions and methods • low expected added value
Consolidation stage	Peripheral conditions	• subsidy • co-operation within working hours	• network costs • co-operation outside working hours • too heavy job load for field worker
	Organisational	• co-operation embedded in organisation	• co-operation at field level
	Institutional	• readiness to invest by institution	• little readiness to invest by institution
	Personal	• well motivated field workers • readiness by field workers to invest • mutual respect • familiarity with other disciplines	• unmotivated field workers • little readiness by field workers to invest • personal antipathy • mistrust, lack of respect • different visions, opinions, methods
	Added value	• added value determined is high	• added value determined is low

Source: Research voor Beleid, 1994.

evident as practical experience is gained with this function and when the first measurements of results have been made.

Specifically institutional factors: The provision of more coherent or integrated services calls for the recognition by those involved that the problems of children and youth at risk and their families cannot be solved by one institution alone. In Emmen, the initiators of MOVE also realised that their attempt to achieve a climate in which education and welfare could reinforce one another must be based on the idea that neither the schools nor welfare institutions could do it alone.

Table 5. **Preschool educational structures: success and failure factors of MOVE as examples of good practice**

	Context	Input	Process	Product

Strategic level
– senior management consultations with covenant partners
– project management
	– basis of support
	  • political
	  • content (via work group)
		– support
		– readiness to co-operate
		– decision to subsidise and concentrate flow of funds
			– co-operation in senior management consultations and project management
			– readiness to invest
			– good substantive underpinning based on existing expertise
			– clear-cut, realistic objectives
			– clear phasing
			– confidence in result of effort
				– covenant
				– co-operation in senior management consultations and in project management
				– concentration of flow of funds

Operational level – programme management	– basis of support	– support – co-operation – subsidy – effort, commitment and flexibility of parties – quality of programme leader *Failure factors:* – getting everyone on one line and attuning tasks and responsibilities took a long time	– co-operation between parties – subsidy – readiness to invest – motivation – clear-cut plan of campaign (objectives, phasing, etc.) – confidence in result	– co-operation – cohesion between content, policy, organisation and (evaluation) research – new methods developed
Field level – contact mothers and neighbourhood mothers – institutions	– basis of support *Failure factors:* – scepticism at neighbourhood level	– support – co-operation – subsidy – "tempt and demand" strategy: offer to and demand from parties	– alderman makes appearance at field level – co-operation with help of contact mothers – subsidy – readiness to invest – motivation – clear-cut implementation plan and plans per neighbourhood – clear work agreements – sound division of tasks – concrete activities – dare to look and step beyond own boundaries – confidence in result	– co-operation under the direction of programme leader with help of contact mothers – input from all institutions

Client
– children
– parents
	– parents who make no use of service offered	– need of more attention to parents' own questions and needs
		– importance of participation in programmes by parents and children
			– stage of contact with parents has still to get going
			  • objective is: teach parents and let them experience that they themselves are important and that it is a question of their choices
			  • strategy: "tempt and demand"
				– MOVE project has not yet reached effects stage
				  • objective is: more cohesion in services on offer and more co-operation in offering them, in short more integrated services and better attuned to the demand

Table 6. **School phase: success and failure factors of FAO as examples of good practice**

	Context	Input	Process	Product
Strategic level – FAO board and FAO bureau	– basis of support: readiness to co-operate on part of municipality, school boards and OVG *Failure factors:* – ineffective application of OVG subsidy – laws and regulations are not failure factors, but on contrary success factors	– subsidy: *i.e.* concentration of the available subsidies in one fund: FAO – readiness to invest: transfer of funds from schools to the joint fund – support and co-operation: municipality, school boards and one welfare body in FAO-board *Failure factors:* – co-operation at policy level (problems with top-down approach)	– subsidy and readiness to invest: concentration of financial resources in FAO – co-operation in FAO-board – co-ordinator: FAO bureau – good substantive underpinning: FAO policy plans – clear, realistic objectives: FAO – clear-cut phasing	– co-operation in FAO board: municipality, school boards, welfare body – subsidy: budget management by FAO bureau *Failure factors:* – unbalanced management situation (position of De Meeuw)
Operational level – school management team – project management team	– basis of support: insight into necessity of co-operation between schools and welfare bodies	– readiness to co-operate within own sector and outside – subsidy: readiness to transfer responsibility for part of budget to FAO	– co-ordinators: school management team and project co-ordinators – objectives aligned to own school situation – clear-cut plans of campaign per project – mutual respect – good motivation	– co-ordination in FAO-bureau – clear phasing – clear-cut plan of campaign: four-track policy (facilitation, exchange of practical experience, evaluation, projects)
Field – co-operative projects	*Failure factors:* – no basis of support on account of differences in culture	*Failure factors:* – lack of motivation in field workers – mistrust, lack of respect – different visions, opinions, methods – low expected added value	– clear, realistic objectives: project plans on basis of FAO objectives – growing readiness from various sectors to co-operate in projects	– co-operation in projects (4th track) – good motivation field workers – readiness by workers to invest – growing familiarity with other disciplines – co-operation embedded in organisation (De Meeuw) – high expected added value *Failure factors:* – job load to heavy in various projects
Client level – pupils and parents	– needs of one talking point: parents came to the school with their general problems			

This applies, moreover, not only to institutions, but also to projects. There have been many (national) projects which were only directed towards education or to the situation at home. In Emmen on the other hand the choice was made for a two-track policy of family-oriented and institution-oriented projects and services. Centre-oriented policy is directed to stimulating the development of young children, for example in preschool playgroup, crèche, or school. Family-oriented policy is directed to increasing the parents' possibilities of bringing up their children, to empowerment. Strengthening these two policy fields calls for a great deal of attunement, consultation and the goodwill of the participants, if only because the number of institutions concerned in providing institution-oriented and family-oriented services is so large. In Emmen too, those involved in the MOVE project have come up against institutions with their own vested interests. Ultimately, however, the institutions concerned were prepared to invest in MOVE.

Specifically personal factors: In co-operation between sectors such as education and welfare a great deal is asked of the professionalism of the staff at all levels. This too was the conviction in Emmen. For example, the leader of the preschool playgroup was at least expected to be able to recognise and refer the presence of developmental delay; and a teacher should essentially be expert in reporting and (to some extent) diagnosing educational disadvantage.

Policy workers are often in agreement on the content and necessity of integrated policy, but at the management level institutional interests come into the picture. The experience in Emmen is that co-operation and the achievement of integration at all levels calls for people whose heart is in the project, people who will really make an effort to achieve integrated policy and make it work on the ground. There must be a broad foundation of support. The various levels cannot do without one another. In a process of change it is important that all levels are – and remain – well informed, and that all those involved regard one another as full partners.

In contacts during the study it was apparent that those involved at various levels were highly motivated and prepared to commit themselves; at the field level, for instance, this was evident among the participants in the discussion at the preschool playgroup. With regard to mutual respect it is only possible to report (positively) on those interviewed; as far as familiarity with other disciplines is concerned, not enough data have been collected to make any pronouncement.

Rotterdam

For general conclusions on the FAO see the section on Rotterdam entitled "Case product" which contains the results of the co-operation between education and welfare work. As mentioned earlier, what matters here are the factors which were important in achieving the results. Following on from Table 6 it should be noted that the FAO is in the consolidation stage, but that factors from earlier stages will also be discussed here.

Peripheral conditions: The peripheral conditions for co-operation within the FAO are favourable, but all those involved have had to work hard to achieve this.

The policy (including decentralisation, Educational Priority Policy and social renewal) of both national and local authorities gave a considerable stimulus to the development. The municipality and the school boards managed to create a clear-cut financial situation and to set up a workable organisational structure.

Furthermore, it should be noted that before the FAO got under way, the factors concerned with peripheral conditions were not really very favourable at all. There were more failure than success factors. Yet it is precisely the factors which could lead to the failure of the co-operation, which have led to success. The ineffective way in which the OVG funds were used ultimately led to a strong desire, on both the strategic and the operational level, to combine the financial sources in the FAO and set up a clear-cut organisational structure.

The support for the co-operation is particularly strong on the part of the municipality and the school boards. The municipality was prepared to deploy extra funds to ensure the success of the collaboration and the schools and school boards were prepared to transfer part of their subsidy to the FAO.

One of the serious failure factors is still the compromise model with its unbalanced managerial situation. Education has a greater say in the matter than welfare, but in practice the situation has remained productive through the constructive attitude of those involved. In this context financial obstacles formed by differences in budgetary flow also play a part. The funds come from different subsidisers, national and local authorities for education and boroughs for welfare work.

At the strategic and operational level, the co-operation between education and welfare work is considered of such importance that care is taken to provide good peripheral conditions for the workers in the field. The co-operation at the implementation level takes place in projects, which means that it is precisely the co-operation which occupies the central position in the activities. One of the failure factors at the field level is the heavy job load.

Organisational factors: In the organisational field, mainly success factors are to be reported. At the strategic level there is a clear and sturdy structure, at the operational level the co-operation is well directed and the different agencies collaborate successfully in the projects. In this connection the central position of the FAO bureau with a capable co-ordinator has been important. The FAO bureau was able to achieve cohesion and a certain consensus in the integrated projects. Very important factors here were joint substantive underpinning, clear objectives and tasks, resulting in an agreement and clear policy plans.

Clear objectives and tasks were also found to be of importance at the field level. The common culture within the FAO of setting out plans (school work plans and project plans) as clearly and concretely as possible has had a positive influence on the way in which the integrated projects progressed.

The extent to which these new arrangements need to become part of the structure and regular functioning of the organisation to be successful differs for each project. The school social work is well embedded in the schools and the same applies to the contacts with welfare bodies other than those which deal with social work. A project such as the Broad School, as the sequel to the Extended School Day, still has to win itself a place in the school.

Continuity is also well regulated in the school social work, while that still remains to be seen in the Broad School project.

Taken across the board, the FAO activities are well anchored in the totality of activities directed towards diminishing the deprivation problems in the city of Rotterdam.

Specifically institutional factors: One of the most important success factors of the co-operation within the FAO is the common interest of all those involved. After the major discussions had taken place and the greatest disagreements resolved, the policy of most schools was constructive co-operation. Only a few schools were not – at their own request – resourced for activities for disadvantaged pupils.

It was also important that institutions – and that applies in particular to schools – were prepared to invest time, money and human resources in the co-operation.

One of the failure factors to be noted is the great difference in the culture of education and that of welfare. That was why institutions were initially reluctant about co-operation within one project. Through the strong motivation at all levels to nevertheless get something going in a co-operative effort, that particular failure factor has not really posed a threat. Because the preconceived ideas about each other's methods are disappearing, people have a more positive attitude to one another and that can only benefit the client.

Specifically personal factors: Both at the strategic level and also at the operational and field level the personal motivation is exceptionally strong, not only to participate in the co-operation, but also to make an extra investment in it, be it in time or money. Real involvement was evident in the discussions at every level; people were enthusiastic about what had been set in motion and on the other hand they were concerned about the obstacles. They were indeed prepared to do everything possible to get rid of them.

At the strategic level personal preferences were shown, but these were expressed in more general terms. At the operational level, and more evidently at the field level, personal preferences were shown to a greater extent. At the start of the co-operation there was a degree of resistance in schools to collaboration with welfare. And both in education and in welfare bodies misunderstandings and incomprehension existed with regard to methods. Because of unfamiliarity with each other, there was disagreement about the other party's supposed views on how to deal with groups at risk. Through getting to know one another and each other's methods mutual trust and respect grew up. The personal involvement to make a contribution to the co-operation developed and even led to enthusiasm. The school management team of *De Beukelburg* and field workers of the Extended School Day project are examples of this.

Second line of approach: municipal management and educational priority network

In both locations the municipal management had largely been transferred to a co-ordination point, in which the educational priority area occupies an important place.

In Emmen the Educational Priority Bureau plays a central role. The Bureau comes under the Foundation for Educational Priority in Drenthe, in which all those concerned participate (including educational and welfare bodies as well as the municipality). The municipality has indicated that in the preschool field it sees a major role for (the Bureau of) the Foundation as regards innovation and co-ordination. Other bodies should be given more responsibility for implementation. In the case of MOVE the Bureau seems in practice to have a mainly pioneering role; apart from co-ordination the Bureau also provides an innovative impulse. Thus the role of the Bureau in the development process weighs heavier than that of the covenant partners Thuiszorg Drenthe and SKGE/Opmaat. The Bureau and the municipality often act as joint managers, for example in the expansion of MOVE Emmen to MOVE Drenthe.

In Rotterdam the municipality has transferred the management to the FAO, in which education and a welfare body are represented, as well as the municipality itself. In the day-to-day running much of the management work is delegated to the FAO Bureau.

That is why we do not only look at the municipality itself in connection with the management functions, but also at the co-ordination point in which the municipality participates.

Emmen

The managerial role of the municipality in Emmen constituted something of a problem, at least as regards the context of national and provincial policy within which this role had to be played. In the first place a municipality does not have a grip on all policy fields, as for example youth services, where the province develops the policy and distributes the funds. Another point is that a municipality which wants to pursue local policy is confronted with an enormous choice of programmes from local, regional and provincial bodies as well as from the national authorities. In a medium-sized municipality such as Emmen the scale is not large enough to introduce, for example, all the projects offered by the Ministry of Health, Welfare and Sport. A choice has to be made for a programme such as *Opstapje*, *Opstap* or *Klimrek* (a home intervention programme to help mother and child, aged 1 to 2 years, play and learn together), for which the number of families is one of the criteria for participation. Local problems are, however, extremely diverse and rather call for a little bit of *Opstap* or a little bit of *Klimrek*, since the number of families qualifying for the project does not always reach the required minimum. Thus integrated policy at the local level requires a great deal of consultation, attunement and agreement with the authorities at the provincial and national level.

Where it is a question of the management in the preschool realm within the municipality of Emmen, there is very close co-operation between the municipality and the Educational Priority Bureau. An important factor here is that there are also excellent person-to-person relations, particularly at strategic level. Partly on this account co-ordination and attunement can be swiftly and flexibly realised.

In the case of MOVE the municipality and the Educational Priority Bureau made use of existing networks and followed that up with the development of their own network and organisational structure. In the newly developed network the project management of MOVE, in which the municipality and the Bureau are also represented, was given a central position.

Following on from the general observation that the municipality and Bureau mostly co-manage where MOVE is concerned, the following more specific remarks can be made with regard to some of the six different management functions:

- Middleman in the process: municipality and the Bureau stimulate participation by institutions concerned and carry on consultations with them.

- External management: municipality and Bureau together develop preschool policy regarding MOVE, but also involve other institutions (see for example recommendation from the Working Group on Educational Support).

- Internal management: within the municipality the municipality naturally does that itself, the alderman's basic principle is that "problems which have arisen integrally should also be dealt with integrally"; within MOVE the Bureau again plays a role.

- Regional management: the introduction and supervision of MOVE in the province of Drenthe is also a joint activity of the municipality of Emmen and the Educational Priority Bureau whereby use is made of contacts within the existing provincial networks.

Rotterdam

It is essential for the success of the FAO construction that the central direction of the policy in the framework of educational priority and the combating of educational disadvantages is delegated to the board of the FAO. The municipality, education and welfare participate in the board. Almost all OVB schools in Rotterdam are directly represented or represented by mandate and one welfare foundation, which was specially established for the co-operation construction, sits on the board. The De Meeuw foundation maintains pragmatic contacts with other welfare bodies but does not represent them.

The power relation between municipality and education has been laid down in a covenant in a pragmatic, workable manner. The FAO board is free to determine policy, but must account for it to the town council of Rotterdam (and thereby according to an agreement also to the Ministry of Education). The steering group is formed by a municipal committee, that is to say that the town council has empowered the committee. This committee must also account to the town council.

The fact that the FAO board is responsible for the central direction of the educational deprivation policy, makes it possible for so many projects, including integrated projects for education and welfare, to get off the ground. If there were no central direction, a great deal of time and energy would be lost in trying to get matters aligned. For example, consultations with all the boroughs would take up a great deal of time. The schools do not need to carry on all the discussions with the authorities and other bodies, for they have given the FAO board a mandate to act for them in this respect.

Of the six management functions previously mentioned, that of middleman deserves special mention in the process of co-operation. This function is fulfilled by the FAO board, supported by the FAO bureau, at policy level. Moreover, it is most important that all those involved have confidence in both the FAO board and the FAO bureau. De Meeuw also has a middleman function. In the first place because it forms the link between policy and practice; on the authority of the FAO board De Meeuw develops, co-ordinates and implements projects. In the second place De Meeuw forms the link between education and welfare. There too the intermediary role of De Meeuw is not to be underestimated. Since 1996, the function of FAO has essentially been extended in a different administrative structure, namely the Rotterdam Education Form.

In conclusion

The two lines of approach, which have been used here to indicate the strong and weak sides of the analysed examples of good practice, would seem to be very suitable for municipalities which want to improve their activities for youngsters at risk in the direction of more cohesion and integration. The list of success and failure factors can be used by these municipalities as a checklist for analysing the state of affairs in their own municipality and for action points for improvement. The CIPP model and the distinction between strategic, operational and field level can be helpful in setting up and analysing the process of improvement. This can be based on the situation, questions and needs at client level, as well as on the client's possibilities.

At the same time the various different roles in the local management can facilitate a choice for ones own role, activities and key partners.

In this way municipalities receive the tools to go their own way in providing services in a more effective, efficient and above all, more coherent or more integral manner for groups at risk. The experiences in Emmen and Rotterdam are thereby intended as examples, no more and no less. The analysis of these experiences can give other municipalities ideas and alert them to opportunities and dangers. Our expectation is that the examples of good practice and the instruments mentioned will facilitate the process in other municipalities which, proceeding on the basis of their own situation, wishes and potential, will take steps towards integrated services for children and youth at risk and their families.

Annex

ABBREVIATIONS

AMW	Social work
BOA	Out-of-School Care for non-Native Speakers
Boddaert	Out-of-School Care for Children at Risk
CERI	Centre for Educational Research and Innovation
CIPP	Context, Input, Process, Product
FAO	Fund for the Reduction of Educational Disadvantages
GGD	See GG and GD
GG&GD	Municipal Medical and Health Service
HBO	Higher Professional Education
ISEO	Institute for Sociological and Economic Research of the Erasmus University Rotterdam
INSTAPJE	A programme teaching parents to foster the development of children 0-2 years.
KLIMREK	A home intervention programme to help mother and child (1-2 years old) to play and learn together.
LBO	Junior Vocational Education
MBO	Senior Secondary Vocational Education
MOVE	Model for the Development of Policy and Activities in the Field of Preschool Education
NIZW	National Institute for Care and Welfare
OCW	Ministry of Education, Culture and Science
O&W	Ministry of Education and Science
OPSTAP	Fostering language and cognitive development as well as social-emotional development for 4-6 year-olds
OPSTAPJE	Support for parents of preschool children 2-4 years
OVB	Educational Priority Policy
OVG	Educational Priority Area
RIAGG	Regional Institute for Outpatient Mental Health Care
S&O	Centre for Information on Play Activities and Parenting
SARDES	Organisation for Research, Development and Advice in the Educational Sector
SES	Socio-economic Status
SKGE	Foundation for Socio-cultural Work Municipality of Emmen
VBO	Pre-vocational Education
VNG	Association of Netherlands Municipalities
VWS	Ministry of Health, Welfare and Sport
WVC	Ministry of Welfare, Health and Cultural Affairs

LIST OF INTERVIEWEES

For the preschool case study

– D. van de Bout, co-ordinator of the Drenthe Educational Priority Area

– Y. Boxem, educational advisor for the age group 0-7 years for the municipality of Emmen

– J. van Donk, head Learning and Care sector, municipality of Emmen

– R. Fijen, parent of child at Nieuw Dordrecht preschool playgroup

– T. de Graaf, board member at Nieuw Dordrecht preschool playgroup and parent of a toddler

– T. Lambers, leader of Nieuw Dordrecht preschool playgroup and "Fun with Books" supervisor

– J. Muskee, parent of child at Nieuw Dordrecht preschool playgroup

– P. Reuver, alderman for education, municipality of Emmen

– J. van de Waarsenburg, staff member Drenthe Educational Priority Area, responsible among other things for co-ordination and innovation in the preschool field

For the school case study

– Th. Magito, co-ordinator City Fund for Reduction of Educational Disadvantages Rotterdam (FAO)

– J. Kriens, policy officer FAO bureau

– J.T.C.M den Oudendammer, alderman for Education, Sport and Recreation, Social Services (Urban Welfare Facilities) of the municipality of Rotterdam

– F. van der Matten, director of Foundation De Meeuw

– C. Langstraat, director Protestant Educational Services Foundation, Rotterdam (DCO)

– R. Schouten, director, De Beukelburg, VBO school

– W.D. Greeven, member senior management team of De Beukelburg

– M. Blok, child welfare officer Foundation for Welfare in Afrikaanderwijk

– P. Dubbeldam, Foundation De Meeuw, project leader Extended School Day

REFERENCES

English language publications

EURYDICE (1994), *Preschool and Primary Education in the European Union*, Brussels.

GEELEN, H., VAN UNEN, A. and WALRAVEN, G. (in coll. with C. Buis) (1994), *Services Integration for Children and Youth at Risk: A country report for the Organisation for Economic Co-operation and Development*, SARDES, The Hague.

KLOPROGGE, J., MULDER, G., WALRAVEN, G. and Van der WERF, G. (1995), *Developments in the Dutch Educational Priority Policy: Expectations and Reality Are Slowly Converging*, SVO, The Hague.

MINISTRY OF WELFARE, HEALTH AND CULTURE AFFAIRS (1993), *Youth Deserves a Future*, Government memorandum on inter-sectoral youth policy summarised.

STICHTING EXIS (1994), *Being Young in the Netherlands: An Introduction to Youth, Youth Services and Facilities, and Youth Policy*.

VEENMAN, J. et al. (1995), *Best Practices: Transition from School to Work for Youth at Risk in the Netherlands*, ISEO, Rotterdam.

VOLPE, R. (1996), "The CIPP model and the case study approach", in OECD (1996), *Successful Services for our Children and Families at Risk*, Paris.

VAN DER WERF, M.P.C. (1995), *The Educational Priority Policy in the Netherlands: Content, Implementation and Outcomes*, GION, Groningen.

WOTHERSPOON, T. and JUNGBLUTH, P. (1995), *Multicultural Education in a Changing Global Economy, Canada and the Netherlands*, Waxman, Munster/New York.

Dutch language publications

General

JACOBS, E. et al. (1995), *Lokaal Onderwijsbeleid En Onderwijsverzorging*, SAC, Utrecht.

KLOPROGGE, J. et al. (ed.) (1995), *Integraal Op Schaal: Een Handreiking Voor Gemeentelijk Educatief Beleid*, SARDES, The Hague.

MINISTERIE VAN BINNENLANDSE ZAKEN (1995), *Veiligheidsbeleid 1995-1998: Veiligheid Door Samenwerking*, The Hague.

MINISTERIE VAN ONDERWIJS EN WETENSCHAPPEN (1995), *Een Impuls Voor Het Basisonderwijs*, Zoetermeer.

MINISTERIE VAN VOLKSGEZONDHEID (1995), *Welzijn en Sport/Ministerie van Justitie, Rijksplan jeugdhulpverlening 1995-1998*, Rijswijk.

MINISTERIE VAN VOLKSGEZONDHEID (1995), *Welzijn en Sport/Ministerie van Onderwijs, Cultuur en Wetenschappen*, Beleidsreactie Commissie voorschoolse educatie, Zoetermeer.

MINISTERIE VAN VOLKSGEZONDHEID, WELZIJN EN SPORT (1995), *Perspectief voor Jeugdigen, Kansen Voor Gemeenten: Lokaal Preventief Jeugdbeleid*, Rijswijk.

MINISTERIE VAN VOLKSGEZONDHEID, WELZIJN EN SPORT/MINISTERIE VAN JUSTITIE/MINISTERIE VAN ONDERWIJS, CULTUUR EN WETENSCHAPPEN (1995), *Preventieve En Curatieve Jeugdzorg: Beleidskader 1996-1999*, Rijswijk.

MINISTERIE VAN WELZIJN, VOLKSGEZONDHEID EN CULTUUR/MINISTERIE VAN ONDERWIJS EN WETENSCHAPPEN (1994), *Allochtone Kleuters Meer Aandacht*, Advies van de Commissie (voor)schoolse Educatie, Rijswijk.

MINISTERIE VAN WELZIJN, VOLKSGEZONDHEID EN CULTUUR (1993), *Jeugd Verdient De Toekomst: Nota Inter-sectoraal Jeugdbeleid*, Rijswijk.

MINISTERIE VAN WELZIJN, VOLKSGEZONDHEID EN CULTUUR (1994), *Perspectief Voor Jeugd En Beleid: Debatten Rond Jeugd Verdient De Toekomst,* Rijswijk.

MINISTERIE VAN WELZIJN, VOLKSGEZONDHEID EN CULTUUR/MINISTERIE VAN JUSTITIE (1994), *Regie in de jeugdzorg: standpunt van de Ministers van Welzijn, Volksgezondheid en Cultuur en Justitie,* Rijswijk/The Hague.

NETELENBOS, T. (1995a), *Lokaal onderwijsbeleid,* Ministerie van Onderwijs, Cultuur en Wetenschappen, Zoetermeer, Sdu DOP, The Hague.

NETELENBOS, T. (1995b), *De School Als Lerende Organisatie: Kwaliteitsbeleid Op Scholen Voor Primair En Voortgezet Onderwijs,* Ministerie van OCW, Zoetermeer.

RESEARCH VOOR BELEID (1994), *Intersectoraal samenwerken rond jeugd: inventarisatie en analyse,* Leiden.

SCHUYT, C.J.M. (1995), *Kwetsbare Jongeren En Hun Toe-komst: Beleidsadvies Gebaseerd Op Literatuurverkenning,* Amsterdam.

VERENIGING NEDERLANDSE GEMEENTEN (VNG) (1995), *Lokaal Jeugdbeleid: Handleiding Voor Een Geïntegreerd Beleid,* The Hague.

Preschool phase and case study – Emmen

BALAGEUR, I., MESTRES, J. and PENN, H. (1992), *Kwalitatieve Dienstverlening aan Jonge Kinderen: een Discussie-Document,* Commissie van de Europese Gemeenschappen, Netwerk Kinderopvang, Brussels.

BURO ONDERWIJSVOORRANG DRENTHE (1993), *Evaluatie Buurtnetwerken Jeugdhulpverlening, Seizoen 1992-1993,* Emmen.

BURO ONDERWIJSVOORRANG ZUID-OOST DRENTHE (1992), *Advies Over Het Beleid Voorschoolse Periode In De Gemeente Emmen,* Emmen.

BURO ONDERWIJSVOORRANG DRENTHE (1994), *Move Model Ontwikkeling Voorschoolse Educatie In Het OVG Drenthe,* Emmen.

BURO ONDERWIJSVOORRANG DRENTHE (1994), *Move Emmen: Concept Uitvoeringsplan Project Move Emmen,* Emmen.

ELDERING, L. and CHOENNI-GOBARDHAN, S. (1990), *Interventieprogramma's Voor Jonge Kinderen Uit Kansarme Groepen: Een Verkennende Studie,* DSWO Press, Leiden.

JANSZEN, C. and de BOER, N. (1994), *Peuterspeelzalen In De Lift; Werkboek Voor Peuterspeelzalen,* Nederlands Instituut voor Zorg en Welzijn, Utrecht.

LINDIJER, H., POEL, J. and SMINK, G. (1993), *Vroeg Beginnen: Programma's Voor Het Jonge Kind,* CPS, Hoevelaken.

LOGGEM, D. and Van BEKKERS, B. (ed.) (1994), *Het Jonge Kind Tussen Onderwijs En Welzijn; Verslag van het Averroes-Congres Over De Samenwerking Tussen Onderwijs En Welzijn in de Voor- En Vroegschoolse Periode,* Averroes Stichting, Amsterdam.

MOSS, P. (coord.) (1990), *Kinderopvang En-Verzorging In De Europese Gemeenschap 1985-1990,* Commissie van de Europese Gemeenschappen, Netwerk Kinderopvang, Brussels.

POT, E.M. (1994), *Daar Doen Ze het zo! Een Reisverslag Van Inspirerende Voorzieningen Voor Jonge Kinderen,* Utrecht.

RAAD VOOR JEUGDBELEID (1993), *Kinderbeleid: Een Advies Over De Versterking Van De Positie Van Kinderen,* Amsterdam.

VEEN, A. (1994), *Doelgericht En Samen. Condities Waaronder Peuterspeelzalen Een Rol Kunnen Spelen In Het Voorkomen En Bestrijden Van Achterstanden,* WVC, Rijswijk.

School phase and case study – Rotterdam

Contouren van de Brede School (1995), Stichting de Meeuw, Rotterdam.

Drie Jaar FAO: Terugblik en Uitzicht, Stedelijk bureau FAO Rotterdam, Rotterdam, August 1994.

DUBBELDAM, P. (1994), *Gidsproject: Eindverslag,* de Meeuw, Rotterdam.

KRIENS, J. and LAKENS, P. (1994), "Rotterdam and the education of immigrant children", paper presented to the conference on Language Teaching in Multi-Cultural Schools, FAO, Rotterdam.

Op Weg Naar Het 2e Meerjarig Beleidsplan FAO (1995-1999) (1994), Stedelijk bureau FAO, Feiten en cijfers 1994, Sectie Voorlichting, Bestuursdienst Stadhuis, Rotterdam.

Speurtocht Door Een Landschap: Kansen, Ideeën En Bondge-noten Van Het Voorbereidend Beroepsonderwijs In Rotterdam (1994), Stichting de Meeuw/Stedelijk Bureau FAO, Rotterdam.

Uitgangspunten Voor Beleid: Beleidsnotitie Stichting De Meeuw, Stich-ting Voor Wlezijn In Onderwijsvoorrang (1991), Stichting De Meeuw, Rotterdam.

OECD PUBLICATIONS, 2, rue André-Pascal, 75775 PARIS CEDEX 16
PRINTED IN FRANCE
(96 98 01 1 P) ISBN 92-64-16038-8 – No. 49923 1998